Issues in TESOL

Issues in TESOL
A Primer for Teaching English to Speakers of Other Languages

David Kent

Copyright © 2021. All rights reserved.

No part of this publication may be reproduced, distributed, or transmitted in any form or by any means, including photocopying, recording, or other electronic or mechanical methods, without prior written permission, except in the case of brief quotations embodied in critical reviews and certain other noncommercial uses permitted by copyright law.

Distributable Content: The author, and the publisher, grant permission for the copy and distribution of handouts and photocopiable material from the book for any and all instructional purposes.

Trademark Notice: Product or corporate names may be trademarks or registered trademarks, and are used only for identification and explanation without intent to infringe.

Phonetic Font: Doulos SIL 5.000

Phonetic Use: The use of phonetics in this book follows that of the IPA (revised to 2015) under a Creative Commons Attribution-ShareAlike 3.0 Unported License (CC-BY-SA).

Text Illustrations: All images in text are Public Domain unless other permissions are noted.

Although every precaution has been taken to verify the accuracy of the information contained herein, the editor and publisher assume no responsibility for any errors or omissions. No liability is assumed for damages that may result from the use of information contained within.

A catalogue record for this book is available from the National Library of Australia

ISBN: 9781925555592

Pedagogy Press. Sydney, Australia.
www.pedagogypress.com

Second Edition.

DEDICATION

For the teacher in all of us.

CONTENTS

ACKNOWLEDGMENTS	xxi
PREFACE	xxiii
PART ONE: PERSPECTIVES AND PRACTICE	1
1. Second Language Acquisition (SLA) Aspects, Frameworks, and Influences	2
Overview	2
Learning Outcomes	2
SLA Aspects	3
The Place of the Brain	4
Neuroplasticity	4
Brain Architecture	4
The lobes.	6
Language and the Brain	7
Neurocognitive research – Benefits of bilingualism.	8
Memory.	10
Affective Factors	12
Language Ego	12
State Anxiety	13
Inhibition and Self-Esteem	14
Risk Taking	16
Attribution Theory and Self-Efficacy	16
Motivation	17
Environmental Influences (Social and Educational Contexts)	20
Myths and Misconceptions	20
Myth 1: Children Acquire Languages Better Than Adults	21
Myth 2: You Are Unable to Lose Your Accent After Becoming an Adult	22
Myth 3: You Can Acquire a Language Just by Listening or Reading	23
Myth 4: I Am Too Old to Learn a New Language	23
Myth 5: Immersion is Key to Fluency	24
Stages of Language Acquisition	24
Second Language Acquisition (SLA)	25
Initial Language Acquisition (ILA)	25
Sign Language Acquisition	26
Artificial Intelligence and Language Acquisition	26
SLA Frameworks	27

Concepts	28
Interlanguage	28
Fossilization/Stabilization	28
Interference	29
Contrastive Analysis	29
Method, Approach, and Technique Distinction	29
Mistake, Error, and Attempt Differentiation	30
Memory and SLA	30
Cognitive Semantics	30
Ambiguity Tolerance-Intolerance	30
Connectionism and SLA	31
Mediation, the Zone of Proximal Development (ZPD), and Scaffolding	31
Willingness to Communicate (WTC)	32
Models	32
Semantic Cognitive Model	32
Models of Communicative Competence	33
Competition Model	35
Psychological Model	35
Attention Processing Model	35
Classroom Model	36
Declarative/Procedural Model	37
Pyramid Model of Second Language Use	37
Theories	38
Nativist Theory and Universal Grammar	38
Processability Theory (PT)	38
Automaticity: The Adaptive Control of Thought – Skills-Based Theory	39
Semantic Theory	39
Sociocultural Theory (Interactionist Approach)	40
Complex Dynamic Systems Theory (CDST)	40
Hypotheses	40
Critical Period Hypothesis (CPH)	40
Markedness Differential Hypothesis	41
Emergentism, the Amelioration Hypothesis, and the Mapping Assumption	41
Input Hypothesis (aka Monitor Model)	41
Acquisition/Learning Hypothesis	42
Monitor Hypothesis	43
Natural Order Hypothesis	43
Affective Filter Hypothesis	43
Noticing Hypothesis	43

Interaction Hypothesis	44
Output Hypothesis	44
SLA Influences	44
Language	45
Pidgins, Creoles, and Lingua Francas	46
Linguistic Imperialism and the Native- Versus Non-Native Teacher Debate	48
World Englishes	49
Language Planning and Policy	52
Culture and Cultural Parameters	53
Identity	54
Intercultural Competence	56
Intercultural Language Learning (IcLL) and Teaching	56
Summary	57
Review	58
Content Quiz	58
Multiple-Choice	58
True or False	70
Quiz Answers	79
Suggested Readings	80

2. Educational Paradigms, Classroom Management Theories, and Educational Leadership — 88

Overview	88
Learning Outcomes	89
Educational Paradigms	89
Andragogy and Pedagogy	90
Behaviorism	93
Cognitivism	94
Humanistic Learning	94
Constructivism	96
The Sociocultural Theory of Cognitive Development	96
Transformative Learning	97
Poststructuralist and Critical Pedagogical Theory	98
Connectivist Learning	99
Educational Neuroscience	100
Developmental Stage Theory	101
Hierarchy of Needs Theory	102
Domains of Learning	104
Cognitive Domain	104
Affective Domain	108
Psychomotor Domain	108

Structure of Observed Learning Outcomes (SOLO) Taxonomy	109
Conditions of Learning	110
Spiral Curriculum	112
Experiential Learning	114
Subsumption Learning	116
Psychosocial Development	118
The Banking Model of Education and Problem-Posing Education	120
Phenomenon-Based Learning	122
Dual Coding, the Promise of Multimedia, and Cognitive Load Theory	124
Sensory Stimulation Theory and Multimodal Learning	127
Digital Nativism, Twenty-First Century Core Skills and Competencies, Personal learning Networks, and Community of Practice	128
Classroom Management Theories	133
Applied Behavior Analysis (ABA)	134
Assertive Discipline	135
Behaviorist Classrooms	136
Choice Theory	137
Democratic Classrooms	138
Non-Adversarial Method	139
Pragmatic Method	139
Response Thinking Process (RTP)	141
The Token Economy	141
Unconditional Positive Regard	142
Educational Leadership	142
Teacher leadership	143
The teacher leader	144
Student Leadership	146
The student leader	147
Wellbeing	149
Enhancing Staff Wellbeing	151
Enhancing Teacher Wellbeing	152
Enhancing Student Wellbeing	153
Ethics, Laws, Rights, and Responsibilities	154
A Personal Ethics Code	156
Summary	157
Review	158
Content Quiz	158
Multiple-Choice	158
True or False	176
Quiz Answers	188
Suggested Readings	189

3. Language Teaching Methods, Approaches, and Techniques
197

- Overview — 197
  - Learning Outcomes — 197
- Methods, Approaches, and Techniques — 197
  - Methods — 198
    - The Classical Method (Grammar-Translation) — 198
    - The Direct Method — 198
    - The Audiolingual Method (Army Method) — 199
    - The Silent Way — 200
    - Total Physical Response (TPR) — 201
    - Community Language Learning (CLL) — 204
  - Approaches — 204
    - The Oral Approach (Situational Language Teaching) — 204
    - The Structural Approach — 205
    - Cooperative language learning — 206
    - Suggestopedia (Desuggestopedia) — 206
    - Competency-Based Language Teaching (CBLT) — 207
    - The Natural Approach — 208
    - Content-Based Instruction (CBI) — 209
    - Lexical Approach — 210
    - Communicative Language Teaching — 210
    - Multiple Intelligences — 211
    - Dogme — 212
    - Data-Driven Learning (DDL) — 213
  - Techniques — 214
    - Authentic Learning — 214
    - Task-Based Language Teaching (TBLT) — 214
    - Present, practice, produce (PPP) — 214
    - Engage Study Activate (ESA) — 215
- The Eclectic Era (Post-Methods Period) — 216
  - Post-Method Pedagogy — 217
    - Post-method pedagogical parameters — 217
    - Strategies for post-method teaching — 218
  - Post-Pandemic Pedagogy and the Future of Instruction — 219
- Summary — 220
- Review — 221
  - Content Quiz — 221
    - Multiple-Choice — 221
  - Quiz Answers — 232
- Suggested Readings — 233

PART TWO: IMPLEMENTATIONS	236
4. Lesson Framing	**237**
Overview	237
Learning Outcomes	237
Techniques behind Language Teaching	237
Language Teaching Principles	238
Cognitive Aspects	238
Socioaffective Aspects	239
Linguistic Aspects	240
In the Classroom	240
Learner Motivation	241
Classroom Management	243
Teacher Presence	244
Seating Plans	246
Content Delivery	248
Student work groups.	*253*
Staging lessons.	*255*
Teaching Varying Ages	256
Young Learners	256
Teens	257
Adults	257
Teaching Varying Proficiencies	258
Teaching Beginners	260
Teaching at the Intermediate Level	261
Advanced Level Teaching	262
Summary	263
Review	263
Content Quiz	263
Multiple-Choice	263
True or False	267
Quiz Answers	270
Suggested Readings	271
Photocopiable Content	272
Sample Seating Chart – Rows	273
Sample Seating Chart – Roundtable (Circle)	274
Sample Seating Chart – Horseshoe (Semi-circle)	275
Sample Seating Chart – Double Horseshoe	276
Sample Seating Chart – Pods (Groups)	277
Sample Seating Chart – Pods (Pairs)	278

5. Developing Great Lessons — 279
Overview — 279
- Learning Outcomes — 279
The Teaching and Learning Context — 279
- Understanding Students — 280
- Understanding Yourself as a Teacher — 281
  - Teacher Talk — 281
  - Balancing the Use of the L1 in the Classroom — 282
- Scaffolding and Differentiation — 283
  - Scaffolding Strategies — 284
  - Differentiation Strategies — 284
- The Place of Textbooks and Supplementary Material — 286
- Developing Active Learning — 287
  - Teaching Active Language skills — 288
    - *Speaking.* — *288*
    - *Writing.* — *292*
  - Teaching Receptive Language Skills — 294
    - *Listening.* — *294*
    - *Reading.* — *298*
  - Supporting Grammar, Pronunciation, and Vocabulary — 300
    - *Grammar.* — *300*
    - *Pronunciation.* — *301*
    - *Vocabulary.* — *305*
- Testing Students — 305
- Incorporating Games and Songs — 309
  - Games — 309
  - Songs — 310
- Incorporating Technology — 312
  - Evaluating and Assessing Technology Use — 312
    - *The SAMR model.* — *313*
  - Teaching Tools: An Overload — 314
    - *Class-management/economy.* — *315*
    - *Speaking – presentations.* — *315*
    - *Listening – videos/songs.* — *316*
    - *Reading – data-driven learning (DDL).* — *317*
    - *Writing – stories/comics.* — *317*
    - *Games – language fun.* — *318*
    - *Assessment – interactive quizzes.* — *318*
    - *Voice-activated learning.* — *319*
    - *Community of practice (COP) – knowledge, practice, and craft.* — *320*
Teaching Challenges — 320
- Teaching English for Specific Purposes (ESP) — 321

Teaching with Limited Resources	321
Teaching Large Classes	322
Teaching Mixed-Level Classes	322
Dealing with Speedsters	323
Working with Uncooperative Students	323
Continuing Professional Development (CPD)	325
Summary	326
Review	326
Content Quiz	326
Multiple-Choice	327
Quiz Answers	334
Suggested Readings	335
Photocopiable Content	337

6. Lesson Planning — 365

Overview	365
Learning Outcomes	365
The Lesson Plan	365
Initial Considerations and the Lesson Plan Foundational Framework	365
Rationale	366
Learning context	366
Materials and Resources	367
Aims and goals.	367
Implementation.	367
Outcomes and implications.	367
Developing the Lesson Plan	368
Teaching Context	368
Teacher Preparation	368
Procedure	369
Further Considerations	369
Mind Mapping a Lesson Plan	370
Summary	372
Review	373
Content Quiz	373
Multiple-Choice	373
True or False	374
Quiz Answers	375
Suggested Readings	376
Photocopiable Content	377

PART THREE: SOUND, MEANING, AND FORM — 384

7. Pronunciation in Teaching — 385
- Overview — 385
  - Learning Outcomes — 385
- Pronunciation – Phonology, Stress, Intonation — 386
  - Phonology — 386
  - Stress — 388
  - Intonation — 392
- Pronunciation in the Classroom — 394
  - Drawing Attention to Pronunciation Features — 395
    - Minimal Pairs — 396
    - Tongue Twisters — 397
    - Poems, Songs, and Texts — 397
  - Pronunciation Games and Activities — 399
  - Testing Pronunciation — 401
- Summary — 403
- Review — 403
  - Content Quiz — 403
    - Multiple-Choice — 404
    - True or False — 407
  - Quiz Answers — 409
- Suggested Readings — 410
- Photocopiable Content — 411

8. Vocabulary in Teaching — 425
- Overview — 425
  - Learning Outcomes — 425
- Vocabulary – Items, Tiers, and Lists — 425
  - Items — 425
  - Tiers — 426
  - Lists — 427
  - Vocabulary in the Classroom — 428
    - Vocabulary Teaching Strategies — 428
    - Vocabulary Games and Activities — 432
  - Testing Vocabulary — 440
- Summary — 442
- Review — 443
  - Content Quiz — 443
    - Multiple-Choice — 443
    - True or False — 446
  - Quiz Answers — 448

Suggested Readings	449
Photocopiable Content	450

9. Grammar in Teaching — 466

Overview	466
Learning Outcomes	466
Grammar – Types, Rules, Focus	466
Types of Grammar	467
Rules of Grammar Teaching	469
The Focus of a Pedagogical Grammar	470
Grammar in the Classroom	472
Teaching Grammar	472
Grammar Games and Activities	475
Testing Grammar	487
Summary	489
Review	489
Content Quiz	489
Multiple-Choice	490
Quiz Answers	498
Suggested Readings	499
Photocopiable Content	501

PART FOUR: CAPSTONE PROJECTS — 533

10. Practicum — 534

Overview	534
Learning Outcomes	534
The Practicum	534
Advisors	535
Academic Advisor	535
Supervisory Teacher	536
Practicum Project Completion	536
Requirements	536
Tasks	537
Task 1. Self-Reflection – Logging to Learn	537
Task 2. Peer Observation and Evaluation	538
Task 3. Clinical Supervision – Observation by a Peer	539
Task 4. Pedagogy Project – Lesson Plan Development	539
Task 5. Professional Development – Lifelong Learning	540
Evaluation	542
Summary	543
Review	543

Content Quiz	543
Multiple-Choice	543
Quiz Answers	546
Suggested Readings	547
Photocopiable Content	548
11. Portfolio	**605**
Learning Outcomes	605
The Portfolio	605
The Advisor	606
Time Requirements	606
The Portfolio Project	606
Preparation	606
Work Product Selection	607
The Importance of Reflection	609
Model Portfolio	609
Portfolio Tasks	609
Portfolio Layout	610
Title Page and Table of Contents	610
Task 1: Introductory Reflection	610
Task 2 to Task 4: TESOL, MALL, and CELT Components	611
Task 5: Summary Reflection	611
Checklist and Declaration	611
Submission	612
Evaluation	612
Summary	613
Review	613
Content Quiz	613
Multiple-Choice	613
True or False	615
Quiz Answers	616
Suggested Readings	617
Photocopiable Content	618
12. Thesis	**627**
Overview	627
Learning Outcomes	627
The Thesis Project	627
Completion Timeline	628
Advisors	628
Academic Advisor	628
Thesis Advisor	628

Developing a Proposal	629
Ethical Considerations	630
Citation and Copyright	631
Thesis Layout	632
Title Page	633
Signature Page	633
Abstract	633
Definition of Terms	634
Acknowledgements	634
Introduction	634
Background/Literature Review	634
Methodology	634
Findings	635
Conclusion	635
References	635
Glossary	635
Appendices	635
The Thesis Defense	636
The Defense Committee	636
The Oral Defense	636
Evaluation	637
Defense Debrief	638
Summary	639
Review	639
Content Quiz	639
Multiple-Choice	640
True or False	645
Quiz Answers	648
Suggested Readings	649
Photocopiable Content	650
Glossary	**702**
Useful Resources	**759**

LIST OF TABLES

Table 1.1 Traits of the Hemispheres of the Human Brain	6
Table 1.2 Perspectives and Attributes of Motivation	17
Table 1.3 Extrinsic and Intrinsic Motivational Drivers	19
Table 1.4 Attention Processing Model Examples	36
Table 2.1 A Comparison of Learning Theory Paradigms	91
Table 2.2 The Assumptions of Andragogy and Pedagogy	92
Table 2.3 Knowledge Dimension Matrix – Cognitive	105
Table 2.4 Knowledge Dimension Matrix – Artifacts	107
Table 2.5 Knowledge Dimension Matrix – Artifacts Completed	107
Table 2.6 Learning Outcome and Associated Domain	110
Table 2.7 Instructional Events and Associated Cognitive Processes	110
Table 2.8 Gagne's Conditions of Learning (with descriptor)	111
Table 2.9 Benefits and Limitations of the Spiral Curriculum	113
Table 2.10 Kolb's Learning Style Matrix	115
Table 2.11 Erickson's Eight Stages of Psychological Development	119
Table 2.12 Banking Model of Education	120
Table 2.13 Problem Posing Approach	121
Table 2.14 Phenomenon Based Learning Theory	123
Table 2.15 Sixteen Skills Required by the 21st Century Learner	129
Table 2.16 Categories of Classroom Management Theories	134
Table 2.17 Applying Assertive Discipline Theory in the Classroom	135
Table 4.1 Language Learning Proficiency Levels	259
Table 5.1 Reductions in English	303
Table 5.2 Five Aspects of Testing and their Focus	307
Table 7.1 The Four General Rules of Word Stress	390
Table 7.2 Changing Meaning by Shifting Word Stress	391
Table 7.3 Linking Rules	393
Table 7.4 Improving and Teaching Pronunciation	394
Table 8.1 Vocabulary Teaching Strategies	429

LIST OF FIGURES

Figure 1.1 The Lobes of the Brain	7
Figure 1.2 Levels of Processing Model of Human Memory	11
Figure 1.3 Locus of Control and Stability	17
Figure 1.4 Components of Communicative Competence	34
Figure 1.5 Components of Language Competence	34
Figure 1.6 Kachru's Three Concentric Circle Model	50
Figure 2.1 Maslow's Hierarchy of Needs	103
Figure 2.2 A Revised Taxonomy, 2001	106
Figure 2.3 Kolb's Experiential Learning Cycle	114
Figure 2.4 Eight Key Competencies for Lifelong Learning	130
Figure 2.5 See-Saw Model of Wellbeing	150
Figure 3.1 The DIKW Pyramid	213
Figure 5.1 Example Stress Practice Activity	304
Figure 5.2 The SAMR Model	313
Figure 6.1 Mind Mapping a Lesson Plan – General Guide	371
Figure 7.1 The IPA Chart Consonant Diagrams	387
Figure 7.2 The IPA Chart Vowel Trapezium	388
Figure 7.3 Example Waveform	389
Figure 7.4 Stress Practice Word Web	396
Figure 7.5 Syntactic Word Structure Diagram	399
Figure 8.1 Example Gap-Fill Vocabulary Exercise Using Antonyms	433
Figure 8.2 Example of English and Korean False Friends	436
Figure 9.1 A Grammar Teaching Continuum	471
Figure 9.2 Continuum of Focus – Form to Meaning	471
Figure 9.3 Sentence Diagrams Using the Reed-Kellogg System	474
Figure 9.4 A Constituency Sentence Tree	474
Figure 9.5 A Dependency Sentence Tree	474
Figure 9.6 A Hybrid Dependency-Constituency Sentence Tree	475
Figure 9.7 Past Grammar Tense Using a Timeline	483
Figure 9.8 Simple Verb Tenses Using Timelines	484
Figure 9.9 Progressive Verb Tenses Using Timelines	484
Figure 9.10 Perfect Simple Verb Tenses Using Timelines	485
Figure 9.11 Perfect Progressive Verb Tenses Using Timelines	485
Figure 12.1 Plagiarism Levels	631

ACKNOWLEDGMENTS

I wish to extend my deepest appreciation to my wife *Hyunhee* who has been very patient and understanding throughout the entire process involved with the production of this book. I would also like to thank *Noel David* for his suggestions regarding this text and for his patience.

PREFACE

Serving as a general overview to the field, *Issues in TESOL: A primer for teaching English to speakers of other languages,* aims to deliver insight into the many varied concepts and practices involved in the teaching of English to speakers of other languages (TESOL). It focuses on those particular issues of TESOL that are important over the various stages of a career. Of significance, the book emerges to fill the needs of those who come to the education field from other disciplines; for those who may find themselves teaching without experience; for those interested in beginning a career in teaching English; as well as those in-service teachers looking to reground; or for those who are about to embark on TESOL certification. The intent is to provide an overview of the field that will help readers make connections between the various theoretical discourses, research, and teaching practices that are involved in the craft of teaching of English to speakers of other languages.

Organization of the Text

The book consists of four parts with the intent of introducing readers to TESOL theories, methods, and approaches, along with the basics of classroom management and lesson plan development, establishing a foundation in pronunciation, vocabulary, and grammar teaching, while also introducing how to benefit from engaging in classroom observation and other professional development endeavors.

Part one, *perspectives and practice* centers on aspects of second language acquisition and the place of educational theories in teaching. It also reviews the methods, approaches, and techniques applied to the teaching and learning of languages over time, particularly those that provide us with an understanding of how best to teach today. Those influences affecting second language acquisition from language, planning and policy, to culture, identity, and intercultural communication are also touched upon.

Chapter one, *Second Language Acquisition*, explores the place of the brain in the language learning process by emphasizing brain architecture (particularly language areas), and the role of neuroplasticity in second language acquisition (SLA). Benefits of bilingualism are also presented, as are the different types of memory and their role in terms of language learning. A number of myths and misconceptions regarding the SLA process are then underscored so that their fallacies can be highlighted and in turn debunked. The stages of language acquisition are then examined in terms of initial and second language acquisition, alongside a brief discussion on sign language acquisition and the acquisition of language by artificial intelligence. This is so that the similarities and disparities between each can be recognized before moving on to provide a comprehensive listing of the contributions to the field in terms of theories, models, hypotheses and concepts. All of these have formed, to one degree or another, the basis for the methods, approaches, and techniques that are discussed throughout the remaining chapters of the text, and make up those that we use to best teach human languages today. A number of influences on second language acquisition are then presented, from the types of English that exist to language learning and policy. The place of culture and identity, linguistic relativism, and how language and thought operate together are then considered, as is the role of intercultural competence in the teaching and learning of languages.

Chapter two, *Educational Paradigms, Classroom Management, and Educational Leadership*, examines the place of some of the most prominent and prevailing principles influencing the development and teaching of lessons, the supervision of students, and the running of classrooms. Aspects of andragogy and pedagogy, behaviorism, cognitivism, humanism, constructivism, socio culturalism, transformativism, poststructuralism, connectionism and educational neuroscience all serve to establish an avenue from which a plethora of learning theories are explored. Providing teachers with an understanding of a wide range of learning theories can assist them in being able to better their craft, and to implement methods, approaches, techniques, and strategies that come to underpin their curriculum or lessons in order to support learning and knowledge development. Also important, is the ability to consider the role of classroom management, and in particular, the means of encouraging and promoting positive learner behavior from within the classroom and among students. In this regard, examining theories emerging from behaviorist, cognitive, democratic, humanist, and psychoanalytic paradigms aim to assist teachers in keeping learners on task, giving them the skills necessary to preempt any potential problems, and to deal with any issues that may impinge upon a lesson during class time in ways that are swift, effective, and appropriate. The chapter is not meant to be a definitive or comprehensive exploration, but instead one that offers a general introduction, it also focuses on aspects of educational leadership, and how teacher and student leadership can be fostered, and what those roles mean, along with the importance of wellbeing in the school community and how this can be enhanced. The significance of ethics and a moral code in guiding leadership in relation to the laws, rights, and responsibilities placed on stakeholders is also discussed.

Chapter three, *language teaching methods, approaches, and techniques*, considers language learning and teaching to be a very complex process, and one where the best methods, approaches, and techniques are those that create conditions inducive for learning to occur. In many teaching contexts, the language learning classroom will consist of diverse learners from diverse backgrounds, and classes may be large or small and consist of learners of various skill levels and academic ability. Identifying the methods, approaches, and techniques suitable for a particular class, and those that are easily adaptable by the teacher, allows for the various methods, approaches, and techniques to be best employed while simultaneously making best use of content and materials that cater to the immediate needs of learners.

Part two, *implementations* focuses on those practical aspects of concern to teachers. Such as how to frame lessons to engage students, the basics of classroom management, the delivery of appropriate teaching content, and the development of effective lesson plans. This part covers chapters four through six.

Chapter four, *lesson framing*, places emphasis on understanding the guiding principles behind the teaching of English to speakers of other languages. Also covered are the means of how teachers can determine, prior to entering the classroom, how they will conduct themselves professionally. How to manage the classroom for maximum benefit when required to teach students of varying ages, proficiencies, and motivational levels, while understanding how to best deliver content and provide correction.

Chapter five, *developing great lessons*, covers a range of important concepts and aspects involved with the roles of teachers and students, and the place of the textbook and various other resources in the classroom. The skills required to teach, as well as the types of activities and techniques often employed while teaching various language skills are discussed, as are many of the challenges that teachers can undoubtedly expect to face. This section then closes by examining the place and importance of engaging in continued professional development to maintain and improve upon teaching skills.

Chapter six, *lesson planning*, introduces the necessary frameworks and considerations to take into account during the development and delivery of a comprehensive educational plan. A comprehensive lesson plan outline for new teachers to familiarize themselves with, and to easily follow when starting out teaching, is provided. A method for more seasoned teachers to follow is also presented.

Part three, *sound, meaning, and form* covers those concepts that are of most importance for teaching the 'what' of language (pronunciation, vocabulary, grammar) as opposed to the 'how' (listening, speaking, reading, writing). The focus is on developing a means of understanding as to how to best teach these aspects, along with how to best provide learners with the means of improving them. Relevant to this are key teaching strategies and techniques, along with efficient and effective assessment of learner knowledge and linguistic production.

Chapter seven, *pronunciation in teaching*, focuses on delivering a background of support for teachers in terms of developing their understanding of pronunciation. To do this, the chapter explores aspects of the international phonetic alphabet chart, as it is these symbols and representations that are used to denote the sounds of a language. This then leads to a discussion involving an exploration of those aspects of stress and intonation that relate to how sounds are formed and altered. Relevant to this are the ways and means of drawing learner attention to pronunciation features while incorporating into the classroom both direct and indirect methods, approaches, and techniques of teaching that address them. This is then coupled with the delivery of tasks and activities central to the testing of pronunciation in teaching.

Chapter eight, *vocabulary in teaching*, sees emphasis on the place and importance of vocabulary in the language teaching classroom, and how it links sound, meaning, and form. Aspects of what constitutes vocabulary items, and how these are broken down into a variety of tiers and lists, are examined along with the practicality of using such content with learners, particularly for data-driven learning. A variety of teaching strategies are then explored to provide a means of both effectively presenting and efficiently teaching vocabulary items. A number of means for teaching and testing vocabulary are then outlined.

Chapter nine, *grammar in teaching*, highlights a number of different types of grammar before focusing on a pedagogical grammar from a form-meaning-use paradigm. A number of rules from which to teach grammar are then introduced, including those that consider context, use, economy, relevance, nurture, and appropriateness. A variety of teaching strategies are then detailed to provide a means to effectively and efficiently teach various facets of grammar in relevant, timely, and engaging ways. A number of means for testing grammar are then uncovered.

Part four, *capstone projects* highlights the expectations and steps required to complete some of the final projects often linked to TESOL certification, from the practicum through to the portfolio and thesis. This will help any educator if they wish to engage in further education at the graduate level as well as those who may have colleagues or family members beginning academic studies to become an educator.

In chapter ten, *practicums* are covered. A practicum experience involves a combination of class observation, providing classroom assistance, as well as the teaching of classes. It typically serves as the capstone project to a certificate or diploma in TESOL. During the initial stages of a practicum prospective and in-service teachers simply watch classes, record their observations, and ask questions of their supervisory teacher outside of class time. The practicing teacher will then provide guided assistance to their supervisory teacher, and then move on to ultimately teach a series of classes that involve supervisory teacher observation. This part of the book provides one means to achieve this process, and along with an accompanying series of templates in the appendices, it aims to help guide the practicing teacher through completion of a practicum process. The goal behind completion of the practicum presented in this book is to help pre-service and existing teachers partner with others who can provide mentorship by directing their activities and giving them appropriate feedback on any work they may perform. The objectives of this section include: providing readers with a means of being able to critically analyze and evaluate the delivery of learning, demonstrate effectiveness in developing students competence through TESOL, showing that they can incorporate materials and resources into lessons to create a dynamic teaching environment appropriate to the language level and cultural context for language learners, and to show how they are able to engage in life-long learning by seeking out and undertaking their own professional development.

In chapter eleven, *portfolios* are covered. The portfolio typically serves as a capstone project to courses such as a Masters in TESOL, and it is typically undertaken by those students who do not wish to complete a thesis. It serves as a means for prospective, and in-service teachers, to showcase their learning, consider their competency as a classroom teacher, and engage in the reflection of their learning, and of the coursework they have competed while undertaking graduate study. The chapter focuses on the importance of a portfolio, and the place of reflection in its development. Also considered are the place of the advisor, and the time requirements for portfolio submission. The very basics of what is involved in developing a portfolio is provided, with particular emphasis on the kind of work products that might be included, as well as the need to contextualize the teaching philosophy and goals, teaching methods and strategies, activities undertaken to improve teaching, and future goals within those reflections. An example portfolio, with the means used to evaluate and submit it to one particular graduate program, is also presented.

In chapter twelve, *theses* are covered. The thesis track in a Master's graduate program typically consists of four basic components: successful completion of coursework, candidacy examination, the formation of a thesis committee and the writing and oral defense of a thesis project that follows a specific timeline. This track is typically undertaken by those students who intend to go on to doctoral level studies. The completion of a thesis, as the capstone project, to a degree serves as a means for prospective, and in-service teachers, to conduct an original study and perform critical analysis on a topic of their own interest. The chapter covers the rationale behind the writing of a thesis, and the need to follow a strict completion timeline. The role of advisors and students in the development of a thesis are also presented, as is the critical need to consider ethical implications when undertaking research. Scholarly rigor and academic misconduct are also briefly discussed, as is what constitutes a thesis proposal. The typical sequential style thesis layout is then introduced, along with the stages of a typical oral defense, and the means of finalizing the thesis project.

It is hoped that this book will provide both education and something new for all teachers – be they trained or untrained, pre-service, in-service, or retired.

David Kent.

PART ONE: PERSPECTIVES AND PRACTICE

… Issues in TESOL

1. Second Language Acquisition (SLA) Aspects, Frameworks, and Influences

Overview
This chapter consists of three sections: aspects, frameworks, and influences. The first section discusses a number of aspects in relation to second language acquisition, including the place of the brain, a number of affective factors, several myths and misconceptions, as well as the stages of language acquisition for initial language speakers, second language speakers, sign language users, and artificial intelligence. The second section follows, and focuses on a number of frameworks including those theories, models, hypotheses, and concepts that have come to contribute to the development of the myriad methods, approaches, and techniques that assist us in the teaching and learning of languages today. The third section then presents a number of influences on second language acquisition (SLA), from the types of English that exist to language learning and policy. The place of culture and identity, linguistic relativism, and how language and thought operate together are then considered, as is the role of intercultural competence in the teaching and learning of languages.

Learning Outcomes
1. Develop an understanding of brain architecture, particularly regarding language areas.
2. Understand the place of the brain in the language learning process in terms of neuroplasticity.
3. Gain an appreciation for the benefits of bilingualism, and the role of the different types of memory in language learning.
4. Become familiar with a number of myths and misconceptions regarding SLA, and how these have been debunked.
5. Recognize the similarities and disparities behind the stages of language acquisition, and how these stages are relevant in sign language acquisition and to artificial intelligence and language acquisition.
6. Appreciate many of the affective factors involved with SLA, and how these may hinder or contribute to learner linguistic development.

7. Develop a solid understanding of the vast amount of theories, models, hypotheses, and concepts that have contributed to the development of the field of SLA.
8. Distinguish the kinds of English that exist today, and the kind of language that we teach when we teach English to speakers of other languages.
9. Grasp the impact of planning and policy on what, how, and why a language is (or is not) taught, and how it is used.
10. Recognize the influence of culture and identity on individuals in the development of SLA.
11. Comprehend the value and significance of intercultural competence in the teaching and learning of language.

SLA Aspects
The Place of the Brain, Affective Factors, Motivation, Myths and Misconceptions, and the Stages of Language Acquisition

Central to any understanding of second language acquisition is the development of knowledge regarding language and the brain. This is especially true for the place of brain architecture, and the primary importance of neuroplasticity in the development of second language acquisition (SLA). It is also important to understand the role of the different types of memory in this process, along with the emerging benefits of bilingualism. Important here too, is gaining an understanding of the impact of affective factors on the language learning process, especially how these may hinder or contribute to the development of language acquisition in your learners. This will also help you to accept why a number of the myths and misconceptions surrounding the learning of additional languages can be debunked. In further support, the stages of language acquisition are briefly introduced so that similarities and disparities between them can be recognized. Also considered are how these stages relate to sign language acquisition, and to artificial intelligence and its acquisition of language.

The Place of the Brain

The brain is responsible for interpreting all of the sensory data that we receive: visually, auditorily, olfactory, by touch, and from our palate. All of the information that we receive is worked upon or stored by our sensory, short-term or long-term memory so that it has meaning for use and can be recalled and relied upon as required. Our central nervous system (CNS) is comprised of the brain and the spinal cord, with the peripheral nervous system (PNS) comprised of the spinal nerves branching from the spinal cord and the cranial nerves branching out from the brain.

Neuroplasticity

The human brain is a complex organ. It constantly undergoes reorganization, and it is adaptable to change (e.g., after injury). This may see brain activity associated with a given function transferred to a different location, gray matter change, and synapses be rerouted. This adaptability is known as *neuroplasticity*, and it occurs when the brain reorganizes itself by forming new neural connections. It also occurs when you learn something, or need to adjust to a new environment. This restructuring may also be referred to as brain plasticity or neural plasticity. Interestingly, the developing brain tends to exhibit a higher degree of plasticity over the adult brain. So, the brain is made up of dynamic, flexible networks in which diverse regions are recruited according to various task demands.

Brain Architecture

The parts of the brain all work together, but each part can contain its own special properties. The three basic units of the brain are the forebrain, midbrain and hindbrain.

Forebrain. Consisting primarily of the cerebrum and the structures beneath it, this is the largest and most highly developed part. It performs higher functions like the interpretation of sensory input along with speech, reasoning, emotions, learning, and fine motor control. The surface of the cerebrum is called the *cortex*, and it maintains a folded appearance with the folds known as *gyrus* and the grooves between known as *sulcus*. These folds contain billions of neurons, and their gray-brown color gives them their name: *gray matter*. These neurons are connected to axons which are known as *white matter*. The folded structure allows for more neurons to fit inside the skull and enables higher functioning. Pathways known as *white matter tracts* connect areas of the cortex, sending messages from one gyrus to others, and from one lobe to others, and from one hemisphere to the other, and also into the deeper structures of the brain. These deeper structures include the hypothalamus, pituitary gland, pineal gland, thalamus, basal ganglia, and the limbic system.

Midbrain. This is the uppermost part of the brainstem responsible for controlling such things as reflexes and voluntary movements and control of the eye.

Hindbrain. This refers to the cerebellum, the brain stem, and the upper part of the spinal cord. The hindbrain serves to control functions such as heart rate, respiration, and swallowing. The cerebellum also works to coordinate movement, and it is involved in rote movements (e.g., muscle memory), and maintaining posture and balance.

The two hemispheres

The brain is divided into two halves or hemispheres, connected by nerve fibers called the *corpus callosum,* and within each half, certain regions control certain functions. When learning new languages, the left side of the brain is considered the hub of processing. However, the right brain plays a critical role in assisting learners to identify the basic sounds associated with the language(s) that they learn. In other words, the left hemisphere is the language learning side of the brain, but the right hemisphere may help to predict the success a learner may have in learning the language and identifying its phonological elements.

The left brain/right brain theory considers one side of the brain to be more dominant than the other. So, if you are more inclined to be analytical and methodological in your thinking you might be considered left-brained. If you are more creative or artistic, then you would be considered right-brained. Some of these traits are highlighted in Table 1.1. Unfortunately, there is no real proof that this theory is correct. What we see is the two sides working together in a complementary fashion, and not working independently of each other. However, it is known that each side of the brain is responsible for the opposite side of the body. For example, a stroke that injures the left side of the brain might then impact the functionality of the right side of the body (e.g., loss of movement in the right arm). Interestingly, the left hemisphere is dominant in hand use and language in around 92% of people (Hines, 2018).

Left-Hemisphere	Right-Hemisphere
Analysis	Controls left parts of the body
Controls right parts of the body	Drawing
	Dreams
Language skills	Emotion
Detail and fact oriented	Imagination
Logical thinking	Intuition
Memorizing facts and names	Multitasking and parallel processing
Numerical	
Reading and writing abilities	Musicality
Science and mathematical capabilities	Non-verbal information
	See the big picture
Sequential processing	Spatial orientation
Speech	Synthesis
Think in words	Think in pictures

Table 1.1 Traits of the Hemispheres of the Human Brain

The lobes.

Each hemisphere of the brain can be divided into four lobes by distinct fissures (see Figure 1.1). These lobes are known as the frontal lobe, the parietal lobe, the occipital lobe, and the temporal lobe, and they function together, working with the left and right hemispheres of the brain. However, we can further divide these lobes into specific areas that assist in serving particular functions.

Frontal lobe. Tends to be responsible for aspects such as:
- behavior, emotions, personality;
- problem solving, planning, judgements;
- speech – speaking and writing (*Broca's area*);
- body movement (*motor strip*);
- self-awareness, concentration, intelligence.

Parietal lobe. Tends to be responsible for aspects such as:
- Interpretation of language, words;
- Pain, touch, temperature (*sensory strip*);
- Interpreting auditory, visual, motor, sensory and memories;
- Spatial and visual perception.

Occipital lobe. Tends to be responsible for aspects such as:
- interrupting vision (in terms of color, light, movements).

Temporal lobe. Tends to be responsible for aspects such as:
- hearing;
- language understanding (*Wernicke's area*);
- memory;
- organization and sequencing.

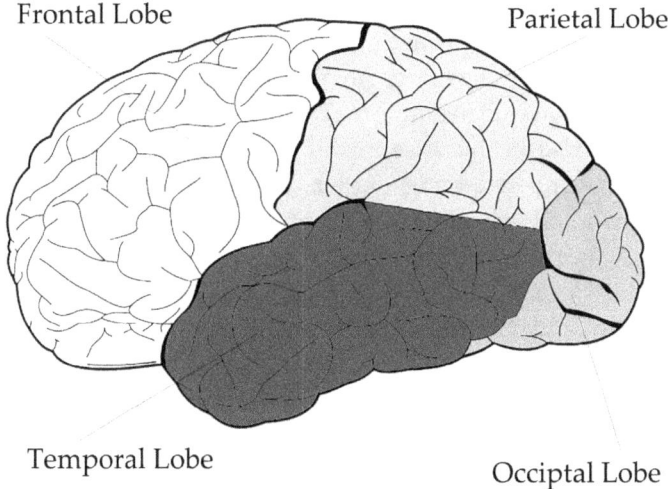

Figure 1.1 The Lobes of the Brain
(Note: Image adapted from that in the Public Domain)

Language and the Brain

In general, it is considered that the left hemisphere is largely responsible for language and speech, and it is usually a person's 'dominant' hemisphere, while the right hemisphere plays a large part in the interpretation of visual cues and spatial processing. In those who are left-handed though, around a third may see speech function located on the right side of their brains (Hines, 2018), and they might require special testing prior to surgery to see if their speech center is located on the left or right side of the brain prior to any operation on the brain. A loss of the ability to understand or express speech, and/or the ability to read and write, is known as *aphasia*.

Broca's area. Located in the frontal lobe of the dominant hemisphere of the brain, usually the left, it is linked to speech production functions. There is typical loss of tongue movement or the facial muscles that assist in producing the sounds of speech if this area is damaged. Such a person will be able to read and understand spoken language but may have difficulty in speaking and writing (i.e., formation of words and letters; not writing within lines. Medically this would be diagnosed as *Broca's aphasia.*

Wernicke's area. Located in the temporal lobe of the brain, this area is important for language development and for the comprehension of speech. Damage to this area might see the person speak in long sentences that have no meaning, or contain novel or unnecessary words. The patient who in this case is able to make speech sounds but has difficulty in understanding speech, and is unaware of their own mistakes, would medically carry a diagnosis of *Wernicke's aphasia.*

Arcuate fasciculus. This is a bundle of axons that connect *Broca's area* and *Wernicke's area* of the brain, as an association fiber tract, which connects the caudal temporal cortex and the inferior frontal lobes.

All of the above present a classical model for language and the brain in neurobiology. The *angular gyrus* is the area that assembles information in order to interpret words and concepts, with the *insular cortex* mediating aspects of speech production and articulatory control. So, it is now known that language function is *"widely distributed throughout the brain with the language connectome extending far beyond the single pathway notion of the arcuate fasciculus and ... Broca and Wernicke's areas"* and that it involves areas *"in the frontal, parietal, and temporal lobes, in the medial hemispheres of the brain, as well as in the basal ganglia, thalamus and cerebellum"* (Tremblay & Dick, 2016, p. 62). A *connectome* is defined as a comprehensive map of neural connections, typically in the brain, but, more broadly, also a mapping of all neural connections with the nervous system.

Neurocognitive research – Benefits of bilingualism.

It has been observed that children who learn an additional language early on in life store it with their native language, but those who learn an additional language later in life store it in a different area of the brain, illustrating cortical adaptation. *Code switching* (CS), or switching from the use of one language to another, or from one dialect to another, or between two registers of the same language has also been shown to produce an additional volume of gray matter. The frontal and parietal regions (involved in executive control) are also larger in those that speak an additional language. Research also shows that the *anterior cingulate cortex* increases in size because it appears to play a role in monitoring which language is being spoken at any given time, and serves to assist in keeping any others from intruding during communication. Research suggests that this area is also responsible for ignoring distractions when completing other tasks (e.g., listening to something in a noisy environment). This implies that bilinguals may then have an advantage over monolinguals in terms of being able to better ignore irrelevant information and focus on what is important. Bilingual children also have the ability to more readily think about language as abstract associations and units over monolingual children. Keep in mind also that bilingual babies may start to develop linguistic abilities at a much slower pace than monolingual babies, and as they become children, start to constantly engage in code switching. This is normal; after all, they are developing *communicative competence* in two (or more) language systems.

No matter the age at which you learn an additional language, you can still enjoy the benefits of better memory, increased cognitive creativity, and mental flexibility over a monolingual. Learning any additional language will increase the size of your brain. Those learning additional languages will see growth in the hippocampus and areas of the cerebral cortex, and development of better overall language skills than other learners who may possess a more developed motor region of the cerebral cortex. Noteworthy is that the areas of the brain that grew are those linked to how easy the learners found languages, with brain development varying according to performance (Mackey, 2014). Brain-based research is starting to show that those people who are talented at picking up sequences and patterns are also able to learn grammar particularly via immersion. Further, those that learn additional languages by immersion over explanation-based teaching of rules construct native-speaker-like brain processes in regards to that language. Additional language speakers are also able to integrate contradictory concepts which may result from linguistic and cultural contexts that allow them to experience and see the world from different perspectives, and to maintain an increased cognitive flexibility over monolinguals as a result.

As we get older, particularly after the age of 25, our brain's abilities (e.g., processing speed, efficiency, and working memory) start to decline. Multiple language use can compensate for this decline through a process known as *cognitive compensation* where the brain begins to use alternative networks and connections over the original pathways that have become damaged or destroyed. Additional language users may also delay the onset of certain types of brain diseases (e.g., Alzheimer's) as a result of having increased white matter. Such an increase allows for messages to travel faster and more efficiently across networks by providing more neurons, and with continued language practice, these connections are strengthened and maintained. Learning additional languages when aging also tasks a great number of areas in the brain, giving them a workout, but research into the ultimate benefits and what types of learning is required is still being undertaken (Skibba, 2018). Of interest, language acquisition has been found to improve all aspects of working memory, even those that are unrelated to languages.

Memory.

Memory is how the brain encodes data or information for storage and retrieval as required. It can be defined as the preservation of information over time for the purpose of influencing future actions (Sherwood, 2015). However, it also involves the processes of encoding and recalling, as well as storing. Different areas of the brain are involved with different types of memory.

Short-term memory. Working memory or short-term memory occurs in the prefrontal cortex. Information is stored for about one minute and its capacity is limited to around seven items. In the case of reading, your working memory will hold the sentence you have just read in mind, in order to assist in you in understanding the one you are currently reading.

Long-term memory. This kind of memory is processed in the hippocampus of the temporal lobe, and it is activated when memorizing something. This memory is believed to have unlimited content and duration capacity. It may contain facts and figures, as well as personal memories.

Skill memory. This kind of memory is processed in the cerebellum, which relays information to the basal ganglia.

An alternative model, the levels-of-processing model, proposed by Craik and Lockhart (1972) considers memory recall and the depth of memorization as a continuum from shallow (perceptual) to deep (semantic) with no distinction between short- and long-term memory (see Figure 1.2).

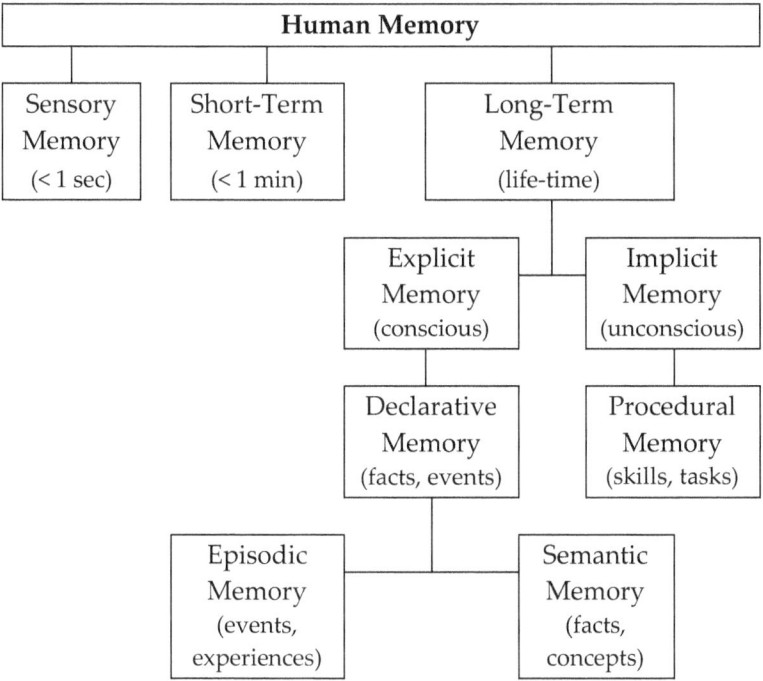

Figure 1.2 Levels of Processing Model of Human Memory

In any case, the native language that you speak does affect the quality of your working memory (Amici, et al., 2019). Those of us who are native speakers of left branching (LB) languages have a significantly better working memory, particularly for items presented early on in a memory task, while those that are native speakers of right branching (RB) languages have far better memory for items presented later. This is the result of the differences in syntax, and how much of a typical sentence a speaker has to hold in mind before they are presented with the main point. LB phrases are those like *a full of people room, a containing private documents briefcase, a born in 2005 Korean boy,* all beginning with details about the subject that lead up to then revealing the subject. RB phrases might include *the man who was sitting at the bus stop,* starting with a subject then expanding into details. The main impact of this study is that it indeed shows that the language that we speak can affect the way that we process, store and retrieve information. While the relationship between language and thought is perhaps still controversial, studies like this one may in the future come to alter how we think about second language acquisition theory.

Affective Factors

The affective domain of language learning involves the emotions and attitudes of the learner(s) towards them self and those around them. The impact of affective factors on the learning process can be a negative or a positive one, depending on the emotion or attitude that the learner maintains regarding the language that they need or may want to learn. The *affective-filter hypothesis* in relation to motivation, self-esteem, and anxiety sees learners with high motivation performing better, those with a good self-image being able to perform better, and learning environments that provide low personal and low classroom anxiety more conducive to language acquisition. Other affective factors include language ego, state anxiety, inhibition and self-esteem, risk taking, attribution theory and self-efficacy, motivation and Ausubel's (1968) list of needs, along with environmental influences.

Language Ego

Those learners who are more comfortable using a second language (taking on the second language identity) are perhaps those without very fixed and inflexible personalities, who are more open to others and are more sensitive, flexible and adaptable, and also more empathic. Learners who hold greater empathy are able to identify more readily with others, and in terms of SLA, this correlates with personality, as the biggest step in taking on another personality when learning a language that involves pronunciation and attempting to sound like a native speaker of a different culture and language. This is an important step, as how we speak and pronounce our native language(s) is an essential feature of self.

The identity that a person develops in reference to the language(s) that they speak is their language ego (Brown, 2014). The term was coined by Guiora, et al. (1972), who sees a new representation of self as necessary during language acquisition, since acquiring a native-like pronunciation is necessary when breaking boundaries of identity related to the L1 (first language), while also recognizing that pronunciation is difficult to lose and hard to acquire. Benveniste (1958) also considers the language ego to involve the learner recognizing that they are a part of the SLA process, as *ego is he who says ego*. Brown also views the language ego as producing an identity that can either inhibit or promote language learning and adjustment to another culture, and the possible feeling that is connected to the target linguistic and cultural environment. The concept of inventing a new self, at times even adopting a new name, can help a learner develop a new sense of self that communicates in a foreign language, and in a way where they can more easily accept their inability to express themselves as much as their normal self, and their normal level of wittiness, irony, and eloquence.

It is not clear if extroversion or introversion assists or hinders the second language acquisition process. It is also apparent that cross-cultural norms vary widely, and what might be considered as introversion in one culture might be considered a state of politeness or respect in another. Extroverts though, are those who need to receive ego enhancement, self-esteem, and a sense of wholeness from others, needing others in order to feel good about themselves. On the other hand, introverts are those that obtain their sense of wholeness and fulfillment from within (Wakamoto, 2009).

State Anxiety

Development of the language ego can also help displace anxiety, as the 'other' persona is the one that is engaging in the new experience and dealing with the anxiety and nervousness involved when in the classroom. As MacIntyre and Gardner (1991) recognize, the language learning classroom is one that can provide students with a stressful and anxiety-provoking experience. This kind of anxiety is labelled *state anxiety*, one that occurs in a particular situation, and it can have a negative experience on the language learning process. Diverse factors can lead to anxiety in learners from social pressure to academically perform (e.g., peer pressure), through to high-stakes testing (e.g., language tests related to permanent residency). However, Bailey (1983) does note that a certain level of anxiety in relation to the completion of tasks, such as those that provide a certain degree of anticipation, curiosity, or concern, can provide a balance that prevents learners from entering a state of being disheartened, or emotionally dull in response to the L2 (second language). Perhaps the most widely used questionnaire for measuring anxiety in the foreign language classroom is the FLCAS – foreign language classroom anxiety scale (Horwitz, et al., 1986). The notion of foreign language anxiety (FLA) is "fundamental to our understanding of how learners actually approach second language learning" (de Dios Martinez Agudo, 2013, p. 832). Anxiety, along with other affective factors like age, falls under the I of the INTAKE acronym provided by Kumaravadivelu (2006):

I – *Individual* (age and anxiety)
N – *Negotiation* (interaction and interpretation)
T – *Tactical* (learning/communication strategies)
A – *Affective* (attitudes and motivation)
K – *Knowledge* (language/metalanguage knowledge)
E – *Environmental* (social/educational context)

This illustrates that anxiety can see attention deficit occur at the level of input. Intake is then affected by a variety of internal and external factors (ibid), with emotion- and task-related cognition coming to interfere with the storage and retrieval of previously learned information, which in turn comes to affect output (Tobias, 1986).

Inhibition and Self-Esteem

Inhibition and self-esteem are linked (i.e., the weaker the learner's self-esteem, the stronger the learner's inhibition). Those learners who possess a thick perfectionist boundary will find language learning more difficult than those learners with a thin boundary who favor attitudes of openness and possess high tolerance to ambiguity. Language learning by its nature will see any learner make mistakes, and this can lead to vulnerability and self-exposure of the learner (Brown, 2014). Depending on teacher attitude, and how the teacher deals with those mistakes in the classroom may see the learner develop feelings of inadequacy and deficiency. This in turn impacts upon the learner's self-esteem, and their overall evaluation or appraisal of self-worth. Self-esteem is reflected in behavior, leading learners to be assertive or shy, and confident or cautious learners. Of note also, those students who feel good about themselves are the ones who are more likely to succeed (Holly, 1987). As teachers, we need to remember that we can influence both the performance of our learners and their wellbeing, with good teachers succeeding because they provide optimal attention to both linguistic goals of the student as well as their person (Brown, 2014).

The self-confidence that the learner develops is that of the trust they have in their own abilities, qualities, and judgments. It also considers personal attributes including those revolving around emotional maturity and the ability to handle criticism, as well as those of pride, independence, trust, affection, enthusiasm, optimism, and assertiveness. In terms of SLA, it relates to the confidence that the learner maintains toward their capability of completing tasks (Brown, 2014). It is strongly linked to motivation, and this sees more capable students profiting from even a minor correction, while those learners who are struggling or are lacking in self-confidence might better perform with only error corrections for major issues. Those more self-confident students tend to be more motivated, and are then able to apply better or newer strategies to learning over others (Oxford & Nyikos, 1989). Oxford (1990) would then develop the *strategy inventory for language learning* (SILL) as a response to the belief that a successful language learner will tend to use good strategies for learning over a less successful learner. This involved direct and indirect strategies in the following ways.

Direct Strategies
- *Memory* (how a learner remembers and retains knowledge)
- *Cognitive* (how a learner thinks about their learning)
- *Compensation* (how learners make up for limited language ability when engaging in communication)

Indirect Strategies
- *Metacognitive* (how learners manage their learning)
- *Affective* (how learners adjust their affective status throughout the learning process)
- *Social* (how learners learn language via social interaction)

Linked to self-confidence, and motivation is the concept of risk-taking.

Risk Taking

Risk taking involves the level of eagerness that a learner holds when trying out the use of new information (lexical terms, grammar, and so on) regardless of embarrassment. These risks, or intelligent guesses, are a crucial and interactive process of learning a language. The downside from engaging in risk taking does of course include being laughed at, or perhaps not being understood at all. The key with learning from risk taking comes from the learner being able to correct any failure that they encounter. This only works in situations where the teacher responds with feedback, or native speakers in the real world provide actual feedback to their interlocutor (although many native-speakers in the real world may rarely do so). In other words, risk taking is most beneficial to students in the SLA process when it is coupled with a learning experience.

Attribution Theory and Self-Efficacy

This theory focuses on how people come to explain their own failures and successes. These explanations align to sets of combinable characteristics:
- *Internal/external*, which are those originating within us or from the environment
- *Stable/unstable*, which are those that will ensure the same outcomes or different ones in the future
- *Controllable/uncontrollable*, which are those we can alter and those that we may not easily be able to alter

Weiner (1980, 1992) sees learners attribute success to their ability, their effort, the perceived task difficulty, or to luck. These factors align to the sets of combinable characteristics above in the following manner:
- *Ability* is an internal and stable factor, which the learner cannot exercise much direct control over
- *Task difficulty* is an external but stable factor that is largely beyond the scope of learner control
- *Effort* is an internal and unstable factor that the learner may exercise a great deal of control over
- *Luck* is an external and unstable factor that the learner is able to exercise very little control over

These factors are outlined in figure 1.3 in terms of a locus of control and stability. They also tie to self-efficacy, as learners' current self-perceptions can be seen to influence the ways in which they interpret their success or failures. It also influences which behaviors that the learner will continue, and as such, the teacher should encourage or motivate.

Locus of Control

	Internal	External
Stable	Ability	Task difficulty
Unstable	Effort	Luck

Locus of Stability

Figure 1.3 Locus of Control and Stability

Motivation

Motivation is a complex psychological construct, and it often emerges as one of the most determinant factors in successful foreign language acquisition (Lagabastar, 2009). The three major schools of thought concerning motivation are that of behaviorist, cognitive, and constructivist (see Table 1.2).

	Perspectives		
	Behaviorist	**Cognitivist**	**Constructivist**
Attributes	External, with individual forces in control	Internal, with individual forces in control	Internal, with interactive forces in control
	- Anticipation of reward - Desire for positive reinforcement	- Needs driven - Effort based	- Social - Community - Security

Table 1.2 Perspectives and Attributes of Motivation

The behavioral perspective sees motivation as anticipation of reward. In other words, positive reinforcement drives future behavior or the development of learned behavior (e.g., Pavlov's dog, Skinner's box).

The cognitive perspective sees motivation in terms of how one views oneself and the environment. That is to say, an individual's choices drive their learning behavior. This might involve a learner approaching or avoiding certain types of tasks, and the amount of effort that the learner is willing to put into one type of task over another. These decisions have been interpreted by some cognitive psychologists as those compelling forces that drive behavior. Those of Ausubel's (1968) list of needs is a good example.

- *Exploration:* The need to see what is on the other side of the mountain
- *Manipulation:* The need to cause a change in the environment or a person
- *Activity:* The need to move or exercise (physically and mentally)
- *Stimulation:* The need to receive stimulus from the environment or people, ideas, or feelings
- *Knowledge:* The need to solve problems, resolve contradictions, and to learn
- *Ego enhancement:* The need to be accepted and approved of by other individuals

The *constructivist perspective* views learners as responsible for the "... active creation and modification of knowledge" as they "strive to make sense of the world" using their background knowledge and previous experience (Palmer 2005, p. 1854); therefore, a constructivist learning environment "requires effort on the part of the learner" (Palmer, 2005, p. 1855), with motivation a key factor as the learner will only put effort into learning if they are motivated in some manner to do so.

Motivation can also be broken down into two main types: intrinsic or extrinsic. These can then be further broken down into various kinds of motivational drivers (see Table 1.3), and teachers are able to use these with their learners.

Intrinsic motivation is simply defined as all of the things that motivate a person which come from internal reward. This kind of motivation can be promoted in the classroom when the goals and rewards of the learning are meaningful, important, assist in obtaining a valued accomplishment, assist in integrating the learner in the world with others, and involve the promotion of self-awareness.

Extrinsic motivation is simply defined as all of the things that motivate a person which stem from an external reward. This kind of motivation can be promoted in the classroom by providing students with prizes, grades, and even positive feedback.

Motivational Drivers	
Extrinsic	**Intrinsic**
Incentive. This provides motivation by promising a specific reward (e.g., a promotion is desired due to receiving higher salary, not because of a want for more responsibility).	*Competence and learning motivation.* This sees people motivated more by the process itself, over the reward (e.g., the act of learning, being able to perform better at a task by engaging with it).
Fear. This is a negative motivator put in place alongside punishment to prevent certain behavior.	*Attitude motivation.* This motivation stems from the desire to positively change how you and others think and/or feel.
Power. People are motivated by control over their own lives or those of others (e.g., the desire to make our own choices).	*Achievement motivation.* This is based on the desire to pursue or achieve a goal in and of itself, not because of any reward attached to it.
Affiliation (social motivation). People are motivated if they feel that they belong and are accepted.	*Creative motivation.* This is based on a desire to express yourself.
	Physiological motivation. This is driven by physiological feelings that are often viewed as primal and unable to be ignored.

Table 1.3 Extrinsic and Intrinsic Motivational Drivers

Environmental Influences (Social and Educational Contexts)
The environmental factors that influence additional language acquisition and teaching are wide and varied, and they include global, national, social, cultural, political, economic, educational, and family contexts. How these overlap in second language contexts is complex, and many have not been fully explored. Factors that have been examined more widely include those of the social and educational contexts for the learner.

The social level may or may not provide learners with the opportunity to engage in L2 communication, not only with each other but with native speakers of the language. The environment in which the learner resides will provide varying degrees of language contact, placing the learner in positions that allow for practice or dismissal of their language use, and in turn influencing their L2 development (Wong-Filmore, 1989).

Educational contexts can also play an affective influence on not only acquisition of the language itself but what kind of language a learner is being taught. This may be guided from the institutional side by aspects of language policy and language planning. It is also, crucially, one of the main avenues for a learner to gain exposure to any L2, but it also comes with exposure to other learners, all of whom may be studying for different reasons. The study cohort may come from a wide variety of socio-economic, political, and educational backgrounds, all of which may impact each learner differently (e.g., one learner may be isolated as they are the only one with that particular ethnic background, or they may be left out from class get togethers due to being unable to afford the dinners and coffees that these may entail).

Myths and Misconceptions
A variety of myths and misconceptions surround the learning of languages (McLaughlin, 1992; Brown and Larson-Hall, 2012). People are sometimes called smart if they possess additional language skills, children are viewed as being able to acquire additional languages better than adults, and immersing in the culture and country of the language is seen to be the best way to improve a language. Some of these myths arise from misconceptions; others from the fact that learning a language takes longer, and is a much harder and more complex process than what many people believe.

Myth 1: Children Acquire Languages Better Than Adults

For a long time, it was believed that the best and only way to learn a language and to obtain native-like proficiency is to do so when very young. However, we now know that adults can learn a language just as well as a child can, and that even accent removal is a possibility. Understandably though, as we age we take on different responsibilities. We are no longer the *tabula rasa*, blank slate, as Locke (1690) proposes, where at birth we are considered to be without built-in mental content, and that all knowledge and ability comes from our individual experiences and perceptions. This is in contrast to epistemological proponents who argue that the mind at birth does possess innate abilities that allows for the acquisition of skills like language. Adults, however, and perhaps those who are parents working two jobs and attending a language class an hour or two a week, will see a different rate of acquisition over a child who is supported and regularly tended to, and who is receiving constant linguistic input from their mother, grandmother, father, and other caregivers. There may also be different levels of plasticity between young learners and adult learners as well as learned versus immersive contexts. Keep in mind that some learners will flourish in one context but others will not be able to learn as effectively when in the same context, and this may be due to their preferred means of learning or working with information. Further, the language that children are expected to be fluent in, and the ways in which they use language are vastly different to that of the expectations of language use that is placed upon an adult.

Aspects of this myth also emerged from Lenneberg (1967) who suggested that an initial language must be learned prior to puberty (around 12 years old) as neurological changes make it impossible to fully learn a language. Evidence for this came from feral children (raised by animals) and from those children who were abandoned, abused, neglected, and/or socially isolated, both groups in particular largely void of human linguistic contact. Some notable cases include Genie who, from the age of 20 months, was strapped and harnessed in confinement before being rescued at age 13 in California in 1970; Isabelle who was illegitimately born in 1932, was raised in silence by an uneducated, deaf, and mute mother until she was rescued at age 6½; Victor of Aveyron in France (*the wild boy*) who was rescued at the approximate age of 12 after he spent an unknown time in the wild, and living from approximately

1788-1828; Prava (the Russian *bird-boy*) who was rescued at age 7 in 2008 after never being spoken to, being surrounded by birds in cages, and raised as a pet bird; Arthur Zverev (*wolf boy*) who was rescued at aged 4 in 2006 after being raised by a pack of 10 wolves; John Ssebunya (*Ugandan Monkey-boy*) who at age 2 or 3 in 1988 spent 3 years in the wild after fleeing to the jungle after his father murdered his mother); the *Gazelle boy* in Spain who was abandoned at 7 or 8 months in 1966, and despite an attempt to capture him, he was never removed from his wild companions; and, Rochom P'ngieng (*the Cambodian jungle girl*) who had spent 19 years in the wild when she was found at the age of 27 in 2007). Genie, in particular, did not acquire language during childhood and grew up almost always bound in place, isolated, and without language contact. Although she was rescued and taken into state care at the age of 13, and did develop nonverbal communication and social skills, she was never able to fully acquire a first language and lacked a true grammar (Curtiss, et al., 2015). Her story, and others like hers, do seem to grant credibility to the critical period hypothesis (CPH), where the time to acquire a first language is between the ages of 2 to puberty, after which the ability is severely hampered and becomes effortful and difficult. The stories also add credence to language development requiring language input, but it may also possibly require human interaction and nurturing combined with the development of other cognitive abilities, a healthy diet, and other factors that these children lacked during their time in the wild, with animals, or in confinement.

Myth 2: You Are Unable to Lose Your Accent After Becoming an Adult

This myth also relates to the CPH, where it is considered that after passing puberty you will carry your native accent for life. By the time that we are aged around 5 or 6, we have acquired most foundational language along with its pronunciation. If you are learning a language twenty or forty years after this, it is going to take time for the mouth, tongue, lips, and ear to adjust to mimicking the sounds and rhythms of a native speaker. Further, when we learn our native language(s), the neurology for these languages are all formed in an interconnected way in the same area of the brain. However, when we acquire languages later in life, they are formed in an adjacent area in our brain. Yet, accent training is possible in a new language, and an accent can be 'lost' to varying degrees. It can be lost entirely allowing you to sound like a native speaker of that language, it can be neutral, or you can retain varying degrees of your native language accent when speaking another language. The secret is practice, mimicry, and in developing the neurological pathways. Some people rely on headphones to help vibrate the auditory nerve as an additional stimulus in this training, others may rely on videos of lip and mouth movements, and there are those that record their own voice and play it back alongside that of a native speaker.

Myth 3: You Can Acquire a Language Just by Listening or Reading

Although input is important, it must also be combined with output and interaction during the language learning process. Students need to do more than practice language, they need to notice new language and how they can use the language that they possess. There is always a gap between what is taught in class and what you as a learner will retain, and the teaching of chunks instead of isolated terms can help you and your learners in retaining the language that they learn, especially when combined with recasting and prompts during correction. Finally, the biggest influence on the learning of a second language is learner independent variables. These include all of the things that make that learner's situation unique, for example: their learning style, personality, motivation levels, socio-economic status, and the time that they have to devote exclusively to study.

Myth 4: I Am Too Old to Learn a New Language
You 'Can't Teach an Old Dog New Tricks'

We now know that our brains are plastic throughout our lives, changing and forming new neurons and connections when undertaking learning. Learning a language when older is not impossible, but it is different, and not acquired in the same manner as when we are younger. There is a need to consider a variety of factors including:

Patience. Learning as an adult is a slower process as there are more demands on our brain and bodies.

Scaffolding. Use a framework for language content to build upon your existing knowledge, and work towards fluency one step at a time. Step back and review topics that are difficult and those that you know require more practice.

Background knowledge. Rely on past experience, memories, and your own knowledge to support the language learning endeavor.

Learning style. As you have learned how to learn, apply those strategies to learning a language and use the techniques that you favor and have found to work. Relating to this point, if you are failing at learning the language, you may be taking the wrong approach.

Remember it takes hours and hours to master a task, and years to become an expert.

Myth 5: Immersion is Key to Fluency

Learning a language in the country of those that speak it can provide an immersive environment that perhaps forces the learner into constant use and exposure to the target language. The notion behind the effectiveness of such a technique is greater time on task. That is to say, the more a learner hears and speaks the language, the faster it will develop. This is not necessarily the case, and it relies on the kind of language that the learner is exposed to, and the chances that they have to effectively engage with speakers of that language. There may be no pressure for you to improve past a certain proficiency in an immersive environment. Native speakers may also accept your limited communicative ability, excusing any mispronunciations and grammatical errors. Alternatively, when interacting in various offices and stores in public, you may simply be grunted at, or native speakers will point to things and communicate non-verbally with those they see as foreigners, and simply be unwilling to engage in verbal communication at all. Further, in an immersive environment, you may only learn and continue to use what you require in order to function, the rest will rely upon your motivation and ability to learn.

Stages of Language Acquisition

The stages of language acquisition all follow a certain generally predictable sequence. This holds true for learners of a second language, for those learning their native language, for those learning sign languages, and for artificial intelligence (AI) when it attempts to acquire and use a language for communication with humans or other AIs. The steps involved in each of these cases are discussed in this section of the chapter.

Second Language Acquisition (SLA)

As we learn additional languages we may go through five stages:

The silent stage, also known as the receptive stage or pre-production period, is where many learners may not produce the target language and rely on the use of non-verbal communication (e.g., pointing, nodding). The focus at this stage is on building the confidence that it takes to speak, and on focusing on acquiring basic vocabulary skills. There is no language fluency at this level.

The early production stage is when learner confidence begins to grow and vocabulary increases, but learners may still not be comfortable with the language enough to produce more than one- or two-word responses or short phrases using a range of around 1,000 words.

The speech emergence stage is when real communication begins to emerge, and where the learner is using sentences and phrases of greater complexity. Although students will be making grammatical errors, their greater comprehension ability will also see an increase in reading and writing skills in the second language.

Intermediate fluency is where learners begin thinking in the second language, with increasing levels of comprehension and fluency emerging as a result.

Advanced fluency is the full mastery of the language, and it can take between two and ten years to reach this stage, although there is no time limit for learning. Individuals will move at their own pace as a result of socialization, and particularly for adults, it depends on the environments in which they live and work and the time and dedication that they are able to put into the second language learning, which in turn present ongoing opportunities to engage in the language to keep it useful, relevant, and current.

It is important to remember that these stages are representative of the general way in which second language acquisition may develop in a learner. There is no set time limit for a learner to stay at each stage, and learners may remain in the first stage for years.

Initial Language Acquisition (ILA)

At this juncture, it may be important to state that, in comparison to the stages of SLA, there are six recognizable stages for first or initial language acquisition (Hutauruk, 2015). A simple breakdown of these are:

Pre-talking stage/cooing (0-6 months). Producing vowel-like sounds in response to human sounds, also chuckling sounds.
Babbling stage (6-8 months). Producing consonant-vowel combinations.
Holophrastic stage (9-18 months). Single word use, produced as a sentence.
Two-word stage (18-24 months). Mini-sentence use with simple syntactic and semantic relations.
Telegraphic stage (24-30 months). Sentence-like utterances with hierarchical constituent structures similar to that of adult grammar.
Multiword stage (30+ months). Utterances have communicative intent, no babbling, understanding of language heard and directed toward them.

Sign Language Acquisition

The acquisition of sign language is also worth a brief mention, as it may be perceived to be acquired differently than that of a first language in babies and children. However, spoken languages while relying on auditory/oral skills initially are different to sign language in that they rely upon visual/manual abilities, but the way that each is acquired is essentially similar. In other words, sign language development mimics that of first language acquisition in babies. For example, from the age of six to ten months, children who are learning to sign begin to produce syllabic babbling after moving from a prelinguistic gesturing phase (Bohren, 2018). This activity is differentiated from other hand activities as it possesses a restricted set of phonetic units, syllabic organization, and it is used without reference or meaning.

Artificial Intelligence and Language Acquisition

In the current era, it would also be amiss not to make brief mention of artificial intelligence (AI) systems and their language learning abilities. AI systems are able to both use any natural language provided to them for communication, as well as create their own languages to communicate with each other. Like humans, when machine translation occurs, an AI generates an interlingua language, and this has been evidenced by Google Translate (Johnson, et al., 2017). Novel language creation constantly occurs between AI systems, as noted by Facebook researchers (Reynolds, 2017) who found that two of their chatbots developed their own language to communicate. The language was based on English but not understandable by English speakers, and it allowed the chatbots to communicate at a faster pace, and to perform their tasks better than when relying upon a natural language.

SLA Frameworks
Concepts, Models, Theories, and Hypotheses

All of the concepts, models, theories, and hypotheses surrounding second language acquisition aim to shed light on how those who know one language are able to become proficient in another. Research on SLA covers a number of diverse fields including those of education, linguistics, sociolinguistics, psychology, cognitive science, and the neurosciences. This illustrates the importance and place of interdisciplinary research approaches to developing an understanding of SLA.

Two seminal papers stand out as marking the emergence of the interdisciplinary field of SLA. These articles revolve around the significance of learners' errors (Corder, 1967), and the development of an interlanguage (Selinker, 1972). In this era, focus on SLA research examined aspects of error analysis, transitional stages, morpheme studies, and naturalistic studies of learning. The following decade then gave rise to notions of input hypothesis (*i+1*; Krashen, 1977), learner competence (White, 1987), speech processing models and lexical functional grammar (LFG; Pienemann, 1998), and connectionism (Smolensky, 1999). Building upon this led to the emergence of the interaction hypothesis (Long, 1996), the output hypothesis (Swain & Lapkin, 1995), and the noticing hypothesis (Schmidt, 1990). Research interest surrounded aspects of universal grammar (Chomsky, 2000) or UG, skill acquisition theories (such as that of Lebiere & Anderson, 1993), along with processability and input processing models (both from connectionism). Aspects of sociocultural theory (VanPatten & Benati, 2010), which focuses on the learner's environment, also rose to the fore at this time. Into the 2000s and beyond, the field relies mainly upon linguistic and psychological approaches to examining second language acquisition. Aspects of all of these concepts, theories, models, and hypotheses are presented in this section, along with others, and a number of the important terms and concepts that they raise.

Concepts

Interlanguage

Interlanguage is an idiolect, an idiosyncratic dialect, consisting of rules that form a temporary systematic grammar for the learner. It is based on the language learners' experiences with the L2, and characterized by the preservation of some features from the learners L1 along with their overgeneralizations of aspects of the L2. Interlanguage rules are shaped by L1 transfer, previous learning, strategies of language acquisition, the learner's L2 communication strategies and their overgeneralization of L2 language patterns. It has its basis in the theory that there is a dormant psychological framework in the human brain that is activated when one engages in second language learning using a separate linguistic system, and this is identified by those utterances that the learner produces that is different from those that native speaker might produce when attempting to convey the same meaning. Interlanguage emerges with production (i.e., learner communication) and not practice (i.e., in repetition of oral drills in the classroom). Selinker (1972) is credited with coining the term interlanguage, as well as the term fossilization.

Fossilization/Stabilization

Fossilization is the argument that a learner's interlanguage will progress to a certain point in their additional language learning endeavors and never go beyond it. They will stabilize at a certain level, or with the use of certain terminology and grammatical structural usage. Reasons for this are varied, and include: learners may not need to acquire native-like proficiency; or they have reached a level where their need to correct the form/structure of language use is unnecessary in the contexts in which they use their additional language(s). It may also happen for other reasons, as the Vigil and Oller (1976) affective and cognitive feedback model illustrates. In this traffic signal metaphor-based model, affective feedback is given to terms and language usage in relation to cognitive feedback. Words or meanings that are understood are given a green light by the listener (correct, grammatical, or neither), and those that are not understood are given a red light. In other words, the focus is on communication over the accuracy of form. This may produce in the Korean context *Konglish* terms being frequently used by Korean speakers of English because the terms are green-lighted as understood by native speakers of English and others who visit the country. Of note, Long (2003) disagreed with the term fossilization, preferring stabilization, as this term provides a future window of opportunity for the language to continue developing if the learner requires it at some point in time. It is also important to recognize that, for those learners who have plateaued in their language learning, that they may backslide.

Interference

This term refers to the influence of features from one language onto another. It can be either beneficial (positive) or negative. It can take place at all levels (i.e., in phonology, morphology, syntax, lexicon). Increasingly, the term transfer is being used due to the negative connotations implied by interference.

Contrastive Analysis

Contrastive analysis assumes that learner errors are caused by the difference between the L1 and the L2. Simply put, it is the systematic study of a pair of languages with a view to identifying the structural differences and similarities between them, and it was used during the 1960s and the 1970s as a means of explaining why some aspects of the TL were more difficult to acquire than others. It was believed at the time that, by mapping out all areas of potential difficulty, that it would be possible to design courses to teach language more efficiently, and that this would come to hold a profound impact on the development of SLA curriculum design and language teacher education. It also became one of the theoretical pillars of the audiolingual method.

Method, Approach, and Technique Distinction

It is important when discussing language learning and education, and when reading and writing for academic journals, that scholars are all using their words both carefully and in the same way. One particularly important distinction is that between what constitutes a method, an approach, and a technique. A method is an overall procedural plan designed for the implementation of approaches which are the practices and principles of language teaching (the ways of looking at teaching and learning). Within one approach, there may be any number of methods (ways of teaching something). Techniques are the means of implementation (the activities), and must be consistent with a method and taught in line with the approach applied.

Mistake, Error, and Attempt Differentiation
No matter the level of the student, when thinking about correcting student use of language, it is important to consider the kind of correction appropriate to the mistake, error, or attempt made. In other words, as Harmer (2010) explains, there are distinctions that can be made: mistakes or slips are those things that students can correct themselves once pointed out to them, but errors are not self-correctable and will need an explanation, while attempts occur when students make an effort to say something which they do not yet know how to verbalize correctly. Each will require a different approach to correction.

Memory and SLA
The role of memory in SLA may be significant. Williams (1999) discovered that there is a positive correlation between verbatim memory functioning and the success of grammar learning. This type of memory is for surface form and it is typically detailed, and it suggests that those individuals who possess less short-term memory capacity may see limitations emerge when attempting to cognitively process linguistic knowledge.

Cognitive Semantics
This is part of the cognitive linguistics movement, and it holds language to be part of a more general cognitive ability that is used to describe the world based upon how people conceive of it. The main tenants are:
- Grammar is the conception of the world held by a culture.
- Linguistic knowledge is acquired and contextual.
- Language ability utilizes cognitive resources.

Ambiguity Tolerance-Intolerance
This is a psychological construct that describes the relationship that an individual may have with stimuli or events that are ambiguous. The stimuli will be viewed in either a neutral/open way or as a threat. In other words, if you are willing to tolerate ideas and propositions that are counter to your own, then you would be considered ambiguity-tolerant, and conversely, ambiguity-intolerant if you reject things that are incongruent or contradictory to your existing systems (Brown, 2014).

When learning a language, a great deal of uncertainty may be encountered (e.g., different grammar, cultural systems), and this also goes for when you use that language with native speakers. For example, those native speakers that are ambiguity intolerant may have difficulty understanding those speaking their native language with an accent.

Connectionism and SLA

This is an approach in the field of cognitive science explaining mental phenomena using artificial neural networks (ANN), and it is an attempt to model the cognitive language processing ability of the human brain by using computer architecture that seeks to make associations between the elements of language, based on frequency of co-occurrence in language input (Christiansens & Chater, 2001). This sees input as being the source of both the units of language and the rules of language. It suggests that learners form mental connections between those items that co-occur, and from input, extract rules of language through the cognitive processes that are common to other areas of cognitive skill acquisition.

Mediation, the Zone of Proximal Development (ZPD), and Scaffolding

The mediating role of language, from a sociocultural perspective, views language as means to control and regulate communicative activity (Lantolfe & Thorne, 2007). L2 learners create new ways of meaning in a similar manner to that of children acquiring their L1 by reshaping biological perception into "cultural perceptions and concepts" (p. 203), moving from object- to other- to self-regulation. This relates well to the zone of proximal development (ZPD), a figurative distance between an existing developmental state and the potential development of the learner (Vygotsky, 1978). It represents "the domain of knowledge or skill where the learner is not yet capable of independent functioning, but can achieve the desired outcome given relevant scaffolded help" (Mitchell & Myles, 2004, p. 196). Scaffolding as a process enables the learner to solve tasks or achieve goals beyond an unassisted effort, allowing for the completion of those elements that are within the range of competence (Wood, et al., 1976).

Willingness to Communicate (WTC)

In SLA, willingness to communicate (WTC) is the notion that a language student who is willing to communicate in the target language not only will do so, but will also actively seek out chances to communicate (MacIntyre, et al., 1998). Specific strategies that teachers might use to promote WTC are those that may include:

- fostering interest in foreign affairs and culture,
- reducing student anxiety by building their confidence in TL usage,
- building upon student knowledge,
- having students perform tasks in pairs prior to performing in a large-group type of setting,
- relying upon authentic content in the classroom,
- depending on a wide variety of tasks and activities, and
- relying on activities and tasks of an appropriate level.

Models

Semantic Cognitive Model

Piaget (1923) theorized that language development is a stage secondary to that of cognitive learning and growth. This contribution to the concept of the semantic cognitive view of linguistic development argues that for a language to be truly generative, it must be able to generate meaning as well as structure. That is where meaning in a language is expressed not only in words but also through syntactic relationships among words. Learners must first familiarize themselves with what they see and experience prior to attaching meaning to things. After recognition and association of objects, learners are then able to relate language to experience. In other words, as learners acquire the ability to express themselves, they then begin to use and apply the language that they possess. The semantic cognitive model was extended by Fillmore (1968) with case grammar theory as a substantive modification to transformational grammar (TG) or transformational-generative grammar (TGG). TG is part of a theory of generative grammar, especially of natural languages, where grammar is considered to be a system of rules that generate all of the combinations of words that form grammatical sentences in any given language, and involve the use of defined operations (transformations) to produce novel sentences from existing ones. Case grammar theory stresses the importance of semantic roles in an effort to make explicit the basic-meaning relationships in a sentence. It explains the importance and influence of semantics on the form of language; that is to say, beneath deep structure is a level of universal concepts that determine how nouns and verbs are related to one another, with semantic concepts independent from surface structure. Case grammar, like many theories, has gone through a number of changes since its original introduction.

Models of Communicative Competence

Coined by Hymes (1966), the term communicative competence, or the ability to communicate using a language, requires grammatical knowledge (e.g., syntax, morphology, phonology) as well as social knowledge (e.g., using utterances appropriately). This ethnography of communication, with communicative form and function in integral relation with one another, emerged as a response to the perceived inadequacy of Chomsky's (1965) distinction between (linguistic) competence and performance. Later, Canale and Swain (1980) argued that communicative competence is a global competence that is comprised of four different sub-competencies:

- *Grammatical competence:* the ability to create grammatically correct utterances
- *Sociolinguistic competence:* the ability to produce sociolinguistically appropriate utterances
- *Discourse competence:* the ability to produce coherent and cohesive utterances
- *Strategic competence:* the ability to solve communication problems as they arise

The above competencies are graphically represented in Figure 1.4.

Bachman (1990) also divided communicative or language competence into subcategories: those of organizational competence (grammatical and textual) and pragmatic competence (illocutionary and sociolinguistic). See Figure 1.5.

Celce-Murcia, Dornyei, and Thurell (1995) provided a model that views communicative competence as including linguistic, strategic, sociocultural, discoursal, and actional competence. Today, communicative competence is one of the theories that underlies the communicative approach to language teaching, and it is the goal of many language learners when studying an additional language.

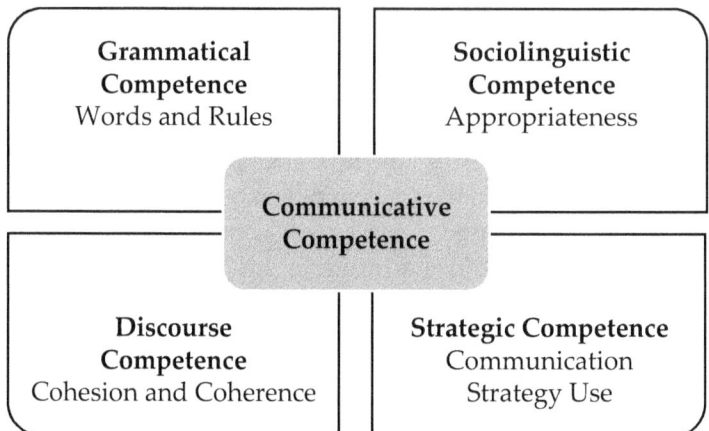

Figure 1.4 Components of Communicative Competence

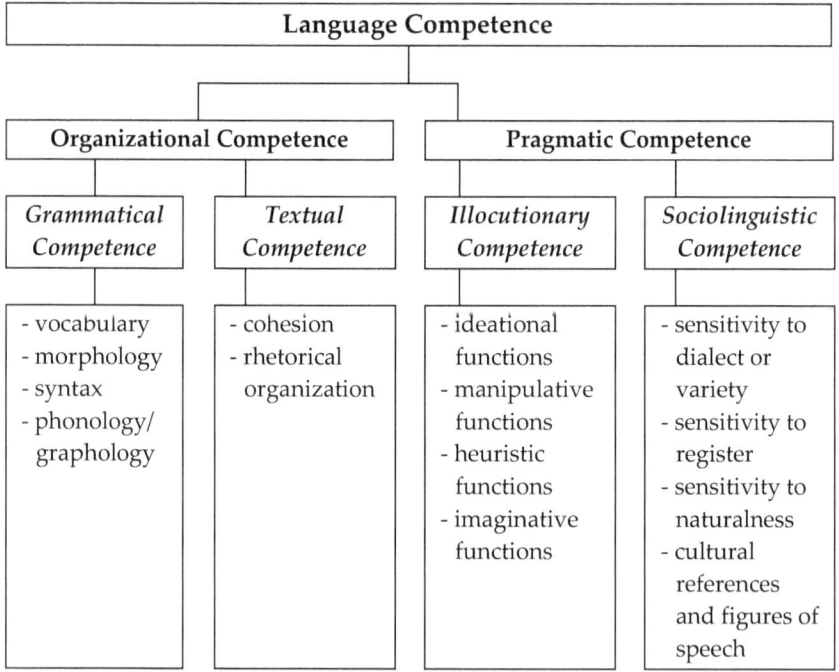

Figure 1.5 Components of Language Competence

Competition Model

This is a psycholinguistic theory of language acquisition and sentence processing (Bates & MacWhinney, 1981), and the model suggests that the meaning of language is interpreted by comparing linguistic 'cues' within a sentence. The cues serve to signal specific functions, with language being learned from a rich linguistic environment and through the competition of basic cognitive mechanisms. It is an emergentist theory, as opposed to an innatist theory or an empiricist theory. It therefore allows language to be acquired over a wide variety of chronological periods, with competitive cognitive processes operating on a phylogentic (evolving), ontogenetic (developmental), and synchronic (time) scale.

Psychological Model

Levelt (1989) provides one of the most influential psycholinguistic models of oral production, and it breaks speech production down into separate cognitive processes: conceptualization, utterance formation, speech articulation, and self-monitoring. The model focuses on speech production in terms of the cognitive steps required to produce a spoken utterance, from intention to articulation.

Attention Processing Model

This model, introduced by McLaughlin, et al. (1983), considers SLA to be a mental process that assumes a hierarchy of complexity of cognitive skills. Involving controlled and automatic processing, structured practice leads to automation and integration of linguistic patterns in the learner. That is where controlled processing relates to the learning of a new skill, where only several elements of that skill can be retained, while automatic processing refers to being able to manage many elements of that skill. Both of these can occur in combination with focal (intentional or explicit) or peripheral (incidental or implicit) attention to task (e.g., focal attention may be on form at times but on meaning at other times). See Table 1.4.

	Focal	Peripheral
Controlled	- Grammar points explained. - Examples of word usage provided. - Prefabricated routines learned. - Copy a model (written or spoken).	- Utilizing simple greetings. - Applying memorized routines in novel situations. - Dialogue memorization. - Undertaking limited conversation.
Automatic	- Monitors output. - Brief attention to form during conversation. - Scanning for keywords. - Editing, writing.	- Open-ended group work participation. - Rapid reading and skimming. - Engaging in freewriting. - Engaging in unrehearsed conversation.

Table 1.4 Attention Processing Model Examples

Classroom Model

This model involves the operationalizing of communication (Lee, 1999); in other words, developing a workable pedagogical activity that is based on real communication. Such tasks would also need to synthesize the many parts of a lesson (e.g., vocabulary, grammar). Such activities also highlight that the way that a task is structured in the classroom can lead to either its success or demise, based on the demands placed on the student when completing it. These demands would include cognitive demands, communicative stress, and linguistic complexity.

- *Cognitive demand.* Familiarity with the topic, memory requirements involved, processing demands of the task, and so on.
- *Communicative stress.* The number of people involved in the task, their relationship to each other, the face threatening nature of the topic or task, and so on.

- *Linguistic complexity.* The vocabulary, grammar, textual/genre conventions, and other aspects that are involved with the task completion.

Declarative/Procedural Model

This model presents the means of understanding how language information may be stored (Ullman, 2001), and it states that declarative knowledge, consisting of arbitrary linguistic information (e.g., irregular verb forms), is stored in declarative memory. This type of memory is explicit, and it involves the conscious and intentional recollection of factual information, previous experience, and concepts. Knowledge regarding the rules of a language (e.g., grammatical word order), considered to be procedural knowledge, is stored in the procedural memory. This is a type of implicit memory or unconscious memory, and it is a long-term memory that aids in the performance of particular types of tasks. So, implicit knowledge is information that one automatically and spontaneously uses, while explicit knowledge includes those things that the learner knows about language (Williams, 2009).

Pyramid Model of Second Language Use

A pyramid model of second language use has been proposed to illustrate the control over communication in the target language that a learner may maintain. The higher the learner climbs up the pyramid, the more control they maintain over communicative acts.

The model consists of six layers and twelve constructs (MacIntyre, et al., 1998). Layers I through III are those that influence SLA at a given time, while those from IV through VI are those that are considered lasting influences. The layers (and constructs) from top to bottom are:
- Layer I: Communication behavior (use)
- Layer II: Behavioral intention (willingness to communicate)
- Layer III: Situated antecedents (desire to communicate with a specific person; state of communicating self-confidence)
- Layer IV: Motivational propensities (interpersonal motivation; intergroup motivation; self-confidence)
- Layer V: Affective-cognitive context (intergroup attitudes; social situation; competence)
- Layer VI: Social and individual context (intergroup climate; personality)

Theories

Nativist Theory and Universal Grammar

The nativist theory suggests that humans are born with genes that allow for language learning to occur, and possess a theoretical component of the brain known as the language acquisition device (LAD). This theory also suggests that there is a universal grammar (UG) that is shared across every language in the world (Chomsky, 1975). UG explains why languages all have a finite amount of rules, but offer ways to structure thought in a manner that allows for the development of an infinite number of novel phrases.

Chomsky has defined UG as "the system of principles, conditions, and rules that are elements or properties of all human languages" (Chomsky, 1975, p.29). In generative linguistic terms, the principles and parameters framework sees the syntax of natural language described in accordance with particular general principles (i.e., abstract rules of grammar) and specific parameters (i.e., markers, switches) that are either turned on or off. In other words, a native speaker of a language knows a set of principles that can be applied to all languages, as well as parameters that can vary from one language to another. From this perspective, the learning of a second language relies on setting principles and parameters for the learner. For example, a parameter can have two values, either on (positive) or off (negative), and the learner needs to set the parameter correctly for the languages they wish to speak. It is considered innate, and therefore does not require specific learning but only exposure to a language. Important to note here is that Chomsky has since come to consider that the domain-specific faculty of language (FLN) comprises of only the property of recursion, and no longer argues for a rich set of innate features and categories (Hauser, Chomsky, & Fitch, 2002).

Processability Theory (PT)

This theory posits that language learners are able to restructure their interlanguage knowledge to be in greater conformity to the language they are learning. That is to say, learners are able to restructure their use of L2, based only on what they can process, at any given stage of their development (Pienemann, 1998). Clahsen (1984) suggested that certain processing principles determine the order. For example, learners follow a series of stages in order to acquire the correct morphological and syntactic forms involved when making English questions by transforming declarative sentences. As a cognitive approach to SLA, it seeks to explain learner variation as well as learner developmental schedules. Essentially, it is based on Levelt's (1989) approach to language generation and is operationalized using lexical-functional grammar (Bresnan, 2001) or LFG. Applying LFG formalisms in EFL/ESL results in an assortment of predictions for developmental schedules in syntax and morphology. Processability Theory (PT) also includes other theoretical models for L1 transfer, linguistic typology, and inter-learner variation, and, coming with detailed morphological tools, it has been applied to linguistic profiling and the additional language classroom.

Automaticity: The Adaptive Control of Thought – Skills-Based Theory

This involves the process of performing a skill without conscious control. The notion of automaticity in additional language learning is that learners acquire their proficiency in language in the same manner as people acquire other complex cognitive skills. That is, resulting from a gradated process of proceduralization, it is a cognitive psychological model of skill acquisition that sees individuals use procedures to apply declarative knowledge about a subject so that they can solve problems (Anderson, 1992). Such procedures, upon repetition, develop into production rules that learners can use to solve problems without accessing long-term declarative memory with accuracy, performance, and speed increasing as learners implement the production rules. In other words, the theory suggests that declarative knowledge can be transformed into procedural knowledge, with knowledge gained through language learning used to initiate speech production. This involves moving through three stages during SLA: declarative to procedural and then to autonomous. This aligns with the three stages of development for skills of any kind: cognitive, associative, and autonomous (Fitts & Posner, 1967).

Semantic Theory

This theory posits that meaning is at the core of a language, and not its sounds or structure. Different types of meaning are seen to contribute to, and result in, integrated second language possession. The different meanings include grammatical, lexical, pragmatic, and semantic.

- *Grammatical:* Sentence meaning determiners (for example, *-ed* used to indicate past simple)
- *Lexical:* Meaning stored in mental lexicon
- *Pragmatic:* Meaning that depends on situational context
- *Semantic:* Word meaning

Sociocultural Theory (Interactionist Approach)

Also known as the interactionist approach, sociocultural theory, coined by Wertsch (1985), derives from the work of Vygotsky and considers the cultural, historical, political, and social contexts in which second language acquisition occurs, and how learners are able to negotiate or resist the diverse options that life presents. In this regard, the distinction between this theory and others is that it argues that SLA is not a universal process. Learners are viewed as active participants who interact with others and the culture of the environment in which they live and learn. To this end, Larsen-Freeman (2011) sees an interplay between four important concepts in language learning and education: the teacher, the learner, the language/culture, and the context. Language learning is therefore dependent upon and emerges from social interaction, and develops out of the desire and need to communicate.

Complex Dynamic Systems Theory (CDST)

This is both a perspective and an approach to the study of SLA. As a term, de Bot (2017) suggests that Complex Dynamic Systems Theory refers to both complexity theory and dynamic systems theory. The theory reflects the current state of thought regarding SLA as a complex dynamic system, where SLA is viewed developmentally, by Larson-Freeman (1997), involving processes of attrition and acquisition. Her argument is that language should be viewed as a system that is adaptive, chaotic, complex, dynamic, feedback sensitive, nonlinear, sensitive to initial conditions, open, self-organizing, and unpredictable.

Hypotheses

Critical Period Hypothesis (CPH)

The notion of a critical period for initial language acquisition to occur, between the ages of 2 and prior to puberty (approximately 12 or 13 years of age), was popularized by Lenneberg (1967), but first put forth by

Penfield and Roberts (1959). This hypothesis sees adequate stimuli being a requirement for language development, as long as it is presented at the right stage of life. If this input is neglected, then the full command of language, especially grammatical systems, will never be achieved. For second language learning, research suggests that how a learner is exposed to an additional language might contribute to how their second language acquisition develops, with second language learning affected by the learners maturational state (Newport, 1990).

Markedness Differential Hypothesis

This states that areas of difficulty that a learner will have can be predicated. These predictions are based upon a systematic comparison of the grammars of the native language (NL) and the target language (TL), and the markedness relations stated in universal grammar.

Emergentism, the Amelioration Hypothesis, and the Mapping Assumption

The emergent nature of language is viewed in opposition to that of the behavioral models. It takes the view that "… not only is there no UG, there is no specialized acquisition device" (p. 116). Language is considered to be an ability that "emerges from a relatively simple developmental process being exposed to a massive and complex environment" (Ellis, 2003, p. 81), and not an isolated ability which is governed by innate and predisposed rules. O'Grady (2012) has come to denote language acquisition as "an accidental side-effect of attempts to improve the ability of a grammatically naïve processor to deal with input" (the Amelioration hypothesis), with the "mapping assumption" seeing language acquisition yielding "… a way to create 'mappings' between form and meaning" (p. 117).

Input Hypothesis (aka Monitor Model)

This hypothesis was put forward by Krashen (1977). It states that learners progress in their language acquisition endeavors when provided with comprehensible input that is slightly more advanced than their current level. This is *i+1*, where the *i* refers to the learner's interlanguage and the *+1* is the next stage of language acquisition. A great deal of research has taken place on input enhancement methods for learners (e.g., bold facing key vocabulary, marginal glosses in reading texts). The hypothesis has been criticized, due to there being no clear definition of *i+1*, and because other factors may inhibit input turning into intake (e.g., learner motivation, presentation of content), that can be then used to generate output.

As an unconscious process of picking up language, Krashen views input as essential to language acquisition in line with connectionism, seeing monitoring as the means by which the learner uses their innate language processing device to regulate their own L2 production, checking for accuracy and adjusting language production as required. Other components of the monitor model (e.g., Bialystok & Smith, 1985) argue that interlanguage should include distinctions between the learner's knowledge of L2 grammar as 'representation' and the ability to use that knowledge to analyze the target language (TL) as 'control'. The argument here is that non-native speakers of a language possess higher representation over their native-speaking counterparts, with language acquisition framed in terms of the interaction between 'analysis' (understanding rules of the TL) and 'control', which in turn can lead to acquisition and greater control over production (Bialystok, 1994).

In addition to the input hypothesis, the learning theory developed by Krashen that would come to underpin the natural approach includes: the acquisition/learning hypothesis, the monitor hypothesis, the natural order hypothesis, and the affective filter hypothesis.

Acquisition/Learning Hypothesis

This involves a distinction between learning and acquisition. Learning refers to the formal knowledge of language, and the process in which conscious rules are formed along with the ability to verbalize them. Formal teaching is necessary for learning to occur, with directed error correction assisting in the formation of rule learning. Alternatively, acquisition refers to the development of competency in the use of a language for real communication. It is seen as paralleling natural language development as it is an unconscious process that leads to proficiency resulting from the continued use of language for meaningful communication.

Monitor Hypothesis

This is the process of using learned knowledge to help correct language production during communication. Three conditions limit the successful use of the monitor: a sufficient amount of time is required before a learner is able to choose and apply a rule as necessary; focus on form and the correctness of the output; and knowledge of rules as a prerequisite for the use of the monitor.

Natural Order Hypothesis

This sees grammatical structures acquired in a predictable order no matter the language. Certain morphemes and grammatical structures are seen to be acquired before others, with learner errors being a result of the natural developmental process.

Affective Filter Hypothesis

This relates to the emotional state or attitude of the learner that can make learning easier, impede it, or block it entirely. Three kinds of attitudinal, or affective, variables are: motivation, seeing learners with high motivation performing better; self-confidence, those with a good self-image are able to perform better; and anxiety, low personal and low classroom anxiety are more conducive to language acquisition. In other words, those with a low affective filter tend to seek out and receive more input, are more receptive to the input they receive, and are able to interact with confidence. Those with a high affective filter, being anxious, fearful or embarrassed to speak, retard or prevent acquisition taking place. Those who have higher levels of empathy may be able to more readily identify with others and accept input as intake. Empathy would also allow them to more readily identify with others.

Noticing Hypothesis

This hypothesis sees the place of attention as key to the development of a second language (Schmidt, 1990) where the learner must notice the ways in which their interlanguage structures differ from target language norms. This *noticing of the gap* allows the learner to internally process language and to restructure their internal representation of L2 rules in order to bring production closer to that of TL native speakers. The theory is consistent with process of rule formation found in connectionism and emergentism.

Interaction Hypothesis

The hypothesis is that the use of the target language in interaction facilitates language acquisition (Long, 1996). In the interaction hypothesis, as with the input hypothesis, comprehensible input is viewed as essential for language learning. In this hypothesis, comprehensible input effectiveness is enhanced when the learner is required to undergo the negotiation of meaning. An example of this is when speakers go through turn-taking to reach an understanding of each other (e.g., asking for clarification, rephrasing, or confirming what is thought to have been understood). For example, when the learner asks or states something, a native speaker of the language then models the correct language form if the learner did not use it. This provides the learner with feedback on their language production, along with provision of grammar that they have not as yet mastered. Such interactions help to focus learner attention on the difference between their current knowledge of the target language and what they see and hear in use, particularly if they clarify those things that they do not understand, and take the time to process the input that they receive.

Output Hypothesis

In this hypothesis, meaningful output is seen to be just as necessary as meaningful input in the language learning process (Swain & Lapkin, 1995). The view today sees meaningful output as being important because output of language can lead to more effective processing of received input as a result. It sees the learner using output as a means of trying out the language to test various hypothesis, and while they do this, they notice erroneous attempts at conveying meaning, with speech and writing offering a means for the learner to reflect upon the language that they are learning while interacting with others.

SLA Influences
Language, Language Planning and Policy, Culture and Cultural Parameters, Identity, and Intercultural Competence

This section examines those aspects of second language acquisition that have come to influence the language that we teach when we teach English to speakers of other languages (TESOL), including those pertaining to language planning and policy. Cultural aspects from linguistic imperialism through to the World Englishes paradigm and the native- versus non-native teacher debate are also highlighted, as are a range of cultural parameters that serve to illustrate how difficult culture can be to define. These parameters also serve to highlight that each individual from a culture should be considered to be unique rather than a stereotype. The place of identity in language learning and the roles of socio(cultural)linguistics and linguistic anthropology in terms of SLA are then discussed prior to aspects of linguistic relativism. With language and thought operating together in many significant ways, these topics are important to consider, as the languages that we speak and learn can modify our positions, attitudes and beliefs, and shape constantly shifting identities (Lopez-Deflory & Juan-Garau, 2017). The section then comes to a close by discussing the importance of intercultural competence when acquiring and teaching a second language, taking the stance of developing second language acquisition in order to become an intercultural speaker.

Language

Today, when teaching English to speakers of other languages, an important question to ask is: What language are we teaching when we TESOL (teach English to speakers of other languages)? The answer to this question is not so straightforward, but we might consider it to be the teaching of English as an international language (EIL). McKay (2018) defines this term as one that ranges from being a way of using language (referring to the use of English by those who speak it as a second/foreign language) to a type of language (the many varieties of English that are spoken across the globe). Discussing the global spread of English in terms of users sees three distinct groups emerge, as Jenkins (2015) highlights:

1. Native language (ENL) users, i.e., those who speak the primary language of the majority population of a nation such as Australia, the United Kingdom, and the United States of America.
2. Second language users, i.e., those who speak English as an additional language for *intra*national as well as *inter*national communication in those communities that are multilingual (e.g.,

India, Nigeria, Singapore), with most of these languages resulting from imperial expansion.
3. Foreign language users, i.e., those who speak English almost exclusively for international communication such as in Korea.

The use of English by these user groups parallels the different varieties of English that have emerged, and have recently been classified as World English, World Englishes, and Global Englishes. Global Englishes refers to the spread of English due to globalization, resulting from the use of World English, which refers to the use of the language as a lingua franca in different spheres of activity (e.g., busines, diplomacy, trade), with World Englishes relating to the different varieties of English and those English-based creoles that have developed in different regions of the world.

Pidgins, Creoles, and Lingua Francas

When people of two or more language groups need to communicate, a pidgin language might develop, which is a grammatically simplified mode of communicating using elements of both languages. A pidgin is not a language that is native to an area or group; rather, it is a language with no native speech community (defined as a group of people who share a common language or dialect). It is a language of necessity that allows speakers of different languages to communicate. The need for a pidgin language is most often associated with trade, such as that which occurred with the development of Chinese Pidgin English when the British began to trade with China during the eighteenth century. With this in mind, pidgins are usually used in a limited fashion, and after their use is served, they often die out. However, if they are used for long enough, they can develop into very rich and structurally complex languages. If a pidgin language becomes nativized (spoken as an L1), then it is known as a creole. A creole, then, is a stabilized natural language emerging from a pidgin. For example, the Gullah language, which is spoken on the South Carolina coast, is a creole derived from the influence of Central and West African languages on English during the transatlantic slave trade, and Tok Pisin (literally, 'bird talk'), the official language of Papua New Guinea and the most widely used in the country, is one which emerged from the extensive multilingualism of the copra and sugarcane plantations to which labor was imported from China, Malaysia, and Melanesia.

European colonization and expansion efforts in more recent history have seen languages such as English, French, Portuguese, Spanish, and Russian established as lingua francas in the colonies or territories that were taken over. A lingua franca is a language or dialect systematically employed to ensure that communication is possible between groups of people who do not share a native language or dialect. The terms 'language' and 'dialect' are not so easily defined, with languages often being demarcated as autonomous and dialects as heteronomous, and in contrast to languages they are mutually intelligible (though not always), are used only in certain domains with a codified form and are characteristically spoken with a variety (Melchers, et al., 2003). In terms of lingua francas, attempts have been made to construct an international auxiliary language including Esperanto which was created by Polish ophthalmologist Ludwik Zamenhof in 1887. The aim was to see the language serve as a universal second language that would foster world peace and understanding while building a speech community. Esperanto did gain significant recognition, but notions of imperialism and concerns of natural language preservation were the primary deterrents that would ultimately come to prevent it from unifying nations and emerging as a lingua franca, many of its advocates still have hope for it to become the universal auxiliary language.

Today, French is still a lingua franca and official language for many Western and Central African countries. Russian is used widely in Central Asia and the Causcasus, and in much of Eastern Europe. Meanwhile, English, which served as the lingua franca of the colonies of the British Empire, has in the post-colonial period been designated an official language of some of the former colonies or newly formed nation states which have multiple indigenous languages. In the modern era, English is arguably the most dominant lingua franca in terms of being the most recognized and used form of communication between non-native speakers of the language. This lingua franca, World English, leads us to now look into the concept of World Englishes and, with the global expansion of English as a primary example, the concept of linguistic imperialism (including the later emerging native- versus non-native teacher debate).

Linguistic Imperialism and the Native- Versus Non-Native Teacher Debate

The notion of linguistic imperialism is tied to the imposition of one language on speakers of other languages, and considered to be a demonstration of power (e.g., military, economic), with aspects of the dominant culture typically transferred along with the language. Phillipson (1992) sees the defining characteristics as:

- Linguicism manifesting favor for the dominant language over another (i.e., in lines similar to racism and sexism, with prejudice leading to endangered languages becoming extinct).
- Structurally manifesting ideas (i.e., more resources and infrastructure are granted to the dominant language).
- Intertwined (i.e., with the same structures as imperialism in culture, education, media, and politics).
- Exploitive essence (i.e., causing injustice and inequality between those who use the dominant language and those who do not).
- Subtractive influence on other languages (i.e., learning the dominant language at the expense of others).
- Contested, and resisted (i.e., due to the factors listed above).

Ultimately, the view is one where the spread of English has served to undermine the rights of other languages and to marginalize the opportunities that should exist for multilingual education, potentially endangering cultural ideals, ways of life and indigenous languages. As such, radical change in terms of language policy was called for to redress the balance and to promote multilingualism in order to reflect a more natural state of global language use. Critics have since argued that a language in itself cannot be imperialistic, and that the notion of linguistic imperialism adopts an attitude that is patronizing toward developing countries, and assumes that they are incapable of making their own decisions in terms of language choice. Around the same time, the native speaking and non-native speaking language teacher debate also spurred productive discussion in the literature. One side of the debate argued that native teachers hold a superior model of oral production of the target language as well as familiarity with the target culture. They were long considered to be the ideal language teacher model which, under linguistic imperialism, is viewed as a hegemonic process. However, it has been argued that non-native teachers offer a number of inherent advantages by having gone through the process of acquiring the target language itself, and with multiple varieties of languages (such as English) now considered legitimate and acceptable, these kinds of instructors are certainly well-equipped to be able to teach target languages. Today, both kinds of instructor are seen to have value and are able to contribute to language teaching in varying and different ways, with their strengths coming to provide learners with a more well-rounded and productive educational experience in terms of the varieties of English that they teach.

World Englishes

Scholars identify varieties of English using different sociolinguistic contexts, historical analyses, backgrounds, functions, and influences. Central to the notion is that languages develop to fulfill the needs of the societies that utilize them, and because such needs are diverse and can differ across cultures and geographies, multiple varieties of English exist. These varieties include those of American English, Australian English, British English, Canadian English, Indian English, and Singaporean English to name a few. There is no recognized single means for a new variety of English to emerge, and so the development of one might best be described as a process of adaptation. That is to say, over time, as variations occur in word choices, spellings, pronunciations, sentence structures, accents, and meanings, a distinct variety of English eventually emerges. When recognizing the emergence of a World English from a variant of the language, a range of different criteria are applied and include, among others, the sociolinguistic contexts of use, the range of functional domains, and the ease to which new speakers become acculturated to its use. Of note, not all of these varieties of English will necessarily be intelligible to each other. Smith (1992) argues that intelligibility, in terms of World Englishes, should be considered as a matter of those in the same speech community being able to understand it, rather than it being understood by a native speaker of English.

The concept of World Englishes first emerged in 1965 with Kachru establishing Indian English as a unique variety of English. Later, he formally introduced the term, along with the global profile of English, and the three concentric circle model (see figure 1.6).

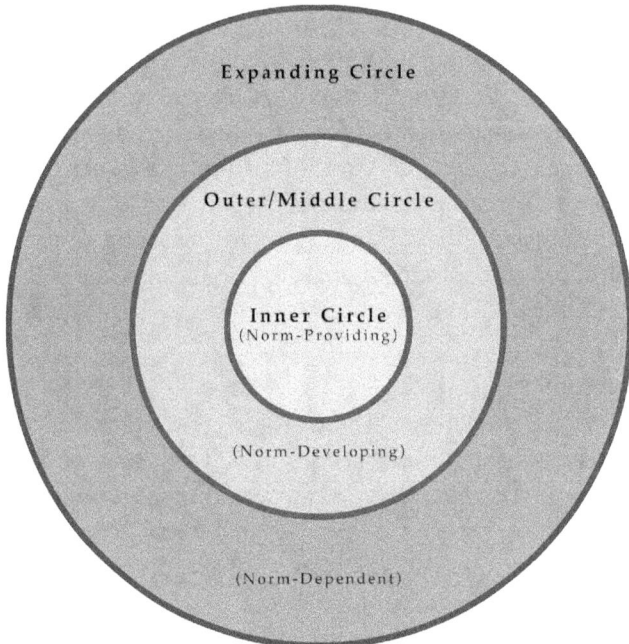

Figure 1.6 Kachru's Three Concentric Circle Model

The three concentric-circle model is comprised of inner circle, outer/middle circle, and expanding circle nations:
- Inner Circle nations: Norm-providing (i.e., varieties in those countries where English is used as the primary language; e.g., America, Australia, Britain, Canada, New Zealand).
- Outer/Middle Circle nations: Norm-developing (i.e., varieties in those countries where English has a colonial history; e.g., Bangladesh, Ghana, India, Kenya, Malaysia, Nigeria, Pakistan, Philippines, Singapore, Sri Lanka, Tanzania, Zambia, Zimbabwe).
- Expanding Circle nations: Norm-dependent (i.e., varieties in those countries where English is spoken but it may not necessarily have a colonial history nor a primary/official language status; e.g., China, Egypt, Indonesia, Israel, Japan, Nepal, Saudi Arabia, South Korea, Taiwan, USSR, Vietnam), any country where English is regularly spoken (even in a limited fashion, e.g., for trade or international business), and one that does not fall into the first two categories.

Lines between those nations in the outer and expanding circles may blur due to demographic shifts, economic motivations, and language education policies, with Kachru (1984) emphasizing that it is important to view each variety of English from its own historical, political, sociolinguistic and literary context. The concept of nativeness, in World Englishes then, is viewed "in terms of both its functional domains and range, and its depth in social penetration and resultant acculturation" (Kachru, 1997, p. 68). In other words, as communities use English in broader and greater societal contexts shaped by the historical role of the language, the interaction between functionality and history then leads to the nativization of English within that particular society or population group. Subsequently, Kachru famously argues that English belongs not only to native speakers but to non-native users throughout the world.

Aside from the three concentric circle model, a number of others have been developed. These include Streven's (1992) world map of English, McArthur's (1998) wheel model of World Englishes, Gorlach's (1990) circle model of English, Modiano's (1999) model of English, and Schneider's (2007) dynamic model of postcolonial Englishes. Taking these models into consideration and conceptualizing the English language in terms of variety from a Global Model perspective, Haswell and Hahn (2016) see it providing administrators, instructors, and learners with a representation of English that can assist them in visualizing an internationalized communicative outlook for the planning, teaching, and learning of the language. In this way all stakeholders are at the forefront of realigning what English means and how it is used and taught in different contexts, with learners themselves taking ownership of the language that they possess, and coming to view themselves as "full participants in global language development" (p. 244). Yet, going forward, the place of English has been questioned, with the increasing soft power of other nations such as China on the rise (Wu, 2019), and with advancements in machine translation and artificial intelligence (Kent, 2020), the rationale for language learning, the means to provide it, the reasons why we use it, and to who we now speak the languages that we know has changed significantly. How these factors are to impact Global Englishes, World English, and the World Englishes paradigm, and in turn, the teaching of English as an international language, will be interesting to see, particularly in regards to language planning and policy.

Language Planning and Policy

Impacting on what language is taught, especially to children, is a matter of language planning and policy (LPP), and it is the LPP field that is concerned with those policies (explicit and implicit) that influence what languages are spoken when, how, and by who, as well as the values and the rights associated with those languages and how those languages will be used in a society. These decisions are often made by political entities (e.g., ministries of education, state boards), and in terms of the teaching of English, the choice may be made between the two main varieties, standard British English (such as in the People's Republic of China) and General American (such as in the Republic of Korea). Each of these varieties have some differences in grammar, vocabulary, spelling, and pronunciation, with the choice as to which to employ often tied to historical or political motivations, as well as that which might be deemed valuable for future generations and voters in a given society (Brown, 2014). For example, in the multilingual nation state of Singapore, top-down language planning by the government influences language acquisition and the respective function of languages in the speech community via the educational system (Kaplan & Baldauf, 2004), and it is certainly dependent on the political and social impact of the colonial and post-independence periods experienced by the nation (Spolky, 2004).

Other choices that are explicitly made after selecting those languages that are available to citizens are when to start instruction with them, and how that instruction is to be delivered. The latter might involve consideration of the methods, approaches, and techniques favored, which can influence the focus of language use (e.g., a competency-based approach for adult migrants versus content-based instruction for migrant children). Considerations include the duration of time spent mandated for study (or available to a learner for study), the type of teacher employed to teach the language (e.g., native- or non-native, trained or untrained), the capabilities of the teachers employed in implementing the polices according to planning, and the types of material developed by planners of the curriculum. Large-scale social and political issues also affect language use in any given society (e.g., by governments in official ceremonies, on street signs, and in public announcements, and by citizens in daily life). This can lead to language variation occurring in individuals from place to place and situation to situation, variance in language interaction, variance in how language is used in different settings for communication, and how cultures privilege certain languages over others.

Culture and Cultural Parameters

Culture, as an umbrella term, encompasses social behavior and the norms found in societies, as well as the arts, capabilities, customs, knowledge, habits, and laws of individuals in these groups. It is communicated across generations, and although relatively stable, it is a dynamic system of rules that are implicit and explicit, and it has the potential to change across time (Matsumoto, 2000).

Brown (2014) presents eight cultural parameters to illustrate the different cohesive values among cultures, highlighting what separates one from another, and how individuals in one may differ to those in others. These aspects should be viewed as appearing on a continuum, rather than attributable to any single individual or group specifically, and include action focus, gender role differentiation, individual/collective, power distance, space distance, tightness, time orientation, and uncertainty avoidance.

1. *Action focus.* Doing cultures value decisiveness and spontaneity, responses may be immediate and impulsive. Being cultures value reflectiveness, contemplation, conformity, and traditions.
2. *Gender role differentiation.* Masculine societies are those that value gender roles that are specific and distinct, with maximal distinction between what is expected between women and men. Feminine societies are those that value relatively overlapping social roles between the sexes.
3. *Individual/collective.* Individualist cultures value personal needs over others, while collectivist cultures value needs of the group, and sacrifice personal wishes.
4. *Power distance.* Large power distance societies value status differentiation, such as those ascribed to various positions, ranks, and occupations in society. Small power distance cultures value achievements over family background or aspects of rank.
5. *Space distance (including eye contact as well as privacy, proxemics, and touching).* Public space cultures accept closer distances, touching, and open doors to homes and offices. Private space cultures value larger space bubbles, minimal touching, and less transparency.
6. *Tightness.* Valuing homogeneity. Tight cultures are highly integrated, with few differences among members. Loose

cultures exhibit diversity, accepting greater divergence (e.g., among beliefs, customs, religions).
7. *Time orientation.* Valuing time. Fixed time cultures place importance on punctuality, are aware of passing time, are goal-fixated, single-focused, and are more interruption intolerant. Fluid time cultures value flexibility with time constraints, are slower paced, and value what occurs during the time taken to reach a goal.
8. *Uncertainty avoidance.* Strong uncertainty avoidance cultures value absolute truths, security, and strict rules. Weak uncertainty avoidance cultures are those more contemplative, more tolerant to change, and more accepting of personal risks.

These aspects also serve to illustrate how difficult culture can be to define, and although stereotypes can be made, individuals from any one particular culture are all different. Aspects such as these, among many others, are all studied via sociolinguistics and linguistic anthropology, which also help to determine the place and influence of identity in regards to second language acquisition.

Identity

In sociolinguistics, identity refers to the ways in which people position or construct themselves, or are positioned or constructed by others, in socio-cultural situations through language, with reference to variables comprising identity markers in each speech community. The acquisition and use of languages occur in social contexts. Identity is a social phenomenon, with a model of sociolinguistic processes informing SLA, viewing L2 input and the processing of it in social settings as socially mediated, with social and linguistic context affecting linguistic use, choice, and development. Learners intentionally assert social identities through L2 communication in social contexts to produce interlanguage based on the interaction of social factors and cognitive processes. Here,

> an important aspect of sociolinguistics is the study of the interdependence between the social contexts in which interlanguage is used and the cognitive processes of the learner that affect learner language variation and change, leading to acquisition ... [In other words, and in a broader sense,] sociolinguistics, as a well-established branch of linguistics focuses on the study of the impact of society, including the impact of social context on the way language is used (Tarone, 2007, p. 837).

Important also, due to the increasingly narrow associations of the term sociolinguistics, sociocultural linguistics is used to refer to the broad range of theories and methods that focus on the study of language from a sociocultural context, with ethnolinguistics used to refer to the study of the relationship between language and culture, and how different ethnic groups perceive the world. In this regard, linguistic anthropology is important to consider as well, in terms of how language forms social identity and group memberships, shapes communication, organizes large-scale cultural beliefs and ideologies, develops a common cultural representation of natural and social worlds, and influences culture, power, thought, and social life. As Brown (2014, pp. 196-197) notes,

> issues of culture, social identity, [and] concomitant ideological ramifications, as ingrained sets of behaviors and modes of perception, become highly important in the learning of an L2 … [as] SLA is intertwined with sociocultural identity … [seeing] language, thought, and culture, a 'package' that an L2 learner must grapple with in the journey to successful acquisition.

He also notes that second language learning is second-culture learning, highlighting aspects of culture shock and social distance as two aspects of importance to consider during acculturation, particularly for those studying in a target language context. Here, culture shock is viewed as the second of four successive stages of cultural acquisition (Brown, 2014, p. 188):

1. Excitement and euphoria.
2. Culture shock/culture stress (erosion of self-esteem and security).
3. Gradual recovery (adjusting to new ways of acting, thinking, feeling).
4. Adaptation/integration (acceptance of a new identity).

These are viewed in light of social distance in terms of (Schuman, 1976):

1. Dominance, or the power relationship between cultures.
2. The extent to which cultural integration is possible.
3. The congruency of the cultures.

The greater the social distance or perceived social distance (Acton, 1979) between cultures, then the greater the difficulty there will be in learning the L2. "Adapting to the new culture without a comparable increase in linguistic ability may give rise to low motivation to improve one's L2 ability" (Brown, 2014, p. 190), with delays in adaptation (synchronization between culture and linguistic development) leading to L2 fossilization/stabilization. In this regard, in addition to teaching communicative competence, instructors need to be mindful of developing intercultural competence in their learners.

Intercultural Competence

The ability to function effectively across cultures, to think and act appropriately, and to communicate and work with people from different cultural backgrounds is intercultural competence (Leung, et al., 2014). In a globalized world, it is a valuable asset as we interact with people from different cultures and countries who have been shaped by different values, beliefs and experiences. The learning of intercultural competence is an experiential process that involves the creation of "shared meaning between cultural representatives and constructing a social identity within the learner's community of practice … over years of language learning, and [it is something which] penetrates deeply into an individual's patterns of thinking, feeling, and acting" (Brown, 2014, p. 197).

Intercultural competence is important because how people think and speak is determined largely by their culture. Although now considered a false hypothesis by modern linguists (Ahearn, 2012), advocates of *linguistic determinism* would argue that language determines thought and that linguistic categories limit and determine cognitive categories. However, *linguistic relativity* advocates view linguistic categories and usage as only influencing thought and decisions, with Comrie (2020) noting that the language(s) that we speak is only one factor influencing our cognition and behavior. These two ideas were previously referred to as the *strong* and *weak* versions of the Sapir-Whorf hypothesis respectively, which is a principle suggesting that the structure of a language affects its speakers' cognition or world view, and thus perceptions are relative to the language(s) spoken by an individual. Explicit teaching can help learners gain cultural knowledge concerning target language(s), as cultural differences may go unnoticed until they create a problem (ALPLP, 2004).

Intercultural Language Learning (IcLL) and Teaching

At the global level, intercultural language teaching and learning throughout the second language acquisition process aims to understand

and value all, one's own, and the target languages and cultures being taught. There is also emphasis placed on how to mediate among languages and cultures, with cultural sensitivity being an ongoing goal of the learner. This paradigm sees a clear shift from that of developing second language acquisition in terms of a native-speaker model to one where the target norm is that of an intercultural speaker, with intercultural language learning developing as a key direction in language education, where the fusing of language, culture, and learning are provided through the lens of a single educative approach (ESA, 2015; McLoughlin & Liddicoat, 2005).

Summary

This chapter highlights the place of the brain in the language learning process by emphasizing brain architecture (particularly language areas), and the role of neuroplasticity in the SLA process. Benefits of bilingualism were also presented, as were the different types of memory and their role in terms of language learning. A number of myths and misconceptions regarding the SLA process were also underscored, so that their fallacies could be highlighted and debunked. The stages of language acquisition were then examined in terms of initial and second language acquisition, alongside a brief discussion of sign language acquisition and the acquisition of language by artificial intelligence. This allowed for the similarities and disparities between these to be discussed prior to providing a comprehensive listing of the contributions to the field in terms of theories, models, hypotheses, and concepts. All of these, to one degree or another, form the basis of a variety of methods, approaches, and techniques that have been developed over time to help learners with second language acquisition. The chapter also highlights those influences that impact the language(s) that we teach, from the types of English that exist, through to those that shape policy and planning and how this influences what languages are spoken when, how, and by who, as well as the values and the rights associated with those languages, and how those languages will be used in a society. Aspects of culture and the place of identity were also considered, as were concepts of linguistic relativism, and how language and thought operate together. The chapter then closes by detailing the importance of intercultural language learning and teaching, highlighting a shift in the target-language model norm to that of becoming an intercultural speaker.

Review

Content Quiz
Second Language Acquisition (SLA) Aspects, Frameworks, and Influences

To help solidify some of the concepts introduced by this chapter the following multiple-choice and true or false quizzes might be helpful for you to undertake. So that you can check the accuracy of your responses, an answer key can be found following the quizzes.

Multiple-Choice

Circle **a**, **b**, or **c** for the answer that best completes the sentence presented in each question.

1. The adaptability of the brain to accommodate changes or injury by reorganizing itself by forming new neural connections is known as …
    a) neuroconnectome.
    b) neuroplasticity.
    c) neurochange.

2. The three basic units of the brain are the …
    a) forebrain, midbrain, hindbrain.
    b) aftbrain, midbrain, sternbrain.
    c) cortex, cerebellum, ganglia.

3. The left brain/right brain theory considers …
    a) people have a split mind.
    b) one side of the brain to be more dominant than the other.
    c) the left side is always more dominant than the right side.

4. Each hemisphere of the brain has been traditionally divided into …
    a) two lobes (frontal, parietal).
    b) three lobes (frontal, parietal, temporal).
    c) four lobes (frontal, parietal, temporal, occipital).

5. Broca's area is located in the frontal lobe of the dominant hemisphere and it is traditionally considered responsible for ...
   a) language ego.
   b) speech production functions.
   c) language development and comprehension of speech.

6. Wernicke's area is located in the temporal lobe of the dominant hemisphere and it is traditionally considered responsible for ...
   a) language ego.
   b) speech production functions.
   c) language development and comprehension of speech.

7. The arcuate fasciculus is a bundle of axons that connect ...
   a) Broca's area and Wernicke's area of the brain.
   b) the two hemispheres of the brain.
   c) Broca's area and Wernicke's area to the angular gyrus and the insular cortex.

8. The angular gyrus is the area that assembles information in order to ...
   a) interpret words and concepts.
   b) determine truth from falsehood.
   c) mediate aspects of speech production.

9. The insular cortex is the area that ...
   a) interprets words and concepts.
   b) determines truth from falsehood.
   c) mediates aspects of speech production.

10. Benefits of bilingualism show that as we age, additional language users may ...
    a) delay certain types of brain diseases.
    b) cause certain types of brain diseases.
    c) cure certain types of brain diseases.

11. Different types of memory are stored in different places of the brain. Short-term memory is in the prefrontal cortex, long-term memory is in the hippocomapus of the temporal lobe, and skill memory is in the …
    a) cerebellum which relays it to the basal ganglia.
    b) cerebellum which relays it to the angular gyrus.
    c) cerebellum which relays it to the insular cortex.

12. The identity that a person develops in reference to the language(s) that they speak is their …
    a) language ego.
    b) language personality.
    c) Language self.

13. The language learning classroom is an environment that can induce in the learner …
    a) a sense of peace, love, and harmony.
    b) a stressful and anxiety-provoking experience.
    c) a stressful but pleasurable experience at all times.

14. Language learning by its nature will see any learner make mistakes, and this can lead to vulnerability in and self-exposure of the learner. This in turn impacts upon the …
    a) learner's self esteem, or their overall evaluation or appraisal of self-worth.
    b) Learner's intelligence level, with the more languages that they speak proving the smarter that they are.
    c) Learner's time, as they must always be learning the additional language in isolation.

15. Risk taking …
    a) is a crucial and interactive process of learning a language.
    b) is to be avoided by learners
    c) needs to be taught out of learners by the teacher during class time.

16. There are three major schools of thought concerning motivation (behaviorist, cognitive, and constructivist), with motivation broken down into two main types (extrinsic/intrinsic). Extrinsic motivation can be promoted in the classroom by …
   a) providing students with prizes, grades, and even positive feedback.
   b) promoting meaningful learning goals that are important.
   c) assisting the learner in obtaining value of accomplishment.

17. In general, the five stages of second language acquisition are …
   a) silent, babbling, holophrastic, intermediate fluency, advanced fluency.
   b) pre-talking, babbling, holophrastic, two-word, telegraphic, multiword.
   c) silent, early production, speech emergence, intermediate fluency, advanced fluency.

18. The nativist theory suggests that humans are born with …
   a) the ability to only ever learn one language.
   b) the inherent ability to learn all languages but only with great difficulty and much effort.
   c) genes that allow for language learning to occur, and that there is a universal grammar (UG) that is shared across every language in the world.

19. A global communicative competence consists of grammatical, sociolinguistic, discourse, and strategic competence. Strategic competence can be defined as …
   a) the ability to produce grammatically correct and sociolinguistically appropriate utterances.
   b) the ability to produce coherent and cohesive utterances.
   c) the ability to solve communication problems as they arise.

20. A method is …
   a) an overall procedural plan.
   b) the practices and principles of language teaching.
   c) the means of implementation.

21. Interlanguage is an idiolect, an idiosyncratic dialect, which consists of rules that from a temporary systematic grammar for the ...
    a) learner.
    b) teacher.
    c) teacher and the learner.

22. Interference refers to the influence of features from one language onto another. It can be either beneficial (positive) or negative. It can take place ...
    a) at all levels of language.
    b) at the grammatical level only.
    c) at the vocabulary level only.

23. In the input hypothesis comprehensible input is viewed as ...
    a) essential for language learning.
    b) non-essential for language learning.
    c) essential or non-essential, depending on learner level.

24. The monitor hypothesis refers to ...
    a) using learned knowledge to help correct language production during communication.
    b) acquiring grammatical structures in a predictable order no matter the language.
    c) the emotional state or attitude of the learner that can make learning easier, impede it, or block it entirely.

25. The natural order hypothesis refers to ...
    a) using learned knowledge to help correct language production during communication.
    b) acquiring grammatical structures in a predictable order no matter the language.
    c) the emotional state or attitude of the learner that can make learning easier, impede it, or block it entirely.

26. The affective filter hypothesis refers to …
   a) using learned knowledge to help correct language production during communication.
   b) acquiring grammatical structures in a predictable order no matter the language.
   c) the emotional state or attitude of the learner that can make learning easier, impede it, or block it entirely.

27. A mistake or slip, an error, and an attempt are all considered different. A mistake or a slip is …
   a) those things that students can correct themselves.
   b) not self-correctable and will need an explanation.
   c) when students make an effort to say something which they do not yet know how to verbalize correctly.

28. In the interaction hypothesis comprehensible input is viewed as …
   a) essential for language learning.
   b) non-essential for language learning.
   c) essential or non-essential depending upon learner level.

29. The psychological model breaks speech production down into separate cognitive processes, which are …
   a) conceptualization and utterance formation.
   b) conceptualization, utterance formation, and speech articulation.
   c) conceptualization, utterance formation, speech articulation, and self-monitoring.

30. The competition model suggests that the meaning of language is interpreted by comparing linguistic 'cues' within a sentence. The cues serve to signal specific functions, with language being learned from a rich linguistic environment and through the competition of basic cognitive mechanisms. It is an …
   a) emergentist theory, as opposed to an innatist theory or an empiricist theory.
   b) innatist theory, as opposed to an emergentist theory or an empiricist theory.
   c) empiricist theory, as opposed to an innatist theory or an emergentist theory.

31. The noticing hypothesis …
    a) views that the place of attention is key to the development of a second language.
    b) sees language learners as able to restructure their interlanguage knowledge to be in greater conformity to the language that they are learning.
    c) presents a means of understanding how language information may be stored.

32. Processability theory …
    a) views that the place of attention is key to the development of a second language.
    b) Sees language learners as able to restructure their interlanguage knowledge to be in greater conformity to the language that they are learning.
    c) presents a means of understanding how language information may be stored.

33. The declarative/procedural model …
    a) views that the place of attention is key to the development of a second language.
    b) Sees language learners as able to restructure their interlanguage knowledge to be in greater conformity to the language that they are learning.
    c) presents a means of understanding how language information may be stored.

34. Semantic theory posits that meaning is at the core of a language, not its sound or structure. The different meanings include those of …
    a) grammatical, lexical, pragmatic, and semantic.
    b) grammatical, lexical, and pragmatic.
    c) grammatical and lexical.

35. The attention processing model involves controlled and automatic processing, and both of these can occur in combination with focal or peripheral attention to the task. Focal attention here refers to ...
   a) incidental or implicit.
   b) intentional or explicit.
   c) controlled or automatic.

36. If you are willing to tolerate ideas and propositions that are counter to your own (including pronunciations and errors in form) then you would be considered to be ...
   a) ambiguity intolerant.
   b) ambiguity tolerant.
   c) ambidextrously talented.

37. Transformational grammar is part of a theory of generative grammar. Transformational grammar ...
   a) explains the importance and influence of semantics on the form of language.
   b) considers that grammar is considered to be a system of rules that generate all of the combinations of words that form grammatical sentences in any given language and involve the use of defined operations to produce novel sentences from existing ones.
   c) considers grammar to be innate to all humans, independent of sensory experience.

38. Case grammar theory stresses the importance of semantic roles in an effort to make explicit the basic meaning relationships in a sentence. Case grammar ...
   a) explains the importance and influence of semantics on the form of language.
   b) considers that grammar is considered to be a system of rules that generate all of the combinations of words that form grammatical sentences in any given language and involve the use of defined operations to produce novel sentences from existing ones.
   c) considers grammar to be innate to all humans, independent of sensory experience.

39. Scaffolding ...
   a) represents the domain of knowledge or skill where the learner is not yet capable of independent functioning, but can achieve the desired outcome given relevant scaffolded help.
   b) is a process that enables the learner to solve tasks or achieve goals beyond an unassisted effort, allowing for the completion of those elements that are within the range of competence.
   c) is the notion that a language student who is willing to communicate in the target language not only will do so, but will also actively seek out chances to communicate.

40. The zone of proximal development (ZPD) ...
   a) represents the domain of knowledge or skill where the learner is not yet capable of independent functioning, but can achieve the desired outcome given relevant scaffolded help.
   b) as a process enables the learner to solve tasks or achieve goals beyond an unassisted effort, allowing for the completion of those elements that are within the range of competence.
   c) is the notion that a language student who is willing to communicate in the target language not only will do so, but will also actively seek out chances to communicate.

41. The notion of linguistic imperialism is tied to the imposition of one language on speakers of other languages and ...
   a) is considered to be a demonstration of power (e.g., military, economic), with aspects of the dominant culture typically transferred along with the language.
   b) although not considered to be a demonstration of power (e.g., military, economic), aspects of the dominant culture are typically transferred along with the language.
   c) is considered to be a demonstration of power (e.g., military, economic), with aspects of the dominant culture not typically transferred along with the language.

42. The native- versus non-native speaking language teacher debate established that …
    a) native-speaking teachers are the ideal language teaching model.
    b) both native- and non-native speaking language teachers provide value.
    c) non-native speaking language teachers are the ideal model as they have learned the language they teach.

43. The use of the English language as a lingua franca in business, diplomacy, trade, and other spheres of global activity is considered to be …
    a) global English
    b) world English
    c) world Englishes

44. The different varieties of English and English-based creoles developed in different regions of the world are considered to be …
    a) global English
    b) world English
    c) world Englishes

45. This refers to the recent spread of English due to globalization resulting from the use of world English is known as …
    a) global English
    b) world English
    c) world Englishes

46. The three concentric circle model is comprised of inner circle, outer/middle circle, and expanding circle nations. The English spoken in those countries in the inner circle consists of …
    a) norm-dependent varieties.
    b) norm-developing varieties.
    c) norm-providing varieties.

47. The three concentric circle model is comprised of inner circle, outer/middle circle, and expanding circle nations. The English spoken in those countries in the outer/middle circle consists of ...
    a) Norm- dependent varieties.
    b) Norm-developing varieties.
    c) Norm-providing varieties.

48. The three concentric circle model is comprised of inner circle, outer/middle circle, and expanding circle nations. The English spoken in those countries in the expanding circle consists of ...
    a) Norm- dependent varieties.
    b) Norm-developing varieties.
    c) Norm-providing varieties.

49. Language planning and policy is involved in deciding ...
    a) the language(s) available to study in school.
    b) the lunch menu available in schools.
    c) the number of administrators assigned to a school.

50. The social behavior and the norms found in societies, as well as the arts, capabilities, customs, knowledge, habits, and laws of individuals in these groups is defined as being ...
    a) culture.
    b) identity.
    c) intercultural competence.

51. In sociolinguistics, the ways in which people position or construct themselves, or are positioned or constructed by others, in socio-cultural situations through language, with reference to variables comprising identity markers in each speech community is defined as being ....
    a) culture.
    b) identity.
    c) intercultural competence.

52. The concept of language determining thought and linguistic categories determining cognitive categories is …
   a) linguistic determinism.
   b) language planning and policy.
   c) linguistic relativism.

53. The concept of linguistic categories and usage influencing thought and decisions is …
   a) linguistic determinism.
   b) language planning and policy.
   c) linguistic relativism.

54. The ability to function effectively across cultures, to think and act appropriately, and to communicate and work with people from different cultural backgrounds is considered to be…
   a) intercultural competence.
   b) intercultural language learning.
   c) identity.

True or False

Circle **a** (true) if you think that the statement is correct, or **b** (false) if you think that the statement is incorrect.

1. A connectome is defined as a comprehensive map of neural connections, typically in the brain, but more broadly also a mapping of all neural connections with the nervous system.
    a) True.
    b) False.

2. We now know that language function is widely distributed throughout the brain, with the language connectome extending far beyond the single pathway notion of the arcuate fasciculus and Broca and Wernicke's areas.
    a) True.
    b) False.

3. Children who learn an additional language early in life store that language with their native language, whereas adults who learn an additional language later in life store it in a different area of the brain from where they store their native language.
    a) True.
    b) False.

4. Code switching means switching from the use of one language to another, or from one dialect to another or between two registers of the same language to another.
    a) True.
    b) False.

5. Memory is how the brain encodes data or information for storage and retrieval as required. It can be defined as the preservation of information over time for the purpose of influencing future actions.
    a) True.
    b) False.

6. The affective domain of language learning involves the emotions and attitudes of the learner(s) toward themselves and those around them.
   a) True.
   b) False.

7. How we speak and pronounce our native language(s) is considered to be an essential feature of self.
   a) True.
   b) False.

8. State anxiety is one that occurs in a particular situation, but it does not have a negative experience on the language learning process.
   a) True.
   b) False.

9. Inhibition and self-esteem are linked (i.e., the weaker the learner's self-esteem, the stronger the learner's inhibition).
   a) True.
   b) False.

10. Risk-taking involves the level of eagerness that a learner holds when trying out the use of new information (lexical terms, grammar, and so on) regardless of embarrassment.
    a) True.
    b) False.

11. Motivation is a complex psychological construct, but it does not often emerge as one of the most determinant factors in successful foreign language acquisition.
    a) True.
    b) False.

12. The environment in which the learner resides will provide varying degrees of language contact, placing the learner in positions that allow for practice or dismissal of their language use, and in turn influencing their L2 development.
    a) True.
    b) False.

13. Children acquire languages better than adults.
    a) True.
    b) False.

14. You are unable to lose your accent after becoming an adult.
    a) True.
    b) False.

15. You can acquire a language just by listening or reading.
    a) True.
    b) False.

16. In any language, immersion is key to fluency.
    a) True.
    b) False.

17. The stages of language acquisition all follow a certain generally predictable sequence.
    a) True.
    b) False.

18. The markedness differential hypothesis states that areas of difficulty that a learner will have cannot be predicted.
    a) True.
    b) False.

19. Language competence can be divided into two sub-categories: those of organizational competence (grammatical and textual) and pragmatic competence (illocutionary and sociolinguistic).
    a) True.
    b) False.

20. Simply put, contrastive analysis is the systematic study of a pair of languages with a view to identifying the structural differences and similarities between them.
    a) True.
    b) False.

21. Fossilization is the argument that a learner's interlanguage will progress to a certain point in their additional language learning endeavors and never go beyond it.
    a) True.
    b) False.

22. The acquisition/learning hypothesis distinguishes between learning and acquisition. Learning refers to the development of formal knowledge regarding the language, and acquisition refers to the development of competency in the use of the language.
    a) True.
    b) False.

23. The interaction hypothesis views the use of the target language in interaction as a means of facilitating language acquisition.
    a) True.
    b) False.

24. The output hypothesis views meaningful output as being necessary as meaningful input in the language learning process because meaningful output can lead to more effective processing of received input as a result.
    a) True.
    b) False.

25. The classroom model views the classroom as a place to deliver pedagogical activities based on real communication, and that the way a task is structured can lead to either its success or demise, based on the demands placed on the student when completing it.
    a) True.
    b) False.

26. The critical period hypothesis is the notion that a critical period for initial language acquisition to occur lies between the ages of 2 and prior to puberty.
    a) True.
    b) False.

27. Emergentism views that not only is there no universal grammar, but that there is also no specialized language acquisition device, as languages emerge from a relatively simple developmental process of being exposed to a massive and complex environment.
    a) True.
    b) False.
28. The amelioration hypothesis denotes that language acquisition as an accidental side effect of attempts to improve the ability of a grammatically naïve processor to deal with input.
    a) True.
    b) False.
29. The mapping assumption views language acquisition as a means of a way to create 'mappings' between form and meaning.
    a) True.
    b) False.
30. Connectionsim is an approach that views input as the source of both the units of language and the rules of language. It suggests that learners form mental connections between those items that co-occur, and from input, extract rules of language through the cognitive processing common to other areas of cognitive skill acquisition.
    a) True.
    b) False.
31. The notion of automaticity in additional language learning sees that learners acquire their proficiency in language in the same manner as they acquire other complex cognitive skills (e.g., from a gradated process of proceduralization).
    a) True.
    b) False.
32. The role of memory in SLA may not be important, as there is no positive correlation between verbatim memory functioning and the success of grammar learning.
    a) True.
    b) False.

33. Cognitive semantics holds language to be a part of a more general cognitive ability that is used to describe the world based upon how people conceive it, with the main tenants being grammar, linguistic knowledge, and language ability.
    a) True.
    b) False.

34. The semantic cognitive view of linguistic development argues that for a language to be truly generative, it must be able to generate meaning as well as structure.
    a) True.
    b) False.

35. Willingness to communicate (WTC) is the notion that a language student who is willing to communicate in the target language not only will do so, but will also actively seek out chances to communicate.
    a) True.
    b) False.

36. A pyramid model of second language use has been proposed to illustrate the control over communication in the target language that a learner may maintain. The higher the learner climbs up the pyramid, the more control that they maintain over communicative acts. It consists of six layers and twelve constructs.
    a) True.
    b) False.

37. In sociocultural theory, SLA is not a universal process, but one where language learning is dependent on and emerges from social interaction, and develops out of the desire and need to communicate.
    a) True.
    b) False.

38. The mediating role of language, from a sociocultural perspective, views language as a means to control and regulate communicative activity.
    a) True.
    b) False.

39. The zone of proximal development (ZPD) is a figurative distance between an existing developmental state and the potential development of the learner.
    a) True.
    b) False.

40. Complex dynamic systems theory is both a perspective and an approach to the study of SLA where language is viewed as a system that is adaptive, chaotic, complex, dynamic, feedback-sensitive, nonlinear, sensitive to initial conditions, open, self-organizing, and unpredictable.
    a) True.
    b) False.

41. A lingua franca is a language that is used for communication between people who do not share a native language.
    a) True.
    b) False.

42. A pidgin is a stabilized natural language emerging from a creole.
    a) True.
    b) False.

43. A creole is a grammatically simplified language emerging for use as communication between people not sharing a common language.
    a) True.
    b) False.

44. A dialect is a form of a language peculiar to a specific region or social group.
    a) True.
    b) False.

45. Languages within a branch that share descent from a common parental or ancestral language are language families.
   a) True.
   b) False.

46. Languages related through descent from a common parental or ancestral language (the protolanguage of that family) are known as a language group.
   a) True.
   b) False.

47. Linguistic variety is a general term for a distinct form of a language or linguistic expression, used to cover overlapping subcategories (e.g., dialect, register, jargon, and idiolect). It is also known as a lect.
   a) True.
   b) False.

48. A speech community is a group of people who share a common language or dialect.
   a) True.
   b) False.

49. The field of language learning and policy is concerned with those policies, explicit and implicit, that influence what languages are spoken when, how, and by whom, as well as the values and the rights associated with those languages.
   a) True.
   b) False.

50. Culture can be communicated across generations, and although relatively stable, it is a dynamic system of rules that are implicit and explicit, and it has the potential to change across time.
   a) True.
   b) False.

51. Linguistic anthropology considers a broad range of theories and methods that study language from a sociocultural context, while sociocultural linguistics considers how language influences social life.
    a) True.
    b) False.

52. Although stereotypes are often made, individuals from any one particular culture are all different.
    a) True.
    b) False.

53. Linguistic determinism and linguistic relativism were previously referred to as the strong and weak versions of the Sapir-Whorf hypothesis respectively.
    a) True.
    b) False.

54. Intercultural language learning is an educative approach where students are provided with the knowledge and the skills to support them in the ability to both understand and interact with people from cultures other than their own.
    a) True.
    b) False.

Quiz Answers
Second Language Acquisition (SLA) Aspects

Multiple-Choice				*True or False*			
1.	b	31.	a	1.	T	31.	T
2.	a	32.	b	2.	T	32.	F
3.	b	33.	c	3.	T	33.	T
4.	c	34.	a	4.	T	34.	T
5.	b	35.	b	5.	T	35.	T
6.	c	36.	b	6.	T	36.	T
7.	a	37.	b	7.	T	37.	T
8.	a	38.	a	8.	F	38.	T
9.	c	39.	b	9.	T	39.	T
10.	a	40.	a	10.	T	40.	T
11.	a	41.	a	11.	F	41.	T
12.	a	42.	b	12.	T	42.	F
13.	b	43.	b	13.	F	43.	F
14.	a	44.	c	14.	F	44.	T
15.	a	45.	c	15.	F	45.	T
16.	a	46.	c	16.	F	46.	F
17.	c	47.	b	17.	T	47.	T
18.	c	48.	a	18.	F	48.	T
19.	c	49.	a	19.	T	49.	T
20.	a	50.	a	20.	T	50.	T
21.	a	51.	b	21.	T	51.	F
22.	a	52.	a	22.	T	52.	T
23.	a	53.	c	23.	T	53.	T
24.	a	54.	a	24.	T	54.	T
25.	b			25.	T		
26.	c			26.	T		
27.	a			27.	T		
28.	a			28.	T		
29.	c			29.	T		
30.	a			30.	T		

Suggested Readings

Acton, W. (1979). *Second language learning and perception of difference in attitude* [unpublished doctoral dissertation]. University of Michigan, USA.

Ahearn, L. (2012). *Living language: An introduction to linguistic Anthropology,* (3rd ed). Wiley Blackwell.

ALPLP. (2004). *Getting started with intercultural language learning.* Asian Languages Professional Learning Project.

Amici, F., Sanchez-Amaro, A., Sebastian-Enesco, C., Cacchione, T., Allritz, M., Salazar-Bonet., Rossano, F. (2019). The word order of languages predicts native speakers' working memory. *Scientific reports 9,* 1124. https://doi.org/10.1038/s41598-018-37654-9

Anderson, J. (1992). *Automaticity and the ACT theory. American Journal of Psychology, 105*(2), 165-180.

Ausubel, D. (1968). *Educational psychology: A cognitive view.* Rinehart & Winston.

Bates, E., & MacWhinney, B. (1981). Second language acquisition from a functionalist perspective: Pragmatic, semantic and perceptual strategies. In H. Winitz (Ed.), *Annals of the New York Academy of Sciences conference on native and foreign language acquisition,* (pp. 190-214). New York Academy of Sciences.

Bachman, (1990). *Fundamental considerations in language testing.* Oxford University Press.

Benveniste, G. (1958). Subjectivity in language. *Journal de Psychologie, 5,* 223-230.

Bailey, K. (1993). Competitiveness and anxiety in adult second language learning: Looking at and through the diary studies. In H. Selinger & M. Long (Eds.), *Classroom oriented research in Second Language Acquisition,* (pp. 67-103). Newbury House.

Bialystock, E. (1994). Analysis and control in the development of second language proficiency. *Studies in Second Language Acquisition, 16*(2), 157-168. https://dx.doi.org/10.1017/S02772263100012857

Bialystock, E. & Smith, M. (1985). Interlanguage is not a state of mind: An evaluation of the construct for second language acquisition. *Applied Linguistics 6,*(2), 101-117. https://dx.doi.org/10.1093/applin/6.2.101

Block, D. (2007). The rise of identity in SLA research, post Firth and Wagner (1997). *Modern Language Journal, 91,* 863-876.

Bohren, A. (2018). Language acquisition theory: A comprehensive guide. *Cognifit.* https://blog.cognifit.com/language-acquisition-theory

Bresnan, J. (2001). *Lexical-functional syntax.* Blackwell.

Brown, H. (1980). The optimal distance model of second language acquisition. *TESOL Quarterly, 14*(2), 157-164.

Brown, H. (2014). *Principles of language learning and teaching: A course in second language acquisition,* (6th ed.). Pearson Education.

Brown, S., & Larson-Hall, J. (2012). *Second language acquisition myths.* Michigan University Press.

Budner, S. (1962). Intolerance of ambiguity as a personality variable. *Journal of Personality, 30*(1), 29-50.

Canale, M., & Swain, M. (1980). Theoretical bases of communicative approaches to second language teaching and testing. *Applied Linguistics 1*(1), 1-47.

Celce-Marcia, M., Dornyei, Z., & Thurrell, S. (1995). Communicative competence: A pedagogically motivted model with content specifications. *Issues in Applied Linguistics, 6*(2), 5-35.

Chomsky, N. (1965). *Aspects of the theory of syntax.* MIT Press.

Chomsky, N. (1975). *Reflections on language.* Penguin Random House.

Chomsky, N. (2000). N*ew Horizons in the Study of Language and Mind.* Cambridge University Press.

Christiansen, M., & Chater, N. (2001). Connectionist psycholinguistics: Capturing the empirical data. *Trends in Cognitive Sciences, 5*(2), 82–88. https://dx.doi.org/10.1016/S1364-6613(00)01600-4

Clahsen, H. (1984). The acquisition of German word order: A test case for cognitive approaches to second language acquisition. In R. Anderson (Ed.)., *Second languages: A cross-linguistic perspective,* (pp. 219-242). Newbury House.

Comrie, B. (2020). *Language and thought.* LSA. https://www.linguisticsociety.org/resource/language-and thought

Corder, P. (1967). The significance of learner's errors. *International Review of Applied Linguistics in Language Teaching, 5*(4), 161-170.

Curtiss, S., Fromkin, V., Krashen, S., & Rigier, M. (1974). The development of language in Genie: A case of language acquisition beyond the critical period. *Brain and Language, 1*(1), 81-107. https://doi.org/10.1016/0093-934X(74)90027-3

De Bot, K. (2017). Complexity theory and dynamic systems theory. In L. Ortega, & Z. Han, *Complexity theory and language development: In celebration of Diane Larsen-Freeman*, (pp. 51-58). John Benjamins. https://doi.org/10.1075/llt.48.03deb

De Dios Martinez Agudo, J. (2013). An investigation into Spanish EFL learners' anxiety. Revista Brasileira de Linguistica Aplicada, 23(3), 829-851.

Donovan, M., Bransford, J., & Pellegrino, J. (1999). *How people learn: Bridging research and practice.* National Academy of Sciences.

ESA. (2015). Intercultural language learning. Language Learning Space – Professional Learning Topics. https://www.lls.edu.au/teacherspace/professionallearning/34

Fitts, P., & Posner, M. (1967). *Human Performance*. Brooks/Cole.

Guiora, A., Beit-Hallahmi, B., Brannon, R., Dull, C., & Scovel, T. (1972). The effects of experimentally induced changes in ego states on pronunciation ability in a second language: An exploratory study. *Comprehensive Psychiatry, 13*(5), 421-428. https://doi.org/10.1016/0010-440x(72)90083-1

Gorlach, M. (1990). *Studies in the history of the English language*. Carl Winter.

Haswell, C., & Hahn, A. (2016). *How a global model can positively influence English language teachers*. In P. Clements, A. Krause, & H. Brown (Eds.), *Focus on the learner*. JALT.

Hauser, M., Chomsky, N., & Fitch, W. (2002). The faculty of language: What is it, who has it, and how did it evolve? Science, 298, pp. 1569-1579. https://dx.doi.org/10.1126/science.298.5598.1569

Hines, T. (2018). *Anatomy of the brain*. Mayfield Clinic. https://mayfieldclinic.com/pe-anatbrain.htm

Holly, W. (1987). Students' self-esteem and academic achievement. *Research Roundup, 4*(1), 3-6.

Horwitz, E., Horwitz, M., & Cope, J. Foreign language classroom anxiety. *The Modern Language Journal, 70*, 125-132.

Hutauruk, B. (2015). Children first language acquisition at age 1-3 years old in Balata. IOSR Journal of Humanities and Social Sciences, 20(8), 51-57.

Hymes, D. (1966). Two types of linguistic relativity. In W. Bright (Ed.). *Sociolinguistics*, (114-158). Mouton.

Jenkins, J. (2015). *Global Englishes: A resource book for students*, (3rd ed). Routledge.

Johnson, M., Schuster, M., Le, Q., Krikun, M., Wu, Y., Chen, Z., Thorat, N., Viegas, F., Wattenberg, M., Corrado, G., Hughes, M., & Dean, J. (2017). Google's multilingual neural machine translation system: Enabling zero-shot translation. Computation and language. *ArXiv*. https://arxiv.org/abs/1611.04558

Kachru, B. (1965). The Indianness in Indian English, *Word, 21*(3), 391-410.

Kachru, B. (1984). World Englishes and the teaching of English to non-native speakers: Contexts, attitudes, and concerns. *TESOL Newsletter, 18*(5), 25-26.

Kachru, B. (Ed.). (1992). *The other tongue: English across cultures,* (2nd ed). The University of Illinois Press.

Kaplan, B., & Baldauf, R. (2004). *Language planning from practice to theory*. Multilingual Matters.

Kent, D. (2020). A room with a VUI – Voice user interfaces in the TESOL classroom. *Teaching English with Technology, 20*(3), 96-124.

Krashen, S. (1977). Some issues relating to the monitor model. In H. Brown, C. Yorio, R. Crymes (Eds.). *Teaching and learning English as a Second Language: Trends in Research and Practice: On TESOL '77: Selected Papers from the Eleventh Annual Convention of Teachers of English to Speakers of Other Languages, Miami, Florida, April 26 – May 1.* (pp. 144 – 158). Teachers of English to Speakers of Other Languages.

Kumaravadivelu, B. (2006). *Understanding language teaching: From method to postmethod*. Routledge.

Lagabastar, D. (2009). English achievement and student motivation in CLIL and EFL settings. Innovation in Language Learning and Teaching, 5(1), 3-18. https://doi.org/10.1080/17501229.2010.519030.

Lantolfe, J., & Thorne, S. (2007). Sociocultural theory and second language acquisition. In B. Van Patten & J. Williams (Eds.), *Theories of second language acquisition,* (pp. 201-224). Erlbaum.

Larson-Freeman, D. (1997). Chaos/complexity science and second language acquisition. *Applied Linguistics, 18*(2), 141-165. https://doi.org/10.1093/applin/18.2.141

Larson-Freeman, D. (1997). Chaos/complexity science and second language acquisition. *Applied linguistics, 18*(2), 141-165.

Larson-Freeman, D. (2011). A complexity theory approach to second language development/acquisition. In D. Atkinson (Ed.), *Alternative approaches to second language acquisition,* (pp. 48-72). Routledge.

Lave, J., & Wagner, E. (1991). *Communities of practice: Creating learning environments for educators.* Cambridge University Press.

Lebiere, C., & Anderson, J. R. (1993). A connectionist Implementation of the ACT-R production system. *Proceedings of the Fifteenth Annual Conference of the Cognitive Science Society.* Erlbaum.

Lee, J. (1999). *Tasks and communicating in the language classroom.* McGraw-Hill.

Lenneberg, E. (1967). *Biological foundations of language.* Wiley.

Leung, K., Ang, S., & Tan, M. (2014) Intercultural competence. *Annual Review of Organizational Psychology and Organizational Behavior, 1*(489-519).

Levelt, W. (1989) *Speaking: From intention to articulation.* MIT Press.

Long, M. (1996). The role of the linguistic environment in second language acquisition. In W. Ritchie & T. Bhatia (Eds.), *Handbook of second language acquisition,* (pp. 413-468). Academic Press.

Lopez-Deflory, E., & Juan-Garau, M. (2017). Going glocal: The impact of CLIL on English language learners' multilingual identities and attitudes in the Balearic Islands. *European Journal of Applied Linguistics, 5*(1), 5-29.

MacIntyre, P., & Gardner, R. (1991). Methods and results in the study of anxiety and language learning: A review of the literature. *A Journal of research in Language Studies, 41*(1), 85-117. https://doi.org/10.1111/j.1467-1770.1991.tb00677.x

MacIntyre, P., Clément, R., Dörnyei, Z., & Noels, K.A. (1998). Conceptualizing willingness to communicate in a second language: A situational model of second language confidence and affiliation. *The Modern Language Journal, 82*(4), 545-562.

McArthur, T. (1988). *The English languages.* Cambridge University Press.

McKay, S. (2018). English as an international language: What it is and what it means for pedagogy. *RELC Journal, 49*(1), 9-23.

McLaughlin, B. (1992). *Myths and misconceptions about second Language Learning: What every teacher needs to unlearn. Educational Practice Report 5.* National Center for Research on Cultural Diversity and Second Language Learning.

McLoughlin, M., & Liddicoat, A. (2005). In the context of intercultural language learning. *Babel, 40*, 5-11.

McLaughlin, B., Rossman, T., & McLeod, B. (1983). Second language learning: An information-processing perspective. *Language Learning, 33*, 135-158.Newport, E. (1990). *Maturational constraints on language learning*. Cognitive Science, 14(1), 11-18.

Melchers, G., Shaw, P., & Sundkvist, P. (2019). *World Englishes*, (3rd ed). Routledge.

Mitchell, R., & Myles, F. (2004). *Second language acquisition theories*. Oxford University Press.

Modiano, M. (1999). Standard English(es) and educational practices for the world's lingua franca. *English Today, 15*(4), 3-13.

Newport, E. (1990). *Maturational constraints on language learning*. Cognitive Science, *14*(1), 11-18.

O'Grady, W. (2011). Language acquisition without an acquisition device. *Language Teaching, 45*(1), 116-130. https://doi.org/10.1017/S026144481000056X

Oxford, R., & Nyikos, M. (1989). Variables affecting choice of language learning strategies by university students. *Modern Language Journal, 73*, 291-300.

Palmer, D. (2005). A motivational view of constructivist-informed teaching. *International Journal of Science Education, 27*(15), 1853-1881.

Penfield, W., & Roberts, L. (1959). *Speech and brain mechanisms*. Princeton University Press.

Phillipson, R. (1992). *Linguistic Imperialism*. Oxford University Press.

Piaget, J. (1923). *Le langage et la pensée chez l'enfant*. Delachaux & Niestlé.

Pienemann, M. (1998). *Language processing and second language development: Processability theory*. John Benjamins.

Reynolds, M. (2017, June 14). Chatbots learn how to negotiate and drive a hard bargain. *New Scientist*. https://www.newscientist.com/article/mg23431304-300-chatbots-learn-how-to-drive-a-hard-bargain

Schmidt, R. (1990). Psychological mechanisms underlying second language fluency. *Studies in Second Language Acquisition, 14*, 357-386.

Schneider, E. (2007). *Postcolonial English: Varieties around the world*. Cambridge University Press.

Schuman, J. (1976). Social distance as a factor in second language acquisition. *Language learning, 26*, 135-143.

Selinker, L. (1972). Interlanguage. *Product Information International Review of Applied Linguistics in Language Teaching, 10,* 209-241. http://dx.doi.org/10.1515/iral.1972.10.1-4.209

Sherwood, L. (2015). *Human physiology: From cells to systems.* Cengage Learning.

Smith, L. (1992). Spread of English and issues of intelligibility. In B. Kachru (Ed.), *The other tongue: English across cultures* (2nd ed.)., (pp. 75-90). University of Illinois Press.

Smolensky, P. (1999). Grammar-based connectionist approaches to language. *Cognitive Science, 23*(4), 589-613.

Spolky, B. (2004). *Language policy.* Oxford University Press.

Strevens, P. (1992). English as an international language. In B. Kachru (Ed.), *The other tongue: English across cultures* (2nd ed.)., (pp. 27-47). University of Illinois Press.

Swain, M., & Lapkin, S. (1995). Problems in output and the cognitive processes they generate: A step towards second language learning. *Applied Linguistics, 16,* 371-391.

Tarone, E. (2007). Sociolinguistic approaches to second language acquisition research – 1997-2007. *The Modern Language Journal, 91,* 837-848).

Tobias, S. (1986). *Anxiety and cognitive processing of instruction.* In R. Schwarzer (Ed.), Self-related cognition in anxiety and motivation, (pp. 35-54). Erlbaum.

Tremblay, P., & Dick, A. (2016). Broca and Wernicke are dead, or moving past the classical model of language neurobiology. *Brain & Language, 162,* 60-71.

Ullman, M. (2001). The declarative/procedural model of lexicon and grammar. *Journal of Psycholinguistic Research, 30(1),* 37-69.

University of Delaware. (2019, May 8). Learning language: New insights into how brain functions. *ScienceDaily.* https://www.sciencedaily.com/releases/2019/05/190508093716.htm

Van Patten, B., & Benati, A. (2010). *Key terms in second language acquisition.* Continuum.

Vigil, N., & Oller, J. (1976). Rule fossilization: A tentative model. *Language Learning, 26,* 281-295.

Wertsch, J. (1985). *Vygotsky and the social formation of mind.* Harvard University Press.

White, L. (1987). Against comprehensible input: The input hypothesis and the development of second-language competence. *Applied Linguistics, 8*(2), 95-110.

Williams, J. (1999). Memory, attention, and inductive learning. *Studies in Second Language Acquisition, 21,* 1-48.

Williams, J. (2009). Implicit learning in second language acquisition. In W. Ritchie& T. Bhatia (Eds.). *The new handbook of second language acquisition,* (pp. 319-353). Emerald Group Publishing.

Wong-Fillmore, L. (1989). Language learning in social context. The view from research in second language learning. *North-Holland Linguistic Series: Linguistic Variations, 54,* 277-302. https://doi.org/10.1016/B978-0-444-87144-2.S50014-8

Wood, D., Bruner, J., & Ross, G. (1976). The role of tutoring in problem solving. *Journal of Child Psychology and Child Psychiatry, 17,* 89-100.

Wu, M. (2019). Will English remain as a lingua franca in the Industry 4.0 era? In D. Kent (Ed.), *The fourth industrial revolution: Digital language learning and teaching,* (pp. 182-219). KOTESOL DCC.

Vygotsky, L. (1978). Mind in society: The development of higher psychological processes. Harvard University Press.

2. Educational Paradigms, Classroom Management Theories, and Educational Leadership

Overview

Serving as *in loco parentis*, it is expected that schools (and teachers) act in the best interest of the learner, and in any way that they see fit, in order to best achieve such interests. Understanding a wide range of learning theories assists teachers in being able to better practice their craft, and to implement methods, approaches, and various techniques to full advantage when seeking to improve student learning. With this in mind, the various learning theories presented in this chapter illustrate a range of philosophies that explain the nature of learning, and how instructors can apply various principles to underpin their curriculum or lessons in order to support learning and knowledge development. Implementation of these theories also forms a part of effective classroom management. Along with which comes the notion of encouraging and promoting positive learner behavior among students and from within the classroom. As such, a variety of techniques that aim to keep learners on task, ones that can be employed to preempt any problems or issues that may impinge upon a lesson, and those that can be used to deal with issues that do arise during class time in ways that are swift, effective, and appropriate are presented. The chapter is not meant to be a definitive or comprehensive exploration, but instead one that offers a general introduction to many of the educational paradigms, learning, classroom management theories, and the educational leadership roles available to educators. It examines the place of some of the most prominent and prevailing principles that influence the development and teaching of lessons, the supervision of students, and the running of classrooms, particularly those ones that you may very well wish to incorporate into your teacher toolkit. It also focuses on how teacher and student leadership can be fostered, and what those roles mean, along with the importance of wellbeing in the school community and how this can be enhanced. The significance of ethics and a moral code in guiding leadership in relation to the laws, rights, and responsibilities placed on stakeholders is then discussed in closing.

Learning Outcomes
1. Comprehend a range of educational paradigms from which a number of educational theories have emerged.
2. Become familiar with a wide variety of learning theories, and how these serve to engage students in learning and promote the acquisition of knowledge.
3. Gain insight into classroom management theories from behaviorist, humanist, democratic, psycho-analytic, and cognitivist perspectives.
4. Explore a range of different theories that encourage and promote positive learner behavior in the classroom.
5. Understand how to preempt various learner behaviors before they occur, respond positively to them as they occur, and deal with any repercussions that may result from them in ways that are appropriate, effective, and swift.
6. Grasp aspects of educational leadership, with particular emphasis on the roles of teacher and student leader.
7. Explore the concept of wellbeing in relation to staff, teachers, and students, and how enhancement of it can positively impact educational settings.
8. Make sense of the place of ethics, laws, rights, and responsibilities in education.
9. Appreciate the need to develop and rely on a moral code in teaching, and when charged with leadership.

Educational Paradigms
There are a number of paradigms that can be applied to the categorization of learning theories, including those of behaviorism, cognitivism, humanism, constructivism, and connectivism (see Table 2.1). From within these paradigms, among others such as andragogy and pedagogy, socioculturalism, transformativism, poststructuralism, and educational neuro-science, a number of learning theories and pedagogical implications emerge. The most pertinent of these educational paradigms and learning theories will be explored in this section of the chapter.

Andragogy and Pedagogy

Andragogy refers to those theories and principles that apply to adult education, as opposed to pedagogy which are those theories and principles that apply to the education of younger learners and children. The term andragogy was coined by Kapp in 1833 but it was popularized and developed into a learning theory by Knowles (2005). Today, however, most people use the term pedagogy to refer to all of the theories and principles of education in a general sense.

Primarily, andragogy relates to the theory and practice of lifelong education in adults, taking the view that self-directed autonomous learning is undertaken by learners with the teacher seen as a facilitator of learning. The assumptions of andragogy and pedagogy (Jarvis, 1985; Yazdani, 2005) are presented in Table 2.2.

There are seven principles of adult learning based on comprehension, organization, and synthesis of knowledge over rote memory. These principles (CLLN, 2014) see that:

- *One must want to learn.* Adults learn effectively when they are able to direct their own learning. A strong inner and excited level of motivation to develop any new skill or knowledge sustains learning.
- *One learns only what one feels that they need.* Knowledge needs to be practical if time is going to be spent developing it. It needs to be relevant and target/goal focused.
- *One learns by doing.* Adolescents learn by doing, but adults learn via active practice and participation, which helps to integrate component skills into a coherent whole.
- *One learns by focusing on problem solving.* While adolescents tend to learn sequentially, adults tend to start with problems and seek solutions. This means that full engagement, achieved by posing and solving real-world problems and questions, is necessary for deep learning to occur.
- *Experience affects learning.* Adult experience can be an asset as well as a liability. Prior knowledge, if inaccurate, incomplete, or naïve can interfere with the integration of later information.

Paradigm	Behaviorist	Cognitivist	Humanist	Constructivist	Connectivist
Timeline	1900s~	1960s~	1960s~	1970s~	2000s~
Focus of Learning	Development of desired behavior.	Acquiring new knowledge and developing adequate mental constructs.	Assist learner in developing self-actualization and personal potential.	Constructing new knowledge.	Connection forming.
Control Locus	Environmental – external.	Learner – internal.	Learner – internal.	Learner – internal.	Mainly learner but also environmental – internal/external.
Learner Role	Passive, responding to external stimuli – instinct driven.	Active and central, learning objective knowledge from the external world – conscious individual.	Active and discovery – conscious individual.	Active, constructing the representation of knowledge using preferred ways of learning – conscious individual.	Knowledge is formed by establishing connection – conscious individual.
Learning Process	External support providing reward or punishment of behavior – environment driven.	Active process of acquiring and processing novel information using prior knowledge and experience – ad-hoc personal processing.	Active learning through experience – ad-hoc personal processing.	Constructing subjective representations of knowledge based on previous knowledge and experience – systematic personal processing.	Learning occurs outside of the learner, and focuses on establishing connections – ad-hoc network processing.

Table 2.1 A Comparison of Learning Theory Paradigms (Based on Biro, 2014)

	Andragogy	**Pedagogy**
Learners	- Self-directed, and move toward independence. - Responsible for their own learning. - Self-evaluation evident.	- Dependent upon the instructor; the teacher schedules all activities, determining the when, how, and where they should take place. - Instructor is responsible for what is taught and how it is taught. - The teacher evaluates the learning.
Learner's Experience	- Large quantities of experience are gained. - Problem-solving, discussion, and service-learning methods.	- Little experience gained. - Didactic methods.
Readiness to Learn	- Application-based curriculum revolving around life.	- Standardized curriculum based on societal need
Orientation to Learning	- Learning to perform tasks and solving problems.	- Learning to acquire subject matter.
Motivation	- Driven by internal motivation (including self-actualization, self-confidence).	- Motivation is by external pressure, grade competition.

Table 2.2 The Assumptions of Andragogy and Pedagogy

- *Informal situations provide the best learning.* Adolescents need a curriculum; often adults can take on the responsibility of becoming an active participant in the learning process to make it more efficient by collaborating and learning within a networking environment to develop their own content to meet specific end goals.
- *Guidance and consideration on an equal level is important.* Adults seek out information that will assist in improving their current situation. They prefer to evaluate what helps and what does not, and not to be told what to do. Providing options and choices based on individual needs provides a meaningful impact on learner engagement, seeing socialization as being important for learning to occur in adults.

Behaviorism

Behaviorism focuses on the use of conditioning paradigms solidified by reward and/or punishment (stimulus-response). Knowledge is seen as external to the learner, and the learner viewed as *tabula rasa* (a blank slate), with all knowledge coming from experience or perception (Locke, 1690). Pavlov is perhaps one of the most well-known behaviorists who viewed the learning process as one consisting of associations between stimuli and reflexive responses, and based on his findings, Watson (1913) coined the term behaviorism. Pavlov was famous for experimenting with dogs, using an unconditioned response in dogs (salivation to the smell of food) with a neutral stimulus (the sound of a bell) in order to eventually develop a conditioned response (salivation at the sound of a bell). Through conditioning, we build a range of stimulus-response connections with complex behaviors learned by building chains of responses. Thorndike (1932) expanded on classical conditioning, showing that stimuli occurring after a behavior had an influence on future behaviors (*the law of effect*). For example, behavior followed by positive responses is likely to be repeated, while behavior followed by negative responses is likely not to be repeated. Skinner would come to define Pavlovian conditioning as *respondent conditioning* as it was concerned with behavior that is elicited by a preceding stimulus, and that this was inferior to *operant conditioning*. He defines *operants* as acts with no observable stimulus, and those that are governed by the consequences that they produce (e.g., lack or provision of reinforcement). The reinforcement provided then strengthens or weakens the probability of a recurrence of the operant. In other words, we are governed by the consequences of our behavior with the absence of reinforcement being the best method of extinction of an operant as opposed to punishment (the withdrawal of positive reinforcement or the presentation of an aversive stimulus). Skinner (1957) viewed language as a system of verbal operants that would impact on language teaching, with the audiolingual method (discussed in the next chapter) an example.

Cognitivism

Emerging as a response to behaviorism, a 'programmed animal' paradigm, cognitivism focused on inner mental activities as valuable and necessary for the development of learning. Knowledge development was seen as the construction of schema or symbolic mental constructions, with learning defined as a change in schemata. The theory posits that humans require active participation in order to learn, with actions being the consequence of thought. This views the learner as an information processor, using the metaphor of mind as computer (information in, then processed, leads to outcome). Cognitivists consider basic mental processing to be genetic or hard-wired, which can be modified or programmed by external factors (e.g., new experiences). Emphasis is on making knowledge meaningful to the learner who then relates this new knowledge to existing/previous knowledge. Ausubel (1965) views this as associating new events with existing cognitive 'pegs'. Due to having a unique perception of the world, each individual is able to generate their own learning experiences and interpret information that may or may not be the same as others. The postcognivist movement came to hold that knowledge of the world is gained directly with cognition being a physical process on which external variables can impact, with mental properties and predicates not required to understand cognition.

Humanistic Learning

In humanistic learning theory, or humanism, the learner is the source of authority, with the focus being on specific human capabilities including those of creativity, personal growth, and choice. In this view, emphasis is placed on learner potential over learner materials, seeing that:

- the learner is trusted to establish their own goals, is presented with options or choices of what to learn (and should have options or choices);
- students set their own standards (e.g., quantity of work to complete), and evaluate their work; and,
- students focus on the development of positive relationships with peers.

The role of the teacher in the above is to facilitate learning, assisting learners in achieving their goals, and designing supportive strategies that are implemented from a non-threatening environment with learning activities related to life experiences. The teaching strategy of a humanist educator will have at its core:
- *Free will.* People have the choice to do and think what they want.
- *Emotions.* People achieve their best when in a positive emotional state.
- *Intrinsic motivation.* People have an internal desire to become the best that they can be.
- *Innate goodness.* People are essentially good at their core.

Essentially, humanist learning theory posits that, once the ideal learning environment has been established, free-willed learners who are fundamentally good are capable of achieving their best (Crain, 2015; Duchesne & McMaugh, 2013; Veugelers, 2011). It is most notably based on the work of Maslow (1954) and that of Rogers (1951) who came to view the teacher as a facilitator over a conveyor of knowledge, with teacher success deriving from their ability to construct positive relationships with learners. The three core attitudinal characteristics that an instructor needs to possess for facilitative learning to be a success derive from being:
- *Real.* Instructors should be themselves, and rely on their own personality when teaching so that an ethos of trust can be fostered between the learner and teacher.
- *Prizing, accepting, and trusting.* Instructors should care about their learners and accept their feelings, regardless of whether they assist or detract from learning, and through such characteristics, develop deep trust and respect.
- *Empathic.* Understand the learner's attitudes and feelings as well as their perception of learning along with their own attitudes and feelings.

Such facilitative learning also requires students to possess a range of certain traits. These include motivation, an understanding of the conditions they have been provided with, and an awareness of how the tasks they are completing are useful, realistic, and relevant to their life.

Constructivism

Constructivism emphasizes the importance of the active involvement of learners in constructing knowledge for themselves, with novel information acquired based on the learner utilizing their background knowledge. This view sees new information present a loss of equilibrium to the learner that the learner seeks to rectify, which demands changes in cognitive structure with these changes combining to create an improved cognitive schema. Contextual constructivism encompasses the effects of culture and society on experience, with radical constructivism considering the subjective interpretation of experience as opposed to objective reality (Bodner, et al., 2001). The instructor acts as a facilitator of knowledge (*a guide on the side*), as opposed to a dictator of knowledge (*a sage on the stage*), with students encouraged to construct their own knowledge by working on problem-solving and answering open-ended questions. Essentially, constructivist theory posits that, because knowledge only exists within the human mind, it does not have to match any real-world reality (Driscoll, 2000).

The Sociocultural Theory of Cognitive Development

Vygotsky (1978) sees social learning as integral to cognitive development, arguing that learning varies across cultures rather than it being a universal process driven by structures and processes such as those proposed by Piagetian theory. Central to this is the notion that for learners, especially children, development is advanced through social interaction, particularly with others who are more skilled than the learner. In other words, social learning comes before cognitive development, with knowledge actively constructed.

One of the main concepts emerging from this line of thought is the *zone of proximal development* or the ZPD which is a figurative distance between an existing developmental state and the potential development of the learner (Vygotsky, 1978). It represents "the domain of knowledge or skill where the learner is not yet capable of independent functioning, but can achieve the desired outcome given relevant scaffolded help"

(Mitchell & Myles, 2004, p. 196). Scaffolding as a process enables the learner to solve tasks or achieve goals beyond an unassisted effort, allowing for the completion of those elements that are within the range of competence (Wood, et al., 1976).

Crucial to the provision of scaffolding is the *more knowledgeable other* (MKO). This is someone, or something (e.g., a software system) that literally knows more than the learner about what is being learned. The learner works with the MKO, operating in a ZPD that enlarges due to the provision of scaffolding, which results in learner development. Central to this is language as it is the primary means for communication of ideas between the learner and the MKO, and internalizing language is an enormously powerful way of cementing understanding and perspectives of the world around us. The internalization of speech (development of an inner voice) becomes private speech, and this is distinct from social speech which occurs between interlocutors. Over time, social speech becomes internalized and, as the learner is now collaborating with themselves to expand their knowledge, this is learning. The richer the sociocultural environment provided to the learner, the more tools will be available to the learner in the ZPD, and the more social speech they will be able to internalize as private speech. Socialization is key to learning (e.g., the learning environment + interaction = learning).

Transformative Learning

This explains how humans revise and reinterpret meaning, while moving learners to a more inclusive, discriminating, self-reflective, and integrative experience of learning. It involves the cognitive process of effecting change in a frame of reference – habits of mind, and points of view (Mezirow, 1997). Habits of mind (including ethnocentrism) are harder to change than points of view (which can change with appropriation, feedback, and reflection). As a theory, it sees the process of perspective transformation occur across three dimensions: psychological (changes in self-understanding), convictional (belief system revision), and behavioral (lifestyle change) (Clark & Wilson, 1991).

Poststructuralist and Critical Pedagogical Theory

With power structures distributed throughout the classroom discourse (i.e., language), the poststructuralist view sees the classroom as a place of inclusion and one in which education is socially just. The focus is on discourse, truth, and power, with discourse meaning the way that language is used, truth being shaped by the dominant discourse presented, and power in the hands of those who shape the truth of discourse and control that discourse. "*Truth* is linked in a circular relation with systems of power that produce and sustain it, and to effects of power which it induces and which extend it – a *regime of truth*" (Foucault, 2002, p. 132). In other words, everywhere we look, power is being exercised to one degree or another. In the classroom, it is found in how women are represented in posters and books. It is found in how minorities are represented in the reading material and the textbooks (i.e., in a positive manner or a degrading and stereotypical manner). It is found in the language that a teacher uses, and if that language reinforces certain values. It is found in the cultural responsiveness of the pedagogy applied in the classroom, and so on. So, poststructuralist theory sees power operating everywhere and reinforcing unjust social disparity "with language a vehicle through which differences between and within identity categories (e.g., gender, race, ethnicity) are created and realized" (Morgan, 2004, p. 949). To challenge such power structures in education, it focuses on, and sees, inclusivity discourse as essential in the classroom. This would include use of inclusive tests, encouraging social critique, challenging gender stereotypes, and amplifying minority voice. Keep in mind that in education, a teacher can present with *deficit discourse*, and this impacts upon how students, coworkers, and others may view themselves. Deficit discourse refers to those disempowering patterns of thought, language and practice which represent people or groups in terms of deficiencies such as absence, lack, or failure, and which can then lead to negativity. For example, a student constantly called dumb might end up believing they are stupid, and as a result, give up on study.

Critical theory, like poststructuralist theory, believes in the importance of critiquing how power operates in the classroom and harms minority learners. However, the critical theory approach focuses on working-class minorities. So, while poststructuralists focus on inclusiveness, critical theorists focus on promotion of the belief systems of those considered to be oppressed. Critical pedagogy in the EFL/ESL context maintains that both language learning and the teaching of it are a political process. Language is not simply a means of expression or communication. It is a practice that constructs, and is constructed by, the ways that language learners understand themselves, their social surroundings, history, and future possibilities (Norton & Toohey, 2004).

Connectivist Learning

Connectivism has been described as a 'learning theory for the digital age' (Siemens, 2005). It attempts to explain how internet technologies (i.e., browsers, search engines, wikis, online chat/discussion, and social networking) have created novel opportunities to learn from others and to share information with them (Siemens, 2005; Downes, 2010). It sees learning occur when knowledge is actuated by the process of a learner connecting to and feeding information into a network or a learning community.

At its core, connectivism is a form of experiential learning that prioritizes actions and experience over the notion that knowledge is propositional. In a classroom context, this may involve encouraging students to use real-world problem-solving skills or to conduct experiments so that they can practice creating knowledge, reflecting upon it, and discussing it in order to process how their understanding is developing. The instructor's role then is one that guides the learner as appropriate, thereby assisting in the construction of knowledge as a more knowledgeable other (MKO).

Not only does connectivism view that learning occurs by engaging with a diversity of ideas and opinions, with new ideas constructed through shared thinking and conversations, but that this knowledge can also reside within machines. Examples are the internet, which is a vast repository of knowledge (perhaps, of variable quality), and WolframAlpha, a computational knowledge engine that relies on curated data (which, digital assistants like Alexa have access to as well as we do). It also includes the ways in which people store knowledge within machines, and how they interact with that knowledge and with other humans as well as AIs (artificial intelligences) in order to take control of their own learning as they retrieve and engage with knowledge. More basic examples include the use of PowerPoints and interactive whiteboards for presenting and interacting with stored knowledge. So, technology is viewed as a resource and as a way to mediate human interactions, with these interactions making use of different connections and different language forms depending on the media. Hence, knowing where to find information is more important than knowing that information, making the ability to see connections between fields, ideas, and concepts a core competency.

The core principles of connectivism are:
- Knowledge and learning rest in the diversity of opinions.
- Learning involves connecting specialized nodes or information sources.
- Learning may reside in machines.
- Learning is more critical than knowing.
- Maintaining and nurturing connections facilitates continuous learning. Learning networks cannot be consolidated when interaction time between actors is not enough (Mena-Guacas & Velandia, 2020).
- Perceiving connections between fields, ideas, and concepts is a core skill.
- Providing accurate and up-to-date knowledge (currency) lies behind the intent of learning activities.
- Decision-making is itself a learning process. Deciding what to learn and interpreting the meaning of incoming information is conducted through the lens of a shifting reality (i.e., the right answer now might be wrong tomorrow due to alterations in further incoming information). Learners constantly assess, gain understanding, and reflect on experience, which further strengthens their ability to integrate new information that they can then assess.

Educational Neuroscience

The practical application of neuroscience to education sees it able to analyze the biological changes in the brain that occur as a result of processing new information. Research involving educational neuroscience attempts to link understanding of brain processes with classroom instruction and experiences (Wolf, 2010). This can help in identifying what environmental, emotional, and social situations may best assist the brain in the processing of novel information. The key here also lies in determining how best to keep dendrites from being reabsorbed and losing information after the linking of neurons have been able to solidify knowledge.

Developmental Stage Theory

This is a comprehensive theory put forth by Piaget (1936) that deals with the nature of knowledge itself, and how we as humans come to acquire, construct, and use it. In this theory, the basic concepts of learning, or development as Piaget refers to it, are schema, adaptation processes, and the stages of cognitive development. It views intellectual growth as a process of adaptation (or adjustment) to the world. This happens through a process of assimilation, accommodation, and equilibration, involving schema and adaptation processes that occur throughout four stages of cognitive development.

Schemata are building blocks of knowledge, and they are clusters of connected ideas concerning the real world that allow people to respond accordingly. *Equilibrium* occurs when schemas can deal with most new information through *assimilation*; that is, where assimilation involves the use of an existing schema to deal with a new object or situation. *Accommodation* happens when existing schema does not work, and needs to be altered in order to deal with a new object or situation.

Adaptation processes allow a transition from one stage to another (equilibrium, assimilation, and accommodation). When a schema is used to deal with a new situation or thing, then that schema is in assimilation, with accommodation occurring once the existing schema is found lacking, and once changed, it then reaches a new level of equilibrium. The force that moves development along is equilibration, with the learner seeking a balance by mastering any new challenges that they are presented with (via accommodation), forming a learning loop (schema → assimilation → accommodation → schema).

Stages of cognitive development are **sensorimotor, preoperational, concreate operational, and formal operational.**
- The *sensorimotor stage* (from birth to around 2 years old) sees children learning basic schemas and project permanence (the notion of something existing even though it is unable to be seen).
- The *preoperational stage* (from 2 to 7) sees the child develop additional schemas and the ability to think symbolically (e.g., understanding that one thing can stand for another). There will

still be a struggle with empathy (Theory of Mind) and understanding the views of other people.
- The *concrete operational stage* (from 7 to 11) is when children begin to think things through and develop the ability to conserve (understand that something stays the same even though it may look different, e.g., the same amount of liquid in a small container appears more than when in a smaller container).
- The *formal operational stage* (from 11 into adulthood) is where abstract thought develops along with logic and hypothesis testing. In educational contexts, a teacher can use Piaget's theory, in terms of syllabus choice, for children at similar levels of cognitive development to perform operations with similar accuracy.

Hierarchy of Needs Theory

This theory lends itself to building student/teacher relationships more so than to curriculum development or lesson planning. It is a popular theory for motivation. The classroom is also viewed by many educators as a place that should meet many of the needs of learners, particularly those that serve to establish a physiological and emotional safe space where students feel that they belong and are comfortable, and one in which their self-esteem can be supported so that they can perform optimally ('self-actualize'). These requirements are all reflected in the hierarchy of needs (see Figure 2.1), which has been revised over time with the hierarchy now perceived to continuously overlap.

The hierarchy of needs (Maslow, 1954) sees those most fundamental requirements labelled as *deficiency needs* (or *d-needs*). These include esteem, friendship and love, security, and physical ones. If these needs are not met, then the learner may feel anxious. The term *metamotivation* refers to those who go beyond the basic needs and strive for self-betterment, although the most basic needs must be met prior to an individual desiring this. Many different motivations from the hierarchy may occur at any time, and concurrently.

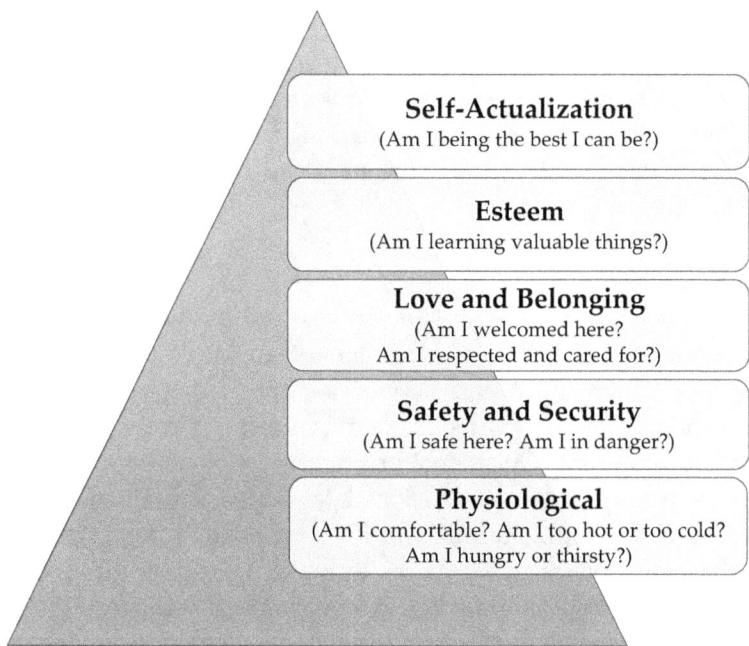

Figure 2.1 Maslow's Hierarchy of Needs

To support students' physiological needs, adequate air-conditioning or heating control should be provided along with adequate access to water and snacks, toilet breaks, and perhaps naps, as appropriate to the learning context. The classroom climate should also be monitored for bullying to ensure that students are in a safe space, one where they feel that they belong, and one where they feel comfortable expressing themselves. This may be supported through the development of family-belonging, and by active seating arrangement that places students in groups where they feel supported by their friends or fellow learners. Self-esteem can be supported through the provision of affirmative, concrete, and transparent feedback (from both instructors and other students) in ways where students can understand their specific strengths and identify the factors that have led to their classroom success. In this way, students will be able to perform at their best potential.

Domains of Learning

Bloom and his colleagues argue that there is a hierarchy of learning. These hierarchies (taxonomies of learning objectives) relate to the development of different kinds of learning skills and are part of either the cognitive (thinking), affective (feeling), or psychomotor (doing) domain (Bloom et al., 1956).

Cognitive Domain

The cognitive domain involves objectives and skills that assist with processing information. Bloom's original taxonomies that describe the processes of learning in this domain are knowledge, comprehension, application, analysis, synthesis, and evaluation. The categories are meant to represent educational activities with increasing complexity and abstraction. These subdivisions later underwent a major revision (Anderson & Krathwohl, 2001) which included a renaming of the subdivisions from nouns to verbs to make them easier to use when designing curriculums and when lesson planning. See Figure 2.2.

- *Remembering.* Retrieving relevant knowledge from long-term memory (e.g., recognizing, recalling).
- *Understanding.* Determining the meaning of instructional messages, including oral, graphic and written. (e.g., interpreting, exemplifying, classifying, summarizing, inferring, comparing, explaining).
- *Applying.* Performing or using specific procedures in given situations (e.g., executing, implementing).
- *Analyzing.* Breaking material into constituent parts and detecting how the parts relate to each other and to an overall purpose or structure (e.g., differentiating, organizing, attributing).
- *Evaluating.* Making judgements based on criteria and standards (e.g., checking, critiquing).
- *Creating.* Putting elements together to form a coherent whole, or to create an original product (e.g., generating, planning, producing).

The order of the top two subdivisions was also reversed. The knowledge dimension of the revised hierarchy shifted from knowledge as specific facts, ideas, and processes (revised category: 'remember') to include awareness of possible actions that can be

performed with knowledge. This second dimension of knowledge brings with it four aspects:
- *Factual knowledge.* The basic elements of a discipline that a learner must be acquainted with in order to solve problems.
- *Conceptual knowledge.* An understanding of the interrelationships among the basic elements of a discipline that operate within a larger structure that enables them to function together.
- *Procedural knowledge.* Understanding how to do something, utilize methods of inquiry, and being able to apply the specific criteria required for using specific sets of skills, algorithms, techniques, and methods.
- *Metacognitive knowledge.* The knowledge of cognition in general as well as an awareness and knowledge regarding one's own condition. When the cognitive and knowledge dimensions are then arranged in a matrix they can be utilized as an aid when creating performance objectives. See Table 2.3.

Knowledge Dimension	Factual	Conceptual	Procedural	Metacognitive
Remember				
Understand				
Apply				
Analyze				
Evaluate				
Create				

Table 2.3 Knowledge Dimension Matrix – Cognitive
(see Clark, 2015)

A similar matrix using five knowledge artifacts (Clark & Chopeta, 2004; Clark & Mayer, 2011) appear in tables 2.4 and 2.5. These knowledge artifacts are broken down as follows:
- *Facts.* Specific and unique instances or data.
- *Concepts.* Classes of items, words, or ideas that are represented by a common name. These would be either concrete or abstract.
- *Processes.* A flow of events or activities describing how things work over how to do something (e.g., work flows, technical processes). It is the big picture of how something works.

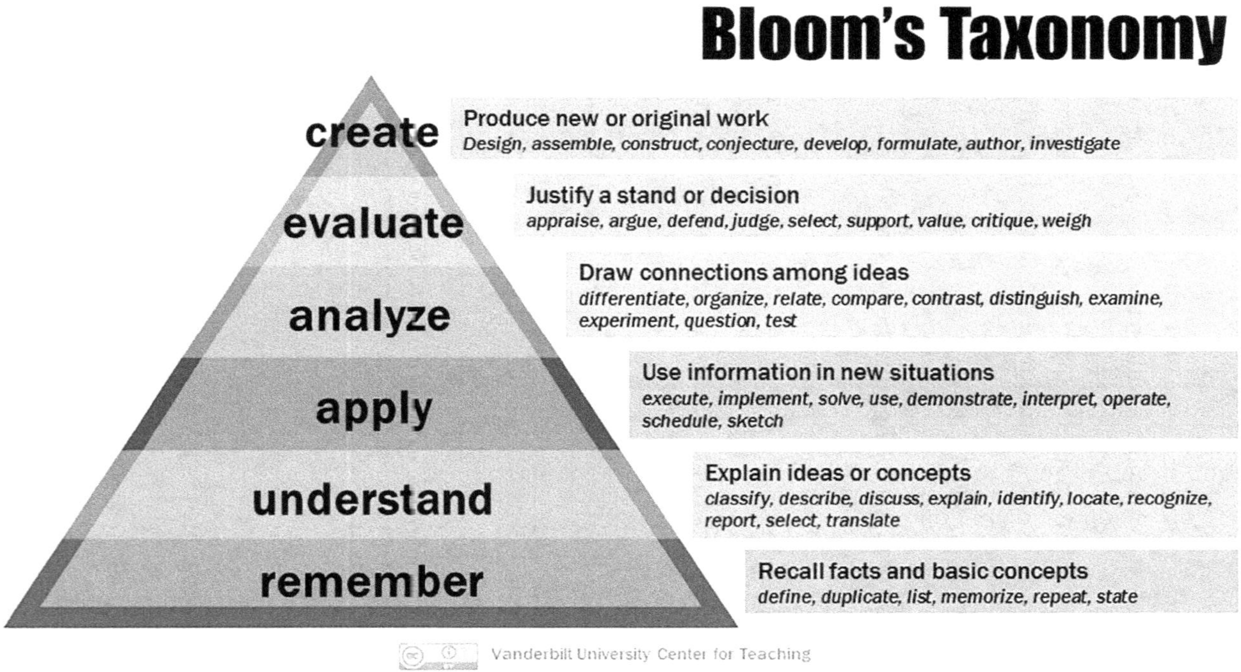

Bloom's Taxonomy

create — Produce new or original work
Design, assemble, construct, conjecture, develop, formulate, author, investigate

evaluate — Justify a stand or decision
appraise, argue, defend, judge, select, support, value, critique, weigh

analyze — Draw connections among ideas
differentiate, organize, relate, compare, contrast, distinguish, examine, experiment, question, test

apply — Use information in new situations
execute, implement, solve, use, demonstrate, interpret, operate, schedule, sketch

understand — Explain ideas or concepts
classify, describe, discuss, explain, identify, locate, recognize, report, select, translate

remember — Recall facts and basic concepts
define, duplicate, list, memorize, repeat, state

Vanderbilt University Center for Teaching

Figure 2.2 A Revised Taxonomy, 2001
(Image reproduced under the Creative Commons Attribution license, courtesy of the Vanderbilt University Center for Teaching)

Educational Paradigms   107

Knowledge Dimension	Facts	Concepts	Processes	Procedures	Principles	Metacognitive
Remember						
Understand						
Apply						
Analyze						
Evaluate						
Create						

Table 2.4 Knowledge Dimension Matrix – Artifacts
(see Clark, 2015)

Knowledge Dimension	Facts	Concepts	Processes	Procedures	Principles	Metacognitive
Remember	List	Recall	Outline	Reproduce	State	Proper use
Understand	Paraphrase	Explain	Estimate	Provide example	Convert	Interpret
Apply	Classify	Show	Produce	Relate	Solve	Discover
Analyze	Outline	Contrast	Diagram	Identify	Differentiate	Infer
Evaluate	Rank	Criticize	Defend	Critique	Conclude	Predict
Create	Categorize	Modify	Design	Plan	Revise	Actualize

Table 2.5 Knowledge Dimension Matrix – Artifacts Completed
(see Clark, 2015)

- *Procedures.* Step-by-step actions and decisions that result in the achievement of tasks. These can be linear or branched.
- *Principles.* Guides, rules, and governing parameters. These include what should be done as well as what should not be done, and allow for predictions and implications, therefore becoming the building blocks of causal or theoretical models and theories.

Affective Domain

The affective domain involves objectives that deal with the development of feelings, emotions, attitudes, appreciation, and preference. The domain subcategories here range from receiving through to characterization as follows:
- *Receiving.* Being aware of external stimuli (e.g., touch, sense, experience).
- *Responding.* Reacting to external stimuli (e.g., contributing, enjoyment, satisfaction).
- *Valuing.* Appropriation of worth (e.g., preferences, respect).
- *Organization.* Conceptualization and organization of values (e.g., clarifying, integrating, examining).
- *Characterization.* Practicing and acting on values (e.g., reviewing, concluding, judging).

Psychomotor Domain

The psychomotor domain includes those objectives relating to the development of motor skills, coordination, and physical movement (kinesthetic action). This might involve reflex actions, interpretive movements, discreet physical functions, and so on. It refers to how we use our body and senses to interact with the world, and how to move within that space. The different types of learning in this domain (Harrow, 1972), moving from those that are reflex to those that require more control, are:
- *Reflex movement.* Appearing at birth and emerging through puberty (e.g., automatic movement, like breathing, shivering).
- *Fundamental movements.* Basic movements that also tend to form more complex actions like those involved in sports (e.g., running, jumping, walking).
- *Perceptual abilities.* Those abilities that allow us to sense the world around us and coordinate our movements in order to

interact with the environment (e.g., auditory, olfactory, tactile, taste, visual).
- *Physical abilities.* Those abilities that allow us to perform a physical act (e.g., dexterity, endurance, flexibility, strength).
- *Skilled movements.* Those that involve 'muscle memory' (e.g., sport, dance, playing a musical instrument).
- *Nondiscursive communication.* That in which writing is absent (e.g., physical actions such as facial expressions, gestures, and posture).

Structure of Observed Learning Outcomes (SOLO) Taxonomy

To further distinguish between increasingly complex levels of understanding, a structure of observed learning outcomes (SOLO) was developed (Biggs & Collis, 1982). The SOLO taxonomy moves from describing what learners do with information to describing the relationship that students articulate between multiple pieces of information. In this model, understanding is conceived as an increase in the number and complexity of connections that a learner makes as they progress from being incompetent to becoming an expert. It is comprised of five levels:

- *Pre-structural.* Learners acquire pieces of unconnected information that have no organization and make no sense. This is a state of ignorance.
- *Unistructural.* Learners make simple and obvious connections, but the significance of these connections is not grasped. This is comprised of surface learning, as is the multistructural level.
- *Multistructural.* Learners make connections but the meta-connections between them are missed as is their significance in relation to the whole.
- *Relational.* Learners are able to appreciate the significance of the parts in relation to the whole.
- *Extended abstract.* Learners make connections within the subject area, and are able to generalize and transfer the principles and ideas that underlie specific instances. Like the relational level, this level is comprised of deep learning.

Conditions of Learning

Eight conditions of learning (see Table 2.8) were proposed by Gagne (1965), and viewed as being hierarchical based on their complexity. These involve learning outcomes that can be categorized into five types (see Table 2.6) that provide the critical conditions required for learning. In order to achieve these learning outcomes, nine instructional events (see Table 2.7), based on the information-processing model of learning and memory (Schunk, 2008), are considered essential. Each type of learning outcome requires a different kind of instruction, and aligns with either the affective, cognitive, or psychomotor domains.

Type of Learning Outcome	Domain
Verbal information	Cognitive
Intellectual skills	
Cognitive Strategies	
Motor skills	Psychomotor
Attitudes	Affective

Table 2.6 Learning Outcome and Associated Domain

Each instructional event provides a hierarchy of learning where learning tasks for intellectual skill development can be organized according to complexity.

Instructional Event	Cognitive Processes
Gaining Attention	Reception
Informing learners of the objective	Expectancy
Stimulating recall of prior learning	Retrieval
Presenting the stimulus	Selective perception
Providing learning guidance	Semantic encoding
Eliciting performance	Responding
Providing feedback	Reinforcement
Assessing performance learning	Retrieval
Enhancing retention and transfer	Generalization

Table 2.7 Instructional Events and Associated Cognitive Processes

Conditions of Learning	Linguistic Application
Signal learning (classical conditioning)	Humans notice and attend to human language.
Stimulus-response learning (operant conditioning)	Noticing and responding to specific sounds, words, and nonverbal gestures, and receiving a reward for the response.
Chaining (complex operant conditioning)	Stringing several sounds or words together to attempt to communicate meaning.
Verbal association (creation of associations using verbal connections)	Assigning meaning to various verbal stimuli. 'Nonsense' syllables become meaningful communication.
Discrimination (learning of responding different to different stimuli)	Noticing differences between/among sounds, words, or phrases that are similar, e.g., minimal pairs (ship/sheep), homonyms (left/left), and synonyms (maybe/perhaps).
Concept learning (learning a general response to a class of stimuli)	The word 'hot' applies to stoves, candles, and irons; young children learn that four-legged farm animals are not all 'horsies'.
Rule learning (a rule is a chain of two or more concepts)	Verbs in the past tense are classified into regular and irregular forms, yet both forms express the concept of tense.
Problem solving. (The application of previously learned rules and concepts to new situations)	Learning that metaphorical language is not simply idiosyncratic, but connected to cultural world views and ways of thinking, thus explaining why a dead person is 'gone'. Also, using language to solve problems, such as information gap exercises in a classroom.

Table 2.8 Gagne's Conditions of Learning (with descriptor) Categorized by Levels of Complexity and Presented with Linguistic Application (based on Brown, 2014, pp. 93-94)

Combined with taxonomies such as those of Bloom, Gagne's nine levels of learning can provide educators with a framework from which to begin planning lessons and topics. This would see Bloom's taxonomy used to set differentiated objectives, with Gagne's providing scaffolding on which to construct a lesson.

Spiral Curriculum

An iterative curriculum that revisits topics, subjects, and themes throughout a course is what lies at the heart of the spiral curriculum. Each revisiting of content is one of deepening learning as the material presented builds upon the previous encounter. The hypothesis behind such a curriculum is "that any subject can be taught in some intellectually honest form to any child at any stage of development" (Bruner, 1960, p. 33). Such a curriculum is based on three main principles:

- *Cyclical.* Learners revisit content multiple times throughout their academic career. This serves to reinforce learning on each revisit.
- *Increasing depth.* Complexity of the content increases upon each revisit. This serves to allow for progression through subject matter as cognitive ability develops.
- *Prior Knowledge.* As learners revisit content matter, new ideas are linked to ones previously met (activation of prior knowledge). This serves to help familiarize learners with keywords and ideas that enable them to grasp more difficult elements of the topic in a deeper manner.

The three principles follow three modes of representation. These modes are sequential, and they also refer to the way that knowledge is stored in memory.

- *Enactive (age 0-1).* Knowledge representation through physical activities – manipulation and interaction with objects.
- *Iconic (age 1-6).* Knowledge representation through visual imagery – manipulation and interaction with images of actual objects or phenomena.
- *Symbolic (age 7+).* Words and symbols used to describe experience – manipulation of representations of actual objects or phenomena.

To design a spiral curriculum, units need to be developed so that there is an increase in complexity from one unit to the next. For example, in the first unit, students may need to simply understand the topic. However, revisiting that unit might see learners' critique or analyze content, with a final revisit to the same unit then seeing learners create content of their own. A number of benefits and limitations exist for such a curriculum as Table 2.9 highlights.

The Spiral Curriculum	
Benefits	**Limitations**
Provides developmentally appropriate learning.	Very time consuming for curriculum designers.
Sees prior knowledge as central to learning.	The curriculum can get very crowded.
Utilizes spaced repetition.	It may lead to the development of a number of irrelevant short courses.
Allows instructors to focus on the structuring of work following a logical progression.	It risks becoming an instructor-centered curriculum.
Allows integration and collaboration to occur (e.g., instructors collaborate to ensure the provision of holistic and coherent learning).	Instructors find themselves reteaching the same content over and over again (e.g., gap-filling over teaching of new knowledge).

Table 2.9 Benefits and Limitations of the Spiral Curriculum (from Drew, 2020a)

An alternative to the spiral curriculum is the strand curriculum (Strand, 2004). Instead of chunking content into topic blocks, this type of curriculum aims to integrate multiple topics into every lesson, every day, in order to slowly but consistently provide work on a given topic over a sustained and extended period of time. This may serve to prevent memory loss and loss of momentum that may occur when a topic is left alone for a period of time before it is revisited.

Experiential Learning

The experiential learning cycle involves four stages (Kolb, 1984), of which the learner can enter at any point, with effective learning occurring as the learner progresses through the cycle. It is built on the premise that learning is the acquisition of abstract concepts that can then be applied to a range of scenarios. Learning can only be achieved if all four stages have been completed. Each stage feeds into the next and are mutually supportive, with learner understanding refined each time they go through the cycle. That said, the first stage is considered to be concrete experience, which leads into reflective observation, then abstract conceptualization, and then on to active experimentation (see Figure 2.3). The learning works in conjunction with learning styles, with each learning style representing a combination of two preferred styles (see Table 2.10).

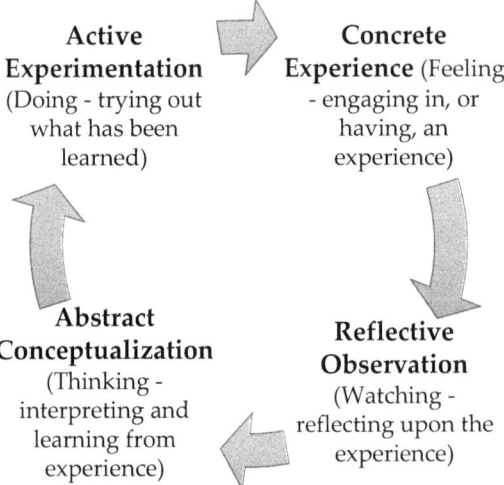

Figure 2.3 Kolb's Experiential Learning Cycle

	Active Experimentation (AE)	Reflective Observation (RO)
Concrete Experience (CE)	Accommodating (CE/AE)	Diverging (CE/RO)
Abstract Conceptualization (AC)	Converging (AC/AE)	Assimilating (AC/RO)

Table 2.10 Kolb's Learning Style Matrix

The learning styles (Lu, et al., 2007) are comprised of:
- *Accommodating* (doing and feeling – Concrete Experience/Active Experimentation). This style relies on intuition over logic. Such learners tend to rely on the analyses of others, preferring practical and experiential approaches.
- *Converging* (doing and thinking – Abstract Conceptualization/Active Experimentation). This style of learner is a problem solver who uses their learning to find solutions to practical issues. They prefer technical tasks, and are less concerned with others and interpersonal aspects of learning, preferring to experiment with new ideas, simulations, and working with practical applications.
- *Diverging* (feeling and watching – Concrete Experience/Reflective Observation). This style of learner is sensitive, and is able to examine things from a variety of perspectives. They observe rather than participate, gathering information and using their imagination to solve problems. These people prefer to work in groups, listen to others with an open mind, and prefer to receive personal feedback.
- *Assimilating* (watching and thinking – Abstract Conceptualization/Reflective Observation). This style prefers concise, logical approaches, with ideas and concepts being more important than others. Clear explanations over practical opportunities are preferred, as they excel at understanding wide-ranging information and at being able to organize it in a clear and logical manner. They prefer readings, lectures, exploring analytical models, and having the time to think things through for themselves.

The learning stages and the cycle can be used by instructors to develop appropriate learning opportunities for students, and to critically evaluate learning provision (McLeod, 2013). Learning content should be developed in a manner that best draws on learner abilities as they pass through each stage of the cycle in sequence, with instructors needing to ensure that there is differentiation of activities so that learners can each engage with each other in the way that suits them best.

Subsumption Learning

This theory is concerned with how individuals learn large amounts of meaningful content from verbal/textual presentations in school contexts (Ausubel, 1962). The process is intended to be one of meaningful learning, as opposed to rote learning, where subsumed items (or meaningfully learned ones) hold greater potential for retention. It is based on the use of expository learning, or reception learning, which is an organized teaching method where information is presented in a specific order to focus attention and promote memorization (e.g., through the use of advanced organizers).

Unlike other educational theories that arose from psychology-based models, subsumption learning theory was developed exclusively for instructional design. It sees the acquisition of knowledge as being successful if it is tied to an existing knowledge base (subsumption), with the information standing out within a lesson being that which is dedicated to memory. In this theory, meaningful learning occurs once subsumed cognitive structures have been fully developed. That is, where cognitive structures are what is left after the learning experience, and once 'cognitive pruning' (Brown, 1972) or forgetting occurs (e.g., when situations, details, and facts all lose their individuality and become integrated into a general notion).

There are two types of subsumption:
- *Correlative.* New material is an extension of content already grasped.
- *Derivative.* New material derives from existing structure, linked to other concepts or new interpretations.

Four key principles involved with subsumption theory are the need to:
- Present learners with general concepts first, and then their analysis.

- Provide instructional material that includes new as well as previously acquired content, with the comparison between old and new concepts viewed as crucial.
- Reorganize existing cognitive structures within learner memory, not develop them.
- See the instructor serve to bridge the gap between what is already known and what is about to be learned.

Implementing subsumption theory within a course may see you need to focus on the provision of key outcomes, and providing a general overview highlighting everything the learner needs to know by the end of the lesson. This allows learners to develop a big picture which they can then relate to existing ideas, theories, and notions, and begin to relate to how these concepts may fit within their existing mental map. Material would then follow a general to a specific sequence ('progressing differentiation'), and as learners progress, they will be able to relate the new information to what they have just encountered, which would help them in categorizing content and aligning it to cognitive structures. This may also assist in encouraging learners to apply previously learned knowledge, and help them to anchor new knowledge to memory in order to improve comprehension and knowledge retention. In this regard, the use and development of comparison and contrast models may prove useful in creating a connection between what is being learned and what can be retained. Another effective means of doing so is to make the learning more personal. This may involve using stories that trigger emotion, or relying on real-world examples that stress the benefits of learning the subject matter, allowing the learner to relate the concepts being learned to actual use in daily life.

It may also be profitable to use advanced organizers with learners in the way that Ausubel has advocated their use

> ... *introduced in advance of learning itself, and are also presented at a higher level of abstraction, generality, and inclusiveness; and since the substantive content of a given organizer or series of organizers is selected on the basis of its suitability for explaining, integrating, and interrelating the material they precede, this strategy simultaneously satisfies the substantive as well as the programming criteria for enhancing the organization strength of cognitive structure* (1963, p. 81).

Advanced organizers fall into one of four categories, and these are
- expository organizers that present descriptions of new knowledge,
- narrative organizers that provide new information in a story-based format,
- skimming organizers that focus on key aspects or the highlights of new information, and
- graphic organizers that represent new information in pictographs, descriptive or conceptual patterns, and concept maps.

Psychosocial Development

Understanding the stages of psychological development helps us as teachers begin to understand what kind of questions students might be asking of themselves and the world around them, and this in turn provides a framework that we can begin to base our teaching upon. According to Erikson's psychosocial theory of development (1993), humans go through eight stages of development during their lifetimes (see Table 2.11), and these are based on the impact of external factors, parents, and society on personality development from childhood through to adulthood. In each stage, there is a dilemma that we all face, and in resolving it, we feel a sense of competence, and develop into a well-adjusted adult.

Stage	Age	Dilemma
Basic Trust vs. Mistrust – Hope	0~1.5	Infants must learn that adults can be trusted. If treated poorly, they may grow up feeling mistrust towards others.
Autonomy vs. Shame – Will	1.5~3	Children start to make decisions, showing preferences (e.g., what clothes to wear, or toys that they enjoy). Children who are not allowed to explore preferences may develop low self-esteem and shame.
Initiative vs. Guilt – Purpose	3~5	Children start to plan and achieve goals involving others.

		Those not supported in doing this will develop a low sense of purpose and lack self-confidence.
Industry *vs.* Inferiority – Competence	5~12	Children start to compare the self to peers. Unable to successfully compare will see a sense of accomplishment lacking in regard to school work, social and family activities, and sport.
Identity *vs.* Role Confusion – Fidelity	12~18	Young adults will consider multiple roles for the self to find a best fit. If not supported here, there will be a lack of ability to defend core beliefs and face others' opinions.
Intimacy & Solidarity *vs.* Isolation – Love	18~35	Those in early adulthood see focus shift to making and maintaining strong, intimate relationships with others. Isolation results if this does not occur.
Generativity *vs.* Stagnation or Self-Absorption – Care	35~55/65	Adults at this stage are concerned with contributing to society through work or parenthood. If this is not supported, there may arise a struggle in finding purpose.
Ego Integrity *vs.* Despair – Wisdom	55~65+	Adults at this point reflect on their life. Those who feel that they are failures will obsess with ideas of what 'could have' or 'should have' been done.

Table 2.11 Erickson's Eight Stages of Psychological Development Matched to Age and the Dilemma

The Banking Model of Education and Problem-Posing Education

A teaching style where the instructor deposits knowledge into the learner's mind, as if they are a 'piggy bank', lies at the core of the banking model of education. It sees students as passive learners with no scope provided for creative freedom or critical thinking (the 'empty vessel'). Freire (1970), in this Marxist model, views instructors as oppressors and learners as the oppressed. He considers the knowledge transmission model to be one that harms students, and purports a model where learning is practical, focuses on problem posing, and alters the instructor role to that of co-learner. The benefits and limitations of the banking model can be seen in Table 2.12.

Banking Model	
Benefits	**Limitations**
- Maintains teacher dominance and control. - Provides an avenue for the reproduction of values and culture. - Delivers direct instruction. - Ensures a structured learning environment.	- Promotes a lack of critical thinking. - Develops a lack of creativity. - Creates a power imbalance.

Table 2.12 Banking Model of Education Benefits and Limitations (based Drew, 2020b).

Ten defining features of the banking model of education (Freire, 1970, p. 73) are:
- The teacher teaches; students are taught.
- The teacher knows everything; students are ignorant.
- The teacher thinks; students are thought about.
- The teacher narrates; students listen.
- The teacher disciplines; students are disciplined.
- The teacher chooses; students comply.
- The teacher acts; students observe.
- The teacher sets the curriculum; students adapt to it.

- The teacher claims authority; students are oppressed by it.
- The teacher is the subject, students are the objects.

Problem Posing Approach	
Benefits	**Limitations**
- Active discovery and examination of new knowledge by learners. - Learner-instructor partnership, giving students a sense of empowerment and ownership of learning. - Instructors do not feel like they need to have all the answers (relinquish being a 'sage on the stage'). - Students learn about phenomena that has relevance to everyday life. - Learners are encouraged to develop problem-solving, along with creative and critical thinking skills. - Open communication and social learning are encouraged, assisting the students to build communication skills and learn from each other.	- Teacher relinquishes control. - Sometimes theoretical ideas need teaching, and must use direct instruction. - Learning is more difficult (students must exercise cognitive strategies, higher-order thinking skills, and active learning strategies that require cognitive load).

Table 2.13 Problem Posing Approach Benefits and Limitations (based on Drew, 2020b)

As an alternative, Freire would suggest a problem-posing approach (see Table 2.13). This active learning strategy was viewed as one that would liberate students and empower them, and in such a classroom, the teacher is no longer the knowledge holder. (No one is.) A problem would be posed by someone in the class, and then the class would need to uncover a solution together. Students are viewed as active learners that are capable of reaching conclusions via the application of cognitive skills. The teacher is seen as a co-learner, with student prior knowledge used to help learners understand new topics. The aim of the approach is to encourage in learners a means of coming to conclusions using logic over rote learning, develop higher-order cognition, embrace the use of prior knowledge to learn new information, and establish a democratic classroom where instructors do not dominate or impose beliefs upon learners.

Phenomenon-Based Learning

This is a holistic approach to education, and one where students learn through topics and themes as opposed to subject areas. It is a rejection of the silo-based approach to learning which sees subjects taught in isolation from each other. Students are expected to apply concepts from a range of disciplines when solving problems that they are studying, and the aim is to teach subject areas concurrently rather than separately. It is grounded in constructivist theory where students learn through 'mulling over' concepts rather than absorbing facts transmitted from the teacher. It involves a student-centered socio-constructivist approach involving active learning, project-based learning, and problem-based learning that provides learners with authentic materials with which to work.

Learning starts with a phenomenon that students begin to explore, and not one particular subject. A topic might be provided to students to research and discover a problem they want to explore or solve. This sees students using inductive and deductive inquiry to reach conclusions (i.e., make predictions and generalizations based on observation, and test these generalizations or hypotheses in order to reach clear conclusions.) The benefits and limitations of this learning theory can be seen in Table 2.14.

Phenomenon Based Learning Theory	
Benefits	**Limitations**
- Students learn how to apply knowledge to real-world circumstances. - Students can see connections between different learning domains. - Students gain the skills required in 21st century workplaces. - Highlights the importance of linking theoretical knowledge to practice. - Holistic perspectives are provided concerning phenomena under analysis. - Enhances engagement, as focus is on problem-solving over repetitive subject-based tasks. - Students rely on group work, problem-solving, communication, and logical reasoning skills to reach conclusions. - Students are encouraged to learn in independent cooperative groups to solve problems. - Educators across different disciplines can collaborate. - Educators can employ flexible classroom layouts.	- Sometimes, there is a need for traditional (direct or modelled) instruction. - Students need to be trained on how to work in groups, identify problems, and conduct research. - Lack of structure in project-based learning approaches may be disconcerting to some learners. - Some phenomena may not need all disciplinary knowledge to solve problems, leaving gaps in learning and practice. - Open-endedness, and student-led nature, presents difficulties for educators to present challenges in the right sequence for optimal learning. - Sufficient resources and support needs to be provided to learners as they go about their work.

Table 2.14 Phenomenon Based Learning Theory Benefits and Limitations (based on Tissington, 2019)

Dual Coding, the Promise of Multimedia, and Cognitive Load Theory

Learning from multimedia occurs when learners are able to build mental representations from words and pictures. This aligns with dual coding theory (Paivio, 1971) which relies on verbal associations and visual imagery for deep learning to occur. In dual coding theory, visual and verbal information are processed differently and along distinct channels in the human mind, which creates separate representations of the same information which is then processed by each channel. The incoming information can then be acted upon, stored, and retrieved as necessary, with either the image, or the word, or both recalled at any given time. If associations between a word and image cannot be formed, it will prove more difficult to recall and remember that word. A limitation of dual-coding theory is that it does not consider the possibility of cognition being mediated by anything other than words and images. In relation to this, the promise of multimedia learning (Mayer, 2003) involves students acquiring knowledge better from messages that consist of words and pictures over words alone. Presented here are fourteen empirically established principles (Mayer & Moreno, 1998; Mayer, et al., 2002; Hasler, et al., 2007; Moreno, 2007; Savoji, et al., 2011; Crookes, et al., 2012; Ibrahim, et al., 2012; Spanjers, 2012; Khacharem, et al., 2013).

- *Multimedia principle.* Students learn more deeply from words and pictures than from just words alone in both text- and computer-based contexts. Yet, combining two of relevant graphics, audio narration, or explanatory text works best over the use of just one or all three.
- *Coherence principle.* Students learn more deeply when extraneous material is excluded rather than included, in both text- and computer-based contexts. In other words, avoid including graphics, narration, and other content that does not directly support learning. This minimizes cognitive load, keeping in mind that the less students know about the topic the easier it is for them to get distracted. On the other hand, those with experience regarding the content may benefit from the addition of some motivational imagery.
- *Contiguity (spatial-contiguity) principle.* Students learn more deeply when printed words are placed near, rather than far from, corresponding pictures in both text- and computer-based

contexts. This also applies for spoken words that are presented simultaneously with graphical content, and with feedback presented next to answers.
- *Temporal contiguity principle.* Students learn more deeply when words and images that support one another are presented simultaneously rather than sequentially.
- *Personalization principle.* Students can learn more deeply when words are presented in a conversational rather than formal style in a computer-based environment which presents content using spoken words with printed words (e.g., captions). In other words, the learner should feel someone is talking directly to them when they listen to narration. A more polite rather than a directive tone of voice also leads to deeper learning for those with a low prior knowledge of the content, over a more directive tone, with the opposite trending for those with high prior knowledge.
- *Modality principle.* Students learn more deeply when graphics are explained by audio narration over text on screen, although exceptions occur when learners are familiar with the content or are not native speakers of the narration language, or when printed words appear on screen.
- *Voice principle.* Students learn more deeply when they are presented with learning content that is presented in a more human sounding voice than a non-human mechanical one.
- *Segmenting principle.* Students can learn more deeply when content is broken down into smaller chunks (e.g., long lessons should be broken down into smaller segments, and long passages of text broken down into multiple shorter ones).
- *Signaling principle.* Students can learn more deeply when presented with auditory, visual, or temporal cues that draw attention to critical elements of a lesson (e.g., use of arrows, circles, highlighting, bold font, pausing). Ending a lesson after providing critical content is also considered a signaling cue.
- *Learner control principle.* Students can learn more deeply when they are able to control their pace of movement through segmented content. This sees learners doing best when narration ceases after a short, meaningful segment of content,

and a learner has to turn a page or click a button to move forward.
- *Pre-training principle.* Students can learn more deeply when key concepts or vocabulary is presented prior to the processes or procedures related to those concepts. This may be more important for those with low prior knowledge than for those with higher prior knowledge.
- *Redundancy principle.* Students can learn more deeply when graphics are explained by audio narration alone, rather than audio narration and on-screen text. The exceptions to this involve those learners who are non-native speakers of the course language, when screens have no visuals, and when there is placement of only a few keywords on screen (i.e., graphics or critical elements are tagged or labeled).
- *Image principle.* Voiceover is adequate; a moving image or a person's face is not necessary to see improvement in learning.
- *Expertise principle.* This sees the above design principles come to contradict when used with those learners who have greater prior knowledge compared to those that have low prior knowledge of the subject matter under study.

It is also important to consider cognitive load theory (Sweller, 1988); that is, the amount of mental effort required to perform a task. There are three categories of this:

Germane cognitive load. The amount of cognitive effort required to process information about the task itself, making sense of it, and accessing and/or storing information regarding it in long-term memory (e.g., with a math problem, identifying the values and operations required to solve it, and understanding that the task is to solve the problem).
- *Intrinsic cognitive load.* The amount of cognitive effort involved in performing the task itself (e.g., solving a math problem).
- *Extraneous cognitive load.* The mental effort arising from the manner in which the task is presented to the learner, such as sorting through other information for what is required to solve a problem (e.g., finding a math problem on a web page that contains advertisements for math textbooks).

Sensory Stimulation Theory and Multimodal Learning

Traditional sensory stimulation theory posits that effective learning occurs when the senses are stimulated – sight, hearing, touch, smell and taste (Laird, 1985). It was found that the predominant way in which learning occurs in humans is by seeing (75%), with hearing the next most effective (13%). Senses are stimulated through the use of colors, volume levels, strong statements, and facts presented in a visual manner along with deployment of a variety of methods, approaches, and techniques as well as media.

At the heart of the theory is the concept that people complete actions in order to receive different kinds of sensory input, and that use of all five senses is natural and should be nurtured for learning. It also allows for the provision of different avenues for learning with those students who experience sensory deficits. It can be used in a variety of ways to help students learn various concepts (e.g., teaching fractions with segmented chocolate bars, and allowing the students to eat the chocolate after the lesson).

Multimodal learning also takes the position that when a number of our senses are engaged when learning, we are better able to understand and remember more (Lawless, 2019; May, 2019). It is often employed with those learners, particularly young ones, who experience learning challenges. There are four main methods involved: visual, auditory, reading and writing, and kinesthetic (VARK).

Visual learning which incorporates artwork, cartoons, diagrams, graphs, illustrations, infographics, videos, and other content that can stimulate the eye. Techniques include using color coding of content, using different fonts, and tagging of different points (e.g., with stickers). Learners favoring this kind of approach retain new information through text, images, and visual representations of concepts.

Auditory learning is mostly concerned with what we listen to or hear, and it may come in the form of an audiobook, song, podcast, or webinar, with group debates or discussion on topics listened to forming part of auditory learning. Learners favoring this kind of approach will take in information through sound, story, discussion, lecture, and so on.

Reading and writing learning is provided by text-based courses, pdfs, documents, and soft- and hard-copy texts. Included here are written assignments and exams (e.g., choice-type and true/false questions).

Learners favoring this kind of approach retain information by making lists, note-taking, reading, and rewriting.

Kinesthetic learning promotes activity, and it may involve off-site visits, demonstrations, and the development of multimedia presentations that can involve video (employing visual, auditory, and kinesthetic skills). Learners favoring this kind of approach learn as a result of physically performing a task, and it may also involve hand-eye coordination, walking or pacing while studying, or making flashcards to help study through a visual learning method.

Ultimately, instructors should try to combine two or more multimodal learning modes to provide a well-rounded educational experience to learners. Perhaps by integrating presentational, interpersonal and interpretive communication modes at the appropriate level of proficiency for the learner.

Presentational involves speaking, writing, and visually representing knowledge with learners presenting information in spoken or written form in a variety of ways including that of a presentation to a group, developing and posting digital content, composing reports or articles.

Interpersonal involves two-way communication, including conversing face-to-face, digital discussion participation, and personal email/letter exchange.

Interpretive involves listening, speaking, reading, writing to demonstrate understanding by learners in a culturally appropriate manner, and this may include having learners show comprehension of digital texts, printed material, audio, and audiovisual content.

Digital Nativism, Twenty-First Century Core Skills and Competencies, Personal learning Networks, and Community of Practice

Prensky (2001) has proposed that those of us growing up with modern technology have seen our use of that technology shape and hardwire our brains differently to those of an older generation who grew up without technology, or with different kinds of it (digital immigrants). The most profound difference for teachers is that digital natives are perhaps more capable of learning from non-linear pathways. Previously, a linear model, with a beginning and an end, was normally presented to learners, and there was limited possibility for the inclusion of hypertext, or the use of integrated multimodal activities utilizing adaptive learning algorithms. Learning from such contexts may also see digital natives possess shorter attention spans, and intrinsically skim material for key information rather than conduct sequential reading of material. Although recent use of the terms digital natives/digital immigrants is starting to wane, in terms of relation to theory, use of the lexicons are still prevalent in describing an older versus younger generational learning style. What is important here is that it shows that the use of technology in the connectivist age is different to the previous ones. Moving into the era of the fourth industrial revolution, all learners now require a range of competencies and skills that come to support education in terms of personalization, equality, collaboration, adaptability, communication, relationships, and technology (Kent, 2019). This sees sixteen skills required of twenty-first century learners (see Table 2.15), eight key skills required for lifelong learning (see Figure 2.3), four digital competency proficiencies, procedural, socio-digital, digital discourse, and strategic (Walker & White, 2013), and the need to develop personal learning networks that include community of practice.

Twenty-First Century Skills		
Foundational Literacies	**Competencies**	**Character Qualities**
How students apply core skills to everyday tasks.	*How students approach complex challenges.*	*How students approach their changing environment.*
- Literacy - Numeracy - Scientific literacy - ICT literacy - Financial literacy - Cultural and civic literacy	- Critical thinking/problem-solving - Creativity - Communication - Collaboration	- Curiosity - Initiative - Persistence/grit - Adaptability - Leadership - Social and cultural awareness

Table 2.15 Sixteen Skills Required by the 21st Century Learner

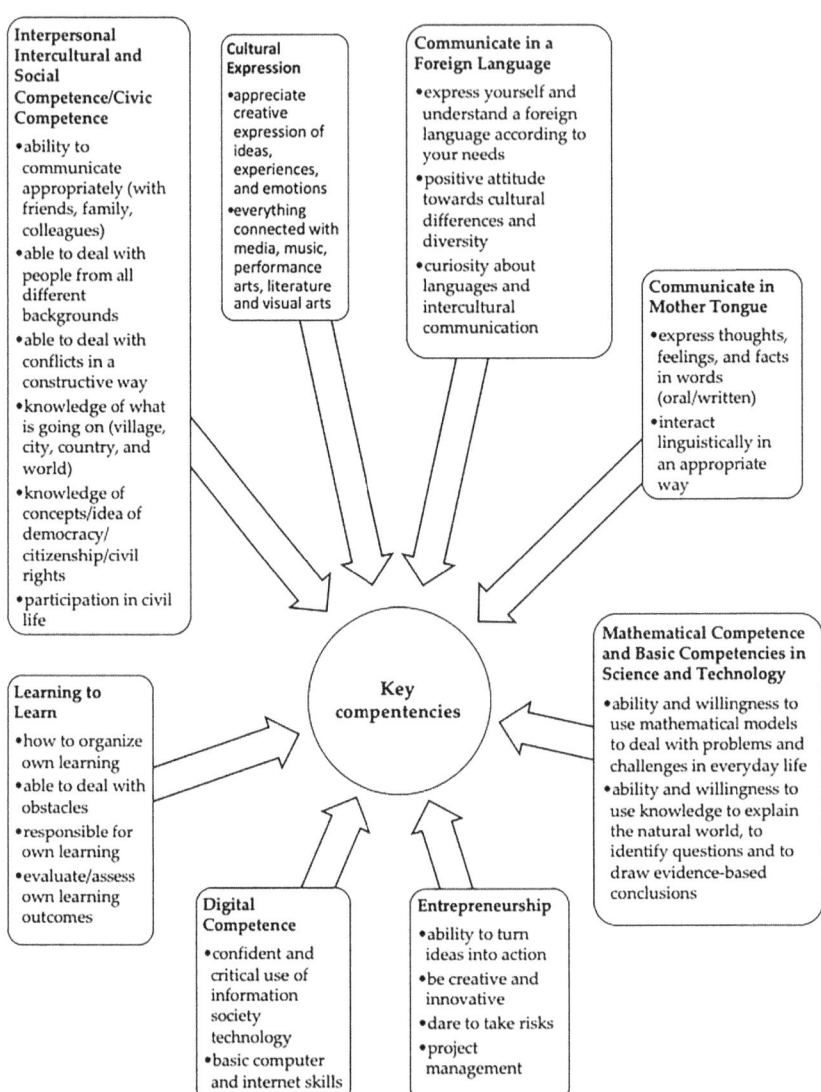

Figure 2.4 Eight Key Competencies for Lifelong Learning

Procedural competence. The ability to manipulate technology (in terms of hardware and software) – knowing how to use technology (e.g., switch it on, the buttons to click). This is similar to the traditional view that to know a language means knowing the grammar and vocabulary, and just as we now know that communicative competence requires more than knowledge of the syntactic, phonological, and lexical, we also need to understand that digital competence requires understanding of how, when, and why to use technologies and how to compensate for gaps in knowledge and skills.

Socio-digital competence. Understanding what is appropriate in different social contexts and knowledge domains in terms of both technology and language; in other words, how technological competence and communicative competence overlap, and the types of language appropriate to use for different audiences in various digital contexts (see Crystal, 2006). For example, deciding on the appropriateness of using social media such as Facebook for business communication, and how it should be used to achieve a desired communicative response.

Digital discourse competence. The ability to manage an extended task, using several applications and/or types of equipment (e.g., recording, editing, and publishing a video, or writing a blog post with photographs). This then includes being able to perform tasks that require a range of skills and technical knowledge, and typically ones that would also require communicative discourse competence in order to structure text, create paragraphs, and sequence and link ideas using appropriate language forms.

Strategic competence. The ability to repair problems and work around the gaps in technological knowledge and skills. This refers to the ability to think of alternate routes or options (e.g., switching channels, contacting someone by email or social media if they don't answer the phone, or knowing how to deal with disruptive online interactions such as 'flaming' or a troll). Linguistically speaking, this is akin to the ability to manage and navigate communication to repair communication breakdowns, and work around unfamiliar areas of language.

A key feature of connectivism is that much learning occurs across online peer networks with students learning as they seek out information on their own, sharing what they find with others, and with teachers guiding students to information and answering key questions as needed. The personal learning network (PLN) that students then forge is created on the basis of how they organize their own connections to learning communities as they transverse networks through multiple knowledge domains. In other words, what constitutes the development of knowledge or understanding is the formation of connections between nodes of information (i.e., networks), with the ability to both construct and transverse those networks then considered to be learning. 'Learning is the network.' This sees connectivism's core concepts stem from socio-cultural learning theories, which argue that learning occurs more effectively when people work together.

Crucial to the development of personal learning networks is learner autonomy and levels of learner confidence as they move from formal settings, teacher-guided/controlled and institutional-based, to environments where they can direct their own learning, find their own information, and create their own knowledge from more knowledgeable others with whom they engage. These networks, based on personal interests and preferences over institutional requirements and choices, may be small or vast but their main characteristics are to support knowledge development by being autonomous, connected, diverse, and open (Downes, 2007).

Although technology including mobile developments make new and different educational structures, organizations, and settings possible, connectivism is not limited to the online environment. The theory also applies to a larger learning environment and helps to inform how we understand our relatedness to the world, and consequently how we learn from it and understand it. Networks should be thought of as the relationship between 'internal' and 'external' physical environments. As a learner engages in creating and recreating their own PLN, understanding arises through the application of meta-cognition to the evaluation of elements that prove useful and those that can be eliminated from the network. The face-to-face as well as online networks that people build up throughout their lifetime will provide them with expertise and knowledge. Learners are at the center of their own learning experience, and instrumental in determining the content of their own learning, how they engage and participate in learning, and who can participate with them.

A community of practice (COP), or affinity spaces as Gee (2004) calls them, are places in which people develop relationships in a discourse community based on their shared interests. A COP is formed from three components – domain, community, practice – which sees a group of people (*the domain*) who share a craft or profession come together (*as a community*) to distribute experience and information, and to learn from each other (*with practice*), which leads to both personal and professional development (Lave & Wagner, 1991). For students, this might mean offline spaces like the traditional classroom, as well as digital spaces from which they may practice English utilizing technology in an interactive, integrated, and normalized way using apps to develop specific skills and practice them with others, and using forums to ask questions and receive answers regarding specific problems. For teachers, a COP might emerge while attending live events such as conferences or workshops from conversations held in teacher's lounges, or as a result of joining online spaces like TESOL association Facebook groups: any place where teachers-as-learners can engage in formal or informal professional development as part of their PLN (personal learning network).

Classroom Management Theories

The term classroom management is typically applied to describe the processes that are involved with running the classroom effectively. This involves the smooth integration and transition among learning activities, arranging the classroom, working with technology and other learning materials (e.g., texts, the board) as well as working with learners. The term also applies to preempting problems and issues, particularly those regarding working with learners, and ensuring that they keep on task, preventing them from disrupting the work of other students or the lesson in general. It also includes being able to effectively respond to such behavior after it occurs. Like learning theories, a wide variety of classroom management theories, procedures, and systematic approaches to discipline abound. A number of the more popular fall into one of the five categories as presented in Table 2.16, and are presented in detail from within this section in alphabetical order.

Classroom Management		
Category	**Focus**	**Theory**
Behaviorist	Fixing behavior.	- Applied behavior analysis. - Assertive discipline. - Behaviorist classrooms. - Non-adversarial method. - The token economy.
Cognitive	Thought, not behavior.	- Response thinking process.
Democratic	Learner empowerment.	- Democratic classrooms.
Humanist	Removal of negative influence.	- Choice theory. - Unconditional positive regard.
Psychoanalytic	Unconscious thought.	- Pragmatic method.

Table 2.16 Categories of Classroom Management Theories (based on Drew, 2020c)

Applied Behavior Analysis (ABA)

This behavioral management theory utilizes learning principles to assist with producing changes in student behavior. It relies upon assessment of the functional relationship between the targeted behavior and the environment to develop socially acceptable alternatives to any aberrant behavior. It is often applied to help those students who present with learning disabilities, and it involves close observation of students to identify the ABC's of misbehavior. These are:

    A – *Antecedents* (What occurred prior to misbehavior?)
    B – *Behavior* (What is the misbehavior?)
    C – *Consequences* (What consequences need follow the misbehavior?)

A data-based approach is taken to correcting any misbehavior among learners from a one-to-one environment. It is from breaking down the ABC's of a (mis)behavior that the educator can establish how to proceed so that:

    Antecedents do not reoccur.
    Behavior strategies can be taught to overcome (mis)behavior.
    Consequences are appropriate and also developed to be ones that work with each individual.

Assertive Discipline

Providing a structured system that enables teachers to manage their classrooms, assertive discipline focuses on the teacher developing a positive behaviorist management strategy over being dictatorial. Canter and Canter (1996) propose that instructors have the right to decide what is best for the learners under their care, and that no learner should prevent any other from engaging in learning. It is an obedience-based discipline approach to classroom management which has the aim of allowing instructors to engage in providing learning that is not interrupted by student misbehavior, and which trains teachers to:

- fix clear behavioral limits and establish consequences;
- follow-through consistently; and
- reward applicable behavior (Moles, 1990).

The system was developed for children with special needs, with rules and consequences developed by authority figures with those who are subordinate expected to follow them. It assumes that there are only three types of teacher (non-assertive, hostile, and assertive), and no other discipline system. It is one of the most widely used classroom management tactics in the entire world (McIntyre, 2020), and the means of applying it are seen in Table 2.17.

Applying Assertive Discipline
Be clear of the consequences for misbehavior, as there are no acceptable reasons for it.
Make rules clear; don't be ambiguous – stick to 4 or 5.
Determine negative consequences for noncompliance – always follow through with the consequences set for rule breaking.
Determine positive consequences for appropriate behavior – 'Catch students being good', be specific with praise and be sure learners know that they are being praised.
List the rules on the board, along with the positive/negative consequences.
Students will write down the rules, take them home, and they will be signed by parents and returned. An attached message can explain the program and request the parents' help with compliance.

Table 2.17 Applying Assertive Discipline Theory in the Classroom

Assertive discipline theory contains several key features:
- The right to learn.
- The right to teach.
- Teachers must maintain control.
- Clear boundaries must be set.
- Positive reinforcement needs providing.
- Positive repetition needs to occur.
- Firm consequences need following through.
- Behavior is taught through modeled and direct instruction.
- It is possible to teach difficult students.
- Proactive discipline is better than reactive discipline.
- Instructors should build and establish relationships with students.

This theory has clear links to behaviorist theory (e.g., student behavior is effectively managed via reward and punishment). It has been challenged by other learning theories. Freire (1970), for example, argues that assertive teaching reinforces unfair power hierarchies, and creates a 'banking approach to education'. This is where students are taught not to think, but to simply comply. Further, if a teacher is cruel or unfair, there is no avenue for students to achieve justice. To resolve these issues, a problem-posing approach to education has been suggested.

Behaviorist Classrooms

In any behaviorist classroom, behaviorism is at the core, which means that rewards and punishments will be central to ensuring that a learner produces the desired behavior. It is a classroom management strategy that necessitates the need for very clear rules and codes of conduct. It is also one that views the need for reinforcement decreasing as time passes, and one that changes the kind of negative reinforcer as students become desensitized to it.

This classroom management style relies on three main factors:
- Learners should respond to each step in turn, receiving immediate and appropriate feedback.
- Performance needs to be paired with secondary reinforcement (e.g., good behavior rewarded with praise, prizes, high grades).

- Instructors should arrange questions by difficulty so that responses are always correct, thereby self-generating positive reinforcement.

Critics of this classroom management style view it as one that does not teach moral values (i.e., right and wrong) or develop critical thinking; instead, students learn that the end goal is one of receipt of reward.

Choice Theory

In this humanist approach, Glasser (1998) sees all behavior as purposeful. Outside influence is rejected with every action seen to be a choice, even if we may not be fully aware of it (internal control). However, most people behave based on the belief that we are not responsible for the choices that we make, and that states of being just happen anyway (external control). How we choose to perceive or filter information that is presented to us, respond to it, and decode it is behavior, and the only behavior that we can control is our own.

Choice Theory recognizes humans as having five basic needs, and although they remain the same throughout life, they may change daily. How we behave reflects our best attempt at meeting our needs. These needs are broken down into those that are genetically driven, psychologically driven, and survival driven.

Genetically driven needs are:
- Belonging and love.
- Freedom.
- Fun.
- Power.
- Survival.

Psychologically driven needs are:
- Belonging/connecting/love.
- Freedom/autonomy.
- Fun/Learning.
- Power/significance/competence.

Survival driven needs are:
- Breathing.
- Clothing.
- Food.
- Personal safety.
- Security and sex (having children).
- Shelter.

The aim of the teacher is to develop a classroom environment and to provide activities and materials that meet all of these needs so that students will be able to connect, feel a sense of competence and power, work with freedom, and enjoy studying in a safe, secure environment. Three common characteristics of a choice theory classroom/school are ones that:

- Create active learning. Develop engaging, exciting and relevant content that students are excited about engaging with (fun and freedom). Focus on quality and providing deep learning through application, while delivering a comfortable and enjoyable classroom.
- Fulfill intrinsic need. Reward and punishment are not used to control student behavior. Rather, instructors foster and maintain positive relationships with their learners with minimal coercion.
- Promote ownership of learning and choice of actions. By ensuring that learners evaluate their own performance, responsibility is placed on the learner as they become skilled-decision makers who are active agents in their own education.

Democratic Classrooms

In the democratic classroom, learner voice is heard and exhibits real influence on the rules of the room. Learners are also allowed to explore those topics that are of most interest to them without worrying about how good they are in the process. Emphasis is on the understanding that not all learners learn at the same pace, and that mistakes provide the teacher valuable input in regard to learner level and occur in a climate of safety in order to ultimately promote successful learning (Kohn, 1997). The classroom environment is therefore one where transfer of power shifts from the educator to the learner, with the goal of promoting deep thought regarding how the classroom should operate. Included within this is the notion of *what* rules to put in place, *why* those rules are required, and *how* those rules should be upheld in order to develop learners that are just and moral critical thinkers.

The democratic classroom, particularly a self-directed one, would feature:

- Multiple activity centers (with classroom structures for group work in place)

- Student project displays
- Students exchanging ideas
- A teacher that mingles with students, and respects their ideas
- Students excited about learning and actively asking questions
- Multiple activities occurring simultaneously.

Non-Adversarial Method

Jones' (1987) behaviorist method is one that advocates for instructors to focus on the provision of positive rewards for their learners. Instructors are expected to assist learners in developing self-control through the use of body language, incentives, and providing help as required. Learning of self-control is seen to empower learners and prepare them for the future, and central to this method is the concept of preferred activity time (PAT).

Preferred activity time is set aside for students to engage in activities that they find enjoyable. These activities are used by the teacher to leverage improvements in behavior from learners by incentivizing:
- Engagement on task in exchange for more 'fun' time
- Shorter and more focused transitioning periods between activities
- Self-regulation, along with the co-regulation of others' behavior.

It is employed by:
- The teacher identifying an activity that learners prefer.
- The teacher then tells students that a given period of activity time has been set aside (e.g., 20 minutes) at the end of the day for them to engage in their preferred activity.
- Students understand that after efficiently completing all of the day's required tasks, more time can be spent on engaging with preferred activities.

Pragmatic Method

This is a psychoanalytic method of classroom management that relies on human beings striving to fit in or belong to a social group, and it views misbehavior as a result of the learner breaking rules in order to achieve, maintain, or protect their status in the group. Misbehaviors are classified as 'mistaken goals' (Dreikur, 1964) which occur when students 'act out', and are viewed in terms of:

- *Attention seeking.* Children who pursue attention might show off, ask irrelevant questions, become disruptive, or be overly eager to please as they seek constant affirmation to affirm their worth. A way to address this is to ignore negative behavior but praise positive behavior, suggest appropriate ways for the learner to get noticed or become special to the group, and point out that their behavior is not achieving results that it is bothersome to others.
- *Power seeking.* This results from students feeling as though they are outsiders or being excluded from their groups, and assisting them in gaining more power may alleviate this behavior. This can be achieved by asking each of them their opinions, and acknowledging or including this perspective into lessons. If the power seeking is inappropriate, then the educator can apply redirection or discipline as appropriate, pointing out that the behavior may alienate the student or to the things that the student might do to become a group leader. Power seeking in children might see arguing, tantrums, lies, stubbornness, and disobedience emerge as they seek control to affirm their worth.
- *Revenge seeking.* Children who are seeking revenge may aim to get even for perceived injustices by destroying property or by publicly casting insults at others as they pursue revenge to affirm their worth. This results from students feeling hurt, and causing this kind of learner more pain reinforces the behavior. Instead, offer understanding and assistance, and encourage them not to retaliate, allowing them chances to express what has hurt them.
- *Failure avoidance (feelings of inadequacy).* Learners pursuing failure avoidance tend to give up, strive to be left alone, and evade participation as they seek to avoid the failures that lead to their feelings of inadequacy. They aim to retain the little self-worth they may have by pushing others away and avoiding any kind of public displays. Educators should tell them that they are alright as they are, and be less critical of them while simultaneously providing support and encouragement. It is also worthwhile to attempt to coax higher performing peers to accept the learner as they are, and allow this kind of learner to begin achieving goals at their own pace.

Response Thinking Process (RTP)

This is a cognitivist method of classroom management that stresses learner thought as a means for students to actively ponder their (mis)behavior and to develop a sense of responsibility and respect for their own lives and those around them (Ford, 1994). It is based on perceptual control theory (PCT) which is designed to assist in making sense of the environment in order to construct a satisfying life (Powers, 1998), with emphasis on:

- Encouraging achievement of goals without harming others.
- Asking 'what' over 'why', rather than telling learners what to do.
- Promoting mutual respect between teachers and students, with educators assisting learners by helping them in the thinking through of moral issues.

If rule-breaking occurs, then a process of mediation between the learner, parents, and educator should be utilized to encourage the learner to set personal standards to adhere to, or to establish a series of goals to strive for.

The Token Economy

This is an approach to classroom management which relies on reward and punishment to produce positive behavior. It utilizes a system of classroom currency where those who do the right thing are awarded with points or tokens, while those who do not may be required to forfeit or rescind them. It is based on the principles of operant conditioning and behavioral economics, with tokens used as reinforcers along with back-up reinforcers (what the tokens may be exchanged for) in order to encourage specific target behavior (Kazdin, 1977).

The encouragement of long-term positive behavior among students is one of the main advantageous of this kind of system. Students are continuously and consistently incentivized to behave positively as they aim to collect as many tokens as possible over time. Tokens can be awarded individually or on a group basis, which sees learners prompt group members to keep in line. Tokens can also be used as part of a trade-in system where learners can cash in their tokens for prizes (e.g., an increase in preferred activity time, small gifts.)

Class Dojo is a popular application that allows educators to use their phones to reward or punish students. Serving as a mechanism for behavior control, the application also allows educators to keep this data in sync with parents and other stake-holders (e.g., principles) through the use of gamification.

Unconditional Positive Regard

This is a humanist approach to classroom management that involves basic acceptance and support of a learner regardless of what they say and do, believing them to be inherently good and encouraging them to do good things (Rogers, 1951). It is a simple process that focuses on:
- Inclusivity of the classroom, where all student's needs are met.
- Providing affirmation that the learner wants to be their best self.
- Addressing the root cause of any misbehavior.

In the classroom, unconditional positive regard would employ such phraseology as:
- Great job last Friday. I'd love to see you do just as well today.
- This is not how I expect you to behave. I know that you can do better.
- Today was a fantastic day for us, but tomorrow, let's both come to class with positive attitudes.

Educational Leadership

School leadership in the United States of America, and what was previously termed educational management in the United Kingdom, is known as educational leadership. It is the process of enlisting and guiding the energies and the talents of staff, teachers, students, and parents toward achieving common educational goals. While interdisciplinary in nature, it distinguishes itself by focusing on aspects of pedagogical (teaching), epistemological (knowledge), and human development.

The style of educational leadership employed by an individual can lead to different practices and actions coming to impact levels of student achievement, teacher job satisfaction, and overall organizational improvement. There are many types of educational leadership, such as instructional leadership (e.g., management of curriculum and instruction by a principal), distributed leadership (e.g., mobilizing leadership expertise across all levels of a school to promote opportunities for change and capacity for improvement), social-justice leadership (e.g., emphasizing democratic beliefs that students can all reach proficiency, and providing equitable learning opportunities to enable this to occur), and transformational leadership (e.g., encouraging growth and development across the educational organization). However, this section will focus on teacher leadership and student leadership, as these are perhaps the most immediate for beginning and career practicing teachers to understand in terms of their own roles, and as the roles of instructor and learner continually adapt to the changing nature of education.

It is also recognized that for teaching and learning to be at its most effective, instructors and learners should maintain a high level of wellbeing, self-efficacy, and self-confidence, and several means for leadership to promote and enhance wellbeing are discussed. The section will then close by considering the ethics, laws, rights, and responsibilities associated with the teaching field, which are important to recognize when in a leadership role before considering the importance of a moral code to assist in guiding instructors and students while in leadership.

Teacher leadership

Teacher leadership is no longer optional (*Teacher leadership competencies*, 2014), and because teachers can lead in various ways, either individually or collectively, they can shape the culture of their teaching context. This is typically achieved by influencing peers, principals, and other members of the school community, with an aim to increase student learning and achievement through individual, collaborative/team, and organizational development. Three key areas that allow organizations to foster the growth of teacher leaders, as noted by the Center for Comprehensive School Reform and Improvement (2005), emerge from school culture and context, from roles and relationships, and from structure.

In terms of school culture and context, learning, inquiry, and reflective practice for teachers should encourage instructors to take the initiative with expectations of teamwork and shared responsibility set, and with decision making and leadership opportunities made available. Teacher professionals should be valued as role models, and there should be an organizational aim to develop a strong sense of community among teachers that fosters professionalism. Roles and relationships should then nurture teacher leadership by encouraging colleagues to recognize and respect those who have subject-area/instructional expertise by promoting an environment of high trust and a positive working relationship among teacher peers and administrators, by continually assigning leadership work relating to the teaching and learning process over that of administrative/managerial tasks, by clearly defining teacher-leader and administrator-leader domains (including those responsibilities of shared leadership), and by encouraging professional interpersonal relationships between teacher leaders and school directors or principals. Structure, coming last, then ensures adequate access to material, as well as the time and the space to engage in activities that facilitate teacher leadership (e.g., professional development opportunities).

The teacher leader

Teacher leaders are facilitators within the school and are important in the spread and strengthening of school reform and improvements, with educational improvement at the instructional level consisting of classroom leadership (e.g., monitoring student learning efforts, developing curriculum, participating in meetings, providing peer coaching, engaging parent/community participation, reviewing new research, and engaging in professional development). As a process, teacher leadership aims to promote the opportunity for voice and shared leadership, where voice refers to the values, opinions, beliefs, perspectives, and cultural backgrounds of the people in a district, school, or school community, especially students, teachers, parents, and local citizens, and how these are considered, included, listened to, and acted upon when critical decisions are being made.

Teacher leaders normally have significant teaching experience and are well respected among peers. They are willing to take on risk and assume responsibility while also being learning and achievement oriented. Teacher leaders take on a wide range of supportive roles, and these may be formally or informally assigned. Such roles help build capacity for the school and learner to improve, and there is no shortage of roles where teachers can establish themselves as a leader both on and off campus. Harrison and Killon (2007) highlight the roles of resource provider, instructional specialist, curriculum specialist, classroom supporter, learning facilitator, mentor, school leader, data coach, being a catalyst for change, and as a learner.

Resource providers share instructional resources with colleagues, including websites, instructional materials, readings, handouts, worksheets, or other resources, including professional resources (e.g., assessment tools, lesson plans, articles, and books).

Instructional specialists help colleagues implement effective teaching strategies, including providing assistance in developing differentiated instruction or planning lessons in partnership with other teachers, studying research-based classroom strategies, exploring which instructional methodologies, approaches, and techniques are appropriate for the school context, and sharing these findings with colleagues.

Curriculum specialists understand content standards, and how various components of a curriculum link together, and how the curriculum is used in planning instruction and delivering assessment to ensure consistent curriculum implementation. They come to agreement with colleagues as to the standards used in the teaching context, follow any adopted curriculum, use common pacing charts, and develop shared assessments with other instructors as well.

Classroom supporters work inside the classroom to assist other teachers in implementing new ideas (e.g., demonstrating a lesson, coteaching, observing, and giving feedback).

Learning facilitators develop and provide professional development opportunities for peers that are central to the teaching and learning context including that of the classroom, the school, the school system, and involvement of students and teachers within the community.

Mentors serve as a role model to novice teachers, acclimate new teachers, and advise all teachers on aspects such as curricula, practices, politics, and procedures.

School leaders share the vision of the school, align their professional goals with that of the workplace, and share responsibility for the success of the school as a whole. They serve on committees, act as heads of department, support school initiatives, and/or represent the school on community committees or district task forces.

Data coaches lead conversations and engage in data analyses that can engage peers in using information to strengthen and drive classroom instruction.

Catalysts for change are teacher visionaries. They contemplate how the status quo can be improved, and show a strong commitment to continual professional improvement, while analyzing ways to develop student learning.

A learner engages in lifelong learning and demonstrates professional development, using what they gain through delivery or participation in these endeavors to help all teachers and students achieve more.

Student Leadership

The rationale behind inspiring student leadership is to create a culture of ownership, collaboration and community. Consequently, it sees students taking on an active role in their education and in that of the wider improvement of the classroom, school, school system, and the community, with the aim of developing positive skills in the process (National College for School Leadership, 2006). Student leadership, then, promotes the opportunity for voice and agency in learning, and this is where student agency refers to learning through meaningful, relevant, interest driven activities that are often self-initiated with teacher guidance. As a process, student leadership allows for meaningful positive changes to occur in the educational environment, and at its core is the concept that leadership is inherent within all. It involves the teacher motivating learners to engage and to develop on a personal level, enabling them to use the right skills, at the right time, and in the right contexts to achieve desired outcomes, and ensuring that students have the ability to set and achieve those goals that make a real-world difference. All of these are aspects which clearly come to redefine the role of the learner today.

Goker (2020) conceptualizes opportunities for student leadership in terms of the community, the school, the school system, and the classroom. At the community level, students can be encouraged to improve and apply to develop community-based projects, particularly those that can help foster their learning, and those that see them participate and communicate with local governments and the wider community in order to do so. At the school level, students can be encouraged to participate in mentor/coaching programs, in becoming school ambassadors/representatives, and/or in becoming active participants in school leadership appointment panels. In this way, learners can be encouraged to engage with projects that develop and implement change in organizational culture, practices, and school operations, and can be encouraged to undertake the necessary research to guide such change and the means of implementing any process of reform. Across the school system, learners can be empowered by being allowed to conduct research targeted at evaluating school systems, and then by being assigned active roles in the process of reforming those systems. At the classroom level, learners can be encouraged to engage in decision making and conversations regarding classroom rules and management, decisions concerning learning, teaching, and evaluation, and to speak out about their own expectations of the class, as well as their opinions regarding issues of current debate.

The student leader

A student leader is any student that takes on responsibility, particularly for spreading knowledge through inspiration, tutoring, and by applying for and being designated to undertake certain leadership roles. Like their teacher counterparts, the roles of a student leader might be formal or informal, official or voluntary. Student leaders are also those learners who strive to see change for the better, and strive to see that changes occur. In the classroom, there are several ways for a teacher to promote student leadership, such as the use of problem-based learning, and by providing the means for students to communicate and learn in those ways in which they feel most comfortable, as well as those ways that mirror real-world issues. To this end, problem-based learning allows for learners to deliver outcomes that can lead to solving real-word issues, and those that might help the local community, reform aspects of the school system, or lead to change in the school or the classroom itself. As a teacher, you should help to inspire the growth of those skills and qualities found in good student leaders among all of your students, no matter how, what, or who you might be teaching. Traits found in good student leaders, as Fulton (2019) presents, are those of being goal-oriented, encouraging, positive, responsible, honest, hard-working, as well as being good listeners, good communicators, good decision makers, and being willing to serve.

Goal-oriented student leaders understand the lesson objective and are driven to get there, as they desire personal success and are able to intrinsically set their own goals beyond that of the teacher. To encourage this kind of student leadership, notice those students who take charge of groups and activities, and inspire others to do the same, and assist them in being able to do so once you designate them with such a role.

Encouraging student leaders recognize the strengths and weaknesses of others, they affirm and utilize group strengths while also providing assistance where there is weakness. To inspire this kind of student leadership you can help learners recognize and delegate activity work based on their strengths and weaknesses. If they are unable to do this, you might need to work with them to identify these aspects.

Positive student leaders believe that whatever the goal may be, it is possible to accomplish it, even if it seems insurmountable, and this confidence can inspire others. To encourage this kind of leadership, support students with phrases that they can, in turn, use to drive their group, and those that are positive instead of negative (e.g., *This is looking pretty good, you're nearly finished* instead of *Oh, you're only half done, better hurry the class is nearly over*).

Responsible student leaders do not pass on blame or make excuses, but accept their roles and learn from them, correct what went wrong, and move forward. They are humble, and recognize the effort of the group, not just their own. To encourage this, provide students with ways to not only shoulder responsibility but in ways to also share group successes (e.g., get them to clean up a mess that they made but also highlight the success that the mess led to, such as completion of a certain activity).

Honest student leaders should be truthful and committed to completing work ethically. The class, and the teacher, can all trust this kind of student. To encourage this, you might like to highlight behavior that students can emulate (e.g., highlight the low amount of plagiarism in one student's work, if you notice a high amount of it in other submissions).

Hard-working student leaders show perseverance, and they inspire and push their classmates to do more. To encourage this kind of student leadership, consider admiring the actions and work of those students exhibiting this kind of behavior while others in the same group might be sitting and doing nothing.

Good listeners are able to listen to the thoughts and concerns of others in their groups they show genuine interest and care about others in their groups, and they want to help them. As a result, they are also more receptive to others' feedback, and they are more willing to compromise. To encourage this kind of student leadership, you may want to help all students to understand how taking into account others' opinions and feedback, as well as compromising, can lead to success.

Good communicators expresses ideas to their groups, and they make their suggestions known in an open and respective manner. Fostering this kind of student leadership behavior and interaction will help learners also respect their peers and you as a teacher, and it is one that you can also model for them.

A good decision maker can evaluate a situation and come to well reasoned conclusions regarding the best course of action to take. Good decision making stems from the ability to think quickly under pressure, a strong sense of direction, and a high sense of responsibility, and these are traits that you would want to encourage to foster this aspect of student leadership in learners.

Students who are willing to serve do what is best for others and go out of their way for those who may be in need. Such students are likely to engage in acts of kindness and selflessness, perhaps going out of their way to clean up or hand out materials to everyone in their group. You might inspire such a student leadership trait by encouraging pupils to not sit idly by if someone is being bullied, to speak up about injustice, and to voluntarily fill needs that they see in the classroom, school context, or community. Inspiring all of these traits in students can help create a good school environment that students will enjoy attending, and be able to effectively learn from, as well as one from which to promote, nurture, and provide a culture of wellbeing.

Wellbeing

A notion critical to being an effective worker, leader, teacher, or student today is wellbeing. Although definitions of wellbeing have long varied, no matter how it is defined, it has over time become recognized as something that is essential to address by educational leadership and policy makers (McCallum, 2017).

Brought into the public and educational domain by positive psychologists such as Seligman (2011), wellbeing is a complex construct to define, covering a wide scope of dimensions including cognitive, psychological, physical, and social (Schleicher, 2018). Taking these factors into account, wellbeing might also be described as the quality of a person's life (DEC, 2015), with Dodge, et al. (2012, p. 130) seeing it as "the balance point between an individual's resource pool and the challenges faced" (see figure 2.5)

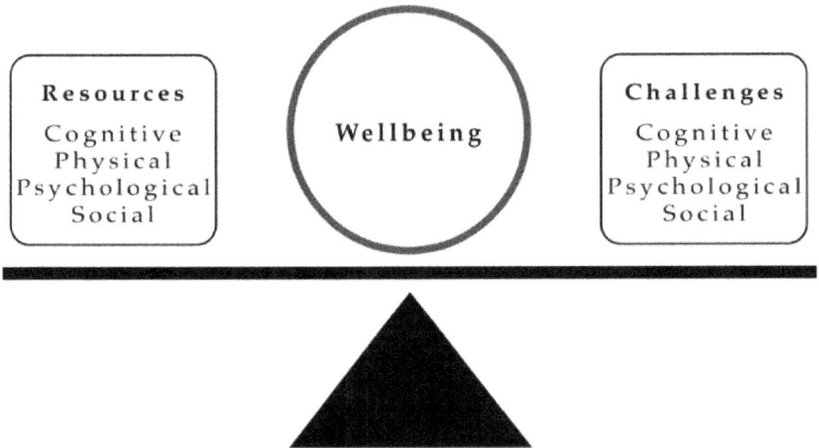

*Figure 2.5 See-Saw Model of Wellbeing
(based on Dodge, et al., 2012)*

Cognitive wellbeing is associated with the sets of skills and abilities required for effective work/study to be conducted, and it is mirrored in self-efficacy (the belief in the ability to perform). Physical wellbeing refers to the health conditions that stem from work and study, including workloads that lead to exhaustion (burnout) or those that allow for a work-life balance. Psychological wellbeing includes those emotions arising from work and study which can lead to depression or to increased commitment. Social wellbeing arises from the levels of collaboration and support that is provided from peers, which in turn impacts on levels of performance and satisfaction.

It is recognized across cultures and languages that working conditions can positively and negatively affect student, teacher, and staff wellbeing (Schleicher, 2018), which in turn impacts the educational system as a whole (McCallum, 2017). Kern et al. (2014) find that when staff members are doing well across multiple wellbeing domains, they are more committed to the school, and they are more satisfied with their health, life, and jobs. Lower levels of student and teacher wellbeing bring with them increased difficulties with misbehavior as both teacher and students become less engaged, increasing pessimism concerning learning as they then become less successful. Coupled with this are then higher levels of stress combined with lower levels of satisfaction (DEC, 2015; Schleicher, 2018). With this in mind, the focus of the remainder of this section will be concerned with aspects of enhancing staff, teacher, and student wellbeing, so that all can flourish.

Enhancing Staff Wellbeing

Any educational organization is a highly interactive community, and all staff should be a focus of wellbeing, from the janitor to the principal, including those specially trained to assist and those that volunteer, including parents. Although teacher wellbeing and staff wellbeing are terms that may be used interchangeably, staff wellbeing in relation to employee wellbeing refers to such considerations as the way that employees' duties, expectations, stress levels, workplace environment, and workload affect their overall health, happiness, and commitment to the organization.

Ways to enhance wellbeing across all staff start with creating a foundation of understanding regarding stakeholder issues and perspectives as presented by Naylor (2019). These include providing a means to engage, collecting data, thinking through the data collected, understanding the context and culture, creating safe spaces, providing lines of communication, and partnering.

Engage with those that hold a stake in staff endeavors (including unions, and any organizations or affiliations) so that they become allies rather than adversarial. Collect data from focus groups so that multiple and widening conversations regarding wellbeing can be broached and lead to wellbeing strategies that are coproduced. Think through the data collected so that any issues raised can be addressed, particularly if relating to, or impacting on, decision making at the local, district, and/or national levels. It is important to understand the school, district, and community contexts and culture, and the various issues that one community or context might have as opposed to another. Some may be positive and supportive while others may show divisions and chasms, and these can be discovered after determining a consensus from among a number of members. Create safe spaces in meetings where people can speak openly, with the freedom to challenge any ideas with civility, and knowing that their views are respected. Communication is central, key information should be available to all, and all involved should be encouraged to engage in follow-ups that help identify any areas of priority action. Clear information should also be available to all if they need help inside and outside of the school environment. Partnering with external organizations to provide collaboration is important, including working with health authorities, governments, and/or community organizations. For example, partnerships might extend to organizing symposia in conjunction with local university departments for professional development purposes.

Other practical strategies to increase the wellbeing for all stakeholders include those of undertaking mindfulness, relaxation and stress management sessions or resilience-based workshops. Peer support networks can also be encouraged, so that a sense of belonging can be established, with expectations set in place which see those in senior positions modeling good/expected behavior (e.g., educational leaders to teacher leaders, teacher leaders to other teachers, all staff/teachers to students, student leaders to other students, and students to students).

Enhancing Teacher Wellbeing

Teacher wellbeing refers to teachers who flourish in the workplace as an individual, and in their relationships with others, by maintaining a sense of balance between their emotional, physical, spiritual and social needs. Focus on the enhancement of teacher wellbeing is also identified as one of the first steps in a whole-school approach to improving the wellbeing of students. Such an approach, as Slemp, et al. (2017) note, stems from combining the concepts and scholarship of positive psychology with that of best educational practice to form positive education (PosEd). Yet, teachers experience ever increasing demands that reside outside the scope of their job description, with the way of working as a teacher establishing the position as particularly demanding. As such, teaching is one of the most stressful and under-supported professions, built on the backbone of unpaid overtime and voluntary labor that involves a variety of stakeholders. Such a reality is shackled to an increasing opinion among teachers of the job being steadily less valued. However, this is a perception that can change for the better when instructors participate in decision-making (Schleicher, 2018). Aside from this, there are a number of other key ways to heighten teacher wellbeing, particularly from an educational leadership perspective. These include providing recognition and respect, supporting professional development and collaboration, and promoting agency (Cann, 2019).

Recognition and respect from teacher leaders, or really the lack of it, can dishearten teachers, leaving them to feel that their contributions are worthless, and that will stifle any future commitment to those endeavors, and then toward the school, to other teachers, and toward students. However, recognizing, valuing, and rewarding teachers for the extra contributions that they make will encourage them to continue to do so, and work with others to do more. This could be as simple as providing them with a respectful thank you, setting time aside in meetings to provide praise and acknowledgement, or formally presenting them with an award. As a peer, you could offer assistance to such coworkers or let them know the ways that you are willing to support them if they should require it. Professional development also allows teachers to grow and experiment in using aspects of best practice, and it is something that needs to be targeted for them to be able to gain those skills from which they can then see both improvement in their teaching and improvement in their students' learning. Promoting agency provides teachers with increased input into decision making and the confidence to approach leaders with suggestions. This can then translate into teachers approaching leadership for assistance when required, in terms of personal and professional support. Further, if teacher views are not taken into account and organizational change is implemented with disregard to teacher input or without a clear rationale, then increased dissatisfaction with the role and workplace may result, divisions amongst staff, teachers, and students may then appear, and teacher attrition results.

Enhancing Student Wellbeing

Student wellbeing refers to the sustainable state of a positive mood and attitude, resilience, satisfaction with the self, relationships, and experiences at school. This can be heightened when schools draw on and connect with the expertise, contributions, and support of their communities, promoted by educational, teacher, and student leadership. In this regard, student wellbeing can be shaped by delivering choice, experience of achievement, the promotion of enjoyment, the formation of positive relationships, room for growth and development and, an environment of health and safety from which learners can actively participate in education (DEC, 2015).

Choice, or the lack of it, impacts student learning and engagement, and it can impact motivation, interest, and commitment to task. The provision of choice supports self-regulation, self-discipline, and achievement levels in a positive manner, particularly when there is opportunity to engage in learning that is of value and interest. Achievement of meaningful goals can lead to increased confidence and self-esteem, fostering self-discipline and effort, along with positive emotions that then allow students to take risks in learning in order to build the traits of engagement and effort. Providing enjoyment allows for more effective learning to occur, as it can promote creativity in learners that can in turn see them innovate and engage in problem solving more effectively. Formation of positive relationships allows learners to establish feelings of belonging and connectedness, particularly if they stem from a basis of constructive interactions emerging from genuine support. This can then lead to social and emotional skills development and the nurturing of positive, caring, respectful, and satisfying relationships with others. Providing room for development and personal growth can also sponsor a greater sense of satisfaction within learners, and one that can contribute to their social competence, self-esteem, and a sense of meaning and purpose. Importantly, environments that support good leaner health and safety can also support optimal learning.

Ultimately, an investment in wellbeing among educational leadership and policy makers leads to improved health among teachers and learners, promotes positive learning outcomes, and, for all stakeholders involved, increased levels of energy, motivation, revitalization, and self-efficacy. Also important to teachers and students, especially those in leadership roles, is the place of ethics, laws, rights, and responsibilities in the school system. The final section of this chapter now turns to these aspects.

Ethics, Laws, Rights, and Responsibilities
Education is full of ethical and legal issues, and instructors need to be aware of how ethics and the law play an integral part in their work, no matter who employs them, in what position they occupy, or wherever they may be posted. It is also important to understand the distinction

between ethics and laws, what ethical teaching and leadership means, and rights (including those of the student).

Ethics is a system of morality embraced by a person or a group, and these include laws which are explicitly written rules that members of a community must follow and are often statements that have been formally produced by authorities. It also includes invisible obligations: those ideas that are less tangible and observable than laws. Rights are moral or legal entitlements. The right to teach, in terms of assignment completion, may include the right to give a zero based on the requirements provided to students when the paper was assigned. Yet, this has to be balanced with the students' right to learn, and any activity on the part of the teacher leading to an adverse impact on student success is certainly something that should be avoided, as it could also be grounds for dismissal due to not meeting responsibilities: things that one is required to do as part of a job, role, or legal obligation. Keep in mind that no matter where you work, there might be laws in place relating to accepting gifts, ethics in place that prevent fraternizing with students, rights in place to assist you to do your job (e.g., *in loco parentis*), and responsibilities afforded to you in order to assist students in meeting theirs. However, over the past few decades, the teaching profession has become less respected in many societies, translating to changes in how all stakeholders now view and treat teaching professionals, and this change has also seen students increasingly focus on their rights with a disregard for classroom and learner responsibilities.

Depending on the country and/or organization in which you work, you will meet a variety of ethical problems throughout your professional career. These will involve stakeholders at all levels, with a few real-world examples including: administrators changing grades of students or attempting to withhold employee passports; workplace discrimination against teachers due to nationality, gender, sexuality, race, or age; and, visa holder human rights violations by issuing authorities (e.g., forcing certain kinds of examinations during mandatory health checks). You may be in an organization that will fire a teacher based on the word of a student (e.g., saying that you taught while drunk, but you might be a teetotaler or have a health condition that doesn't allow you to consume alcohol). There may or may not be any recourse, but you may also have a chance to go through substantive or procedural issues regarding due process (e.g., in the case of a sexual harassment complaint). In some countries, due process may be fair, and in others, the system might be against you from the start. Typically, substantive issues relate to the severity of the issue, and they determine if you should be fired or a student expelled, with the procedural relating to the fairness of the situation, having the fate of the teacher/student predetermined, or even an outcome of administrative incompetence due to a xenophobic chairman, a person not qualified to be in their position such as one who has not graduated high school running a graduate school administration team, or a dean who was awarded the position through nepotism. Issues of legality surrounding such situations will vary depending on the country and perhaps even the state or province in which you work, and they can extend from any of the previous situations through to a student injuring themselves when your back is turned.

A Personal Ethics Code

A code of ethics can help you work more effectively with stakeholders, and when faced with any of the previous kinds of situations, while also helping establish a teacher presence that might prevent many of them. A personal code of ethics is often not written down, but it is something that might be crafted after watching the behavior of others; stem from a religious, spiritual or secular guide; or be developed by adapting to changes in morals among the community in which you live. It may also prove valuable to develop a personal ethics code that helps you employ the six cornerstones of ethical teaching when running into moral issues.

1. *Moral deliberation* – the ability to identify and analyze conflicting and competing moral interests while also adhering to the truth.
2. *Empathy* – the ability to appreciate a situation from the point of view of others, allowing for decision making that aims to be unbiased and of benefit to all involved.
3. *Knowledge* – the acquisition of adequate information of both the situation and what is expected in terms of outcomes, and how the pros and cons of any decision can lead to various consequences for the parties involved.
4. *Reasoning* – the logical and coherent analysis of a given situation, while understanding the perspectives of those involved, considering all aspects while reflecting on the circumstances or

situations, and using moral principles as a gauge for deliberation.
5. *Courage* – the creation of ethical outcomes that are appropriate for all parties involved, including standing by the convictions of various stakeholders (e.g., your students, other faculty members, parents, and the administration).
6. *Interpersonal skills* – the formulation of your stance and the presentation of your position, coming across neither too harsh nor too feeble, in ethically tinged situations.

No matter what your ethical stance may prove to be on issues, your personal moral code can influence your learners as well as those who you may lead, particularly via personal example, through the establishment of an environment of trust and safety, and from any ethical dialogues that you engage in. Personal examples are set by the way that you dress, do your work, and treat people as these all demonstrate your values. Establishing an environment of safety and trust lets students and faculty approach you with their own moral and ethical dilemmas, and allows them to give respect back to you. The ethical dialogues that you engage in can assist students to clarify their own values, and for colleagues to be able to clarify any dilemmas that they may face.

In your career, you may come across daily ethical decisions and issues, from the use of content in class that may breach copyright through to various forms of censorship and other infringements that are placed upon you by administration. You may also face heavier issues relating to the behavior of other faculty members, or the behavior of parents including child abuse cases. No matter how choppy the moral waters may become, a personal code of ethics will help you to navigate them.

Summary

This chapter highlighted a range of educational paradigms from which a wide variety of language theories have emerged to provide educators with ways to better engage learners in the classroom, and to help learners to secure knowledge. The paradigms explored included those of andragogy and pedagogy, behaviorism, cognitivism, humanism, constructivism, socio-culturalism, transformativism, poststructuralism, connectionism, and educational neuroscience. These served to establish an avenue from which a plethora of learning theories could be further introduced. Also considered was the importance of classroom management, particularly the means of encouraging and promoting positive learner behavior among students and from within the classroom. Ten classroom management theories, grounded in behaviorist, cognitive, democratic, humanist, and the psychoanalytic domains, were then detailed. The importance of educational leadership, was then highlighted, with an emphasis on the teacher leader and the student leader. The concept of wellbeing was also explored, along with its impact on educational settings, before introducing several means of enhancing it for staff, teachers, and students, and in terms of the betterment of the educational system as a whole. Finally, the role of ethics, laws, rights, and responsibilities were considered alongside the need for development of a code of ethics to help guide instructors in their daily teaching, and when charged with leadership.

Review

Content Quiz
Educational Paradigms, Classroom management, Theories, and Educational Leadership
To help solidify some of the concepts introduced by this chapter the following multiple-choice and true or false quizzes might be helpful for you to undertake. So that you can check the accuracy of your responses, an answer key can be found following the quizzes.

Multiple-Choice
Circle **a**, **b**, or **c** for the answer that best completes the sentence presented in each question.

1. Andragogy refers to those theories and principles that apply to …
    a) adult and lifelong education.
    b) young learner education.
    c) child education.

2. Behaviorism focuses on the use of …
   a) social interaction, particularly with others who are more skilled than the learner.
   b) the construction of schema or symbolic mental constructions, with learning defined as a change in schemata.
   c) conditioning paradigms solidified by reward and/or punishment (stimulus-response).

3. Cognitivism views that knowledge results from …
   a) social interaction, particularly with others who are more skilled than the learner.
   b) the construction of schema or symbolic mental constructions, with learning defined as a change in schemata.
   c) conditioning paradigms solidified by reward and/or punishment (stimulus-response).

4. Sociocultural theory sees that knowledge results from …
   a) social interaction, particularly with others who are more skilled than the learner.
   b) the construction of schema or symbolic mental constructions, with learning defined as a change in schemata.
   c) conditioning paradigms solidified by reward and/or punishment (stimulus-response).

5. Poststructuralism …
   a) believes in the importance of critiquing how power operates in the classroom in order to harm minority learners.
   b) views that learning occurs when knowledge is actuated by the process of a learner connecting to and feeding information into a network or a learning community.
   c) focuses on, and sees, inclusivity discourse as essential in the classroom.

6. Critical pedagogy …
   a) believes in the importance of critiquing how power operates in the classroom in order to harm minority learners.
   b) views that learning occurs when knowledge is actuated by the process of a learner connecting to and feeding information into a network or a learning community.
   c) focuses on, and sees, inclusivity discourse as essential in the classroom.

7. Connectivism …
   a) believes in the importance of critiquing how power operates in the classroom in order to harm minority learners.
   b) views that learning occurs when knowledge is actuated by the process of a learner connecting to and feeding information into a network or a learning community.
   c) focuses on, and sees, inclusivity discourse as essential in the classroom.

8. In developmental stage theory, equilibrium …
   a) happens when an existing schema does not work, and needs to be altered in order to deal with a new object or situation.
   b) involves the use of an existing schema to deal with a new object or situation.
   c) occurs when schemas can deal with most new information through assimilation.

9. In developmental stage theory, assimilation …
   a) happens when an existing schema does not work, and needs to be altered in order to deal with a new object or situation.
   b) involves the use of an existing schema to deal with a new object or situation.
   c) occurs when schemas can deal with most new information through assimilation.

10. In developmental stage theory, accommodation …
    a) happens when an existing schema does not work, and needs to be altered in order to deal with a new object or situation.
    b) involves the use of an existing schema to deal with a new object or situation.
    c) occurs when schemas can deal with most new information through assimilation.

11. Hierarchy of needs theory is a motivational theory that is often depicted in pyramidic form. From the base to the apex, the five needs are …
    a) self-actualization, esteem, love and belonging, safety and security, physiological.
    b) physiological, esteem, love and belonging, safety and security, self-actualization.
    c) physiological, safety and security, love and belonging, esteem, self-actualization.

12. The domains of learning are cognitive, affective, and psychomotor. The cognitive domain …
    a) involves objectives that deal with the development of feelings, emotions, attitudes, appreciation, and preference.
    b) involves objectives and skills that assist with processing information.
    c) includes those objectives that relate to the development of motor skills, coordination, and physical movement (kinesthetic action).

13. The domains of learning are cognitive, affective, and psychomotor. The affective domain …
    a) involves objectives that deal with the development of feelings, emotions, attitudes, appreciation, and preference.
    b) involves objectives and skills that assist with processing information.
    c) includes those objectives that relate to the development of motor skills, coordination, and physical movement (kinesthetic action).

14. The domains of learning are cognitive, affective, and psychomotor. The psychomotor domain …
    a) involves objectives that deal with the development of feelings, emotions, attitudes, appreciation, and preference.
    b) involves objectives and skills that assist with processing information.
    c) includes those objectives that relate to the development of motor skills, coordination, and physical movement (kinesthetic action).

15. The spiral curriculum is an alternative to the strand curriculum as it …
    a) aims to integrate multiple topics into every lesson every day in order to slowly but consistently provide work on given topics over a sustained and extended period of time.
    b) is an iterative revisiting of topics, subjects, and themes throughout a course.
    c) is based on the use of expository learning, or reception learning, which is an organized teaching method where information is presented in a specific order to focus attention and promote memorization (e.g., through the use of advanced organizers).

16. The strand curriculum is an alternative to the spiral curriculum that …
    a) aims to integrate multiple topics into every lesson every day in order to slowly but consistently provide work on given topics over a sustained and extended period of time.
    b) is an iterative revisiting of topics, subjects, and themes throughout a course.
    c) is based on the use of expository learning, or reception learning, which is an organized teaching method where information is presented in a specific order to focus attention and promote memorization (e.g., through the use of advanced organizers).

17. Subsumption learning …
    a) aims to integrate multiple topics into every lesson every day in order to slowly but consistently provide work on given topics over a sustained and extended period of time.
    b) is an iterative revisiting of topics, subjects, and themes throughout a course.
    c) is based on the use of expository learning, or reception learning, which is an organized teaching method where information is presented in a specific order to focus attention and promote memorization (e.g., through the use of advanced organizers).

18. The banking model of education …
    a) views students as being active learners who are capable of reaching conclusions via the application of cognitive skills.
    b) sees students learn through topics and themes as opposed to subject areas.
    c) sees students as being passive learners with no scope provided for creative freedom or critical thinking (the 'empty vessel').

19. A problem-prosing approach to education …
    a) views students as being active learners who are capable of reaching conclusions via the application of cognitive skills.
    b) sees students learn through topics and themes as opposed to subject areas.
    c) sees students as being passive learners with no scope provided for creative freedom or critical thinking (the 'empty vessel').

20. Phenomenon based learning …
    a) sees students learn through topics and themes as opposed to subject areas.
    b) sees students as being passive learners with no scope provided for creative freedom or critical thinking (the 'empty vessel').
    c) views students as being active learners who are capable of reaching conclusions via the application of cognitive skills.

21. The dual coding theory sees students learn more deeply …
    a) by processing visual and verbal information differently, and along distinct channels in their minds, which creates separate representations of the same information that is then processed by each channel.
    b) from words and pictures rather than just words alone.
    c) when extraneous material is excluded rather than included.

22. The multimedia principle posits that students learn more deeply …
    a) when extraneous material is excluded rather than included.
    b) from words and pictures rather than just words alone.
    c) by processing visual and verbal information differently, and along distinct channels in their minds, which creates separate representations of the same information that is then processed by each channel.

23. The coherence principle states that students learn more deeply ...
    a) when extraneous material is excluded rather than included.
    b) by processing visual and verbal information differently, and along distinct channels in their minds, which creates separate representations of the same information that is then processed by each channel.
    c) from words and pictures rather than just words alone.

24. The continguity (spatial-contiguity) principle suggests that students learn more deeply when ...
    a) printed words are placed near, rather than far from, corresponding pictures.
    b) words and images that support one another are presented simultaneously rather than sequentially.
    c) words are presented in a conversational rather than formal style in a computer-based environment that presents content using spoken words with printed words (e.g., captions).

25. The temporal contiguity principle sees students learn more deeply when ...
    a) printed words are placed near, rather than far from, corresponding pictures.
    b) words and images that support one another are presented simultaneously rather than sequentially.
    c) words are presented in a conversational rather than a formal style in a computer-based environment that presents content using spoken words with printed words (e.g., captions).

26. The personalization principle posits that students learn more deeply when ...
    a) printed words are placed near, rather than far from, corresponding pictures.
    b) words and images that support one another are presented simultaneously rather than sequentially.
    c) words are presented in a conversational rather than a formal style in a computer-based environment that presents content using spoken words with printed words (e.g., captions).

27. The modality principle states that students learn more deeply when ......
   a) they are presented with learning content that is presented in a more human sounding voice than a non-human mechanical one.
   b) content is broken down into smaller chunks. (e.g., long lessons should be broken down into smaller segments, and long passages of text should be broken down into multiple shorter ones).
   c) graphics are explained by audio narration rather than text on screen, although exceptions occur when learners are familiar with the content or are not native speakers of the narration language, or when printed words appear on screen.

28. The voice principle suggests that students learn more deeply when ...
   a) graphics are explained by audio narration rather than text on screen, although exceptions occur when learners are familiar with the content or are not native speakers of the narration language, or when printed words appear on screen.
   b) they are presented with learning content that is presented in a more human sounding voice than a non-human mechanical one.
   c) content is broken down into smaller chunks. (e.g., long lessons should be broken down into smaller segments, and long passages of text broken down into multiple shorter ones).

29. The segmenting principle posits that students learn more deeply when ...
   a) graphics are explained by audio narration rather than text on screen, although exceptions occur when learners are familiar with the content or are not native speakers of the narration language, or when printed words appear on screen.
   b) content is broken down into smaller chunks. (e.g., long lessons should be broken down into smaller segments, and long passages of text broken down into multiple shorter ones).
   c) they are presented with learning content that is presented in a more human sounding voice than a non-human mechanical one.

30. The signaling principle sees that students learn more deeply when ...
    a) presented with auditory, visual, or temporal cues that draw attention to critical elements of a lesson. (e.g., use of arrows, circles, highlighting, bold font, pausing).
    b) key concepts or vocabulary are presented prior to the processes or procedures related to those concepts.
    c) they are able to control their pace of movement through segmented content.

31. The learner control principle suggests that students learn more deeply when ...
    a) they are presented with auditory, visual or temporal cues that draw attention to critical elements of a lesson (e.g., use of arrows, circles, highlighting, bold font, pausing).
    b) they are able to control their pace of movement through segmented content.
    c) key concepts or vocabulary are presented prior to the processes or procedures related to those concepts.

32. The pre-training principle states that students learn more deeply when ...
    a) they are presented with auditory, visual or temporal cues that draw attention to critical elements of a lesson (e.g., use of arrows, circles, highlighting, bold font, pausing).
    b) they are able to control their pace of movement through segmented content.
    c) key concepts or vocabulary are presented prior to the processes or procedures related to those concepts.

33. The redundancy principle posits that students learn more deeply as …
   a) graphics are explained by audio narration alone, rather than audio narration and on-screen text.
   b) voiceover is adequate; a moving image or a person's face is not necessary to see improvement in learning.
   c) many multimedia design principles contradict each other when used with those learners who have greater prior knowledge compared to those that have low prior knowledge of the subject matter under study.

34. The image principle suggests that students learn more deeply when …
   a) graphics are explained by audio narration alone, rather than audio narration and on-screen text.
   b) voiceover is adequate; a moving image or a person's face is not necessary to see improvement in learning.
   c) many multimedia design principles contradict each other when used with those learners who have greater prior knowledge compared to those that have low prior knowledge of the subject matter under study.

35. The expertise principle sees that students learn more deeply when …
   a) graphics are explained by audio narration alone, rather than audio narration and on-screen text.
   b) voiceover is adequate; a moving image or a person's face is not necessary to see improvement in learning.
   c) many multimedia design principles contradict each other when used with those learners who have greater prior knowledge compared to those that have low prior knowledge of the subject matter under study.

36. Behaviorist classrooms rely on a classroom management style that ...
    a) is an obedience-based discipline approach to classroom management which focuses on the teacher developing a positive behaviorist management strategy over being dictatorial.
    b) utilizes learning principles to assist with producing changes in student behavior. It relies upon assessment of the functional relationship between the targeted behavior and the environment to develop socially acceptable alternatives to any aberrant behavior.
    c) necessitates the need for very clear rules and codes of conduct along with the need for reinforcement to decrease as time passes, and one that changes the kind of negative reinforcer as students become desensitized to it.

37. Applied behavior analysis is a classroom management style that ...
    a) necessitates the need for very clear rules and codes of conduct along with the need for reinforcement to decrease as time passes, and one that changes the kind of negative reinforcer as students become desensitized to it.
    b) is a behavioral management theory which utilizes learning principles to assist with producing changes in student behavior. It relies upon assessment of the functional relationship between the targeted behavior and the environment to develop socially acceptable alternatives to any aberrant behavior.
    c) is an obedience-based discipline approach to classroom management which focuses on the teacher developing a positive behaviorist management strategy over being dictatorial.

38. Assertive discipline is a classroom management style that …
   a) is a behavioral management theory which utilizes learning principles to assist with producing changes in student behavior. It relies upon assessment of the functional relationship between the targeted behavior and the environment to develop socially acceptable alternatives to any aberrant behavior.
   b) is an obedience-based discipline approach to classroom management which focuses on the teacher developing a positive behaviorist management strategy over being dictatorial.
   c) necessitates the need for very clear rules and codes of conduct along with the need for reinforcement to decrease as time passes, and one that changes the kind of negative reinforcer as students become desensitized to it.

39. Applied behavior analysis interprets student's behavior from the ABC's of antecedents, behavior, and consequences. The antecedents are those things that …
   a) occur prior to misbehavior.
   b) are the misbehavior itself.
   c) result from student behavior.

40. The democratic classroom is one that …
   a) relies on human beings striving to fit in or belong to a social group. This views misbehavior to be a result of the learner breaking rules in order to achieve, maintain, or protect their status in the group.
   b) advocates positive rewards for learners exhibiting self-control, and utilizing preferred activity time as a means to leverage improvements in behavior.
   c) promotes learner voice, with the learner regularly involved in the decision-making process in terms of establishing the classroom learning environment.

41. Nonadversarial method is a classroom management method that …
   a) relies on human beings striving to fit in or belong to a social group. This views misbehavior to be a result of the learner breaking rules in order to achieve, maintain, or protect their status in the group.
   b) advocates positive rewards for learners exhibiting self-control, and utilizing preferred activity time as a means to leverage improvements in behavior.
   c) promotes learner voice, with the learner regularly involved in the decision-making process in terms of establishing the classroom learning environment.

42. The pragmatic method is a psychoanalytic method of classroom management that …
   a) relies on human beings striving to fit in or belong to a social group. This views misbehavior to be a result of the learner breaking rules in order to achieve, maintain, or protect their status in the group.
   b) advocates positive rewards for learners exhibiting self-control, and utilizing preferred activity time as a means to leverage improvements in behavior.
   c) promotes learner voice, with the learner regularly involved in the decision-making process in terms of establishing the classroom learning environment.

172   Issues in TESOL

43. The response thinking process (RTP) is a cognitivist method of classroom management that …
    a) involves basic acceptance and support of a learner, regardless of what they say and do, believing them to be inherently good and encouraging them to do good things.
    b) stresses learner thought as a means for students to actively ponder their (mis)behavior and to develop a sense of responsibility and respect for their own lives and those around them.
    c) relies on reward and punishment to produce positive behavior. It utilizes a system of classroom currency where those who do the right thing are rewarded, while those who do not may be required to forfeit previous rewards. It is based on the principles of operant conditioning and behavioral economics, with rewards used as reinforcers, in order to encourage specific target behavior.

44. The token economy is an approach to classroom management that …
    a) stresses learner thought as a means for students to actively ponder their (mis)behavior and to develop a sense of responsibility and respect for their own lives and those around them.
    b) involves basic acceptance and support of a learner, regardless of what they say and do, believing them to be inherently good and encouraging them to do good things.
    c) relies on reward and punishment to produce positive behavior. It utilizes a system of classroom currency where those who do the right thing are rewarded, while those who do not may be required to forfeit previous rewards. It is based on the principles of operant conditioning and behavioral economics, with rewards used as reinforcers, in order to encourage specific target behavior.

45. Unconditional positive regard is a humanist approach to classroom management that …
   a) involves basic acceptance and support of a learner, regardless of what they say and do, believing them to be inherently good and encouraging them to do good things.
   b) stresses learner thought as a means for students to actively ponder their (mis)behavior and to develop a sense of responsibility and respect for their own lives and those around them.
   c) relies on reward and punishment to produce positive behavior. It utilizes a system of classroom currency where those who do the right thing are rewarded, while those who do not may be required to forfeit previous rewards. It is based on the principles of operant conditioning and behavioral economics, with rewards used as reinforcers, in order to encourage specific target behavior.

46. A variety of roles that can be taken on formally or informally on a paid or a voluntary basis, and which involve the process of enlisting and guiding the energies and the talents of teachers, students, and parents toward achieving common educational goals is referred to as being …
   a) educational leadership.
   b) student leadership.
   c) teacher leadership.

47. In education, voice refers to …
   a) learning through activities that are relevant and meaningful to learners, driven by their interests, and often self-initiated with teacher guidance, giving them voice and choice in how they learn.
   b) moral guidelines where values, principles, and standards can impact decision making and guide behavior and practice in personal and professional life.
   c) the values, opinions, beliefs, perspectives, and cultural backgrounds of the people in a district, school, or school community, especially students, teachers, parents, and local citizens, and includes how this is considered, included, listened to, and acted upon when critical decisions are being made in a district or school.

48. The student leader process aims to promote the opportunity for …
   a) voice and agency.
   b) voice and shared leadership.
   c) Voice.

49. The teacher leader process aims to promote the opportunity for …
   a) voice and agency.
   b) voice and shared leadership.
   c) voice.

50. The kind of wellbeing that is associated with the sets of skills and abilities required for effective work/study to be conducted, and mirrored in self-efficacy (the belief in the ability to perform) is …
   a) cognitive.
   b) physical.
   c) psychological.

51. The kind of wellbeing which includes emotions that arise from work/study, and which might lead to depression or to increased commitment to work/study is …
   a) cognitive.
   b) physical.
   c) psychological.

52. The kind of wellbeing which refers to health conditions that stem from work/study, including workloads that lead to exhaustion (burnout) or those that allow for a work-life balance, is …
   a) physical.
   b) psychological.
   c) social.

53. The kind of wellbeing that arises from the levels of collaboration and support from peers, and which impacts levels of performance and satisfaction, is …
   a) physical.
   b) psychological.
   c) social.

54. Ethics can be defined as …
   a) a system of morality that is embraced by a person or a group.
   b) explicitly written rules that members of a community must follow.
   c) a thing that one is required to do as part of a job, role, or legal obligation.

55. Laws are …
   a) moral guidelines where values, principles, and standards can impact decision making and guide behavior and practice in personal and professional life.
   b) explicitly written rules that members of a community must follow.
   c) things that one is required to do as part of a job, role, or legal obligation.

True or False

Circle **a** (true) if you think that the statement is correct, or **b** (false) if you think that the statement is incorrect.

1. *In loco parentis* refers to the legal responsibility of an organization or person that takes on some of the functions and responsibilities normally undertaken by a parent.
    a) True.
    b) False.

2. *Tabula rasa* sees the learner as a blank slate, with all knowledge coming from experience or perception.
    a) True.
    b) False.

3. In humanistic learning theory, or humanism, the learner is the source of authority, and the focus is on specific human capabilities including those of creativity, personal growth, and choice. In this view emphasis is therefore placed on learner *materials* rather than learner *potential*.
    a) True.
    b) False.

4. Constructivism emphasizes the importance of the active involvement of learners in constructing knowledge for themselves, with novel information acquired based on the learner utilizing their background knowledge.
    a) True.
    b) False.

5. In transformative learning, the process of perspective transformation occurs across three dimensions: psychological (changes in self-understanding), convictional (belief system revision), and behavioral (lifestyle change).
    a) True.
    b) False.

6. Poststructuralists focus on inclusiveness; critical theorists focus on promotion of the belief systems of those considered to be oppressed. In this light, critical pedagogy in the EFL/ESL context maintains that both language learning and the teaching of it are a political process.
    a) True.
    b) False.

7. Connectivism has been described as a learning theory for the digital age. At its core is a form of experiential learning that prioritizes actions and experience over the notion that knowledge is propositional.
    a) True.
    b) False.

8. Aspects of educational neuroscience are becoming increasingly important because the field attempts to link understanding of brain processes with classroom instruction and experiences.
    a) True.
    b) False.

9. A schema refers to a cognitive framework or concept that helps to organize and interpret information.
    a) True.
    b) False.

10. In developmental stage theory adaptation processes allow a transition from one stage to another (equilibrium, assimilation, and accommodation).
    a) True.
    b) False.

11. The hierarchy of needs theory lends itself to curriculum development or lesson planning more so than to building student/teacher relationships.
    a) True.
    b) False.

12. Bloom and his colleagues argue that there is a hierarchy of learning. These hierarchies (taxonomies of learning objectives) relate to the development of different kinds of learning skills and are part of the cognitive (thinking), affective (feeling), or psycho-motor (doing) domain.
    a) True.
    b) False.

13. The structure of observed learning outcomes (SOLO) describes levels of increasing complexity in learners' understanding of subjects. In other words, understanding is conceived as an increase in the number and complexity of connections that a learner makes as they progress from being incompetent to becoming an expert.
    a) True.
    b) False.

14. Gagne's eight conditions of learning involve five types of learning outcomes that provide the critical conditions that are required for learning, and these are achieved via nine instructional events.
    c) True.
    d) False.

15. Blooms' taxonomy can be used to help teachers in setting differentiated objectives, while Gagne's nine levels of learning can help teachers provide scaffolding on which to construct lessons.
    a) True.
    b) False.

16. Kolb's experiential learning cycle consists of four stages, each feeding into the next and being mutually supportive, with learner understanding refined each time they go through the cycle. The four stages are: concrete experience, reflective observation, abstract conceptualization, and active experimentation. It is built on the premise that learning is the acquisition of abstract concepts that can then be applied to a range of scenarios.
    a) True.
    b) False.

17. Subsumption learning is a process that is intended to be one of meaningful learning, as opposed to rote learning, where subsumed items (or meaningfully learned ones) hold greater potential for retention.
    a) True.
    b) False.

18. According to Erikson's psychosocial theory of development, humans go through eight stages of development during their lifetimes. These are based on the impact of external factors, parents, and society on personality development from childhood through to adulthood. Understanding these stages of development *do not* help us as a teacher begin to understand what kind of questions that students might be asking of themselves and the world around them.
    a) True.
    b) False.

19. In dual coding theory, processing visual and verbal information differently, along distinct channels in the human mind, *does not* create separate representations of the same information which is then processed by each channel.
    a) True.
    b) False.

20. The promise of multimedia learning involves students acquiring knowledge better from messages that consist of words and pictures rather than words alone.
    a) True.
    b) False.

21. Sensory stimulation theory posits that effective learning occurs when the senses are stimulated – sight, hearing, touch, smell and taste.
    a) True.
    b) False.

22. Multimodal learning also takes the position that when a number of our senses are engaged while learning, we are better able to understand and remember more.
    a) True.
    b) False.

23. There are four main methods involved with multimodal learning that result in the VARK model (visual, auditory, reading and writing, and kinesthetic).
    a) True.
    b) False.

24. In multimodal learning, those learners who favor a visual approach tend to retain new information through text, images, and visual representations of concepts.
    a) True.
    b) False.

25. In multimodal learning, learners favoring an auditory approach will tend to take in information through sound, story, discussion, lecture, and so on.
    a) True.
    b) False.

26. In multimodal learning, learners favoring a reading and writing approach will tend to take in information as a result of performing movements.
    a) True.
    b) False.

27. In multimodal learning, learners favoring a kinesthetic approach will tend to take in information by making lists, note taking, reading, and rewriting.
   a) True.
   b) False.

28. Digital immigrants are those of us who have grown up with modern technology, while those that have grown up without it (or with old defunct technology) are classed as digital natives.
   a) True.
   b) False.

29. One of the biggest changes that have occurred in education as a result of digital technology is that of being able to teach and learn using multimodal, non-linear pathways.
   a) True.
   b) False.

30. Moving into the era of the fourth industrial revolution all learners now require a range of competencies and skills that come to support education in terms of personalization, equality, collaboration, adaptability, communication, relationships, and technology. This sees the need for sixteen skills required by twenty-first century learners, along with eight key skills for life-long learning, four digital competency proficiencies as well as the need to develop a personal learning network that includes a community of practice.
   a) True.
   b) False.

31. The sixteen skills required by twenty-first century learners can be broken down into foundational literacies, critical competencies, and character qualities.
   a) True.
   b) False.

32. Of the four digital competency proficiencies (procedural, socio-digital, digital discourse, and strategic), *procedural competence* refers to the ability to manipulate technology (in terms of hardware and software).
   a) True.
   b) False.

33. Of the four digital competency proficiencies (procedural, socio-digital, digital discourse, and strategic), *socio-digital competence* refers to the ability to manage an extended task, using several applications and/or types of equipment.
   a) True.
   b) False.

34. Of the four digital competency proficiencies (procedural, socio-digital, digital discourse, and strategic), *digital discourse competence* refers to understanding what is appropriate in different social contexts and knowledge domains in terms of both technology and language.
   a) True.
   b) False.

35. Of the four digital competency proficiencies (procedural, socio-digital, digital discourse, and strategic), *strategic competence* refers to the ability to repair problems and work around the gaps in technological knowledge and skills.
   a) True.
   b) False.

36. A personal learning network (PLN) refers to the combination of tools, people, and services that an individual utilizes as resources and approaches to learning (personally for enrichment, and professionally for development purposes).
   a) True.
   b) False.

37. Crucial to the development of personal learning networks are learner autonomy and levels of learner confidence as they move from formal settings, teacher-guided/controlled and institutional-based, to environments where they can direct their own learning, find their own information, and create their own knowledge from more knowledgeable others with whom they engage.
    a) True.
    b) False.

38. A PLN, based on personal interests and preferences over institutional requirements and choices, may be small or vast, but the main characteristic is that they are developed in order to support knowledge growth by being autonomous, connected, diverse, and open.
    a) True.
    b) False.

39. A community of practice (COP) is formed from three components – domain, community, and practice – which sees a group of people (the domain) who share a craft or profession come together (as a community) to distribute experience and information, and to learn from each other (in practice), which leads to both personal and professional development.
    a) True.
    b) False.

40. The concept of a COP and PLN see learners at the center of their own learning experience, and instrumental in determining the content of their own learning, how they engage and participate in learning, and who can participate with them.
    a) True.
    b) False.

41. Classroom management theory involves working with learners and focuses on managing their behavior, it is not concerned with the smooth integration and transition among learning activities, arranging the classroom, working with technology and other learning materials (e.g., texts, the board).
   a) True.
   b) False.

42. The assertive discipline classroom management theory was originally developed to work with children with special needs, with rules and consequences developed by authority figures with those who are subordinate expected to follow them.
   a) True.
   b) False.

43. The assertive discipline theory of classroom management assumes that there are only three types of teacher (non-assertive, hostile, and assertive), and that there is no other discipline system.
   a) True.
   b) False.

44. The assertive discipline system is not one of the most widely used classroom management tactics in the entire world.
   a) True
   b) False.

45. Choice theory envisions behavior as a result of being our best attempt at meeting our current needs (genetically, psychological, or survival driven), and changing daily. The aim of the teacher is to develop a classroom environment, and to provide activities and materials, that meets all of these needs.
   a) True.
   b) False.

46. In the democratic classroom theory of classroom management, power shifts from the educator to the learner, with the goal of promoting deep thought regarding how the classroom should operate. Included within this is the notion of *what* rules to put in place, *why* those rules are required, and *how* those rules should be upheld in order to develop learners that are just and moral critical thinkers.
    a) True.
    b) False.

47. In the non-adversarial method of classroom management, preferred activity time (PAT) is set aside for students to engage in activities that they find enjoyable. These activities are used by the teacher to leverage improvements in behavior from learners by providing incentives for good behavior.
    a) True.
    b) False.

48. The response thinking process of classroom management stresses learner thought as a means for students to actively ponder (mis)behavior and to develop a sense of responsibility and respect for their own lives and those around them. It is not based on perceptual control theory but is designed to assist in making sense of the environment in order to construct a satisfying life.
    a) True.
    b) False.

49. The token economy encourages long-term positive behavior among students, as they are continuously and consistently incentivized to behave positively as they aim to collect as many tokens as possible over time. Today, smartphone applications are useful in sharing this data among teachers, parents, and administrators, and also for allowing other teachers to provide rewards to students using the same app (e.g., when on playground duty).
    a) True.
    b) False.

50. In the humanist approach to classroom management, unconditional positive regard involves the basic acceptance and support of a learner, believing them to be inherently good.
    a) True.
    b) False.

51. Teacher leadership is where teacher leaders take on an active role in order to shape the culture of their teaching context, with an aim to increase student learning and achievement through individual, collaborative/team, and organizational development.
    a) True.
    b) False.

52. Student leadership is where a student leader takes on an active role in their education and in the wider improvement of the classroom, school, school system, and community. It aims to develop positive skills in the process, to promote the opportunity for voice and agency in learning, and to allow for meaningful positive changes to occur in the educational environment. At its core is the concept that leadership is inherent within all.
    a) True.
    b) False.

53. Teacher agency refers to the provision of learning through activities that are relevant and meaningful to learners, driven by their interests, and often self-initiated with teacher guidance, giving them voice and choice in how they learn.
    a) True.
    b) False.

54. Student agency, in the context of professional learning, refers to the capacity of teachers to act purposefully and to constructively direct their professional growth and contribute to such growth in colleagues.
    a) True.
    b) False.

55. Teacher wellbeing can be defined as a teacher flourishing in the workplace as an individual, and in their relationships with others, by maintaining a sense of balance between their emotional, physical, spiritual and social needs.
    a) True.
    b) False.

56. Student wellbeing can be defined as the sustainable state of a positive mood and attitude, resilience, and satisfaction with self, relationships. and experiences at school.
    a) True.
    b) False.

57. Positive education refers to the ways in which schools and other educational settings are able to apply the research and practice from positive psychology to their own contexts with the purpose of building positive emotions, engagement, relationships, meaning, accomplishment, and health, in order to boost wellbeing.
    a) True.
    b) False.

58. A code of ethics refers to moral guidelines: the values, principles, and standards that can impact decision making, and those that guide behavior and practice in personal and professional life.
    a) True.
    b) False.

59. Rights are a thing that are required to be done as part of a job, role, or legal obligation.
    a) True.
    b) False.

60. Responsibilities are moral or legal entitlements.
    a) True.
    b) False.

Quiz Answers
Educational Paradigms, Classroom Management Theories, and Educational Leadership

Multiple-Choice

1.	a	31.	b
2.	c	32.	c
3.	b	33.	a
4.	a	34.	b
5.	c	35.	c
6.	a	36.	c
7.	b	37.	b
8.	c	38.	b
9.	b	39.	a
10.	a	40.	c
11.	c	41.	b
12.	b	42.	a
13.	a	43.	b
14.	c	44.	c
15.	b	45.	a
16.	a	46.	a
17.	c	47.	c
18.	c	48.	a
19.	a	49.	b
20.	a	50.	a
21.	a	51.	c
22.	b	52.	a
23.	a	53.	c
24.	a	54.	a
25.	b	55.	b
26.	b		
27.	c		
28.	b		
29.	b		
30.	a		

True or False

1.	T	31.	T
2.	T	32.	T
3.	F	33.	F
4.	T	34.	F
5.	T	35.	T
6.	T	36.	T
7.	T	37.	T
8.	T	38.	T
9.	T	39.	T
10.	T	40.	T
11.	F	41.	F
12.	T	42.	T
13.	T	43.	T
14.	T	44.	F
15.	T	45.	T
16.	T	46.	T
17.	T	47.	T
18.	F	48.	T
19.	F	49.	T
20.	T	50.	T
21.	T	51.	T
22.	T	52.	T
23.	T	53.	F
24.	T	54.	F
25.	T	55.	T
26.	F	56.	T
27.	F	57.	T
28.	F	58.	T
29.	T	59.	F
30.	T	60.	F

Suggested Readings

Amici, F., Sanchez-Amaro, A., Sebastian-Enesco, C., Cacchione, T., Allritz, M., Salazar-Bonet., Rossano, F. (2019). The word order of languages predicts native speakers' working memory. *Scientific reports 9*, 1124. https://doi.org/10.1038/s41598-018-37654-9

Anderson, M. (2015). *Students as leaders.* ICT Evangelist. https://ictevangelist.com/students-as-leaders

Atherton, J. (2005). Learning and teaching: SOLO taxonomy. https://ar.cetl.hku.hk/pdf/solo.pdf

Ausubel, D. (1962). A subsumption theory of meaningful verbal learning and retention. *Journal of General Psychology, 66*, 213-224.

Ausubel, D. (1963). *The psychology of meaningful verbal learning.* Grune & Stratton.

Ausubel, D. (1965). Introduction to part one. In R. Anderson & D. Ausubel (Eds.), *Readings in the psychology of cognition*, (pp. 3-17). Holt, Rinehart & Winston.

Ausubel, D. (1968). *Educational psychology: A cognitive view.* Holt, Rhinehart & Winston.

Biggs, J., & Collis, C. (1982). *Evaluating the quality of learning: the SOLO Taxonomy.* Academic Press.

Blase, J., & Blase, J. (2006). *Teachers bringing out the best in teachers: A guide to peer consultations for administrators and teachers.* Corwin Press.

Bloom, B., Engelhart, M., Furst, E., Hill, H., & Krathwohl, D. (1956). *Taxonomy of educational objectives: The classification of educational goals.* Handbook I: Cognitive domain. David McKay Company.

Bodner, G., Klobuchar, M., & Geelan, D. (2001). The many forms of constructivism. *Journal of Chemical Education, 78*, 1108-1134.

Bohren, A. (2018). Language acquisition theory: A comprehensive guide. *Cognifit.* https://blog.cognifit.com/language-acquisition-theory

Brown, H. (1972). Cognitive pruning and second language acquisition. *Modern language journal, 56*, 2218-2222.

Brown, H. (2014). *Principles of language learning and teaching: A course in second language acquisition*, (6th ed.). Pearson Education.

Brown, S., & Larson-Hall, J. (2012). *Second language acquisition myths.* Michigan University Press.

Bruner, J. (1960). *The process of education.* The President and Fellows of Harvard College.

Cann, R. (2019). *Positive school leaderships for flourishing teachers: Leadership actions that enhance teacher wellbeing.* [Unpublished master's thesis]. The University of Auckland, New Zealand.

Clark, D. (2015). Bloom's taxonomy of learning domains. *Big dog & little dog's performance juxtaposition.*
http://www.nwlink.com/~donclark/hrd/bloom.html

Clark, R., & Chopeta, L. (2004). *Graphics for learning: proven guidelines for planning, designing, and evaluating visuals in training materials.* Jossey-Bass/Pfeiffer.

Clark, R., & Mayer, R. (2011). *E-Learning and the Science of Instruction: Proven guidelines for consumers and designers of multimedia learning,* 3rd ed. Pfieffer.

Clark, M., & Wilson, A. (1991). Context and rationality in Mezirow's Theory of transformational learning. *Adult Education Quarterly, 41*(2), 75-91.
https://doi.org.10.1177/0001848191041002002.

CLLN. (2014). *Seven principles of adult learning.* Principles of adult learning. Canadian Literacy and Learning Network.

Cosenza, M. (2015). Defining teacher leadership: Affirming the teacher leader model standards. *Issues in Teacher Education, 24*(2), 79-99.

Crooks, S. M., Cheon, J., Inan, F., Ari, F., & Flores, R. (2012). Modality and cueing in multimedia learning: Examining cognitive and perceptual explanations for the modality effect. *Computers in Human Behavior, 28*(3), 1063 1071, 2012.

Crystal, (2006). *Language and the internet.* Cambridge University Press.

Cooper, P. (1993). Paradigm shifts in designed instruction: From behaviorism to cognitivism to constructivism. *Educational technology, 33*(5), 12-19.

Corder, P. (1971). Idiosyncratic dialects and error analysis. IRAL: *International Review of Applied Linguistics in Language Teaching, 9*(2), 147-160.

Curtiss, S., Fromkin, V., Krashen, S. & Rigier, M. (1974). The development of language in Genie: A case of language acquisition beyond the critical period. *Brain and Language, 1*(1), 81-107.
https://doi.org/10.1016/0093-934X(74)90027-3

DEC. (2015). *The wellbeing framework for schools.* NSW Department of Education and Communities.

Dodge, R., Daly, A., Huyton, J., & Sanders, L. (2012). The challenge of defining wellbeing. *International Journal of Wellbeing, 2*(3), 222-235.

Downes, S. (2010). New technology supporting informal learning. *Journal of Emerging Technologies in Web Intelligence, 2*(1), 27-33.

Dreikur, R. (1964). *Children the challenge*. Duell, Sloan and Pearce.

Drew, C. (2020a). *Bruner's spiral curriculum | The 3 key principles*. Helpful Professor.
https://helpfulprofessor.com/spiral-curriculum

Drew, C. (2020b). *The banking model of education – pros & cons*. Helpful Professor. https://helpfulprofessor.com/banking-model

Drew, C. (2020c). Thirteen effective classroom management theories. Helpful Professor.
https://helpfulprofessor.com/classroom-management

Erikson, E. (1993). *Childhood and society*. W. W. Norton & Co.

Ford, E. (1994). *Discipline for home and school*. Brandt Publishing.

Foucault, M. (1999). Truth and power. In J. Faubion (Ed.), *Michel Foucault: Aesthetics, essential words of Foucault 1954-1984*. The New Press.

Freire, P. (1970). *Pedagogy of the oppressed*. Continuum.

Gagne, R. (1965). *The conditions of learning and theory of instruction*. Holt, Rhinehart & Winston.

Gee, J. P. (2004). *Situated language and learning: A critique of traditional schooling*. Routledge.

Glasser, W. (1998). *Choice Theory: A new psychology of personal freedom*. Harper-Collins.

Goker, S. (2020). Student Leadership 4.0. In H. Senol (Ed.), *Educational Leadership*. IntechOpen. https://www.intechopen.com/books/educational-leadership/student-leadership-4-0

Fulton, J. (2019). *Ten interesting characteristics of a student leader. Classcraft*.
https://www.classcraft.com/blog/features/characteristics-of-a-student-leader

Harrow, A. (1972). *A taxonomy of the psychomotor domain: A guide for developing behavioral objectives*. Addison-Wesley Longman.

Hasler, B., Kersten, B., & Sweller, J. (2007). Learner control, cognitive load and instructional animation. *Applied Cognitive Psychology, 21*(6), 713-729.

Hecker, D. (2020). *The six domains of effective student leadership*. Leaders of Evolution. https://www.classcraft.com/blog/features/characteristics-of-a-student-leader

Hines, T. (2018). *Anatomy of the brain*. Mayfield Clinic. https://mayfieldclinic.com/pe-anatbrain.htm

Hutauruk, B. (2015). Children first language acquisition at age 1-3 years old in Balata. *IOSR Journal of Humanities and Social Sciences, 20*(8), 51-57.

Ibrahim, M., Antonenko, P., Greenwood, C., & Wheeler, D. (2012). Effects of segmenting, signaling, and weeding on learning from educational video. *Learning, Media and Technology, 37*(3), 220-235.

Jarvis, P. (1985). *The sociology of adult and continuing education*. Croom Helm.

Johnson, M., Schuster, M., Le, Q., Krikun, M., Wu, Y., Chen, Z., Thorat, N., Viegas, F., Wattenberg, M., Corrado, G., Hughes, M. & Dean, J. (2017). Google's multilingual neural machine translation system: Enabling zero-shot translation. Computation and language. *ArXiv*. https://arxiv.org/abs/1611.04558

Kazdin, A. (1977). *The token economy: A review and evaluation*. Plenum Press.

Kent, D. (Ed.). (2019). *The fourth industrial revolution and education: Digital language learning and technology*. Pedagogy Press.

Kern, M., Waters, L., Adler, A., & White, M. (2014). Assessing employee wellbeing in schools using a multifaceted approach: Associations with physical health, life satisfaction, and professional thriving. *Psychology, 5*(6), 500-513.

Khacharem, A., Spanjers, I., Zoudji, B., Kalyuga, S., & Ripoll, H. (2013) Using segmentation to support the learning from animated soccer scenes: An effect of prior knowledge. *Psychology of Sport and Exercise, 14*(2), 154-160.

Knowles, M., Holton, E., & Swanson, R. (2005). *The adult learner: The definitive classic in adult education and human resource development*, 6th ed. Elsevier.

Kohn, A. (1997, September 03). *Students don't work – they Learn*. Education week.

Kolb, D. (1984). *Experiential learning: Experience as the source of learning and development*, (Vol. 1). Prentice-Hall.

Jones, F. (1987). *Positive classroom discipline*. Frederic H Jones & Associates.

Laird, D. (1985). Approaches to training and development. Addison Wesley.

Lave, J., & Wagner, E. (1991). *Situated learning: legitimate peripheral participation.* Cambridge University Press.

Lawless, C. (2019). *Multimodal learning: Engaging your learner's senses.* LearnUpon.
https://www.learnupon.com/blog/multimodal-learning

Locke, J. (1690). *An essay concerning human understanding.* Thomas Basset.

Lu, H., Gong, S., & Clarke, B. (2007). The relationship of Kolb learning styles, online learning behaviors and learning outcomes. *Journal of Educational Technology and Society, 10*(4), 187-196.

Manolev, J. (2018). The datafication of discipline: Class Dojo, surveillance and a performative classroom culture. *Learning, Media and Technology, 44*(1), 36-51.

Maslow, A. (1954). *Motivation and personality.* Harper.

May, M. (2019). *Seven reasons to love – and leverage – multimodal learning in your classroom.* Solid Professor.
https://www.solidprofessor.com/blog/multimodal-approach-learning

Mayer, R. (2003). The promise of multimedia learning: Using the same instructional design methods across different media. *Learning and Instruction, 13*(2), 125-139.

Mayer, R.E., & Moreno, R. (1998) A split-attention effect in multimedia learning: Evidence for dual coding hypothesis. *Journal of Educational Psychology, 83*, 484–490.

Mayer, R., Mathias, A., & Wetzell, L. (2002). Fostering understanding of multimedia messages through pre-training: Evidence for a two-stage theory of mental model construction. *Journal of Experimental Psychology: Applied, 8*, 147-154.

McCallum, F., Price, D., Graham, A., & Morrison, A. (2017). *Teacher wellbeing: A review of the literature.* AIS NSW.

McIntyre, T. (2020). *Assertive Discipline.* Classroom Behavior Management Strategies.
http://www.behavioradvisor.com/AssertiveDiscipline.html

McLeod, S. (2017). *Kolb's learning styles and experiential learning cycle.* Simply Psychology.
https://www.simplypsychology.org/learning-kolb.html

Mena-Guacas, D., & Velandia, R, C. (2020). Interaction through mobile technology in short-term university courses. *Heliyon, 6*(2), e03287.

Moles, C. (1990). *Student discipline strategies: Research and practice.* State University of New York Press.

Moreno, R. (2007). Optimizing learning from animations by minimizing cognitive load: Cognitive and affective consequences of signaling and segmentation methods. *Applied Cognitive Psychology, 21*, 765–781.

McLaughlin, B. (1992). *Myths and misconceptions about second Language Learning: What every teacher needs to unlearn. Educational Practice Report 5.* National Center for Research on Cultural Diversity and Second Language Learning.

Mezirow, J. (1997). Transformative learning: Theory to practice. *New Directions for Adult and Continuing Education, 74*, 5-12.

Morgan, P. (2007). Poststructuralism and Applied Linguistics. In J. Cummins, & C. Davison (Eds.). *International handbook of English language teaching,* (pp. 949-968). Springer International Handbooks of Education.

National College for School Leadership. (2006). *Student leadership: Investing in tomorrow's leaders for schools and communities.* https://core.ac.uk/download/pdf/4152266.pdf

Norton, B., & Toohey, K. (2004). *Critical pedagogies and language learning.* Cambridge University.

Piaget, J. (1936). *Origins of intelligence in the child.* Routledge & Kegan Paul.

Powers, W. (1998). *Making sense of behavior.* Benchmark Publications Inc.

Prensky, M. (2001). *Digital natives, digital immigrants.* On the Horizon MCB University Press, 9(5), 1-6.

Reynolds, M. (2017, June 14). Chatbots learn how to negotiate and drive a hard bargain. *New Scientist.* https://www.newscientist.com/article/mg23431304-300-chatbots-learn-how-to-drive-a-hard-bargain

Rogers, C. (1951). Client-centered therapy: Its current practice, implications and theory. Houghton Mifflin.

Savoji, A., Hassanabadi, H., Fasihipour, Z. (2011). The modality effect in learner-paced multimedia learning. Precedia-Social and Behavioral Sciences, 30, 1488-1493.

Schunk, D. (2008). *Learning theories: An educational perspective,* 5th ed. Pearson.

Selinker, L. (1972). Interlanguage. *International Review of Applied Linguistics, 10,* 209-241.

Sherwood, L. (2015). *Human physiology: From cells to systems*. Cengage Learning.

Schleicher, A. (2018). *Valuing our teachers and raising their status: How communities can help.* OECD Publishing.

Seligman, M. (2011). *Flourish: A new understanding of happiness and well-being – and how to achieve them.* Nicholas Brealey Publishing.

Siemens, G. (2005). Connectivism: A learning theory for the digital age. *International Journal of Instructional technology and Distance Learning, 2*(1), 3-10.

Skinner, B. (1957). *Verbal behavior.* Copley Publishing Group.

Slemp, G., Chin, T., Kern, M., Siokou, C., Loton, D., Oades., Vella-Brodick, D., & Waters, L. (2017). Positive education in Australia: Practice, measurement, and future directions. In E. Frydenberg., A. Marin., & R. Collie (eds.), *Social and Emotional Learning in Australia and the Asia-Pacific: Perspectives, programs, and approaches,* (pp. 101-122). Springer.

Snider, V. (2004). A comparison of spiral versus strand curriculum. *Journal of Direct Instruction, 4*(1), 29-39.

Spanjers, I., Van Gog, T., Wouters, P., & Van Merrienboer, J. (2012). Explaining the segmentation effect in learning from animations: The role of pausing and temporal cueing. *Computers and Education, 59*(2), 274-280.
https://doi.org/10.1016/j.compedu.2011.12.024

Teacher leadership competencies. (2014). Center for Teaching Quality, National Board for Professional Teaching Standards, and the National Education Association. https://www.nbpts.org/wp-content/uploads/teacher_leadership_competencies_final.pdf

The Center for Comprehensive School Reform and Improvement. (2005). *Research brief: What does the research tell us about teacher leadership?* http://www.centerforcsri.org/files/Center_RB_sept 05.pdf

Thorndike, E. (1932). *The fundamentals of learning.* AMS Press.

Tissington, S. (2019). Learning with and through phenomena: An explainer on phenomenon based learning. *ALDinHE 2019: The Learning Development Conference.* Association for Learning Development in Higher Education.

Tremblay, P., & Dick, A. (2016). Broca and Wernicke are dead, or moving past the classical model of language neurobiology. *Brain & Language, 162*, 60-71.

University of Delaware. (2019, May 8). Learning language: New insights into how brain functions. *ScienceDaily*. https://www.sciencedaily.com/releases/2019/05/190508093716.htm

Vygotsky, L. (1978). *Mind in society: The development of higher psychological processes*. Harvard University Press.

Walker, A., & White, G. (2013). *Technology enhanced language learning*. Oxford University Press.

Watson, J. (1913). Psychology as the behaviorist views it. *Psychological Review, 20*(2), 158-177. https://doi.org/10.1037/h0074428

Wilson, L. (2020). *Three domains of learning – cognitive, affective, psychomotor*. The Second Principle.

Wolf, P. (2010). *Brain matters: Translating research into classroom practice*, 2nd ed. ASCD.

Yazdani, S. (2005). *Pedagogy, Andragogy and heutagogy*. Saginaw Valley State University. http://www.svsu.edu/~cagilbre/TE571/TE571%20Session%202/3_Pedagogy__Andragogy___Heutagogy.pps

3. Language Teaching Methods, Approaches, and Techniques

Overview

Methods, approaches, and various teaching techniques help instructors best provide language learning opportunities to students. They also help you as an instructor to provide your students with the means of engaging with language content, and practicing and mastering it in various ways. The use of one language teaching method or approach over another is often reflected in the proficiency that learners need to acquire, the focus behind why they are learning the language, and what they intend to use it for, or changes in language learning or pedagogical theory. This chapter will explore a number of methods, approaches, and techniques that have been used over time, and those which have helped us to develop our understanding of what and how best to teach today.

Learning Outcomes

1. Comprehend the difference between a method, an approach, and a technique.
2. Become familiar with the range of methods, approaches, and techniques that have been applied to the teaching of English.
3. Contextualize the use and application of a variety of methods, approaches, and techniques for language learning, and how each is commonly applied in the language teaching classroom.
4. Understand the learning theories behind the methods, approaches, and techniques used to teach languages, and their relevance to teaching today, and where pedagogical practice is heading in the future.

Methods, Approaches, and Techniques

A method is an overall procedural plan designed for the implementation of approaches which are the practices and principles of language teaching (the ways of looking at teaching and learning). Within one approach, there may be any number of methods (ways of teaching something). Techniques are the means of implementation (the activities), and they must be consistent with a method and taught in line with the approach applied. Some of the more prevalent methods, approaches, and techniques used in language teaching include the oral approach and situational language teaching, PPP (present-practice-produce), the grammar-translation method, the direct method, the audiolingual method, total physical response, the silent way, community language learning, whole language, the lexical approach, competency-based language teaching, communicative language teaching, the natural approach, cooperative language learning, content-based instruction, task-based language teaching, dogme, EAS (engage, activate, study), among others. Today, in the post-methods era, an eclectic approach is often utilized by course books and instructors alike. So, it is very common to see experienced educators applying various methods and approaches in response to the needs analysis of their learners for any given lesson, and this has become increasing relevant as we encourage post-method pedagogical practice and move toward redefining and reorienting education based on what is emerging with the impact of severe acute respiratory syndrome coronavirus 2 (SARS-CoV-2; aka COVID 19, corona virus) as post-pandemic pedagogy.

Methods

The Classical Method (Grammar-Translation)

The traditional teaching technique for the learning of Latin and Greek was the grammar-translation method, and as it was used as the standard method of teaching from the 17th to 19th centuries, it has also become known as the classical method. The goal of language study at this time was to learn languages for reading and for developing mental discipline, leading the method to focus on the memorization of rules and applying those rules in the translation of sentences. Reading and writing was concentrated upon, with speaking and listening overlooked, with textbooks extensively utilized and vocabulary presented in long word lists for students to memorize. Classes were largely conducted in the L1 with accuracy emphasized, grammar taught deductively, and the sentence used as the basic unit of teaching and language practice.

The Direct Method

In contrast to the grammar-translation method, the direct method, also known as the natural method, emerged near the turn of the 19th century, and refrains from the use of a leaners' initial language (L1) when teaching, and relying on the target language (TL) or the second language (L2) being learned. It was a move away from teaching about the language to teaching the language itself. Listening and speaking skills are therefore given a priority, with new vocabulary taught through the use of mime, realia, or visual aids, with grammar being deduced by the learner. As a method for teaching languages it was popularized by Berlitz (a chain of private language schools), and as it has its roots in mimicking the process of first language acquisition, it is sometimes referred to as the natural method (not to be confused with the natural approach discussed later in this chapter). We have this method to thank for ushering in what Richard and Rodgers (2005) refer to as the methods era, a time that held the belief that for language learning to improve, changes and improvements in teaching methodology needed to occur. This is something which is perhaps supported by researchers, teachers, and companies who are all seeking that single 'best' method, approach, or technique to teach a language.

The Audiolingual Method (Army Method)

After the entry of the United States of America into World War II, the emphasis there on utilizing one of either the direct method, a reading-based approach, or a reading-oral approach (Darian, 1972), shifted, with soldiers being posted worldwide requiring a language learning method that gave them, at a minimum, basic verbal communication skills.

A heavy reliance on behaviorism, with training conducted using positive and negative feedback as a reinforcement technique, was then employed with language learning often occurring in a language lab, and with the teacher presenting the correct model of a sentence and students repeating it. New vocabulary was then made available for the student to use in the sample structure being memorized.

The method, while employing a structure-based approach, essentially relies upon dialogues and drills for classroom practice. Dialogues are provided to contextualize key structures and provide situations in which structures can be used, and they are memorized through repetition, with correct pronunciation, stress, rhythm, and intonation emphasized. After the memorization of a dialogue patterns then become the focus of additional drills and pattern-practice exercises. As a teacher-directed method, students have little or no control of their own output, as particular responses are expected.

Like the direct method, students were taught without the use of L1 (first language) to explain grammar and vocabulary, with the teacher making extensive use of drills to present the use of the grammar and language that was memorized. Listening was considered the most important aspect in the development of speaking proficiency, and foundational for it, with speaking viewed as being effective via listening to articulation and the differentiation of speech sounds, and through the memorization and internalization of auditory stimulus.

The Silent Way

The silent way is a method of language teaching that originated in the early 1970s. Devised by Gattegno (1972), it is particularly famous for applying the strategic use of Cuisenaire rods and color-coded pronunciation charts (Fidels) for the teaching of language. The underlying premise is that the teacher should remain as silent as possible, limiting teacher talk time (TTT) with students in order to encourage them to speak as much as possible. The hypothesis behind the method sees learning facilitated by discovery and the creation of language rather than remembering and repeating things that should be learned. The silent way is facilitated by the use of physical objects and by engaging students in problem solving approaches that focus on the content that they need to understand.

In this method a structural approach is taken to the learning of language, with the sentence used as the basic unit of teaching, and the instructor focusing on propositional meaning over communicative value. Learners are presented with structural patterns, learning grammar through an inductive process, with vocabulary selected according to functionality and versatility. Activities are largely teacher-directed, although teacher modeling is minimal, with learning to learn facilitated by the process as students need to develop autonomy, independence, and take increased responsibility for their own learning. In the absence of explanation, learners are principal actors that make their own generalizations who form their own conclusions and rules, and need to work in class in a cooperative rather than a competitive manner, helping and interacting with each other in order to produce language.

Classes often begin by using Fidel charts in the learners' first language with the first part of the lesson focusing on pronunciation.

Rods, pictures, objects, or situations, along with other aids, are used in order to connect sounds to meanings. The leaners' L1 can be used to give instructions when necessary with meaning made clear by focusing student perceptions and not by translating. Teachers will model appropriate sounds after pointing to symbols on the Fidel chart. This can be followed by the teacher pointing to symbols and eliciting student response, and then pointing to a variety of symbols in a row to have students string utterances together. Intonation and phrasing can be demonstrated by tapping on the chart to the rhythm of the utterance, and stress shown by touching symbols more forcefully.

Following the practice of sounds is that of sentence patterns, structure, and vocabulary where the teacher models an utterance while creating a visual representation of it with Cuisenaire rods. After that, a student is chosen to follow suit. If necessary, the teacher may need to reshape the utterance or have it modeled by another student. After a particular structure is understood, the teacher can then manipulate the rods in order to practice a variety of structures.

In today's classroom, the silent way can still hold a place, and the technique can be adapted if you have a cold (or laryngitis) and are unable to talk. In this case, teachers may need to develop their own charts, using pointers to provide instruction and modeling appropriate to the lesson and the typical classroom commands that they need to use.

Total Physical Response (TPR)

Asher (1965) developed the method of total physical response (TPR) to language teaching as a way to learn languages through physical (motor) activity. It is based on several traditions from developmental psychology, learning theory, humanistic pedagogy, and language teaching procedures where successful adult second language acquisition is seen to parallel that of child initial language acquisition (ILA). With this method, the role of affective (emotional) factors are considered, by use of game like movements, to reduce learner stress in order to then facilitate learning. The method is also linked to the trace theory of memory, which holds that the more intensively or more often a memory connection is traced, the stronger that memory association will become and the more likely it will be recalled. It considers the use of bio-programming, brain lateralization, and stress reduction as key to the language learning process.

Bio-programming is the view that the brain and nervous system are biologically programmed to acquire language skills, and these should be developed in second language learning using activities surrounding natural childhood-esque learning patterns such as building commands that promote action. Keeping in mind that as children develop language skills, they are able to respond verbally to adult commands, and develop listening competence at a higher level than speech production. Once a foundation in listening comprehension exists speech evolves out of it.

Brain lateralization in this method relies on the use of motor movement as a right-hemisphere activity being combined with language learning to become a left-hemisphere activity. In this way, a stimulus response model is also put into place with the teacher providing commands with the students responding to them so that a cognitive map that is essential for language retention can be developed. In other words, the view is that once a sufficient amount of right-hemisphere learning has been undertaken, the left-hemisphere will initiate language production and language processes.

Stress reduction is seen as important in this method of language teaching as the first language acquisition context is viewed as one undertaken from a stress-free context. The key behind lesson implementation then is to provide learners with a relaxed and pleasurable context that focuses on meaning interpreted through movement.

The cornerstones of TPR are the use of non-abstractions and abstractions, speech acts, and a lexical approach to vocabulary acquisition. Non-abstractions would include development of a cognitive map for students with simple commands (e.g., *stand up and touch your head*), before moving on to abstractions (e.g., *stand up and talk to your partner about what they plan to do today*). As such, speech acts and role plays become are a large part of the method. Vocabulary in this approach is taught in chunks rather than a single word at a time (e.g., by compounding nouns and verbs through commands and actions). The essentials for learners are that they should listen before speaking and learn through commands, and that target language (TL) speech evolves from listening.

To put TPR into practice, a stress-free environment needs to be established by keeping the material and information presented to the learner simple at first, and by demonstrating commands before giving them and expecting them to be carried out. Building from simple to more complex commands allows for students to develop a cognitive map based upon non-abstractions before moving onto more complex routines and language use that involves abstraction. As such, the role of the student is to listen intently, respond physically, and speak when ready. The role of the teacher then is to use this process to instill confidence in the learner and to develop a fun learning environment that focuses on simplicity and the provision of feedback that allows students to grow as they listen, respond, and speak at their own pace. For beginner level students, this may involve simple commands and the use of songs such as *'Heads, Shoulders, Knees, and Toes'*. For more advanced students, the use of props may be necessary and can involve the use of the classroom (pens, books, light switches, windows, doors) through to teacher-prepared pictures and other items of realia.

A basic implementation of TPR might follow after a lesson consisting of practicing the names of body parts and the actions involved when listening to the song *'Heads, Shoulders, Knees, and Toes'*. In this case, focus is placed on the use of the verb 'touch', and practice after listening to the song can involve students standing in a circle and the instructor calling out 'Touch your {body part}' as an introduction to the game *'Simon says …'*. The aim is to produce sentence-based learning, and to use commands as a sequence and building from one to another. In this case, when focusing on the verb 'hold' the sequence might follow: *'Everyone hold up your hands, Put your hands down, Stand up, Hold up your hands, Put your hands down and sit down, Student A hold up your left hand, Student A hold up your pencil in your left hand, Student A stand up and move to student B's desk and hold up their pencil, Student B hold up student A's pencil'*. In a lesson based on maps and navigation, TPR can be used to give students increasingly complex directions with one chained to another. In a classroom setting, you can use desks as blocks, the aisles between them as streets, students as landmarks (e.g., gas station, hotel, supermarket, library, park) with one student then standing and being designated as a car. The teacher can then demonstrate the activity by directing the car to a particular landmark, and on arrival, the car takes a seat to become the landmark, swapping roles with the seated student who then becomes the car. The seated student can then direct the car to the next landmark.

Community Language Learning (CLL)

In this method, Curran (1972) sees the teacher as serving as a facilitator (a 'knower') who is an empathic helper (counselor), aiming to lower the affective filter of students as they learn. It is based on the counselling approach that views learners as client/collaborators. The approach emphasizes interaction as a vehicle for learning and seeks to establish a sense of community for students where learners use their first language to communicate and the teacher translates for them. The intent is that, over time, learners become independent of the teacher and are able to converse and use language without the need for translation. To aid in this process, students may work together in groups, or as individuals recording conversations and transcribing them to analyze their language use, which they can then reflect on and discuss. Students may also listen to teacher monologues involving elements of classroom interactions, and engage in free conversation with the instructor or other learners. As students develop their skills, they move from being able to apprehend the sound system of the language to assigning fundamental meaning to lexical units and be able to construct a basic grammar. This sees them go from birth (feelings of security and belonging) to achieving a measure of independence, to then speaking independently, and then taking criticism and correction, before blossoming into an adult (the knower of the language).

Approaches

The Oral Approach (Situational Language Teaching)

Arguing for a sound methodological basis for teaching techniques, linguists from the 1920s onward developed general principles that would serve as the oral approach to language learning. These involved selection (choosing lexical and grammatical items to teach), gradation (sequencing and organizing content), and presentation (techniques utilized to present and practice language). The approach was popular in Australia and Britain through to the middle of the 19th century, and developed by Tate into a set of teaching materials based on a situational approach, emphasizing that language teaching begins by speaking, with material being taught orally before being presented in a written form; that the language of the classroom is that of the TL; that new language points are to be introduced and practiced situationally; that vocabulary selection ensures that general service vocabulary is covered; that grammar is graded with simple forms being taught prior to complex ones; and that only when a sufficient grammatical and lexical basis has been established can reading and writing be introduced. With new language points being introduced situationally which was a key feature of the approach during the 1960s, it has since also been referred to as situational language teaching as well as the structural-situational approach. Aspects of this approach continue to be widely used today, particularly in countries where syllabuses are grammatically-based, with essential features of the situational approach also found in the widely-popularized PPP technique.

The Structural Approach

The structural approach having emerged in the 1950s stresses the teaching of language through the systematic selection and graded structuring of the language. The aim is to increase student command of the use of structures (phrase patterns, sentence patterns, formulas, and idioms) over vocabulary, with structure defined as the arrangement of words into patterns as opposed to a grammatical ordering of words into a sentence. In other words, word order (e.g., *Cindy broke her toy* versus *The toy broke Cindy*), the presence of function words (e.g., *I kill a spider, I am killing a spider, I shall kill a spider, I have killed a spider, I have to kill a spider*), and the use of inflections (e.g., *great-greater-greatest*) or the pattern of form is important when making meaning. Every clause or sentence is learned according to its structure.

Certain principles, such as framing language habits for the effective use of speech, see the approach rely on oral work and student activities, with the active teaching of structure over grammar undertaken through meaningful situational use of language, and the teaching of one item at a time with an emphasis on mastery. Students are actively involved in the learning process, with aspects of dramatization, facial expressions, and actions often relied upon to create or represent situations in the classroom (e.g., a facial expression might be used by the teacher to indicate that a correction in student language production is required). This approach is also known as the aural-oral approach, and stresses habit formation through the use of intensive drills.

Cooperative language learning

Although the origins of cooperative language learning may date back centuries, little research was conducted on it until the 1960s (Jacobs & Hall, 2002). The philosophy behind this approach is that heterogenous classes (a mixture of strong and weak learners) can raise the achievement levels of all students if they work together (cooperatively) in pairs or small groups. The intention is to establish a student-centered classroom where learners are able to benefit by supporting each other rather than competing against each other.

Learning theories behind this approach stem from Vygotsky and Piaget, where social interaction is viewed as necessary for language learning to occur, which sees 'think', 'pair' and 'share' activities being common to this kind of classroom. *Think* seeing students first concentrate on the material, working to understand it at their own pace. *Pair* sees one student then work with another to compare their results or discuss content. *Share* then sees the students present/discuss their results or content with others (in groups or to the whole class). Advantages are the involvement of all students, and active use of the target language throughout the lesson, with stronger students solidifying and practicing their language by teaching/helping lower level students improve. This is opposed to a teacher-focused classroom where these weak students may be left behind or alone while stronger students lead the room.

Suggestopedia (Desuggestopedia)

The power of positive suggestion lies behind this unconventional approach which was developed by Lozanov (1978). Here students are made to feel relaxed and comfortable so that they can be more receptive to learning. There are no tables or chairs in the classroom, instead there are armchairs, or cushions with students lounging around the floor. A drawback to this approach is its reliance on infantilization as the teacher-student relationship is viewed as akin to parent-child and relies on the absolute authority of the teacher for the power of suggestion. It draws on elements of Soviet psychology and yoga, and ultimately consists of lessons that are conducted in four stages where the 'introduction' sees the teacher playfully present material. The 'concert' then sees the teacher read with intonation and rhythm matched to selected music. 'Elaboration' then requires personal participation from students, as they sing songs and play games, with 'production' then seeing students spontaneously speak and interact without correction or interruption by the teacher.

Looking back at suggestopedia (suggestion + pedagogy) today, music and rhythm are key elements of the approach, and we can use these to great advantage when teaching songs, and using chants, rhymes, and rounds with young learners and beginner level students. The approach also helps us consider physical elements of the classroom. Is where you teach conducive to learning? Do you need to use the curtains to ensure no reflections shine onto the board? Do you need to arrange the chairs in the room to make the activities flow more smoothly? Can all students see the board from their seats? Do you need to rethink how you use or lay out the board? Another element to consider may be classroom ambience. Background noise, such as classical music or the sounds of the rainforest, and the dimming of the classroom lights may help to generate a peaceful and calming mood.

Competency-Based Language Teaching (CBLT)
Originating in the 1970s (see Bataineh & Tasnimi, 2014), and initially adopted for vocational training, CBLT is an outcome-based approach, and as a result, the type of syllabus used with this approach revolves around the kinds of assessment that rely on a criterion-based assessment method over a norm-referenced one. This sees students needing to perform specific language skills during the course which are required in order to effectively perform a real-world task. Learning activities therefore revolve around those that are systematically designed to see students achieve a certain competence, and typically revolve around those oriented to survival- or work-related situations (e.g., buying train tickets, applying for a library card, opening a bank account, understanding a work schedule, applying for a job, undertaking a job interview).

The focus of this approach is to help learners successfully function in society with a focus on life skills, with language always taught as a medium of communication using concrete tasks. This means that the focus is placed on what students can do with the language that they are learning over knowledge of the language itself, relying on modularized instruction with competencies taught systematically and separated into manageable units with outcomes clear to all stake-holders. It involves a need for continuous and ongoing assessment based on students being able to demonstrate mastery of a competence from a variety of means that allow for the possibility of individualized, differentiated, and student-centered instruction.

The Natural Approach

Krashen and Terrel (1983), like Asher (1965), feel that language learners benefit from delayed production until speech emerges spontaneously as the learner 'picks up' the language naturally, which is akin to initial language acquisition.

In the natural approach, TPR style activities are utilized at the beginning level, with the focus placed on everyday language situations (e.g., shopping, health). The most important aspect of this approach is the use of teacher-delivered *comprehensible input*, and in this sense, language is viewed as a means of communicating messages and meaning using lexical content, and acquisition takes place only when learners can understand the message behind the target language being used, despite not understanding all the words and structures in it. For learners to move to the next stage of language development, they need to be presented with input that contains structures that are to be a part of the next stage. This is known as the *input hypothesis*, i+1 (i.e., input plus content slightly beyond current comprehension leads to acquisition).

In addition to the input hypothesis previously mentioned, the other learning theories underpinning the natural approach include: the acquisition/learning hypothesis, the monitor hypothesis, the natural order hypothesis, and the affective filter hypothesis.

The acquisition/learning hypothesis involves a distinction between learning and acquisition. *Learning* refers to the formal knowledge of language, and the process in which conscious rules are formed along with the ability to verbalize them. Formal teaching is necessary for learning to occur, with directed error correction assisting in the formation of rule learning. Alternatively, *acquisition* refers to the development of competency in the use of a language for real communication, and it is seen as paralleling natural language development as it is an unconscious process that leads to proficiency resulting from the continued use of language for meaningful communication.

The monitor hypothesis is the process of using learned knowledge to help correct language production during communication. Three conditions limit the successful use of the monitor: a sufficient amount of time is required before a learner is able to choose and apply a rule as necessary; the focus is on form and the correctness of the output; and that knowledge of rules is a prerequisite.

The natural order hypothesis sees grammatical structures acquired in a predictable order no matter the language. Certain morphemes and grammatical structures are seen to be acquired before others, with learner errors a result of the naturalist developmental process.

The affective filter hypothesis relates to the emotional state or attitude of the learner that can make learning easier, impede it, or block it entirely. Three kinds of attitudinal, or affective, variables have been identified: motivation, where learners with high motivation are able to perform better; self-confidence, where those with a good self-image are able to perform better; and anxiety, where low personal and low classroom anxiety are more conducive to language acquisition. In other words, those with a low affective filter tend to seek out and receive more input, are more receptive to the input they receive, and are able to interact with confidence. Those with a high affective filter, being anxious, fearful, or embarrassed to speak, prevent acquisition from taking place.

Teaching according to the natural approach involves focusing on learner communicative abilities, with vocabulary concentrated on syntactic structures and provided to the learner by means of comprehensible input and visual aids to assist in comprehension. As a result, focus is often placed on listening and reading, with speaking expected to emerge later with the high affective filter reduced by placing focus on meaningful communication over form, and providing interesting comprehensible input. To achieve this, the approach incorporates aspects of TPR command drills, direct method activities (like miming, gesturing, and context to elicit questions and answers), and communicative language teaching techniques where group work activities are relied on to see learners share information to complete tasks such as retelling activities.

Content-Based Instruction (CBI)

Emerging in the 1980s content-based instruction sees the language being learned also become the medium through which something new is being learned (see Brinton, 2003; Villalobos, 2013). It is also strongly tied to project-based work, task-based learning, and it is a holistic approach to language instruction. It is increasingly popular across the educational sector and it utilizes authentic language and texts with a top-down approach, seeing that the curriculum is based on subject matter and communicative competence that is acquired in the context of learning about certain topics in that area. The theory behind this method or philosophy of teaching is that intrinsic motivation can be provided to learners as they are interested in engaging with content that they find stimulating, with the content in turn promoting language learning through the use of advanced level thinking skills over focusing on the structure of language. Although students need to be independently motivated, as language is not taught directly, the language that they are exposed to is immediately useful to context and can be connected to prior knowledge.

Lexical Approach

The lexical approach places emphasis on the use of language through lexical units over grammatical structures. Lexical units are chunks of collocations (e.g., *fast + asleep*) or fixed phrases (e.g., *salt and pepper, agree to disagree*) including idioms (e.g., *time flies*). The approach emerged in the early 1990s (Lewis, 1993) and was later expanded (Lewis, 2000). In language teaching today, we recognize lexis as one component of communicative competence, often relying on the use of set or fixed phrases and collocations, and actively teaching them and guiding our students in identifying them as they read texts and practice speaking. We can also guide our students and classroom work with collocations and word lists such as that of the British National Corpus (BNC), the New General Service List (NGSL), the New Academic Word List (NAWL), and the Corpus of Contemporary American (COCA). A number of tools are electronically available that teachers can employ to parse dialogues or reading content in order to see the types of words used, and modify material to the level of the student as desired (see the *Compleat Lexical Tutor* website for such tools).

Communicative Language Teaching

Communicative language teaching is an approach to the teaching of target language (TL) through the use of authentic communication and active student interaction in order to achieve communicative competence in the target language across all four skills (reading, writing, listening, speaking). It supports the idea that learners are able to acquire language while communicating with others (socialization) with fluency being more important than accuracy, and that they should be learning a language for a meaningful purpose. Criticisms of the approach have centered around its lack of explicit grammar teaching, and that less teacher feedback and correction may lead to the stabilization (or fossilization) of student mistakes.

At the syllabus level, it follows a functional-notional approach using real-life situations in which people communicate, using authentic language (notions) which is further broken down into specific aims for communicating language use (functions). It also consists of a strong and a weak form. The weak version, learning to use language, stresses a communicative purpose behind language learning and integrates activities to achieve this purpose into a wider program of study, while the strong version, learning English to learn English, focuses on stimulating the language system itself so that language can be acquired through the use of the language being studied (communication). In both versions, exposure to the target language is important, with opportunities for it use (socialization) being the key to its maintenance and development.

Multiple Intelligences

This is an approach to teaching that was developed by Gardner (1993) and it takes into account his belief that a learner's intelligence is not simply an intelligent quotient (IQ) but that there are different types of intelligences which some have argued might be best called abilities. The intelligences initially identified are linguistic, visual-spatial, bodily-kinesthetic, interpersonal, logical-mathematical, musical, intrapersonal, and environmental-naturalist, and have since been extended to include spiritual and existential. In this approach, the teacher recognizing that these intelligences exist in their students, and that every learner is unique, makes use of all of them in the design and incorporation of activities and exercises that students complete when engaging in language learning. A proposed means for learners to identify their intelligences is to make use of a learner inventory.

The most important intelligence for language learning is the linguistic one, and all task types that deal with reading, writing, listening, and speaking are a part of this intelligence. The use of a variety of tasks suited to each intelligence in the classroom may lead to increased intrinsic motivation in students, especially when the tasks are suited to their particular intelligence. Essentially, teaching to verbal/linguistic intelligence would mean explaining and understanding through the use of words. Visual/spatial oriented intelligence may require explanation and comprehension through the use of pictures, graphs, maps, and drawing. Bodily/kinesthetic intelligence relates to using the body to express ideas, accomplish tasks, and engage in activities like 'Simon says'. Interpersonal intelligence is based on the ability to get along with others, and working with them to accomplish tasks. Logical/mathematical intelligence relates to working with ideas. Musical intelligence involves the ability to recognize and communicate using melody, rhythm, and harmony, and the use of chants, songs, tongue twisters, and the practice of stress and intonation lends nicely to this intelligence. Intrapersonal intelligence makes use of self-knowledge that leads to understanding of motives, goals, strengths, and weaknesses. Finally, environmental-naturalist intelligence recognizes elements of the natural world and learns from it.

Although no syllabus has been developed for the use of this approach, it has been adopted by a number of educational institutions. Lazear (1991) has also developed a basic sequence for its application that moves from awakening (providing sensory input regarding the lesson) to amplifying (students sharing their own experiences), then teaching with the intelligence (applying group/project work to solve tasks based on the amplification that previously occurred), and transferring the intelligence (where students reflect and relate the lesson experience back to other life or school situations). A more specific means of using the approach aimed at language teaching, which was developed by Nicholsen-Nelson (1998), sees it used to play to student strengths (structuring learning material to the intelligences), incorporating variety (let all students participate in tasks using as many intelligences as possible), linking the use of the intelligences to the aspects or functions being taught, aiming to develop all the intelligences with students, and being mindful of cultural differences in the valuing of intelligences.

Dogme

This approach, suggested by Thornbury (2000), is against resource-heavy classrooms and generally relies on material that is leaner-directed and learner-generated and that which can be easily used and implemented, particularly in a one-to-one teaching context. The philosophy behind the method is that teaching should focus on learner needs and objectives, relying on real language stemming from a need to communicate, with grammar explanations arising naturally and in context. To this end, lessons on nature should be taught outside, and lessons that involve cars require being next to or in one. Essentially, it is a conversation-driven teaching approach with focus on the discourse level over the sentence, with the teacher's role being one of facilitating the emergence of language.

Data-Driven Learning (DDL)

This is an approach to foreign language learning where language is treated as data and learners as researchers who undertake guided tasks. Underpinning this approach is the data-information-knowledge-wisdom paradigm (DIKW) which is often depicted as being a hierarchical model with wisdom at the apex, below it knowledge, then information, and data at the base. It describes structural or functional relationships with the lower levels comprising the material of the higher ones. This sees data (given context) becoming information (given meaning) becoming knowledge (given insight) becoming wisdom (see Figure 3.1). The basic task of DDL is identifying patterns, and the role of the learner is discovering grammatical patterns, word meanings, and/or other aspects of language by searching through linguistic data and examining large amounts of authentic language. In other words, it consists of using the tools and techniques of corpus linguistics for pedagogical purposes. Gilquin & Granger (2010) see DDL as offering authentic content that can serve to provide a corrective function, elements of discovery, and the development of learning skills when engaging in activities that apply the approach.

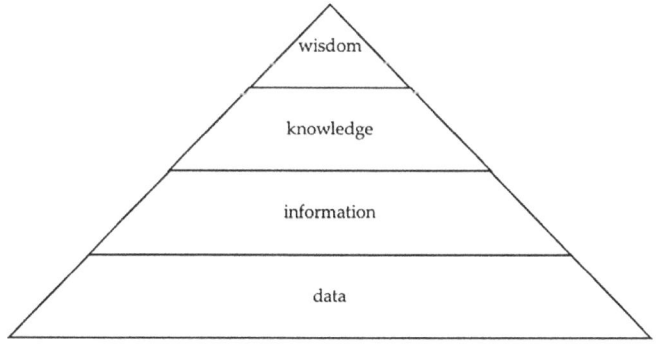

Figure 3.1 The DIKW Pyramid

Techniques

Authentic Learning
The intent behind the use of realia, or authentic materials from the real world, is to include aspects of authentic learning into the language learning classroom. It is an instructional approach aimed at seeing students explore, discuss, and meaningfully construct concepts and relationships that involve real-world problems, tasks, and applications that are relevant to the learner (Dononvan, et al., 1999).

Task-Based Language Teaching (TBLT)
Also known as task-based instruction (TBI), task-based language teaching revolves around the use of authentic language to undertake meaningful tasks such as seeing a doctor, conducting an interview, or calling a customer service center. The approach draws on a number of principles that also formed the communicative language teaching approach such as those that view real communication as essential to language learning, that use of language that is meaningful promotes learning, and that language that is meaningful to learners supports the learning process. Tasks become central to the syllabus, and these may form either real-world or pedagogical tasks (e.g., jigsaw, information-gap, problem-solving, decision making, opinion exchange).

Present, practice, produce (PPP)
Elements of the situational approach that have more recently been popularized by those studying for the Cambridge Certificate in TEFL (teaching English as a foreign language), is the PPP technique which sees an instructor *present* the content to be learned, *practice* examples with the students, and then have students *produce* the language while working as a class, in groups, or in pairs. Sometimes a fourth P might be included for *personalization*.

Present refers to providing learners with aspects of language in a context that students are familiar with, and an analogy is how a swimming instructor may demonstrate how to perform a certain stroke outside of the pool. An in-class example when conducting teaching a unit on travel might be describing an itinerary, and practicing 'going to', e.g., *She is going to Paris; She is going to visit the Louvre.*

Practice is where students are able to begin using the material for themselves with minimal or appropriate assistance from the instructor, an analogy being the swimming instructor having a student practice the stroke in the pool and offering support as needed. Language examples: *I am going to the movies on the weekend; I am going to the library after class.*

Produce refers to the stage of the lesson in which students use the language in context and in activities that the teacher has set up for them, and this is akin to students then practicing a stroke that they have been taught and completing laps of the pool using it. For language learners, using a travel unit example, this may see students preparing their own itinerary using 'going to' for all of the things that they will do and the places that they will visit.

Personalization involves incorporating into the classroom the reasons why we are learning the language, making the content personal and more meaningful for students will also help increase their willingness to communicate (WTC) as it connects them to what they are learning. For example, students may present an itinerary of a trip that they have been on with family or friends, replacing 'am/are going to' with 'went to'.

The PPP (or PPPP) approach is based on the behaviorist method where knowledge can be provided in discrete chunks for learners to engage with. Its popularity stems from it being very easy to implement, as an instructor can provide language in a linear method from easy to difficult (moving from controlled to less controlled, and then to free language practice), and it can be used to provide learners with skills that they can use later in language development. Unfortunately, this also limits the language that learners are exposed to, being comprehensible input exposure which relies on noticing opportunities and, as such, incidental language learning to occur in learners.

Engage Study Activate (ESA)

The engage, study, activate technique consists of three stages. Stage one attempts to engage students physically and emotionally at the beginning of the lesson, arousing a personal interest in the content.

The second stage (study) focuses on the language and the structures to be taught. Although a variety of activities can be used in this stage of the technique, the focus is on the language (or information) that students need to acquire and how it is constructed. This may involve the practice of a single sound, or see the teacher explain a grammar point, and students looking at a text to discover it for themselves. In any case the focus is on the construction and practice of language.

The third stage (activate) sees students undertake activities where they move from practice to use, and this may involve those such as role plays, debates, storytelling (or writing). It is important to note that a test-teach-test paradigm may be required for students here as well, and this may see a classroom using the ESA technique following the sequence engage-activate-study-activate-study-engage-activate. In this way, the three concepts of engaging students, helping them study content, and then activating and using that content is a process that is not linear but one where all three opportunities are provided to learners throughout a lesson as the content, material, and the students' use of it allows.

The Eclectic Era (Post-Methods Period)

Today, we teach in what is known as the post-method era (Richards and Rogers, 2005) where we recognize that comprehensible input for learners is important to help them practice and progress, and that many learners (aside from young learners) appreciate that an understanding of form and its use is extremely helpful to the language acquisition process. Often lessons are designed in a way where a structure and vocabulary are presented alongside the opportunity to use these in a communicative manner. Particularly one that revolves around the completion of task-based activities in a way that moves from controlled practice to free language use while allowing the learner to use the language skills that they currently possess. In other words, we choose elements from the various methods, approaches, and techniques that have come before, and use parts of all of them to best benefit our students learning while keeping in mind our teaching style, aspects of student variables and readiness (including age, level, interests, language needs), and the type of content/lesson being taught (such as focus of language, grammar points, vocabulary practice, debating, test taking). The risk here is that lessons may become disorganized and incoherent, so a principled eclecticism, one that makes use of an underlying teaching and learning philosophy to support language acquisition, is important to follow, particularly one where students are first exposed to the language they will need to learn, then provided with the motivation to learn it before being given the opportunity to practice it. A scaffolded lesson that delivers learning in this way is one that would follow the engage, study, activate paradigm proposed by Harmer (2007).

Post-Method Pedagogy

The notion of the educator as a person who values their own beliefs, experience, and knowledge, and uses this to support their learners is at the heart of post-method pedagogy, as it is the instructor who is the one who understands their teaching practices, their learners, and their teaching contexts better than any other stakeholder. Such an understanding allows instructors to engage in a reflective approach to their teaching, analyze and evaluate their teaching acts, and initiate change while also monitoring the impact of such changes in learners (Wallace, 1991). Kumaravadivelu (1994), the one who first put forward the concept of a post-method pedagogy, views it as relying on the implementation of 10 macrostrategies and any number of microstrategies across a three-dimensional system revolving around the replacement of method with the pedagogic parameters of particularity, practicality, and possibility (Kumaravadivelu, 2001).

Post-method pedagogical parameters

1. Particularity arises from situational understanding (Elliot, 1993), viewing language pedagogy as being relevant and sensitive "to a particular group of teachers teaching a particular group of learners pursuing a particular set of goals within a particular institutional context embedded in a particular sociocultural milieu" (p. 538). In essence, pedagogy is local.
2. Practicality focuses on the relationship between theory and practice as being one that "encourage[s] and enable[s] teachers themselves to theorize from their practice and practice what they theorize" (p. 541). Basically, teachers can improve upon their craft through the implementation of action research elements (theorize/plan, implement/act, reflect/observe, self-evaluate/revise plan).
3. Possibility, developing from the relations of power and dominance in pedagogy, is an aspect concerned with the impact of pedagogical practice on individual identities, as it can situate not only our sense of selves but also our subjectivity. Essentially then, instruction should be based on minimizing those aspects that create and sustain any social inequalities (p. 542-44).

Strategies for post-method teaching

The post-method strategic framework for language instruction consists of 10 macrostrategies implemented within the classroom by relying on any number of microstrategies. Such microstrategies refer to "classroom procedures that are designed to realize the objectives of a particular macrostrategy", and depend on local learning and teaching contexts, with endless possibilities (Kumaravadivelu, 2006). The 10 macrostrategies listed below are presented with potential microstrategies from Kumaravadivelu (as highlighted in Chen, 2014).

1. *Maximize learning opportunities* by recognizing that teaching is a process of creating and utilizing learning opportunities. The instructor here is viewed as a creator of learning opportunities for students, and as a utilizer of learning opportunities that are created by students. Microstrategies would involve opportunities outside of the classroom.
2. *Minimize perceptual mismatches* by recognizing potential perceptual mismatches between intentions and interpretations of the learner, the teacher, and the teacher educator. Microstrategies here would center on learner training and learner perception.
3. *Facilitate negotiated interaction* through meaningful learner-learner and learner-teacher classroom interaction where learners are entitled and encouraged to propose topics and initiate talk; not simply expected to react or respond. Microstrategies here include those centered on intensive teacher-learner communication.
4. *Promote learner autonomy* to assist learners in learning how to learn, while equipping them with learner autonomy (the means to self-direct and self-monitor their own learning). Microstrategies would revolve around those of learner preference that leads to learner autonomy.
5. *Foster language awareness* using any attempt to draw learner attention to the formal and functional properties of their second language in order to increase their degree of explicitness that is required to develop acquisition. Microstrategies here involve language use and language awareness.
6. *Activate intuitive heuristics* by providing rich textual data so that learners can infer and internalize underlying rules that govern

grammatical usage and communicative use. Microstrategies here would also involve language use and language awareness, as with the previous strategy.
7. *Contextualize linguistic input* by highlighting how language use and its usage are shaped by linguistic, extralinguistic, situational, and extrasituational contexts. Microstrategies would involve contextualizing linguistic input.
8. *Integrate language skills* that are traditionally separated, and which sequence listening, speaking, reading, and writing. Microstrategies would rely on various kinds of raw materials.
9. *Ensure social relevance* by being sensitive to the societal, political, economic, and educational environment in which the language learning and teaching occurs. Microstrategies would revolve around social and cultural relevance.
10. *Raise cultural consciousness* by treating learners as cultural informants so that they are encouraged to engage in a process of classroom participation that puts a premium on their power/knowledge. Microstrategies would also revolve around social and cultural relevance.

Post-Pandemic Pedagogy and the Future of Instruction

As teachers taught through the global pandemic that began in Asia during the later months of 2019, and has since gripped the world, they have employed technology and their training to lead educational change. They have achieved this by riding the wave of a paradigm shift for the mainstream provision of education, predominantly by rising to the challenge of adapting to and delivering emergency remote teaching. Changes moving forward will likely continue with the ever-increasing digitalization of education, the hybridization of education on return to the classroom, and the possible increase of blended and distance learning offerings institution-wide (along with an increasing need to develop asynchronous and synchronous online and offline learning activities and opportunities for learners).

Teaching today would not be possible without the onset of the fourth industrial revolution, which also brings with it many changes and challenges for educators (Kent, 2019). It is now impossible to teach students all of the content that they need to learn, and so emphasis needs to be placed on the need to teach our students aspects of 21st century skills, digital citizenship, and most importantly, those soft skills that will allow them to adapt and to change their approaches, their thinking, and their ways of implementing and completing any project that they approach, and the learning that they need to develop in order to perform any work or tasks required of them, or any hobbies that they may wish to enjoy. Learning these skillsets also sees students needing to engage with content in increasingly different ways to achieve their learning goals. For instructors, also, it may very well come to change with who we will teach, and how we might best need to begin the integration of AI-based content and assistants into our classrooms (Kent, 2020). So too, as language teachers, we need to understand that with this new phase of education comes a fundamental change in the nature of how we may begin to use the languages that we learn, and also why we may need to learn them, and this will also impact significantly on how we should be teaching them (Underwood, 2018). Essentially then, what is important to recognize at this stage is that what this disruption offers us as educators is an opportunity. It is a chance to reorient how we deliver instruction and reach our students, with it coming at a time where we must also rely heavily on our training to guide and teach our learners as we expand ourselves and expand our repertoire.

Summary

This chapter offers a glimpse into how pedagogical practice has evolved over time and where it is heading into the future. By doing so, it highlights that language learning and teaching can be a complex process, and that the best methods, approaches, and techniques to use are those that create conditions that induce learning to occur. In many teaching contexts, the language learning classroom will consist of diverse learners from diverse backgrounds, and classes may be large or small and consist of learners of various skill levels and academic ability. Identifying the methods, approaches, and techniques suitable for a particular class, and those that are easily adaptable by the teacher, allows for the various methods, approaches, and techniques to be best employed while simultaneously making the best use of content and materials that cater to the immediate needs of learners.

Review

Content Quiz
Language Teaching Methods, Approaches, and Techniques

To help solidify some of the concepts introduced by this chapter the following multiple-choice quiz might be helpful for you to undertake. To check the accuracy of your responses, an answer key can be found following the quizzes.

Multiple-Choice

Circle **a**, **b**, or **c** for the answer that best completes the sentence presented in each question.

1. A method is …
   a) a way of teaching something.
   b) a way of looking at teaching and learning.
   c) a way of using activities.

2. An approach is …
   a) a way of teaching something.
   b) a way of looking at teaching and learning.
   c) a way of using activities.

3. A technique is …
   a) use of activities for learning.
   b) the plan for the lesson.
   c) the style of the teacher.

4. If the teacher tells a story about animals and then asks students to make the noise of the animal each time that they hear its name, this is an example of …
   a) communicative language teaching.
   b) grammar-translation.
   c) total physical response.

5. Students ask their classmates when their birthdays are, write them down, and gather responses for each month of the year. This is an example of using …
   a) the audiolingual method.
   b) total physical response.
   c) communicative language teaching.

6. A classroom without chairs and using music to control the ambiance of the room so that students can study in a relaxed environment is an example of …
   a) suggestopedia/desuggestopedia.
   b) audiolingual method.
   c) direct method.

7. A teacher-directed class that is heavily dependent on imitating language models and undertaking memorization of dialogues is an example of …
   a) competency-based language learning.
   b) the silent way.
   c) the audiolingual method.

8. A classroom activity that views collocations, idioms, and vocabulary as key to learning a language would rely upon …
   a) multiple intelligences.
   b) A lexical approach.
   c) task-based language teaching.

9. Vocabulary taught through the use of mime, realia, or visual aids, with grammar deduced by the learner is popular with the…
   a) direct method.
   b) oral approach.
   c) structural approach.

10. If you are using Cuisenaire rods and Fidel charts with your students, then you are practicing the …
    a) classical method.
    b) silent way.
    c) community language learning.

11. The need for comprehensible input is considered to be a part of …
    a) the natural approach.
    b) multiple intelligence.
    c) the classical method.

12. Speech, structures, and a focus on a set of basic vocabulary items are viewed as the basis of language teaching from …
    a) an oral approach.
    b) a structural approach.
    c) cooperative language learning.

13. A communicative approach to teaching without the use of a textbook, and making all learning relevant to surroundings is one of …
    a) dogme.
    b) multiple intelligences.
    c) an oral approach.

14. If you are focusing not on the language itself but on what is being taught, and viewing language as the medium through which something is learned, you are likely employing …
    a) community language learning.
    b) content-based instruction.
    c) competency-based language learning.

15. If you are focusing on the what learners are expected to do rather than what they are expected to learn, and you are assessing learners based upon what they are able to accomplish in the real-world, then you are likelyemploying …
    a) cooperative language learning.
    b) the silent way.
    c) competency-based language teaching.

16. A method that focuses on the literature of the target language and includes the process of translating into and out of the L1 is …
    a) classical method/grammar-translation.
    b) cooperative language learning.
    c) community Language Learning.

17. An approach that emphasizes interaction as a vehicle for learning where learners use their first language to communicate and the teacher translates for them is ...
    a) task-based instruction.
    b) community language learning.
    c) competency-based language teaching.

18. If you are using a jigsaw activity (one where each student is required to research one section of the material and then teach it to other members of the group), then you would be employing an aspect of ...
    a) the classical method.
    b) community language learning.
    c) cooperative language learning.

19. A brain-based perspective of teaching language which focuses on using different tasks to appeal to different abilities in students is ...
    a) multiple intelligences.
    b) the classical method.
    c) content-based instruction.

20. The intent behind the use of realia or authentic materials from the real world is to ...
    a) include aspects of authentic learning into the language learning classroom.
    b) allow teachers to create a curriculum using content that is of interest to them.
    c) discourage the development of student real-world language use.

21. Focusing on the authentic use of language, and on asking students to engage in tasks from which they learn language, involves the application of ...
    a) competency-based language teaching.
    b) cooperative language learning.
    c) task-based instruction.

22. The hypothesis which holds that language input plus content slightly behind current comprehension leads to acquisition is …
    a) affective filter hypothesis.
    b) input hypothesis.
    c) monitor hypothesis.

23. The process of using learned knowledge to help correct language production during communication can be defined as the …
    a) acquisition/learning hypothesis.
    b) monitor hypothesis.
    c) natural order hypothesis.

24. The hypothesis that views grammatical structures acquired in a predictable order no matter the language is the …
    a) input hypothesis.
    b) monitor hypothesis.
    c) natural order hypothesis.

25. The emotional state or attitude of the learner that can make learning easier, impede it, or block it entirely is related to the …
    a) acquisition/learning hypothesis.
    b) affective filter hypothesis.
    c) input hypothesis.

26. The hypothesis that involves a distinction between learning and acquisition (that learning requires formal teaching while acquisition is the unconscious process of learning) is the …
    a) acquisition/learning hypothesis.
    b) monitor hypothesis.
    c) natural order hypothesis.

27. If you are teaching grammar in a way that learners must discover the rules in context for themselves while reading or listening, then you are employing …
    a) a deductive approach.
    b) grammar/translation.
    c) an inductive approach.

28. What does the acronym PPP stand for?
    a) practice, PowerPoint, presentations.
    b) present, practice, produce.
    c) practical principles paradigm.

29. The tools and techniques of corpus linguistics are used for pedagogical purposes when applying …
    a) data-driven learning.
    b) present, practice, produce principles.
    c) The monitor hypothesis.

30. A teacher who finds a way for students to engage with a subject emotionally before focusing on studying the construction of the target language, and then activating learning through engaging activities, is employing …
    a) engage, study, activate.
    b) estimate, situate, activate.
    c) elaborate, solidify, achieve.

31. At the heart of post-method pedagogy is …
    a) the notion of the educator as a person who values their own beliefs, experience, and knowledge, and uses these to support their learners.
    b) the notion of the instructor as a *sage on the stage*, and not a *guide on the side*.
    c) the notion of the learner as an instructor.

32. Post-method pedagogical parameters are those of particularity, practicality, and possibility. Particularity arises from ...
   a) the relations of power and dominance in pedagogy. This aspect is concerned with the impact of pedagogical practice on individual identities, as it can situate not only our sense of selves but also our subjectivity. In essence then, instruction should be based on minimizing those aspects that create and sustain any social inequalities.
   b) the relationship between theory and practice as being one that encourage[s] and enable[s] teachers themselves to theorize from their practice and practice what they theorize. In essence, teachers can improve upon their craft through the implementation of action research elements (theorize/plan, implement/act, reflect/observe, self-evaluate/revise plan).
   c) situational understanding, viewing language pedagogy as being relevant and sensitive to a particular group of teachers who are teaching a particular group of learners who are pursuing a particular set of goals within a particular institutional context that is embedded in a particular sociocultural milieu. In essence, pedagogy is local.

33. Post-method pedagogical parameters are those of particularity, practicality, and possibility. Practicality arises from …
   a) from the relations of power and dominance in pedagogy, see this aspect concerned with the impact of pedagogical practice on individual identities, as it can situate not only our sense of selves but also our subjectivity. In essence then, instruction should be based on minimizing those aspects that create and sustain any social inequalities.
   b) the relationship between theory and practice as being one that encourages and enables teachers themselves to theorize from their practice and practice what they theorize. In essence, teachers can improve upon their craft through the implementation of action research elements (theorize/plan, implement/act, reflect/observe, self-evaluate/revise plan).
   c) situational understanding which views language pedagogy as being relevant and sensitive to a particular group of teachers who are teaching a particular group of learners who are pursuing a particular set of goals within a particular institutional context that is embedded in a particular sociocultural milieu. In essence, pedagogy is local.

34. Post-method pedagogical parameters are those of particularity, practicality, and possibility. Possibility arises from ...
    a) the relations of power and dominance in pedagogy. This aspect is concerned with the impact of pedagogical practice on individual identities, as it can situate not only our sense of selves but also our subjectivity. In essence then, instruction should be based on minimizing those aspects that create and sustain any social inequalities.
    b) the relationship between theory and practice as being one that encourage[s] and enable[s] teachers themselves to theorize from their practice and practice what they theorize. In essence, teachers can improve upon their craft through the implementation of action research elements (theorize/plan, implement/act, reflect/observe, self-evaluate/revise plan).
    c) situational understanding, viewing language pedagogy as being relevant and sensitive to a particular group of teachers teaching a particular group of learners pursuing a particular set of goals within a particular institutional context that is embedded in a particular sociocultural milieu. In essence, pedagogy is local.

35. Post-method pedagogy relies on the implementation of macrostrategies and microstrategies across a three-dimensional system revolving around replacement of method with the pedagogic parameters of particularity, practicality, and possibility. There are ...
    a) 10 macrostrategies and 10 microstrategies.
    b) 10 macrostrategies and an infinite number of microstrategies.
    c) an infinite number of macrostrategies and an infinite number of microstrategies.

36. In post-method pedagogy, microstrategies that match with the macrostrategy that maximizes learning opportunities are those that revolve around ...
    a) intensive teacher-learner communication.
    b) learner training and learner perception.
    c) opportunities that are outside of the classroom.

37. In post-method pedagogy, a microstrategy that matches with the macrostrategy that minimizes perceptual mismatches is one that revolves around …
    a) intensive teacher-learner communication.
    b) learner training and learner perception.
    c) opportunities that are outside of the classroom.

38. In post-method pedagogy, a microstrategy that matches with the macrostrategy that facilitates negotiated instruction is one that revolves around …
    a) intensive teacher-learner communication.
    b) learner training and learner perception.
    c) opportunities that are outside of the classroom.

39. In post-method pedagogy, a microstrategy that matches with the macrostrategy that promotes learner autonomy is one that revolves around …
    a) language use and language awareness.
    b) learner preference that leads to learner autonomy.
    c) social and cultural relevance.

40. In post-method pedagogy, a microstrategy that matches with the macrostrategy that fosters language awareness is one that revolves around …
    a) language use and language awareness.
    b) learner preference that leads to learner autonomy.
    c) social and cultural relevance.

41. In post-method pedagogy, a microstrategy that matches with the macrostrategy that activates intuitive heuristics is one that revolves around …
    a) language use and language awareness.
    b) contextualizing linguistic input.
    c) various kinds of raw materials.

42. In post-method pedagogy, a microstrategy that matches with the macrostrategy that contextualizes linguistic input is one that revolves around …
   a) language use and language awareness.
   b) contextualizing linguistic input.
   c) various kinds of raw materials.

43. In post-method pedagogy, a microstrategy that matches with the macrostrategy that integrates language skills is one that revolves around …
   a) language use and language awareness.
   b) contextualizing linguistic input.
   c) various kinds of raw materials.

44. In post-method pedagogy, a microstrategy that matches with the macrostrategy that ensures social relevance integrate language skills is one that revolves around …
   a) contextualizing linguistic input.
   b) various kinds of raw materials.
   c) social and cultural relevance.

45. In post-method pedagogy, a microstrategy that matches with the macrostrategy that raises cultural consciousness is one that revolves around …
   a) contextualizing linguistic input.
   b) various kinds of raw materials.
   c) social and cultural relevance.

Quiz Answers
Language Teaching Methods, Approaches, and Techniques

Multiple-Choice

1.	a	21.	c	41.	a
2.	b	22.	b	42.	b
3.	a	23.	b	43.	c
4.	c	24.	c	44.	c
5.	c	25.	b	45.	c
6.	a	26.	a		
7.	c	27.	c		
8.	b	28.	b		
9.	a	29.	a		
10.	b	30.	a		
11.	a	31.	a		
12.	b	32.	c		
13.	a	33.	b		
14.	b	34.	a		
15.	c	35.	b		
16.	a	36.	c		
17.	b	37.	b		
18.	c	38.	a		
19.	a	39.	b		
20.	a	40.	a		

Suggested Readings

Asher, J. (1965). The strategy of total physical response: An application to learning Russian. *International Review of Applied Linguistics, 3,* 291-300.

Auerbach, E. (1986). Competency-based ESL: One step forward or two steps back? *TESOL Quarterly, 20*(3), 411-415.

Bataineh, K., & Tasnimi, M. (2014). Competency-based language teaching. *Express, An International Journal of Multi-Disciplinary Research, 1*(7).
https://www.researchgate.net/publication/330088979_Compe tency-Based_Language_Teaching

Brinton, D. (2003). Content-Based Instruction. In Nunan, D. (Ed.), Practical English Language Teaching. McGraw-Hill Contemporary.

Chen, M. (2014). Postmethod pedagogy and its influence on EFL teaching strategies. *English Teaching, 7*(5), 17-25.

Compleat Lexical Tutor.
https://www.lextutor.ca

Curran, C. (1972). *Counseling-learning: A whole-person model for education.* Grune and Statton.

Darian, S. (1972). English as a foreign language: History, development, and methods of teaching. University of Oklahoma Press.

Gardner, H. (1983). *Multiple intelligences: The theory and practice.* Basic books.

Gattegno, C. (1972). *Teaching foreign languages in schools: The silent way* (2nd ed). Educational solutions.

Gilquin, G., & Granger, S. (2010). How can data-driven learning be used in language teaching? In A. O'Keefe & M. McCarthy, *The Routledge handbook of corpus linguistics,* (pp. 359-370). Routledge.

Harmer, J. (2007). *How to teach English, New Edition.* Pearson Education Ltd.

Jacobs, G. M., & Hall, S. (2002). Implementing cooperative learning. In J. C. Richards & W. A. Renandya (Eds.), *Methodology in language teaching: An anthology of current practice* (pp. 52-58). Cambridge University Press.

Kent, D. (2019). *The fourth industrial revolution and education: Digital language learning and teaching.* KOTESOL DCC.

Kent, D. (2020). A room with a VUI – Voice User Interfaces in the TESOL classroom. *Teaching English with Technology: A Journal for Teachers of English, 20*(3), 96-123.

Kumaravadivelu, B. (1994). The postmethod condition: Emerging strategies for second/foreign language teaching. *TESOL Quarterly, 28,* 27-47.

Kumaravadivelu, B. (2001). Toward a postmethod pedagogy. *TESOL Quarterly, 35*(4), 537-560.

Kumaravadivelu, B. (2003). Beyond Methods: Macrostrategies for language teaching. Yale University.

Kumaravadivelu, B. (2006). *Understanding language teaching: From method to postmethod.* Lawrence Erlbaum Associates.

Lazear, D. (1991). *Seven ways of teaching: The artistry of teaching with multiple intelligences.* Basic Books.

Lewis, M. (1993). The lexical approach: The state of ELT and a way forward. Heinle ELT.

Lewis, M. (2000). *Teaching collocations: Further developments in the lexical approach.* Language Teaching Publications.

Lozanovv, G. (1978). *Suggestology and outlines of suggestopedy.* Gordon and Breach.

Mackay, A. (2014, September 04). What happens in the brain when you learn a language? *The Guardian.* https://www.theguardian.com/education/2014/sep/04/what-happens-to-the-brain-language-learning

Nicholson-Nelson, K. (1988). *Developing students' multiple intelligences.* Scholastic.

Richards, J., & Rodgers, T. (2005). *Approaches and methods in language teaching.* Cambridge University Press.

Scrivener, J. *Learning teaching: The essential guide to English language teaching* (3rd Ed.). MacMillan. [Chapter 6].

Skibba, R. (2018, November 29). How a second language can boost the brain. *Knowable Magazine.* https://www.knowablemagazine.org/article/mind/2018/how-second-language-can-boost-brain

Thomas, S. (2019). *ELT resources and lesson ideas.* http://eltresource.com

Thornbury, S. (February-March, 2000). A dogma for EFL. *IATEFL Issues,* 153, 2. http://nebula.wsimg.com/fa3dc70521483b645f4b932209f9db17?AccessKeyId=186A535D1BA4FC995A73&disposition=0&alloworigin=1

Underwood, J. (2018). *Using voice and AI assistants for language learning*. British Council Teaching English Webinar. Retrieved from https://www.teachingenglish.org.uk/article/using-voice-ai-assistants-language-learning

Villalobos, O. (2013). Content-based instruction: A relevant approach of language teaching. *Innovaciones Educativas XV* (20), 71-83. https://dialnet.unirioja.es/descarga/articulo/5181354.pdf

Wallace, M. (1991). *Training foreign language teachers: A reflective approach*. Cambridge University Press.

PART TWO: IMPLEMENTATIONS

4. Lesson Framing

Overview

In order to deliver great lessons, you need to have an understanding of all the techniques that can be utilized while teaching, and be guided by a well-developed lesson plan. However, prior to that, you need to have a solid means of framing your lessons. To do this competently, you need to possess an appreciation of the principles behind how you can approach the teaching of English to speakers of other languages. This includes knowing how to handle yourself in the classroom, and how to use the classroom to maximum benefit when required to teach students of various proficiencies and ages, while simultaneously delivering content and providing correction.

Learning Outcomes

1. Grasp the basic techniques and principles behind the teaching of English to speakers of other languages.
2. Gain insight into aspects of student motivation.
3. Appreciate the basics of classroom management techniques.
4. Recognize the difference that a classroom layout can produce.
5. Appreciate a range of content delivery techniques.
6. Be able to identify the difference between a mistake, slip, error, and attempt.
7. Understand what it means to teach various ages and proficiency levels.

Techniques behind Language Teaching

There are a number of methods, approaches, and techniques that have been developed to provide students with the practice of language in the classroom. The ways in which we implement any of these is guided by the principles behind our individual approach to teaching, as well as the ways that we go about explaining meaning and helping our students to practice language. The first section of this chapter will detail these language teaching principles before moving on to take into consideration other aspects of importance to teachers 'in the classroom'.

Language Teaching Principles

Brown (2007) describes 12 principles of language teaching that are split into cognitive, socio-affective and linguistic aspects. He suggests that teachers can use these aspects to help them develop their own core techniques to the teaching of an additional language with students.

Cognitive Aspects

1. *Automaticity*: focus on the meaningful use of language so that it can be absorbed subconsciously by the learner, with a movement to a focus on purpose and fluency and away from analysis of form.
2. *Meaningful learning*: appeal to student interests (e.g., academic goals, career goals, social goals, and so on), anchor new topics to existing knowledge and student background to associate it with something already known, and avoid the pitfalls of rote learning.
3. *Reward anticipation*: be enthusiastic and provide a level of excitement in the classroom, provide short-term reminders of progress so students perceive development, provide immediate verbal praise and encouragement to students as short-term rewards to keep them confident in their abilities, and point out to students what they can do so that they can see the long-term rewards regarding their use of language.
4. *Intrinsic motivation*: use tasks that have a greater success rate and learners will engage with them more readily. This includes those that are perceived as being self-rewarding by learners and are the kinds of tasks that are fun, useful, interesting and challenging.
5. *Strategic investment*: provide as much attention as possible to each individual student; focus on the class as a whole, but provide the opportunity for students to engage in strategies for learning and communication; assist individual learners in becoming aware of their strengths, weaknesses, and the actions that they can take to engage in better learning, while sensitizing students to take on the responsibility for their own learning (build learner autonomy); and provide opportunities that assist students in engaging in a variety of language learning strategies.
6. *Autonomy*: move learners toward autonomy through guided practice of language use; allow activities that use creativity but are not beyond the capacity of students to successfully complete; engage in appropriate pair/group work; encourage and praise

students in trying language that is slightly beyond their current capacity; provide constant feedback on speech production but not to a stifling extent; and provide suggestions individually for the use of the language (e.g., movies, songs, television shows, or magazines that would be of interest).

Socioaffective Aspects

7. *Language ego:* provide cognitively challenging activities in a supportive manner, and understand that students may go through a moderate identity crisis as they develop a 'second-self' that speaks another language and deals with another culture. They may decide to give this second-self a second name in the new language, and this may require patience and understanding on the part of the teacher. Considering language-ego states of particular students and classes can direct you in regards to who to call upon, when to correct speech errors, how much to explain, how structured or planned activities need to be, who to place together, and how 'tough' you can be with your students.

8. *Willingness to communicate (WTC):* is 'the intention to initiate communication, if given a choice', and it is perhaps in contrast to unwillingness to communicate (shyness). This involves aspects of both the language ego and student confidence, along with self-efficacy and levels of anxiety and confidence in using the new language. It is important then to provide verbal and non-verbal assurance to learners to help them to stop avoiding certain areas of language use or to break them out of a shyness routine. Sequence techniques to achieve language outcomes and to build self-confidence, encourage an atmosphere of response, provide reasonable challenges that allow for risk-taking, and respond with positive affirmation and praise toward any attempts that students make to communicate.

9. *Language-culture connection*: highlight cultural differences using activities and materials that connect the language to the culture but screen content that may be culturally offensive, assist students in understanding acculturation, and be aware of students who are discouraged with learning and provide your best assistance.

Linguistic Aspects

10. *Native language effect*: be aware of interference (positive/negative) from the initial language. Help learners to understand the importance of thinking in the new language in order to minimize interference errors, and to move away from translating sentences and words from one language to another (the 'language crutch syndrome').
11. *Interlanguage.* Understand that the variance of this among individual students can be considerable, distinguish between interlanguage and actual errors in usage of the new language, and exercise tolerance to interlanguage forms but still point out the logical difference of usage with appropriate feedback techniques. Further, be aware that mistakes are an indication that aspects of the new language are still developing. As such, assist students with self-correction rather than providing the correct form, particularly through the use of affective (verbal and non-verbal) feedback.
12. *Communicative competence*: covers developing aspects of organizational competence (grammar and discourse), encouraging pragmatic competence (functional and sociolinguistic uses of the language), and developing psychomotor skills (e.g., pronunciation aspects) and strategic competence, encouraging fluency through the use of authentic content, and preparing learners to be independent language users who are able to use the skills that you provide in the classroom to continually develop their language ability once they leave the learning environment.

In the Classroom

After a teacher has a solid understanding of the principles that guide them as a language educator, and how they might go about teaching, they will then need to consider a range of aspects before stepping into the classroom for the first time. Perhaps the most critical of these is understanding learner motivations, followed by the knowledge of what to expect when presented with varying ages and the proficiency of each learner. Teachers also need to understand the importance of error correction and how to implement it.

Learner Motivation

Another key issue in the classroom is that of motivation which includes attitude, and this can be broken down into: integrative, instrumental, intrinsic, and extrinsic. Gardner and Lambert (1972) focus on the integrative and instrumental. Integrative motivation includes integrative orientation or a willingness to be like members of the language community of the second language (L2), while the more practical instrumental motivational concerns involve getting a job, passing an exam, and commitment to learning the L2 (including holding a positive attitude toward the target language and community). Brown (2007), on the other hand, highlights the intrinsic and extrinsic. Intrinsic motivation (enjoyment of learning the language itself) and extrinsic motivation (driven by external factors, e.g., academic requirements, parental pressure, societal expectations, and so on) play a role in how effective engagement and the learning of the L2 will be with any given student.

Sources of motivation for many students will depend on a range of factors such as age, sociocultural background, economic status, friends, and interests. It can also stem from the use of teacher activities, tasks, and teaching style. Aspects of this are reflected in the Gardner (1985) socio-educational model of motivation which is made up of:

- *Cultural belief*, with L2 learning taking place in a specific cultural context.
- *Individual learner differences* that are determined by intelligence, language aptitude, and motivation (the desire to learn, the effort put in toward achieving the goal, and the satisfaction achieved from learning).
- *Learning acquisition contexts*, which are the settings in which the L2 is learned: a combination of formal training (e.g., classroom) and informal training (e.g., natural settings).
- *Language learning outcomes* involving linguistic skills or linguistic competence (involving vocabulary, knowledge of grammar, pronunciation, and so on) and non-linguistic skills (affective components like attitude and values of the target language and community).

Skehan (1989) has also distinguished four main sources of motivation in educational contexts:

- *Learning and teaching activities* which generate an interest to learn (intrinsic motivation).
- *Learning outcomes* with success reinforcing motivation and failures diminishing it (along with expectations, sense of efficiency, and global motivation).
- *Internal motivations* which are those that students arrive to class with (developed due to the influence of other motivations).
- *Extrinsic motivation* which are those that result from the influence of external incentives on learner behavior (e.g., rewards or punishments).

In many cases, a student's motivation might be very low, especially in a formal learning environment where language study is compulsory. Teachers may then likely have to resort to relying on their skills, the implementation of tasks and activities and the use of extrinsic motivation to help produce intrinsic motivation in their learners. However, language learning not only depends upon the methods, approaches, and techniques that a teacher uses but the learners' attitude towards them. Students who have a positive attitude regarding the language being learned are more willing to communicate in the classroom, as opposed to those that have a more pessimistic view of the language (including toward that of the people who use it natively). This kind of attitude towards language may be seen in learners who need to study language as a compulsory part of formal schooling, while those learners who have a clear focus for why they want/need to learn a language tend to view it more favorably. Attitude toward the language is therefore seen as a key factor in success. Helping to stimulate a positive attitude in your students is therefore important, and this can be achieved by using those activities and resources that fit with your teaching style, and are ones that you enjoy using. The enjoyment that teachers have (teacher attitude) when teaching a class spreads to learners who will then view the class as a positive environment for learning, with Dornyei (2001) identifying four strategies to generate a positive attitude in learners:

1. Enhance the learners' language-related values.
2. Increase learner goal orientation.
3. Make the curriculum learner relevant.
4. Establish realistic learner beliefs.

The power dynamic between student and teacher in the classroom, and this dynamic along with student-teacher rapport, a supportive classroom atmosphere, group cohesion and seeing a class begin to work together based on excellent classroom management techniques is also important for any motivational framework to begin to work.

Classroom Management

Key to ensuring a great class is classroom management. In the language classroom, the aim should be to establish a climate that optimizes effective teaching and learning instead of one that is focused on utilizing discipline, order, or control. That said though, the teacher is an authoritative figure in any classroom, and this position comes with its own responsibilities and student expectations, and ones that students, especially young children, might try and test in the first week or so. For many learners, a stern look or a simple 'Stop!' might be enough to then be able to continue smoothly with the lesson. If a student cries, it might be better to leave them be (if they are not hurt) to sulk. Children may also act out to get your attention and in such cases, it may prove better to target the child near the misbehaver, and praise them for doing what you would like the misbehaver to do (e.g., sitting down, or working on a task). However, what may work with one student, or even one class, may not necessarily work with another, and so, it is important to establish and maintain clear expectations from the start.

The first step in taking charge of a class occurs well before entering it. You need to ensure that you are fully prepared before entering the classroom, be ready to implement the lessons that you have developed. Be armed with a means of providing clear learning objectives and ways for students to achieve them, and have sufficient resources and activities to keep students engaged throughout the lesson. This means having a well-organized lesson plan that maintains appropriate levels of time-on-task with clear transitions between activities and tasks while holding contingency plans in reserve (e.g., offline activities ready to use in case the website that was working before class is suddenly inaccessible, or additional worksheets for any students requiring additional work).

Consistency is also important for students. They need to know what to expect from you and your classes; in other words, develop a routine. Part of this might be the need to establish class rules, and discussing classroom/student expectations along with any necessary consequences for misbehavior or disruptions. This might involve a point system (e.g., using apps like *Class Dojo*) that sees the teacher provide and remove points for certain task completion or behaviors. For young children, the points might be enough on their own, but for older learners, you might use points as rewards to leave the classroom first, and for adults these might come with a prize or punishment attached (e.g., a final class party with those on a team with less points bringing the food). Other techniques might involve calling out positive behavior when others are disruptive (e.g., 'MinSoo, it looks like you are ready to begin. Great to see.') and awarding a point to that student to foster both expected behavior, while using modeling on the part of a student, and aspects of extrinsic motivation. For young learners, puppets might be employed to whisper into the teacher's ear, or write a message to the class. No matter what the issue might be in the classroom, you should act on it in a calm and rational manner, and plan ahead to deal with common problems that you know a particular class or student could present. The environment established in the room is also important, and this can be developed in a number of ways from teacher presence right through to the use of seating charts and seating plans to focus on the various aspects of content delivery while staging a lesson.

Teacher Presence

Part of teaching is about being confident in yourself, and knowing your limitations as well as your strengths. Teach to your strengths and engage in professional development to help address your weaknesses. Also, focus on student strengths and provide leadership in the classroom, but don't be afraid to say that you don't know something and that you need to look it up (and do so). Be enthusiastic, use materials that consistently work well for you, while also trialing and integrating new tasks and activities into lessons.

Try to maintain a pleasant expression when teaching, and wear clothes that are appropriate to your teaching environment or ones that align to the workplace dress code if one is in place. Look around the room as you teach, and try to keep your gaze constantly going from one student group to another so that all of the learners feel included in the lesson.

Also, be mindful of the positions you take at different parts of a lesson, and how close you are standing or sitting when monitoring students or helping with written corrections. Are you always behind the lectern, or standing on a raised dais, or do you sit on the edge of a desk more often? One may prove to be distancing for students while the other might make them feel the class is too informal. You may also stay in one place while teaching, instead of moving around the room to see if students are spending time-on-task and offering assistance as required. Perhaps you also tend to stand on one side of the classroom instead of the other, in which case, some students might feel that you are teaching to one side of the room and neglecting them. Of course, this may be due to the sun shining in your eyes when positioned on that other side of the room, and you have not realized that the blinds need to be drawn. Regardless, the way that students interpret your physical location in the room may or may not impinge on how they view you as a teacher, which could then affect the rapport that you need to develop with them. Always try to maintain a better position to be aware of what is going on in the room.

You also need to use your voice to establish presence, and this is perhaps the most important tool accompanying you into the language classroom. You will need to learn how to project your voice at a level appropriate to each of the classrooms that you find yourself scheduled, and in ways where all students in the room (or in the group that you are helping) can hear you and in a way where they can understand you. This means adjusting volume, intonation, tone, speed, vocabulary, and form, as well as introducing physical movement, and the use of facial expressions along with physical gestures (which you may need to overly exaggerate). This also highlights that variety in the use of voice and body is important: the way that you present instructions, model an activity or expression, provide feedback, and being different in how you use your voice and body when assisting individuals, pairs, groups, or the class as a whole. Sometimes, using a small voice, or a whisper, can be as important as using a loud voice, or a shout when getting attention, particularly if students know that you are going to be talking about something important (such as an upcoming exam). You might need to clap your hands a few times to get attention, or rely on a seating chart to be able to loudly call out a student's name, or direct praise towards them.

Seating Plans

A seating chart labeled with student names can enable you to recognize easily who is absent or who you might want to call on, particularly if you have not yet learned student names. A seating plan could also prove useful when rearranging chairs and desks to best suit tasks, activities, games, or other lesson plan aspects. The way that you make use of seating charts and plans can vary from school to school, room to room, and activity to activity, and each comes with its own advantages and disadvantages.

A way to help you move around the room more effectively, and to implement different types of lessons, is to make use of both a seating chart and a seating plan to organize where students sit. It has long been known that how students interact with one another and how the instructor communicates with students can be impacted by the layout of the chairs and desks in the classroom, influencing aspects of engagement, motivation, and focus (McCorskey & McVetta, 1978). Students tend to prefer flexible seating, preferring rooms with mobile versus fixed chairs and trapezoidal tables compared to rectangular tables and immobile chairs (Harvey & Kenyon, 2013). Yet, no matter the type of table or chair, and no matter where in the room they sit, students should ideally have a clear and unobstructed view of the board. The photocopiable content section of this chapter contains sample seating charts that you might like to use with your classes.

Rows. The traditional room is often set up consisting of rows of desks that may or may not be fixed, and supports a *sage on the stage* rather than a *guide on the side* type of learning environment. It supports learning and engagement with the teacher from the students in the first rows or along the middle of the classroom, with students in the back less likely to be engaged. In this kind of room, desks are usually aligned in a grid like fashion. Students will typically be able to collaborate with the person next to them when working in pairs, but it is slightly harder with larger groups (although pairs in front can work with pairs behind). While teachers can move between the rows, it still may prove difficult with bags blocking pathways, with groups working together also inhibiting teacher movement and allowing for pockets of students receiving less direct interaction and attention from the teacher. Nonetheless, this kind of layout can prove very useful depending on the type of lesson delivered (e.g., watching a video, delivering sets of instructions, teaching a grammar point, practicing drills/chants, and so on). To create a cohesive atmosphere, the teacher will need to try and move around the room, walking up and down the aisles, and remembering to call on students at the back of the room as well as the front – randomly rather than one student and then the next in sequence.

Roundtable (circle). Students sitting around a single large table, or with singular desks placed into the shape of a circle, sees them facing each other, and this arrangement can be used to support whole-class as well as pair-wise dialogue.

Horseshoe (semi-circle). The arrangement of chairs into a semi-circle, or a horseshoe shape, modifies the roundtable format to allow all students to face each other while the instructor is free to walk around the room. It can encourage more discussion between students and the instructor, but it supports higher engagement between the instructor and those students sitting directly opposite, coming at the cost of less interaction with those students sitting adjacent to the instructor.

Double horseshoe. This seating arrangement is a semi-circle with an inner and outer grouping of chairs, and it can invite greater discussion over the conventional horseshoe pattern. Its limitation is that it has the backs of the inner semi-circle students facing those of the outer semi-circle students, but the benefit is that students may more easily interact with those nearest to them, including those who they can turn around to and face.

Pods (groups/pairs). The most flexible seating arrangement is that of grouping pods of desks together. This can be in pairs with two student desks together, or in groups with several desks clustered together around the room. This kind of layout is especially advantageous for encouraging interaction, and it assists with establishment of a learning community among students where they are expected to work together and with one another to complete tasks. It is also beneficial for the teacher, as it is easier to move around the room and monitor several students at one time, paying close attention and providing individual support, while students at other tables who are not struggling can get on with their work without disruption. In a mixed ability class, it also allows the teacher to pair or mix stronger students with weaker ones, or to develop content-based activities that include differentiation tasks with one level, or one type of learner, working on different tasks in each grouping.

Content Delivery

It is important to understand that, even if you are teaching an intermediate level class, students are unique and each one of them will be at a different language level. So too, when teaching classes of different sizes, different dynamics come into play. The number of students and desks might impact your seating arrangements, and the size of the room can impact on the kind of language games that you might be able to play. With increasing class sizes, it is also not uncommon to be confronted with students sitting in rows of desks that are unmovable and all in a room designed for far less learners. Important in this respect will be use of the board, as well as how you give instructions to student groupings, stage your lessons, prepare work for early finishers, and establish contingency plans.

Board use. No matter where students are sitting, ensure that all of them are able to see the board. If you are blocking their line of sight, move; if the sun is shining through the window, draw the blinds. Realize that from a seated position, much of the lower half of the board might be obscured for students who sit in the back rows. Perhaps also, use a layout for your board. Lesson objectives and learning outcomes might go on the right-hand side, new vocabulary might go in a column down the left-hand side, leaving the area in the upper middle for instructions and examples, and the lower half for student use, checking, and modeling. Ideally, you may not want to erase anything from the board, or you may designate a work area on the board where things from that section only get removed. You may also want to get into the habit of asking students if it is okay to erase something from the board before you move on to something else. So too, occasionally go to the back of the room to make sure that you are consistently writing large enough so that all students can clearly see the content you are or other learners are providing. An example of what you expect the board to look like at the end of a lesson might be included in your planning, and an imaginary walk through of the lesson that includes writing things up on the board will help you refine the lesson as you develop it.

Giving instructions. Keep instructions precise and concise; they should be as simple as possible. Make sure that they tell students how to successfully complete the activity, and that they are presented in the correct order. It is also important to check that they have been understood, and that all students know what is expected of them and how they are going to accomplish the task. You might consider presenting instructions in two modalities (e.g., spoken and written), having another student explain how to complete the activity in the native or target language (TL) after you have provided the instructions, or model the activity yourself before calling on students to demonstrate the activity for the class to then follow. In either case, giving instructions is an important step prior to working with students in different groups, and it may require you to check answers, and to ask students questions to ensure that they have understood what you are expecting of them.

Answer checking. It is often not wise to call on a whole class to provide an answer to a single question, as a single voice might consistently provide answers while other students may either be unwilling to share their answer, may not know the correct answer, or have nothing written down at all. *Do you understand?* is nearly always a question to be avoided in front of a class. Instead, rely on concept checking questions (CCQ). This means that you need to put yourself in the place of the student, speak at their level and required speed, and check with questions using vocabulary and structures that are already familiar to the learner. Avoid using target words in the questions you ask. Ask yes/no questions when you are sure that the students really do know what you require as a response, as closed questions take pressure off students to provide a full-length answer. Use pictures and mime to encourage language production and a response, along with synonyms and antonyms for quick comprehension checks.

Alternate Questions. Having some alternate questions is important, particularly if you are met with blank stares or you find that students are not doing as directed and so you need to clarify things. Here are some questions that should be avoided.

Do you understand? Asking this question and receiving a *yes* from a student might mean that they comprehend in full; that they think they comprehend, but actually do not; that they partly understand, but think they understand it all; or perhaps, that they understand the last thing spoken about, but nothing before that. Learners might also answer in an affirmative manner if they have lost interest and want you to move onto something or to someone else, they just want to begin the task, or they are ashamed to admit that they do not understand. Even a negative response here might be ambiguous: the learner might think they do not understand but actually have a full comprehension of what you are asking about.

What does this mean? This is a very general open-ended type of question that could be met with a myriad of responses depending on what it is that you are trying to elicit information regarding. Although such a question might be effective with a very high-level student, its value decreases as student levels decrease. It is much better to ask for more precise information. To find out if students know what a word means, you can ask *What is a synonym/antonym for this word?* This will provide additional vocabulary practice and also provide a short answer. You can also have one student mime or draw a picture, and have another learner produce language about what is being acted out or shown.

Why?/How do you know? Although it is great to have students provide reasoning for their answers, you need to be specific as to what you are asking and do so in a way where the question can check if the students have really figured out the answer or if they have perhaps made a random guess and happen to be correct (or perhaps have had a peer whisper the answer into their ear). So, a question such as *What did you read/hear?* might be better, or asking something like *What sentence has the answer/gave you the answer?* or *Does X mean Y or Z?* and so on.

Is this difficult?/Is this interesting? Asking this kind of question might see students unwilling to admit that they are having an issue or do not like the activity chosen by the teacher, or they may simply be unable to express an answer. It is better to go around the room and monitor how students are progressing on the task, and you can then see what parts of the material that they are struggling with, see how many need the same kind of help (which you can then look at later in review), and read the non-verbal cues such as laughter, engagement, and the willingness to communicate (WTC) during time-on-task (TOT).

Any questions? Instead of asking this general open-ended question, make it closed and specific, e.g., *How many words do you need to memorize for homework/need to write? Do you need to complete the listening task?*

Elicitation. Eliciting techniques are used when you want students to give answers rather than giving them yourself. Elicitation can create a more student-centric atmosphere, and it can be used for checking quiz answers, garnering vocabulary definitions, encouraging the use of a grammar structure, for the provision of synonyms and/or antonyms, and to collect background information regarding student opinions, feelings, ideas, thoughts, and so on. It gets students involved in lessons because they are actively producing speech and providing feedback to the teacher. Learners become active responders rather than passive listeners, and it allows teachers to assess student knowledge and adapt the lesson accordingly. When eliciting, give students time to respond so that they can think of an answer, if there is a slow response, provide slightly more input to help guide or shape the kind of response that you are looking for. Key to the benefit of elicitation is to provide students with a means of utilizing what you have elicited so that it can then be solidified.

Vocabulary. The need to elicit vocabulary comes after you have taught a word and need to review it, and also when you want to determine if learners already know the vocabulary you are going to teach during any given lesson. One technique used is that of providing a definition to students and asking for a word that means the same thing, another technique is that of providing a range of vocabulary items and asking students to provide a synonym and antonym for each of the terms on the list. You might also use direct questions when asking students to describe what can be seen in a picture, photo, or video, or when asking them to describe their feelings about a headline or a title. Mind maps and the use of word clusters might also work, and for younger students, the use of flashcards and pictures prove helpful.

Grammar. Providing situational dialogues, drawings, or models to follow is useful when eliciting structural or grammar-based responses from students. It is then important to establish a context and check understanding from which learners can begin to provide answers (e.g., working with a reading text that utilizes the same structure). Asking questions that require a response in the form being practiced is also important.

Reading. Techniques to elicit when providing a reading task to students involve asking them to provide information on what they think the story/topic of the reading might be from the title, headline, or a picture in the text. This will see students beginning to think about the kind of vocabulary, and the forms of language that might be used, and you can then model and introduce the type of language that they will meet during the reading exercise.

Background Knowledge. If you are providing a topic-based lesson, it is a good idea to have the students provide their background knowledge regarding the topic. As with other forms of elicitation, any ideas or vocabulary items that have been provided, and which you know are useful to the task, can be written on the board. Aspects often used for this include mind maps, pictures, titles, telling your own story about the topic, and having a brainstorming session among small groups of students who could then report back to the class in a short word association type activity based on the topic of the lesson/task.

Post-Activity. In some classes stronger learners may dominate while weaker ones remain silent, and a way to alleviate this in a group-based activity is to have students in each group number themselves from 1 upwards. At the end of any activity during a whole class answer check, a teacher can then randomly call on, say, group five and student three to provide an answer. This should motivate each student in a group-based activity to actively engage with the material as they will never know who might be called on later, and it allows a chance for all students to be able to practice the language they are studying. Random number generators are also useful when employing this kind of technique.

Providing Correction. No matter the level of the student, when thinking about correcting student use of language, it is important to consider the kind of correction appropriate to the mistake, error, or attempt made. In other words, as Harmer (2010) explains, there are distinctions that can be made. Mistakes or slips are those things that students can correct themselves once they are pointed out, but errors are not self-correctable and will need to be explained, while attempts occur when students make an effort to say something which they do not yet know how to verbalize correctly. Each will require a different approach to correction.

Mistakes or slips will see the teacher need to encourage the learner to repeat what they have said (perhaps by echoing what the student has said and using a questioning intonation), or if it was an error, turning to a peer to provide the correct language and then following this through with an explanation. It could then be put on the board if it is a common mistake or slip being made by the learners in the room, and perhaps also gone over as part of a lesson review.

Praise can also be used when dealing with correction. For example, you might ask a student to use a new structure along with some new vocabulary that you have been teaching throughout a lesson. However, the student responds with correct use of vocabulary and language use, but without employing the structure. In this case you could recognize the correct use of language and the vocabulary with both praise and correction, stating *That's right, good job, but let's try and fit the vocabulary to this structure. How might we say that?*

Ultimately, when you hear an error in the classroom, model a correction (as a group or individually) and encourage peer correction during activities and answer checks. So too, listen for errors throughout a lesson and review them at the end of the class. Throughout the lesson, and depending on the kind of class that you are teaching, you may need to provide a listing of the usual kind of corrections that editors make to written material, and provide it to the students so that they can begin to use them, and so that they understand your feedback on their content. A color other than red may be more suitable and less depressing for corrections, such as green. Also, a simple technique that some teachers use to help with spoken errors, and correcting an individual one-on-one, is fingering, or finger correction. That is to say, they use a finger to represent each word in a sentence, and indicate the wrong word or error by indicating the 'problem' finger while encouraging the learner to self-correct. Further, the board can be used to review errors, presenting structure practice, or having students write their answers. To help you consider more approaches to correction, think about how you can use the board to demonstrate the revision of errors. You might also use different wording, as discussed in the answer checking section of this book, or rely on peer correction, depending upon how you have grouped your students for the lesson.

Student work groups.

Individuals. Solo work in the classroom, and in the completion of homework, has its place. Students who work by themselves are able to complete tasks at their own speed, giving them the thinking time that they need to work with the language that they are gaining in class. The kinds of in-class tasks suited to this will vary, but they can involve online work by those who finish early, or review work where students need to undertake a quiz or complete surveys and polls.

Pairs and groups. Placing students into pairs and groups helps to foster collaborative activity, and it ideally should be used to see students work together to complete a task, allowing them to engage in communication with each other, and to practice using the language that they already know. Suitable tasks might revolve around discussion of a topic, asking and answering questions, retelling activities, working online together, competing against other teams when playing games, or working on different WebQuest components as part of a major classroom activity. Developing role plays also works well to help students engage in both the creation and practice of dialogues (e.g., between customer and shop assistant, doctor and patient, and so on). All of these activities then help to involve and motivate learners, particularly if you are able to pair stronger learners with weaker ones.

With students working together in pairs or groups, the teacher is then free to monitor students on a walk around the room, and to provide assistance to those who may require it. In most cases students will be able to pair up successfully with friends, but sometimes they might end up in groups where they do not like who they have to work with and may be more comfortable after changing partners or teams. Another issue to pay attention to after arranging students into pairs or groups is reversion to use of the native language (L1) as they work together. So, in the English as a second language setting (ESL) it is often important to ensure that different language speakers sit with each other, and in the English as a Foreign Language (EFL) setting, engage in techniques such as only responding to students when they use the target language (TL), and to refocus students by talking to them in the TL, and directing attention back to the task at hand when appropriate. It is also important to understand that some students may simply be checking on instructions and seeking to clarify their understanding of a task from peers, in which case you might allow a stronger student to repeat activity instructions in the L1 to weaker students at the start of working together.

Whole class work. Teachers will often work on a whole class level to present learners with information (e.g., giving instructions, answer checking a quiz, and so on), and when engaging in controlled practice (e.g., to practice chants and drills, and to model examples for learners). Whole class activities and games can lead to class cohesion, but it limits participation of all individuals, and some may be left at the end of the lesson having never spoken aloud at all by the end of class due to shyness or other aspects stemming from their cultural background that might prevent or inhibit them from doing so, in which case, smaller groups may then prove more effective. You may also wish to finalize such lessons or classes by conducting an exit ticket activity where each learner needs to respond before being able to leave the class.

Class-to-class work. On a number of occasions, it may also prove beneficial for whole classes to interact with each other in a class-to-class activity. These activities would depend on the size of the classes (e.g., two smaller classes merging for a debate) and the focus of language being learned (e.g., two writing classes sharing letters to each other in a pen-pal situation, or a speaking class sharing short video diaries or digital stories with each other). Such interactions can often prove difficult to organize and coordinate, and it might also be time-consuming to prepare, but they do work well by providing students with exposure to unique situations and authentic tasks in which they can then practice and make use of the language skills that they possess.

Staging lessons.

The staging of a lesson is important for students to understand what is expected of them and what will be conducted during the lesson. At the start of class, you likely want to arouse interest and try and engage students through some kind of warm-up activity that may involve a review, aspects that reflect the learning objectives of the day, what students will be focusing on throughout the lesson, or discussing with them what they might be wanting to achieve that day. When transitioning to the next activity, it is important to make this clear by drawing attention to yourself so that you can explain what students need to do next or by refocusing attention onto something else (e.g., pointing to a student to begin answer checking). You will also need to set time limits for each stage of the lesson, and inform students of how long they have to complete an activity.

Keep in mind that no matter what task or activity you provide, there will nearly always be some students that will finish earlier than others, whether it be a minute or two or somewhat longer. One way to provide these learners with work is to ensure that you are building extension activities or 'early-finisher tasks' into all of the activities that you create or choose to use with learners. Also, get into the practice of developing a contingency plan for the lesson or aspects of activities that you know might fail (e.g., the website or internet access may go down, the video that you have chosen may become inaccessible, you may not have enough spare worksheets for students who have made mistakes). In this case, a contingency plan could simply involve moving onto another lesson that you have planned, replacing the activity with another, or skipping that activity for the day and moving onto the next. You might also rely on alternate methods of presentation (e.g., a music video replaced by an audio file, an online quiz replaced by a handout or vice versa).

It is also important to finalize lessons, making it clear that the lesson is over. Often the best way to do this is to review what students have achieved, and what will be conducted in the following lesson (more of the same or a different topic), and perhaps a reminder to do homework. By presenting students with an idea of what will be completed in the next lesson, it might be possible to create a level of enthusiasm for it, and that would help to foster a positive attitude in students toward coming to class. Keep in mind though that what you do in one class, which may work well, may not work in another class with a different group of students. You will also need to adapt your classroom management techniques and the ways that you teach when addressing different age groups and different language levels.

Teaching Varying Ages

Depending on the age of the learners that you find yourself teaching, there are some broad special considerations that should be kept in mind. These include classroom management techniques and language learning activities, as well as the verbal register and body language that needs to be used with learners, all resulting in very different teacher-student and classroom dynamics emerging. Age is only one learner variable that a teacher has to consider; others are those that include language proficiency, motivations for learning, and the context from which students learn (a native language or immersive environment), and what may be impinging on their learning (physically, economically, socially, psychologically).

Young Learners

Attention spans can vary among learners, and for the young, any material that is perceived as boring, useless, or difficult will see them lose focus. Children are often centered on the here and now, so activities need to capture their immediate interest. A lesson needs variety to keep this interest, and needs to also place attention on keeping activities alive.

To help keep activities within the attention span of young learners maintain a time on task of double their age minus two.

Teachers need to be animated, lively, and enthusiastic about what they teach. A sense of humor will help to keep children laughing and happy, which can then promote learning as they become comfortable with you and begin to allow their natural curiosity to emerge.

Language needs to be contextually embedded using familiar contexts, characters, and story lines. Try not to engage in explanations but in practice and repetition instead. Drills and chants, sing-alongs, and read-aloud story times are all popular means of going over language and the forms that it uses. Also focus on function, and what language can be used to do, and design tasks and activities that lead to an immediate outcome or a reward.

Children also require all five senses to be stimulated. Physical activities, such as role play, games, and total physical response activities and other hands-on tasks can help children internalize the language that they are exposed to and are using. Sensory aids can also help them internalize concepts by smelling flowers, touching fruits or eating them, along with the use of audiovisual content from videos, songs, and pictures. Nonverbal language is also important, and children may react sensitively to facial features, gestures, and body language.

Teens
Attentions spans for teenagers are longer than those for children, as a result of a maturing intellect, which also allows for abstract operational thought and complex problem solving utilizing logical thinking skills. The increasing capacity for abstraction by such learners also allows for less of a focus on stimulating the five senses, but this is still regarded as being important. Other issues of importance are needing to take into account the emerging physical and psychological changes that are occurring in the lives of teenagers, and the need to keep the self-esteem of such students high by avoiding embarrassing students, by affirming their personal talents and strengths, by allowing mistakes and other errors to be accepted, and by deemphasizing competition between classmates, and encouraging work that allows for risks to be taken more comfortably.

Adults
Understand that adults are not children, and you should not call them your 'kids'. Do not use caretaker talk (e.g., like parents talk to children)

or talk down to them. Discipline them as adults, reason with them first if there is any disrespect or disruptions in class. Keep in mind that, even though they may not be able to express complex thinking in the new language, they possess mature cognition, and fully developed emotional and intelligent abilities that require stimulating activities. These activities need tailoring to the learning context, as well as scaffolding and differentiation, just as teens and young learners would need.

Allow adults to work with you by providing them many opportunities to practice the language, and to have input into the kind of classes, activities, and learning opportunities that you present. They will enjoy input to the five senses, and they require you to have stimulating activities to maintain their attention and to generate motivation and interest – just like teens and young learners. Although they may be able to use their cognitive abilities to learn better than teens or children, they may also be shier and need more lowering of the affective filter to be willing to communicate through the use of authentic materials and the use of realia.

Teaching Varying Proficiencies

Regardless of the age range that you teach, try to remember your students' names. This will help you to establish a personal connection and to develop a rapport with your learners. Young students especially will feel that the teacher cares about them, and is working with them. Particularly useful on the first day are 'getting-to-know-you' activities (ice-breakers), establishing classroom rules, and setting up routines. Also important on the first day is understanding the proficiency level of the students that you are about to teach, and what this means for you as a teacher.

Language proficiency is officially rated by the Common European Framework of Reference (CEFR), by the American council on the teaching of foreign languages (ACTFL), by the Canadian language benchmarks (CLB), and by international second language proficiency ratings (ISLPR) in other countries like Australia. Language institutes, colleges, and universities providing language education may also have their own level testing procedures to ensure that their students are then separated into general levels such as beginner, elementary, pre-intermediate, intermediate, upper intermediate, advanced, and proficient. Students may also be considered false beginners meaning that they are at the beginner level of language study, but they have been

General Levels	ACTFL	CEFR	CLB	ISLPR
Beginner	Novice low			
Elementary	Novice (mid/high)	A1	Initial basic proficiency, developing basic proficiency.	Formulaic proficiency (0+), Minimum 'creative' proficiency (1-).
Pre-intermediate	Intermediate (low/mid)	A2	Adequate basic proficiency, fluent basic proficiency.	Basic transitional proficiency (1), Transactional proficiency (1+).
Intermediate	Intermediate (high)	B1	Initial intermediate proficiency, developing intermediate proficiency.	Basic social proficiency (2).
Upper Intermediate	Advanced (low/mid/high)	B2	Adequate intermediate proficiency, fluent intermediate proficiency.	Social proficiency (2+).
Advanced	Superior	C1	Initial advanced proficiency, developing advanced proficiency.	Basic 'vocational' proficiency (3), Basic 'vocational' proficiency plus (3+).
Proficient	Distinguished	C2	Adequate advanced proficiency, fluent advanced proficiency.	'Vocational' proficiency (4), Advanced 'vocational' proficiency (4+).

Table 4.1 Language Learning Proficiency Levels

exposed to the language for some time and they know the alphabet, the sounds of the language, and the use of basic survival phrases. As such, they are not true beginners who have almost zero or no knowledge of the language. These proficiency levels and how they relate to each other are presented in Table 1.1.

Teaching Beginners

A beginner level learner can be a challenge for many instructors as these students may have very little knowledge of the language that they are studying, or very little ability with it. It is at this level that the materials and techniques used in the classroom can be crucial to the success of students in obtaining lesson learning outcomes. The primary focus needs to be placed on the use of a limited range of words, phrases, and sentences, with the aim being to engage learners with peripheral processing and encouraging them to use practiced language for meaningful purposes. Students will likely be highly dependent on you to model language for them, and this requires more teacher-focused delivery than other levels. You will need to be vigilant regarding time-on-task, the development and practice of student constructions and their use of language while helping them to engage in noticing, and providing comprehensible input. All of this requires the modification of your own speech patterns and speed. So too, correction is important but it should be provided in ways that do not discourage student language production.

Language that students are exposed to at this level should be authentic and should include simple greetings and introductions that rely on the use of simple and short phrases, and other limited utterances that can produce fluency, with attention being given to practicing grammatical, phonological, and discourse elements. Fluency refers to the ability of being able to convey language in a meaningful, natural, and reasonably lengthy way without much hesitation. Pronunciation practice is critical at this stage with phonemes, phonemic patterns, intonations, rhythm, and stress being important to focus on. Short, simple techniques, such as chants and drills can prove useful along with group and pair work that is structured and clearly defined by outcome. Due to the limited amount of language that students are practicing and working with, a variety of activities is essential in providing engagement with the material and drawing focus to what needs to be learned.

Meaningful and authentic communication tasks should be used for listening and speaking activities with limits placed on the type of grammar, vocabulary, and the length of utterances used, but not by communicative function. Reading and writing tasks can take on the form of lists, notes, recipes, and the completion of simple forms. In the communicative classroom, a typical inductive approach to grammar is used with all levels, particularly if the teacher is unable to provide explanations in the first language (L1). The type of grammar learned at this level typically involves the use of personal pronouns, definite and indefinite articles, singular and plural nouns, and simple verb forms.

Teaching at the Intermediate Level

Working with intermediate level learners involves teaching those who are able to engage in basic communicative tasks, self-correct, employ compensatory strategies (e.g., guessing meaning in context, using gestures to explain and describe a concept, and so on), and use the language beyond survival level. Students should be encouraged to engage with you by asking questions, making comments, and negotiating learning tasks and outcomes. Learner-centered tasks and activities will see students being able to increasingly work in pairs and groups or as a whole class on varying activities.

Learners will be diverse and may require increasingly differentiated and scaffolded content to focus their attention, help them engage in learning activities that lead to successful outcomes, and engage them in language production. Speech interactions will be at an increasingly natural and normal pace, with some students wanting increased correction and more precise grammatical explanations of language functions. Some students may also require more attention on certain areas than others (e.g., pronunciation for one, and grammar for another). The goal is to keep students focusing on fluency, using the language that they possess with enough attention to aid correction to keep them encouraged and engaged. This should then lead to increasing interlanguage being produced by students, and you will be able to lead them in an increasingly diverse range of activities from chain stories, surveys, paired interviews, group problem solving tasks, role plays, storytelling, and so on.

Students will progressively produce novel sentences, be able to participate in short conversations, ask and answer a range of questions, and find alternative ways to convey meanings and solicit information from others. They will also be able to read paragraphs and short simple stories, and start to use skimming and scanning techniques when presented with reading material. The types of grammar employed at this level could include progressive (continuous) verb tenses and clauses.

Advanced Level Teaching

Students at an advanced level are increasingly native-speaker like and possess a high functioning command of the language in social and professional contexts. They are able to readily engage in the negotiation of meaning and are able to convey their thoughts and feelings in interactive communication. There is still need for correction and refinement in language as well as focus on continued practice and use of the language at normal and natural speeds. Teachers need to engage learners with higher level vocabulary, the use of idioms, and more advanced grammatical structures and language features. Students are expected to be the main producers of language at this level, with the teacher providing learner-centered tasks and activities that allow for optimal production as well as feedback and correction for learners as appropriate. Students at this level have likely all passed through the breakthrough stage: that stage of language learning where a student may still be translating from one language into the other in order to facilitate their communication.

Materials and activities would rely on authentic content, as with previous levels, with almost anything being usable as long as it is classroom-appropriate. Typical activities can include debates, complex role plays, scanning and skimming of reading material to determine author intent, and the writing of essays and short stories. Focus by the teacher may need to be placed on aspects of targeted grammar, and helping students to produce and comprehend language in terms of register, style, interlocutor status, conversational exchange, turn taking, topic nomination, topic changing, and culturally conditioned language constraints.

Summary

This chapter places an emphasis on developing the guiding principles surrounding the teaching of the English language, and to working out, prior to entering the classroom, how you will conduct yourself professionally, and be able to best manage and make use of the classroom to learner advantage. In addition to this, aspects of content delivery, learner motivation, and the teaching of various ages and skill levels have been presented, along with the important distinction between mistakes or slips, errors, and attempts. The next step is to use these skills to think about what you will need to teach in order to develop and then deliver great lessons, and this is dealt with in the following chapter.

Review

Content Quiz
Lesson Framing

To help solidify some of the concepts introduced by this chapter the following multiple-choice and true or false quizzes might be helpful for you to undertake. So that you can check the accuracy of your responses, an answer key can be found following the quizzes.

Multiple-Choice

Circle **a**, **b**, or **c** for the answer that best completes the sentence presented in each question.

1. The meaningful and subconscious use of language is …
   a) meaningful learning.
   b) automaticity.
   c) autonomy.

2. Delivering meaningful learning is an attempt to …
   a) associate learning with what students are familiar with.
   b) constantly test student knowledge of vocabulary.
   c) test the meaningful and subconscious use of language.

3. Moving students toward autonomy might involve techniques using activities that are fun, interesting, and challenging …
   a) but decrease goal-orientedness.
   b) that provide prizes.
   c) to engage learners.

4. The language ego can be described as …
   a) a mental breakdown that the language learner undergoes when learning a language, from which they go crazy.
   b) the identity that a person develops based on the language(s) that they speak.
   c) a language student who sees themself as being important.

5. If a student has willingness to communicate, then they will be eager to …
   a) engage in using the language that they have, and in practicing the language that they are learning.
   b) engage in homework and watching videos instead of using and practicing the language that they know.
   c) disengage from using the language that they have learned and no longer want to practice the language that they are learning.

6. Interlanguage can be described as …
   a) the learner's current version of the language that they are learning.
   b) a way of looking at teaching and learning languages.
   c) the language that a teacher uses when in the classroom.

7. Communicative competence covers aspects of organizational, pragmatic, and strategic competence along with the development of psychomotor skills. An example of organizational competence would involve …
   a) the grammar and discourse functions of language.
   b) fluency and social knowledge of how the language works.
   c) the functional and sociolinguistic uses of language.

8. Communicative competence covers aspects of organizational, pragmatic, and strategic competence along with the development of psychomotor skills. An example of pragmatic competence would involve the …
   a) grammar and discourse functions of language.
   b) functional and sociolinguistic uses of language.
   c) pronunciation aspects of the language.

9. Communicative competence covers aspects of organizational, pragmatic, and strategic competence along with the development of psychomotor skills. An example of strategic competence would involve …
   a) the grammar and discourse functions of language.
   b) fluency and social knowledge of how the language works.
   c) the pronunciation aspects of the language.

10. Communicative competence covers aspects of organizational, pragmatic, and strategic competence along with the development of psychomotor skills. An example of psychomotor skills would involve …
    a) the functional and sociolinguistic uses of language.
    b) fluency and social knowledge of how the language works.
    c) the pronunciation aspects of the language.

11. The four types of learner motivation are integrative, instrumental, intrinsic and …
    a) extrinsic.
    b) existential.
    c) esoteric.

12. An example of intrinsic motivation is a technique that uses activities that are fun, interesting, and challenging …
    a) but decreases goal-orientedness.
    b) that provides prizes.
    c) to engage learners.

13. An example of extrinsic motivation is a technique that uses activities that are fun, interesting, and challenging …
    a) but decreases goal-orientedness.
    b) that provides prizes.
    c) to engage learners.

14. Integrative motivation includes …
    a) learning a language to get a job.
    b) learning a language for fun.
    c) a willingness to be like members of the language community of the L2.

15. Instrumental motivational concerns would include learning a language to …
    a) get a job.
    b) have fun.
    c) keep parents happy.

True or False

Circle **a** (true) if you think that the statement is correct, or **b** (false) if you think that the statement is incorrect.

1. Planning a holiday is an example of an authentic activity.
    a) True.
    b) False.

2. Mistakes are self-correctable.
    a) True.
    b) False.

3. Errors are self-correctable.
    a) True.
    b) False.

4. A mistake and a slip are considered to be the same thing, and both are self-correctable.
    a) True.
    b) False.

5. A false beginner has a low level of proficiency but may not have zero knowledge of the language, having been exposed to it for some time, knowing the alphabet, the sounds of the language, and the use of basic survival phrases.
    a) True.
    b) False.

6. Placing students into pairs helps to foster collaborative activity.
    a) True.
    b) False.

7. Students should always be seated so that they have a good view of the board.
    a) True.
    b) False.

8. An example of a contingency plan would be preparing extra handouts of worksheets in case students require more work.
   a) True.
   b) False.

9. On the first day of class, there is no need for ice-breaker activities.
   a) True.
   b) False.

10. The most flexible seating arrangement in a classroom is that of grouping pods of desks together.
    a) True.
    b) False.

11. Eliciting answers from students is a good way of getting them involved in lessons because they are actively producing speech and providing feedback to the teacher.
    a) True.
    b) False.

12. Individual work in the classroom is just as important as pair and group work as it allows students to work at their own speed.
    a) True.
    b) False.

13. When teaching beginners, the focus should be on practicing a lot of speaking rather than focusing on a limited range of words, phrases, and sentences.
    a) True.
    b) False.

14. Pronunciation practice is critical at the beginner stage of language learning.
    a) True.
    b) False.

15. Fluency refers to the ability to convey language in a meaningful, natural, and reasonably lengthy way without much hesitation.
   a) True.
   b) False.

Quiz Answers
Lesson Framing

Multiple-Choice		*True or False*	
1.	b	1.	T
2.	a	2.	T
3.	c	3.	F
4.	b	4.	T
5.	a	5.	T
6.	a	6.	T
7.	a	7.	F
8.	b	8.	T
9.	b	9.	F
10.	c	10.	T
11.	a	11.	T
12.	c	12.	T
13.	b	13.	F
14.	c	14.	T
15.	a	15.	T

Suggested Readings

Brown, H. (2007). *Teaching by principles: An interactive approach to language pedagogy*. Longman Pearson.

Dornyei, Z. (2001). *Motivational strategies in the language classroom*. Cambridge University Press.

Gardner, C. (1985). *Social psychology and second language learning: The role of attitudes and motivation*. Edward Arnold.

Gardner, C., & Lambert, W. (1972). *Attitudes and motivation in second language learning*. Peter Lang Publishing.

Harmer, J. (2010). *How to teach English*. Pearson Education Limited.

Harvey, J., & Kenyon M. (2013). Classroom Seating Considerations for 21st Century Students and Faculty. *Journal of Learning Spaces, 2*(1). https://files.eric.ed.gov/fulltext/EJ1152707.pdf

McCorskey, J., & McVetta, R. (1978). Classroom Seating Arrangements: Instructional Communication Theory Versus Student Preferences. *Communication Education, 27, 99-111*. https://dx.doi.org/10.1080/03634527809378281

Skehan, P. (1989). *Individual differences in second language learning*. Edward Arnold.

Turula, A. (2002). Language anxiety and classroom dynamics: A study of adult learners. *English Teaching Forum, 40*(2), 28-37. https://americanenglish.state.gov/files/ae/resource_files/02-40-2-g.pdf

Photocopiable Content
Lesson Framing

This section of the text includes a variety of material that is free to photocopy. It contains examples of the following content:

- Sample seating charts – rows
- Sample seating charts – roundtable (circle)
- Sample seating charts – horseshoe (semi-circle)
- Sample seating charts – double horseshoe
- Sample seating charts – pods (groups)
- Sample seating charts – pods (pairs)

Lesson Framing 273

Sample Seating Chart – Rows

Front of Room

Photocopiable Content – Lesson Framing

Sample Seating Chart – Roundtable (Circle)

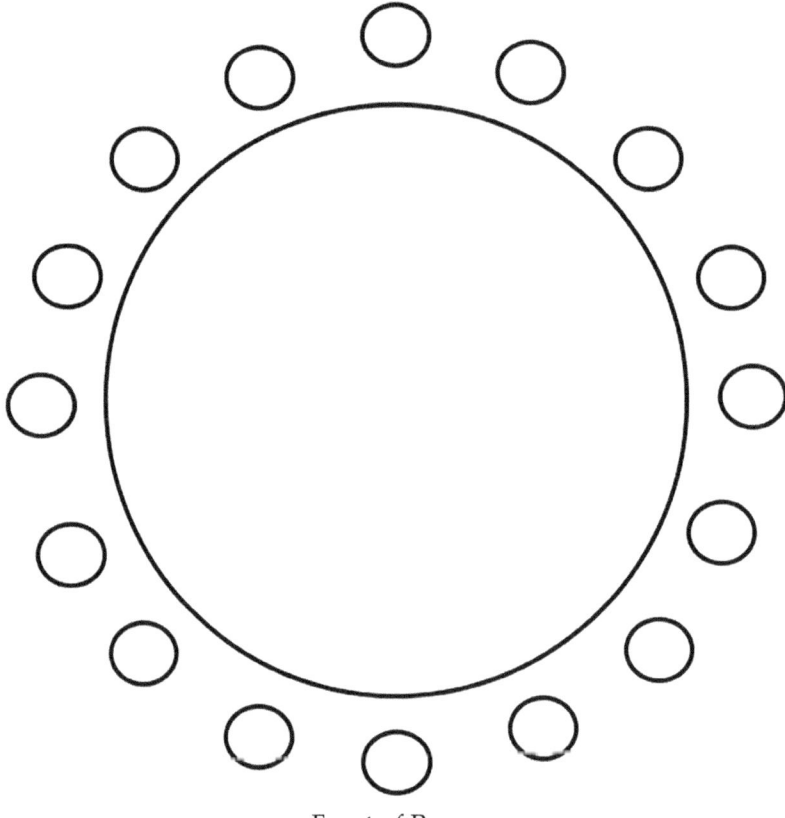

Front of Room

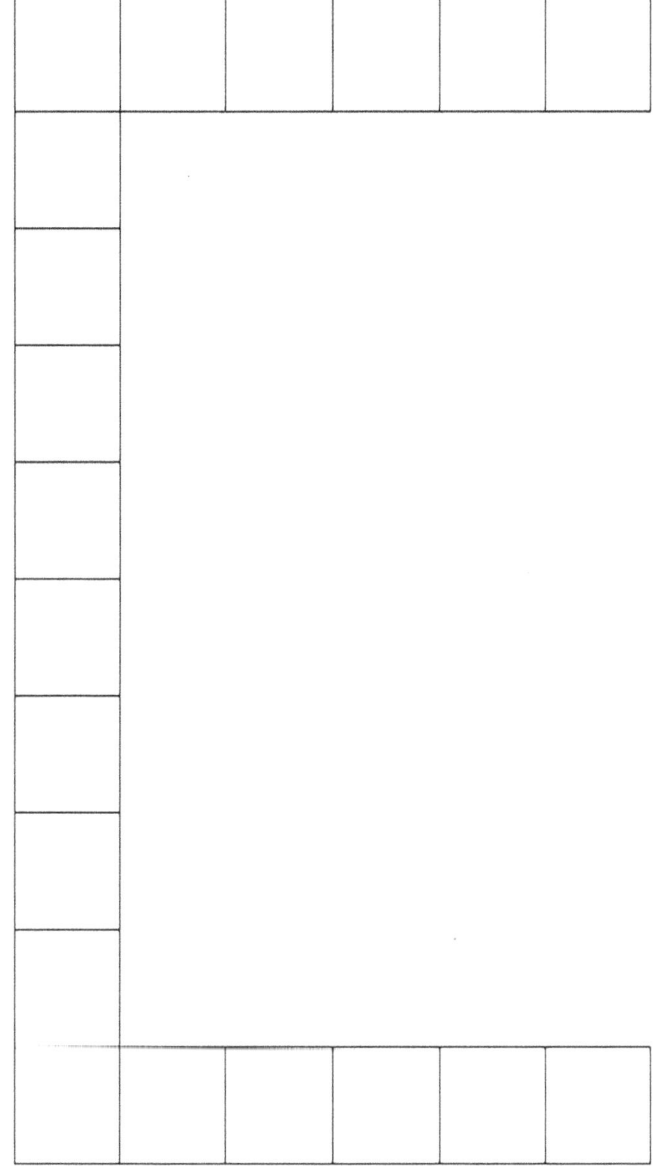

Sample Seating Chart – Double Horseshoe

Front of Room

Photocopiable Content – Lesson Framing

Lesson Framing 277

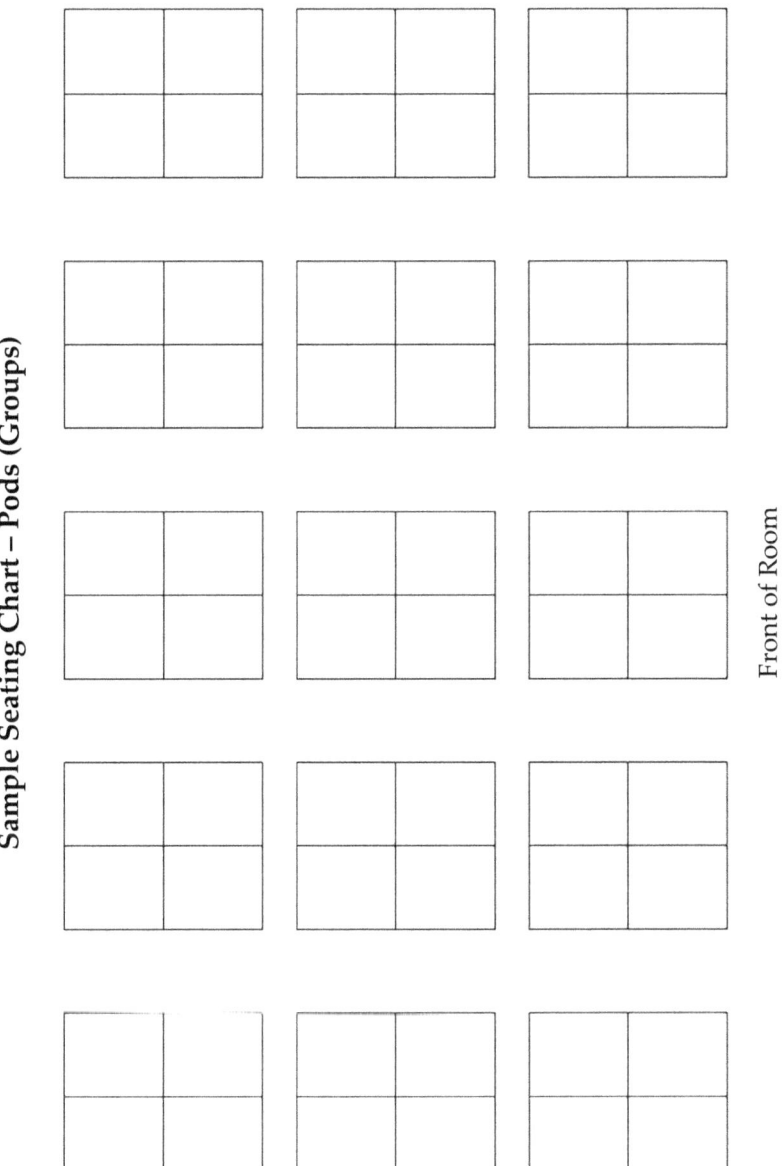

Photocopiable Content – Lesson Framing

278 *Issues in TESOL*

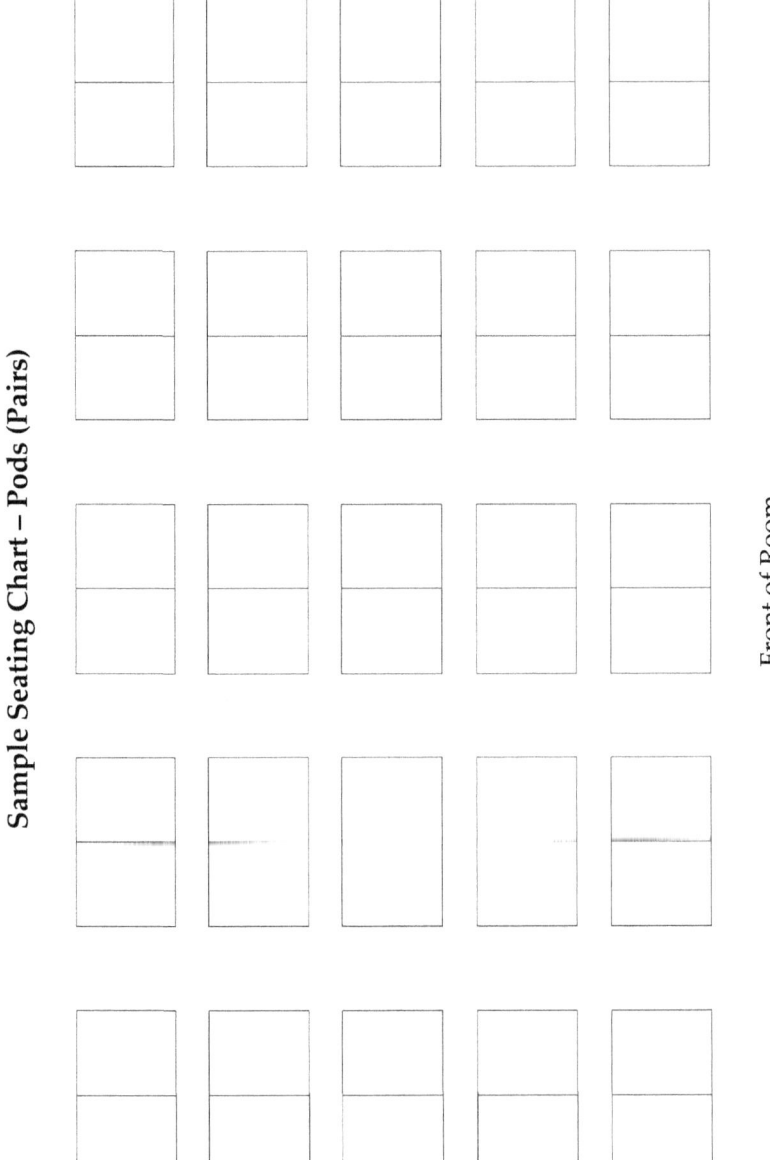

Photocopiable Content – Lesson Framing

5. Developing Great Lessons

Overview

The key to the construction of a great lesson is understanding the teaching and learning context well, and it may be important to conduct a needs analysis to determine what your students want to learn, and how. Needs analyses are also useful to see how you may need to scaffold and differentiate content for learners and the techniques that may prove essential in maintaining student motivation. Another key to developing great lessons that this chapter presents is getting to know the environment that you will teach in as well as the students that you will teach. In order to do this, you will need to have a solid understanding of the principles behind the application of a range of techniques that you can use for the teaching of various language skills. A range of aspects that teachers might need to confront, both inside and outside of the classroom, along with a guide to combat any of the challenges that a teacher might face are also presented, as is the need for teachers to continually engage in professional development in order to upskill.

Learning Outcomes
1. Comprehend the varying roles and responsibilities of students and teachers in the language learning classroom.
2. Understand the importance behind scaffolding and the differentiation of learning, and the place of textbooks and supplementary material.
3. Identify a range of techniques appropriate for the teaching and testing of a variety of language skills.
4. Gain understanding of the various challenges that can arise in the classroom, and ways to approach them.
5. Appreciate the need to engage in continued professional development.

The Teaching and Learning Context

Teaching involves gaining an understanding of your students as well as yourself as a teacher, and how you are developing and improving your craft over time as well. It also involves the use of a number of frameworks, the application of a wide variety of techniques, and the successful use of materials and content in order to provide scaffolded and differentiated lessons to learners that can lead them to practice and develop their communicative abilities and fluency in the language that they are learning. To this end, it is also important to understand the types of activities that can be relied on when developing student language skills.

Understanding Students

A needs analysis is often conducted at the start of a course, and it is one way to understand why your students want to learn English or how they want to apply it, for example, providing them with a simple survey to complete. However, analyses can be much more complex than this and if being created from scratch, you may want to consider why you need to undertake it in the first place, the ways for students to undertake it (on paper, online), how you will identify student language needs in terms of function, how you will word questions to fit in with the restrictions of the workplace (e.g., there is no need to ask students if they don't like textbooks if you must use one and they all say no), examine a mix of skills in the analysis, and try to make it as interactive as possible by including it as a classroom activity so that you can also use it to help students learn something new or in a way where they can practice their existing language skills. It is also important that the needs analysis provides you with a written record that you can use to make your classes more focused, and perhaps also to use as part of a level testing or language diagnostic check.

Conducting needs analyses is one technique among many that you can use to find out more about your students. Another is for students to write personal profiles to be posted on the classroom wall. This could also be a pair activity using a worksheet.

It might also prove useful to ask each learner to write down on a slip of paper the kinds of language activities that they enjoy doing, along with the ones that they do not, and then place the slip of paper into a 'hat' on the way out of class, allowing you to develop activities for the class that are more preferred. An example of this activity can be found at the end of this chapter.

These simple techniques can be done electronically using an online survey or poll system that can tally the results, and which you can then use to provide feedback to the class concerning the types of activities that they like and what you can focus on as a whole. Incorporating the activities that students like and concentrating on the aspects of language use that they want or feel that they need is one simple technique that is likely to lead to increased learner engagement and potentially increased learner motivation.

If you are in a teaching context that requires the use of a core text with flexibility, you may be able to find supplementary materials that you can employ in this manner. You can also discuss the topics and units of the text with students during the first class so that you can complete the book in the order that students may want to approach it, and undertake the textbook activities that students want to focus on first.

An example of a basic needs analysis survey, a student profile handout, and language learning activity likes/dislikes handout are provided in the photocopiable worksheets section of this chapter.

Understanding Yourself as a Teacher

You may wish to keep a teaching diary or a reflective journal regarding your lessons. It can be as simple as a few notes regarding your teaching for the day, or a more complex breakdown and analysis of your lessons. In either case, aspects to include are: techniques that you trialed that worked well (or didn't work, but you have identified ways to improve them); a problem that arose with students in a particular class (e.g., a classroom management problem, and the best way to resolve it in the future); questions that you may have about teaching or that students have asked that you could not answer and need to research (e.g., those focusing on form, certain structures, or the use of vocabulary); and ideas that you gained from the use of certain course materials, or ideas for modifying and implementing these materials differently; along with ideas gained from other teachers that you might like to implement. In other words, focus on particular aspects of the lesson such as the objectives, activities and material usage, student responses, classroom management, and so on. A range of questions that can be used to help begin dairy writing can be found in the teaching diary outline in the photocopiable section of this chapter.

Teacher Talk

Teacher talk time (TTT) is the time that a teacher spends talking during a lesson, and it can be compared to student talk time (STT). Key elements of many methods, approaches, and teaching techniques aim to minimize TTT and focus on STT in order to provide learners with opportunities to practice their speaking and learn from engaging with other learners.

Naturally, depending on the type of lesson being provided the amount of TTT will vary. For example, a teacher mentoring students who are working in pairs or groups will limit themselves to clarification and the answering of language requests, or to providing corrections if any are required. The same teacher leading an inductive grammar presentation will talk more as they explain, illustrate, and check understanding.

The importance of STT is to help students not only engage with the language they are learning, but to practice its use in ways where they can notice their mistakes, and by working with other language learners the class can maintain a student-centered focus. However, this needs to be balanced by TTT as the teacher, particularly in the English as a foreign language (EFL) context, may be the only effective language user students can access. This also means that the talk that teachers engage in needs to be at a level, speed, and volume suitable to the room and students. The quality of teacher responses are also important, as you need to not only be understood but provide timely and accurate feedback that students can understand and work with, and in this way you will be able to interact and engage more with learners. In this regard, especially in an EFL context, the judicial use and application of the students first language (L1) is also important to consider, and one consideration of teacher-talk that has been much debated.

Balancing the Use of the L1 in the Classroom

In an EFL context, instead of that of English as a second language (ESL), the use of the L1 may be more problematic unless you are teaching in a community setting where there are students from one language group that make up a significant portion of the class. There should be a balance between student L1 use and their production of the target language (TL) in the classroom.

Some signs that you may not have the right balance of L1 and second language (L2) use are that the use of the L1 is consistent across all the classes that you teach, and that the student use of L1 does not lessen as the term or semester continues, or as the level of the student changes. Another is that you do not have a clear understanding of when you allow use of the L1 and L2 in the classroom, and when you may wish to curb the use of the L1 among students.

You may begin to realize that there is too much L1 use if students (and even yourself as the teacher) begin to say things in the L1 that you know can be said in the L2, or that the L1 is being used without a clear purpose (e.g., for general chatter instead of explaining task instructions to those who did not comprehend them in the L2). Understand, however, that never being able to use the L1 will make students feel stressed and unhappy, and that using the L1 can sometimes allow more time to be spent on students producing the L2. Provide instructions to all tasks and activities in the target language, and modify these as the lesson progresses if you find that they are not at the appropriate level for the class. Understanding what is at the appropriate level for your students is important both in terms of the materials and content being used as well as the types of tasks and activities that you employ.

Scaffolding and Differentiation

In education, scaffolding refers to a variety of instructional techniques that are used to move learners progressively toward stronger understanding, and ultimately, greater independence in the learning process. It is best provided in a way that breaks learning into chunks, with concrete structures used in the teaching of each chunk. For example, in the case of reading, you might do this by previewing text with learners and discussing key vocabulary, or by chunking the text into paragraphs and conducting reading and discussion of each in turn. In differentiation, you might provide each learner with a different piece of text to read, shorten it or alter the vocabulary or even modify the writing assignments or homework activities that follow, basing these on the language needs or language levels of each learner. In other words, scaffolding is what you are doing first, to ensure that learners are able to manage and digest the content in a manner that leads to understanding and language use, while differentiation is what you do in order to accommodate individual learner needs and continued learner practice with the language content being provided. Differentiation then, is a supportive framework that is put into place by a teacher in order to accommodate the different capabilities of each learner in the class.

Scaffolding Strategies

Scaffolding is also known as 'instructional scaffolding' or 'Vygotsky scaffolding', and it relies on a student working with others (peers or teachers) who possess a wider range of skills and knowledge than the student and can help the learner to expand their learning boundaries and learn more than they would be able to learn on their own. It relies on the concept of a zone of proximal development (ZPD) in which learning takes place. This is an area between where the learner can do things by themselves and an area where they cannot do things at all. For the technique to be effective teachers need to know their students' current level of knowledge, and by building on that knowledge to help them achieve tasks that they would not have been able to perform without assistance. Two means of providing scaffolding with a class are that of verbal and procedural scaffolds.

Verbal scaffolds are those that are provided during instruction. These might include modeling, thinking aloud, slowing speech and enunciating, reinforcing concepts with contextual definitions, simplifying questions that you ask students, and engaging in read-alouds to model correct pronunciation and intonation.

Procedural scaffolds are those that are ones designed to support students in accessing learning, making use of visuals, gestures, and realia (e.g., to pre-teach or as a show-and-tell technique), student manipulation of information with tools like visual organizers, using wait-time to give adequate opportunity for all students to think and respond, use of pause-question-pause-review to solidify information and for students to engage use of prior knowledge, providing a series of discussion prompts (sentence frames) to support dialogue or discussion practice, and allowing students to collaborate with others as they discuss their learning.

Differentiation Strategies

Differentiation is effective for all levels as well as those with mild to severe disabilities. It helps to produce a more autonomous learner who is more engaged in learning, which can in turn lead to fewer disciplinary problems. However, its implementation needs to be balanced with the increasing workload that it produces.

In the differentiated classroom, educators need to provide clear guidelines for all activities, and maintain an active and engaged role with students in a flexible learning environment. This can be done by focusing upon choices, outcomes, and tasks, as well as the content, process, product, and learning environment.

In terms of *choice*, students could be provided with a variety of assignments on a topic from which they can apply a range of skills.

Outcomes would see teachers assigning the same material to all students, but accepting and encouraging a range of results by employing open-ended questions, writing prompts, and discussion topics.

Task differentiation needs to be based on student learning speed or difficulties, age ranges, and levels. Worksheets could be color-coded by level (e.g., beginner, intermediate, advanced) or coded to skills (e.g., reading, writing, listening, speaking).

Content refers to the kind of concepts that the lesson covers, knowing that students will understand, remember, apply, and organize content with different abilities. Differentiation can be established by using a range of activities that cover the various levels present in Bloom's Taxonomy (a higher-order/lower-order thinking skills classification system) covering remembering, understanding, applying, analyzing, evaluating, and creating. Such a lesson might involve activities that include vocabulary matching (words to definitions), the reading of a passage of text and answering related questions, thinking through a situation that happened to a character in a story and developing a different outcome, separating fact from fiction in the same story, identifying an author's position and providing evidence to support the viewpoint, or creating a presentation that summarizes the story.

Process is how students learn (e.g., auditorily, kinesthetically, visually, or through words), and how much support they require of the teacher in order to achieve learning or lesson goals (one-on-one instruction, pair-/group-work, independent work). It might involve providing textbooks for word learners and videos for visual learners, while allowing auditory learners to listen to audio books and kinesthetic learners to engage with an interactive online assignment.

Product is the result of student learning and how they demonstrate that they have gained knowledge. It could involve students taking a test or some other form of activity such as conducting book reports for reading and writing learners, development of mind maps of a story for visual learners, oral reports of a story given by auditory learners, and the building of a diorama to illustrate a story by kinesthetic learners.

Environment refers to the physical and the psychological learning space that should be relaxed and comfortable and allow for varied educational work to be performed by individuals, pairs, and groups. Grouping strategies could address distinct learning needs by providing, for example, areas for groups to discuss work, areas for individuals to conduct solo work or activities, and quiet spaces with no distractions. This may then see a class with some students working individually, some working in small groups, and some working in pairs, all at the same time. Some of these groupings can be teacher assigned, others made by student choice, and some based on common learning needs. Some groups would be working closely with the teacher while others would work more independently. Essential to this is the layout of the classroom, and this needs to be flexible, along with the use of classroom management techniques to provide a safe and supportive learning environment that keeps the learners on task.

The Place of Textbooks and Supplementary Material

Often teachers are provided with a textbook that they must follow when working with students. If you are new to teaching you may not know that many textbooks also come with a teacher's guide, and this can prove invaluable in directing how each activity and task should be presented.

Sometimes the textbook is comprehensive and comes with supplementary material, and a great deal of additional content available over the internet. Other times, it might prove to be lacking in many ways. It might be an inappropriate choice for the length of time that has been assigned to the course, or it may not go into the right level of detail for the type of students enrolled. In these cases, you will need to rely on supplementary material that builds on what is provided by the textbook while matching any additional content to both your teaching style and the interests of your learners.

Supplementary material for textbooks may prove to be as unique and varied as each teacher, yet choices need to be based on the core text content. For example, you may use a real menu from a restaurant to help students engage in a customer-waiter role play to extend the one provided by the book. You might augment and extend each of the review activities found in the text with language games, and rely on different songs as transitions from one unit or chapter to the next. You may decide to rely on material that other teachers have made, tweaking or enhancing it as necessary, or you may develop content from scratch. Regardless, it is important that you add such material to your portfolio of teaching tricks over time. This is important as you will not only have an arsenal of good supplementary material that you know works with learners, but because you also need to maintain and develop a series of go-to lessons and activities that you can rely on at a moment's notice and put to good use in those times in which you need to enact a contingency plan.

Keep in mind that if students have purchased a book, then they will expect to use it and get their money's worth out of it. So, it is important that you cover content from the text that is not only the minimum expected of you by your place of employment, but that which is expected by the students themselves.

Developing Active Learning

No matter how good the teacher may be, there will always be some students who do not understand what the instructor would like them to do, what the meaning or use of some vocabulary is, or some grammar concepts. At the beginner level, this may then see a great deal of gesture and mime use, and the possible use of the L1. You might then need to develop a series of gestures that your students can become familiar with, e.g., cupping your hand to your ear might mean that you want students to begin repeating after you. You might also tug on your ear, and point to specific words that you want a student to practice. However, instructors need to be mindful that gestures may mean something completely different in another culture. Examples of this is pointing directly at someone or gesturing for someone to follow you, as, in parts of Asia and Africa, beckoning with the palm facing up is used with animals and facing down with humans.

In order to help learners internalize language, teaching and learning needs to be scaffolded, and various differentiation strategies may need to be applied. You will also need to decide what method, approach, or technique is appropriate for the content and activities that you will use throughout a planned lesson. Then, if it is appropriate, provide guided practice or controlled practice, and move to freer practice so that students can use the language that they possess while incorporating the use of new vocabulary and grammatical structures at the level of *i+1*. This is relying on the input hypothesis by providing comprehensible language input plus content that is slightly beyond current comprehension levels to promote language acquisition in the learner. At times also, teaching various skills involves particular types of activities, with certain techniques more suited to the development or practice of one skill over another. The chapter will now briefly look at a few of these and consider aspects of incorporating games and technology into the classroom, and some of the challenges that teachers can face.

Teaching Active Language skills

Speaking.

As a productive task, students need to first hear clear, slow, and simple words in order to repeat them. Although they can learn several words in a single lesson, a successful speaking exercise is one where the class and students want to engage in speaking and saying sentences out loud. This can be a satisfying experience to learners in that it helps to build confidence and lets them use the language in a familiar and well understood manner. The three main reasons for getting students to speak in the classroom are:

- rehearsal – providing real-life speaking opportunities in a safe environment;
- feedback – the teacher can provide guidance as students try to use the language that they know, and practice the new language that the teacher provides, so that they can then understand what problems they are experiencing and the potential ways to move forward.
- Activating knowledge – moving learners toward becoming more autonomous language speakers who can use the language without need for constant translation or conscious thought.

The best way to develop activities for the above purposes is to step from controlled practice to providing purpose behind activities that require learners to use speaking as a skill to foster better communication, rather than speaking to practice specific language constructions. In these kinds of lessons, it is important to strike a balance between prompting, correcting, and pushing activities forward. You also need to pay attention to students as they speak to note any language issues that you might want to review as a whole class or have learners practice for homework.

The activities that you can use to provide students with the opportunity to practice speaking as a skill are many and varied.

A popular kind of activity to support speaking practice is the *information gap*. An example of this is where one speaker or group has some information and another speaker or group has the rest of it. The intent is to have the groups work together to combine the information to create a whole, such activities should be demonstrated first with one of the groups or students in the class.

Examples of activities that can use information gap tasks are those that involve completing text, describing and drawing, finding differences, and giving directions. Storytelling tasks, surveys and polls, presentations, and games can also be adapted to the completion of an information gap.

Completing text. Students work together with two different versions of a story where one version might have missing character and location names (proper nouns) while the other story might omit adjectives and adverbs. Students keep their version of the story a secret, and ask questions of each other to complete the version of the story that they have.

Describing and drawing. In this activity, students can work in pairs or groups, with one pair or group handed a picture and the other pair or group then needing to draw the picture without seeing it. Select pictures that can help students practice the vocabulary or language they have been using in class. For example, to help students focus on using color vocabulary, you could use pictures with people wearing bright colors. This activity can also be turned into a class challenge to see who can develop the closest drawing to the original picture.

Finding differences. In this kind of activity students can work in pairs or groups, where each has a picture that is very similar. Learners then need to describe their pictures and ask lots of questions about the other picture in order to find the differences between them.

Giving directions. This activity can see one student be provided with a map of a city or town, and another provided with a list of the locations that are shown on their partners map. The locations can include those from the textbook being used in class, such as a bank, library, hospital, park, police station, and so on. The map can be one of a fictional or real location. The student without the map then asks the one with the map how to get from one location to another. They might be directed to use a question format such as: 'How do I get from the (*bank/library/hospital*) to the (*park/police station*)?, and you could write it up on the board. With the other student then providing the correct directions, with a list of these also written on the board if necessary. Dialogue and role play practice could also be provided using an example such as the following:

A: Excuse me, can you help me?
B: Sure.
A: Can you tell me, where is the library?
B: Yes, it's on Third Street.
A: Okay. How do I get there?
B: Go straight (*one/two/three*) block(s) and turn (*left/right*) at the (*park/hospital*). Then, go straight and you'll see it on the (*left/right*).
A: Thank you. Have a good day.
B: You too.

This kind of role play activity can also be modified for many other kinds of popular units in a textbook like a unit on food or cooking. For example, one student can take on the role of a grocery store shop assistant and the other that of a customer. This would see student A have a recipe and need certain foods in order to prepare a particular dish. Student B then needs to tell the other student where the ingredients are located in the store in order to help the customer complete their shopping. Another alternate would see student A provided with a list of interview questions, and acting as an employer. Student B would then reply using set backstories based on different professions, and student A would note these answers. In addition to swapping roles, students can continuously swap partners around the room if they have been provided with different locations, ingredients, or professions/backstories.

Storytelling can also be adapted to information gap and other speaking activities in a number of ways. This can include giving a sequence of pictures to one student who then describes the pictures to another student to make a story. The same task could be modified so that the pictures are out of sequence, and the students need to work together to create a sequence that works. Alternatively, one student could be given the first half of the pictures and the other student the second half so that they can work together to create a whole story. This kind of retelling task can then be extended to other activities, like that of watching a short animation and then telling the story to the other student. An alternative can be with souvenirs or cherished artifacts, where students would tell where it was purchased and why it is so important to them (i.e., as in show-and-tell)..

Surveys and polls can be used to get students mixing with others around the room and talking to those that they may not normally interact with. This can involve students in activities such as *someone who*, where students would need to go around the room asking various questions to each other to find out which of them has performed a certain activity that is on their list (e.g., climbed a mountain, did bungee jumping, rode a horse, and so on). These can be real activities that the students have done, or they can be fictional ones that you can assign each person (e.g., walked on the moon, lived on the international space station), and depending on the nature of the topic in the book you are working on (e.g., fantasy, travel).

Presentations are also a good way for students to practice speaking, and are a good way for students to give a talk on a specific topic, person or event. These can also be used to develop types of presentations focusing upon aspects of informative, demonstrative or persuasive speech. It can also be helpful during such activities to focus on presentation delivery skills (eye contact, gestures, body language) as well as working with students prior to the presentation so that they understand the different stages involved with planning and delivery, and perhaps also focus on providing useful phrases that can be used. Those listening to the presentation might then be required to take notes or complete an information gap activity sheet containing questions similar to 'Who is the presenter talking about?', 'When where they born?', 'What are they famous for?', and so on.

Games like *Twenty Questions* can be conducted as a whole class, small group, or pair situation. One student might think of an item or object while other students need to ask questions that require a yes or no answer in order to figure out what that item or object is. The limit of questions is twenty, and the winner is the person who can guess the item or object that the first student is thinking of. As a whole class activity, the teacher should count the questions being asked, and if conducted in pairs or groups the student thinking of the item or object should be the one keeping tally. *What am I?* is an alternative that sees students think of something that others need to guess, but they provide a series of sentences as clues to help people guess the item. The limit of sentences might be set to five, and students may work in groups to prepare their clues. The activity could then be completed as a whole class, with either the teacher or group leader reading the clues to the class, and the students trying to guess the answer.

Writing.
Depending on what kind of level your students are at, writing could involve the very basics of drawing the shapes of letters (particularly if they do not use an alphabet or a letter-based script in their first language), and involve lots of pronunciation practice, matching words to pictures, word bingo, and studying the sequence of the alphabet. Alternatively, it might involve the teaching of English for academic purposes (EAP) and the structuring of sentences, paragraphs, and essays, or the nuances of formal and informal writing when typing emails for business purposes. In either case when writing, students have more time to think about the language to use, and how they will use it more than other language skills (like speaking and listening). It is classed as an active skill because it requires students to process language, or to think about the language that they will use before they produce it.

Writing can focus on facts (expository writing), a story (narrative writing), expressing an opinion (persuasive writing), or providing a vivid picture (descriptive writing). No matter the type, when reviewing student work, you may need to use the kind of corrections that editors make to written material, and provide a listing of these to students so that they can begin to use them, and so they understand your feedback on their content. These might be signs and squiggles of varying kinds drawn directly over the issue that needs addressing, or they may be abbreviations that you list in the columns next to sentences that need attention (e.g., *Sp* for spelling, *Gr* for grammar, *WO* for word order, and so on). Traditionally the red pen has been used to provide corrections, but another color such as green may be more suitable and less depressing, particularly if you are correcting every error instead of those that interrupt the flow of writing or the understanding of its content. Once students are familiar with annotated corrections and ways to go about correcting some of the issues their writing might contain, you might then decide to have them engage in simple peer correction of their cohorts written work.

Writing tasks can involve different genres, and this can also dictate the kinds of writing activities that you might decide to use with students, as will learner language levels and their academic background. Irrespective of the task or activity you might like to encourage developing a writing habit within students (writing for the sake of writing), and one that they can use in planning what to write, drafting, reviewing, and then editing when participating in guided writing activities.

Moving to a writing task during a lesson might require bridging tasks as a transition, and these might include cloze exercises, open-ended dialogues, and gap writing (i.e., filling in the middle, but providing an end and a beginning paragraph). If teaching vocabulary from a unit or reviewing it, teachers might also use dictation as a method to transition to a writing task. Such an activity might then see the teacher write the spelling of certain words, or write the word provided in a sentence to show its use. This kind of activity can also be extended through instant writing techniques such as dictating half sentences that students then write and complete (e.g., *My favorite color is _____*.)

You might also have students write a tweet about the day's activity or how they feel right now where the language should be casual and the content can be fun. These kinds of activities may help lower level students, or those less practiced in writing, start to feel more comfortable with the writing process. A tweet activity can also involve showing a movie trailer, discussing it briefly, and working through questions that you have prepared to make it a communicative activity. The follow-up writing activity is tweeting about different topics regarding the movie, which could include an actor/actress (e.g., how they look, their attitude, their role), the genre (e.g., the kind of movie that it is, and whether that genre appeals to them). Another could be about how the students feel about the movie (e.g., if they are looking forward to seeing it, and who they might see it with, as well as if they might think it will be good/bad).

Picture use could also do the same thing as students can write a descriptor (vocabulary, or more detailed information like the taste of a food). They can also sequence photographs in an order, and write a series of instructions regarding them (e.g., for making a cup of tea), and if they are at a more advanced level, these could be extended into how-to article writing to practice expository writing (e.g., how to fold paper into a crane, how to prepare a favorite dish).

Correspondence like postcards and emails are other good ways of practicing descriptive, persuasive, or narrative writing styles. The use of emails might also involve keypals (an exchange of emails with students in the same class, or other classes in the same school or a different region or country). Reports also offer students a chance to engage in writing and might cover the development of a book report based on a graded reader where they need to either work together or by themselves. They could also focus on a movie or a TV show, and make written notes as a short report that can then be developed into an oral presentation. This can involve jotting down information on the title, characters, the genre/mood of the plot, the main plot points, aspects of the story that make it compelling and the hook, along with why someone would want to read the book or watch the TV show or movie, before giving their final recommendations. An example worksheet for this purpose can be found in the photocopiable section of this chapter. This could be continued into storytelling or essay writing activities. Other similar tasks include keeping a diary or log for each day or week, and then using that, along with additional research, to build a biography about the learner or about a fictional character which can then be useful for article writing on specific topics for a class newspaper or magazine. This could then lead into the development of different types of city or tourist guides as well as product brochures or advertisements for various products or venues (e.g., gyms, health clubs, bowling alleys, cinemas, and so on).

Teaching Receptive Language Skills

Listening.

This is an important skill because it allows students to be able to engage in speaking as they become familiar with the pitch, intonation, stress, and pronunciation of the language, as well as the sounds of individual and blended words. Students should be encouraged to listen to a variety of material as much as possible, and this should include extensive and intensive listening material. Extensive listening includes the audio from radio and television programs, listening to music, watching movies with subtitles for enjoyment, and listening to audio books that may come with a matching graded reader. Intensive listening, on the other hand, involves students listening in a specific order to study the way that language is spoken and to work on developing their listening skills. The teacher can also use listening to present aspects of language to students and employ audio as a vehicle to present new words and grammatical structures to learners. To this end, listening tasks should be developed to meet a purpose so that students know what they are listening for, and like reading tasks, it is important to pre-teach and contextualize these activities in order to help focus student attention.

During the pre-listening stage of a listening lesson, it is important to focus the students' attention on the material by providing a play through of the audio. In this first listening, you are preparing students to hear what the audio is like, and introducing them to the general topic before having them focus on particular points in a subsequent listening. Attention can also be drawn to an associated worksheet which contains information that learners can use to help them understand the audio better (e.g., instructions, questions, and so on). Pre-listening tasks can involve brainstorming on the topic with students, and eliciting vocabulary that they will meet during the main focus of the task. This could be achieved by discussing pictures of relevance to the topic or unit of study. Essentially, you are attempting to motivate in students a desire to listen to the content presented, contextualizing it for them so it is easier to approach, and preparing them to focus on completing the activity easily.

The while-listening stage of the lesson might then involve focusing on listening for the main idea or gist of the audio, listening for specific information or for certain keywords, phrases, or specific details, and making inferences from the audio and gaining information from it that has not been explicitly stated. The audio might need to be played twice or three times during these tasks, depending on the complexity and speed of the audio extract being presented. In this case, the second listening will help students to complete and finalize their answers or the task at hand, and the third listening can offer them a chance to double check their responses. During this stage, the audio could also be paused at key points in order to draw attention to certain elements or only at a key extract that could become the focus. It is also important to help students to respond to the content and not just to the language (e.g., ask questions such as *Do you agree with the speaker? What language did she use with her mother?*). You can also match the audio to three to five graded questions (e.g., a gist-type question, detail-oriented questions, and then a single follow-up inference-style question).

The post-listening stage should be used as a means of springboarding students into further language practice, and involve extensive use of the information that they have heard (e.g., developing a schedule, writing a report). Students might also want to have a copy of the transcript to look over for vocabulary that they may have missed, or for grammar structures that they may not have been introduced to previously. A transcript can also be provided as a pre-listening activity, and as one that provides a different kind of introduction to the material instead of just playing it aloud for students.

There are a number of ways to practice listening. Some activities might involve distinguishing sounds as in the teaching of minimal pairs (e.g., ship/sheep), games like Whispers with students verbally and aurally passing a sentence from one to another, whole-class dictation-based activities, pair-work with students describing pictures to each other, gap-fill activities based on news, weather reports, broadcasts, announcements, lectures, phone conversations, as well as content involving the playing of songs, listening to music, and the showing of a variety of video (audio-based, caption-based, and so on). Whatever the audio content, when choosing your own listening material for use with a class, such as music videos/songs or news reports, it is important to ensure that the audio is clear, and that any authentic content is appropriate for the classroom and at the intended level for students. Some activities that can be completed with music include live listening (bringing in guests to the classroom) or when the teacher role-plays different personas for students to interact with. This is more dynamic than the use of recorded extracts, but may not always be appropriate.

Songs are a rich source of authentic content that a teacher can use in a lesson, and they offer learners a break from the usual material found in the course book or work that they need to do to pass a class. If teaching a song as a listening activity, the pre-listening stage might involve brainstorming different kinds of songs for a topic or theme, having students describe their favorite artists/songs and why they like them, or having learners predict words and expressions based on a songs' title. The while-listening stage can then involve cloze-type gap-filling or sentence slip ordering of the lyrics. The post-listening stage can then involve a check of the while-listening activity answers, explaining vocabulary and idiom meanings, discussing how the song made students feel and what they liked about it, as well as writing additional verses for the song, and so on.

Listening activities with video can also be a rich source of learning content for students, particularly since the audio can be removed and focus placed on interlocutor body language, and the clothing worn, in order to then develop dialogues for the characters on screen. Similarly, video can be used to have students predict the content of conversations, with audio playback then used to verify the accuracy of such predictions. Video might also be paused with the teacher asking students to guess what will happen next, and the type of vocabulary and language that the characters on screen might use. Material from movie trailers, short films, and silent movies can all be adapted to suitable listening tasks and learner levels. For example, two infomercials could be played with students comparing the two products to determine which is of better value. Most of this content is freely available on sites such as YouTube but should always be vetted and watched in full before being used with a class to ensure that the quality of the content is good, and that there are no surprises like missing audio or blank video halfway through the content.

Other activities can include jigsaw listening. This is where students each listen to different content on a similar topic (e.g., different news stories on the same event, or different clues to a mystery). They then come together to compare what they have heard with the aim of solving the mystery or preparing a comprehensive news report with graphs or charts developed from the details provided in each of the audio reports. Other listening activities might include sequencing tasks where students working in groups follow verbal instructions (e.g., you might hand all students a piece of paper, and then if they follow each instruction as they hear it, they should be able to successfully fold that piece of paper into a certain shape). Message taking is also a popular activity where students are played short recordings of information, and they jot it down. Calling the cinema for movie show times is a good example of the kind of authentic material that can be used for this kind of task. A longer extension of this kind of activity can involve lectures, speeches, and interviews.

Reading.
There are a number of reasons that students might need to be taught reading, including for their jobs, to fit in better in society, or it may be one of the only ways a student can consistently interact with the language that they are learning. It is also a very useful means of practicing and assisting with language acquisition, as students will often meet various uses of grammar, and unfamiliar vocabulary or expressions that they may then begin to use. It can also improve other aspects of language such as spelling, and punctuation, which in turn can help in the development of writing skills. In other words, reading material can serve as a model for good writing in many ways, from whole text layout through to the type of vocabulary used, and the structure and paragraph construction applied. Reading material can also serve as a vehicle to introduce interesting topics and ideas for later discussion and speaking activities.

The kind of reading normally engaged in within the classroom is often that of intensive reading (as opposed to extensive reading). It involves a detailed focus on set readings, accompanied by specific aims and tasks, and would normally see students examine extracts of authentic content suitable to their level and coming from sources such as magazines, the internet, novels, newspapers, plays or poems, as well as those from other genres such as technical manuals for classes teaching English for specific purposes (ESP).

Extensive reading, on the other hand, involves reading for enjoyment and for the betterment of reading skills in general. In the classroom, this could involve the teacher reading a story to learners as they follow along, look at any associated graphics, and listen. In this case graded readers might be used with learners, with students actively choosing what they are interested in reading.

Pre-reading tasks can involve pre-teaching vocabulary, skimming, provocation, mind maps, show and tell, prediction, and scanning.

Pre-teaching vocabulary involves the selection of key words from the text that you feel could prove difficult for the student, and this is sometimes provided by the textbook author. However, you could be using material that has no such provision, or something that you have written yourself. One way to determine the level of the text, and to determine the words that might prove difficult for different levels of learner, is to use aspects of data-driven learning and vocabulary profiling. The *Compleat Lexical Tutor* website has such tools, and these can be used to determine which words in a text may align to different types of word lists, such as that of the British National Corpus (BNC), the New General Service List (NGSL), and the academic word list (AWL).

Skimming would involve students looking over the text and highlighting the words that they might not be familiar with, and you then providing the definitions. A matching activity could then be conducted with students, for example linking newspaper headlines to matching articles.

Provocation encourages students to discuss ideas behind readings with you, creating an interest in the topic that might then spur students to use their background knowledge to help them prepare for readings. One way to extend such discussions is to develop a mind map centering around what an expected reading might involve, or discussing what the reading might be about based on an accompanying picture. Other means of extension engage students in thinking about readings, such as articles, based on the words and vocabulary presented in their titles. Scanning can then be used with learners looking quickly over the text to find key pieces of information, such as dates, names, and numbers.

While-reading tasks could involve model reading, silent reading, and reading aloud. Model reading could see you read a phrase or sentence, and have students repeat it. Silent reading would see students reading at their own pace, in order to identify any terms and structures that they do not know. Reading aloud activities could see each learner take a turn in reading out loud a single sentence or paragraph, which would allow you to then check student pronunciation and assist with enunciation. More interactive reading tasks could involve jigsaw reading activities where each student reads different content about the same topic or story, and after coming together, begin to compile it. For example, different eyewitness accounts of an event might be provided to each student, and they then have to combine these to understand what is most likely to have happened. Such an activity can then be extended into those used while and after reading, including that of puzzle-based reading tasks where texts have been chopped, and students then need to arrange them in sequence (e.g., ordering a text that details the steps in making a cup of tea). This kind of activity is also particularly interesting when using poems, as it can see radically different versions emerge over the original to which students can later compare their arrangements. Puzzle-reading activities can also be useful in teaching ESP where the same email (written in formal and informal speech) needs to be unjumbled.

Post-reading tasks can see learners complete comprehension questions, fill in cloze exercises, engage in retelling tasks, or perform a series of speaking activities like those discussed in the speaking section (i.e., presentations, role plays, and so on). Comprehension questions involve students writing down answers to questions related to the text, with such activities checked over as a whole-class. In the same way, cloze exercises, where students perform gap-fill activities, can also be used to practice comprehension, along with the vocabulary and structures presented by the reading. These can also be checked over as a whole class, possibly with students writing answers on the board. Retelling tasks, on the other hand, can see students work together in pairs where one retells their reading to another who then writes it down using their own words. This could then be extended to a variety of other speaking-based activities that have already been outlined. (See the speaking section earlier in this chapter.)

Supporting Grammar, Pronunciation, and Vocabulary

Grammar.

One way to teach grammar is by using an explain-and-practice process. For example, to teach the present simple you might show a picture of someone running. You would ask questions such as *Do you exercise? Would you like to run?* You can also use a series of pictures for a morning routine, pointing to the first picture and modeling a sentence such as: *She gets up at 7 o'clock*. You might then use answer-checking: *Does she get up at 7 o'clock on Monday?* and isolate words such as *get* to show that an *s* is added to the verb (except the modal auxiliaries) for *he, she,* and *it* (and any other singular pronoun except *I* and *you*, and any singular noun) when answering: *Yes, she gets up at 7 o'clock*. After modeling the sentence have students chorally and individually practice it. A second picture could then be provided with a time in the corner of the picture, and you would begin to elicit the sentence being modeled using different times, e.g., *He gets up at 6 o'clock*, before moving on to another part of the morning routine with another picture and eliciting answers such as: *She has breakfast at 7:30.* You would then isolate *has* and present the question: *What time does she have breakfast?* You can then contrast *he/she/it has* with *they have,* and you might like to, depending on the level, extend this contrast to: *Someone has* with *Some have*, and: *My brother has* with *My brother and sister have*.

Alternatively, a discovery approach to teaching grammar could be required if the focus is on reading and writing. In this case, students are not directly provided with a target structure or rule to practice or memorize. They should be able to work out the rule for themselves by being presented with content in which the target structure is repeatedly used, and you can then use activities directed at getting students to notice and practice the target structure. An example of this is using words written on single cards, with students moving the cards around to form sentences demonstrating target grammatical sequences.

Pronunciation.

Problems with pronunciation may emerge from interference from the student's native language, some may be 'stress deaf' or speak languages that do not have consonant clusters, or a language may be absent the sound that a learner now needs to produce. Getting pronunciation right is important because students who know the grammar and vocabulary but are unable to pronounce words correctly may not be understood, or they may make others feel uncomfortable by not sounding natural.

Flow of speech and linking. It is important for you as a teacher to keep the flow of your speech, although you might slow down the pace. Of note, when slowing down speech you may lose linking (or liaisons). For example, you may pronounce each word separately. *How ... much ... is ... it.* This is compared to it sounding more like *How muh_chi_zit*? The underscore here shows how the words are being linked for ease of faster pronunciation in normal conversation, causing reduction. There are three types of linking. The first is consonant-vowel, this sees words ending with a consonant linked to words ending with a vowel sound (e.g., turn off becomes turn_off). The second is consonant-consonant, where words ending with the same consonant sound are connected when the next word starts with a consonant in a similar position. The third is vowel-vowel, where words ending with a vowel sound are linked to those beginning with a vowel sound. In this case words that end in *a, e,* and *i* see a *y* sound inserted at the beginning of the next word e.g., the$_y$end. If the first word ends in an *o* or *u* sound then a *w* sound is inserted at the beginning of the next word e.g., too$_w$often. Reductions also occur when we speak, seeing many words collapsed into each other. These include *word + have, word + to, word + me, word + you, word + of, did*

+ *you* + *word*, and *do* + *not* + *know*. See Table 2.1 for examples. A blank of this table is also included in the photocopiable section of this chapter for use with students if you so choose.

Word and sentence stress. Words with two or more syllables will have one syllable stressed more than others, and words spelled and pronounced the same will change meaning based on stress placement. A syllable is a unit of sound, and it may be a vowel, diphthong, or one or more vowels combined with one or more consonants. When concentrating on listening, and teaching stress patterns, the key is to listen for and emphasize tone, length of time, and loudness. Dictionaries will mark the stress on words using a vertical line before the syllable to be stressed, with ' for primary stress and ˌ for secondary stress, and show the division of syllables using a dot or space between the syllables (e.g., ex'it /ˈegzət,ˈeksət/, in·cred·i·ble /inˈkredəb(ə)l/, pres·en·ta·tion ˌprez·ənˈtā·SH(ə)n, ˌprēˌzenˈtāSH(ə)n/.) Sentences also have stress patterns, with some words not so important to hear, being reduced in time, loudness, and tone. In general, this sees content words spoken louder, longer, and higher in tone (e.g., nouns, main verbs, adjectives, adverbs), over function words (e.g., pronouns, helping verbs, conjunctions, prepositions).

Stress can also be taught by exaggerating the stressed syllable, using the hands to beat stress timing of words and sentences. A simple technique is to use a vocabulary box containing three- and four-syllable words which students can then sort into one of four columns depending on the placement of stress. See Figure 2.1.

Minimal pairs are often taught together, so that students can gain practice in hearing and pronouncing the differences. Such pairs are those that differ in only one phonological element (e.g., phoneme, toneme or chroneme), and have distinct meanings. These are a source of confusion for many learners of English, and they need to take note of lip positions for vowels and voiced and voiceless consonants Examples of minimal pairs include *fan–van, hat–hut, heart–hard, sip–ship, ship–sheep, sea–she*. In teaching these kinds of words, flashcards are very helpful along with block building (teaching by phrases instead of word by word). The teacher or other students may then say the words aloud, with classmates guessing the sounds or running to different sides of the classroom depending on what sound they believe that they have heard.

Practicing Reductions in English

What + is + *word*	
What is up	*Whassup*
What is her	*Whatser*
What is his	*Whatsiz*

Word + me	
Give me	*Gimme*
Let me	*Lemme*

Word + have	
Could have	*Coulda*
Might have	*Mighta*
Must have	*Musta*
Should have	*Shoulda*
Would have	*Woulda*

Word + to	
Going to	*Gonna*
Got to	*Gotta*
Have to	*Hafta*
Has to	*Hasta*
Ought to	*Oughta*
Want to	*Wanna*

Did + you + *word*	
Did you eat	*Jeet*
Did you have	*Jev*
Did you ever	*Jever*

Word + you	
Bet you	*Betcha*
Don't you	*Doncha*
Get you	*Getcha*
Got you	*Gotcha*
How are you	*Howarya*
How do you	*Howdya*
How did you	*Howjya*
How would you	*Howujya*
Did you	*Jya*
What are you	*Whaddaya*
Want you	*Wancha*
What did you	*Whajya*
When did you	*Whenjya*
Where did you	*Wherejya*
Who did you	*Whojya*
Would you	*Woujya*

Word + of	
Front of	*Frunna*
Kind of	*Kinda*
Kinds of	*Kindsa*
Lot of	*Lotta*
Lots of	*Lotsa*
Out of	*Outta*
Sort of	*Sorta*
Type of	*Typea*

Do + not + know	
Do not know	*Donno*
or	*Dunno*

Table 5.1 Reductions in English

Stress Practice Activity				
Instructions: Read the word in the vocabulary box below. Then, decide if the stress is placed on the first, second, or third syllable. Write the word in the appropriate column A, B, C, or D.				
Vocabulary: audience assistant	audition employee		composer interview	conductor manager
A •••	B •••	C •••		D ••••

Figure 5.1 Example Stress Practice Activity

Other ways to teach pronunciation and intonation involve playing back (or having the teacher speak aloud) the same sentence differently. Students then decide if they should put a period, a question mark, or an exclamation mark at the end of the sentence. The same technique could be used to have students get practice in using the same sentence in different situations. Songs and chants are also particularly useful to practice the rhythm of the language, and because they use repetition, they also help to solidify vocabulary and the use of grammar structures. Some teachers use jazz chants where words and sentences are spoken to the accompaniment of clapping or stamping. Intonation can also be illustrated by moving your arm through the air in a wave type motion. So too, tongue twisters are also a popular way of having students practice speech production, pronunciation, stress, and specific sounds, and these can be practiced, like many sentences, using a technique called back chaining where the end of the sentence is given to students (either in chunks or word by word) e.g., *last Thursday; the thick thorny thicket last Thursday; rushed through the thick thorny thicket last Thursday; thirty-three thieves rushed through the thick thorny thicket last Thursday.* Twenty-four English tongue twisters ranging from beginner through medium to difficult are included in the photocopiable section of this chapter for use with your students.

Vocabulary.

A popular technique, using an explain and practice procedure for the teaching of vocabulary involves flashcards. This might involve holding up a picture of a car and saying 'car', or a picture of expressions (e.g., happy, sad) and pointing to each in turn, modeling what each is before eliciting the vocabulary from students. This could then be followed by a cue-response drill with the teacher holding up a card and students using the words they have learned, students would then be prompted to use the words in sentence form.

When introducing a new topic, it might also be helpful to use mind maps (or vocabulary trees as they are sometimes known) where, for example, you might have a unit on the home. The word 'household' could be written in the center of the board with the names of various rooms elicited from the class as a whole, with the teacher or students writing these on the board (e.g., kitchen, bathroom, bedroom). You can then elicit further vocabulary regarding what could be found in each room, and adding additional lexical items to the vocabulary students are learning for the unit. Alternatively, students could be placed in groups and assigned a room each, brainstorming the vocabulary associated with and then writing it up on the board. If jobs is the topic and a phrase such as 'caring professions' needs explaining, then we can list the relevant jobs (e.g., counsellors, nurses, social workers).

Testing Students

The language classroom is full of tests: placement tests before a student enters the class in order to determine their language level and to match them with others of the same level; progress tests (continuous assessment) throughout the course to determine how students are learning and if they are improving; and achievement tests or exit tests at the end of the course to determine how well students have learned. Development of a portfolio can also be used for students to showcase their linguistic ability as well as their experience and progress in learning. There are also proficiency tests which are available from external organizations such as the International English Language Testing System (IELTS), the Test of English as a Foreign Language (TOEFL), and the Test of English for International Communication (TOEIC).

Washback (or backwash effect) for a teacher can also come into play when deploying tests. For students, a test might encourage more engagement and motivation (positive washback or washforward) or it might lead to demotivation if they constantly receive low scores (negative washback). Negative washback on the part of the teacher might see tests failing to mirror the content being studied and focusing on how to answer question types. Any test that you create or provide to students needs to be valid, meaning that it tests what it states that it will test. Sometimes, this involves face validity, meaning that the test on face-value looks like a good test, and this is why many multiple-choice tests still rely on three or more distractors when two and a keyed answer is more optimal. Reliability is also important in testing, meaning that it should be graded in the same way irrespective of the grader. Practicality is also important and this involves the length of time that the test will take, and how long it will take to grade. Spin-off is also something to consider. This can be positive spin-off which could see the test being useful for application in remedial teaching and review, or it could be negative spin-off which could see the test demotivate learners if their grades are low or they find it difficult to complete.

If you are designing a test, prepare a list of the items that you want it to focus on (e.g., the present continuous) and then construct the test items with the best ways for students to respond. You will also need to prepare an answer key, with each item weighted or assigned a score, and each section of the test given a time limit. Many course books contain test generation software, but you may still need to tailor to suit what you have been teaching and the focus of the language that you are going to test. You can show and share your test with colleagues to not only generate feedback but to develop resources that your school community can recycle and continually develop and improve on. Thornbury (2008) reminds us of how the focus of each aspect might look in a well-designed and well-delivered quiz or exam (see Table 2.2).

When developing your own test, you will also need to decide if you will focus on discrete or indirect aspects of testing, and if the test can be an integrative one. Discrete item testing involves the testing of one thing at a time, and it can involve integrative testing where students use a variety of language and skills to complete a task successfully. Essentially, it focuses on student knowledge of language rather than their use of the language. In either case, students need to be presented with the kind of tasks and language that they have been introduced to during their lessons. Indirect tests are employed to test performance, and these can involve writing based on supplied information and transactional writing to refer back to the information that is provided. Reading and listening tests using discrete testing can include asking learners to select the best summary of what they have read or heard, or to put pictures into a sequence based upon a listening or reading. Integrative testing can combine both discrete and indirect testing with the aim of assessing multiple skills. For speaking, students can be interviewed or put into pairs in order to perform a provided task (role play) while their use of a grammar point is assessed, or to discuss the similarity and differences between two pictures while focusing on their pronunciation as well.

Aspect	Focus
Practicality	The test is easy to administer, set up, and correct.
Reliability	The test provides consistent results when graded by different people, and when taken by the same level of student.
Validity	The test actually tests for what it was designed to test, and it looks like a good test (e.g., face-validity).
Washback	The test provides a positive experience.
Spin-off	The effect of the test (e.g., it can be used for remedial teaching or for review).

Table 5.2 Five Aspects of Testing and their Focus

Discrete-item testing is most commonly conducted to test knowledge through the use of multiple-choice (including true/false), gap-fills, cloze exercises, and also transformation tasks where students are usually asked to change the form of words and phrases, which helps to illustrate their knowledge of specific syntax and word grammar. This can include rewriting sentences and replacing a word in bold with another one; replacing the form of an underlined word in a sentence; reordering the jumbled words of a sentence; make questions sentences, and sentences questions; or have students identify and correct mistakes purposely placed into a sentence. Gap-fill, or selective cloze, involves the use of one or more gaps in a sentence that have been selectively (or randomly) removed, with students needing to fill in or gap-fill an appropriate word or phrase (which may or may not be provided). Cloze procedure, where a gap is made in a text every so many words (e.g., every fifth, sixth, or seventh) can also be used if it is suitable for the level, otherwise a modified cloze exercise can be developed. Modified cloze exercises can focus on creating gaps in the text that revolve around what is being tested specifically, and ones that present students with the best chance of completing the exam or quiz successfully. Multiple-choice tasks usually consist of a descriptor followed by a keyed answer and a number of distractors. The best design is to rely on a single clearly wrong response matched to a clearly correct response that is tempered by an almost correct response. Use of the phrase 'all of the above' should be avoided, although it is common to see, as is long lists of distractors along with questions that don't ask for the correct response but the best response. Most problems with multiple-choice development come in the construction of the descriptor, and it is important that the descriptor and the answer match well to what you have taught and what you are trying to discover learners understand. Multiple-choice questions can also be presented in a true or false format and can be used in a number of testing situations from reading to listening. They are usually reliable in terms of scorer reliability or in grading.

To test performance in the classroom, we can involve role plays or ask students to perform specific real-world tasks (e.g., filling out an application for a library card and receiving it, ordering takeaway food on an app or the phone and having it delivered). This kind of test has a useful backwash effect for teachers in that it serves to remind us that we are typically teaching for the purpose of seeing our students communicate to achieve real-world outcomes. Testing for this context can involve the use of a rubric that involves a Likert scale for assessment. This is a scale that employs a measure for each assessment item (e.g., a 1-5 point scale) and assigns a specific level of competency accordingly. An example of an oral testing procedure and its associated rubric is available from the photocopiable materials section of this chapter.

Grading quizzes, tests, and exams in a timely manner is important in order to provide feedback to students. This feedback can be the score itself, or it can be actual feedback on specific items that were graded incorrect so that students can attend to them in future. You may have to design a simple key, such as a transparent overlay, if grading multiple-choice items.

Incorporating Games and Songs

The use of games and songs allow students to practice the target language in ways that are fun and often non-threatening, they also allow for the use of language that is repeated. Many games and songs can be used in review, to practice production, or as a warm-up to a lesson. Songs and games can also become part of your contingency toolkit, or part of a go to bag if you need to fill in for another teacher who has not left a lesson plan. You should consider having a number of songs and games ready that work with minimal preparation, and resources and that can be easily adapted to a variety of lessons.

Games

For games, there are a number of applications, websites, and basic classroom activities that a teacher can turn to for use in any given lesson. These can be especially important during the first lesson when a number of ice-breaker or getting-to-know-you activities are going to be required. These types of games will help you to establish a rapport with the class, and if students have never met, it also gets them knowing each other while they collaborate and communicate. These games also help to establish a classroom environment where students can relax, are having fun, and can practice their language skills.

Ice-breakers need to have as few instructions as possible and be appealing to students. A popular ice-breaker is Ball Toss which can be adapted to a large range of uses. It is played by having one student toss the ball to another and asking a question such as *What's your name? What's your major?* or *What's your job?* The student who catches the ball answers the question, and then asks a different question to another student. Alternatives are spelling words one letter at a time, or telling a story one sentence at a time, or stating minimal pairs (the pitcher saying *ship* and the receiver saying *sheep*).

Another game is Touch which is Simon Says without the *Simon says* where students move around the room and touch things that the teacher has called out, e.g., *Touch green, Touch your head*.

You might also play a numbers game like Bottletops where all of the students stand and take it in turns to count upwards, but in multiples of 3 (3, 6, 9 …) being *bottles*, multiples of 4 (4, 8 …) being *tops*, and multiples of both (12, 24 …) being *bottletops*. Those who get it wrong sit down and are out for that round, and the one who hasn't got any wrong is the winner.

Yet another game is to have students stand in a circle and a theme given to them, such as *beach* where each student provides a word associated with the theme. If they are unable to state a different word or take too long thinking of one, then they are out and have to go and sit down. Again, the game continues until there is one person remaining – who is the winner!

Sketch is another game, with the teacher showing a word to one student who then draws it on the board while the other students begin to guess the word as it is drawn. The student who guesses correctly is the next to play. This game can use vocabulary from the current lesson as a review, or a past lesson as a warm-up.

Other word games like Hangman can be quickly turned to, and there is a variety of worksheet generators available on the internet that you can use to create staples such as word puzzles and crosswords, particularly if you prefer seated activities that students can work on either individually or in pairs if they have finished tasks early.

Songs

Like games, songs and how they are used will vary among different levels and age ranges of students, and the type of song chosen will depend on the intent behind its use. Songs contain authentic language and provide a range of vocabulary, grammar, and cultural aspects that you can present in fun ways to learners depending on the activities that you implement to go alongside use of the song. The activities that you plan for use of the song can also vary in length from a full-lesson to just five or ten minutes.

For adults and teenagers, use of popular songs are a good choice, while young learners will prefer those songs that use a lot of action and repetition such as *Heads, Shoulders, Knees, and Toes* and *Wheels on the Bus*. Small rhyming chants can also be used to mark common lesson transitions for such learners, e.g., *Books out, toys away! It's time to play another day*. For young learners, lyrics need to be quick, clear, and simple. Songs also need to be easy to remember, and suitable in terms of age, speed, content, and similarity to the ones that they already know and can use often in other parts of the class or when outside the classroom.

So, planning to use a song can be complex and involve thinking about the level of your students, their age range, any cultural issues or sensitivities, and of course the type of language that the song will support students in learning. Once these factors have been determined, you will need to think about access to the song and how you will present the song in the classroom. This may be from an internet portal, relying on audio or video, or by offline means. No matter the means, you need to make sure that it will be accessible on the day, that the speakers are connected to appropriate devices and are working, and that the song is audible enough for all to hear it but not too loud so as to disturb other classes.

Steps to introduce a song to students involve listening to it or showing the video clip. You may use it as a means to transition into the next activity, or ask students what the song is about, if they have heard it before, or if they recognize any vocabulary, idioms, or structures from it. You can then begin to ask directed questions, perhaps about the title of the song. If the song is based on a theme of some kind, this could be an opportunity to put students in groups to work on an activity or game related to that theme, e.g., *champions* might be a theme associated with the Queen song *We are the champions*. The theme of other songs, like that of Johnny Cash's *Hurt*, come from the chorus and highlight heavier topics such as self-harm which could be appropriate for a group of nurses or psychology majors when teaching English for specific purposes (ESP).

The next step can involve listening to the song with lyrics that appear as captions underneath the video, or are projected in a browser window, and students could focus on the words that they do not understand. The lyrics can also be turned into a worksheet where students need to complete a gap-fill activity or put sentence strips in order. You might also direct students to apps that play video of the song and provide gap-fill activities that they can complete as they watch. *LyricsTraining* is an app and website that allows you to create such activities for songs and to use those that others have created. It is useful for pre-class (active listening for tense/parts of speech), in-class (splitting the class into teams to compete), and homework (to reinforce grammar/vocabulary). Be sure to focus on the use of any unique use of vocabulary, idioms, and other expressions. This could springboard the lesson into the teaching of similar language items, and the same could be done after focusing on particular grammar points that the song uses often.

Follow-up activities for songs that can be adapted to various levels might include continuing the song with another verse, or creating a parody based on the lyrics as Weird Al Yankovic is famous for doing.

Students might also write a response to the singer. For example, what advice and help could be provided to the singer if they engage in self harm (e.g., in *Hurt* by Johnny Cash), or if they have been framed for a murder (e.g., in *Hazard* by Richard Marx). A diary entry for one of the characters in the song could also be developed (e.g., for the fireman in the Beatles song *Penny Lane*).

Incorporating Technology

We no longer talk about technology replacing teachers, or even teachers who use technology replacing those that do not (Wheeler, 2013). We expect to be incorporating technologies into our classrooms in ways that are engaging, motivating, and opportunistic for learning. Instructors need to be able to competently apply the technology of their choice in order to best achieve the learning objectives that need to be attained in their individual teaching contexts. To do this, teachers need to be able to competently and continually assess and evaluate the technologies that they use and consider others that could be more suitable.

Evaluating and Assessing Technology Use

Ultimately, digital language learning and teaching should today be focusing on being used to significantly enhance learning (e.g., motivating students), adding value to the classroom (e.g., improving the quality of education), usefully engaging learners (e.g., focusing on learning outcomes), and providing leverage (e.g., working for you; saving you time). To help you determine if the technology that you are using does all of this, the technology integration evaluation rubric (TIER) found in the photocopiable worksheets section of this chapter could prove useful.

The goal is to introduce technology in a way that allows its use to redefine the learning space for students, and you as a teacher, by replacing traditional teaching methods or learner interactions with alternatives that add value. Keeping a framework such as the substitution augmentation modification redefinition (SAMR) model (Puentedura, 2006) in mind when reviewing different technology for use with students will help you to understand how you can capitalize on providing learning within your specific educational context, and if the technology you have chosen is in fact worthwhile implementing.

The SAMR model.

One means of determining if the content that you are looking at integrating into the classroom is worthwhile is to apply a framework like the SAMR model. This model consists of four segments with substitution and augmentation considered to be the enhancement sections of the model, while modification and redefinition are considered to be the transformational (see Figure 2.2).

Substitution is the utilization of technology in a way that simply replaces or directly substitutes a non-technological implementation. Here, you have to ask yourself what the gains can be for replacing the traditional teaching tool or technique with a technological one. For example, digital assistants could be used to spell out a word and provide its definition, synonym, antonym, and translation.

Enhancement	**SUBSTITUTION** Technology directly replaces an old way of teaching (direct substitute, no functional change)	S
	AUGMENTATION Technology provides improvement (direct substitute, with functional change for the better)	A
Transformational	**MODIFICATION** Technology allows for significant task redesign (presents learning in a new way)	M
	REDEFINITION Technology allows for the creation of new tasks (implements something previously inconceivable)	R

Figure 5.2 The SAMR Model

Augmentation also sees technology directly substitute traditional tools or techniques with technological substitutes, but a significant enhancement in the use of the technology should result. Here, you would consider if using the technology being considered will augment or increase learning potential or student productivity in any way. For example, digital assistants provide all the facts that once needed to be learned, and they can be used when students create posters in order to conduct research that provides real-time information. They also provide real audio (animal noises), games (e.g., Twenty Questions, Jeopardy!), and quizzes, all of which result from the use of voice-driven interactions and turn-takings that can help students practice both their active (speaking) and passive (listening) skills.

Modification, instead of replacement or enhancement, looks at the design of a lesson or task and how technology use may provide increased learning outcomes. Here, you would need to ask yourself if this use significantly alters the task for the better. For example, students can engage with a digital assistant for just-in-time learning where they use it to complete or check homework answers or to review content in a way that also provides additional language practice (speaking and listening) to assist with the development of fluency.

Redefinition, the final segment of the model, looks at using technology to promote a learning paradigm that is not possible to achieve without the incorporation of technology into the teaching and learning space. Here, you need to consider how the technology has helped the instructor or learner to engage with content in a manner that would be previously inconceivable. For example, if students can use a digital assistant to check their pronunciation and develop their fluency, they can rely on it to provide them with one-on-one individualized support for engaging in language learning and language practice, and be provided a device where they can also interact not just with an artificial intelligence (AI) but with other language learners as well (via voice chat).

Teaching Tools: An Overload

The problem today is that there is an overload of technology available for teaching, ranging from apps and websites, to digital assistants and chatbots. It is often hard to disseminate what might prove best to use with your students, and by the time that you do, the technology may be outdated or nor longer supported. To help you understand how best to approach technological choice, the following examples present a range of use cases centering on *application, usability, implementation,* and *example use* that are then tied to a technological framework (*the SAMR model*).

Class-management/economy.
Applications: Class Dojo and Class123.
Usability: both provide a point behavior system for classroom management and establishing good behavior (group/team, or individual based), with syncing available from app/phone to web/computer.
Implementation: helps teachers establish expected behavior with positive reinforcement e.g., getting students involved in teamwork, helping others, stopping bullying.
Use case examples:
- Activity cards – track/reward completion points (in-class, homework, reflection, exit tickets).
- Classroom management tools – timers, group makers, noise meter, student selector, messaging (especially to parents with privacy, no phone number, and night mode).
- Portfolio development – students/teachers uploading completed class work with each other and to parents.

Technology framework fit (SAMR model):
- Substitution – digitizes wall star charts.
- Augmentation – provides a unique means of showcasing work for all stakeholders, with report card summary.
- Modification – redefines report card possibilities, and expectations of parent-teacher meetings.
- Redefinition – helps to establish learner autonomy, and responsibility for actions/learning.

Speaking – presentations.
Applications: Glogster and Padlet.
Usability: both focus on digital literacy, multimodal approaches, collaboration with pair/group work, and skill development for individuals.
Implementation: practice speaking for presentations, reading for content searches, writing for summarizing, listening for audio/video choice/summary, and collaboration for undertaking pair/group work.
Use case examples:
- One-pagers – students share their most important takeaways on a single digital page.
- Online bulletin boards, poster presentations, portfolios, resource curation, mind-mapping, timelining, summaries, and topic development e.g., timelines of a trip, a life, or a how to; a topic like

animals with the audio of the sound a particular animal makes, an image of what it looks like, and a video of how it does something; or, summaries of other sites, such as newspaper/Wikipedia articles, or summaries of books set for holiday reading.

Technology framework fit (SAMR model):
- Significance – allows for curation of content that can be worked on inside/outside class.
- Augmentation – use in place of other content such as handouts or paper posters.
- Modification – produces always accessible multimodal documents that contain audio, video, text, hyperlinks, PDFs, and so on.
- Redefinition – digitizing posters/notices and making them shareable.

Listening – videos/songs.

Applications: EDPuzzle and LyricsTraining.
Usability: focus on listening and reading skills.
Implementation: practice language/grammar points and encourage comprehension skills development while also encouraging speaking/singing, and pronunciation development.
Use case examples:
- LyricsTraining – pre-class active listening for tense/parts of speech, in-class: games or challenges (splitting the class into teams to compete), and for homework to reinforce grammar/vocabulary.
- EdPuzzle – pre-class/warm up to introduce concepts, in-class comprehension checks, and revision to solidify concepts, and apply learning.

Technology framework fit (SAMR model):
- Substitution – questions prompted simultaneously with content, but not all at once.
- Augmentation – enhances video with narration to clarify concepts/key points; or you might develop vocabulary specific cloze tasks (after profiling).
- Modification – students develop cloze or multiple-choice/open-ended questions for videos and after sharing them complete peer challenges and follow leader boards.
- Redefinition – provides student-centered engaging ways of working with audio/video tasks.

Reading – data-driven learning (DDL).
Applications: Rewordify and VP-Kids.
Usability: both focus on reading, grammar, and vocabulary skills.
Implementation: Rewordify – practice listening skills, work on word definitions and parts of speech; VP-Kids – develop skills based on data-driven learning using the BNC 1,000 and AWL (for adults), Kids 1-10, and off-list words.
Use case examples:
- Formative assessment.
- Creating cloze exercises.
- Generating vocabulary lists.

Technology framework fit (SAMR model):
- Substitution – provides audio and definitions for easy/difficult words.
- Augmentation – identifies all parts of speech.
- Modification – instant printables such as vocabulary lists, and cloze/matching exercises.
- Redefinition – regrades text instantly.

Writing – stories/comics.
Applications: Story maker (ABCya.com) and Toondoo maker.
Usability: both focus on the creation and printing of short stories, and adding words/sentences/dialogues, pictures, layout, and drawings to them.
Implementation: practice writing and typing skills, and moving work from paper to digital contexts, or working digitally only.
Use case examples:
- Summarizing scenes or characters from books.
- Creating dialogues for particular scenarios.
- Copying out parts of a text such as lines from dialogues or song lyrics.

Technology framework fit (SAMR model):
- Substitution – students are able to demonstrate knowledge through literacy games and digital drawing boards instead of crayon, pencil, and paper.
- Augmentation – students can demonstrate their understanding of concepts by successfully completing tasks during game play.
- Modification (differentiation) – students can work according to

their individual ability levels (e.g., spelling the words, or relying on the identification of the letters of the alphabet that they know)
- Redefinition – students use the applications as homework practice tools.

Games – language fun.
Applications: Vocabulary Spelling City and Flippity.
Usability: both focus on aspects of spelling, writing, phonics, and vocabulary use.
Implementation: practice words alone or in example sentences, using individual or group-based games.
Use case examples:
- Spelling City – four free games that provide targeted listening practice and can be played with custom vocabulary items, giving word and sentence practice.
- Flippity – More than twenty games are available, with all created using teacher or student developed gsheets. Games include those such as Jeopardy, Hangman, interactive flashcards, crosswords, word searches, online Bingo boards, and quizzes (with certificates).

Technology framework fit (SAMR model):
- Substitution – instantly digitize paper-based activities from cross-platform and other content.
- Augmentation – provides reusable activities, with instant feedback.
- Modification – students and teachers can use their own content to create activities.
- Redefinition – use cross-platform and user creations to engage in on-demand learning, with Spelling City providing novel audio and definitions.

Assessment – interactive quizzes.
Applications: Plickers and Kahoot!
Usability: both focus on providing engaging, interactive, motivating, collaborative, tailored, and differentiated content.
Implementation: practice listening/reading to develop quiz content, place emphasis on speaking/reading for question discussion, and undertake reading/writing for question creation.

Use case examples:
- Warm-up – to introduce concepts.
- Main lesson (question creation) – to maintain active involvement, and conduct competency checks.
- Revision – to solidify concepts.
- Exit tickets – to synthesize knowledge, and to show application of learning.
- Other – to assess vocabulary definitions, reading comprehension, rate the homework of other students, and so on.

Technology framework fit (SAMR model):
- Substitution – replaces paper-based formative assessment. Plickers also eliminates hand raising and offers anonymity.
- Augmentation – video and images can be used during quizzes, and students can compare their responses to others instantly.
- Modification – teachers and students are able to visualize answers in real time, and rethink/react accordingly.
- Redefinition – there is real time review of all responses, available to the teacher only or to all students, and there is no longer a need to call out individuals to provide answers one at a time as individual group responses can be highlighted for the whole class.

Voice-activated learning.

Applications: Google assistant – templates and add-ons.

Usability: the focus is on natural interaction with authentic content for classroom management, and interactive learning.

Implementation: practice speaking and listening skills with access to real-time data and authentic content, and for 'asking three (others) before me'.

Use case examples:
- Classroom management – set timers/reminders, choose volunteers/team leaders, stream content, and so on.
- Speaking/listening – ask questions (such as those about time, weather, air quality, definitions, antonyms/synonyms, translations), access interactive game-play, and stories for interactive learning (e.g., Akinator – Twenty Questions, and Story Speaker – a choose-your-own-adventure game).

Technology framework fit (SAMR model):
- Significance – provides voice-driven learning.
- Augmentation – provides all the facts once needed to be learned, provides access to authentic content, real-audio, and real-time information.
- Modification – provides voice-activated just-in-time learning for completing/checking homework or reviewing content.
- Redefinition – uses AI to check pronunciation, develop fluency, and provide one-on-one support for learning.

Community of practice (COP) – knowledge, practice, and craft.
Applications: (Self) lifelong learning and participation in massive open online courses (MOOCs).
Usability: the focus is on (self) lifelong learning and professional development.
Implementation: practice just-in-time learning, and just-in-time downloads for classroom use.
Use case examples:
- Learning new ways of providing education.
- Completing courses that can lead to degrees, promotion, and learning how to implement new techniques.

Technology framework fit (SAMR model):
- Substitution – replaces the traditional ways of learning and providing knowledge.
- Augmentation – delivers online learning that replaces physical textbooks and face-to-face lectures.
- Modification – provides just-in-time learning, and learning for current needs.
- Redefinition – open to all, and often free to learn (with payment for recognition or class credits to obtain certificates or degrees).

Teaching Challenges

Teaching, like many other professions, offers a range of unique challenges to those who are employed in the industry. A few of the ones that are dealt with here, include: teaching English for specific purposes (ESP), teaching with limited resources, teaching large classes, teaching mixed-level classes, dealing with speedsters, and working with uncooperative students.

Teaching English for Specific Purposes (ESP)

Many occupational specialties require specific vocabulary and the use of specific phraseology in day-to-day communication, and this is in contrast to the type of language typically taught in English for general purpose (EGP) courses. Depending on the level of English for specific purposes (ESP) being taught, you may need to have worked in the industry previously, or to have some familiarity with it, and this is because ESP courses often involve utilizing language in ways that will ensure that jobs are done correctly and that on-the-job training and instructions can be delivered accurately.

ESP courses include those for occupational purposes, and for business English (general business) or English for specific careers like those in aviation, engineering, law, medicine, or tourism. English for science and technology, which might also involve aspects of research teaching that would be involved in the teaching of English for academic purposes (EAP), would also be considered ESP. As such, ESP can be more challenging to teach than general English as it concentrates more on language in context than the teaching of grammar, language structures, and everyday conversation. It also involves a combination of subject matter and English language teaching, which may lead to a class that is more motivated, and one where the student knowledge and application of the subject matter might far exceed yours. This can make designing lessons more difficult, but it allows you to draw on this as a strength of your students and one that you can apply during lessons to stimulate an effective learning environment.

Teaching with Limited Resources

Sometimes you might find yourself working in an environment where you will need to provide almost all of the teaching resources yourself. You may need to ensure that you have your own markers or chalk and an eraser, and take these with you to every lesson. You may not be able to photocopy at the school or have access to a printer or computer. Students may not even have textbooks, pens, or paper.

The focus in this kind of context would need to be on games and activities that involve a lot of speaking, and this is likely to involve vocabulary and spelling practice, describing things with gestures and mime, and whole class collaboration and competitive group work. Consider also running role-plays, dialogue-based conversations, and drama activities. You will need to be prepared to copy dialogues to the board for students to all see what needs to be modeled and practiced, and design these to maximize word and phrase substitution.

It could also mean getting creative with the resources that you do have, for example, you might need to scrunch up a piece of paper in order to make a ball to play a game during class. This would then be perfect for use in an icebreaker activity to practice the structure: *My name is* _____. *What's your name?* This is helpful for students to get to know each other, and for the teacher to remember students' names. In this game, the teacher uses the structure and tosses the scrunched-up piece of paper to a student, who then uses the structure before tossing the 'ball' to another student, and so on. The same kind of 'ball' could be used in games of Hot Potato and other activities that you might like to engage with on the fly.

Teaching Large Classes
It is now the norm for class sizes to be increasing, and in such classes in a large room, it could be difficult to engage with those at the back. You may need to speak louder, or students may not be able to see the board or hear the audio, so you will have to rely on worksheets or other methods of presenting content. On the other hand, if everyone is crammed into a small room, then movement around the class to check on individuals could prove difficult, and more whole-class activities over pair and group work might be required. In either case, combine students into manageable groups. It is important that you then explain what you want students to do very clearly, as you do not want to spend the remainder of the lesson going between groups to re-explain what it is that they should do. You also need to establish a good method for conducting answer checks, and this could involve random number generators to choose a group whose leader could then provide a response. The same leaders could also prove useful when handing out or collecting worksheets, as well as explaining the activity to those in a group who do not understand it.

Teaching Mixed-Level Classes
In many cases almost all classes will be those that consist of students of mixed-level abilities. In this case, it is important to use a range of differentiated content and work with students in different groupings,

providing different types of tasks for each group. Activities can also be developed with the understanding that slower students are to concentrate on the first one or two exercises while a third activity would be for those at a higher level, or reserved for those who finish earlier. Often, it is also beneficial to use the stronger students in helping the weaker ones, as they will be able to provide examples of modeling. The danger is that some students might get bored as they wait for peers to catch up to them if they decide not to provide such support, or they might get frustrated with always having to help weaker students. When conducting answer checks, you also need to be mindful of student levels and call on those who are capable of providing modeling or able to provide what you are attempting to elicit from them.

Dealing with Speedsters

There can be those students who genuinely complete the work early, or those that do the minimum and complete a question sheet by providing one-word answers instead of full sentences. One way to deal with this is to provide two sections for every activity: the first containing the required work for all students; the second an extension activity for those who complete the required task early. The intent here is to have no student complete all of the activities in the time allotted, but all students should be able to complete the required section before you bring the activity to a close or move on to another task. Such activities can also be used for homework completion by all students or covered as part of a follow up classroom review. Alternatively, you may keep a series of additional language worksheets, puzzles, or readings handy, and pass these out to those who have finished early, so that they do not get bored or become a distraction to other students.

Working with Uncooperative Students

We may encounter students who do not do homework, do not want to speak, or who do want to speak but just not in the L2. Of course, the use of the L1 is at times beneficial for clearer explanations, but there can be those who fall back to it out of frustration as they may not have enough language skills to effectively communicate in the target language. This is understandable, but it does become a problem if students are talking to each other off topic rather than focusing on the material that they need to study. Ways to focus students are to talk to them directly about the issue and try to get them to understand when it is best to use English for practice and when the L1 might be appropriate, e.g., responding to L1 use with: *Oh, do you need help?* This could help center students back onto task and make them realize that using the L1 draws your attention. So too, you might only respond to them if they use the target language to engage with you. Constant reminders also help them to get into the groove of speaking in the target language when prompted.

Keep in mind that some students will feel apprehensive about using the target language. They may be shy, worried about making mistakes, or feel intimidated by others who dominate activities or can clearly use the target language very well. To help with this, pair work could prove essential as students can then speak more freely with one or two others rather than in a large group setting. Providing support for controlled practice is also key, perhaps getting learners to fill in a word from a sentence that you practice with them before engaging in techniques like back chaining. Use role plays to engage in dialogue practice as well, but it may prove more important to provide good coaching in terms of intonation, stress, and pronunciation for this type of student if you do. You may also want to set speaking activities for homework and provide feedback that can be used to develop learner speaking ability, thereby encouraging them to be more productive in class.

Not all students like homework, or they may not have the time to complete it if they are older learners who work, study, and look after family members. In other cases, students might be required to complete homework as this is mandated by the school, with parents needing to sign off on it. If possible, you can negotiate what constitutes homework, and how much can or should be set directly with the students. Keep in mind that learners who consider the homework useful and appropriate are going to more likely complete it, and if it is made fun or engaging, they will want to be involved in undertaking it as well. It is also important that, if you have set a deadline for homework, you stick to it, and that you provide feedback on all homework set in an appropriate period of time. The feedback should be useful for students, and more than something they simply read once and then forget. In this regard, you may decide that, instead of grading homework at home and just handing it back to students the next day or outside of class, you go through the homework as a whole class activity. In this way, you can review content to see where students still require help, while also providing some suggestions on what they can do to improve any problem areas.

No matter the issue in the classroom, it is always better to be preemptive rather than deal with a surprise or something that could have been a non-issue from the start. Set the rules at the beginning, and ensure that standards are maintained as you go (e.g., consistent use of the L2, and appropriate monitoring and use of the L1; deducting points for the non-completion of homework or non-participation in activities, and so on). When a problem does occur, deal with it or the behavior that led to it rather than the student, and enlist assistance from other teachers if required. Examples are asking students why they are constantly late (e.g., they might come straight from work to class, and are therefore constantly missing out on review, so you might need to provide worksheets that they can use to undertake review before they arrive).

It is important to determine if any students have special needs, and if these are being catered to by the school. In this regard, changing the method and approaches that you are using, and trying out the use of different pre-activity engagement tasks, different practice tasks like jigsaw tasks, or providing single tasks with a single focus, could be helpful. Identifying such students may also mean that you need to consider undertaking continuing professional development (CPD) so that you can begin to learn how best to accommodate these types of learners in the future.

Continuing Professional Development (CPD)

Continual professional development (CPD) may be organized by your workplace or it may not. Regardless, it is important for you to keep up to date with the various materials and resources that you can develop and obtain to assist you in teaching. This will help you to not only add new and interesting activities to your teaching repertoire but become a better teacher, particularly if engaging in self-reflection activities and lesson implementation evaluation techniques such as those outlined in this book.

You can join organizations such as the TESOL association in your local area, as well as attend their conferences and workshops. You can also read about new activities and techniques from teacher magazines, journals, and websites, and participate in a number of social media forums over the internet to learn new implementation techniques.

Performing these activities will keep you in touch with peers, help you to network, and because of the pace of change today, it will also allow you to constantly engage in best practice. It will give you the knowledge and opportunities to perform a range of old things in new ways (e.g., learning how to present grammar or discussion activities in more interesting ways) as well as learning how to use equipment that has recently been developed or popularized. Keeping up to date will help you as a teacher answer any questions that students may ask, and if you are unable to do so, you would either know where to go to find out the answer, or know how to direct the student to go about finding out the information for themself.

Summary

This chapter covered a range of important concepts and aspects that involve the roles of teachers and students, and also looked at the place of the textbook and various other resources in the classroom. A number of the skills required, as well as the types of activities and techniques that are often employed while teaching were presented along with many of the challenges that teachers can undoubtedly expect to face in and out of the classroom. It was also pointed out that students rightly expect you to be familiar with how to address these challenges, and to engage in continued professional development to maintain and improve your skills. They will also expect that you have carefully looked over the material that you are teaching, and that you have developed a plan for its best use. This aspect of teaching, *planning lessons*, is dealt with in the following chapter.

Review

Content Quiz
Developing Great Lessons

To help solidify some of the concepts introduced by this chapter the following multiple-choice and true or false quizzes might be helpful for you to undertake. So that you can check the accuracy of your responses, an answer key can be found following the quizzes.

Multiple-Choice

Circle **a**, **b**, or **c** for the answer that best completes the sentence posed in each question.

1. Needs analysis can help you understand why your students want to learn English, and it can be undertaken by …
    a) pronunciation practice.
    b) a language learning activity likes/dislikes handout.
    c) grammar testing.

2. The aim of minimizing teacher talk time is …
    a) so that students can practice their speaking.
    b) to keep from getting a sore throat.
    c) so that more audio activities can be conducted.

3. Teaching that uses scaffolding is best provided in a way that …
    a) provides all learning content to students at one time, and they then organize it in a way to suit their own learning style.
    b) sees all learning occur at home with only practice provided during class sessions.
    c) breaks learning into chunks, with concrete structures used in the teaching of each chunk.

4. Providing differentiation is effective for producing an environment that has less disciplinary problems, while also producing a …
    a) more autonomous learner who is more engaged in learning.
    b) more spoiled learner who wants everything done to suit themself.
    c) lot of teacher time wasted on developing demanding tasks for every single learner in the classroom.

5. It is important to supplement the textbook because …
    a) students get bored easily, and they enjoy making their own content instead of using a book that they have purchased.
    b) students never bring it to class.
    c) it allows for additional use of realia and the tailoring of content to student interest.

6. Controlled practice might be defined as the stage of a lesson where students …
   a) are producing target language content on their own.
   b) practice the new language in a limited form.
   c) engage in a speaking test.

7. Writing is classed as an active skill because it requires students to …
   a) process language, or think about the language that they will use before they produce it.
   b) move their hands.
   c) actively engage in constant translation and dictionary work.

8. Intensive listening involves students listening …
   a) to audio from radio and television programs, listening to music, watching movies with subtitles for enjoyment, and listening to audio books that might come with a matching graded reader.
   b) to music while camping.
   c) in order to specifically study the way language is spoken and to work on developing their own listening skills.

9. In-class pre-reading tasks can involve …
   a) pre-teaching vocabulary, skimming, provocation, mind map development, show and tell, prediction, and scanning.
   b) model reading, silent reading, and reading aloud after class.
   c) completing comprehension questions, filling in cloze exercises, undergoing a quiz, engaging in retelling tasks, or performing a series of speaking activities.

10. A good technique to use, among others, when teaching stress could be …
    a) to use the hands to clap out the stress timing of words and sentences.
    b) to have students hit each other whenever they think a syllable should be stressed.
    c) not teaching this actively, since most students are stress-deaf anyway.

11. Reliability in testing (for example, the test can be marked the same way by anyone) is an important factor to consider when designing tests for use with students. Validity is also important because …
    a) the test needs to test what it states it will test.
    b) tests should be designed to always be usable no matter how old they are.
    c) the type of test is not important. Teachers just need to record numbers for grading purposes.

12. Games are great ways for students to use and practice language because …
    a) life is a competition and students have to learn to lose sometimes.
    b) they are well suited to engaging students in a fun way with the material that they need to learn.
    c) you cannot be serious in class all of the time because this can lead to lower student evaluations.

13. Teaching brings with it many challenges, so it is always better to be …
    a) preemptive, handling problems straight away, and, if necessary, seeking assistance from other teachers or the administration.
    b) laissez-faire, letting things go to see if they resolve themselves, and not reporting anything.
    c) unconcerned, as the challenges of the classroom are not your responsibility.

14. The SAMR model is a framework used to categorize classroom technology integration. The acronym stands for …
    a) substitution, augmentation, modification, redefinition.
    b) subtraction, addition, multiplication, randomness.
    c) speech, audio, microphone, redefinition.

15. It is important to engage in CPD because it allows you to …
    a) add new and interesting activities to your teaching repertoire.
    b) get time off work, in order to recuperate from teaching and give your voice a rest.
    c) tell other teachers how great a teacher you are, and let them know you are expecting a teaching award.

True or False
Circle **a** (true) if you think that the statement is correct, or **b** (false) if you think that the statement is incorrect.

1. An example of a basic needs analysis survey could involve a student profile handout or by student completion of a language learning activity likes/dislikes handout.
   a) True.
   b) False.

2. Based on the content taught, the amount of teacher talk time compared to student talk time will vary between lessons.
   a) True.
   b) False.

3. Scaffolding is what you do first to ensure that learners are able to manage and digest the content in a manner that leads to understanding and language use.
   a) True.
   b) False.

4. Differentiation is what you do in order to accommodate individual learner needs and continued learner practice with the language content being provided.
   a) True.
   b) False.

5. Textbooks do not often come with a support website that provides additional content and supplementary material for teachers to use with their students.
   a) True.
   b) False.

6. Speaking, as a productive task does not need students to first hear clear, slow, and simple words in order to repeat them. Words and sentences should be spoken as fast as possible so that students can get used to engaging with native-speakers of the language as soon as possible.
   a) True.

b) False.

7. Writing for low level students could involve the very basics of drawing the shapes of letters, and involve lots of pronunciation practice, matching words to pictures, word bingo, and studying the sequence of the alphabet.
   a) True.
   b) False.

8. Extensive listening includes audio from radio and television programs, listening to music, watching movies with subtitles for enjoyment, and listening to audio books that might come with a matching graded reader.
   a) True.
   b) False.

9. Reading in the target language, particularly if reading aloud and reading often, can also improve other aspects of language such as writing skills (e.g., spelling, and punctuation) as well as speaking skills (e.g., pronunciation and fluency).
   a) True.
   b) False.

10. Practicing tongue twisters can support student pronunciation, fluency, and vocabulary practice.
    a) True.
    b) False.

11. Negative washback on the part of the teacher might see tests failing to mirror the content under study and focusing on how to answer question types.
    a) True.
    b) False.

12. Games and songs are important as they provide target language practice in fun and often non-threatening ways. They are also an important part of any contingency kit, and it is always handy to have one or two ready to go at any given time.
    a) True.
    b) False.

13. The best way to deal with early finishers is to let them do homework from other classes.
    a) True.
    b) False.

14. In the SAMR model there are four steps. Two steps are classed as enhancement, and the other two as transformation. The substitution and augmentation steps are classed as transformation.
    a) True.
    b) False.

15. A simple means of engaging in CPD is to join a local TESOL association, and read their newsletter and journal articles in order to keep up with latest trends and teaching techniques.
    a) True.
    b) False.

Quiz Answers
Developing Great Lessons

Multiple-choice		*True or False*	
1.	b	1.	T
2.	a	2.	T
3.	c	3.	T
4.	a	4.	T
5.	c	5.	F
6.	b	6.	F
7.	a	7.	T
8.	c	8.	T
9.	a	9.	T
10.	a	10.	T
11.	a	11.	T
12.	b	12.	T
13.	a	13.	F
14.	a	14.	F
15.	a	15.	T

Suggested Readings

Ashman, A., & Elkins, J. (2005). *Educating children with diverse abilities* (2nd ed.). Pearson.

Bailey, K. (2005). *Speaking*. McGraw Hill.

Brown, H. (2007). *Teaching by principles: An interactive approach to language pedagogy*. Longman Pearson.

Celce-Murcia, M., Brinton, D., Goodwin, J. (1999). Teaching pronunciation: A reference for teachers of English to speakers of other languages. Cambridge University Press.

Compleat Lexical Tutor. https://www.lextutor.ca

Crystal, D. (2004). *Rediscover grammar*. Longman.

Dudeney, G. (2007). *The internet and the language classroom: A practical guide for teachers* (2nd ed.). Cambridge University Press.

Fotos, S., & Browne, M. (2004). *New perspectives on CALL for second language classrooms*. Routledge.

Graves, K. (2000). *Designing language courses: A guide for teachers*. Thomson Heinle.

Harford, N., & Baird, N. (1996). *How to make visual aids*. Heinemann Books.

Harmer, J. (2010). *How to teach English*. Pearson Education Limited.

Hedge, T. (2005) *Writing* (2nd ed.). Oxford University Press.

Hubbard, P., Jones, H., Thornton, B., & Wheeler, R. (1991). *A training course for TEFL*. Oxford University Press.

Hughes, A. (2003). *Testing for language teachers*. (2nd ed.). Cambridge University Press.

Jones, T. (2016). *Pronunciation in the classroom: The overlooked essential*. TESOL Press.

Kent, D., (2017). *Teaching with technology: Integrating technology into the TESOL classroom*. Pedagogy Press.

Kent, D., (2017). *Internet in education: Integrating the internet into the TESOL classroom*. Pedagogy Press.

Kippel, F. (1985). *Keep talking: Communicative fluency activities for language teaching*. Cambridge University Press.

Leech, G. (2001). *An A – Z of English grammar and usage*. Addison-Wesley Longman.

Matthews, A., Spratt, M., & Dangerfield, L. (Eds.). (1991). *At the chalk face: Practical techniques in language teaching*. Nelson Publishing.

Maxwell, T., & Ninnes, P. (2004). *The context of teaching* (2nd ed.). Kardoorair Press.

Mayer, R. (2009). *Multimedia learning* (2nd ed.). Cambridge University Press.

McNamara, T. (2008). *Language Testing.* Oxford University Press.

Nation, I. (2003). *Learning vocabulary in another language.* Cambridge University Press.

Nation, I. (2009). *Teaching ESL/EFL reading and writing.* Routledge.

Nunan, D., & Miller, L. (Eds.). (2002). *New ways in teaching listening.* Teachers of English to Speakers of Other Languages, Inc.

Puentedura, R. (2006). Transformation, technology, and education. Retrieved from http://hippasus.com/resources/tte

Sion, C. (2004). *Recipes for tired teachers.* Alta Book Centre.

Skehan, P. (1989). *Individual differences in second language learning.* Edward Arnold.

Son, J. (2004). *Computer-assisted language learning: Concepts, contexts, and practices.* iUniverse.

Swan, M. (2017). *Practical English usage*, (4th ed.). Oxford University Press.

Thompson, A., & Martinet, A. (1986). *A practical English grammar.* Oxford University Press.

Ur, P. (2009). *Grammar practice activities: A practical guide for teachers* (2nd ed.). Cambridge University Press.

Ur, P. (1992). *Five-minute activities: A resource book of short activities.* Cambridge University Press.

Ur, P. (1981). *Discussions that work: Task-centered fluency practice.* Cambridge University Press.

Walker, A., & White, G. (2013). *Technology enhanced language learning.* Oxford University Press.

Wharton, S., & Race, P. (2016). *Five hundred tips for TESOL teachers.* Routledge.

Wright, A. (2003). *One thousand plus pictures for teachers to copy.* Thomas Nelson Publishers.

Wright, A., Beveridge, D., & Buckby, M. (2006). *Games for language learning.* Cambridge University Press.

Photocopiable Content
Developing Great Lessons

This section of the text includes a variety of worksheets that are free to photocopy and use with your classes. It contains examples of the following content:

- Needs analysis survey
- Personal profile task – Teacher notes
- Personal profile task
- Delayed feedback worksheet
- Language learning activities likes and dislikes
- Teaching diary outline
- Practicing reductions in English
- Stress practice activity
- English tongue twisters
- Book/movie/TV show presentation report
- Example oral interview testing procedure - Teacher notes
- Oral exam interview testing scale
- The technology integration evaluation rubric (TIER)

Needs Analysis Survey

Name _____

A. Why do you want to learn English? (Tick the response that matches why you want to learn English, or write in a new response if yours is not listed.)
___ To find work
___ To do further study
___ To do volunteer work
___ To watch English TV shows/movies
___ To listen to English songs
___ To read English material on the internet

Other: _____

B. Rank your skills from 1 (the strongest) to 7 (the weakest).
___ grammar   ___ listening
___ pronunciation   ___ reading
___ vocabulary   ___ writing
                        ___ speaking

C. Rank the activities below from 1 (the most helpful when learning English) to 7 (the least helpful when learning English).
___ conversation practice   ___ pronunciation drills
___ grammar exercises   ___ reading activities
___ listening activities   ___ vocabulary practice
___ pair or group work   ___ working individually

Personal Profile Task – Teacher Notes

Materials
- One worksheet (double-sided) per student
- Four large pieces of paper to hang around the room
- Markers for groups of students (four to a group)

Warm-up
To use this activity, begin by writing on the board or by dictating a question that students need to unscramble (e.g., *are English learning Why you?*). Then, ask the class to answer this question in pairs. Providing a minute or two for students to talk about the question together before eliciting an answer from one learner, or have one learner write their answer on the board. After checking the answer, explain that during this lesson the class will explore what students want from their English classes, and how they are going with their language study. At this point you can hand out the accompanying worksheet to each student with the side showing activities a, b and c facing up.

Worksheet Activity
After students receive their worksheet, ask them to write their name and the date on it, and to begin activity A by unscrambling the words to create sentences.

A few minutes later, ask students to check their unscrambled sentences with peers. Then, elicit correct answers. You could write these on the board, or you may call on random students to come out and write their answers up.

Answers might include:
  a) How can you improve your English outside the classroom? (homework, motivation)
  b) What activities do you like to do the most when learning English in class? (motivation)
  c) What about your English would you like to improve the most?/What would you like to improve the most about your English? (your needs, motivation)
  d) What do you find the most difficult about learning English? (weaknesses, your needs)

Photocopiable Content – Developing Great Lessons

Next, check that students understand the meaning of each of the words in the Activity B section, eliciting answers from the class as you go. Then, ask students to match each word to a question in Activity A (example answers are in brackets next to the unscrambled answers above). Once this is complete ask students to work in pairs to finish Activity C by having them create additional questions about their English classes using the following categories: homework, motivation, weaknesses, your needs.

At this point, you may want to have pairs swap their sheets with another pair so that they can undertake peer correction of the content. Students can then check the grammar/spelling of the sentences as well as the match to each category, ticking the question(s) that they like the most. After they complete this task, put students into groups of four (with the pair that they swapped their worksheets with). Ask students to point out the questions that they liked to the other pair, and they can explain why as you set up the next stage of the activity.

While students get into groups of four, put up four large pieces of paper around the room. Each piece should have a title at the top in large letters that corresponds to each of the categories from Activity B (homework, motivation, weaknesses, your needs). Hand out a marker to each group of four students. You can have one student from each group stand up in turn, and have that group dictate a question for the student to write up, or have one group have a student do this with the next group dictating and so on around the room. After each question is written, you can correct it for errors or have students undertake that task. Alternatively, if you have four groups of four in the class, you can have each group write their questions for each category on the sheets of paper. Students can then as a group decide which of all the questions they like and tick those. They can also error correct any of the sentences if the teacher has not done so already.

Ask students to find a new partner, and ask them to look at the different sheets around the classroom walls and decide which questions they would like to ask their partner. After they have chosen their questions, they should write their partner's name under Activity D, and write the questions along with their partner's answers to the questions in the space provided. As students undertake this activity, take down the sheets from around the room, and go around monitoring student's language use and activity progress. After the activity is complete (e.g., 20 minutes later), you can elicit some answers from different students about their partner for each of the categories from Activity B. These could be written on the board by the teacher as a summary.

Follow up/Review
Collect the students' worksheets and identify the questions with grammar or spelling errors. You can then use these sentences in a review lesson to provide delayed feedback. In this case, prepare a worksheet for students with the sentences listed in a column mixed with questions that are both grammatically error free and with all words spelled correctly. You can then use this worksheet in a competition style betting game.

For the game, you will need to provide students with $1,000 of imaginary money, printed classroom dollars, or points, then use the delayed feedback handout. Students then need to look over all of the sentences on the worksheet you have provided, and decide which of them are free of both grammatical and spelling errors, and then write these in the ten spaces provided on the handout. They need to bet their entire $1,000, and they can place the amount they want to bet for each sentence under the Bet heading. Explain that for each sentence that they get right, they will win double the amount of their initial bet for that sentence. After students have made their bets and corrections, collect the papers and redistribute them to the class (ensuring that no student receives their own). After that, go through the sentences with the class, eliciting the corrections as necessary and ensuring that students total the money gained or lost for each bet, writing this in the Gain/Loss column. The student whose paper has the highest grand total at the end of the activity is the winner. This lesson can also be adapted and played in groups. You may want to give the winning group/student a small prize (e.g., a candy, a token gesture like a paperclip, or add points to their avatar if using a system such as *Class Dojo*).

Personal Profile Task

Instructions: Work in pairs or a group.

Activity A.
Work together to unscramble the following words to make questions about learning English that you can ask your classmates.

   a) can English How you improve your outside the classroom?
   b) activities What you like do you to do when learning English the most in class?
   c) about your English you like to improve What would the most?
   d) the most difficult What do you find about learning English?

Activity B.
Match each question in activity A with a category in Activity B, write the letter of the question in the brackets next to the categories below:

   ( ) homework   ( ) motivation   ( ) weaknesses   ( ) your needs

Activity C.
Work with your partner and create four questions about English language learning and your classes, one question for each category in Activity B.

   a. _____
      _____

   b. _____
      _____

   c. _____
      _____

   d. _____
      _____

Activity D.

Partner's Name _____

a. _____

b. _____

c. _____

d. _____

Delayed Feedback Worksheet

Instructions: Look at each of the sentences below and correct the sentences that have grammatical mistakes or spelling errors with a pen or pencil. Then decide how much you want to bet that your corrections are correct and write this amount in the bet column. Finally, ensure that the grand total adds up to $1,000

Sentence		Bet	Win/Loss
1.			
2.			
3.			
4.			
5.			
6.			
7.			
8.			
9.			
10.			
	Grand total	$1,000	_____

Photocopiable Worksheets – Developing Great Lessons

Language Learning Activities Likes and Dislikes

Instructions: For the activity that you like, and the activity that you do not like:
1. Tick the focus you like or don't like the most.
2. Tick the type of activity you like or don't like the most.
3. Write one example of the activity that you like or don't like the most.
4. At the end of the lesson, cut the worksheet in half on the dotted line.
5. Hand the slips of paper to the teacher.

What kind of language learning activity <u>do</u> you like?

Focus:
( ) speaking, ( ) listening, ( ) reading, ( ) writing,
( ) pronunciation, ( ) grammar, ( ) vocabulary

Type:
( ) teacher-led class, ( ) pair activity, ( ) group work,
( ) worksheet, ( ) online activity, ( ) physical activity

Example: (e.g., flashcards, quizzes)
_____
_____

- -

What kind of language learning activity <u>don't</u> you like?

Focus:
( ) speaking, ( ) listening, ( ) reading, ( ) writing,
( ) pronunciation, ( ) grammar, ( ) vocabulary

Type:
( ) teacher-led class, ( ) pair activity, ( ) group work,
( ) worksheet, ( ) online activity, ( ) physical activity

Example: (e.g., flashcards, quizzes)
_____
_____

Teaching Diary Outline

Lesson

_____
_____

Objectives

1. Did students understand what to do in the lesson? If not, how can this be addressed in the future? Is there any need for improvement?

   _____
   _____
   _____
   _____
   _____
   _____

2. Was the lesson too easy or too difficult? What aspects made it as such?

   _____
   _____
   _____
   _____
   _____

3. What problems did students have during the lesson? Were these out of your control? Did you respond appropriately in helping to rectify these problems?

   _____
   _____
   _____
   _____
   _____
   _____

4. Did students achieve the learning outcome of the lesson? If not, why not? How can this be resolved in the future?

_____
_____
_____
_____
_____
_____
_____

5. What did students learn and practice that is useful for them? How do you know? How can content be modified in the future?

_____
_____
_____
_____
_____
_____
_____

Activities and Materials

1. Were the different materials and activities that you used appropriate for this lesson? If not, how can they be improved? Can you identify any other materials or activities that could have worked better than those used to teach the lesson?

_____
_____
_____
_____
_____
_____
_____
_____
_____
_____
_____

2. Did the materials and activities utilized during the lesson maintain student interest? If not, why did they lose interest? Can learner motivation be increased by the use of any other kind of material/activity?

_____
_____
_____
_____
_____
_____
_____
_____
_____

Students

1. Were all of the students consistently on task? If not, how can distractions be minimized and time on task increased?

_____
_____
_____
_____
_____
_____
_____

2. What aspects of the lesson did these students enjoy the most/least? What lead to this level of enjoyment? How can student enjoyment of lessons be maintained or increased?

_____
_____
_____
_____
_____
_____
_____
_____

3. Did the students engage in target language practice, using it in appropriate ways and in the intended manner? Was there too much TTT? Could it be minimized and STT increased?

_____
_____
_____
_____
_____
_____
_____

Classroom Management

1. Did activities run to time? Are any adjustments required for the pacing of the lesson? Can you better leverage your time?

_____
_____
_____
_____
_____
_____
_____

2. Were your instructions clear? Did all of the students understand what to do as the lesson progressed? Were transitions between phases of the lesson smooth?

_____
_____
_____
_____
_____
_____
_____
_____

Photocopiable Content – Developing Great Lessons

3. Did you provide an opportunity for all of the students to participate in the lesson? If not, are there any reasons for this, and can these be mitigated in the future?

_____
_____
_____
_____
_____
_____

4. Were you aware of student progress throughout the lesson? Were you able to help the slower students and provide additional content for those who finished the work early? If not, what preparations are required to address this?

_____
_____
_____
_____
_____
_____

5. Were there any behavioral, attitudinal, or other issues during the lesson? Did you handle these in an appropriate manner according to school policy? Was the outcome a satisfactory one? How can such incidences be handled better, or even be prevented?

_____
_____
_____
_____
_____
_____
_____
_____

Overall

1. Taking all of the above aspects into consideration, what facets of the lesson need to be addressed, or modified for future delivery? Essentially, what do you consider doing differently when teaching the lesson again?

   _____
   _____
   _____
   _____
   _____
   _____
   _____
   _____
   _____
   _____
   _____
   _____

2. What aspects of teaching this lesson has made you a better teacher? What aspects of the lesson did the students enjoy the most/least? What lead to this level of enjoyment? How can student enjoyment of lessons be maintained or increased?

   _____
   _____
   _____
   _____
   _____
   _____
   _____
   _____
   _____
   _____
   _____
   _____
   _____

Practicing Reductions in English

What + is + *word*	
What is up	
What is her	
What is his	

Word + me	
Give me	
Let me	

Word + have	
Could have	
Might have	
Must have	
Should have	
Would have	

Word + to	
Going to	
Got to	
Have to	
Has to	
Ought to	
Want to	

Did + you + *word*	
Did you eat	
Did you have	
Did you ever	

Word + you	
Bet you	
Don't you	
Get you	
Got you	
How are you	
How do you	
How did you	
How would you	
Did you	
What are you	
Want you	
What did you	
When did you	
Where did you	
Who did you	
Would you	

Word + of	
Front of	
Kind of	
Kinds of	
Lot of	
Lots of	
Out of	
Sort of	
Type of	

Do + not + know	
Do not know	
or	

Photocopiable Worksheets – Developing Great Lessons

Stress Practice Activity

Instructions: Read the words in the vocabulary box below, and decide if the stress is placed on the first, second, or third syllable of each word. Then, write the word in the appropriate column A, B, C, or D.

Vocabulary:

| audience | audition | composer | conductor |
| assistant | employee | Interview | manager |

A ●••	B •●•	C ••●	D •●••

Photocopiable Content – Developing Great Lessons

English Tongue Twisters

Easy

Big black bear: A big black bug bit the big black bear, but the big black bear bit the big black bug back!

Clam cream can: How can a clam cram in a clean cream can?

Four furious friends: Four furious friends fought for the phone.

Green glass globes: Green glass globes glow greenly.

Ice cream: I scream, you scream, we all scream for ice cream!

Noddy needed noodles: Noddy needed noodles in Neverland at noon to 'nom, nom, nom'.

Red leather: Red leather, yellow leather.

Spell New York: Knife and a fork, bottle and a cork, that is the way you spell New York.

Medium

Fuzzy wuzzy: Fuzzy Wuzzy was a bear, Fuzzy Wuzzy had no hair, Fuzzy Wuzzy wasn't very fuzzy, was he?

Good cook: How many cookies could a good cook cook if a good cook could cook cookies? A good cook could cook as many cookies as a good cook who could cook good cookies.

I have got a date: I've got a date at a quarter to eight. I'll see you at the gate, so don't be late.

I thought of thinking: I thought, I thought of thinking of thanking you.

One-one: One-one was a race horse. Two-two was one too. One-one won one race. Two-two won one too.

Peter piper: Peter Piper picked a peck of pickled peppers. A peck of pickled peppers Peter Piper picked. If Peter Piper picked a peck of pickled peppers, where's the peck of pickled peppers that Peter Piper picked?

Seven slick snails: Seven slick slimy snails, slowly sliding southward.

Thirty-three thieves: Thirty-three thieves rushed through the thick thorny thicket last Thursday.

Two witches: If two witches would watch two watches, which witch would watch which watch?

Whether the weather: Whether the weather be fine or whether the weather be not, whether the weather be cold, or whether the weather be hot, we'll weather the weather whether we like it or not.

Difficult

Betty butter: Betty bought some butter, but the butter that Betty bought was bitter, so Betty bought some better butter, and the better butter that Betty bought was better than the bitter butter that Betty bought before.

Biscuit mixer: I bought a bit of baking powder and baked a batch of biscuits. I brought a big basket of biscuits back to the bakery and baked a basket of big biscuits. Then I took the big basket of biscuits and the basket of big biscuits and mixed the big biscuits with the basket of biscuits that was next to the big basket and put a bunch of biscuits from the basket into a biscuit mixer and brought the basket of biscuits and the box of mixed biscuits and the biscuit mixer to the bakery and opened a tin of sardines.

David Drank: David drank a drink in downtown Denpasar at daylight to de-stress.

Doctor doctoring: When a doctor doctors a doctor, does the doctor doing the doctoring doctor as the doctor being doctored wants to be doctored, or does the doctor doing the doctoring doctor as he wants to doctor?

Mary Mac: Mary Mac's mother is making Mary Mac marry me. My mother is making me marry Mary Mac. Will I always be so Merry when Mary is taking care of me? Will I always be so merry when I marry Mary Mac?

Wish to wish: I wish to wish the wish that you wish to wish, but if you wish the wish the witch wishes, I won't wish the wish that you wish to wish.

Book/Movie/TV Show Presentation Report

Group Members _____
_____
_____

The Book/Movie/TV Show
Title _____

Characters _____

Genre/Mood _____

What is it about?
Plot Points _____
_____
_____
_____

Hook _____
_____
_____

Why would someone want to read or watch it?
Persuade _____
Interest _____
Engage _____

One thing that is
Exciting _____
Interesting _____
Funny _____

Overall recommendation _____
_____
_____
_____
_____

Example Oral Testing Procedure – Teacher Notes

The example below is a simple testing procedure that EFL teachers may choose to apply when conducting oral tests with their young adult students. It may prove particularly useful for those EFL teachers undertaking compulsory freshmen English conversation classes at college and university level in places like the Republic of Korea.

Exam Objectives
Primary Objective: To assess the oral skill level of students in a pre-planned communicative context, as well as testing listening comprehension through question-/answer-based tasks.
Secondary Objective: To allow students to expand their use of language centered on a theme of their own interest, and to engage in oral communication on a familiar topic covered by the class syllabus.

Exam Approach
Students sign up for the exam, in class, one week prior to the testing date. Students should be allowed to select their own partner, and to come in pairs to the exam. As a result, students will feel more comfortable and relaxed during the testing process.

The exam structure is 'semi-free'. Students should be informed that chapter headings of the course syllabus provide the topics for the exam, and that they can discuss any one area of relevance to each topic. Typical topics covered by course syllabuses include the following: around the community, eating, education and school life, friends and family, the global village, health, homes, love and dating, nature, work and lifestyles. As example areas that are relevant to school life, the instructor may provide the following suggestions of topic areas: activities and membership of school clubs, participation and impressions of the university festival, and a comparison between high school and university life. Students should then be tested for approximately 10 minutes per pair.

Exam Method
Initially, students should engage in a prepared conversation for around five minutes. At this point, the examination criteria (see

below) should be checked by the instructor at the relevant points of the students' conversation. As students should have pre-planned their conversations, they should be expected to exhibit a high degree of familiarity with the topic material.

Secondly, after they have completed their paired conversation, the instructor should ask several questions of each learner, and the points of evaluation for each examinee can then be further completed or re-evaluated as necessary. At this phase of the test, the instructor's approach should be based upon the selected topic of the student pair. For example, if students elect to discuss a topic such as their hometown, then the instructor's line of questioning might revolve around asking the students to persuade the instructor that it is a good place to visit for a few days holiday. This phase of testing should be planned to take around five minutes per student.

Exam Critique
Overall, students should be able to complete a pre-planned conversation of the appropriate length for the test conditions. Some students may want to read all of their pre-planned conversation, even though the evaluation is not a reading test. As appropriate, instructors can allow students to bring notes or memory cards along with them to the test.

Further, familiarity with the topic material selected by students should allow them to adequately respond to the questions asked by the instructor in the second phase of testing. Even those students who never speak in class should be able to interact, to a higher or lesser degree, with the instructor at an appropriate level for the line of questioning.

The downside to this kind of testing in large class environments where an instructor has more than 200 students, and up to 300 students to test, is that both students and instructors feel rushed especially with only 10 minutes per exam. Therefore, times should not be indicated on the exam sign-up sheet; only number order should be provided. In this way, students know that they can take as long as they need, as the next pair will enter only after they complete the exam. This approach will see students generally keep to the set five minutes for their prepared conversation but with some going over and some going under. The instructor can the control the line of questioning to see the pair finish up on schedule.

Exam Evaluation

Evaluation should be conducted when students engage in their prepared conversations. Revision of the instructor's evaluation can be conducted, if necessary, during the question/answer phase of the exam. For each point of evaluation, students are graded on a Likert-type scale (1 being poor through to 5 being excellent). The comments section of the exam evaluation sheet can be used to record points of feedback for each student, for example, problematic points of pronunciation or their recurrent grammar errors.

Fluency of Speech. This point of evaluation should be based on the smoothness of speech rather than speed, and with consideration of the normal use of hesitancy in conversation. If students pause their conversation to giggle, or if they have memorized their conversation and do not utilize their inherent communication skills, then this should reflect in a lower rating. Students who speak efficiently and without awkwardness should in turn be granted a higher rating.

Grammar Use. It is unrealistic to expect that any EFL student will come to an exam and speak without any grammar problems, so emphasis should be placed on being able to understand the student's communicative intent even if grammar errors are present in sentence structures. However, continual use of the same grammar errors, such as the use of simple past for all past tense terms, should reflect in a lower rating. Alternatively, those students who are able to recognize that they have made a grammar error, and correct it during conversation, should be given a higher rating.

Listening Comprehension. This phase of evaluation is initially tested during the prepared conversation section of the exam. As some students will not understand what their partners are saying, they will remain silent and wait for their partner to repeat their statement, and this should reflect in a lower rating. At other times, a student could ask for clarification or ask their partner to repeat what they had said, and this should reflect in a higher rating. Furthermore, this section of evaluation should be applied in the question/answer tasks of the exam. Some students may not understand the instructor's question, even after rewording, whereas other students will understand it immediately.

Photocopiable Content – Developing Great Lessons

Pronunciation. As native English speakers possess a high degree of tolerance to ambiguity accent is not considered a viable point of exam evaluation except where it hinders communicative understanding. In situations where continual mispronunciation occurs, or understanding is lost due to incorrect pronunciation of terminology, students should be given a lower rating. Alternatively, if students correct their mispronunciation, or attempt to correct it throughout the exam, then this should reflect in a higher rating.

Vocabulary Appropriateness and Complexity. Depending on the student choice of topic, certain terms or vocabulary items can be selected from the course materials and incorporated within student conversational presentations. If students use higher level vocabulary and select terms taught from the textbook, then they should receive a higher rating. If students employ very simple vocabulary terms for a complex topic, such as health, then this should reflect in a lower rating.

Example Exam Evaluation Scale and Rubric

The following is an example of how you can go about assessing students on the fly. The *oral exam interview testing* scale provides space to write the name and number of each student. Following this is the range of criteria that the assessor is evaluating with ratings from 1 to 5. There is also space for additional comments or observations that the examiner may like to make after they have provided each student's total score. To guide an assessor in using the ratings correctly, they should refer to the following descriptions regarding the ratings for each category.

Fluency
5. The speaker is confident, speaks naturally with no hesitations, and ideas run smoothly together.
3. The speaker hesitates, with pauses in thought natural but distracting.
1. The speaker hesitates and the flow of sentences and that of speech is interrupted.

Grammar
5. The speaker uses the correct form of grammar throughout, especially the structures that have been specifically taught during lessons.
3. The speaker tends to use the correct form of grammar throughout, and applies a number of structures that were taught to students throughout the course.
1. The speaker struggles to use the correct form of grammar, and there is no use of the structures that were taught to students during class time.

Listening Comprehension/ Interactive Communication
5. Students understand what is being said and asked of them and are able to take an active part in the conversation as a result.
3. Students understand most of what is being said and asked of them, and they are able to use language to ask for repetition or rewording.
1. Students do not understand much, if anything, of what is being said or asked of them.

Pronunciation
5. The speaker uses the correct intonation, stress, rhythm, tone, and intonation patterns of the language.
3. The speaker engages in some mispronunciations, but the intonation, stress, rhythm, and tone makes the speaker clear even though they may be hard to understand at times.
1. The speaker often mispronounces words or is difficult to understand due to rhythm or the wrong use of stress or intonations, or is misunderstood due to tone.

Vocabulary Appropriateness and Complexity
5. The speaker's vocabulary range is sufficient, and words taught are being used appropriately.
3. The speaker's vocabulary range is sufficient, but there is no use of words that were taught to the student. Some words are used with correct meanings but there may be occasional issues.
1. The speaker relies on a clearly limited use of vocabulary that may also be incorrect.

Oral Exam Interview Testing Scale

Student Name: _____ **Number:** _____

Fluency of Speech

1	2	3	4	5
Poor	Weak	Average	Strong	Excellent

Grammar Use

1	2	3	4	5
Poor	Weak	Average	Strong	Excellent

Listening Comprehension

1	2	3	4	5
Poor	Weak	Average	Strong	Excellent

Pronunciation

1	2	3	4	5
Poor	Weak	Average	Strong	Excellent

Vocabulary Complexity

1	2	3	4	5
Poor	Weak	Average	Strong	Excellent

TOTAL: _____

Comments: _____

_____

_____

_____

_____

_____

_____

_____

_____

_____

_____

\multicolumn{3}{	c	}{**The Technology Integration Evaluation Rubric (TIER)**}
Aspect	Criteria	Score
The Technology (hardware or software)	Matches with core learning objectives (e.g., developing fluency, increasing listening practice, practicing vocabulary)	1 2 3 4 5
	Content assists with learner development (e.g., provides communicative fluency, grammar-based activities)	1 2 3 4 5
	Meshes well with the instructor (e.g., teaching style, classroom management techniques, time for development and incorporation into lesson plans)	1 2 3 4 5
	Appropriate for use with the target learner (e.g., age, language level, motivation)	1 2 3 4 5
Content	Content and software is error-free (e.g., no bugs; no spelling, grammar, or pronunciation errors)	1 2 3 4 5
	Provides relevant content and topics (e.g., authentic, timeless, up-to-date, holistically useful)	1 2 3 4 5
	Content can be modified, tailored, or guided for effective use (e.g., add content on demand, rework content to a lesson)	1 2 3 4 5
	Content is reusable (e.g., with the same students, across classes, across the curriculum)	1 2 3 4 5
	Content is shareable (e.g., not locked to a single student/class, distributable to other stakeholders)	1 2 3 4 5
Resources	Community of content (e.g., a range of resources exist that can be adapted or used as-is)	1 2 3 4 5
\multicolumn{3}{	c	}{*Ratings*: 1 Poor 2 Fair 3 Average 4 Good 5 Excellent}

Photocopiable Content – Developing Great Lessons

Reflection	Instructor use of the technology provides growth (e.g., leads to action research, pedagogical improvement)	1 2 3 4 5
	Easy to teach others how to apply the technology (e.g., develop a walkthrough)	1 2 3 4 5
	Variable assessment types (e.g., poll or multiple-choice for either formative or summative use)	1 2 3 4 5
	Reviewability (e.g., if assessable: grades can be seen and reviewed; work can be resubmitted by students)	1 2 3 4 5
Usability	Provides a learning shift (e.g., creates multi-modal learning, meets set standards; provides completion of competency pathways)	1 2 3 4 5
	Improves on past learning experiences (e.g., easier distribution or revision of content)	1 2 3 4 5
	Usefulness (e.g., provides formative/summative assessment; can be utilized for revision, homework, skills targeting)	1 2 3 4 5
	Distinctive, provides something old in a new way (e.g., polls students instantly with anonymity)	1 2 3 4 5
	Suitable for — in-class work	1 2 3 4 5
	Suitable for — out-of-class work	1 2 3 4 5
	Suitable for — individual work	1 2 3 4 5
	Suitable for — pair work	1 2 3 4 5
	Suitable for — group work	1 2 3 4 5
	Suitable for — use with accompanying handouts	1 2 3 4 5
	Suitable for — use alongside other technologies (phone/website/etc)	1 2 3 4 5
Score	Obtain a total across all aspects to compare between various application types, websites, or other digital language learning technologies	_____

Ratings: 1 Poor 2 Fair 3 Average 4 Good 5 Excellent

6. Lesson Planning

Overview
The lesson plan serves as the cornerstone of teaching. Well-developed lesson plans provide what becomes the essential elements of the classroom experience for both teachers and students. The material under focus is just as important as the delivery structure, and the way that your lesson plan is laid out should serve to provide an optimal learning environment for your students. Essential to it then is determining what you will be teaching, how you will teach it, what the learners and you will achieve by the end of it, and how you know the lesson has been successful.

Learning Outcomes
1. Understand the basics of lesson plan development.
2. Develop comprehensive lesson plans.
3. Consider the importance of using lesson plans as a means of engaging in reflective teaching.

The Lesson Plan
The lesson plan is evidence of the thinking process behind content delivery, and it is used as a guide to keep you and your students on track throughout a lesson or unit. For those who are just starting out in teaching, these may need to be comprehensive and extremely detailed, and that is why they are practiced and developed in this way in this book, but to those more seasoned educators, a lesson plan may simply consist of a few notes or a mind map of how the lesson could develop. In either case, when it comes to implementation, and when in class, first and foremost is to teach the lesson and not the plan!

Initial Considerations and the Lesson Plan Foundational Framework
A few things to consider before you begin to create a lesson plan are perhaps the following:
1. Will you review content that you have already been teaching or will you begin to teach new content? If the target content is new, ensure that it is appropriate, at the correct level for students, and follows on from previous learning tasks, objectives, and content.

2. What will be the linguistic focus of the lesson? Will it be one of the four skills (reading, writing, listening, speaking) or will it be aspects of pronunciation or grammar, and what are the activities and learning objectives that students will need to achieve to ensure success.
3. Will you teach alone or will you have an assistant? Determine how best to maximize your time and student time when delivering and practicing the content of the lesson. Can you use your assistant to help with group and pair checks, deliver instructions and handouts, and so on, or will you be using class leaders to help with these processes?

With the above in mind, you need to have a framework to begin developing a lesson plan, and to incorporate these considerations into its initial development. It may be useful to use an outline or guide with the following headings (matching that found in the photocopiable section of this chapter).

Rationale

The rationale behind the teaching process should be brief and define any terminology from the literature that you may be using. It will ideally be based on your theory of teaching and learning or that expected by the school where the lesson is being provided. For example: How to tell the time, with a presentation, practice and production (PPP) approach to be used as part of a communicative language teaching (CLT) lesson that employs total physical response (TPR). PPP is being applied to move learners to understanding by presenting the material, helping them practice it, and then having them produce it using CLT to emphasize socialization and collaboration in pair and group work, while TPR is used to help engage young learners further with the content.

Learning context

This is particularly useful if the lesson plan is being produced as part of a formal course and for submission as part of teacher training. Here, you should provide a description of your teaching and learning environment using the following subheadings.

The practitioner (years of teaching service, number of years in present position, what classes have been taught, to who, and at what levels, and the usual teaching style).

The students (age range, gender, total number, practitioner perceptions of the actual language level, learning styles, classroom behavior of the students, and differentiation requirements).
The school situation (how many teachers and students, courses provided, location).
The classroom context (length of lessons, and the kind of activities usually completed and why).

Materials and Resources
These need to be listed so that you can prepare them in advance, and this is particularly useful if the lesson is being delivered as one section of a multi-lesson unit. Here, you should describe in detail the materials and resources that you will use throughout the lesson using the following subheadings. (Be sure to include the nature and usage of the material, and any personal expenses required.)
Pre-prepared material.
In-class material.
Homework and follow-up materials.
Additional or supplementary material.

Aims and goals.
These also need to be described, and here, you should identify the aim(s) of the lesson (tied to the rationale, with one or two clear statements).

Implementation.
Detail the procedure(s) and/or method(s), e.g., if you are using the lesson plan over several class periods, then this can be outlined by stages such as: Lesson 1 to Lesson 5, or Step 1 to Step 5.

Outcomes and implications.
The expected outcomes and implications of the lesson are also useful to document as these can then be revisited after the lesson is taught. This serves to help you identify what worked for you and your students, or what might not have worked, and how these things might then be improved during future implementations. Here, you should provide a brief commentary using the following subheadings.
Anticipated versus actual outcome(s). What actually happened at the end of the day? Did the project work or not (including to your satisfaction)?

What contribution did the use of technology provide over non-technology use (if any)? What major problems emerged? What might solve those problems in the future? What would you change the next time you teach this lesson?

Implications. Where will this lesson go in the future (both for the class/students and you)? Can you develop an action plan for the future based on the content or language skills that students have gained during the lesson?

Developing the Lesson Plan

This can be a detailed written guide that you, or another instructor if they have to teach on your behalf, will follow when delivering the actual lesson. In the photocopiable section, you can find a general guide with the following headings and subheadings.

Teaching Context

This section of the lesson plan details information regarding the learners, along with the purpose and intent of lesson delivery.

Levels of language proficiency and student maturity. Student language level, e.g., beginner, intermediate, advanced. Student age range, e.g., young learners, adults.

Lesson length. Time allotted for the class, e.g., 35-45 minutes.

Lesson topic. Major theme or focus of the lesson, e.g., numbers and time.

Objectives. Lesson aims, e.g., to teach students how to tell the time and date accurately.

Outcomes. Learning outcomes, e.g., students will be able to read analog and digital timepieces.

Relevant prior learning. Anything that the students need to know before starting work on this lesson's content, e.g., students need to have completed Chapter Two of the book, and have previously met language associated with appointments, calendars, and timekeeping.

Teacher Preparation

This section of the lesson plan details information regarding the necessary teacher requirements regarding the appropriate and effective delivery of lesson elements.

Hardware. Types of computer or peripherals required, e.g., USB sticks, tablets.

Software. Name of software used, e.g., Photo Story 3, Microsoft Word.
Webpage links. Hyperlink to web resources, e.g., www.google.com
Additional resources. Other necessary materials for the lesson, e.g., handouts, worksheets, textbooks.

Procedure

This section of the lesson plan details the actual stages of the lesson, and what is expected of the instructor and the learner during each. Here are examples of the objectives (and focuses) in each stage:

Review stage (if required, 5 minutes). Encourage the use of previously acquired language.

Warm-up stage (10 minutes). Introduce new concepts and language to students in a meaningful manner.

Main stage (20 minutes). Allow students to utilize technology to become familiar with and apply the concepts and language content introduced in the lesson.

Practice stage (15 minutes). Allow learners to utilize the skills and language that they are expected to acquire during the lesson in a practical way.

Lesson summation stage (10 minutes). The instructor reinforces the importance of language concepts and skills acquired, stating how they will be useful in forthcoming lessons.

Further Considerations

This section of the lesson plan provides a means for the teacher to reflect on the lesson, place back-up plans to turn to if things go awry, prepare those activities that will incorporate lesson outcomes into future activities, and to remind themselves of how they may use resources in the room such as the board.

Follow-up activities. Suggest material that can be applied in a follow up class. Also, be ready with activities for students who complete their class work earlier than expected.

Contingency plan(s). Always prepare an alternate teaching scenario in case of any problems, e.g., a sudden power outage, or a timetabling issue could make the assigned room unavailable.

Evaluation (students). Determine how you will assess students on what they have learned throughout the lesson, e.g., provide exit tickets, a short review quiz, and so on.

Evaluation (teacher). Reflect on what worked well and what did not, and how you might deliver the lesson differently or improve upon it when running it again.

The board. Ideally, throughout the lesson, you will use the board in a specific way. Use this space to draw what will appear on the board, and how you might use it throughout the lesson. You could write the outcomes or points to be covered on the far left, and the lesson roadmap, new vocabulary and words introduced to students throughout the lesson on the right. The center part of the board can be reserved for core parts of the lesson at the top, the structures to be practiced or learned in the middle, with the area below then being for student use if asked to write or draw.

Mind Mapping a Lesson Plan

As you get more experienced, you can begin to develop your own method for constructing lesson plans that is suitable to both your own teaching context and style, and no longer need to write everything out. A fast method, once you gain the necessary skills and practice, is to develop lessons following a mind map. The subsequent example is similar to that previously presented, but it is graphically represented rather than in table form.

To help you think about what to include in such a mind map, you may want to consider the following, and then review Figure 3.1 which is based on the five-minute lesson plan technique developed by Morrison (2019).

Aims/Big Picture. How does the lesson fit overall into the syllabus/course objectives?

Objectives/Outcomes. What language points will students practice during the lesson, what should they be learning throughout?

Engagement. How will you keep the learners focused at each stage of the lesson? What special activities will you use? How do you transition from one to the other?

Stickiness. What points do you want students to remember from the lesson and be able to always apply later? How will you make this happen? If students have to remember only one thing from this lesson, what is it?

Linkage. How does this lesson tie into past lessons, or future ones? How can this lesson (or the activities applied within it) be used to review or to introduce new topics/units?

Lesson Planning 371

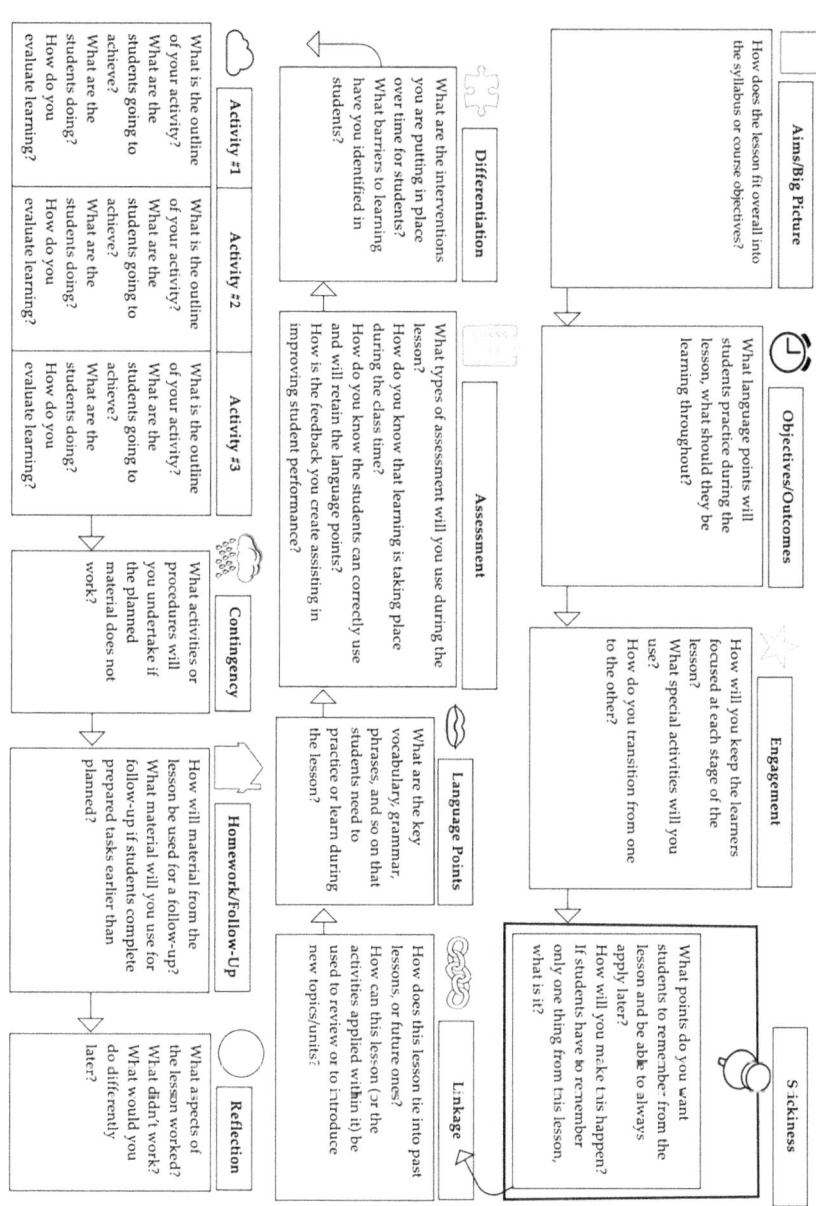

Figure 6.1 Mind Mapping a Lesson Plan – General Guide

Language Points. What are the key vocabulary items, grammar points, phrases, and so on that students need to practice or learn during the lesson?

Assessment. What types of assessment will you use during the lesson? How do you know that learning is taking place during the class time? How do you know the students can correctly use and will retain the language points? How is the feedback you create assisting in improving student performance?

Differentiation. What are the interventions you are putting in place over time for students? What barriers to learning have you identified in students?

Activity 1 to Activity 3. What is the outline of your activity? What are the students going to achieve? What are the students doing? How do you evaluate learning?

Contingency Plans. What activities or procedures will you undertake if the planned material does not work?

Homework/Follow-up. How will material from the lesson be used for a follow-up? What material will you use for follow-up if students complete prepared tasks earlier than planned?

Reflection. What aspects of the lesson worked? What didn't work? What would you do differently later?

Summary

This chapter focuses on the importance of a lesson plan, and outlines the basics of lesson plan development, the rationale for creating and using lesson plans, both as a guide for teaching and as a means of analyzing classes while conducting a process of self-reflection. To this end, a comprehensive lesson plan template for new teachers to familiarize themselves with, and to easily follow when starting out teaching was provided. A method for more seasoned teachers to follow was also presented.

Review

Content Quiz
Lesson Planning

To help solidify some of the concepts introduced by this chapter the following multiple-choice and true or false quizzes might be helpful for you to undertake. So that you can check the accuracy of your responses, an answer key can be found following the quizzes.

Multiple-Choice

Circle **a**, **b**, or **c** for the answer that best completes the sentence posed in each question.

1. Clear teaching goals help ...
   a) improve academic performance and student motivation.
   b) students to get better grades.
   c) the teacher to be more prepared.

2. A very basic lesson plan would include ...
   a) learning objectives, teaching and learning activities, as well as assessments.
   b) content, learning objectives, and assessment.
   c) content, context, assessment, and learning objectives.

3. Strategic lesson planning helps lessons to ...
   a) become more interesting.
   b) connect to form meaningful learning experiences for students.
   c) keep teachers bored.

4. The most important element of a lesson plan is ...
   a) clear learning objectives.
   b) the inclusion of fun activities.
   c) appropriate differentiation.
   d)

5. A lesson plan must be ...
   a) standard testing that is focused and coherent.
   b) rigid and inflexible.
   c) flexible, coherent, and student centered.

True or False

Circle **a** (true) if you think that the statement is correct, or **b** (false) if you think that the statement is incorrect.

1. Lesson plans can contain as many activities as a teacher desires as long as they are relevant to the lesson and appropriate to the learner, and can be completed in the time available.
    a) True.
    b) False.

2. The number of activities will be limited by the amount of class time that you have unless the activities have been set for homework, in which case you should be mindful of the time it will take students to complete them (particularly if they are also working or studying fulltime).
    a) True.
    b) False.

3. A list of materials is not required on a lesson plan as long as you know what these are and can remember them.
    a) True.
    b) False.

4. A warm up activity should be a long and complicated one that tests the students' prior knowledge on any new topic introduced.
    a) True.
    b) False.

5. It is good practice to aim for more student talk time than teacher talk time.
    a) True.
    b) False.

Quiz Answers
Lesson Planning

Multiple-Choice
1. a
2. a
3. b
4. a
5. c

True or False
1. T
2. T
3. F
4. F
5. T

Suggested Readings

Brown, H. (2015). *Teaching by principles: An interactive approach to language pedagogy.* Pearson.

Brunn, P. (2010). *The lesson planning handbook: Essential strategies that inspire student thinking and learning.* Scholastic Teaching Resources.

Morrison, R. (2019). 5-Minute Lesson Plan. Pedagogy Blog. https://pedagogy.blog/2015/12/06/5-minute-lesson-plan-by-ross-morrison-mcgill

Riddell, (2014). *Teach EFL: The Complete Guide* (4th ed.). Teach Yourself.

Skowron, J. (2015) *Powerful lesson planning: Every teacher's guide to effective instruction.* Skyhorse.

Scrivener, J. *Learning teaching: The essential guide to English language teaching* (3rd Ed.). MacMillan. [Chapter 6]

Thomas, S. (2019). ELT resources and lesson ideas. http://eltresource.com

Walker, L. (2008). *The essential guide to lesson planning.* Pearson.

Photocopiable Content

This section of the text includes a variety of material that are free to photocopy and use with your planning. It contains examples of the following content:
- Lesson plan development and reflection guide template
- Lesson plan template
- Lesson plan mind map template

Lesson Plan Development and Reflection Guide Template

Rationale	

Learning Context	
The Practitioner	
The Students	
The School Situation	
The Classroom Context	

Materials and Resources	
Pre-Prepared Material	
In-Class Material	
Homework/Follow-up Materials	
Additional Supplementary Material	

Aims and Goals

Implementation

Reflection: Outcomes and Implications

Anticipated Versus Actual Outcome(s)

Implications

Lesson Plan Template

Teaching Context	
Level of proficiency and maturity	
Lesson length	
Lesson topic	
Objectives	
Outcomes	
Relevant prior learning	

Teacher Preparation	
Hardware	
Software	
Webpage links	
Additional resources	

Photocopiable Templates – Lesson Planning

Procedure
Review Stage (if required: 5 minutes)   *Objective:*   *Teacher:*   *Students:*
Warm-up Stage (10 minutes)   *Objective:*   *Teacher:*   *Students:*
Main Stage (20 minutes)   *Objective:*   *Teacher:*   *Students:*
Practice Stage (15 minutes)   *Objective:*   *Teacher:*   *Students:*
Lesson Summation Stage (10 minutes)   *Objective:*   *Teacher:*   *Students:*

Further Considerations	
Follow-Up Activities	
Contingency Plan(s)	
Evaluation	
The Board	

Lesson Plan Mind Map Template

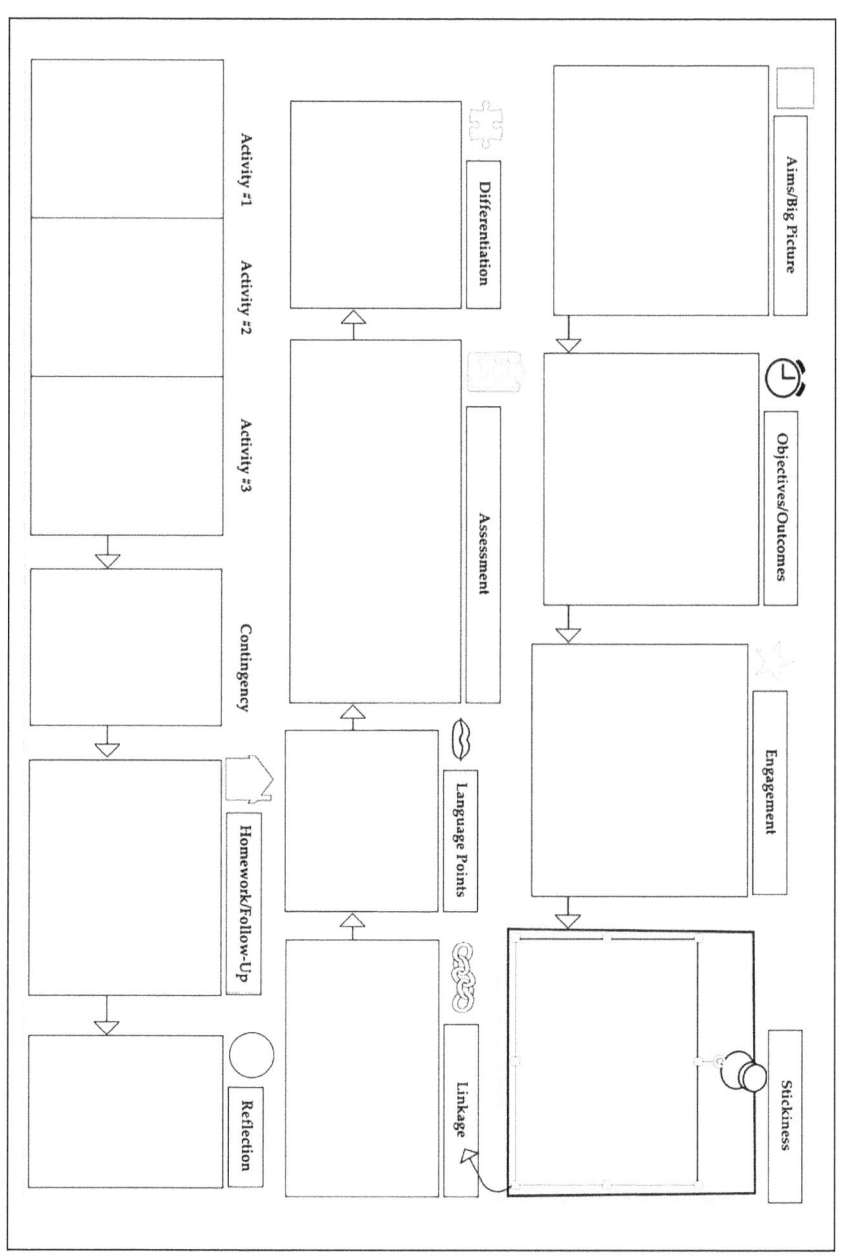

Photocopiable Content – Lesson Planning

PART THREE:
SOUND, MEANING,
AND FORM

7. Pronunciation in Teaching

Overview

At its core, pronunciation is one of the most important aspects of learning an additional language, as it is the way in which the words and the language is spoken. For teachers, accurate pronunciation and the ability to teach it accurately are equally important, and this is especially so in an English as a foreign language (EFL) context as you may be the only speaker of the target language that the learner interacts with. Unfortunately, it is also an aspect of language learning that is often neglected in many teaching programs, or one thought to emerge or improve as students engage in the practice of the four skills (reading writing, listening, speaking), even though it is an aspect of language that is central to communicative competence. This chapter therefore presents the most important aspects of the international phonetic alphabet (IPA), as it is these symbols and representations that are used to denote the sounds of a language. This then leads to a discussion involving an exploration of those aspects of stress and intonation that relate to how sounds are formed and altered. Relevant to this are the ways and means of drawing learner attention to features of pronunciation aspects that incorporate both direct and indirect means of teaching pronunciation are then coupled with the delivery of tasks and activities central to the testing of pronunciation in teaching.

Learning Outcomes

1. Gain a basic working understanding of phonology, stress, and intonation.
2. Comprehend and be able to read components of the international phonetic alphabet chart.
3. Distinguish how best to impart your knowledge of pronunciation onto learners.
4. Discover a number of means for drawing student attention to specific features of pronunciation.
5. Understand how to apply various games and activities with learners when explicitly or implicitly teaching pronunciation.

6. Uncover a number of activities that you can adapt to the testing of pronunciation, along with aspects of their practicality, reliability, validity, backwash, and spin-off.

Pronunciation – Phonology, Stress, Intonation

Phonology

Pronunciation covers aspects such as phonology (the sounds of a language), stress rhythm, and intonation. The international phonetic alphabet (IPA) is an alphabetic system of notation developed in order to illustrate the standardized representations of the sounds of spoken languages. Here, the sounds of all human languages are represented by the term *phonetic,* with *phonemic* used to refer to the transcriptions of a specific sound system. For your reference, the full IPA chart can be found in the photocopiable section of this chapter. There are also a number of websites and applications that provide interactive charts for teachers and learners to utilize, as well as those that will transcribe any word or phrase into phonemics (see the IPA listing in the useful resources section of this book).

The IPA chart contains several diagrams including those for consonants, vowels, diacritics, suprasegmentals, and other symbols. Of note, diacritics are those symbols, or glyphs, that are used to indicate that a particular pronunciation (in terms of accent, stress, tone) or meaning might change. Suprasegmentals are those markers that denote specific features of consonants and vowels (e.g., ' for stress, and : for a long sound). Perhaps the most important aspects of the IPA chart to understand for teachers of English to speakers of other languages are those sections pertaining to consonants and vowels.

The IPA consonant chart (see figure 1.1) arranges consonants in columns according to their *place* of articulation in the mouth, with the rows of the chart indicating the *manner* of articulation. *Voicing* is also shown in the chart by the placement of symbols to the left or right of a cell in the table. Those sounds placed to the left are voiceless, while those to the right are voiced. The consonants also range from the front of the mouth on the left of the chart, to the back of the mouth on the right. When describing a consonant segment, it would typically be described in the order of voicing, then place of articulation, followed by the manner of articulation (e.g., /p/ is a voiceless bilabial stop). Of note, the shaded area of the table represents those sounds that have been determined to be impossible to pronounce.

	Bilabial	Labiodental	Dental	Alveolar	Postalveolar	Retroflex	Palatal	Velar	Uvular	Pharyngeal	Glottal
Plosive	p b			t d		ʈ ɖ	c ɟ	k g	q ɢ		ʔ
Nasal	m	ɱ		n		ɳ	ɲ	ŋ	N		
Trill	B			r					R		
Tap or Flap		ⱱ		ɾ		ɽ					
Fricative	ɸ β	f v	θ ð	s z	ʃ ʒ	ʂ ʐ	ç ʝ	x ɣ	χ ʁ	ħ ʕ	h ɦ
Lateral fricative				ɬ ɮ							
Approximant		ʋ		ɹ		ɻ	j	ɰ			
Lateral approximant				l		ɭ	ʎ	ʟ			

Figure 7.1 The IPA Chart Consonant Diagrams
(see the appendix for the full chart, and license for use)

The IPA Chart vowel diagram arranges vowel sounds on a trapezium, with the important aspects to note being those of highness, backness, and lip rounding. Looking closely at figure 1.2, it can be seen that the vertical axis of the vowel trapezium illustrates vowel closeness, with the horizontal axis denoting vowel *backness*, with front vowels appearing to the left of the diagram. In other words, the vertical axis (up-down) and the horizontal axis (left-right) pertain to the position of the tongue in the mouth when a vowel is pronounced. Up-down relates to how high or low your tongue is in the mouth, the *highness*, or the proximity of the tongue to the roof of the mouth, and how open or closed your mouth will be when pronouncing that vowel sound. The mouth will be relatively wide and open when pronouncing those sounds at the bottom of the chart and relatively closed when pronouncing those words at the top of the chart. So, left-right relates to how far forward or backwards your tongue sits in the mouth when producing a particular sound on the chart. The third aspect of the chart to note is the pronunciation of the first or second vowel in a pair. The first in the pair does not have *lip rounding*, while the second of the pair is pronounced with it (i.e., the lips of the mouth will make an 'o'-shape when producing lip rounding). When describing a vowel, it would typically be described in the order of height, rounding, backness (e.g., /i/ is a high unrounded front vowel).

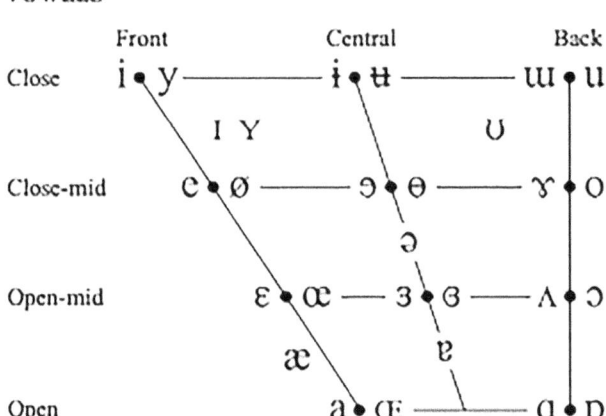

*Figure 7.2 The IPA Chart Vowel Trapezium
(see the appendix for the full chart, and license for use)*

In the teaching of language, and when using the IPA chart, pronunciation is typically written between slashes (i.e., //.) The chart provides one symbol per phoneme, where the word 'example' would be written in American English as /ɪɡˈzæmpəl/ and in British English as /ɪɡˈzɑːmpl/. Depending on the variety of English you might be teaching there will be a range of differences in the pronunciation of the speaker, and there are different charts available for specific languages. For example, there are those for Received Pronunciation (RP), otherwise known as standard British pronunciation, those for General American English (GA or GenAm) which has fewer vowel sounds, and so on (see Thornbury, 2010).

Stress

In English, speech rhythm utilizes tone units, where a word or group of words carries a single stressed syllable with the others lightened (Ur, 2002). This stress is often indicated in dictionaries and in phonemic transcription with a short vertical line above (ˈ) and before the stressed syllable, and can also be indicted to learners using capitals (e.g., the ˈ before pyoo in kəmˈpyoodər shows that syllable to be stressed). Word stress usually sees that part of the word pronounced with a louder, longer, and higher pitch than the unstressed parts (e.g., using the visual system of representing stress we see that with the word 'comPUter', the middle part of the word is stressed and indicated by placing it in bold and uppercase lettering, while in '**SEN**tence' the first syllable is stressed, and in **pre**sen**TA**tion [ˌprez·ən·ˈtā·SH(ə)n, ˌprēˌzenˈtāSH(ə)n] the third of four syllables is stressed with secondary stress indicated by bold underling of the first syllable or 'ˌ' if using the phonemic system).

Word stress can also be viewed graphically when looking at the waveform of recorded words. Using an application that shows audio waveforms is one way that a student can see where they tend to place stress on certain words, or sentences, and seeing if this matches with those of native speaker stress placement. Figure 1.3 shows the waveform for the word 'computer', as spoken by a male native speaker of English, and illustrates the primary stress and aspiration very well. In some cases, students may need to be taught how to read such waveforms if they are unfamiliar with them. Of note, word stress is also closely related to vowel reduction (i.e., a vowel sound like /ə/ or /ɪ/ is pronounced instead of another full vowel).

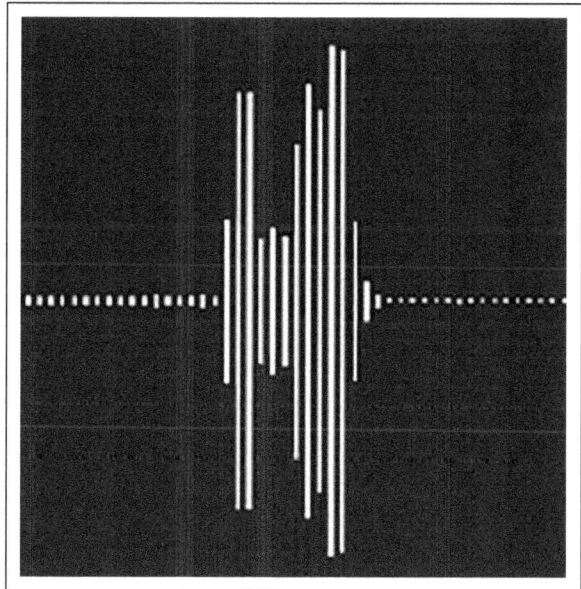

Figure 7.3 Example Waveform
Illustrating Word Stress and Aspiration for the Word Computer
as Spoken by a Male Native-Speaker of English

A means of using such a waveform with students can see you provide a worksheet where they are able to write vocabulary items in one column and the phonemics for them in another, and then after recording these words, identifying where there may be a need for correction. Such a worksheet is provided in the photocopiable section of this chapter. Students will be able to use the sheet when speaking vocabulary aloud, particularly in combination with applications that show the waveform of the recorded voice (e.g., GoldWave). The sheet could also be used with students in a classroom setting, with the teacher identifying where there may be areas to work on to help the learner identify where they can improve upon their pronunciation. During such a time you might also like to remind students that in general there are four rules for word stress (see Table 1.1).

General Word Stress Rules		
Syllable	When to Stress	Examples
First	Most two-syllable nouns and adjectives.	CLImate, KNOWledge, FLIPpant, SPAcious.
Second	Most two-syllable verbs.	acQUIRE, deCIDE.
Second to last	Words ending in: -ic, -sion, -tion, -cion.	ecSTATic, geoGRAPHic, exTENsion, retriBUtion.
Third from last	Words ending in: -al -cy, -ty, -phy, -gy.	deMOCracy, unCERtainty, geOGraphy, geographical, radiOLogy, exCEPtional.
Note. These are general rules only. You may also remind learners that the schwa sound (/ə/) is never stressed in a sentence, so they know that it isn't where stress falls in a sentence.		

Table 7.1 The Four General Rules of Word Stress

Sentence level stress creates the rhythm of a language. Most sentences will contain content words, or key words (e.g., those that carry meaning), and structure words that make the sentence grammatically correct (e.g., those of form). Word stress is placed on one syllable within a word, while sentence stress is placed on certain words within a sentence. Sometimes sentence stress changes the meaning of the sentence as well (see Table 1.2 for an example).

Shifting Stress – Sentences	
Example	Possible Meaning
I don't THINK he will listen to her.	I don't think that, but I might be wrong.
I don't think HE will listen to her.	I think that someone other him will listen to her.
I don't think he WILL listen to her.	I think that he will not be willing to listening to her.
I don't think he will LISTEN to her.	Instead of listening, he might talk to her
I don't think he will listen to HER.	I think that he will listen to someone else over her.

Table 7.2 Changing Meaning by Shifting Word Stress

When teaching sentence stress it can also be important to keep up the flow of speech and linking, especially as the learners you teach move from the beginner to more advanced levels. This is important as you may lose linking (or liaisons) when slowing down your speech, and begin to pronounce each word by themselves (e.g., *How. Much. Is. It.*) This is compared to it sounding more like *How muh_chi_zit?* The underscore here shows how the words are being linked for ease of faster pronunciation in normal conversation, causing reduction. There are three main types of linking. The first is consonant-vowel, this sees words ending with a consonant linked to words ending with a vowel sound (e.g., turn off becomes turn_off). The second is consonant-consonant, where words ending with the same consonant sound are connected when the next word starts with a consonant in a similar position. (It should also be kept in mind that this also occurs when pronouncing numbers and acronyms.) The third is vowel-vowel, where words ending with a vowel sound are linked to those beginning with a vowel sound. In this case words that end in *a, e,* and *i* see a *y* sound inserted at the beginning of the next word e.g., the$_y$end. If the first word ends in an *o* or *u* sound then a *w* sound is inserted at the beginning of the next word e.g., too$_w$often. Reductions also occurs when we speak seeing many words collapsed into each other. These can also be taught as a series of general rules for learners of American English, that involve the *d, t, s, z* and the *y* sound, along with consonant and vowel, consonant and consonant, and vowel and vowel combinations (Cook, 2018). These rules can be found in Table 1.3 and they can be combined for teaching purposes with a worksheet similar to that found in the photocopiable section of this chapter.

Intonation

In some languages, intonation also includes tones, which means that the same word when spoken with a different tone changes the meaning of the word. In English, intonation can be used to make a difference in meaning or implication. Intonation markers to indicate this are: rising ↗, falling ↘, a fall-rise ↘↗, or a rise-fall ↗↘. An example of intonation usage in English can be seen in the following authoritarian-style sentence:

      ↘↗   ↘   ↗
Peter, get in here, now!

Teaching how to hear this kind of intonation may involve playing back (or having the teacher speak aloud) the same sentence differently. Students then decide if they should put a period, a question mark, or an exclamation mark at the end of the sentence. These can be practiced with question, sentence, or dialogue-based sentence-step activities to practice pitch. Such activities could also be extended by increasing dictation difficulty levels by having students write the sentences that they hear with intonation markers, and then the appropriate grammar markers. Example activities can be found in the photocopiable section of this chapter.

So, it is important to be aware of the way that sounds, stresses and intonations all interact, as sounds when pronounced can alter the way another sound is articulated. That is to say, one sound spoken aloud can be influenced by what other sounds are around it (for linking examples see Table 1.3). Intonation can influence how we hear stress (i.e., tone levels), and changing the stress pattern of a word will alter its sounds as well. For example, the word 'subject' pronounced with the first syllable stressed is a noun, while pronounced with the second syllable stressed makes it a verb, which also changes the vowel sound in the word from /ˈsəbjekt/ to /səbˈjekt/.

Linking Rules
Consonant + Vowel Words ending in a consonant sound, with the next word starting with a vowel sound (including the semivowels *W*, *Y*, and *R*), are linked. (e.g., My name is Ann [my nay mi zæn].)
Consonant + Consonant Words ending with the same consonant sound are linked when the next word starts with a consonant in a similar position. (e.g., I've been late twice [äivbin la(t)twice], LA [eh lay], 5068 [fäi vo sick sate].)

	Lips	Behind Teeth	Throat
Voiced	B, V	D, J, Z, Zh	G, Ng, R
Unvoiced	P, F	T, Ch, S, Sh	K, H

Vowel + Vowel Words ending with a vowel sound are linked to those beginning with a vowel sound. (e.g., Go away [go(w)away].)
D, T, S, Z + Y Words ending with the letter or sound of *D*, *T*, *S*, or *Z* are linked to those starting with *Y* or its sound. These rules, with several examples, are:

d + y = j	Graduation [graju(w)ation] Did you like it? [Didja like it?] What did you do [Whajoo do?]
t + y = ch	Actually [achully] Can't you do it? [Canchoo do it?] What's your name? [Whacher name?]
s + y = sh	Insurance [inshurance] Sugar [shüg'r]
z + y = zh	Casual [kazhyoow'l] Who's your friend? [hoozhier friend?]

Table 7.3 Linking Rules
(based on Cook, 2018)

Minimal pairs are a great way to see if learners are able to perceive and produce the sounds of the language that they are learning. A chart of the mouth and a description of where to place the lips, tongue, and teeth may also be useful. You might also direct students to videos on YouTube or to artificial intelligence applications that support pronunciation; for example, typing a word that you want to pronounce into the Google search engine will allow you to hear and see how it is pronounced. An audio file can be played, and the pronunciation studied as the shape of the lips is also provided for you to view as you hear the term pronounced. Learners are also able to record their own pronunciation for analysis, with instant feedback provided both in a written and auditory form along with suggestions for correction. Several means of providing improvement to learners from within the class, along with some suggestions for explicitly teaching pronunciation, can be seen in Table 1.4.

Pronunciation	
Improving	Teaching
- Modeling of sounds, words, and sentences. - Comparing teacher and student. - Self-correction (listening to recorded audio). - Drills and dialogues (repetition of sounds, words, sentences; vary speed, volume, mood). - Jazz chants – rhymes, jingles, songs, tongue-twisters.	- Dictation tasks. - Reading-aloud activities. - Discrimination Tasks (e.g., minimal pair games and activities; false-friend games and activities). - Predication tasks. - Letter-combination games; rule-based spelling activities to introduce new vocabulary.

Table 7.4 Improving and Teaching Pronunciation (based on Ur, 2002, pp. 58, 54)

Pronunciation in the Classroom

In general, you can teach pronunciation in any language learning class, but it is most often taught when the focus is on speaking, and also reading (as students will be given practice in reading terms aloud).

There is a variety of activities and means of drawing attention to the specific features of pronunciation, and this chapter will now provide several of them as well as a number of games and activities that can help learners focus on improving their pronunciation.

Drawing Attention to Pronunciation Features

Instead of tapping a finger or a pencil, you may wish to use your whole hand and open the fingers wide when stress is required and doing the same thing but not as wide when less stress is required (i.e., like a puppet's mouth). Fingers can also be used to indicate the syllable or the word of a sentence that needs to be stressed. Other ways of using body language to teach pronunciation can include using your index finger in front of your mouth to indicate the *sh* from *sheep*. You can move your finger from your mouth and outstretch it as far as you can when pronouncing a long vowel, but only halfway out while pronouncing a short vowel sound. You might open a fist rapidly to indicate explosive sounds like the *p* in *pan*, or use some paper and show how the paper moves as you speak. You can move your hands like a wave in order to show the rising and falling stress patterns of words and sentences. You can also perform dramatic actions such as leaning back as if to sneeze but pronouncing the *ch* of *church*. Other dramatic actions can include hitting the table or clapping with a stressed syllable and only hitting the air for other syllables, and this is particularly useful when conducting jazz chants using rhymes, jingles, or even tongue-twisters. These can be practiced like many sentences using a technique called back chaining where the end of the sentence is given to students either in chunks or word by word. (e.g., *last Thursday; the thick thorny thicket last Thursday; rushed through the thick thorny thicket last Thursday; thirty-three thieves rushed through the thick thorny thicket last Thursday.*)

Your face and lip shape can also be used in an exaggerated manner to help students understand how to make the sounds of any new terms. The hand and fingers can also be used to help illustrate the place of the tongue and where the teeth are positioned when making certain sounds. It is likely best to contrast sounds and use gestures that also contrast in order to get the message across in a fun and interactive way that can be used to later provide simple corrective feedback during a lesson. Any or all of the above can then be combined with a simple technique that employs a vocabulary box containing three- and four-syllable words which students can then sort into one of four columns depending on the placement of stress. An example is provided in the photocopiable section of this chapter, and such an activity can be extended by using each vocabulary item from it in a word-web activity. Such an activity places a single base word and its stress pattern in the center and derived words on the periphery, and it is the students' tasks to indicate the stress patterns of these words. Figure 1.4 illustrates a completed example that starts with the word *photo*.

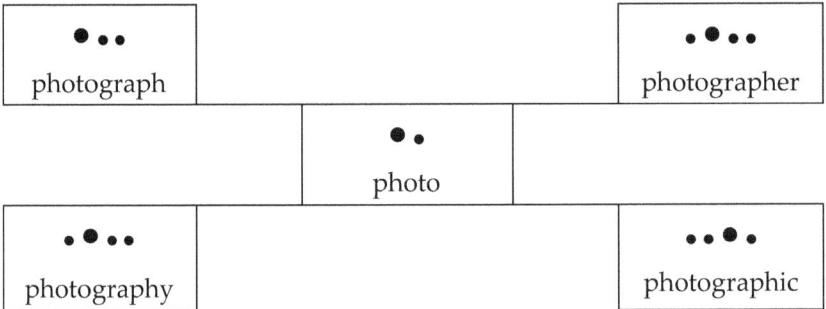

Figure 7.4 Stress Practice Word Web

Minimal Pairs

Minimal pairs are often taught together, so that students can gain practice in hearing and pronouncing the difference between them. Such words, or phrases, differ in only one phonological element (e.g., phoneme, toneme or chroneme), and have distinct meanings. These can be a source of confusion for many learners of English, and when these pairs are taught, students can gain practice in hearing and pronouncing the differences and taking note of lip positions for vowels and voiced and voiceless consonants. Examples of minimal pairs include *fan–van, hat–hut, heart–hard, sip–ship, ship–sheep,* and *sea–she*. In teaching these kinds of words flashcards are very helpful, along with block building (teaching by phrases instead of word by word). The teacher or other students may then say the words aloud, with classmates guessing the sound or running to different sides of the classroom depending on what sound they believe they have heard.

Tongue Twisters

In many cases tongue twisters consist of phonetically similar words, and minimal pairs can be used to help learners in differentiating similar-sounding words and pronouncing them. Tongue twisters can also stretch the muscles involved when producing speech in a new language, and strengthen them as well. Muscle exercises like these may lead learners to clearer pronunciation and speech patterns, and assist in rectifying pronunciation of some of the more difficult sounds of the target language, twenty-seven different tongue twisters are included in the photocopiable section of this chapter, arranged from beginner through medium to advanced. These can be used in a variety of ways from simple dictation, in games such as Whispers (where each student whispers a particular phrase to the next), or in drills where the tongue twister is practiced three to five times after modeling provided by the teacher or via YouTube videos. If using tongue twisters in drilling, then choose those that are short but direct and focus on particular sounds that students have trouble pronouncing, and perhaps its minimal pair (e.g., /b/ and /p/), vowel sounds (e.g., a/e/i/o/u), consonant blends (e.g., ch, sh, th), or focus on the sounds that your class is having difficulty with (e.g., r/l, b/v). Model the tongue twister for learners either by using your own voice or a video, then have learners practice pronouncing it in pairs before they perform the tongue twister one at a time. You might only choose to use one-line tongue twisters for drills, or incorporate tongue twisters into classes when there are special events during the year, such as Halloween or Christmas (e.g., *two witches*, or *romping reindeer*), or when seasons change (e.g., in summer you can use *she sells sea shells*, and in winter, *whether the weather*). A particular unit of study might see you introduce tongue twisters (e.g., a food/cooking unit might see you use the *Peter Piper* or *Betty Botter* tongue twisters together to differentiate the /b/ and /p/ sounds for learners.) You may also have students work on creating their own tongue twisters, and an example activity for this is available from the photocopiable section of this chapter.

Poems, Songs, and Texts

Aside from drawing attention to the features of different sounds with tongue twisters, there are ways to do this with poems, songs, and other short texts. These can be developed into a variety of pre-, while- and post-reading/listening tasks to teach aspects such as assimilation, classifying, connected speech, linking, minimal pairs, phonemic transcription, reductions, and syntactic word structure analysis.

Assimilation. Provide text/lyrics or content that uses assimilation (i.e., the process that sees a speech sound become similar or identical to a neighboring sound), and indicate where this occurs for learners. Then, get them to identify the corresponding sounds that they hear, writing these in the spaces provided at the end of the lyric line or line of text.

Classifying. A selection of text or lyrics could be used to help students classify vowel sounds (e.g., a close-back rounded vowel /u:/ as in *fool* and the near-close near-back rounded vowel /ʊ/ as in *full*). A table could be provided for students to write in the vowel sounds, with the teacher underlining key words in the text/lyrics that require sorting into one of two columns in the table.

Connected speech. Text/lyrics that use connected speech can be made into a fill-in-the blank activity that requires students to write in the separate words that form the connected speech.

Linking. Students can use an underscore to illustrate where linked sounds occur in provided text/lyrics, and then classify these into one of the three types (i.e., consonant + consonant, vowel + vowel, consonant + vowel).

Minimal pairs. The minimal pairs can all be identified for a particular text/song. Students could then sort these into matching pairs.

Phonemic transcription. Text/lyrics can be provided to students, with each phonemically transcribed line on a slip of paper that requires sorting into order. You might also provide students with text/lyrics as a cloze exercise with the vocabulary box filled with words in phonemic transcription. Alternatively, one word in each line of the text/lyrics could be phonemically transcribed but with a target sound as the blank to fill in, allowing you to focus learners on specific sounds (e.g., the voiced dental fricative /ð/ as in *this*, or the voiceless dental fricative /θ/ as in *thing*.)

Reductions. Text/lyrics that use reductions can be made into a fill-in-the-blank activity that requires the reduction heard by students to then be written in full.

Syntactic word structure analysis. Finally, you might like to engage students with word trees to illustrate the function of words or phrases that they are pronouncing. These are similar to sentence diagramming and syntactic trees and can be undertaken with worksheets or by introducing examples to the class while drawing on the board. It may prove to be beyond the scope and the desire of many learners, but it could appeal to some others that you may end up teaching during your career. It is also especially useful when teaching grammar. An example is provided in Figure 1.5, to demonstrate how suffixes are capable of changing the grammatical function of a word. The same kind of diagram could also be constructed as a simple table with headings, rows, and columns.

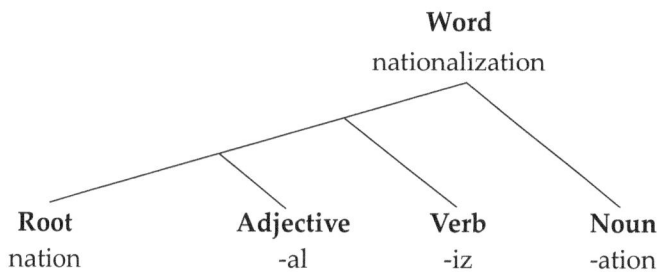

Figure 7.5 Syntactic Word Structure Diagram

Pronunciation Games and Activities

There are many other activities that can be used to help you teach pronunciation to learners, such as a variety of games and different styles of dictation. In the case of dictation, this generally means providing activities that see you or someone else speak vocabulary items or sentences aloud, with learners writing down or completing actions based upon what they hear.

Minimal pairs dictation. Prepare a list of minimal pairs for students. Each minimal pair has a blank line next to it, where students write the word they hear being modeled. Say the chosen word three times aloud, first slower then faster. This could be turned into a pictorial-based activity as well.

Picture dictation. This kind of pictorial-based activity for very young learners would see the minimal pairs represented by graphics, with students coloring in the ones that they hear the teacher speak. Another type of extension is a B*ingo* activity.

Bingo. Here, a bingo card (e.g., a 5 × 5 sheet with 12 minimal pairs of 24 words with a 'free' spot) is provided to students. There are a number of apps or websites on the internet that can create the cards for you if you provide the words (e.g., ESL Activities). In this kind of game, students would use objects as markers to 'stamp' the words that they hear a caller say and are, in this way, able to use the same card to play the game again. The first student to get five markers in a row, in any direction, can call 'Bingo!' to win the round. The winner of the round can then take over from the teacher as the bingo caller. After a round or two, students can swap cards so that they are then using a new arrangement of words. If you have laminated the cards, you will be able to reuse them with other learners. This particular activity gives students the opportunity to hear and recognize sound differences, and provides pronunciation practice when being the caller, especially if a student who wins twice can then nominate another student as the bingo caller so that everyone has a chance to speak.

Relay dictation. In this activity students work in pairs to read words or sentences from one of several stations on the other side of the room, before going back across the room to their partner to dictate what they have read. The dictations could be single words, minimal pairs, sentences, or tongue twisters. The students then swap with the previously seated partner going across the room to the next station, and returning to dictate to the first student. The process repeats until all stations have been visited. The activity could then be checked, with feedback provided, as a whole-class group.

Sound dictation. This kind of total physical response-based activity is a good one for young learners and those who cannot yet write, as you can assign activities to the sounds, words, or phrases that you dictate. This may see learners clap or jump, with older learners perhaps using the same actions that you have been using to teach pronunciation (e.g., drawing the hand away from the mouth a certain distance when they hear short/long vowel sounds).

Tag dictation. In this activity two words or phrases are written on the board. Students then line up around the room in two teams with a pair consisting of one student from each team standing at the center-back of the room. The teacher then calls out one of the words or phrases written on the board with the two students from the back of the room then running up to the board. The first student to touch the word or phrase spoken aloud wins, earning a point for their team. The winning student can then write up a new pair of words or phrases and call out one of them for the next pair of students. Once all students have had a turn, the winning team is announced.

Basketball. Although not a dictation task per se, this is a fun total physical response kind of activity that can also be used as an exit ticket. Here, students line up to leave the room, but they must first pass a table containing scrap pieces of paper that have words or phrases written on them. The first student in the line takes a piece of paper and reads it aloud but if it is not read correctly, they return the piece of paper to the table, and head to the back of the line to try again. If the paper is read correctly, then they can crumple it up into a ball and shoot it into the trash can. If they make the shot, they can leave, otherwise they return to the end of the line.

Testing Pronunciation

Celce-Murcia, Brinton, and Goodwin (1999) suggest a variety of testing methods to check learner knowledge and performance regarding pronunciation. Primarily, these revolve around either listening- or speaking-based diagnostic passages, gap-fills, highlighting, presentations, multiple-choice tests (including true or false exercises), and sorting-style tests.

Diagnostic passages. These are written in a way that, when read aloud, force the reader to engage in the production of a wide range of pronunciation features that they may otherwise not produce in free speech. Such passages are typically used for needs-analysis purposes and to diagnose issues of pronunciation that are unique to individuals. They should be heard first, and either played as audio or read aloud by a native speaker of the language, with the learner then given time to practice reading the passage before they are recorded speaking it aloud. The same procedure and reading passage might be used at the beginning and the end of a course to determine where the learner needs improvement and to illustrate where they have improved. As reading a text is different to speaking in conversation, it might be useful to compare student recordings to samples of their free speech (i.e., where learners record audio of themselves talking about a familiar topic). This will ensure that more natural evidence of learner pronunciation is collected for analysis.

Gap-fills. This type of test typically presents a sentence, or a series of sentences, with words or a series of words removed. For pronunciation, these can be used to test reduced speech with the commonly reduced and unstressed words selectively removed. Students would then listen to a speaker, and fill in the missing words that they have heard. This might involve the use of one or more words removed per gap.

Highlighting. In this kind of test, students need to circle, underline, or otherwise highlight particular points of a sentence. Such a test is useful for indicating word stress or those words that can be reduced. A multiple-choice variant can consist of providing different options to highlight, with students selecting the one of, say, three that might have been presented in a sentence or series of sentences.

Oral proficiency tests. A number of means for undertaking the formal testing of pronunciation exist. Students may be interested in taking such tests that would involve them reading aloud, describing images and/or objects, completing sentences, expressing opinions, and presenting in order to receive a standardized score of pronunciation and fluency. If interested in such a test then students might, for example, undertake the speaking component of the Test of English as a Foreign Language (TOEFL). One test that you might consider obtaining for use in your class, although there are no longer any new versions being developed, is one that was popularly used for assessing pronunciation, and that is the Speaking Proficiency English Assessment Kit (SPEAK).

Sorting Tasks. These kinds of tasks can provide a range of words to students along with a table with three columns that are each labeled with different vowel sounds. Students would then need to write the appropriate words under each heading. A variant would provide the table only, with students listening to audio and writing the words that they hear under the appropriate heading.

True or false. This kind of test is a variant of multiple-choice which provides the correct response along with a single distractor. For pronunciation, this kind of test could be applied to minimal pairs (e.g., consonant-vowel use) or the discrimination of intonation patterns (e.g., rising and falling tones to indicate questions or statements), with students listening to a speaker either saying individual words aloud or speaking out the whole sentence before making their choice. Alternatively, two images could be provided (e.g., one of a sheep and the other of a ship, or one of a rising and one of a lowering tone), with the student needing to then select the image matching the audio that they hear. This technique could also be used with learners who may be unable to read, and with those who have reading difficulties (e.g., dyslexia).

Summary

This chapter highlighted the most important aspects of the IPA chart for teachers of English to understand so that they can become familiar with phonetics, and with reading the consonant table and vowel trapezium. It also provided a way to become familiar with the variety of markers (such as diacritics and suprasegmentals) that are used to indicate changes to the pronunciation of a sound or a word. In line with this, some of the most important aspects related to phonetics, stress, and intonation were introduced. The focus of the chapter then turned to provide ways for teachers to highlight such features of pronunciation for learners, and the means to draw learner attention to pronunciation issues during the classroom context through the use of elements such as word webs, minimal pairs, tongue twisters, as well as poems, songs, and texts and covering assimilation, classifying, connected speech, linking, phonemic transcription, reductions, syntactic word structure analysis, and more. A number of means for teaching and testing pronunciation were then covered, including the use of dictation, diagnostic passages, oral proficiency tests, sorting and highlighting.

Review

Content Quiz
Pronunciation in Teaching

To help solidify some of the concepts introduced by this chapter the following multiple-choice and true or false quizzes might be helpful for you to undertake. So that you can check the accuracy of your responses, an answer key can be found following the quizzes.

Multiple-Choice
Circle **a**, **b**, or **c** for the answer that best completes the sentence presented in each question.

1. The word *phonemic* is used to refer to …
   a) the transcriptions of a specific sound system.
   b) the sounds of all human languages.
   c) the accent, stress, or tone markers of a language.

2. When using the IPA chart and describing a consonant segment, it would typically be described in the order of …
   a) the place of articulation, then manner of articulation, followed by voicing.
   b) voicing, then place of articulation, followed by the manner of articulation.
   c) the manner of articulation, then place of articulation, followed by voicing.

3. When using the IPA chart and describing a vowel, it would typically be described in the order of …
   a) backness, height, rounding.
   b) rounding, height, backness.
   c) height, rounding, backness.

4. Linking describes the technique for smoothly moving from one word to another during …
   a) pronunciation.
   b) stress placement.
   c) intonation.

5. In teaching minimal pairs, flashcards can be most helpful, especially when combined with
   a) teaching by phrases instead of word by word.
   b) teaching the spelling of each word.
   c) teaching word by word instead of by phrases.

6. If using tongue twisters in drills, choose those that are …
   a) long and complex, and focus on many sounds.
   b) short but direct, and focus on particular sounds.
   c) medium length, with simple and repetitive vocabulary.

7. In phonetics, assimilation can refer to the process where …
   a) words join together in a continuous sequence of sounds.
   b) a speech sound becomes similar or identical to a neighboring sound.
   c) there are changes in the acoustic quality of vowels in relation to stress, duration, loudness, and articulation.

8. In phonetics, connected speech can refer to the process where …
   a) words join together in a continuous sequence of sounds.
   b) a speech sound becomes similar or identical to a neighboring sound.
   c) there are changes in the acoustic quality of vowels in relation to stress, duration, loudness, and articulation.

9. In phonetics, reduction can refer to the process where …
   a) words join together in a continuous sequence of sounds.
   b) a speech sound becomes similar or identical to a neighboring sound.
   c) there are changes in the acoustic quality of vowels in relation to stress, duration, loudness, and articulation.

10. A dictation activity sees you or someone else speak vocabulary items or sentences aloud. These are valuable when teaching English, as they …
    a) provide for needs-analyses, and diagnose those issues of pronunciation that are unique to individuals.
    b) can be used as time killers when teachers need to fill in the extra time of a lesson.
    c) easily see the kind of content that learners write down, or the actions that they complete based on what they hear.

11. Diagnostic passages are written in a way that, when read aloud, force the reader to engage in the production of a wide range of pronunciation features that they may otherwise not produce in free speech. They are often used …
    a) to easily see the kind of content that learners write down or the actions that they complete based on what they hear.
    b) for needs-analysis purposes, and to diagnose those issues of pronunciation unique to individuals.
    c) as time killers when teachers need to fill in the extra time of a lesson.

True or False
Circle **a** (true) if you think that the statement is correct, or **b** (false) if you think that the statement is incorrect.

1. A syllable is a unit of pronunciation having one vowel sound.
   a) True.
   b) False.

2. A consonant can be combined with a vowel to form a syllable.
   a) True.
   b) False.

3. A vowel is produced by changing the shape of the area in the mouth above the tongue.
   a) True.
   b) False.

4. In the IPA chart, diacritics refer to those markers that denote specific features of consonants and vowels.
   a) True.
   b) False.

5. In the IPA chart, suprasegmentals refer to those symbols, or glyphs, that are used to indicate that pronunciation (in terms of accent, stress, and tone), or meaning, might change.
   a) True.
   b) False.

6. The IPA consonant chart arranges consonants in columns according to their place of articulation in the mouth, with the rows of the chart indicating the manner of articulation.
   a) True.
   b) False.

7. Voicing of consonants is not shown in the IPA chart.
   a) True.
   b) False.

8. Stress of a word is indicated in most dictionaries, or phonemic transcriptions, with a short vertical line above and before the stressed syllable.
   a) True.
   b) False.

9. Minimal pairs are a great way to see if learners are able to perceive and produce the sounds of the language that they are learning.
   a) True.
   b) False.

10. Minimal pairs are often taught together so that students can gain practice in hearing and pronouncing the difference between the two words.
    a) True.
    b) False.

11. Tongue twisters are useful to stretch the muscles involved when producing speech in a new language, and for strengthening those muscles as well.
    a) True.
    b) False.

Quiz Answers
Pronunciation in Teaching

Multiple-Choice		*True or False*	
1.	a	1.	T
2.	b	2.	T
3.	c	3.	T
4.	a	4.	F
5.	a	5.	F
6.	b	6.	T
7.	b	7.	F
8.	a	8.	T
9.	a	9.	T
10.	c	10.	T
11.	b	11.	T

Suggested Readings

Brazil, D., Coulthard, M., & Johns, C. (1980). *Discourse intonation and language teaching*. Longman.

Celce-Murcia, M., Brinton, D., & Goodwin, J. (1999). *Teaching pronunciation: A reference for teachers of English to speakers of other languages*. Cambridge University Press.

Collis, H. (1999). *101 American Customs*. McGraw-Hill Education.

Collis, H. (2007). *101 American English idioms*. McGraw-Hill Education.

Collis, H. (1990). *101 American English proverbs*. McGraw-Hill education.

Cook, A., (2018). *American accent training with audio*, (4th ed.). Barrons Educational Series.

Esling, J. (1999). *Handbook of the international phonetic association: A guide to the use of the international phonetic alphabet*. IPA Association.

Harding, G. (2013). *Great English pronunciation – move your mouth for clear English*. https://www.youtube.com/watch?v=mfZscA9V6nU

Hughes, A. (1989). *Testing for language teachers*. Cambridge University Press.

Jenkins, J. (2009). *The phonology of English as an international language: New modals, new norms, new goals*. Oxford University Press.

Roach, P. (1991). *English phonetics and phonology: A practical course*, (2nd ed.). Cambridge University Press.

Thornbury, S. (2010). *P is for phonemic chart. An A-Z of ELT*. https://scottthornbury.wordpress.com/2010/08/08/p-is-for-phonemic-chart

Ur, P. (2002). *A course in language teaching: Practice and theory*. Cambridge University Press.

Photocopiable Content
Pronunciation in Teaching

This section of the text includes a variety of content that is free to photocopy and use with your classes, as long as appropriate copyright or licensure is displayed. It contains examples of the following content:

- The international phonetic alphabet (IPA chart)
- Linking rules activity
- Pitch practice – Sentence stairs – Worksheet
- Pitch practice – Sentence stairs – Answer key
- Stress practice dictation
- Stress practice worksheet
- Stress practice activity
- English tongue twisters
- Tongue twister activity – Teacher notes
- Tongue twister activity – Make your own tongue twister

The International Phonetic Alphabet

CONSONANTS (PULMONIC) © 2015 IPA

	Bilabial	Labiodental	Dental	Alveolar	Postalveolar	Retroflex	Palatal	Velar	Uvular	Pharyngeal	Glottal
Plosive	p b			t d		ʈ ɖ	c ɟ	k ɡ	q ɢ		ʔ
Nasal	m	ɱ		n		ɳ	ɲ	ŋ	ɴ		
Trill	ʙ			r					ʀ		
Tap or Flap		ⱱ		ɾ		ɽ					
Fricative	ɸ β	f v	θ ð	s z	ʃ ʒ	ʂ ʐ	ç ʝ	x ɣ	χ ʁ	ħ ʕ	h ɦ
Lateral fricative				ɬ ɮ							
Approximant		ʋ		ɹ		ɻ	j	ɰ			
Lateral approximant				l		ɭ	ʎ	ʟ			

Symbols to the right in a cell are voiced, to the left are voiceless. Shaded areas denote articulations judged impossible.

CONSONANTS (NON-PULMONIC)

Clicks	Voiced implosives	Ejectives
ʘ Bilabial	ɓ Bilabial	ʼ Examples:
ǀ Dental	ɗ Dental/alveolar	pʼ Bilabial
ǃ (Post)alveolar	ʄ Palatal	tʼ Dental/alveolar
ǂ Palatoalveolar	ɠ Velar	kʼ Velar
ǁ Alveolar lateral	ʛ Uvular	sʼ Alveolar fricative

OTHER SYMBOLS

ʍ Voiceless labial-velar fricative   ɕ ʑ Alveolo-palatal fricatives
w Voiced labial-velar approximant   ɺ Voiced alveolar lateral flap
ɥ Voiced labial-palatal approximant   ɧ Simultaneous ʃ and x
ʜ Voiceless epiglottal fricative
ʢ Voiced epiglottal fricative   Affricates and double articulations can be represented by two symbols joined by a tie bar if necessary. t͡s k͡p
ʡ Epiglottal plosive

VOWELS

Front — Central — Back
Close: i y — ɨ ʉ — ɯ u
Close-mid: e ø — ɘ ɵ — ɤ o
Open-mid: ɛ œ — ɜ ɞ — ʌ ɔ
Open: a ɶ — — ɑ ɒ

Where symbols appear in pairs, the one to the right represents a rounded vowel.

SUPRASEGMENTALS

ˈ Primary stress   ˌfoʊnəˈtɪʃən
ˌ Secondary stress
ː Long   eː
ˑ Half-long   eˑ
˘ Extra-short   ĕ
| Minor (foot) group
‖ Major (intonation) group
. Syllable break   ɹi.ækt
‿ Linking (absence of a break)

DIACRITICS Some diacritics may be placed above a symbol with a descender, e.g. ŋ̊

̥	Voiceless	n̥ d̥	̤	Breathy voiced	b̤ a̤	̪	Dental	t̪ d̪
̬	Voiced	s̬ t̬	̰	Creaky voiced	b̰ a̰	̺	Apical	t̺ d̺
ʰ	Aspirated	tʰ dʰ	̼	Linguolabial	t̼ d̼	̻	Laminal	t̻ d̻
̹	More rounded	ɔ̹	ʷ	Labialized	tʷ dʷ	̃	Nasalized	ẽ
̜	Less rounded	ɔ̜	ʲ	Palatalized	tʲ dʲ	ⁿ	Nasal release	dⁿ
̟	Advanced	u̟	ˠ	Velarized	tˠ dˠ	ˡ	Lateral release	dˡ
̠	Retracted	e̠	ˤ	Pharyngealized	tˤ dˤ	̚	No audible release	d̚
̈	Centralized	ë	̴	Velarized or pharyngealized	ɫ			
̽	Mid-centralized	ė	̝	Raised	e̝ (ɹ̝ = voiced alveolar fricative)			
̩	Syllabic	n̩	̞	Lowered	e̞ (β̞ = voiced bilabial approximant)			
̯	Non-syllabic	e̯	̘	Advanced Tongue Root	e̘			
˞	Rhoticity	ɚ a˞	̙	Retracted Tongue Root	e̙			

TONES AND WORD ACCENTS

LEVEL		CONTOUR	
ə̋ or ˥	Extra high	ě or ˨˦	Rising
é ˦	High	ê ˥˧	Falling
ē ˧	Mid	e᷄ ˦˥	High rising
è ˨	Low	e᷅ ˩˨	Low rising
ȅ ˩	Extra low	e᷈ ˧˦˨	Rising-falling
↓ Downstep		↗ Global rise	
↑ Upstep		↘ Global fall	

* IPA Chart, http://www.internationalphoneticassociation.org/content/ipa-chart, available under a Creative Commons Attribution-Sharealike 3.0 Unported License. Copyright © 2018 International Phonetic Association.

Linking Rules Activity

Instructions.

Read the rules. Then look at the example. Finally, write how you think you would pronounce the example on the appropriate line in the pronunciation column.

Rules.

a. Consonant + Vowel

Words ending in a consonant sound, with the next word starting with a vowel sound (including the semivowels *W*, *Y*, and *R*), are linked. (e.g., My name is Ann [my nay mi zæn].)

b. Consonant + Consonant

Words ending with the same consonant sound are linked when the next word starts with a consonant in a similar position. (e.g., I've been late twice [äivbin la(t)twice], LA [eh lay], 5068 [fäi vo sick sate].)

c. Vowel + Vowel

Words ending with a vowel sound are linked to those beginning with a vowel sound. (e.g., go away [go(w)away].)

d. d, t, s, z + y

Words ending with the letter or sound of *D*, *T*, *S*, or *Z* are linked to those starting with *Y* or its sound. This sees:

$d + y = j$ $t + y = ch$ $s + y = sh$ $z + y = zh$

Activity

Example		Pronunciation
1.	772582	
2.	Usual	
3.	My name is John.	
4.	I just didn't get the chance.	
5.	Sugar	
6.	Don't you like it?	
7.	Would you help me?	
8.	I also need the other one.	

Pitch Practice – Sentence Stairs – Worksheet

Instructions.

Look at the example dialogue below, and see how intonation is used within sentences. Then, mark the intonation used in the sentences found in the activity section of the worksheet.

Example.

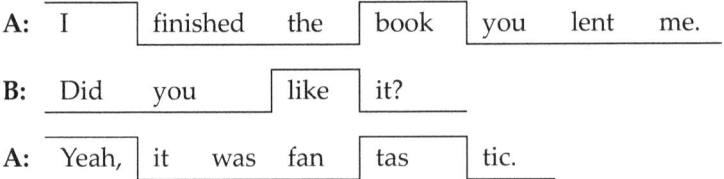

Activity.

Draw a line to indicate the intonation used in the sentences below.

1. Did you understand that?

2. Do you have their phone number?

3. Are you going on vacation?

4. Are you hungry?

5. What's your name?

6. A: Would you like coffee or tea?

   B: I'll have tea.

Pitch Practice – Sentence Stairs – Answer Key

Teacher notes.

Below is the answer key to the pitch practice – sentence stairs activity which can be used as a warm-up prior to the use of the stress pattern dictation worksheet. It can also be modified to have students indicate the stress of words, or parts of words, in a sentence. Ideally, it would be best if you can modify the worksheet so that you are using sentences familiar to your students, perhaps those coming from dialogues in the textbook that you are using with them in class.

Example

A: I — finished the — book — that you — lent me.

B: Did you — like — it?

A: Yeah — it was fan — Tas — tic.

Activity.

Draw a line to indicate the intonation used in the sentences below.

1. Did you under — stand that?

2. Do you have their — phone num — ber?

3. Are you going on — va — ca — tion?

4. Are you hun — gry?

5. What's your — name?

6. A   Would — you like — cof — fee or — tea?

    B   I'll — have tea.

Stress Practice Dictation

Instructions.
Listen to your teacher very carefully, then do the following:
1. Write the sentences that you hear in the space provided.
2. On top of the sentence, mark the words with the type of intonation that you hear (rising ↗, falling ↘, a fall-rise ↘↗, or a rise-fall ↗↘).
3. Place the appropriate grammar marker at the end of the sentence.
4. Circle the words, or parts of words, that are stressed in each sentence.

	Sentence with Intonation	Grammar Marker (. ? !)
a.		
b.		
c.		
d.		
e.		
f.		
g.		
h.		
i.		
j.		

Photocopiable Content – Pronunciation

Stress Practice Worksheet		
Recorded Word	**Word Phonemics**	**Area to Work On**
Presentation	**pre**sen**TA**tion /ˌprezənˈtāSH(ə)n/	Place greater stress on second syllable, not first.

Stress Practice Activity

Instructions.
Read the words in the vocabulary box below. For each of them, decide if the stress is placed on the first, second, or third syllable. Then, write the words in the appropriate column A, B, C, or D.

Vocabulary.

| audience | audition | composer | conductor |
| assistant | employee | interview | manager |

A ●••	B •●•	C ••●	D •●••

Extension activity.
Using the vocabulary items above create word webs as shown in the example below. For each base word, aim to create some derived words and indicate their stress patterns. Draw your word webs on a new sheet of paper, or use the blank word webs overleaf to get you started.

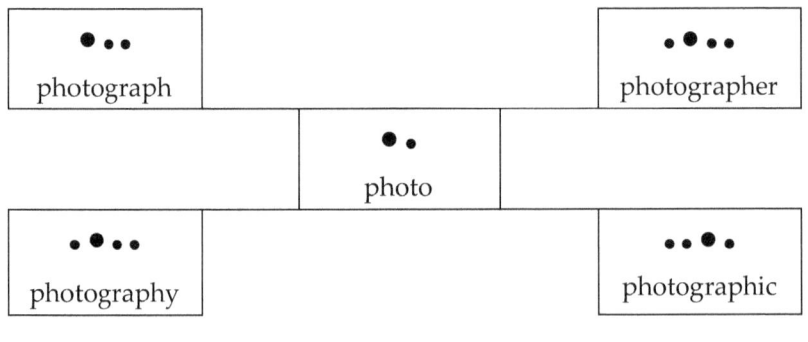

Blank word webs.

Use the three blank word webs below to help you get started on the extension activity.

a.

b.

c.

English Tongue Twisters

Easy

Annie: Annie ate eight Arctic apples.

Big black bear: A big black bug bit the big black bear, but the big black bear bit the big black bug back!

Bragging Baker: A bragging baker baked black bread.

Clam cream can: How can a clam cram in a clean cream can?

Coffee pot: A proper copper coffee pot.

Daddy: Daddy draws doors.

Fatty Fish: Fatty freshly fried fish, freshly fried for the dish.

Four furious friends: Four furious friends fought for the phone.

Green glass globes: Green glass globes glow greenly.

How much wood: How much wood would a woodchuck chuck, if a woodchuck could chuck wood?

Ice cream: I scream, you scream, we all scream for ice cream!

Mumbling mice: Many mumbling mice are making merry music in the moonlight.

Noddy needed noodles: Noddy needed noodles in Neverland at noon to 'nom, nom, nom'.

Noisy noise: A noisy noise annoys an oyster.

Red leather: Red leather, yellow leather.

Six Socks: Six socks sit in a sink, soaking in soap suds.

Seven Snails: Seven slippery snails slid slowly seaward.

Smelly shoes: Smelly shoes and socks shock sisters.

Spell New York: Knife and a fork, bottle and a cork: that is the way that you spell New York.

Synonym: A synonym for cinnamon is a cinnamon synonym.

Thrusts his Fists: He thrusts his fists against the posts, and still insists he sees the ghosts.

Zithy's Zipper: Zithy's zippy zipper zips.

Medium

Dog: If a dog chews shoes, whose shoes does it chose?

Frantic Frogs: Five frantic frogs fled from fifty fierce fish.

Fuzzy Wuzzy: Fuzzy Wuzzy was a bear, Fuzzy Wuzzy had no hair, so Fuzzy Wuzzy wasn't very fuzzy, was he?

Good cook: How many cookies could a good cook cook if a good cook could cook cookies? A good cook could cook as much cookies as a good cook who could cook cookies.

I have got a date: I have a date at a quarter to eight. I'll see them at the gate if their not late.

I thought of thinking: I thought, I thought of thinking of thanking you.

Imagine: Imagine and imaginary manager managing an imaginary manager.

Night light: No need to light a night light on a light night like tonight.

One-one: One-one was a race horse. Two-two was one too. One-one won one race. Two-two won one too.

Peter piper: Peter Piper picked a peck of pickled peppers. A peck of pickled peppers Peter Piper picked. If Peter Piper picked a peck of pickled peppers, where's the peck of pickled peppers that Peter Piper picked?

Romping reindeer: Romping reindeer running 'round red wreaths.

Seven slick snails: Seven slick slimy snails are slowly sliding southward.

Slit sheet: I slit a sheet, a sheet I slit. Upon the slitted sheet I sit.

Thirty-three thieves: Thirty-three thieves rushed through the thick thorny thicket last Thursday

Two witches: If two witches would watch two watches, which witch would watch which watch?

Yak: How many yaks could a yak packer pack if a yak packer can pack yaks?

Difficult

Betty Botter: Betty Botter bought some butter, but the butter that Betty Botter bought was bitter, so Betty Botter bought some better butter, and the better butter that Betty Botter bought was better than the bitter butter that Betty Botter bought before.

Biscuit mixer: I bought a bit of baking powder and baked a batch of biscuits. I brought a big basket of biscuits back to the bakery and baked a basket of big biscuits. Then I took the big basket of biscuits and the basket of big biscuits and mixed the big biscuits with the basket of biscuits that was next to the big basket and put a bunch of biscuits from the basket into a biscuit mixer and brought the basket of biscuits and the box of mixed biscuits and the biscuit mixer to the bakery and opened a tin of sardines.

Creepy Crawler: Creepy crawler critters crawl through creepy crawly craters.

David Drank: David drank a drink in downtown Denpasar at daylight to destress.

Doctor doctoring: When a doctor doctors a doctor, does the doctor doing the doctoring doctor as the doctor being doctored wants to be doctored or does the doctor doing the doctoring doctor as he wants to doctor?

Mary Mac: Mary Mac's mother's making Mary Mac marry me. My mother's making me marry Mary Mac. Will I always be so Merry when Mary's taking care of me? Will I always be so merry when I marry Mary Mac?

Thought: I thought a thought but the thought I thought was not the thought I thought I thought.

Wish to wish: I wish to wish the wish you wish to wish, but if you wish the wish the witch wishes, I won't wish the wish you wish to wish.

Whether the weather: Whether the weather is fine, or whether the weather is not. Whether the weather is cold, or whether the weather is hot. We'll weather the weather whether we like it or not.

Tongue Twister Activity – Teacher Notes

Warm-up.

Select some tongue twisters from the previous lists, and write these on the board for your learners.

Ask students to read the tongue twisters aloud, or model them and have them repeat as a group. Then have the learners read them again as fast as they can, three times in a row.

At this point, you may want to ask about any famous tongue twisters in the learner' L1. If their level is high enough you might also ask them to try and translate them, and you may even try to say them. (This will make the activity more interactive, and show that everyone has problems with tongue twisters.)

You can then continue with drills, tongue-twister games or engage in a make your own twister with students.

The make-your-own tongue-twister activity ideally requires students to be in groups of five with each person answering the following questions. The following questions should be provided on a handout such as the one found overleaf:

1. What is your first name?
2. What did they do?
3. Where did they do it?
4. When did they do it?
5. Why did they do it?

Tongue Twister Activity
– Make Your Own Tongue Twister –

Instructions.

In this activity, you will create your own tongue twister.

A. Get into teams of around five and sit in a circle
B. Read question one below, and in the space provided write your answer. Then, give this piece of paper to the person on your left.
C. After you receive the piece of paper from the person on your right, answer question two in the space provided below. Then, pass this piece of paper to the person on your left. Follow this procedure until you receive the piece of paper with your name as the answer to question one.
D. Take turns reading your new tongue twister to the other members of your group. Vote for the best tongue twister and share this with your teacher and the rest of the class.

Questions.
1. What is your first name?
2. What did they do?
3. Where did they do it?
4. When did they do it?
5. Why did they do it?

Answers

1. _____

2. _____
   _____

3. _____
   _____

4. _____
   _____

5. _____
   _____

8. Vocabulary in Teaching

Overview

One of the most important aspects of being able to speak a foreign language is the learning of vocabulary items, for without them, a learner is unable to express or articulate themself. Vocabulary then plays an important role across all four skills, and it is an aspect of language that links pronunciation, meaning, and form. Notably then, what constitutes vocabulary is important to understand, as is how vocabulary items can be broken down for use in teaching and learning material. Coupled with this is the development of strategies that can be best employed by instructors to deliver effective and efficient lessons. Relevant to this are those aspects of incorporating both direct and indirect means of teaching vocabulary into the classroom context, as are the means of being able to practically, reliably, and validly engage learners in assessment.

Learning Outcomes

1. Gain an understanding of what constitutes a vocabulary item.
2. Appreciate the ways in which vocabulary is separated into tiers.
3. Discover the adaptability and usability of various word lists for learners of English, and in the provision of data-driven learning.
4. Uncover a number of instructional strategies to use while teaching vocabulary.
5. Understand how to apply various games and activities with learners when explicitly or implicitly teaching vocabulary items.
6. Uncover a number of activities that you can adapt to the testing of vocabulary while considering aspects of practicality, reliability, validity, backwash, and spin-off.
7.

Vocabulary – Items, Tiers, and Lists

Items

In the teaching of vocabulary, we refer to vocabulary items. These consist of single words (e.g., *father*), compound words (e.g., *post office, middle class*), set phrases (e.g., *salt and pepper*), and other expressions like idioms (e.g., *don't bite the hand that feeds you*) where meaning cannot be derived by simply understanding each of the component words. With this in mind, Ur (2002) reminds us that vocabulary items over vocabulary words need teaching, and when teaching vocabulary in an additional language classroom, the elements that the learner needs to understand are the following.

- Pronunciation and form, and how that form may change (e.g., *think, thought; mouse, mice; advise, advice*).
- Aspects of meaning including collocations (e.g., indicate that a *decision* or a *conclusion* is *taken* or *made* and that it can be *come to*, and that while things like *dead tired* work, *dead fatigued* does not); denotation (real world meaning); connotation (associations of a word, e.g., *dog* arouses positive feelings of friendship or loyalty in some, but negative feelings of inferiority and dirtiness in others); appropriateness (e.g., noting word use that is taboo, or those that are used in writing but not in conversation, and with formal or informal uses); and meaning relationships (e.g., synonyms, antonyms, hyponyms, co-hyponyms, superordinates, relationships (such as *tractor-farmer-agriculture*), and possibly translations.
- Word formation (e.g., components such as prefixes *dis-*, *sub-*, and *un-*, suffixes such as *-able, -ist,* and *-tion*; and compound and hyphenated words such as *bookcase* and *single-sided*.)

Tiers

Vocabulary can also be thought about as being arranged into one of three tiers.

Tier one – Common. These words are the words of everyday language, and form most native-speaker children's conversational repertoire. This covers around 8,000 word families in English, and includes sight words, adjectives, nouns, verbs, and early reading words. (e.g., *dog, book, girl*).

Tier two – High frequency. These vocabulary items are those that play important roles in specific content areas such as academic language, and are those that can be applied across a wide range of contexts and topics. They are found in most native-speaker adult conversations as well as in works of literature. This covers around 7,000 word families, and includes words like *benevolent, explain, fortunate, industrious, justify, masterpiece,* and *summarize*.

Tier three – Low frequency. These vocabulary items are domain-specific words and are generally specialized to specific content areas or fields. The remaining words of English are those that fall into this tier, and this includes words such as *asphalt, circumference, crepe, economics, etymology, orthography*, and *quantum*. It is important to note that some of the words in this tier may also appear as tier one or two words, but possess a specific use, purpose, or capitalization (e.g., *culture* versus *Culture* in sociology; *substitute* and *expression* in mathematical contexts).

Lists

For teaching and learning purposes, it may be necessary to simplify these tiers into various types of word lists. A number of word lists may be developed, or you may wish to use some of the pre-existing ones in many different ways. Your own word lists may be created during lessons, and these might contain those items that have emerged from explicit or implicit teaching. They can also be those provided in the back of a textbook by a publisher, covering what they consider to be the key terms for students using that particular content for learning. You may create or use preexisting word lists for students preparing to sit specific exams or rely on those provided as a concordance alongside specific texts such as graded readers or other works of literature. Some of the pre-existing word frequency lists that you might like to consider are the following.

The *British National Corpus (BNC)* contains around 100-million-word words of written and spoken English that have been drawn from a variety of sources. It is often broken down further into different word lists. For example, the BNC 1,000 consists of the first 1,000 most commonly used English words, the BNC 2,000 consists of the second 1,000 most commonly used English words, and so on.

Corpus of Contemporary American English (COCA) is a 1.1 billion word corpus of American English from eight genres of content including academic texts, blogs, fiction books, magazines, newspapers, spoken words, web pages, and subtitles from both television shows and movies. It can be browsed by frequency up to the top 60,000 words, including word forms, parts of speech, and by pronunciation. Individual word searches are possible, as is a search for phrases and strings.

The *New General Service List (NGSL)* is a list of high frequency words for learners of English, and it contains terms that cover about 92% of most general texts.

The *New Academic Word List (NAWL)* consists of 288 million corpora from academic text books, the British Academic Spoken English (BASE) list, the Michigan Corpus of Academic Spoken English (MICASE) list as well as academic discourse, academic journals, textbooks, non-fiction works, and student essays. It was developed to work in conjunction with the New General Service List (NGSL), and it is available in alphabetical order, by inflected forms, with a standard frequency index (SFI) and as part of the ANTWordProfile text analysis tool (http://www.laurenceanthony.net/software/antwordprofiler). It is provided for use under a Creative CommonsAttribution-ShareAlike 4.0 International License (https://creativecommons.org/licenses/by-sa/4.0).

Other lists. These include the Business Service List (BSL), the New general Service List Spoken (NGSL-S), and the TOEIC Service List (TSL). All of these lists are part of the public domain and can be used in various ways for teaching, and analysis. This is particularly true when combined with data-driven learning (DDL) in combination with applications such as Vocabprofile (https://www.lextutor.ca/vp).

Vocabulary in the Classroom

Vocabulary Teaching Strategies

When you provide new vocabulary items to learners, or come across them in the course of a lesson, it is often a good idea to always write them in the same place (e.g., on the right-hand side of the board). You may wish to write these words or expressions in various colors to indicate the phonemics, parts of speech, and so on. Writing words up will assist late-comers as well as those students who do not have time to write the items down when you first introduce them. Both types of students can then take a photo of the list with their smartphones at the end of the class. Students will also know where to look for any vocabulary items that were introduced by you during the delivery of any given lesson, and it will also allow students to create their own personal list of vocabulary related to the course, particularly regarding items that they were unfamiliar with. Vocabulary may emerge during explicit instruction (e.g., when introducing items directly from the textbook), or implicitly through in-class discussion or contextual use. Although not an exhaustive list, a number of effective vocabulary teaching strategies are presented in Table 2.1.

Vocabulary Teaching Strategies	
Presenting	**Teaching**
Provide concise definitions.	Deliver in context, and make meaning memorable (perhaps by miming definitions).
Use relevant examples.	Present these in ways that are applicable to the students' lives, and in ways that encourage noticing and recycling.
Present multimodal descriptions.	Define with imagery.
Demonstrate.	Practice (elicitation, pronunciation, miming definitions, and so on).
Associate.	Use word clusters/word webs.
Use lesson lists.	Create personalized lists.
Further expand on examples.	Use phrases, collocations, synonyms, antonyms, hyponyms, root words, and so on.
Analysis.	Employ DDL tools.
Translation/translanguaging.	Rely on dictionary use, machine translation, redefinitions, and semantic maps.

Table 8.1 Vocabulary Teaching Strategies

When introducing new vocabulary items, aim to be precise with the definitions that you use, even if you are not introducing all of the meanings associated with them. One way to introduce various definitions is through active learning and the use of context in order to then associate these definitions with meaningful memories. For example, you may use authentic materials and an interesting story (spoken, read, written, watched, or heard), or use a series of role plays

Photocopiable Content – Pronunciation

and practice dialogues to assist students in noticing new words and understanding the meanings in context.

To introduce and practice new terminology, you may also need to demonstrate the meaning, or elicit the meaning from the students. This can be done by miming the definition (or having learners mime), or by concisely providing a written or pictorial-based definition, and solidifying it by then introducing the form of the vocabulary item, a number of ways in which to use it, and just as importantly, by practicing the pronunciation aloud by drills and then through the use of dialogues, activities, games, or while checking over worksheets. This will also help to situate vocabulary items in ways that students can then see the relevance of examples. This is important as the vocabulary items that you actively teach should be relevant to not only the lesson, but to the students' daily lives. In this way, the words that they discover during class can then be put to immediate and potentially repetitive use (recycling).

Associating words using word webs is a good way to revise vocabulary and introduce associated terms as well as brainstorm the words and vocabulary items that students already know. Even though the focus of such an activity is on the meaning of isolated items, it is an exercise that could prove useful in getting students thinking about a topic or applied as a warm-up to the use of a song, or even when writing a poem or starting to read a book on a certain theme. It can also function as a way to provide a simple recall activity that relies on synonyms that can be adapted to focus on antonyms as well as other grammatical constructs (adjectives, verbs, nouns, prefixes and suffixes). An example word web that you can use with students can be found in the photocopiable section of this chapter. Other similar means to produce noticing in students when reading is to have them highlight passages by underlining words and phrases, or by using a marker to highlight all of the words that they do not know. In groups of two or three, they can then compare each other's passage and, where necessary, explain the terms and expressions. The items can then be looked over as a class after the students have tried to determine the meanings for themselves. The activity proves useful as it stresses what students know, and it helps peers mentor others through peer teaching.

Other effective ways to introduce vocabulary items is through multimodal activities or contexts, including the use of illustrations, video, realia, or by having the students themselves produce drawings. If you do choose to search for images during a lesson, you would need to ensure that 'safe search' is turned on to avoid exposing students to any unforeseen and unprofessional imagery. This is also a reason to always prescreen any videos or media that you may want to use with learners. Also, an interesting way of using multimodal learning with learners is to create an animated or a consistent drawing of a range of characters that will guide them in their learning journey through the class, and for young learners a puppet might be useful. If teaching a unit on cooking, you may also want to introduce some realia by having students prepare a dish or bring in some traditional foods and explain how to make them as they share them around. You could also simply bring in a range of spices and describe the tastes as students try them, smell them, or just look at them.

Translation still has a place in the classroom, and it can be used in many ways. Students may simply look up words in a bilingual dictionary, or they may engage in the use of machine-translation (which you can later utilize for teaching purposes, in translation correction activities). Having access to a dictionary yourself will also ensure that you will be able to define words that you may not know the meaning of, and it can prove useful when you tell students that 'you will get back to them' to explain a definition. You might also have students provide a list of words from their own language that they would like to know the meaning of in English, with learners creating their own worksheet for use with others in the class. Redefinition-style activities might also be used with actual English expressions or words that learners would like to have explained to them if they have not been able to come to understanding of the terms by themselves or if you have noticed that they have been using them inappropriately. This could require expanding on examples that you may need to provide, particularly by using vocabulary-building techniques that could rely on the use of synonyms and antonyms, and a variety of activities.

Tied to such a notion is translanguaging. This is the use of language, by multilingual speakers, as an integrated communication system (Garcia, 2009). It is an extension of languaging, the discursive practice of language speakers, with the addition of using more than one language simultaneously. An effective way of incorporating translanguaging techniques into lessons for vocabulary learning is with semantic maps.

Such maps can be developed in the learners first language, and used in ways that enable them to use their full linguistic repertoire while allowing them to develop and apply the target language in context. This allows students to establish links between the language they feel secure in using and the one(s) that they are learning in the classroom. In terms of vocabulary development, it also allows for the establishment of mental schema around lexical items while allowing leaners to link new words to the language that they already know.

Vocabulary Games and Activities

Depending on the focus of your teaching (e.g., speaking, listening, reading, writing), the way that you introduce new vocabulary items, the ways in which students will practice them, and how they end up being recycled will vary. So too, the activities that you choose to apply in each of the aforementioned cases will also vary based on the size and levels of the classes that you teach, the focus of the lesson that you have planned, the aims of the learners, and a myriad of other factors that may impinge or facilitate student learning (e.g., learner variables). As such, this section of the chapter aims to provide you with a number of activities to use with your learners to help them focus on vocabulary item development, noticing, and recycling.

Antonyms and Synonyms. When introducing vocabulary items to learners it is often beneficial to teach those that have a similar meaning (e.g., synonyms) as well as the opposite meanings (e.g., antonyms). The benefit of this is that you can then use these terms as part of gap-fill activities or question answer activities. For example, teaching *day/night* with *sun/moon*, and extending this to include *on/off* and *open/close* not only provides students with the order for these terms, but also their opposites. Teacher-guided practice can be provided using short gap fills to introduce the concept and vocabulary as in figure 2.1.

Such an activity may then be extended by changing the sentences into questions, and eliciting student responses. For example, the questions can be asked using a number of different patterns:

> *Do you see the sun during the day, or during the night?*
> *Do you turn on the lights during the day?*
> *When do you turn off the lights?*
> *When do you open/close your windows?*

Vocabulary: *day/night, open/close, on/off, sun/moon.*
    Model: The <u>sun</u> is in the sky during the <u>day</u>, and
    Elicit: the _____ is in the sky during the _____.
    Elicit: Turn the lights _____ during the _____, and turn the lights _____ during the _____.
    Elicit: _____ the windows during the _____, and _____ the windows during the _____.

Figure 8.1 Example Gap-Fill Vocabulary Exercise Using Antonyms

An accompanying worksheet could then be provided to continue working with antonyms, synonyms, or both, as well as serve as a means of introducing some new ones with space provided for learners to add ones of their own. A worksheet focusing on vocabulary use and antonyms with an extension activity is provided in the photocopiable section of this chapter.

Vocabulary (Word Wheel) Spinner. Bittman (2020) introduces this concept for vocabulary practice on her blog. An adaptation of her activity uses a range of vocabulary words (e.g., flashcards) that are placed face down on a table, along with a laminated spinner which can be created by drawing a large circle on an A4 piece of paper, dividing it into eighths, and labeling the sections with a variety of tasks suitable for vocabulary practice. She suggests: *Draw it!, Part of speech?, Act it out!, Say a synonym!, Define it!, Use it in a sentence!, Rhyme time!,* and *Give an antonym!* Once the circle is printed, laminated, and cut out, you would be able to use a paperclip inserted through the center to act as the spinner. It works by placing the wheel face up on a table, having a student flick the spinner (paperclip), and where the spinner points is the activity that the students must perform. Prior to spinning, they can draw a flashcard from the table to know the vocabulary that they need to use when performing the task, and they can use a worksheet to record the vocabulary (see the photocopiable content section of this chapter). Alternatively, if using this activity in groups, each with their own spinner, you might prefer that every group completes each activity at least once before they can be declared the class winner.

Hangman. This is another learner favorite, and it is a great activity that can be performed at any time, using very few resources. There are a variety of ways to play it, from teacher-directed and as a whole class activity through to groups and to student-directed activities. Traditionally, the game is played with vocabulary items, but the vocabulary could be provided and the word to guess could include antonyms or a phrase like the definition or an idiom. The number of blank spaces in the vocabulary item is revealed for players by using one dash for each letter. For example, the word *secret* would be indicated using six dashes thus: __ __ __ __ __ __. Beginners would likely need to focus on vocabulary lists and the items under study, but here also, the student/team that wins might be required to provide the definition of the term, an antonym, a synonym, and so on before being able to claim the point. Gaining a point or not, they may then become the game host whose job it is to select a word or phrase for other players/teams to guess. In this way, all teams can play the game, but not all teams may win points for guessing the word. Limiting point provision in this way might prove handy if you are using points for prizes, or as part of a classroom management system. Every wrong guess that other players/teams make brings them closer to losing. Traditionally, a hangman figure is drawn in twelve steps, but the figure drawn could be anything (e.g., flower, pumpkin, snowman). Each time that a correct guess is made, the game host will write that letter in the space provided. If a wrong guess is made, a line is drawn to create the figure. If the full figure is revealed before a player/team can guess the word, the game is over. Games like this can also be set as homework with vocabulary items uploaded to sites such as Flippity (https://flippity.net), using content that is created in a gSheet that you or your students can prepare as part of a class activity or on your/their own. Other games that you may wish to create using Flippity are those like crosswords, word jumbles, word searches, and among others, Bingo.

Bingo. Although discussed in the pronunciation section of this book, it is worthwhile mentioning again here, particularly since it is a game that young learners really enjoy. It is also a game that appeals to a wide range of learners and it lends itself to several different varieties of play. Younger learners who are unable to read may require the use of pictures on their cards, marking vocabulary items once they hear the description. You can also have students create such cards in a previous activity (e.g., one that teaches colors, so that they can make and decorate their own cards). If the vocabulary on the card relates to animals, you might have young learners make the noise of the animal as they hear it called, and when looking to mark it on their card. For older learners, images pertaining to a certain theme of study would be worthwhile when using a picture-based card (e.g., vegetables when engaging in a unit on food; pictures of clock faces that show the time). Alternatively, the caller may rely on the definition of words if the card is text-based. Students may also be required to reproduce a certain pattern on their card, such as a diagonal line, or an X, before they are able to say 'Bingo!' in order to win the game. Alternatives for older learners are using the bingo card as a worksheet where each space on the card is a question, and having them go around the room to find others who can answer the questions positively. Such an activity could be used as part of a review, and to solidify sentence patterns and the kinds of grammatical patterns that might be used with them. In terms of vocabulary and grammar practice, the caller could use the present tense, with students marking irregular past simple verb tense vocabulary items on their cards (e.g., *go/went, see/saw, say/said, buy/bought,* and *take/took*). For a list of irregular past verbs that could be incorporated across Bingo cards, refer to the photocopiable section of this chapter.

Draw it! In this activity, students need to draw the meaning of vocabulary items. This is a very interesting game to play with learners, especially if their language contains a number of false friends which will see you end up drawing an image to represent the vocabulary item, and your students drawing one that looks very different, even though the word or expression that you are drawing is the same. This is a stark way of drawing attention to the difference of meanings between languages, and works to seize advantage of the users' first language (L1) if it shares cognates with the target language, and potentially serves to work as a mnemonic key. Examples of a few of these terms from Korean can be seen in Figure 2.2.

Flashcards. These have been the basis of self-study for vocabulary, and the memorization of new vocabulary items for a long time, and they have also been used to great effect by teachers in the classroom. Flashcards can be created in a multitude of ways. They may contain a target word, expression, or an image on one side, and perhaps a translation into one or more target languages on the flipside. The flipside may also contain additional information (e.g., definitions, phonemics, example sentences). During class, a teacher can use flash cards to drill students, quiz students, or as part of a language game.

436 *Issues in TESOL*

	Student	**Teacher**
Picture		
Word	Manicure	
Meaning	Finger nail polish.	Beauty treatment for the hands and fingernails.
Picture		
Word	Mansion	
Meaning	A luxury apartment for many families.	A house for a single family.
Picture		
Word	Punk	
Meaning	A puncture, as in a flat tire.	A genre of music.
Picture		
Word	Sofa	
Meaning	Any large padded chair, including those designed to seat one person.	A couch, or a padded chair for seating two or more people.

Figure 8.2 Example of English and Korean False Friends
(Note: Images are Public Domain)

Photocopiable Content – Pronunciation

Some language games involving flashcards include pair-matching activities; for example, two sets of the same flashcards in a *memory* or *concentration* pair-matching activity, where all cards are face down and learners would turn one over to reveal a definition or an image, and then turn over another card in order to find the match to the first card. If the learner succeeds in finding a match, those two cards are removed, but if the cards do not match, they are then turned face down and another learner takes a turn. The game continues until all cards are paired. This game might be easily played to practice pronunciation as well as vocabulary with students matching a series of minimal pair flash cards. (See the photocopiable content section for an example.)

You can also have students play card games such as *Fish* where one learner asks another, *Do you have a ____?*, in an attempt to match a word or image on a card that they are holding, to one that another learner is holding. If the other learner does not have such a card, then they say *Go fish*, and the first student then takes a card from the deck. A version of *Pictionary* with flashcards is also popular, with learners taking a card and then drawing an image on the board of the word or definition that is on the card for other learners to try and guess. This can also easily be turned into a game of *Charades*.

Flash cards can also be used as an exit ticket. In this case, the teacher might hold up a card with the facing side showing an image which might then require spelling of the target language word, or a word/expression which might then require students using it in a sentence before they can leave the room. Also, if you have very young learners with a lot of energy, then flash cards can be placed around the walls of the room and total physical response style activities can be relied on. Here, you call out a word and students run to an image, or you may state a definition and students run to a word, making it a race. This activity can also be extended with the teacher asking students to perform various actions as well (e.g., *gallop* to the *horse* while you *neigh*, *run* to the *dog* while you *woof*, *pounce* on the *cat* while you *meow*, *swim* to the *fish* while you *blow bubbles*.)

A number of applications exist today that are useful for creating and studying with flashcards via a smartphone. These applications extend paper-based flash cards by allowing for the use of multimodal content (e.g., embedded audio, high resolution graphics), and they can make learning fun by turning it into a game. Many of these applications will also track your progress, prevent any cheating glimpses, and recycle those vocabulary items that you are having the most difficulty practicing. They also bring portability with them so that learners can study when they feel like doing so. Popular, and free applications, are *Quizlet*, *Memrise*, and *Tinycards*, with each having sets of user-developed cards that you can access for practice – or you may wish to develop some of your own.

Songs. Using music and songs with students provides a break from the textbook, and it is a good way to introduce a range of cultural elements to lessons as well as engage in the use of authentic language. Depending on the level of students and the type of song, the ways to teach it vary as do the type and range of activities that you may want to develop for its use. Even your focus for use of the song will alter these activities (e.g., pronunciation, vocabulary, or grammar). For young learners, one song that is popular and allows for kinesthetic, visual, verbal and aural activities, strong repetition, and specific vocabulary is *Heads, Shoulders, Knees and Toes*. To use this song you might follow a sequence such as:

- Play the song and allow the class to listen to the words as they follow along.
- On a second listening, while performing the actions, have the students show the body parts, and elicit the name of the body part as they do so. (You may or may not need to pre-teach these.)
- On a subsequent listening, have students perform the actions along with you as you sing.
- After practicing several times, draw an outline of a body on the board, and elicit the names of the various parts of the body from students. Follow the sequence of the lyrics as you do this.
- You may then have students copy the outline and the words from the board into their books, or provide them with a worksheet to color.
- Extend the activity by providing homework or group work where learners write one sentence for each of the body parts, and describe what they are used for (e.g., head for thinking, toes for walking).

Word games and worksheets. These can include crossword puzzles, find-a-words, and matching activities (e.g., words to definitions). There are a number of websites that can generate such worksheets if you provide the language content, and all that you then need to do is print them. These kinds of worksheets are very useful to keep ready for use as time-killers, and not only promote recycling and practice of key lesson or unit vocabulary items, but they are good for setting as homework activities as well. Time killers are those kinds of activities that you can draw upon to keep students busy, engaged, and practicing language if they have finished the set work early and there is still time before the end of the lesson. These are also very useful to have as part of your ready-to-go teacher toolkit, so that you can provide them to any early finishers if you are working with a mixed ability class or learners who breeze through activities doing the bare minimum. There is also a number of applications and software packages, like Hot Potatoes (https://hotpot.uvic.ca) that you can use to create such content and then provide it to students online.

Word webs. This includes activities involving the use of mind maps and brainstorming, and one way to use a word web has already been presented along with its associated resources in the photocopiable section of this chapter. Other ways include simply having students work together to create them, and for vocabulary, this might mean developing synonyms for the center word only or moving outwards from the center to categories and then word associations (e.g., weather to spring, summer, fall, winter and then to warm, hot, windy, cold). Word webs can also be employed to help learners revise the vocabulary of a unit that they have just studied, and in this case, they can be created as a class, with peers, or as homework, and all with teacher guidance. The structure of the word webs is not necessarily important; what is important is that students are using the vocabulary items that they have learned, and that they are categorizing and/or are associating this vocabulary with other lexical items. Students may then be asked to present their word webs to the class or be chosen to lead a whole-class word web revision activity. A number of applications such as *MindMeister* can help teachers and learners develop word webs using images, links, notes, or vocabulary as they work either by themselves or in collaboration with others.

Visual dictionaries. Depending on your learners, you may be able to go further than the simple fun-and-basic game and worksheets as well as the song-and-mime style activities above, and undertake root analyses of individual words, as discussed in the pronunciation section of this chapter. You may also introduce other means of data-driven learning with students, or make use of it for yourself. For example, employing the use of concordances, developing word/sentence tree worksheets and vocabulary profiling texts. You may even want to make use of visual dictionaries/thesaurus. Ones like *Visuwords* (https://www.visuwords.com) are ideal to provide learners with the means to explore the relationship between vocabulary items, while others offer more traditional illustrative depictions of lexical content.

Compleat Lexical Tutor (https://www.lextutor.ca) is a website that provides a range of tools that allow for the analysis of text so that you can develop data-driven learning content that can then be used with your students. It allows users to test their vocabulary level so that they can then work on words at the level where they may prove weak. There is a wide selection of tools available for use from concordancing through to vocabulary profiling (using the BNC, COCA, and the NAWL) and this makes it one of the more powerful resources for the teaching and learning of vocabulary available. For example, teachers are able to use *Vocabprofile* to analyze and produce a cloze text that will remove specific words (e.g., those from the NAWL, or the BNC 1,000). The analysis of the text can also help new teachers decide if the reading might prove too difficult for learners as well as highlight for them the kind of words that learners are likely to find difficult when reading the passage. *GroupLex* is a collaborative vocabulary builder in which learners can input words, example sentences, definitions, and so on, and store them under their own name. The entries can then be used to create multiple-choice quizzes. The final tool to highlight here, although the others are all worth exploring on your own time, is *Corpus Correct* which allows learners to evaluate sentences for accuracy, and this requires students to begin to think inductively about how the vocabulary is being used among the examples provided.

Testing Vocabulary

A wide variety of tasks suitable for the testing of learner vocabulary knowledge and use exist. Ur (2002) considers several of them important, including those revolving around dictation, gap-fills and matching, multiple-choice, odd-one-out, sentence completion, and sentence writing.

Dictation. This can see you read words aloud for learners to then write down, which will test their aural skills along with the recognition of terms/phrases and their spellings. It is a test that is relatively simple to develop, administer, and correct.

Dictation-translation. This is similar to the preceding dictation task except that the test items are spoken in the L1 and students write them down in the target language. Leading to the meaning and spelling of the items being tested. Issues of validity might arise if there is no exact translation or if there is misinterpretation. However, if the words or phrases are relatively simple, and equivalent, then the test may have practicality in terms of being easy, quick, and convenient to administer and check.

Gap-fills. This kind of test typically involves the use of meaning, spelling, and to some extent grammar and collocation use. Using blank spaces means that the learner can include anything that makes sense to them, and you would need to decide prior to testing if you will accept those items or are going to focus only on the words/phrases that you intend for the learner to place in the gap. Such a decision can be avoided by providing an answer pool to learners.

Gap-fills with vocabulary box. Like the aforementioned test, meaning, spelling and to some extent grammar, as well as collocation use, will be examined by this kind of test. It may prove easier to mark and deliver over a simple gap-fill, as students are provided with the terms/phrases or other options that they should use to complete the spaces in the passage or sentences provided. One danger here is that the final item can be completed correctly by simply leaving it to last if there are an equal number of test items. This can be avoided by adding more items than there are blank spaces, and asking students to use those that they think are the best suited to complete the gaps in the test sentences or passage.

Matching Exercises. This type of activity is often provided with two components, a vocabulary item and a definition that must be matched together to test understanding of meaning. If even numbers of vocabulary items and definitions are provided the learner may be able to get the final item correct by simply leaving it to complete last, this can be avoided by adding more definitions than there are vocabulary items.

Multiple-choice. This kind of test examines denotative meaning and it can be difficult and time-consuming to create as each question must be understood well by all who take the test. Components of such a test involve the stem (the question, problem, or incomplete sentence that needs to be completed by selecting one of the available choices). The choices include the correct item and a series of distracters which are incorrect. If using this kind of test with learners to exam knowledge, then having one response and two distractors is probably best as you can provide one choice that is completely wrong, one that is similar to the correct response (but is still incorrect), and of course the correct response. You may use three distractors and choices such as 'none of the above' to increase face-validity (e.g., making it look harder), but it is best to avoid these. If composed well, this kind of test is very quick and easy to correct but it also offers a chance of getting an item right by simply randomly selecting or by guessing the answer. A variant of multiple-choice is a true or false test which offers a 50% chance of being correct if learners guess the answer.

Odd-one-out. Provides a range of vocabulary items with students needing to underline or circle the one that does not belong. Again, this predominantly tests understanding of meaning, but there is no way of knowing if all the items are understood by the learner.

Sentence completion. This test involves providing half a sentence, typically the first half, with learners needing to complete it. This allows for a wider interpretation of language and more thought on the part of students to be able to use their own language, but it essentially only tests denotative meaning. An alternative is gap-writing where the beginning and ending of the sentence are provided, and the learner completes the middle.

Sentence Writing. This kind of task can present learners with vocabulary items that they then need to use in a sentence. As a test it can examine a range of skills except for spelling of the vocabulary items provided, and pronunciation if you do not have students read their sentences aloud.

Translation. Translation can test a number of aspects, particularly if learners are translating whole sentences rather than single vocabulary items or expressions. It can be difficult to grade as validity issues might arise in terms of misinterpretations.

Summary

This chapter focused on the place and importance of vocabulary in the language teaching classroom, and how it links pronunciation, meaning, and form. Aspects of what constitutes vocabulary items, and how these are broken down into a variety of tiers and lists is examined along with the practicality of using such content with learners, particularly for data-driven learning. A variety of teaching strategies were then explored to provide a means of both effectively presenting and efficiently teaching vocabulary items. This involved the use of antonyms and synonyms, word wheels, games (*Hangman, Bingo*), false friends, flashcards, songs, worksheets, word webs, as well as visual dictionaries, and data-driven learning. A number of means for teaching and testing vocabulary were then covered, including diction, dictation-translation, gap-fills, gap-fills with vocabulary box, matching exercises, multiple-choice, odd-one-out, sentence completion, sentence writing, and translation.

Review

Content Quiz
Vocabulary for Teachers
To help solidify some of the concepts introduced by this chapter the following multiple-choice and true or false quizzes might be helpful for you to undertake. So that you can check the accuracy of your responses, an answer key can be found following the quizzes.

Multiple-Choice
Circle **a**, **b**, or **c** for the answer that best completes the sentence presented in each question.

1. Vocabulary can be arranged into one of three tiers. Tier two words include vocabulary items that are …
   a) domain-specific words and are generally specialized to specific content areas or fields.
   b) the words of everyday language, and form most native-speaker children's conversational repertoire.
   c) those that play important roles in specific content areas such as academic language, and are those that can apply across a wide range of contexts and topics.

2. Word lists like the BNC 1,000 show the …
   a) words that are misspelled the most often.
   b) most frequently used words in spoken English.
   c) most frequently used words in spoken and written English.

3. When introducing new vocabulary items to learners, it is a good idea to …
   a) only dictate vocabulary items to learners, and never write them anywhere.
   b) always write them in the same place (e.g., on the right-hand side of the board).
   c) sometimes write them in random places.

4. When introducing vocabulary it is important to associate the meaning of terms with meaningful memories, and this can be best achieved through …
   a) passive learning activities.
   b) no learning activities.
   c) active learning activities.

5. The best teaching strategy to help learners associate meaning with vocabulary is …
   a) the use of translation and a bilingual dictionary.
   b) data-driven learning.
   c) activities such as mime, drawing, or the use of word clusters or word webs.

6. Denotation refers to the …
   a) feeling that the word invokes.
   b) way in which a word is pronounced.
   c) literal meaning of a word or name.

7. Connotation refers to the …
   a) literal meaning of a word or name.
   b) feeling that word invokes.
   c) way in which a word is pronounced.

8. Prefix refers to …
   a) an element placed at the beginning of a word to adjust or qualify its meaning.
   b) a morpheme added at the end of a word to form a derivative.
   c) an additional element placed at the beginning or at the end of a root, stem, or word, or in the body of a word, in order to modify its meaning.

9. Suffix refers to …
   a) an element placed at the beginning of a word to adjust or qualify its meaning.
   b) a morpheme added at the end of a word to form a derivative.
   c) an additional element placed at the beginning or at the end of a root, stem, or word, or in the body of a word, in order to modify its meaning.

10. When introducing relevant examples of vocabulary items to learners, it is best to …
    a) provide those that are applicable to student lives, and in a way that encourages noticing and recycling.
    b) use phrases, collocations, synonyms, antonyms, hyponyms, root words, and so on.
    c) have students use dictionaries or machine translation as you continue teaching something else.

True or False

Circle **a** (true) if you think that the statement is correct, or **b** (false) if you think that the statement is incorrect.

1. Vocabulary plays an important role across all four skills, and it is an aspect of language that links pronunciation, meaning, and form.
   a) True.
   b) False.

2. When thinking of vocabulary, we think of vocabulary items. These include single words and compound words, but not set phrases or other expressions.
   a) True.
   b) False.

3. A number of word lists exist, including those of frequency (e.g., the BNC 1,000), and these can be used to help you develop readings and quizzes that are suitable to your learners.
   a) True.
   b) False.

4. Techniques to introduce and practice new terminology include demonstrating the meaning (e.g., by miming), or eliciting the meaning from various students (e.g., by having them draw an image).
   a) True.
   b) False.

5. When presenting concise descriptions of vocabulary items, it is not important to deliver them in context and attempt to make the meaning of them memorable.
   a) True.
   b) False.

6. To further expand on vocabulary-item examples, you might use phrases, collocations, synonyms, antonyms, hyponyms, or root words.
   a) True.
   b) False.

7. The ways in which students practice vocabulary items, and how they end up being recycled, varies depending on the focus of your teaching.
   a) True.
   b) False.

8. When introducing vocabulary items to learners it is often beneficial to teach those that have a similar meaning (e.g., synonyms) along with those that have the opposite meaning (e.g., antonyms).
   a) True.
   b) False.

9. False friends are those words or phrases that are pronounced the same in one language and another but have different meanings.
   a) True.
   b) False.

10. A gap-fill quiz can test a learner's use of vocabulary items, but to prevent many different answers being written into each gap, and to test specific meanings, it may be best to use gap-fills with a vocabulary box.
    a) True.
    b) False.

Quiz Answers
Vocabulary in Teaching

Multiple-Choice		*True or False*	
1.	c	1.	T
2.	c	2.	F
3.	b	3.	T
4.	c	4.	T
5.	c	5.	F
6.	c	6.	T
7.	b	7.	T
8.	a	8.	T
9.	b	9.	T
10.	a	10.	T

Suggested Readings

Allen, J. (1999). *Words, words, words. Teaching vocabulary in grades 4-12.* Stenhouse Publishers.

Beck, I., McKeown, M., & Kucan, L. (2008). *Creating robust vocabulary: Frequently asked questions and extended examples.* The Guildford Press.

Bittman, E. (2020). Word Wheel. *E is for Explore!* http://eisforexplore.blogspot.com/2012/05/word-wheel.html

Carlton, L., & Marzano, R. (2013). *Vocabulary games for the classroom.* Marzano Research Laboratory.

Clark, C. (2013). *Speech and language therapy guide: Step-by-step speech therapy activities to teach speech and language skills at home or in therapy.* The SLP Solution.

Garcia, O. (2009). *Bilingual education in the 21st century: A global perspective.* Blackwell.

Hughes, A. (1989). *Testing for language teachers.* Cambridge University Press.

Kucan, L., McKeown, M., & Beck, I. (2013). *Bringing words to life,* (2nd ed.). The Guildford Press.

Marzano, R. (2009). *Teaching basic and advanced vocabulary: A framework for direct instruction.* Heinle.

Shemesh, R., & Waller, S. (2000). *Teaching English spelling: A practical guide.* Cambridge University Press.

Ur, P. (2002). *A course in language teaching: Practice and theory.* Cambridge University Press.

Photocopiable Content
Vocabulary in Teaching

This section of the text includes a variety of material that is free to photocopy and use either by yourself or with your classes. It contains examples of the following content:

- Word wheel – Spinner
- Word wheel – Worksheet
- Word web activity – Teacher notes
- Word web activity – Worksheet
- Vocabulary activity – Antonyms worksheet
- Minimal pairs – Flashcards – Teacher notes

Word Wheel – Spinner

Instructions.
1. Print the circle below, laminate it, and cut around the edges.
2. Straighten one edge of a paperclip, and poke it through the center of the circle from the reverse side.
3. Place the circle on a table face up, and flatten the straight edge of the paperclip down.
4. Flick the paperclip, using it as the pointer/spinner.
5. Use the spinner in conjunction with the word wheel worksheet and vocabulary flashcards that are placed face down on a table.

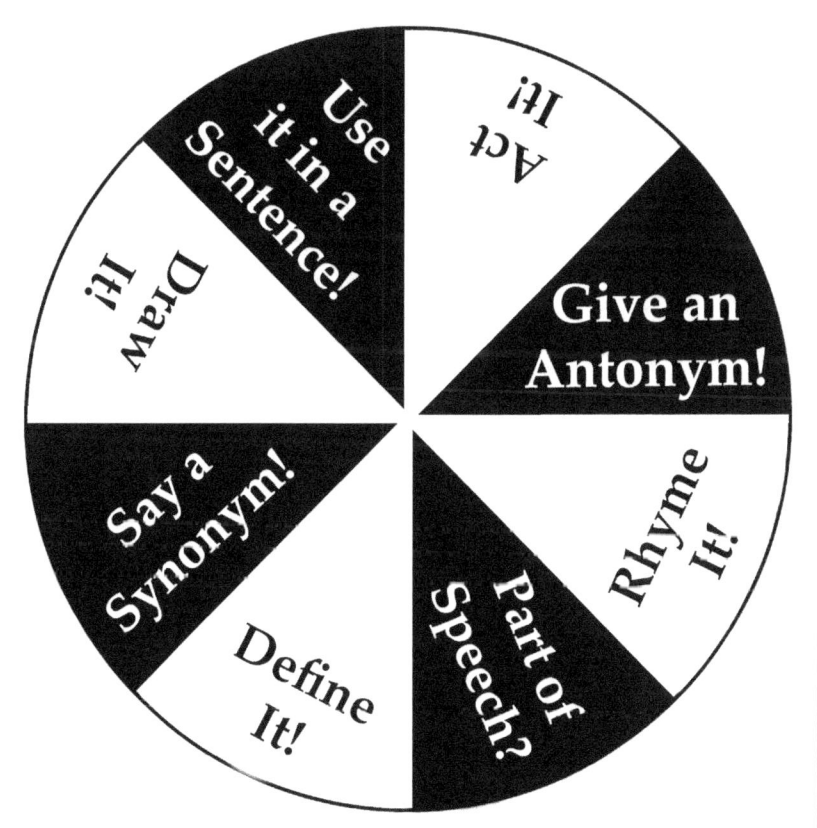

*based on Bittman (2020).

Word Wheel – Worksheet	
Flip over a vocabulary flash card, and spin the wheel! Perform the action that the wheel tells you to do, and write the vocabulary word under the heading below.	
Act It!	Define It!
Draw It!	Give an Antonym!
Part of Speech?	Say a Synonym!
Rhyme it!	Use it in a sentence!

Word Web Activity – Teacher Notes

A. Prior to starting the activity, draw a word web on the board.
B. Label each of the periphery circles with headings (see below). This will help focus student attention on identifying aspects of the center vocabulary item, and in responding when you start to elicit vocabulary items to fill in the word.
C. Use a combination, or all, of the following example headings, and any others that you might consider appropriate for your learners.
D. Provide the *Word Web Activity – Worksheet* to students. They can then complete this worksheet by themselves or as a group using different vocabulary items at the center.

Heading	Elicit from students
Antonyms.	The words or expressions that mean the opposite of the center vocabulary item (e.g., *night/day*).
Category.	The kind of category in which the center vocabulary item might belong (e.g., *fruit, vehicle.*)
Descriptor.	The words or expressions that can describe the center vocabulary item (e.g., actions, colors, and so on).
Function.	The function of the part of speech of the center vocabulary item (e.g., nouns are words that identify people, places, and things).
Parts of speech.	The part of speech the center vocabulary item belongs to (e.g., adjectives, adverbs, conjunctions, interjections, nouns, prepositions, verbs).
Synonyms.	The words or expressions that mean the same as the center vocabulary item (e.g., *baffle/confuse*).
Word parts.	The words that the center vocabulary item can be split into that then form new words (e.g., *butterfly* will break into *butter* and *fly*).
Other.	Other things that use the center vocabulary item (e.g., idioms, proverbs tongue-twisters, and so on).

*based on an activity by Clark (2013).

Word Web Activity – Worksheet

Instructions.

In this activity, you will develop a word web.

1. Choose a vocabulary item, and write it in the center of the word web.
2. Fill in the surrounding squares, writing on the lines provided.
3. Aim for at least one item per square.

Word Web

Antonyms	Category	Descriptor
Function	Center Word or Expression	Word Parts
Parts of Speech	Synonyms	Other

Photocopiable Content – Vocabulary

Vocabulary Activity – Antonyms Worksheet

1. Vocabulary.

Look over the following vocabulary where each pair is an antonym. Make sure that you understand the meaning of each.

| hot/cold | save/spend | stay/go |

2. Sentences.

Fill in the gaps below with the vocabulary above.

    a) Do you like to _____ home, or do you like to _____ out?

    b) Do you like to _____ money, or do you like to _____ money?

    c) Do you like _____ weather or _____ weather?

3. My Vocabulary and Antonyms.

After completing the sentences above, think of some new vocabulary (e.g., from your text book), and pair this new vocabulary with its antonym. Write the vocabulary and its antonym on the lines below.

Vocabulary	Antonym
a. _____	a) _____
b. _____	b) _____
c. _____	c) _____
d. _____	d) _____

4. Your sentences.

Use your vocabulary and antonym pairs above to make sentences of your own. Write your sentences on the lines below.

    a. _____

    b. _____

    c. _____

    d. _____

5. Extension Activity – *wh*-questions.

Make some *wh*-questions (who, what, when, where) using any of the vocabulary or antonyms from this worksheet. Write these questions on the lines below. Then, ask the questions to your partner, and write their answer on the lines provided.

a. **Who?**
   Question _____
   _____
   _____
   Answer _____
   _____
   _____

b. **What?**
   Question _____
   _____
   _____
   Answer _____
   _____
   _____

c. **When?**
   Question _____
   _____
   _____
   Answer _____
   _____
   _____

d. **Where?**
   Question _____
   _____
   _____
   Answer _____
   _____

Irregular Past Verb List

The intention of this list is to show past verbs that are usually or always irregular in **both** *British and American English, except for compounds and prefixed forms that modify meanings. For example,* stand *and* understand *are both listed as* under *does not modify the meaning of* stand *(even though the irregularity is the same), but* misunderstand *is not listed as* mis *modifies the meaning of* understand. *Note that the past simple form of* show *is regular (*showed*) but the past participle is usually irregular (*shown*). Note also that* be *is the only verb with two irregular forms in the past simple. Further, words in brackets indicate meaning, with the words in italics in brackets providing additional information. When two words are provided with* or *between them, the first is that of American English and the second is that of British English.*

Base Form	Past Simple	Past Participle
be	was *and* were	been
bear (give birth)	bore	born
bear (carry)	bore	borne
beat	beat	beaten
become	became	become
beget	begat	begotten
begin	began	begun
bend	bent	bent
bid (direct)	bid *or* bade	bid *or* bidden
bid (make an offer)	bid	bid
bind	bound	bound
bite	bit	bitten
bleed	bled	bled
blow	blew	blown
break	broke	broken
breed	bred	bred
bring	brought	brought
build	built	built
burst	burst	burst
buy	bought	bought
cast	cast	cast

Photocopiable Content – Vocabulary

catch	caught	caught
choose	chose	chosen
cling	clung	clung
come	came	come
cost (have a price)	cost	cost
creep	crept	crept
cut	cut	cut
deal	dealt	dealt
dig	dug	dug
do	did	done
draw	drew	drawn
drink	drank	drunk
drive	drove	driven
eat	ate	eaten
fall	fell	fallen
feed	fed	fed
feel	felt	felt
fight	fought	fought
find	found	found
flee	fled	fled
fling	flung	flung
fly (move quickly)	flew	flown
forbid	forbid *or* forbade	forbidden
forget	forgot	forgotten
forsake	forsook	forsaken
freeze	froze	frozen
get (have *or* have to)	got	got
get *(other meanings)*	got	got *or* gotten
give	gave	given
go	went	gone
grow	grew	grown
hang *(something)*	hung	hung
have	had	had
hear	heard	heard
hide (move from sight)	hid	hidden
hit	hit	hit

Photocopiable Content – Vocabulary

hold	held	held
hurt	hurt	hurt
keep	kept	kept
know	knew	known
lay	laid	laid
lead	led	led
leave (depart)	left	left
lend	lent	lent
let	let	let
lie (not move)	lay	lain
lose	lost	lost
make	made	made
mean	meant	meant
meet	met	met
pay	paid	paid
put	put	put
read	read	read
rend	rent	rent
rid	rid	rid
ride	rode	ridden
ring *(bell)*	rang *or* rung	rung
rise	rose	risen
run	ran	run
say	said	said
see	saw	seen
seek	sought	sought
sell	sold	sold
send	sent	sent
set	set	set
shake	shook	shaken
shed	shed	shed
shoot	shot	shot
show	showed *(regular)*	shown
shrink	shrank *or* shrunk	shrunk
shut	shut	shut
sing	sung	sung
sink	sunk	sunk

sit	sat	sat
slay	slain	slain
sleep	slept	slept
slide	slid	slid
sling	slung	slung
slit	slit	slit
smite	smitten	smitten
speak	spoken	spoken
spend	spent	spent
spin	spun	spun
spit (eject suddenly)	spat *or* spit	spat *or* spit
split	split	split
spread	spread	spread
spring	sprung	sprung
stand	stood	stood
steal	stole	stolen
stick	stuck	stuck
sting	stung	stung
stink	stank *or* stunk	stunk
stride	strode	stridden
strike	struck	struck *or* stricken
string	strung	strung
swear	swore	sworn
sweep	swept	swept
swim	swam	swum
swing	swung	swung
take	took	taken
teach	taught	taught
tear	tore	torn
tell	told	told
think	thought	thought
throw	threw	thrown
thrust	thrust	thrust
understand	understand	understand
wake	woke	woken
wear	wore	worn
weave (*material*)	wove	woven

Photocopiable Content – Vocabulary

weep	wept	wept
win	won	won
wind	wound	wound
wring	wrung	wrung
write	wrote	written

Minimal Pairs – Flash Cards – Teacher Notes

Teacher notes.

The following lists group minimal pairs according to sound.

Matching pairs are on the same row, with the sound focus for each pair highlighted in bold on the top row of each group.

The pages can be photocopied, and you can cut each word out to create a series of small cards to use with your learners.

To extend the life of the cards, you may wish to laminate them.

Please keep in mind that the intention here is not to provide an extensive listing of minimal pairs, but rather to provide a grouping of some common ones in order to assist you in getting started on creating a series of your own.

Example activity.

Use the cards in any kind of matching activity, such as a game of memory or concentration.

How to play:
1. Place all cards face down on the table in a random order. If not placed randomly, you can shuffle their position around as long as the cards remain face down.
2. The first student will select a card, turn it over, read the word on the card aloud, and then turn over a different card. If the two minimal pairs on the card match, then that student collects the two cards, wins the round, and continues playing. If the cards do not match, the student turns both of the cards face down, and it is the next student's turn to play.
3. When all cards are removed from the table, the game is over, and the student with the most cards wins!
4. Cards can be reshuffled, and the game played again.

Extension activity.
1. Match the words with images or definitions and play a variant of the concentration or memory game where learners match the image/definition with the term.
2. Use the cards as an exit ticket by showing students the word and having them pronounce it, spell it, and use it in a sentence.

Minimal Pairs – Flash Cards

/b/ and /v/

ban	**v**an
berry	**v**ery
best	**v**est
bet	**v**et
boat	**v**ote

/e/ and /æ/

bet	bat
dead	dad
bed	bad
beg	bag
gem	jam

Photocopiable Content – Vocabulary

/ɪ/ and /iː/	
chick	cheek
slip	sleep
lip	leap
pick	peek
ship	sheep

/l/ and /r/	
belly	berry
lamp	ramp
light	right
lock	rock
fleas	freeze

/p/ and /f/	
copy	coffee
pat	fat
pride	fried
pan	fan
pull	full

/r/ and /w/	
rail	whale
rig	wig
rich	witch
rest	west
ring	wing

9. Grammar in Teaching

Overview
The knowledge of grammar can assist a learner in the correction of a mistake, and may help them in improving their communicative ability as well as their in-class work. The question then, is not that of how important is grammar to the learning of an additional language, but how we as a teacher present it to our learners during the classes in which we teach. In order to do this, we need to understand the various types of grammar that are available to us, and appreciate how such grammar should be introduced and used, particularly that of a pedagogical grammar. Important too, is understanding how to apply those strategies that enable the efficient and effective teaching of grammar in ways that are relevant, timely, and engaging for our learners. Pertinent to this is being able to develop testing procedures that allow our learners to demonstrate their levels of knowledge and performance.

Learning Outcomes
1. Gain an understanding of the various types of grammar that exist.
2. Appreciate the rules behind the teaching of grammar.
3. Comprehend the focus of a pedagogical grammar.
4. Discover a number of means for drawing student attention to specific features of grammar while teaching.
5. Understand how to apply various games and activities with learners when explicitly or implicitly teaching grammar.
6. Uncover a number of activities that can be adapted to the testing of grammar, along with aspects of test
7. practicality, reliability, validity, backwash, and spin-off.

Grammar – Types, Rules, Focus
For some, the place of grammar teaching in the language learning classroom is a controversial topic, but it is recognized that "knowing a language means, among other things, knowing its grammar" (Ur, 2002, p. 76). Indeed, Thornbury (2008) argues that there is a very clear role for grammar to play in the language learning classroom. Yet, it may prove difficult for a native speaker of a language to be able to explain their

grammar to a non-native speaker, and difficult for non-native speakers to familiarize themselves with the grammar of any additional language(s) they may choose to learn. Grammar can be considered something that is straightforward, but also something that is complex, as it is both a part of natural language systems as well as a highly technical academic subject (Taylor, 2016).

Types of Grammar

When most people think of grammar, they could be thinking about the type that linguists and grammarians use. However, there are many other types, classifications, and categories of grammar. These include descriptive, prescriptive, traditional, generative, transformational(-generative), mental (competence), universal (UG), case, dependency, lexical-functional, comparative, performance, role and reference, and, of course, a pedagogical grammar for foreign language teaching.

Descriptive grammar refers to the structure of a language as it is used by speakers and writers, while *prescriptive grammar* refers to the structure of a language as certain people think that it should be used. Both kinds are concerned with rules, but in different ways. Specialists of descriptive grammar (linguists) study the rules or patterns underlying the use of grammar (e.g., words, phrases, clauses, sentences), while prescriptive grammarians lay out the rules (e.g., what is to be considered correct or incorrect).

Traditional grammar is typically taught in schools, and it relies on imparting the prescriptive rules and concepts concerning the structure of language.

Generative grammar is a set of rules that indicates the structure and interpretation of sentences that a native speaker of a language accepts as belonging to the language. Areas of study in generative grammar include the sound patterns of language (phonology), the structure and meaning of words (morphology), the study of sentence structure (syntax), and the study of linguistic meaning (semantics).

Transformational grammar or *transformational-generative grammar* is part of the theory of generative grammar, and it is a system of performing analyses to examine the relationship among various elements of a sentence, and among the possible sentences of a language, along with the use of processes or rules (some known as transformations). Essentially, it is a theory of grammar where constructions of a language emerge from linguistic transformations and phrase structures. Rules are viewed as unconscious and regularly followed principles internalized by a native speaker.

Mental (competence) grammar refers to the grammar that is stored in the brain, and allows a speaker to produce language that other speakers can understand. The *language faculty* is the capacity to construct a mental grammar as a result of linguistic exposure.

Universal grammar (UG) is a theory of human languages where the system of categories, operations, and principles are considered to be innate. UG attempts to explain why languages all have a finite amount of rules, but offer ways to structure thought in a manner that allows for the development of an infinite number of novel phrases.

Case grammar is a theory that stresses the importance of semantic roles in an effort to make explicit the basic meaning relationships in a sentence.

Dependency grammar is a class of modern grammatical theories based upon the dependency relation, as opposed to phrase structure (constituency grammars). Dependency is the notion that linguistic units (e.g., words) are connected to each other by directed links.

Lexical functional grammar is a declarative, constraint-based framework for analyzing the various components of grammar, including, crucially, syntax.

Comparative grammar seeks to provide an analysis and comparison of the grammatical structures of related languages. It is concerned with providing an explanatory basis for how humans each acquire their first language in order to develop a theory of grammar that is a theory of human language, and one that establishes a relationship among all languages.

Performance grammar refers to the description of syntax as it is used by speakers in dialogues. The focus is on language production in the belief that production problems need to be dealt with prior to those of reception and comprehension.

Role and reference grammar is a prose-like description of the major grammatical constructions in a language that are illustrated with examples. It incorporates aspects of a number of functional grammar theories to provide a description of the grammar of a language with explanations of the principles governing word, phrase, clause, and sentence construction.

Finally, in the teaching of other languages a *pedagogical grammar*, primarily dealing with word-level rules (morphology) and sentence-level rules (syntax) is used to provide descriptions (to language learners) of how to use grammar to communicate. It can be contrasted with other types of grammar, as pedagogical grammars have different functions and uses which may be influenced by instructor cognition, beliefs, assumptions, and attitudes concerning the teaching of grammar. For Davies (2007), a pedagogical grammar is based on grammatical analysis and description, a particular grammatical theory, and the study of grammatical problems of learners, or a combination of approaches.

Rules of Grammar Teaching

Thornbury (in Taylor, 2016) presents six rules for the teaching of grammar. These are the rules of context, use, economy, relevance, nurture, and appropriacy.

1. *Context.* This involves teaching grammar in context, and if taking form out of context to focus upon it, then it should be recontextualized as soon as possible. In this way, form is always associated with the meaning of the speaker or author.
2. *Use.* Grammar is used to improve learner understanding and to help them produce language, but not as an end in itself. In other words, always provide opportunities for learners to use grammar communicatively in practice.
3. *Economy.* This refers to economy of time. Minimize the time spent on presenting form and provide direct explanations to maximize the time that is spent on practicing so that students are able to concentrate on the language as they communicate, and to solidify and remember the language. Teacher talk time (TTT) should be far less than student talk time (STT).
4. *Relevance.* If students already know the form of grammar items or rules, do not waste time on teaching it. A quick revision should be sufficient. In the teaching English to speakers of other languages (TESOL) context, allow the knowledge from the first language to facilitate learning objectives in the target language.
5. *Nurture.* Teaching does not cause learning, but it can provide opportunities for learning to develop, and for language learning, knowledge and skills to emerge from a long, slow and deliberate process of study and practice from environments that are conducive to it. Use noticing techniques.
6. *Appropriacy.* Consider all of the rules according to the teaching and learning context. Determine the needs, interests, and

expectations of learners, and work at their level. This may mean that, for one class, you need to focus on explicit grammar teaching, but for another, not at all.

The Focus of a Pedagogical Grammar

The teaching of grammar in the foreign language classroom has traditionally focused on form and a sentence-based approach. However, this can be balanced with meaning and use, and taught from a contextualized content- and discourse-based approach (Celce-Murcia, 1991). By combining form with meaning for practical use and language practice, meaning can be used to stimulate learning. Providing context for form can also provide layers of meaning to support learning, and this is because the presentation of meaningful language in context with form can prove more relevant to learners than the isolated discussion of form by itself (e.g., the labels of metalanguage, and the presentation of decontextualized words and sentences as linguistic exercises).

Moving to a form-meaning-use paradigm for a pedagogical grammar requires the focus of the teaching of grammar to occur along a continuum. This could see you teach one class, or even one form of grammar in a particular class, using a deductive (rule-driven) means, where there is a focus on accuracy over fluency and constrained examples are used, rather than an inductive one (rule-discovery). This would mean that you are focusing on correct forms and/or error correction in some classes, or at particular times during a lesson, rather than allowing learners to use their own language creatively and accepting their errors as long as understanding and communication is occurring. In the classroom, there is always a shifting of demand between the need to focus on the accuracy of a speaker and to focus on their message, the explicit teaching of rules and an approach of rule-discovery, and a bottom-up provision of learning and one that presents it top-down. This kind of grammar teaching continuum is illustrated by Figure 3.1.

Such an approach views the traditional focus on form to the contemporary focus on meaning as a continuum, and one that a variety of content and class work might shift between. Such a continuum is illustrated by Figure 3.2.

Grammar Teaching Continuum

inductive	↔	deductive
fluent	↔	accurate
creative	↔	constrained
acceptable	↔	correct
implicit	↔	explicit
bottom-up	↔	top-down

Figure 9.1 A Grammar Teaching Continuum

FORM

1. *Non-communicative learning*	Focus on language structure (e.g., substitution exercises, grammar exercises).
2. *Pre-communicative language practice*	Practice language with some attention to meaning but not for communicating new messages to others (e.g., question and answer practice).
3. *Communicative language practice*	Practice pre-taught language in context where it communicates new information (e.g., information-gap activities, personalized questions).
4. *Structured communication*	Use language to communicate in situations that elicit pre-learned language, but with some unpredictability (e.g., structured role play and simple problem-solving).
5. *Authentic communication*	Use language to communicate in situations where the meanings are unpredictable (e.g., creative role play, more complex problem-solving, and discussion).

MEANING

Figure 9.2 Continuum of Focus – Form to Meaning (based on Littlewood, 2004)

Grammar in the Classroom

Teaching Grammar

Grammar teaching in the language classroom has generally taken one of five approaches each with their own aim. These are:
- deductive (rule-driven).
- inductive (rule-discovery).
- interactive.
- text and writing.
- sentence diagramming.

Deductive approach. When applying this top-down approach, you would present a grammar rule and then engage learners with practice and manipulation of it by employing a large number of examples. In other words, explain the grammar rules first, and then present lessons using those rules. After lessons like this, you could provide students with worksheets or exercises to practice what they have learned in a mechanical manner. These are the kind of activities that are perhaps most familiar to teachers, and are those often found as part of the grammar section of a textbook.

Inductive approach. This approach aims to expose learners to many examples from which the intent is that they are able to come to an understanding of how the rules work for themselves. This involves no explanation of form as students are expected to recognize or notice the rules of grammar in a natural way as they use the language and engage in activities such as reading and writing. It is a discovery process of bottom-up learning where learners notice how grammar rules function as they complete various exercises that apply them. For example, you may use lessons that focus on the simple past to illustrate how grammar functions when discussing time.

Interactive approach. This kind of approach employs a number of means to involve students more actively and in more engaging ways than in traditional lessons. This could include the use of games or those kinds of activities that require movement, both of which need a high level of engagement on the part of learners. An example of this is providing each student with a word from a sentence on a large flashcard, and then asking them to arrange themselves into grammatical order. A teacher could then have students use or practice the grammar point by employing a pronunciation activity where students say sentences aloud using the grammar rules as they practice pitch and intonation by walking up and down stairs.

Text and writing. This involves the use of creative writing and reading activities in an inductive fashion, where learners are exposed to grammar rules through use. Any particular problems that emerge would need to be teacher-addressed as part of a more structured lesson. This approach places emphasis on acquisition over learning with an aim of providing students with the opportunity to use the language as they write, and therefore the rules that they have been exposed to while reading. The use of creative or personal writing tasks is a means of providing repeated practice.

Sentence diagramming. One of the oldest methods of approaching the teaching of grammar includes the diagramming of sentences. Sentence diagrams, or working with sentence trees, is a visual mapping process that aims to show the relationships between parts of a sentence. It is not often used in the language learning classroom today, but it is used in many linguistics courses. There are many different forms of diagramming that can be used to map out sentences, such as the use of constituency-based grammar and dependency grammar to show sentence structure based on word order, or the Reed-Kellogg system where sentences are mapped according to word function.

In the Reed-Kellogg system of sentence diagramming, the functions of each word in a sentence are highlighted over that of traditional sentence word ordering (see Figure 3.3).

To start diagramming, you would draw a horizontal line which is then divided by a short vertical line. The subject of the sentence is placed to the left of the dividing vertical line. Sentence modifiers (e.g., adjectives, articles, adverbs) are then placed on a diagonal line below what they modify (e.g., noun, verb). The predicate of the sentence is placed to the right of the dividing line, linking verbs would be placed to the left of it to connect the subject to the predicate and separated by a slanting line. Once again, any modifiers of the predicate are placed on a diagonal line below what it is they modify.

474   Issues in TESOL

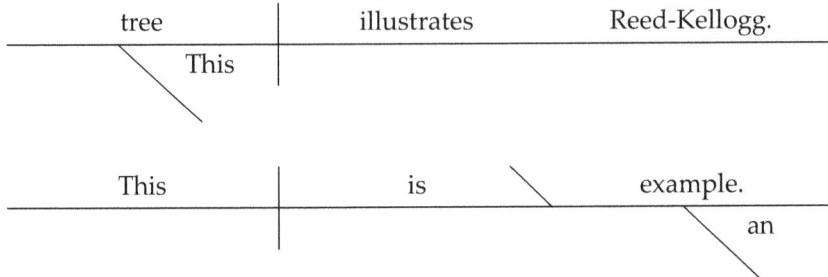

Figure 9.3 Sentence Diagrams Using the Reed-Kellogg System

In the dependency and constituency method of sentence diagramming, sentence trees are used with every word in a sentence corresponding to one or more nodes in the diagram (see Figures 3.4 and 3.5). Acronyms are used to label the nodes of a tree (e.g., D = determiner, N = noun, NP = noun phrase, S = sentence, V = verb, VP = verb phrase). A hybrid dependency-constituency sentence tree can also be diagrammed when rendering a sentence using this system (see Figure 3.6).

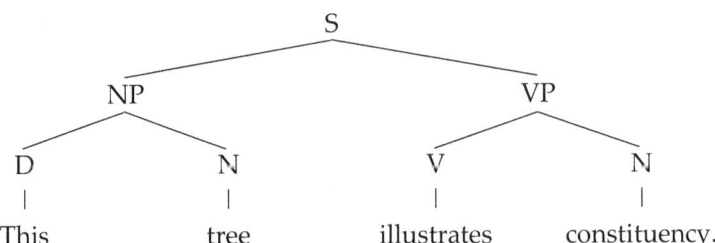

Figure 9.4 A Constituency Sentence Tree

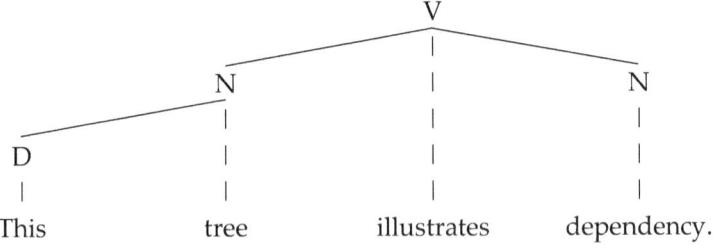

Figure 9.5 A Dependency Sentence Tree

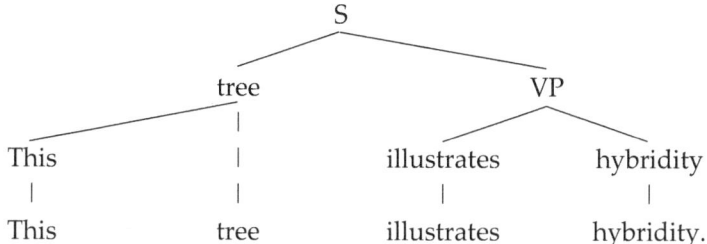

Figure 9.6 A Hybrid Dependency-Constituency Sentence Tree

Grammar Games and Activities

Teaching grammar in context helps to solidify usage, and incorporating its use across a variety of skills will help students understand this usage better. Applying the use of grammar from within thematic units, or introducing it with a supporting overarching lesson or activity concept, will then help students make long-lasting connections between grammar and content, and assist them in being able to recall what they have learned. With this in mind, Taylor (2016) suggests implementing lessons that present grammar using a goal-content-process cycle. This is one that relies on presenting material to contextualize content, awareness raising to produce focus, tasks to present goals, and production to ensure that meaningful practice and recycling occurs. In other words, grammar lessons should see students engage with authentic content to perform a practical task, or work with interesting material in situations that provide purpose for the homework or activities that are set for learners to complete. A number of games and activities can be used for such a manner.

Dictoglosss. As an activity, a dictogloss can integrate listening, speaking, reading, and writing skills and it can also be used to teach grammar in a communicative manner. In the first instance, the teacher will read a short (five-sentence) text twice, once slightly slower and then at normal pace, with students listening for the overall meaning. The intent is for learners to then reformulate what they have heard and understood, using their own words, to provide practice in developing the ability to cope with rapid native-speaker speech, and to focus on those words that impart meaning. Learners then work together and compare their notes with peers in order to discuss and more fully reconstruct the passage. They may write out the main ideas, note keywords, and while doing so, they are engaging in proof-reading and editing of their work. Additional writing activities on the same theme can then be explored with the teacher. In this case, if the dictogloss is about your morning routine, then the students might need to write about their morning routine or that of their partners, and then present these to the class. This could involve the use of guided questions that target specific grammatical form and functions (e.g., simple verbs). An example of such an activity is in the photocopiable section of this chapter.

Songs. Music is a way to change the pace of a class, and its focus, and can be used to introduce activities that are both engaging and entertaining. Lyrics to songs also use particular points of grammar that can be made the focus of a lesson and to either reinforce the concept or introduce it for the first time. A listing of song titles with artist matched to grammar points is available from the photocopiable section of this chapter. If using a song's audio or the official music video, it should also be prescreened to see if it is appropriate for the age and maturity level of your learners. Many professional organizations do not allow you to use profanity in the classroom, nor material that might promote certain kinds of behavior (e.g., drinking or smoking). Sometimes, artists will use grammatically incorrect phrases, and these are also good teaching points that can be put on the board for students to correct, or you could ask learners to identify these as they listen. Focusing lessons and activities on grammar points also means that you can recycle any material that you develop with songs.

For learners to practice with the song outside of the classroom, a number of websites and applications such as LyricsTraining (https://www.lyricstraining.com) offer the ability to link YouTube (https://www.youtube.com) videos to gap-filling tasks, or they may already house links to such content. These activities can then be practiced on smartphones for learner reinforcement, with students either typing in the words or selecting them from a series of those provided as they hear the song, watch the video, and see the lyrics on screen.

In the classroom, when using a song for grammar teaching, students should be familiar with the majority of the vocabulary in the lyrics. If not, then some pre-teaching of vocabulary along with some matching and underlining activities could prove useful. It is also important to anticipate the vocabulary that students might not know, and provide a means of helping them learn it, see its use in a number of contexts, and practice it as well.

It is also important to decide on the focus of the lesson that you are using a song for, and this can include reviewing perfect modals (*must have* + past participle) in order to speculate about past events (guessing what happened), and providing pronunciation practice of past participles and simple past regular verbs (e.g., -ed) along with the weak version of 'must and 'have'. To introduce such a focus to learners you might begin by handing out flashcards that contain different actions or objects. The song by ABBA, *The Day Before You Came*, might be suitable for this purpose.

Students could be provided with flashcards at the start of a lesson, and then use these to state what the teacher might have done on the weekend. For example, a student holding a card with a movie ticket on it might see another student need to respond with, *You watched a movie.* The teacher might then point out that there is only one ticket, and introduce the phrase *You must have gone alone as there is only one ticket.* The idea here is to present a model for students to use with the other cards, and provide students with a means to practice using *must have* + past participle before moving on to discuss what students themselves did last weekend. This ensures that learners are starting to talk about the themes of the song, which relate to routines and boredom. As students do this, more examples of target language from the song that they can practice in this kind of discussion can be written on the board.

The song can then be introduced with lyrics and also any vocabulary that you might want to pre-teach. One way of teaching the vocabulary is to write any new terms on the board, and then hand the definitions to students to match to the vocabulary items. If each student has one definition, they can then attempt to match it with the vocabulary item written up on the board, and be called on to use the vocabulary item in a new sentence. The teacher can extend this activity by asking how these terms might relate to the theme of the song, and how students think the singer may feel.

The entire song can then be played once through, and students may be asked about the song itself. Is it a happy song or a sad one? How do they know? What lyrics help them to know this? On subsequent listening, you could play the song in chunks and focus on different types of tasks. When playing the first audio chunk you could have students attempt to choose the right word (e.g., *gone/conned, made/named*); they could recite or even sing the lines; and they could offer interpretations of the meaning or message of that chunk. You could then practice the pronunciation of these lines with learners, and elicit the terms that students have heard. The next chunk could involve matching, where students could match two halves of a lyric line together from cutout song strips. Another chunk of listening might then involve learners reading the lyrics of the entire song, and attempting to underline all of the regular verbs that they can find (i.e., simple past and participle forms). As students listen again, they would need to separate the verbs into two columns that match a /d/ or a /t/ sound. Prior to such an activity you might need to elicit, or remind students that those verbs ending in a voiced sound see *-ed* pronounced with a final /d/, and those ending with a voiceless sound see it pronounced with a final /t/. Following on from this, you might direct students to underline all of the examples of 'must have' in the lyrics, and elicit the rule that 'must' and 'have' being weak words are not stressed, but that the stress lies on the main verb, the past participle. You might also take this opportunity to explain that *must* + *have* = *mustav* when spoken quickly, seeing the /h/ sound disappear. You could then drill these examples with students practicing the reduction.

Finally, you might play the entire song once more as students read through the lyrics. Then, ask learners to work in groups to make a sentence to best describe the meaning of the song. Students can work together, with these sentences later written on the board and the best might be voted upon. Some songs, like this one, also lend themselves very well to various extension activities. Such activities might involve the writing of short stories or comics that pertain to the themes and imagery introduced by the song, and aim to practice use of the vocabulary and grammar points presented by it.

Short Stories. Always a good choice for learners are stories that are engaging, and on themes and topics that are of relevance to their age, abilities, and interests. Short stories for English as a foreign language (EFL) and English as a second language (ESL) learners often come with accompanying audio, and are written in many different genres. Stories are adaptable to teaching many of the skills or a variety of skills at one time, and not just grammar. To start with any story, you might provide the title of the story and show a picture of the main character or characters, and have students come up with a backstory for them. This can be undertaken as a whole class activity, with students then split into groups to create backstories for a supporting character (one character per group), and then present these to the class. Such an activity can ensure that learners are invested in the story. As you teach grammar from the story, you can use the characters' names in the sentence examples that you provide, and in future lessons where students need error correction on grammar you can then refer back to the character(s) using aspects of familiarity to assist students in remembering the examples. After learners have developed character backstories, you might also introduce the use of adjectives to compare different characters. The comparisons will vary based on the backstories, but learners might develop a character profile that details the characters physical appearances (e.g., eye/hair color, strong/weak), likes and dislikes, personality, and the challenges that they face in the story and how they overcome them (e.g., what the character does). An example character profile sheet is included in the photocopiable section of this chapter. You could then use these profiles to demonstrate an array of grammar. For example, adjectives: Jack is strong (T: *How strong?* S: *90% strong*). Jill is strong too (T: *How strong?* S: *80%*). Jack is strong*er* than Jill. Jack is smart (T: *How smart?* S: *80%*). Jill is smart too (T: *How smart?* S: *90%*). Jill is smart*er* than Jack.

Moving on to the actual story, especially if it also comes with audio, allows for the use of a 'context, analysis and practice' approach. Context being provided by listening allows students to focus differently than by just reading the story by themselves. You could also have students read the story aloud in turn, rather than just listening to the teacher read it or listening to an audio file being played. Taking turns going around the classroom with students reading one sentence at a time, or one paragraph at a time, will help learners keep focus and practice pronunciation. The danger here is that students won't listen and count to their sentence or paragraph to practice reading it before speaking it. To avoid this, you might play or read the story once as all listen, and then have them read it silently or aloud either together or in turn. An understanding of the context could then be checked using comprehension questions specific to the details of the story. Analysis in the form of noticing and understanding is then developed by having students review a script of the story, and underline the key words, tenses, and sentences that you guide them to notice. You may also ask them to circle the ones that they would like to ask you about, which you can then note for discussion when appropriate. Such an activity also checks the level of understanding of your learners, and this may lead you to adjust your future lessons.

After this activity, practice in the form of using the story in different activities such as a gap-fill could be completed without reference back to the story. This gap-fill could be used along with substitution vocabulary. For example, students can replace *taller* with *shorter, slimmer* with *fatter*, and so on in sentences like *He is ___ than her*. You might choose to use this kind of activity as a review in a follow-up lesson, and if focusing on the actual characters of the story with lower level learners, you might put all alternatives as choices in the gap with the learner circling the one that is factual e.g., circling *smarter* in *Jill is slower/faster/smarter/stronger/taller than Jack*, and *stronger* in *Jack is slower/faster/smarter/stronger/taller than Jill*. Extension activities such as asking learners to write an alternate ending for the story are possible, and this could be set as a homework task. For speaking practice, students could retell the story (with one thing changed that other students need to identify), or develop role plays that are based on scenes from the story with each student taking on the persona of a different character.

Comics. Similar to short stories, comics also have appeal for learners, and they provide short chunks of dialogue that is usually easy to read and follow. There is a variety of ways to use these with learners. Comic strips as gap-fill activities with specific grammar of focus set as the blanks are ideal for intermediate and advanced learners, for beginners a word-choice gap-fill may prove better. As an activity then, learners could receive a comic strip with some of the dialogues removed, and they could work in pairs or groups to complete it. They could also receive a comic strip with blank speech and thought bubbles throughout, so that they can create the entire dialogue, and if using realia, their comics could be compared to the original. For extension and homework activities, students could generate their own animations or comic strips using online apps. If in class, and without access to technology, you could provide worksheets for this purpose (see the example in the photocopiable section of this chapter). Worksheets like these can be simply blank squares, or they may be squares that contain various thought and speech bubbles. Any student-created comic could then be ported to the learner management system (LMS), shared with other students, and added to the learner's portfolio. Such portfolios can also be shared with other interested stakeholders such as parents.

Movies/TV Shows and Cinematic Trailers. Using movies and TV shows with learners is, like songs, very popular. It is also much like using short stories in that the intent is not to simply play what the students can engage with on their own time, but to select key pieces of the movie/show/trailer for a teaching purpose. This could involve playing the video as well as relying on use of the script, and there are a number of ways to use both with any grammar focus. For example, if students have practiced the use of a specific form, then you might have them underline its use in a transcript before playing the video and checking their answers. Movies and a number of TV shows are also very useful for not only showing what constitutes real-life grammar use, but also how people speak in various situations (e.g., formal or informal, and when *not* relying on the correct form). Any of these cases might also be selected to use as a short example when introducing a grammar point. For instance, the use of *either* versus *neither*: an example transcript that illustrates the use of *neither* can be seen in bold in the following excerpt from Moffat and McGuidan (2012).

> *Holmes:* My brother has the brain of a scientist or a philosopher and yet he elects to be a detective. What might we deduce about his heart?
>
> *Dr. Watson:* I **don't** know.
>
> *Holmes:* **Neither** do I. But initially, he wanted to be a pirate.

The use of short clips to provide examples adds an element of realism to the classroom, along with practical use of the target grammar for learners. As always though, copyright issues need to be considered when rebroadcasting commercial content, however there is an element of 'fair use' for educational purposes. In cases of doubt, do write and request permission for use (e.g., email the BBC or the Disney Corporation to obtain permission to rebroadcast or reprint elements of their movies for use in the face-to-face and, particularly, the online classroom). Aspects to assist you in determining 'fair use' can include the following.

- Purpose of use. (e.g., the material has a clear educational purpose for being brought into the lesson, students are not being charged a fee for use or access to content, and the material is to be used in classes only for the purpose of a specific educational need.)
- Nature of use. (e.g., there is to be no free distribution of material that is of a consumable nature, such as handing out an entire book or playing an entire movie that a student could buy or stream.)
- Amount of use. (e.g., limited use of excerpts from very long works, such as 10% of a chapter or one chapter if it is less than 25% of a book, or a few lines from one particular scene of a movie/TV Show.)
- Effect of use. (e.g., Will instructional use cause harm to the marketing/sale of the material? Is a source to the original and appropriate citation or copyright notices included, particularly for images?)

Cinematic trailers that offer short clips which are publicly available may lead to actual consumption of the product that they are advertising. The downside to using them is that they are often presented with much of the language decontextualized, but they can be played with the sound muted, with students then writing what they think is the voice over. You could also have students develop their own trailers with a specific grammar focus by developing a 1-minute digital story in groups or by themselves, curating images/videos and providing their own voiceover. Such content could then be watched during class for review and assessment, and like any other student produced content it could be uploaded to the course LMS and used to form part of their portfolio. An example storyboarding handout for digital storytelling purposes is included in the photocopiable section of this chapter. If moving on to short stories and books/texts with learners, the digital storytelling activity could be turned into a WebQuest on book trailer development (Kent, 2017). An example WebQuest, and associated handouts, are included in the photocopiable section of the chapter.

Timelines. An integrated activity that uses timelines will help learners to use the active and passive past as they work on assigned activities. Such a task might involve students creating timelines, with major events from history, as well as generating a personal timeline for themselves, and placing their major life events on it. You can provide an example, perhaps highlighting some of your own significant life events and achievements (e.g., birth, graduation, marriage, having a baby, obtaining a license, winning an award). Students would then need to create their own timeline using the past tense. (e.g., I was born in _____, I graduated high school in ___, and so on).

A simple use of timelines is to show two photos or illustrations of people, and tell students that each person likes to travel: Liam to Australia and Portugal, and Emma to Thailand and Korea. These can then be used with a timeline to illustrate grammar (e.g., irregular simple verbs with example sentences such as: *Liam went to Portugal in 2005* and *Emma has been to Thailand.* This could be drawn on the board as in Figure 9.7. Timelines can also be used in other ways to help learners visualize and conceptualize the appropriate context for different aspects of grammar. This includes the simple, progressive, perfect simple, and perfect progressive verb tenses (see figures 3.8, 3.9, 3.10, and 3.11).

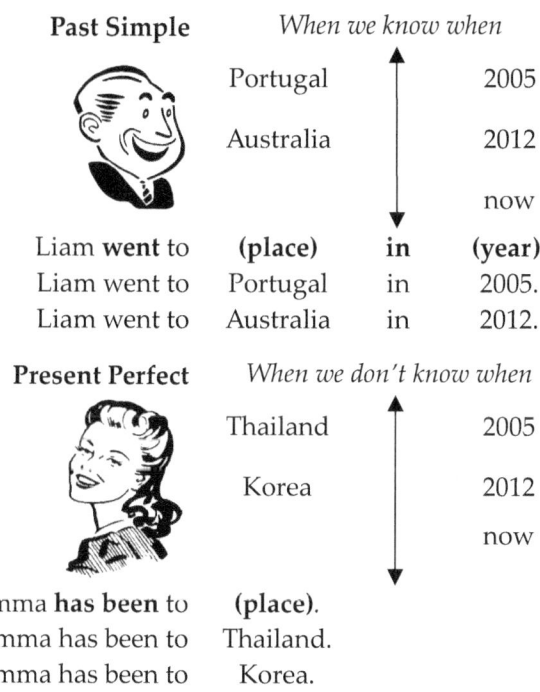

Figure 9.7 Past Grammar Tense Using a Timeline
(Note: Images are Public Domain)

484 *Issues in TESOL*

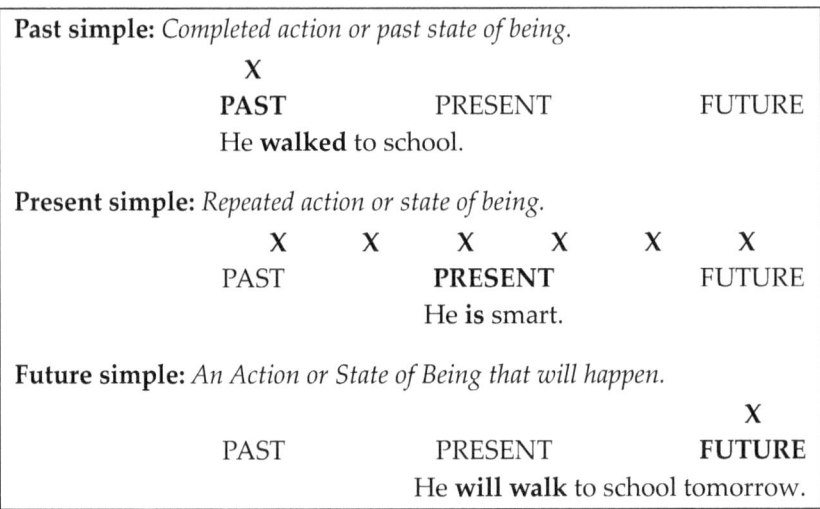

Figure 9.8 Simple Verb Tenses Using Timelines

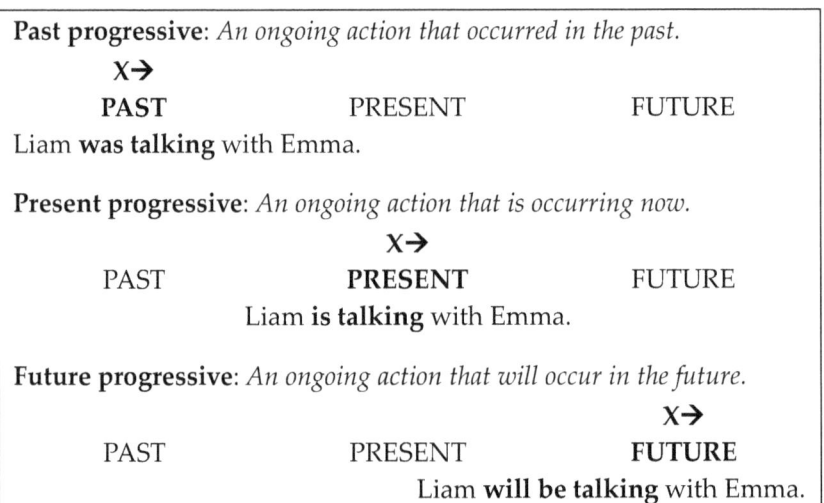

Figure 9.9 Progressive Verb Tenses Using Timelines

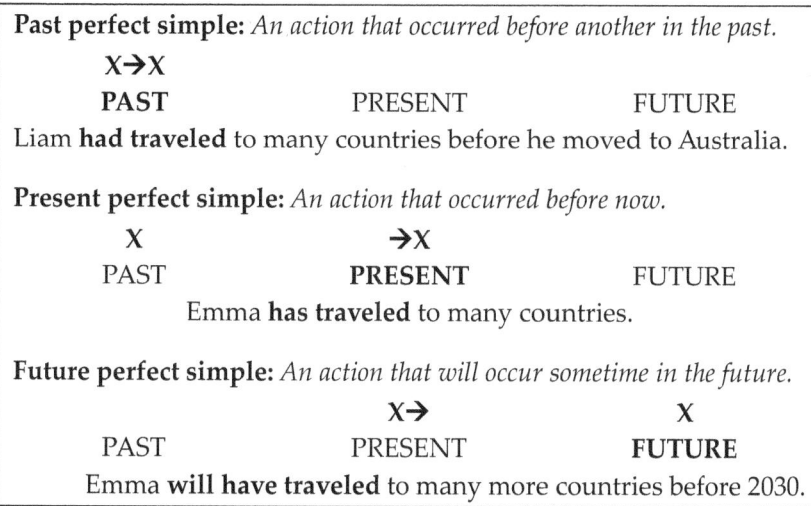

Figure 9.10 Perfect Simple Verb Tenses Using Timelines

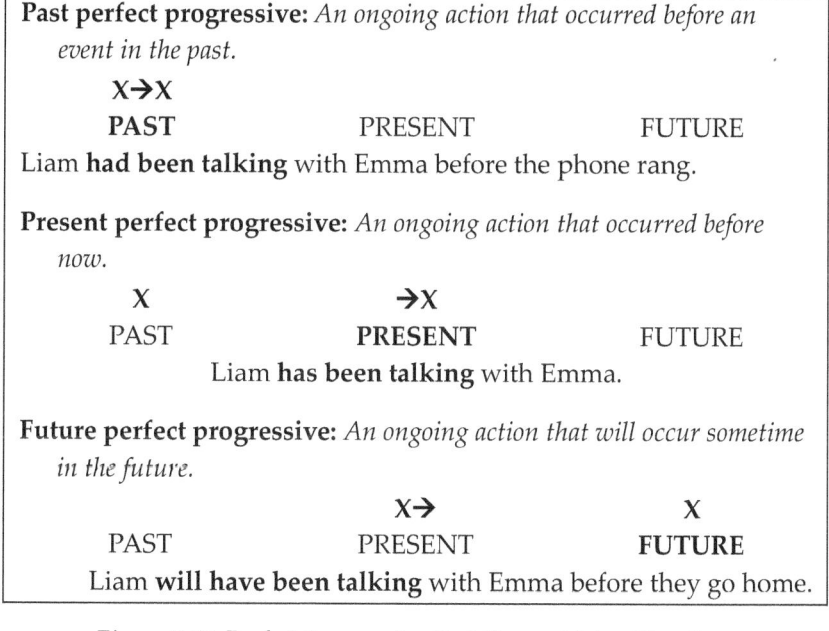

Figure 9.11 Perfect Progressive Verb Tenses Using Timelines

Games. Using games in the classroom encourages personal involvement, lowers learners' affective filters, increases their student talk time, can involve all members of a class and perhaps also motivates learners while also allowing you to engage in formative assessment, and for the fun practice of language. The use of games is also an excellent way to review content and to review what it is that learners have been taught.

An easy game to play at any time is one of questions, particularly those that require answering in a certain tense, and if you carry a blank game board or have students make their own during class, then you can hold a game at any time. A sample blank game board is included in the photocopiable section of this chapter. Player game pieces can be anything from an eraser to different colored paperclips. A dice can also be created from paper (see the photocopiable section of this chapter), or alternatively, even a pencil that has a hexagonal shape can be marked as a die and rolled along a table.

Bain and Witaker (2017) highlight a number of good grammar games including *Have you ever …? What someone does,* and *The truth about me,* and these can all be played by students in groups of three or four using makeshift game pieces and a blank game board. In each case, you can provide students with a list of questions to write in each square, or they can make their own.

Have you ever … ? focuses on use of the present perfect (e.g., each question starts with *Have you ever* and ends with one of: eaten spicy food, slept in, cooked dinner for someone, been late for class, travelled to another country, lost your cell phone, worn a hat, seen a ghost, watched a baseball game, climbed a mountain). As each player lands on a square they then read the question to their group. Each student in the group then replies to the question in turn. If they reply positively, they should describe the last time they performed the activity. If they answer negatively, then they should describe a related activity that they have done.

What someone does focuses on the present simple. As each player lands on a square, they then read the phrase to their group, and say three things that you can do when at that place or in that condition. Question topics might cover: on vacation, at a birthday party, in Daejeon, at a mountain, on a tropical island, when sick, when in love, when hungry, at the cinema, in a bus, when late for school.

The truth about me focuses on use of the past simple. As each player lands on a square they then read those words to their group, using them to create a true sentence about themselves. Question topics might include: yesterday, pets, beach, cinema, last weekend, and museum.

After playing any of the above games with the game board handout from the photocopiable section of this chapter, you can then direct students to create their own grammar games. This would see learners selecting a focus (e.g., a grammar point), an objective behind game-play (e.g., 'the truth about me'), develop several rules for the game, and then work on creating questions/prompts for the game spaces. All students in the class working in groups of three or four on such a project would see enough prompts generated to fill a game board, and swapping and sharing these to create their own board game would ensure that students meet unexpected prompts or questions as they play. A handout for learners to use for this purpose can be found in the photocopiable section of this chapter. You may also wish to assess these worksheets via a rubric if desired.

Testing Grammar

Thornbury (2008) notes that discrete-point tests typically prove to be the best when attempting to ascertain learner knowledge of grammar points, while an indirect test could focus on how learners use grammar when they communicate or produce language. Although there is a wide variety of testing options available to test grammar knowledge and performance, he suggests relying upon gap-fills, sentence completion, writing tasks, and the use of rubrics, depending on the focus behind the test (i.e., assessing knowledge or performance).

Gap-fill. This kind of test typically presents learners with one or more items that they need to place into a gap or point in a sentence that has been pre-selected or randomly chosen, and an answer pool can be provided. This can also be applied to a passage of text, and the learner has to consider the meaning of the text. These are also popular progress tests to measure student learning. The alternative to a gap-fill is the cloze test which is more appropriate for use as a placement test as it is more effective in testing a wider range of competences (e.g., grammar, vocabulary, and discourse) rather than specific or selective aspects of one key language point.

Multiple-choice gap-fill. This kind of test typically presents learners with one or more items that they need to place into a gap or point in a sentence, with the options provided as to where the item may be placed. This type of test for grammar is limited in that it is essentially testing for knowledge of word-order constraints.

Rubrics. In the language classroom, these kinds of assessment tools can prove very useful when evaluating performance, particularly in role plays, conversations, and in an oral testing context. They can be deployed to test aspects of not only grammar but that of vocabulary and pronunciation as well. The main problem comes with deciding on the appropriate criteria, and how that criteria will be applied, and this could affect the validity of the scoring system, and the reliability of using the rubric for a particular test (e.g., avoiding overlapping criteria). The face validity of the test might also be questioned if the learner believes that the instructor is not a competent assessor. Practically, rubrics are also more difficult to use for assessment over a discrete-point test.

Sentence completion. These kinds of tasks involve the completion of half a sentence, usually the last half (it might also be the middle in gap-writing). When used for testing grammar, they tend to provide a less-contrived testing context that requires production along with comprehension. However, if an even number of split sentences are provided the learner may be able to simply match the last one.

True or False. In this kind of test, students are presented with information in the form of a chart, sentence, statement, and so on, and they need to decide if the information being presented is correct or incorrect. This is a variant of a multiple-choice test in that there is clearly one response that is right with the other being a distractor. When relied upon to test aspects of grammar, such tests assess the understanding of meaning or comprehension rather than the use of form.

Writing tasks. These types of tasks often involve free writing (e.g., write a 100-word letter using the simple past to a friend telling them some news). This allows great freedom of imagination and allows learners to use the knowledge of the language that they possess, but it does tend to favor good writers with a large vocabulary. In the grading of such a task, it is important to focus only on the target language being tested (e.g., use of the simple past), and not taking off points for other errors. It is a very time-consuming type of test to grade, particularly if you are going to provide feedback on all of the errors, yet it is the type of test that can show both production and comprehension of the grammar point(s) being tested.

Summary

This chapter highlighted a number of different types of grammar, before coming to focus on a pedagogical grammar from a form-meaning-use paradigm, and introducing a variety of rules from which to teach, including the consideration of the context, use, economy, relevance, nurture, and appropriacy of any grammar being taught. The nature of grammar teaching from a deductive (rule-driven), inductive (rule-discovery), interactive, text and writing, and a sentence diagramming perspective was then explored. A variety of teaching strategies were then detailed to provide a means of effectively and efficiently teaching various facets of grammar in relevant, timely and engaging ways. This involved the detailing of a variety of activities including that of dictogloss, songs, short stories, comics, movies/TV shows, and cinematic trailers, as well as timelines and board games. A number of means for testing grammar were then uncovered, including how to approach the use of gap-fill and multiple-choice gap-fill, true or false, and sentence completion along with the use of rubrics and writing tasks for best results.

Review

Content Quiz
Grammar in Teaching

To help solidify some of the concepts introduced by this chapter the following multiple-choice and true or false quizzes might be helpful for you to undertake. So that you can check the accuracy of your responses, an answer key can be found following the quizzes.

Multiple-Choice

Circle **a**, **b**, or **c** for the answer that best completes the sentence presented in each question.

1. Generative grammar refers to …
   a) the grammar that is stored in the brain, which allows a speaker to produce language that other speakers can understand.
   b) a grammar (set of rules) that indicates the structure and interpretation of sentences that a native speaker of a language would accept as belonging to the language.
   c) a theory that stresses the importance of semantic roles in an effort to make explicit the basic meaning relationships in a sentence.

2. Mental (competence) grammar refers to …
   a) the grammar that is stored in the brain, which allows a speaker to produce language that other speakers can understand.
   b) a grammar (set of rules) that indicates the structure and interpretation of sentences that a native speaker of a language would accept as belonging to the language.
   c) a theory that stresses the importance of semantic roles in an effort to make explicit the basic meaning relationships in a sentence.

3. Universal grammar (UG) is …
   a) a class of modern grammatical theories based upon dependency relations as opposed to phrase structure (constituency) grammars).
   b) a declarative, constraint-based framework for analyzing the various components of grammar, including, crucially, syntax.
   c) a theory of human languages where the system of categories, operations, and principles are considered to be innate.

4. Case grammar is a …
   a) grammar that is stored in the brain, which allows a speaker to produce language that other speakers can understand.
   b) grammar (set of rules) that indicates the structure and interpretation of sentences that a native speaker of a language would accept as belonging to the language.
   c) theory that stresses the importance of semantic roles in an effort to make explicit the basic meaning relationships in a sentence.

5. Dependency grammar is a …
   a) class of modern grammatical theories based upon dependency relations as opposed to phrase structure (constituency grammars).
   b) declarative, constraint-based framework for analyzing the various components of grammar, including, crucially, syntax.
   c) theory of human languages where the system of categories, operations, and principles are considered to be innate.

6. Lexical functional grammar is a …
   a) class of modern grammatical theories based upon dependency relations as opposed to phrase structure (constituency grammars).
   b) declarative constraint-based framework for analyzing the various components of grammar, including, crucially, syntax.
   c) theory of human languages where the system of categories, operations, and principles are considered to be innate.

7. Performance grammar refers to …
   a) a prose-like description of the major grammatical constructions in a language that is illustrated with examples.
   b) an analysis and comparison of the grammatical structures of related languages.
   c) the description of syntax as it is used by speakers in dialogues.

8. Role and reference grammar is ...
   a) a prose-like description of the major grammatical constructions in a language that is illustrated with examples.
   b) an analysis and comparison of the grammatical structures of related languages.
   c) the description of syntax as it is used by speakers in dialogues.

9. Comparative grammar seeks to provide ...
   a) an analysis and comparison of the grammatical structures of related languages.
   b) a prose-like description of the major grammatical constructions in a language that is illustrated with examples.
   c) the description of syntax as it is used by speakers in dialogues.

10. A deductive approach to grammar teaching involves ...
    a) presenting a grammar rule and then engaging learners with practice and the manipulation of it by employing a large number of examples.
    b) exposing learners to many examples from which the intent is that they are able to come to an understanding of how the rules work for themselves.
    c) employing a number of means of involving students more actively, and in more engaging ways, than traditional lessons.

11. An inductive approach to grammar teaching involves ...
    a) presenting a grammar rule and then engaging learners with practice and the manipulation of it by employing a large number of examples.
    b) exposing learners to many examples from which the intent is that they are able to come to an understanding of how the rules work for themselves.
    c) employing a number of means of involving students more actively, and in more engaging ways, than traditional lessons.

12. An interactive approach to grammar teaching involves …
    a) presenting a grammar rule and then engaging learners with practice and the manipulation of it by employing a large number of examples.
    b) exposing learners to many examples from which the intent is that they are able to come to an understanding of how the rules work for themselves.
    c) employing a number of means of involving students more actively, and in more engaging ways, than traditional lessons.

13. Dictogloss involves …
    a) the use of a classroom dictation activity in which learners are required to reconstruct a short text by listening and then noting down key words to use as a base for use when later reconstructing the text.
    b) the use of one or more gaps in a sentence where each word has been selectively removed.
    c) the use of one or more gaps in a sentence, where every n^{th} word is removed (e.g., every 5th, 6th, or 7th).

14. A cloze exercise involves …
    a) the use of a classroom dictation activity in which learners are required to reconstruct a short text by listening and then noting down key words to use as a base for use when later reconstructing the text.
    b) the use of one or more gaps in a sentence where each word has been selectively removed.
    c) the use of one or more gaps in a sentence where every n^{th} word is removed (e.g., every 5th, 6th, or 7th).

15. A gap-fill activity involves …
   a) the use of a classroom dictation activity in which learners are required to reconstruct a short text by listening and then noting down key words to use as a base for use when later reconstructing the text.
   b) the use of one or more gaps in a sentence where every n^{th} word is removed (e.g., every 5th, 6th, or 7th).
   c) the use of one or more gaps in a sentence where each word has been selectively removed.

True or False

Circle **a** (true) if you think that the statement is correct, or **b** (false) if you think that the statement is incorrect.

1. *Descriptive grammar* refers to the structure of a language as certain people think that it should be used, while *prescriptive grammar* refers to the structure of a language as it is used by speakers and writers.
   a) True.
   b) False.

2. Traditional grammar is the type of grammar that is typically taught in schools. The basis of this grammar relies on imparting the prescriptive rules, as well as concepts concerning the structure of language.
   a) True.
   b) False.

3. A *pedagogical grammar*, primarily dealing with word-level (morphology) and sentence-level (syntax) rules is used to provide descriptions of how to use grammar to communicate, and may be influenced by instructor cognition, beliefs, assumptions, and attitudes concerning the teaching of grammar.
   a) True.
   b) False.

4. If form is removed from context, then it should not be recontextualized as soon as possible.
   a) True.
   b) False.

5. Grammar is used to improve learner understanding and to help them produce language, but not as an end in itself.
   a) True.
   b) False.

6. Maximize the time spent on presenting form and providing direct explanations to minimize the time that students spend on practicing the language.
   a) True.
   b) False.

7. If students already know the form of grammar items or rules, then language teachers do not need to spend more time on it other than a quick revision.
   a) True.
   b) False.

8. Teaching can provide opportunities for learning to develop, and for language learning, knowledge and skills to emerge from a long, slow and deliberate process of study and practice from environments that are conducive to it.
   a) True.
   b) False.

9. When teaching grammar, or anything else, it is important to determine the needs, interests, and expectations of your learners and work at their level. This may mean that, for one class, you need to focus on explicit grammar teaching, but for another, not at all.
   a) True.
   b) False.

10. Moving to a from-meaning-use paradigm for a pedagogical grammar requires the focus of the teaching of grammar to occur along a continuum. In the classroom then, there is always a shifting of demand between the need to focus on the accuracy of a speaker to focusing on their message, from the explicit teaching of rules to an approach of rule-discovery, and from a bottom-up provision of learning to one that presents it top-down.
    a) True.
    b) False.

11. Sentence diagrams, or working with sentence trees, is a visual mapping process that aims to show the relationships between parts of a sentence. In the Reed-Kellogg system of sentence diagramming, the functions of each word in a sentence are highlighted more than that of traditional sentence word ordering.
    a) True.
    b) False.

12. In the dependency and constituency method of sentence diagramming, sentence trees are used with every word in a sentence corresponding to one or more nodes in the diagram.
    a) True.
    b) False.

13. The use of short media clips to present language examples to students adds an element of realism to the classroom, along with practical use of the target grammar for learners.
    a) True.
    b) False.

14. Timelines are useful ways of helping learners visualize and conceptualize the appropriate context for different aspects of grammar.
    a) True.
    b) False.

15. Using games in the classroom encourages personal involvement, lowers learners' affective filters, increases student talk time, can involve all members of a class and perhaps also motivate them, allows you to engage in formative assessment, and allows for the fun practice of language. Unfortunately, formative assessment is not a useful means for you to assess the grammar use of students, and summative assessment should always be used in this regard.
    a) True.
    b) False.

Quiz Answers
Grammar for Teachers

Multiple-Choice		*True or False*	
1.	b	1.	F
2.	a	2.	T
3.	c	3.	T
4.	c	4.	F
5.	a	5.	T
6.	b	6.	F
7.	c	7.	T
8.	a	8.	T
9.	a	9.	T
10.	a	10.	T
11.	b	11.	T
12.	c	12.	T
13.	a	13.	T
14.	c	14.	T
15.	c	15.	F

Suggested Readings

Bain, K., & Witaker, L. (2017). *Fun with grammar: Bringing language learning to life through games.* American English. https://americanenglish.state.gov/files/ae/resource_files/5.1_presentation_slides_0.pdf

Butt, D., Fahey, R., Feez, S. Spinks, S., & Yallop., C. (2000). *Using functional grammar: An explorer's guide.* NCELTR: National Centre for English Language Teaching and Research.

Celce-Murcia., M. (1991). Grammar pedagogy in second and foreign language teaching. *TESOL Quarterly, 25*(3), 459-477.

Celce-Murcia, M., & Hilles, S. (1988). *Techniques and resources in teaching grammar.* Oxford: Oxford University Press.

Coats, J. (2017). *A sentence diagramming primer: The Reed and Kellogg system step-by-step.* Page Publishing Inc.

Davies, A. (2007). *An introduction to applied linguistics.* Edinburgh University Press.

Hadfield, J. (2001). *Elementary grammar games: A collection of grammar games and activities for elementary students of English.* Longman.

Hughes, A. (1989). *Testing for language teachers.* Cambridge University Press.

Johnes, A. (2001). *Games for grammar practice – A resource book of grammar games and interactive activities.* Cambridge University Press.

Kent, D. (2017). *WebQuests: TESOL strategy guide.* Pedagogy Press.

Melissa. (2020). *Teaching verb tenses using timelines.* Upper Elementary Snapshots. https://www.upperelementarysnapshots.com/2019/06/teaching-verb-tenses-using-timelines.html

Murphy, R. *Advanced grammar in use* (3rd ed.). Cambridge University Press.

Murphy, R. *Basic grammar in use* (3rd ed.). Cambridge University Press.

Murphy, R. *Essential grammar in use* (3rd ed.). Cambridge University Press.

Murphy, R. *Grammar in use intermediate* (3rd ed.). Cambridge University Press.

Taylor, (2016). *Teaching Grammar in context: Basic principles and concepts – 'doing grammar'.* Saturday Seminar Series in Grammar. Education University of Hong Kong.

Thornbury, S. (2019). *Scott Thornbury's 101 grammar questions.* Cambridge University Press.

Thornbury, S. (2008). *How to teach grammar*. Pearson Education Limited.

Rinvolucri, M., & David, P. (1995). *More grammar games: Cognitive, affective and movement activities for EFL students*. Cambridge University Press.

Ur, P. (2002). *A course in language teaching: Practice and theory*. Cambridge University Press.

Ur, P. (2009). *Grammar practice activities: A practical guide for teachers* (2nd ed.). Cambridge University Press.

Photocopiable Content
Grammar in Teaching

This section of the text includes a variety of content that is free to photocopy and use with your classes, as long as appropriate copyright or licensure is displayed. It contains examples of the following content:

- Dictogloss activity – Teacher notes
- Dictogloss – Worksheet
- Grammar points matched to various song titles and artists
- Character profile
- Blank comic strip
- Digital storytelling resource notes
- Digital storytelling handout
- WebQuest example – Book trailers
- WebQuest example – Handouts
- Blank card game
- Dice templates
- Create your own board game – Activity

Dictogloss Activity – Teacher Notes

Teacher notes.
Read the dictogloss below to students twice. Note that the focus is on simple verbs, and that these are in bold. Ensure that the students are prepared to complete the activities on the accompanying worksheet. This may require pre-teaching some of the vocabulary as well as introducing grammar concepts, and perhaps also introducing sequencing.

After students have listened to the passage, they can work in pairs to reconstruct the text. If you feel that this is too difficult for them, you could create a gap-fill exercise for learners to work on after the listening instead. You can then check this section as a whole class group to ensure that students have got the meaning, and that they are working with the target grammar.

After completing exercise one, learners can then ask their partners guided questions concerning their morning routine, and then use these in the third exercise to write out a passage that uses simple verbs to present to the class. Students should have their partners check their passage for accuracy (both factually and grammatically).

If some pairs finish before others, you can have them write out their own morning routine as an extension activity. Alternatively, you can set the extension activity for all students to complete as homework.

Dictogloss text.
I **live** in a studio apartment, I **wake** up every morning at 6 o'clock. I **do** a little bit of stretching, then I **make** some coffee. Scientists **say** that a small amount of coffee **is** good for you. Then, I **go** to my computer and **read** my emails, and I **watch** the news on TV. After that, I **make** breakfast. I **think** that it**'s** important to eat a big breakfast. I usually **eat** an omelet or some cereal for breakfast. Then I **study** Korean for a little while before I **take** a shower, **shave**, and **brush** my teeth. After I **get** dressed, I **leave** for work. As you can **see**, I **am** a simple man, and my morning routine **uses** simple verbs.

Dictogloss Activity – Worksheet
– My Simple Morning Routine –

1. Listen and write.

Your teacher will read you a morning routine. Listen carefully, then, working with a partner, write down what you can recall in the following space.

_____
_____
_____
_____
_____
_____
_____
_____

2. Ask and answer.

Ask your partner the following questions about their morning routine. Write their answers in the space provided.

a. What time do you wake up?
_____

b. What do you eat for breakfast?
_____

c. Do you exercise?
_____

d. Do you listen to the radio, watch TV, or read?
_____

e. What time do you leave for work/school?
_____

3. **Read, Write, and Present.**

Use the answers above to write a short passage to describe your partner's routine. Ask your partner to check it for you to make sure that it is correct. Be prepared to present your partner's morning routine to the class.

_____

Extension Activity/Homework.

If you finish before others, start to write a second passage detailing your morning routine.

_____

Photocopiable Content – Grammar

Grammar Points Matched to Various Song Titles and Artists

Past Perfect	Past Continuous	Past Simple
Somebody that I used to know – Gotye.	*Call me maybe* – Carly Rae Jepsen.	*Seasons in the sun* – Terry Jacks.
Present Perfect	**Present Perfect Continuous**	**Present Continuous**
Still haven't found what I'm looking for – U2.	*Left outside alone* – Anastacia.	*Tom's dinner* – Suzanne Vega.
Present Simple	**Future Perfect**	**Future Continuous**
She loves you – The Beatles.	*You will be mine* – Faith Hill.	*Every breath you take* – The Police.
Used to	**Going to**	**Will**
She used to love me a lot – Johnny Cash.	*We're going to be friends* – White Stripes.	*I will survive* – Gloria Gaynor.
1st Conditional	**2nd Conditional**	**3rd Conditional**
If I were a carpenter – Johnny Cash ft. June Carter.	*If I could turn back time* – Cher.	*Rolling in the deep* – Adele.
Passive Voice	**Reported Speech**	**Modal verbs**
Get the party started – Pink.	*Somebody told me* – The Killers.	*It must have been Love* – Roxette.
Comparatives/ Superlatives	**Adjectives**	**Prefixes/ Suffixes**
The best – Tina Turner.	*True colors* – Cyndi Lauper.	*Shake it off* – Taylor Swift. *Unbreak my heart* – Toni Braxton.
Wanna	**Gotta**	**Gonna**
I want to hold your hand – The Beatles.	*You gotta be* – Des'ree.	*I'm gonna love you* – Meghan Trainor.

Photocopiable Content – Grammar

Character Profile

Character Name
_____

Appearance _____

_____

_____

_____

Likes _____

_____

_____

_____

Dislikes _____

_____

_____

_____

Character Sketch
(sketch your character here)

Personality _____

_____

_____

_____

Challenges
What does your character do in the story?
(e.g., What problem does your character have? How is the problem overcome?)

_____

_____

_____

_____

_____

Blank Comic Strip

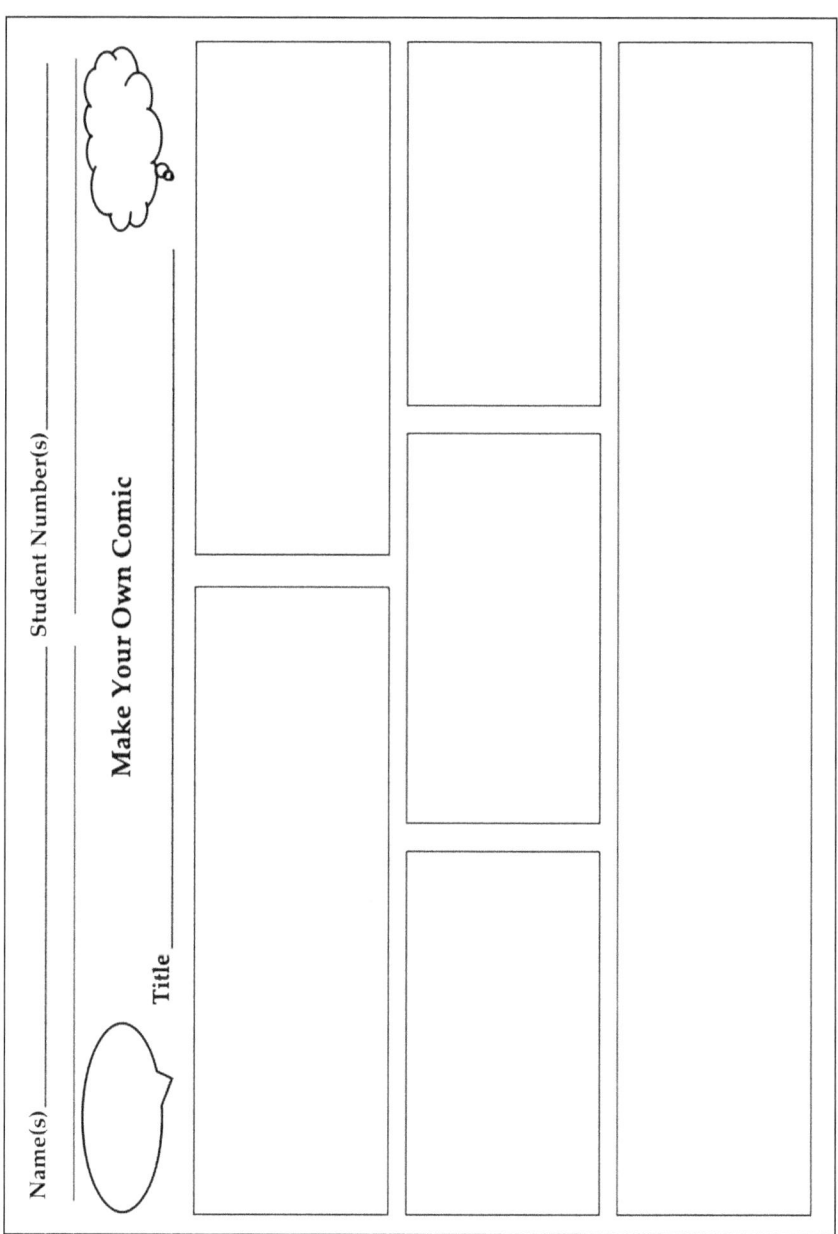

Digital Storytelling Storyboarding Resource Notes

Digital Story Title	Group Members
A title is chosen by students, and written here.	Student names are listed here.

Image	Description	Media Resources
Students sketch an example image (or paste one) here that reflects what will appear at this point in their digital story.	Students will answer one or all of the following questions here: 1. What will your audience see? 2. What will your viewers hear? 3. What are you trying to communicate or achieve?	Students list all of the media that they will need in order to construct this part of their digital story. This will help them later search for the right material. They will need to consider: 1. Music, songs, sound effects, voice recordings. 2. Photo/video, images, diagrams. 3. Text, titles, transitions, motion.

Narration

Students will write their accompanying narration here.

As many frames (including image, description, media resources, and narration) can be added as necessary, with images displayed for around 5-10 seconds each.

Digital Storytelling Storyboarding Handout		
Digital Story Title		**Group Members**
Image	**Description**	**Media Resources**
Narration		
Image	**Description**	**Media Resources**
Narration		

WebQuest Example – Book Trailers

Introduction

The world of book publishing can be an exciting place, and this is where you and your team work – in the offices of one of the world's most famous book publishers. There is an upcoming book launch, and your boss needs an award-winning book trailer.

Task

There is a book launch scheduled for next month, and the author needs a book trailer specifically developed for their book. You will work in a team to prepare a book trailer for the author.

You will need to do the following:
- Review several successful book trailers.
- Learn how to create a successful book trailer.
- Present and pitch your book trailer.
- Evaluate and critique other book trailers.
- Vote on the best book trailer to represent the book on launch day.

Process

Step one – What is a book trailer?
Review existing book trailers:
1. Watch at least five different book trailers.
2. List five things that you think make for a good book trailer.
3. List five things that you think make for a bad book trailer.

Step two – Creating a book trailer
Understand the process behind making a book trailer:
1. Identify the stages behind creating a book trailer.
2. Select software to create a book trailer.

Step three – Producing a book trailer
Create a unique book trailer by working through:
1. Brainstorming.
2. Storyboarding.
3. Script development.
4. Media collection.
5. Trailer finalization.
6. A checklist.

Step four – Presenting a book trailer
In this step, you will need to present and pitch your book trailer:
1. Play it – share your book trailer.
2. Pitch it – 'sell' your book trailer.

Step five – Evaluating and critiquing
In this step, you will need to evaluate and critique peer book trailers:
1. Evaluate – peer book trailers.
2. Write up – the good and the bad.

Step six – Vote
In this step you will need to vote for the best trailer using a classroom response system such as Plickers (https://www.plickers.com).
1. Vote for the best book trailer.

Resources

Step one

In this step you will use several web resources, and an in-class handout to view several book trailers, identify what makes a book trailer good or bad, and prepare a list of the good and bad aspects of a book trailer.

1. Go to Book Trailers for Readers (http://www.booktrailersforreaders.com), and watch at least five different book trailers.
2. Then, think about what makes the good trailers good and the bad trailers bad. How did they captivate you? Did the trailers make you really want to read those books? Think about these kinds of questions while you review the following web sites:
    a) Fantastic book trailers and the reasons why they're so good (https://therumpus.net/2013/06/fantastic-book-trailers-and-the-reasons-theyre-so-good).
    b) Most book trailers are awful but here's how yours can be different (https://goinswriter.com/book-trailer).
    c) What makes a good book trailer (https://youtu.be/wYQCaolRQ4g).
3. Finally, list five things that make for a good book trailer, and five things that make for a bad book trailer.
    a) Handout one – 'Book trailers: The good and the bad'

Step two

In this step, you will identify the various stages behind creating a book trailer, identify appropriate software to help you create one, and detail these aspects on the in-class handout.

1. Identify the stages behind a book trailer.
    a) Book trailers for readers (https://www.digitalbooktalk.net/browse-books/book-trailers-for-readers).
    b) How to make a book trailer: 6 tips (https://www.writersdigest.com/whats-new/how-to-make-a-book-trailer-6-tips).

c) How to make a book trailer for free (that looks professional) (https://www.powtoon.com/blog/book-trailer-free-professional).
   d) 12 easy steps to the making of a book trailer (https://www.thebookdesigner.com/2011/05/12-easy-steps-to-the-making-of-a-book-trailer).

2. Identify the software available to create a book trailer
   a) How to make a book trailer in minutes (https://animoto.com/blog/guides/how-to-make-a-book-trailer).
   b) Book trailers: 11 Steps to make your own (https://bookmarketingmaven.typepad.com/book_marketing_maven/2009/10/book-trailers-11-steps-to-make-your-own.html).
3. Detail the steps that your group will follow when creating a book trailer, along with the applications available and what makes these good choices to use when producing a book trailer. Finally, decide upon an application that your group will use to produce a book trailer.
   a) Handout two – 'Book trailers: Steps to create a book trailer'.
   b) Handout three – 'Book trailers: Applications to use'.

Step three
Now you will produce your book trailer. You need to consider script development, storyboarding, media collection, and trailer finalization before conducting a checklist to ensure that you have met the production criteria as set by your teacher.

1. *Brainstorming*
Prior to starting out, start thinking about the book. Who are the main characters in the book? How do you feel when you think about them? What is the mood of the book? How does this mood make you feel? What images come to mind when you feel this way? What is the plot of the book? What captured you about the plot the most? Why would someone want to read this book? How would you persuade them to read the book? How would you

interest them in the book? What images or video could you use to engage or connect them to the book? What details from the book did you find to be the most exciting, interesting, and funny? What other details could make someone want to read the book?

    a) Handout four – 'Book trailers: brainstorming'.

2. *Script development*

You will need to develop a short narration for your book trailer, as well as think about any on-screen captions that you may want to use. You can use the blurb of the book to help you prepare a summary. Try to use vocabulary that will persuade the viewer to read the book, engage them in the story, and keep them interested until the end. Start by thinking of an interesting 'hook' or captivating question based on a plot point to draw in the viewer. Use the appropriate handout to write out your summary and any desired on-screen captions.

    a) Handout five – 'Book trailers: Summary'.

3. *Storyboard*

The summary that you use for narration, along with any captions that you want to include in your trailer, will need to match any images, music, or video clips that you may also want to use for your book trailer. You also need to see how long your book trailer will be, based on the recording of your summary and how long you think each image, music clip, or video clip will play for.

    a) Handout six – 'Book trailers: Storyboard'.

4. *Media collection*

You will need to find images, music clips, video clips, and other media to use in the development of your book trailer. Pay attention to copyright, and only use images, music clips, or video clips that are in the public domain or are usable when crediting the creator.

    a) Images: Pics4Learning (https://www.pics4learning.com).
    b) Music: Free music archive (https://freemusicarchive.org).
    c) Video: Mazwai (https://mazwai.com).

5. *Trailer finalization*

Use the application that you selected to produce and finalize your book trailer. Reviewing a tutorial on how to use the application to make a book trailer can help you get started and get finished much more quickly.

    a) Book trailer tutorial using (Windows) Movie Maker (https://www.youtube.com/watch?v=7LIP_3qIumk).

    b) How to create an Animoto book trailer (https://www.youtube.com/watch?v=mUWjNHs7c5c).

6. *Checklist*

Ensure that your group has met the minimum production, language use, and playback requirements as set by your teacher.

    a) Handout Seven – 'Book trailers: Trailer finalization checklist'.

Step four

This is where you will need to present your book trailer to the class, and it involves playing the book trailer, and then speaking about it. You need to pitch the trailer as being the best to represent the book on launch, and each group member must give at least one reason for this trailer to be chosen as the best.

1. Play it.
       a) Upload your video to a site such as YouTube for online sharing and playback, or
       b) Upload your video to a USB drive to play back locally.

2. Pitch it.
       a) How to do a presentation in class (https://www.wikihow.com/Do-a-Presentation-in-Class).
       b) Handout eight – 'Book trailers: Pitch it!'

Step five

In this step, you need to evaluate and critique the book trailers produced by each class group. You should do this in two ways.

1. Use the rubric to help you think about the book trailers as you watch them, then complete the associated handout after each book trailer has completed playing.
    a) Handout nine – 'Book trailers: Book trailer evaluation rubric'.

2. After watching all of the other groups' trailers and listening to their presentations, write a paragraph to identify at least one good and one bad aspect of each trailer, and submit these to your teacher for review.
    a) Handout ten – 'Book trailers: Critique'.
3. At the same time that you are doing all of this, your teacher will evaluate your book trailer.
    a) Handout nine – 'Book trailers: Book trailer evaluation rubric'.

Step six

Here, you will watch each trailer again, one by one, and then vote for the one that you think is the best. A classroom response system will be used by the teacher to gather the votes anonymously.

1. Playback.
    a) YouTube or USB.
2. Voting.
    a) Plickers classroom response system (https://www.plickers.com).

Evaluation

Any book can be used for this WebQuest. However, it would be best if it is a novel that students have been studying recently or, perhaps for older students, a popular movie that is based on a book.

1. The completed book trailer can be evaluated using:
    a) Handout nine – 'Book trailers: Book trailer evaluation rubric'.
2. The completed WebQuest can be evaluated using:
    a) Handout eleven – 'Book trailers: WebQuest evaluation rubric'.

Conclusion

Students

1. Each group of students completes and presents a book trailer to the class as a group, and pitches why it is the best one for the author to use for their book.
2. Students write a one-paragraph critique of each book trailer, including their own, and are able to identify what makes for good and bad book trailers. The paragraph is submitted as a writing sample for the teacher to review.
3. Students use a rubric to identify the best class-produced book trailer, and the one that they think would be best used to sell the book.

Teacher

1. The teacher closes the WebQuest with a summary of the topic and the goals achieved by the students throughout its completion.
2. The best book trailer, as voted by the class, is identified.
3. The entire WebQuest is assessed by the teacher using Handout eleven: 'Book trailers – WebQuest evaluation rubric'.

WebQuest Example – Handouts

1. The good and the bad
2. Steps to create a book trailer
3. Applications to use
4. Brainstorming
5. Summary
6. Storyboarding
7. Trailer finalization checklist
8. Pitch it!
9. Book trailer evaluation rubric
10. Critique
11. WebQuest evaluation rubric

1. Book Trailers: The Good and the Bad

Group Members:

Good book trailers …

1. _____

2. _____

3. _____

4. _____

5. _____

Bad book trailers …

1. _____

2. _____

3. _____

4. _____

5. _____

Photocopiable Content – Grammar

2. Book Trailers: Steps to Create a Book Trailer
Group Members:

Steps to Create a Book Trailer

Step 1. _____
Description _____
_____

Step 2. _____
Description _____
_____

Step 3. _____
Description _____
_____

Step 4. _____
Description _____
_____

Step 5. _____
Description _____
_____

Step 6. _____
Description _____
_____

(Add more steps if you need them).

3. Book Trailers: Applications to Use
Group Members:

Applications to use to create a book trailer

Application 1. _____

Reasons for choosing this application _____

_____

_____

_____

Application 2. _____

Reasons for choosing this application _____

_____

_____

_____

Application 3. _____

Reasons for choosing this application _____

_____

_____

_____

4. Book Trailers: Brainstorming
Group Members:

The Book
Title _____

Characters _____

Genre/Mood _____

What is the book about?
Plot Points _____
_____
_____

Hook _____
_____
_____

Why would someone want to read the book?
Persuade _____
Interest _____
Engage _____

Other details from the book
Exciting _____
Interesting _____
Funny _____
Other _____

5. Book Trailers: Summary

Group Members:

You will need to develop a short narration for your book trailer, as well as think about any on-screen captions that you may want to use. You can use the blurb of the book to help you prepare a summary of at least five sentences.

Summary

On-screen captions

6. Book Trailers: Storyboarding

Group Members:

Scene Number _____

Image or Video	Music _____

On-screen caption _____

Summary sentence _____

Scene Number _____

Image or Video	Music _____

On-screen caption _____

Summary sentence _____

7. Book Trailers: Trailer Finalization Checklist	
Group Members:	
Minimum requirements have been met, and at least:	
Production	☐ Five images have been used. ☐ One video has been used. ☐ One song has been used.
Language Use	☐ A five-sentence summary was developed. ☐ One sentence is spoken by each group member.
Playback	☐ A trailer has been uploaded to YouTube, or it has been saved to a USB drive. ☐ The trailer has been tested in the classroom for playback.

8. Book Trailers: Pitch it!

Group Members:

Use notes and keywords as prompts on your cards for your presentation, so that you can recall the information and keep looking at the audience instead of just reading from a piece of paper. Remember that your aim is to sell your book trailer as being the best. Try to use vocabulary to persuade, engage, and keep your audience interested.

Card 1. _____

Card 2. _____

Card 3. _____

Card 4. _____

Card 5. _____

Card 6. _____

Card 7. _____

Card 8. _____

Card 9. _____

Card 10. _____

9. Book Trailers: Book Trailer Evaluation Rubric		
Group Members:		
Plot Hook	A captivating question is used, and the plot is not fully exposed.	1 2 3 4 5
Summary	The summary is concise and does not overwhelm the trailer; any on-screen captions are not overused.	1 2 3 4 5
Language	Appropriate vocabulary is applied to help persuade, engage, and keep the audience interested.	1 2 3 4 5
Images	Any images used relate well to the narration, and are also representative of the plot.	1 2 3 4 5
Music	The genre of music chosen is reflective of the book.	1 2 3 4 5
Video	Video use relates well to the narration, is representative of the plot, and works well with the accompanying soundtrack.	1 2 3 4 5
Production	The length is appropriate (under 90 seconds), the voice is not overpowered by music, and the video has a logical progression.	1 2 3 4 5
Copyright	The material used is copyright free or cited appropriately.	1 2 3 4 5
	TOTAL	/40

Ratings: 1 Poor 2 Fair 3 Average 4 Good 5 Excellent

10. Book Trailers: Critique

Group Members:

Write a paragraph that identifies at least one good and one bad aspect of the book trailers that your classmates have prepared.

Paragraph 1. _____

Paragraph 2. _____

Paragraph 3. _____

Paragraph 4. _____

11. Book Trailers: WebQuest Evaluation Rubric		
Group Members:		
Introduction	Goal of WebQuest achieved.	1 2 3 4 5
Task	All tasks completed, and well executed.	
	☐ Reviewed five trailers	1 2 3 4 5
	☐ Created a successful trailer	1 2 3 4 5
	☐ Presented/pitched a trailer	1 2 3 4 5
	☐ Evaluated/critiqued others	1 2 3 4 5
	☐ Voted on the best trailer	1 2 3 4 5
Process	Students worked well as a team, and the final product is a result of equal collaboration.	1 2 3 4 5
Resources	Ideas expressed are based on all the resources provided, but they demonstrate originality.	1 2 3 4 5
Evaluation and Conclusion	Students were able to achieve the final WebQuest goals.	
	☐ Presented as a group, and pitched successfully	1 2 3 4 5
	☐ One-paragraph critique of other written trailers	1 2 3 4 5
	☐ Rubric used to identify the best trailer; vote submitted	1 2 3 4 5
	TOTAL	**/ 55**

Ratings: 1 Poor 2 Fair 3 Average 4 Good 5 Excellent

Blank Game Board

				FINISH
Move forward one space.				Go back one space.
		Move forward one space.		
Go back one space.				
		Miss a turn.		
START				

Dice Templates

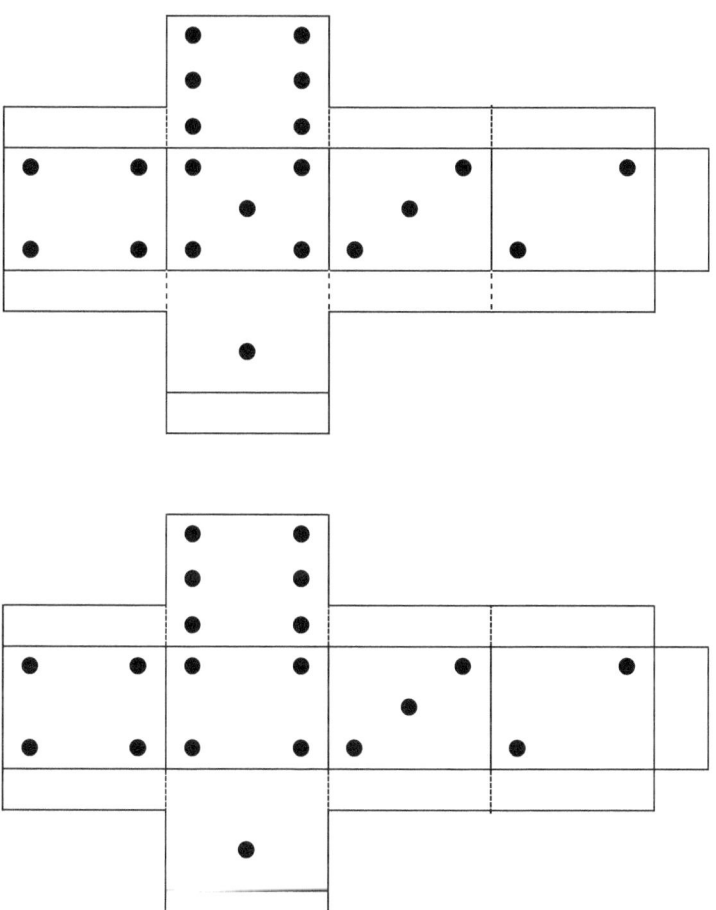

Photocopiable Content – Grammar

Create Your Own Board Game – Activity

Instructions.
Work in groups to prepare the focus, aim/title, and rules for your own board game. Then, prepare a number of prompts/questions to write inside the game space squares.

Grammar focus. Write down the grammar focus behind your game.
_____

Aim/Title. Write down the aim of your game as a title.
(e.g., *The truth about me*).
_____

Rules.
Write down the rules of game-play.
1. _____
2. _____
3. _____
4. _____
5. _____

Prompts/Questions (for the game spaces).
1. _____
2. _____
3. _____
4. _____
5. _____
6. _____
7. _____
8. _____
9. _____
10. _____
11. _____
12. _____

PART FOUR: CAPSTONE PROJECTS

10. Practicum

Overview

The practicum typically serves as a capstone project to courses such as a certificate or diploma in the teaching of English to speakers of other languages (TESOL). It serves as a means for prospective and in-service teachers to showcase their learning, exhibit competency as a classroom teacher, participate in professional dialogues with cooperating teachers, and engage in professional development to assist in life-long learning and ongoing teacher development. Ultimately, the practicum component assists prospective and in-service teachers in identifying their limitations while exploring and developing the skills to overcome these during the perfection of their craft.

Learning Outcomes
1. Understand what constitutes a practicum, and critically analyze and evaluate the delivery of learning.
2. Know the role of the academic advisor and supervisory teacher in practicum work, while demonstrating effectiveness in developing students' competence through TESOL.
3. Incorporate materials and resources in order to create a dynamic teaching environment, and design appropriate language lessons in accord with learning and cultural contexts.
4. Be able to show progress toward the development of a personal learning network through engagement in professional development activities.

The Practicum

The goal behind completion of the practicum presented in this chapter is to help pre-service and existing teachers to partner with others who can provide mentorship by directing their activities and giving them appropriate feedback on any work that they may perform. This chapter provides one means to achieve this process, and along with an accompanying series of templates, it aims to help guide prospective and in-service teachers through completion of the practicum process. If you are working, then you would be able to use the associated chapter templates to engage in a practicum aiming to develop your current teaching skills. If you are not currently working, then the same templates could be used if you were to volunteer with an organization offering free English language teaching services (such as a religious organizations), assisting you to develop confidence and competency while working alongside a teacher in a guided capacity.

A practicum experience involves a combination of class observation, providing classroom assistance, and teaching classes. During the initial stages of a practicum, prospective and in-service teachers simply watch classes, record their observations, and ask questions of their supervisory teachers outside of class time. The practicing teacher will then be provided with guided assistance by their supervisory teacher, and move on to ultimately teach a series of classes that involve supervisory teacher observation. If your practicum is part of a university degree, then it may also contain a link back to the relevant theory that you have covered in courses, and might involve the development of a pedagogy project in addition to the observational experience. Such programs also have students demonstrate how they will continue to engage in professional development once they leave such a program, and these components are also covered by this chapter.

Advisors

Academic Advisor

A faculty member will serve as your advisor, and will be available to help guide you in the completion of your practicum by answering any questions that you may have about the process. They will help you to understand the tasks that you need to complete, and when the practicum is due. It is also the responsibility of the advisor to perform a final check of your submission, ensuring that everything has been completed satisfactorily. Once the completed practicum has been approved by your advisor, it will then be evaluated. In the case of a practicum, the submission is typically pass/fail but it may also be a graded pass. This evaluation would then accompany the bound submission of the practicum that you would need to provide to the graduate department office.

Supervisory Teacher

The supervisory teacher is the one that you will observe, the one who will observe you, and the one who will also comment on your practice and development as a teacher. They will prove invaluable to you as you can see how another teacher approaches the art of teaching and because they will also provide you with guidance and feedback on your own teaching. As each practicum can vary, this teacher may be a colleague that you trust and have asked to perform the duty, someone assigned by the principal of a school, or someone that you may have had to organize yourself by offering to volunteer with an organization or getting permission from an organization to deliver practice teaching in exchange for observing their teachers. Each particular organization will have its own privacy and confidentiality guidelines that you may need to follow.

Practicum Project Completion

There is a range of forms that need to be completed as you work through a practicum, and they a serve as proof of practicum completion. Once complete, they can be collated into a practicum portfolio, or become the basis of a teaching portfolio which instructors can then use to highlight their instructional abilities.

Requirements

Observation time requirements may vary from one academic institution to another, and from one degree program to another. For the examples provided in this text, the specified time of observation is a minimum of 15 hours (see Task 1) and this is split into 5 hours of self-observation, 5 hours of peer observation, and 5 hours of observation by a peer. How these hours are split is often negotiated with the supervisory teacher who you have chosen to help guide you through the completion of the practicum components. To help keep you on track, and to show how you have fulfilled these requirements, a timesheet such as that found in part A of the photocopiable section of this chapter would need to be completed.

Tasks

The tasks to complete for the practicum outlined in this text are:
1. Self-observation, and critical reflection
2. Peer observation, and evaluation
3. Clinical supervision (observation by a peer)
4. Pedagogy project (lesson plan development)
5. Engagement in professional development

Task 1. Self-Reflection – Logging to Learn

In environments where videotaping lessons is not appropriate (due to privacy or other ethical concerns), paper or electronic logs and checklists, as a form of teaching diary and feedback, can prove useful for gathering information and for being reflective in regards to your teaching. They can all allow you to keep track of what you do in your class, and how you do it.

In addition to completing the practicum observation hours timesheet for this task, you will need to keep a series of logs of how you perform as a teacher for at least five hours of class time and complete the appropriate section of the practicum template for this task (see the photocopiable section of this chapter).

    1.1 You may decide to keep electronic or paper-based notes for your log, but you must complete the teaching log sheets with your practicum submission. So ensure that, however you keep your log, it can easily be transferred to these documents.

    1.2 Select any lesson during which you teach normal classes (i.e., not an exam week, and probably not during the first few or last few weeks of the term or semester).

    1.3 Select only one class that you teach, and focus on this class for the purpose of monitoring your teaching for this task.

    1.4 Set aside a particular time of day when you can spend fifteen minutes completing your log. The best time might be directly after the class, or at the end of that work day. It is important to keep the log before you forget what has happened in the class. You may find it useful to take notes during the class, and refer back to these when preparing the log itself.

    1.5 Try to be as specific as possible in your responses.

- **1.6** After completing the logs, distribute the student appraisal form to the same class (if the class is very large you can limit this to at least 5 students), and complete the self-evaluation checklist.
- **1.7** Take a close and critical look at all of your log entries, in light of the responses to the student appraisal form and the self-evaluation checklist, in order to get a clear and coherent picture of your teaching acts during the period of task one completion.
- **1.8** Engage in self-reflection, and complete the self-reflection questions form.
- **1.9** All forms required for completion of this task are found in the photocopiable content section of this chapter under part A (timesheet) and part B (task one).

Task 2. Peer Observation and Evaluation

Peer observation provides both the observer and the observee with the opportunity to mutually enhance the quality of their teaching practice. It also provides teachers with a chance to share good practice methods, approaches, and techniques, while also sharing their thoughts on the practice of teaching and supporting each other in the development of their instructional skills. As with task 1, for this task, you will need to complete the appropriate practicum sections of the observation hours timesheet, and the practicum template.

- **2.1** Find a teacher, or teachers, who will allow you to observe a total of five hours of their class time.
- **2.2** You will need to inform each teacher of the things that you will be doing while you are observing them, and share with them your observations post-lesson.
- **2.3** You will need to complete a series of nine worksheets during this observation period. The first five worksheets can be completed across a single lesson if desired, and will likely take an hour and a half of observation time. The remaining four worksheets can be completed over one hour of observation time each.
- **2.4** All forms required for completion of this task are found in the photocopiable content section of this chapter under part A (timesheet) and C (task two).
- **2.5** In addition, information on the observation process has been included in the photocopiable content section of this chapter

under part D. It would prove worthwhile to have all of the teachers that you observe, and those who intend to observe you, read over this information.

Task 3. Clinical Supervision – Observation by a Peer

Clinical supervision is a process by which a teacher receives individualized support to enhance their instruction in order to improve education for their learners. It is often used as a term to mean the coaching of novice teachers. In this process experienced teachers are relied upon as trusted colleagues rather than as evaluators.

   3.1 Find a teacher, or teachers, who are willing to observe five hours of your class time and complete the appropriate sections of the practicum template.

   3.2 Each teacher that observes you will need to complete an a) pre-observation feedback form and a b) peer observation form for each lesson that they observe.

   3.3 You will need to complete the pre-observation feedback form in advance so that the teacher who is observing you can make appropriate comments on it.

   3.4 The clinical observation form can be completed by the teacher observing you as they sit in upon your lesson.

   3.5 You should aim to discuss the comments on both forms with the teacher that is observing you, and this should occur in a pre-lesson observation briefing and in a post-lesson discussion. These discussions do not have to be lengthy but they give you the opportunity to understand the comments and to ask questions of the teacher observing you, as you go through the process of observation.

   3.6 All forms required for completion of this task are found in the photocopiable content section of this chapter under part E.

Task 4. Pedagogy Project – Lesson Plan Development

Learning to plan and evaluate an effective lesson is an essential skill of being a teacher. This task will engage you in the development of a lesson of your choosing. However, you will need to demonstrate how you can adapt the concepts touched upon during your TESOL coursework to your specific teaching/learning context. You will then need to teach this lesson, and perform an appropriate evaluation and assessment of the

lesson and your teaching effectiveness prior to completing the appropriate sections of the practicum template.
- 4.1 Use the provided templates to help you complete this project.
- 4.2 Develop a comprehensive lesson plan, modifying the templates as required to suit your teaching context and learner needs.
- 4.3 Link the implementation of the lesson plan to theory.
- 4.4 Reflect on the implementation of the lesson, and provide an evaluation of the created content and its use as part of a pedagogy project report.
- 4.5 All forms required for completion of this task are found in the photocopiable section of this chapter under part F.

Task 5. Professional Development – Lifelong Learning

The challenge for many practicing teachers, especially those in the English as a foreign language (EFL) teaching context, is a lack of exposure to professional development during their career. A means of obtaining professional development, and ways to interact with fellow teachers are to join local language teaching organizations or groups, to attend or present at their conferences, and to engage with group members in online forums or special interest groups. All of this will form part of your personal learning environment; in other words, the way that you organize professional development and the system that you put in place to manage your own learning over time.
- 5.1 For this task you will need to show progress toward the development of a personal learning network (PLN) through engagement in professional development activities, or through participation or involvement in a local teaching organization or group (either online or in person), documenting this in the appropriate section of the practicum template.
- 5.2 Choose an organization that you will begin to interact with. In the Republic of Korea for example, there are KOTESOL (Korean Organization for Teaching English to Speakers of Other Languages), KATE (Korean Association for Teaching English), and STEM (Society for Teaching English through Media) to name a few.
- 5.3 Decide which component of this task you will complete: conference attendance, conference presentation, or online

participation. Conference attendance is advised, and many universities put these on for free to the public after registration. Sydney University in Australia hosts their annual TESOL colloquium for such purposes. Other institutions and professional organizations may host conference presentations online, and you may choose to view one, or some, of these.

5.4 All forms required for completion of this task are found in the photocopiable section of this chapter under part G.

Undertake **one** of **5.5**, **5.6**, or **5.7**.

5.5 Conference Attendance Steps
   a. Attend a conference, physically or virtually, and take notes from the presentations that you attend. You should attend at least three presentations.
   b. Prepare a summary of each of the presentations with an associated learning comment that details something new that you learned from the presentation, points that you found interesting, and something that you found that you could apply with your learners or adapt to your teaching context (current or potential). The summary should be in point form with the learning comment in either point or paragraph form.
   c. Use the forms in part G1 to help you complete this task, and submit the certificate of conference attendance (if you have been provided one).

5.6 Conference Presentation Steps
   a. Prepare an abstract to submit to one of the local organizations for potential presentation. You will need to review the specific calls for papers on their websites for the details regarding this.
   b. Once your abstract has been approved for presentation, prepare the paper and PowerPoint according to the organization's guidelines.
   c. Present the paper, and include both a copy of it and the certificate of presentation within your practicum portfolio as proof of completing this task.

5.7 Online Forum Participation Steps
   a. If you are unable to attend or present at a conference then the online forum participation option is available to you.
   b. Join an organization forum, a special interest group (SIG), or Facebook group.
   c. Post a number of questions related to your current teaching context, and answer the responses from group members. Questions might include aspects of classroom management, dealing with disruptive students, and managing teacher-talk time. These will depend on individual teachers, and will likely stem from identified shortcomings or other aspects related to the observation tasks. You will need to post a minimum of ten questions, add the screenshots of the post and any associated responses to your practicum template.
   d. You can use posts made to the learner management system during completion of your coursework for this component of the practicum, as that is considered a community of practice/organization forum.

Evaluation

The practicum component of a course is often evaluated by the head professor of a degree program or a designated faculty member who is known as your advisor. Often, practicums are graded simply as pass/fail but, as in the case for the practicum provided as an example in this text, they can also be graded based on performance and the proofs provided for each of the sections completed. An example grading form that might be used in conjunction with any practicum that you undertake can be found under part H of the photocopiable content of this chapter. This evaluation would also accompany bound submissions of the practicum that you would need to provide to your graduate program department office.

Depending upon the requirements of your graduate program, you may need to present five bound copies of the practicum to the department which will then lodge these with the university on your behalf, and house a copy in the department office. This will then see you officially complete all requirements of the program, allowing you to receive graduand status and to become eligible for the award of your certificate or degree. The practicum can then also serve as proof of your abilities to any prospective employee.

Summary

This chapter defined and explained the nature of a practicum, which is to assist you in developing confidence and competency while working alongside a teacher in a guided capacity. Although practicums may vary, there are some core components to each, and you were provided with an example that contains five tasks. Explanation of these tasks then went into detail regarding the time requirements and the logging of teaching, observing and evaluating lessons required, as well as aspects of completing professional development and engaging in lifelong learning.

Review

Content Quiz
Practicum

To help solidify some of the concepts introduced by this chapter the following multiple-choice and true or false quizzes might be helpful for you to undertake. So that you can check the accuracy of your responses, an answer key can be found following the quizzes.

Multiple-Choice

Circle **a**, **b**, or **c** for the answer that best completes the sentence presented in each question.

1. The purpose behind the practicum is to help pre-service and existing teachers …
   a) partner with others who can provide mentorship by directing their activities and giving them appropriate feedback on any work that they may perform.
   b) undertake original research and perform critical analysis of a topic while adhering to scholarly rigor.
   c) collect and evaluate student work that has been undertaken at key points throughout their academic career.

2. A practicum experience may involve …
   a) developing a rationalized reflective narrative that captures the scope, progress, and value of student learning, with student reflections supported by concrete evidence.
   b) a combination of class observations and providing classroom assistance as well as teaching classes, developing lesson plans, and providing supportive evidence of the ability to undertake lifelong learning.
   c) the undertaking of original research and performing critical analysis of a topic while adhering to scholarly rigor.

3. The role of your practicum advisor is to …
   a) help you solve unexpected academic problems, and resolve class issues that might impact your on academic path, while offering advice to keep you academically on track.
   b) provide mentorship, feedback, observation, and guidance during peer and clinical observations.
   c) ensure that you understand the tasks expected, that you have completed all tasks satisfactorily, and to give the practicum portfolio an evaluation.

4. The role of the practicum supervisory teacher is to …
   a) help you solve unexpected academic problems, and resolve class issues that might impact on your academic path, while offering advice to keep you academically on track.
   b) provide mentorship, feedback, observation, and guidance during peer and clinical observations.
   c) ensure that you understand the tasks expected, that you have completed all tasks satisfactorily, and to give the practicum portfolio an evaluation.

5. The purpose behind self-observation is to …
   a) gather feedback on your teaching practice for reflective purposes, and to evaluate if what you are doing as a teacher is successful.
   b) provide only the observer with the opportunity to enhance the quality of their teaching practice.
   c) Establish a process of practice where you can successfully observe others, and to offer mentorship, feedback, and guidance on others' teaching performance.

True or False

Circle **a** (true) if you think that the statement is correct, or **b** (false) if you think that the statement is incorrect.

1. Practicum requirements are standard across the educational field, and they do not vary from one academic institution to another or from one degree program to another.
    a) True.
    b) False.

2. Peer observation is all about being observed by a colleague or peer that your trust, so that they can offer you mentorship, feedback, and guidance on your teaching performance.
    a) True.
    b) False.

3. Peer observation provides teachers with the opportunity to share good practice methods, approaches, and techniques, while also sharing their thoughts on the practice of teaching and supporting each other in the development of teaching skills.
    a) True.
    b) False.

4. In the clinical observation process experienced teachers are relied upon as trusted colleagues rather than as evaluators.
    a) True.
    b) False.

5. A personal learning network or PLN can be defined as the way that you organize professional development and the system that you put in place to manage your own learning over time.
    a) True.
    b) False.

Quiz Answers
Practicum

Multiple-Choice		*True or False*	
1.	A	1.	F
2.	B	2.	T
3.	C	3.	T
4.	B	4.	T
5.	A	5.	T

Suggested Readings

Celce-Murcia, M. (Ed.). (2001). *Teaching English as a second or foreign language* (3rd ed.). Heinle and Heinle.

Crookes, G. (2003). *A practicum in TESOL: Professional development through teaching practice.* Cambridge University Press.

Kumaravadivelu, B. (2003). *Beyond methods: Microstrategies for language teaching.* Yale University Press.

Kumaravadivelu, B. (2012). *Language teacher education for a global society: A modular model for knowing, analyzing, recognizing, doing, and seeing.* Routledge.

Lynch, B., & Shaw, P. (2005). Portfolios, power, and ethics. *TESOL Quarterly, 39*(2), 263-297.

Richards, J., & Crookes, G. (1988). The practicum in TESOL. *TESOL Quarterly, 22*(1), 9-27.

Richards, J., & Lockhart, C. (1994). *Reflective teaching in second language classrooms.* Cambridge University Press.

Richards, J. & Renandya, W. (Eds.). (2002). *Methodology in language teaching: An anthology of current practice.* Cambridge University Press.

Scrivener, J. *Learning teaching: The essential guide to English language teaching* (3rd Ed.). MacMillan. [Chapter 16]

Ur, P. (2012). *A course in English language teaching* (2nd ed.). Cambridge University Press.

Woodward, T. (2001). *Planning lessons and courses.* Cambridge University Press.

Photocopiable Content
Practicum

This section of the chapter includes a variety of material that is free to photocopy. Use it to help you complete a practicum. It contains the following content provided under different parts from A through H.

Part A
A1.   Practicum observation hours – Timesheet

Part B
B1.   Self-reflection – Teaching logs
B2.   Student appraisal form
B3.   Self-evaluation checklist
B4.   Self-reflection questions

Part C
C1.1   Observation worksheet 1a – Classroom snapshot 1 (Impressions)
C1.2   Observation worksheet 1b – Classroom snapshot 2 (Interactions)
C1.3   Observation worksheet 1c – Classroom snapshot 3 (What helps people learn?)
C1.4   Observation worksheet 1d – Classroom snapshot 4 (Errors and correction)
C1.5   Observation worksheet 1e – Classroom snapshot 5 (The learners)
C2.   Observation worksheet 2 – Teachers and learners
C3.   Observation worksheet 3 – Options and decisions
C4.   Observation worksheet 4 – Thoughts, questions, and appropriation
C5.   Observation worksheet 5 – Influencing the learning environment

Part D
D1.   The observation process

Part E
E1. Pre-observation feedback
E2. Clinical observation form

Part F
F1. Lesson plan development and reflection guide
F2. Lesson plan structure general guide

Part G
G1. Professional development – Conference attendance
G2. Professional development – Conference presentation
G3. Professional development – Online participation

Part H
H1. Practicum evaluation sheet – Task requirements

A1. Practicum Observation Hours – Timesheet			
Date	Class	Focus	Length
(YYYY-MM-DD)	(Name and type of class, e.g., GTC23 – Sophomore Reading, English minors)	(Practicum stage, e.g., self-observation, peer observation, clinical supervision/peer observed)	(e.g., 60 minutes)
	Total self-observation hours:		
	Total peer observation hours:		
	Total clinical supervision hours:		
	TOTAL HOURS:		

Practicing teacher:
I, _____, certify that the above hours are correct.

Signed _____.

Clinical supervisor/Peer observer
I, _____, certify that I have observed the person named above for the hours specified in this time sheet.

Signed _____.

Photocopiable Content - Practicum

B1. Self-Reflection – Teaching Logs

Name:	Type of class:
Date:	Age:
Number of students:	Level:

1. Provide a brief explanation of the lesson and students (e.g., What are they working on during the lesson? What progress is being made to accomplish the learning objectives of the day?)

2. List the teaching techniques that you were able to use in the lesson, and why you found them to be especially useful.

3. Were you able to identify any individual student needs or issues during the class? If so, please list them.

4. What syllabus elements were incorporated into this lesson? How did you identify which are the most appropriate for your learners to concentrate upon during the class?

5. Did you use any supplementary resources during the lesson? If so, please list what you used.

6. Which teaching methods, approaches, or techniques did you use with students in this lesson? List each with a reason why you chose to employ it.

7. Did you have any problems with student behavior during the class? If so, list the steps that you used to overcome these problems.

8. Provide a brief summary of how you feel the lesson went, and what you might do differently if teaching the same material again?

9. Consider any other comments you might want to note regarding the lesson and make them here.

B2. Student Appraisal Form

Explanation: The purpose of this questionnaire is to provide the teacher with feedback on their teaching performance. Your feedback is important as it can help improve the lessons that you receive from your teacher. Please think carefully as you answer each question, and answer as honestly and as best as you can. Keep in mind that all of your answers will remain anonymous.

I have found that this teacher …	*Strongly disagree*	*Disagree*	*Neither*	*Agree*	*Strongly agree*
1. communicates class material clearly.	1	2	3	4	5
2. is well prepared for class.	1	2	3	4	5
3. organizes class time effectively.	1	2	3	4	5
4. stimulates my interest in the subject.	1	2	3	4	5
5. is responsive to student problems.	1	2	3	4	5
6. can teach well.	1	2	3	4	5

B3. Self-Evaluation – Checklist					
	\multicolumn{2}{l	}{A **No** answer means that improvement is possible. **N/A** means not applicable.}	Yes	No	N/A
Language content	1	Did you teach any specific language items during your classes?			
	2	If so, did you find out how many students grasped the meaning?			
	3	Did enough students get the chance to re-use these target language items?			
	4	Did students use these language items to say anything meaningful?			
	5	Do students have a written record of new learning?			
Skills practice	1	Were you trying to practice one specific skill or a mixture of skills?			
	2	Were some tasks, or parts of tasks, appropriate for weak students and some for better ones?			
	3	Did students find the activities motivating?			
	4	Did most students receive some practice in the use of target skills?			
Correction	1	Did you concentrate on relevant points and avoid overcorrecting mistakes?			
	2	Did you only focus on students' communication abilities and ignore errors of form?			
	3	Was there a satisfactory level of accuracy in language practice?			
	4	If not, were you able to identify or provide a solution?			
	5	Did you provide students with scope for self- and peer-correction?			

		A **No** answer means that improvement is possible. **N/A** means not applicable.	Yes	No	N/A
Stages in lesson	1	Did you try to do too much or too little?			
	2	Could the activities have been better sequenced?			
Class management	1	Did you generally keep control of who spoke, and when (not too much calling out)?			
	2	Did you make sure some reluctant students (non-volunteers) participated?			
	3	Was there more student talk than teacher talk?			
	4	Did students speak English with each other?			
	5	Did you do anything to leave students with a feeling of achievement (e.g., use of exit tickets to evaluate, summarize, review)?			
Lesson structure	1	Did you include a variety of activities?			
	2	Were tasks and instructions clear to students?			
	3	Did you utilize visuals, realia, or other supplementary material?			
	4	Did you incorporate student experience, knowledge, and aspects of their own lives into the lesson?			

Photocopiable Content - Practicum

A **No** answer means that improvement is possible. **N/A** means not applicable.			**Yes**	**No**	**N/A**
New language items	1	Did you present new language items in an understandable way?			
	2	Did you provide comprehension checks for students?			
	3	Did you recycle vocabulary throughout the lesson?			
	4	Did you recycle vocabulary from previous lessons?			
	5	Did you ensure students recorded new vocabulary in a notebook or elsewhere?			
Skills practice	1	Did you focus on the participation of weak students?			
	2	Did you adjust the level of difficulty of tasks as required?			
	3	Did you provide repetition and mechanical practice for students?			
	4	Did you provide meaningful practice for students?			
	5	Did you ensure student-to-student work occurred?			
Class management	1	Did you have to nominate any students to speak?			
	2	Did you utilize non-volunteers?			
	3	Did you use student names?			
	4	Did you limit teacher talk time?			

Photocopiable Content - Practicum

B4. Self-Reflection – Questions

1. What was one great thing that you particularly noticed about your teaching?

2. What was one big weakness that you noticed regarding your teaching?

3. What was one thing that you really wanted to do or achieve with this class but could not do?

4. What is one reason why you could not do that one thing that you really wanted to do?

5. What aspect(s) of your teaching would you really like to keep and why?

6. What aspect(s) of your teaching would you particularly like to change and why?

7. What do you consider the most important thing that you have learned by completing this practicum task?

C1.1 Observation Worksheet 1a
Classroom Snapshot 1 (Impressions)

Obtain permission to visit a class for around 10–15 minutes. Your aim is to gain a general snapshot of what occurs. While you are in the room, answer the following questions. For the first few questions aim to be descriptive, but for the final question aim to answer more subjectively.

1. Describe how the learners are positioned (seated/standing) in the room.

2. Describe in general what is happening (e.g., 'an audio recording is being played, learners are listening for answers to fill in a blank on a worksheet')

3. Who is doing the speaking? Who is doing any other thing?

4. Describe a) the feeling; and b) the level of engagement in the room.

C1.2 Observation Worksheet 1b
Classroom Snapshot 2 (Interactions)

Obtain permission to go into a teacher's classroom for around 10–15 minutes. Your aim is to gain a snapshot of what is occurring in the lesson. Ask the instructor not to prepare any special activities for the time you will be observing. While in the room the aim is to consider speaking and interaction patterns.

1a. Who speaks?

Consider:

i. Who does the speaking?

ii. Who do they speak to?

iii. Who does not speak?

Photocopiable Content - Practicum

1b. The who speaks sketch

In the space below, sketch the classroom and mark the seating positions of students and the position of the instructor in the room (standing or sitting). Then, over a two-minute period at the start of the lesson, or any new activity, put a mark (e.g., a tick) next to anyone who speaks. Using different colored ink, repeat this during another one or two points in the lesson, and see how the results might differ.

2. Interaction patterns

In the space below, draw another sketch of the classroom layout. Then, choose a two-minute period during a whole-class speaking activity. Add arrows to the diagram to indicate who speaks to whom.

C1.3 Observation Worksheet 1c
Classroom Snapshot 3 (What helps people learn?)

Obtain permission to go into a teacher's classroom for around 10–15 minutes. While observing the classroom, the activities employed, the teacher, and the student interaction aim to answer:

- What can you identify occurring that establishes a good atmosphere for effective learning to occur?
- What can you identify that might be inhibiting any learning from occurring?

The Physical Classroom

Make notes regarding seating, sight lines, the board, the temperature, free space, lighting conditions, equipment, and so on.

The Activities

Make notes on the kind of activities employed by the instructor, the student involvement, and the balance of student and teacher interaction.

Photocopiable Content - Practicum

The Teacher

What personal qualities does the instructor have that you think are well suited to teaching)? What kind of rapport does the instructor possess with students? What kind of classroom atmosphere does this instructor generate? What do you think it would feel like to be a student of this instructor?

The Learners

How motivated are these students? Why? To what extent are they active participants in their own learning? To what extent are they expecting the instructor to do everything for them?

C1.4 Observation Worksheet 1d
Classroom Snapshot 4 (Errors and correction)

Obtain permission to go into a teacher's classroom for around 10–15 minutes. While observing, note down some student errors and how the instructor deals with them. Categorize each error (e.g., wrong tense, wrong phoneme, meaning unclear, and so on). Describe in detail what happens.

Examples

Error: I am agree. *Type of error:* unnecessary word.
Indication/correction: Teacher holds up three fingers (representing words of the sentence), throws away the middle finger. Student looks puzzled, then says the sentence again without the middle word. The teacher acknowledges this is correct with a smile and by saying, 'Good!'.
Error: Give me that pen. *Type of error:* Rude. *Indication/correction:* not commented upon or dealt with.

Considerations

Did anyone notice that there was an error? Who?
Did the teacher do anything?
Did the student do anything?
Did the other students do anything? Who?
Did anyone indicate that there was an error? Who?
Did anyone correct the error? Who?
How was it corrected?

Error:
Type of error:
Indication/correction:

Error:
Type of error:
Indication/correction:

Error:
Type of error:
Indication/correction:

Photocopiable Content - Practicum

C1.5 Observation Worksheet 1e
Classroom Snapshot 5 (The learners)

Obtain permission to go into a teacher's classroom for around 10–15 minutes. While observing, consider the lesson from the student's point of view. To do this, choose (secretly) one student to focus on and make notes about them below.

1. Choose a random two-minute period. Write a narrative description of what the student does.

2. Choose a random two-minute period. Write a narrative description of what you imagine the student is thinking or feeling.

3. Towards the end of the lesson write down what you think might be the student's description of what has happened in the lesson.

    i.   Did you enjoy the class?

    ii.   Did you learn anything from it?

    iii.   Did the teacher help you in anyway?

    iv.   Did you talk to the teacher or other students at all?

    v.   Did you expect anything to happen during the class that did not happen? (e.g., different activities used).

C2. Observation Worksheet 2
Teachers and Learners

Obtain permission to observe a teacher's class for a whole lesson. As you observe, decide if the statement on the left or right best fits the teacher and the learners, or is it somewhere in the middle.

The teacher			
Instructor often uses expressions (e.g., smiles).			*Instructor does not often use expressions.*
Instructor is too loud or too quiet.			*Instructor uses a natural conversational volume appropriate to the room.*
Instructor acts naturally (as they would outside the classroom).			*Instructor is distinctively 'teacherly'.*
Instructor speaks excessively.			*Instructor speaks very little.*
Instructions are clear.			*Instructions are unclear.*
Instructor makes mainly open-ended inquiries.			*Instructor makes mainly close-ended inquiries.*
Instructor comes across as impatient.			*Instructor comes across as patient.*
Clear dissemination of information, understood by learners.			*Information conveyed unclearly, misunderstood by learners.*
Instructor is oblivious to learner feedback throughout the lesson.			*Instructor notes learner feedback throughout the lesson.*
Instructor does not adjust to learner response.			*Instructor adjusts to learner response.*
Instructor works at own pace.			*Instructor works at learner pace.*

Comments on the instructor

The learners

Generally engaged.			Not generally engaged.
Take a passive role.			Take an active role.
Mainly follow instructions.			Remain largely anonymous.
Balanced participation levels.			One or two learners dominate.

Comments on the learners

C3. Observation Worksheet 3
Options and Decisions

Obtain permission to observe a teacher's class for a whole lesson. As you observe, consider aspects of classroom management. 'Classroom management' refers such things as the moment-to-moment decisions made by the teacher, as well as the actions that the instructor takes throughout a lesson when dealing with material and students, e.g., writing on the board, giving instructions, organizing the class into pairs or groups. For every decision made, there will have been other options that the teacher may not have chosen. For each of the following headings:

1. Note specific examples of classroom situations, and state how the instructor responded.
2. Note alternate options that the teacher might have adopted instead.

Example: Dealing with unexpected problems
Situation: A student arrives twelve minutes late.
Action: Teacher said 'hello'. (The student sat down quietly and asks what is going on in the class from their partner).
Other options: The instructor might have asked why the student arrived late. The instructor may have also pointed out the time to the student.

Student participation in lesson

Situation:

Action:

Other options:

574 *Issues in TESOL*

Grouping of students, arrangement of seating

Situation:

Action:

Other options:

Set up of activities, instructions

Situation:

Action:

Other options:

Board use/layout; classroom equipment; visual aids; realia

Situation:

Action:

Other options:

Dealing with unexpected issues

Situation:

Action:

Other options:

Instructor's role and participation

Situation:

Action:

Other options:

Other notes concerning the lesson

C4. Observation Worksheet 4
Thoughts, Questions, and Appropriation

Obtain permission to observe a teacher's class for a whole lesson. As you observe, note a few things that you observe, and record your own thoughts, questions, or suggestions regarding them. Also note down several things that you consider worthy of appropriating (i.e., something you would like to borrow for use in your teaching – personal qualities, teaching skills and techniques, activities, classroom atmosphere). Finally, choose something that you feel that you would like to suggest for this teacher to change, or to use later in their teaching (e.g., a different way to deliver an activity).

During the lesson
I noticed …
I wondered …

During the lesson
I noticed …
I wondered …

During the lesson
I noticed …
I wanted to ask you …

Appropriated item
Description of the item …
I like this because …

Appropriated item
Description of the item …
I like this because …

Appropriated item
Description of item …
I like this because …

Suggestion
I'd like to suggest …
I think you will like this because …

C5. Observation Worksheet 5
Influencing the Learning Environment

Obtain permission to observe a teacher's class for a whole lesson. As you observe, consider some ways in which the teacher may influence what occurs during the lesson. Select four or five of the following aspects, and consider the teacher's role in regards to each.

Aspects of the learning environment	Instructor role
Classroom atmosphere	Does the teacher establish and maintain a friendly and engaging learning environment?
Organization	Does the teacher take an active role in how the materials, free space, and time on task is utilized throughout the lesson?
Encouragement and support, promoting participation	Does the teacher provide positive support, promote realistically achievable lesson goals, and a means for students to take on an active role in the classroom?
Promoting guided discovery	Does the teacher use elicitation techniques, (elicit answers, construct questions, offer partial examples, encourage hypotheses, and so on) that lead the students to their own conclusions or to use their own language?
Presenting content information	Does the instructor appropriately explain, lecture or answer student questions regarding specific learning content?
Provision of samples of language	Does the instructor provide appropriate target language exposure to students when providing instructions, comments, and answering questions, and so on?
Materials and tasks	Does the teacher use appropriate materials and tasks suitable for the teaching or practice of the language points being presented?
Monitoring	Does the instructor constantly monitor what is occurring throughout the lesson?

Aspects of the learning environment	Instructor role
Informative feedback	Does the instructor provide useable and understandable feedback that supports the learning process? (e.g., draw on peers to assist in providing information about any mistakes or errors made, provides information about language forms and/or uses, demonstrates how to perform a task in a different manner, suggests additional work for early finishers.)
Learning habits	Does the instructor provide a sense of a timed lesson that occurs seamlessly, and seems to provide a formless learning process?
Selecting and presenting	Does the instructor introduce content in ways that are manageable for learners, seeing them work effectively or do students end up struggling with it?
Structuring and sequencing	Does the instructor sequence activities appropriately, or allow students to help select an activity that they want and how they will complete it?
Authority	Does the instructor use their authority appropriately and effectively? (e.g., closing activities or discussions, requiring certain actions from individual students.)
Raising awareness	Does the instructor increase learning by encouraging the students to notice language points, mistakes/errors, new vocabulary, and so on?
Guidance and direction	Does the instructor use their knowledge and experience to best guide, direct, or counsel students?
Learner training	Does the instructor increase learner awareness regarding their own learning processes, and provide any means for developing them more effectively or efficiently?

Aspects of the learning environment	Instructor role
Democracy and personal responsibility	Does the instructor ensure that all students are treated equally, and that each is held accountable for their own learning/participation in the lesson?
Natural motivation	Does the teacher encourage lessons to flow naturally, and encourage the continued use of language if it emerges spontaneously?

Aspect chosen	Instructor role – comments
Area 1:	|//
Area 2:	

Area 3:

Area 4:

Area 5:

D1. The Observation Process

Pre-Observation Meeting

In order for observation to be effective, it is necessary to have consultations prior to the observation so that the observer has some background on the class. It also gives the person being observed a chance to provide some input into the observation. For these reasons then, it is a good idea to hold a pre-observation meeting and discuss:

- the time and place of the observation (which obviously should be arranged so as to minimize any potential impact on student learning),
- the status/history of the learning group (year/degree, level, any other significant information),
- the location of the class,
- how the lesson fits within the course/module/program,
- the aims and objectives of the specific lessons,
- learning outcomes (what students are intended to learn),
- potential difficulties or areas of concern (an opportunity for the observee to flag any specific areas that they would particularly appreciate feedback on),
- any specific focus for the observation, aside from those areas of concern (e.g., classroom management, questioning techniques),
- assessment instruments used, and
- any particular concerns that the observer might have in terms of confidentiality and feedback.

Preparing the Students

It can be disconcerting for students if someone else attends the class without warning. So, it is sensible to explain to learners that a colleague will be attending the class, that they will be there to help you review your teaching, and that they will not be playing a part in class proceedings.

Observing the Class
The observer should:
- be unobtrusive, i.e., not in the direct line of vision of the teacher or students, but able to view both,
- be discreet, e.g., not leap in to correct what may be an obvious error,
- focus upon the teaching and learning processes, rather than the content of the lesson,
- continuously check the level of interaction between teachers and students, and
- aim to gather evidence for later interpretation and discussion.

The Recording Process
Depending upon what stage of the practicum you are completing, the recording process for the observation will be different. For the purposes of this practicum, a number of pre-prepared forms have been provided to make things easier for the observer and the observee, although it is understood that observers often do feel constrained by these.

Checking with Students
At the end of the class, it can prove useful for an observer to check with students about how they felt the lesson went for them. This could be completed in a small group, taking the form of a short-structured session after the teacher has left. Aspects that the observer can bring up may include asking students for their opinions on the teaching and observation process, and their understanding of the material, i.e., learning outcomes. In a larger group (e.g., lecture), a few minutes of conversation with two or three students can at least give the observer a flavor of how the lesson has gone over for them.

Reflecting on the Teaching
The final part of the observation process is to reflect on the evidence gathered during the lesson. To this end, you will try to identify strengths and those areas in which colleagues or you may be encouraged to consider improvements.

E1. Pre-Observation Feedback Form

(to be completed before teaching a lesson and given to the observer)

Instructor: Class:
Observer: Level:
Date: Time:

Teacher's Outline of Lesson to be Observed

1. **Specific aspects of the curriculum taught in the lesson**
   (e.g., competencies, learner objectives)

2. **Instructional strategies used in the lesson**
   (e.g., lecture, small group discussion, cooperative groups, technology integration, and why)

Photocopiable Content - Practicum

3. **Learning activities**
   What learning activities will the students be engaged in?

4. **Learning outcomes**
   How will lesson learning outcomes be achieved? How will you know if they have been achieved?

5. **Specific performance areas/criteria**
   List anything specific that you want the observing teacher to look for or to comment on during the lesson.

Photocopiable Content - Practicum

6. **Student differences**
   How will you accommodate different learners, those at different levels, differentiated instruction, etc?

7. **Sample materials**
   Attach a copy of any additional content used during the lesson (e.g., handouts).

8. **Observer comments** (if any)

E2. Clinical Observation Form

Instructor: Class:
Observer: Level:
Date: Time:

---

1. **Aims and objectives**
   Were the aims and objectives of the lesson clearly explained or presented to students? Did the lesson have a clear focus?

2. **Appropriateness of materials**
   How appropriate were classroom activities in achieving the aims and objectives of the lesson? How effective was the content presented for helping students obtain the stated learning outcomes? Was the material/content provided to learners too much or too little for the lesson?

Photocopiable Content - Practicum

3. **Organization of the lesson**
   How appropriate was the organization of the lesson?

4. **Stimulating learner interest**
   To what extent was the instructor able to stimulate and sustain learner interest throughout the lesson?

5. **Opportunities for learner participation**
   Did students have enough opportunities to participate in learning activities effectively?

6. **Use of teaching aids**
   How effectively were teaching aids (handouts, whiteboard use, and so on) utilized throughout the lesson?

7. **Explaining difficult concepts**
   To what extent was the instructor able to explain difficult concepts to learners?

8. **Effectiveness**
   Was the lesson effective? Why or why not?

9. Any other general observations

10. Observed instructor's response

F1. Lesson Plan Development and Reflection Guide

Rationale

The rationale behind the teaching process should be brief, and define any terminology from the literature that you may be using. It will ideally be based on your theory of teaching and learning or that expected by the school where the lesson is being provided. For example, a presentation, practice, production (PPP) approach will be used as part of a communicative language teaching lesson that employs total physical response as a means of teaching how to tell the time. PPP is being applied to move learners to understanding by presenting the material, helping them practice it, and then having them produce it using CLT to emphasize socialization and collaboration of students in pair and group work, while TPR is used to help engage young learners further with the content.

Learning context

Provide a description of your teaching and learning environment using the subheadings below.

- The Practitioner (years of teaching service, number of years in present position, what classes have been taught and to who and at what levels, usual teaching style).
- The Students (age range, gender, total number, practitioner perceptions [of the actual language level, learning styles, and classroom behavior of the students, differentiation requirements]).
- The School Situation (how many teachers/students, courses provided, location).
- The Classroom Context (length of lessons, kind of activities usually completed and why).

Materials and Resources

Describe in detail the materials and resources that you will use throughout the lesson using the subheadings below.

- Pre-Prepared Material (explain the nature of the material, usage, and any personal expenses required).
- In-Class Material.
- Homework/Follow-up Materials.
- Additional Supplementary Material.

Aims and Goals
Identify the aim(s) of the lesson (tied to the rationale in one or two clear statements).

Implementation
Detail the procedure(s)/method(s) of implementation taken by the instructor. (If you are using the lesson plan over several class periods then this could be outlined by stages such as: lesson 1 to lesson 5, or step 1 to step 5.)

Reflection: Outcomes and Implications
Provide brief commentary on the outcomes and implications of the lesson using the subheadings below:

- *Anticipated versus Actual outcome(s)* (what actually happened at the end of the day?, Did the project work or not [including to your satisfaction]?, What contribution did the use of tech provide over non-tech [if any]?, What major problems emerged?, What could solve those problems in the future?, What would you change next time you teach this lesson?)
- *Implications* (Where will this go in the future [both for the class/students and you]? Can you develop an action plan for the future?)

Lesson Structure
This consists of a detailed lesson plan, and one that can be constructed using the general guide on the following page. It is the actual plan that you would use to guide your lesson, and the one that could be handed to another teacher to follow if they had to teach the lesson on your behalf.

Photocopiable Content - Practicum

F2. Lesson Plan Structure General Guide

Teaching Context	
Levels of language proficiency and student maturity	Student language level, e.g., beginner, intermediate, advanced. Student age range, e.g., young learners, adults.
Lesson length	Time allotted for the class, e.g., 35-45 minutes.
Lesson topic	Major theme or focus of the lesson, e.g., numbers and time.
Objectives	Lesson aims, e.g., to teach students how to tell the time and date accurately.
Outcomes	Learning outcomes, e.g., students will be able to read analog and digital timepieces.
Relevant prior learning	Anything that students need to know before starting work on this lesson's content, e.g., students need to have completed Chapter Two of the book, and have previously met language associated with appointments, calendars, and timekeeping.

Teacher Preparation	
Hardware	Types of computer or peripherals required, e.g., USB sticks.
Software	Name of software used, e.g., Microsoft PowerPoint, Microsoft Word, Zoom.
Webpage links	Hyperlink to web resources, e.g., www.google.com.
Additional resources	Other necessary materials for the lesson, e.g., handouts, worksheets, textbooks.

Procedure

Review stage (if required: 5 minutes)

Objective: e.g., encourage the use of previously acquired language.

Teacher: Indicate what the teacher says and does.

Students: Provide expected examples of student behavior.

Warm-up stage (10 minutes)

Objective: e.g., introduce new concepts and language to students in a meaningful manner.

Teacher: Indicate what the teacher says and does.

Students: Provide expected examples of student behavior.

Main stage (20 minutes)

Objective: e.g., allow students to utilize technology to become familiar with and apply the concepts and language content introduced in the lesson.

Teacher: Indicate what the teacher says and does.

Students: Provide expected examples of student behavior.

Practice stage (15 minutes)

Objective: e.g., allow learners to utilize the skills and language that they are expected to acquire during the lesson in a practical way.

Teacher: Indicate what the teacher says and does.

Students: Provide expected examples of student behavior.

Lesson summation stage (10 minutes)

Objective: e.g., instructor reinforces the importance of language concepts and skills acquired, stating how they will be useful in forthcoming lessons.

Teacher: Indicate what the teacher says and does.

Students: Provide expected examples of student behavior.

Further Considerations	
Follow-up activities	Suggest material that can be applied in a follow-up class. Also, be ready with activities for students who complete their class work earlier than expected.
Contingency plan(s)	Always prepare an alternate teaching scenario in case of any problems. For example, a sudden power outage, or a timetabling issue that could make the assigned room unavailable.
Evaluation	*Teacher:* Reflect on what worked well, and what did not, and how you might deliver the lesson differently or improve upon it when running it again. *Students:* Indicate how you assess learners to determine if what they have learned throughout the lesson meets the learning objectives.
The board	Ideally, throughout the lesson, you will use the board in a specific way. Use this area to draw what will appear on the board, and how you might use the board throughout the lesson. (e.g., outcomes or points to cover on the far left – the lesson roadmap, new vocabulary and words introduced to students throughout the lesson on the right. The center part of the board may be reserved for core parts of the lesson at the top and the structures to be practiced or learned, with the area below for student use when being asked to write answers).

G1. Professional Development – Conference Attendance

Organization Name of conference and organization.

Topic Name of the presentation.

Date/Time Date and time **Number** e.g., 1 of 3

Summary

Learning Comment *(Identify anything new that you have learned from the presentation, this can be something academic (e.g., a new language learning theory) to anything practical (e.g., a new method, approach, or technique that you might like to employ with your learners).*

G2. Professional Development – Conference Presentation

Organization *Name of conference and organization.*
Topic *Name of the presentation.*
Date/Time *Date and time.*
Abstract *Insert copy of abstract here.*

Insert copy of presentation here.

Insert PowerPoint slides of your presentation here.

Insert certificate of presentation here.

Photocopiable Content - Practicum

G3. Professional Development – Online Participation

Organization — *Name of the organization.*
Post Topic — *Title of the post.*
Post Location — *e.g., Facebook permalink, forum URL.*
Number — *e.g., 1 of 3.*
Post — *Insert the text of your post here.*

Replies *(Insert an example of replies to your post here).*

H1. Practicum Evaluation Sheet – Task Requirements	
Section and Evaluation	Comments
1. Layout and logs *Evaluation:*	
2. Self-observation, and critical reflection *Evaluation:*	
3. Peer observation, and evaluation *Evaluation:*	
4. Clinical supervision (observation by a peer) *Evaluation:*	
5. Pedagogy project (lesson plan development and implementation) *Evaluation:*	
6. Professional development and engagement (lifelong learning) *Evaluation:*	

Worksheets

1. Logs – minimum of five hours for each of the following
- ☐ Self-observation
- ☐ Peer observation
- ☐ Observation by a peer (clinical supervision)

2. Self-reflection, student appraisal, self-evaluation
- ☐ Self-reflection – Teaching logs
- ☐ Self-evaluation checklist
- ☐ Student appraisal forms
- ☐ Self-reflection questions

3a. Peer observation
- ☐ Observation worksheet 1a
- ☐ Observation worksheet 2
- ☐ Observation worksheet 1b
- ☐ Observation worksheet 3
- ☐ Observation worksheet 1c
- ☐ Observation worksheet 4
- ☐ Observation worksheet 1d
- ☐ Observation worksheet 5
- ☐ Observation worksheet 1e

3b. Clinical supervision
- ☐ Pre-observation feedback
- ☐ Clinical supervision

4. Pedagogy project
- ☐ Pedagogy project development
- ☐ Lesson plan

5. Professional development and engagement – lifelong learning [One of]
- ☐ Conference attendance [certificate of attendance provided, along with summary and learning comments of at least three presentations attended]
- ☐ Conference presentation (including ppt/paper presented, and certificate of presentation)
- ☐ Online participation (posts to professional forums)

Worksheet Comments:

Summary Comments:

Grade:	Date:

Supervisor:	Signature:

11. Portfolio

Overview

The portfolio typically serves as a capstone project to courses such as a master's in TESOL and it is usually undertaken by those who do not wish to complete a thesis. It serves as a means for prospective and in-service teachers to showcase their learning, consider their competency as a classroom teacher, and engage in the reflection of their learning and of the coursework that they have competed while undertaking graduate study.

Learning Outcomes

1. Understand what constitutes a portfolio, and the importance of reflection in its development.
2. Know the role of the advisor in portfolio development, and the time requirements associated with its construction.
3. Gain an appreciation of the preparatory steps of portfolio development, and identify what constitutes as work product.
4. Discover the guiding aspects behind the reflection and selection of work products to include in a portfolio.
5. Contextualize how a portfolio may be evaluated.
6. Comprehend how a portfolio should be completed.
7. Gain insight into how a particular portfolio should be developed and completed for submission to one specific graduate program.

The Portfolio

Most commonly, portfolios are used to collect and evaluate students' work that has been undertaken at key points in their academic career. There is no single way to develop a portfolio, and many different types of portfolio exist. Nonetheless, the portfolio should consist of a rationalized reflective narrative that captures the scope, progress, and value of student learning, with student reflections supported by concrete evidence (i.e., work products). In any well-developed portfolio, students should not simply construct a scrapbook or collage of course assignments. Instead, they should be reflecting upon all the work that they have undertaken during a program of study, and begin to selectively organize their program work products (assignments, presentations, and so on) in a way that provides evidence of documented academic growth and pedagogical skill achievement. By its very nature then, portfolios are very individual, varying from one person to another, one department to another, and one institution to another. It is therefore important to become familiar with the portfolio that you are expected to develop where you are enrolled.

The Advisor

Your advisor will be available to help guide you in the completion of your portfolio, answering any questions that you may have about the process. In some programs, they may closely mentor the development of the portfolio, particularly if it is undertaken as part of a class project. It is also the responsibility of the advisor to perform a final check of your submission, ensuring that everything has been completed satisfactorily, prior to granting approval for it to be submitted to the graduate team. In the case of a portfolio, the submission is typically pass/fail, but it also may be a graded pass.

Time Requirements

The completion time for the portfolio can vary from one university to another. You may have one year (two semesters) in which to complete it, or you may be given one semester. It may be a part of your final class, or it may be an additional project that you need to complete.

The Portfolio Project

Preparation

It is never too early to begin collecting items that you may want to include in a portfolio. Steps to consider from the very first graduate class might be:

Filing. Establish a system that specifically focuses on your portfolio. This means keeping a duplicate set of the work that you have submitted to individual courses and storing these as a portfolio record set, thus ensuring that you not only have a series of content that will be easily accessible, but one that may also illustrate a clear developmental perspective. This process also serves to provide a backup of your work and would ideally be stored separately, such as on a cloud-based storage system rather than a hard drive.

Contemplating. Think about your teaching beliefs, strategies, and values, how these relate to the content studied throughout your graduate program, and how these could develop into a coherent statement of educational philosophy. It is this statement that can help guide your reflection and selection of work products from your portfolio record set.

Networking. Talk to other students, teachers, and faculty about their approaches to teaching. Such conversations can often help to stimulate your own reflective processes, allowing you to better articulate them.

Diary keeping. Write down your goals for professional development and determine how completing work throughout the graduate program can meet these goals.

Workshopping. Consider presenting at and/or attending symposiums and workshops to expand your professionalism and help develop those critical and reflective skills which can prepare you for lifelong learning as well as those that are required for portfolio development and completion. This will help to develop your educational philosophy and goals, the teaching methods and strategies that you may want to apply with learners, and also the activities that you later engage in to improve on your own teaching when leaving the graduate program. All of these are important to weave throughout any reflective narrative that is being developed in a portfolio.

Work Product Selection

There is a range of work products that need to be included within a portfolio. These include any material that you have developed as a student during your course of study, which may range from a conference, class, symposium, or workshop presentation; a literature review; an annotated bibliography; a research project; or a pedagogy project/lesson plan.

The selection of work products, as well as your reflection on them, will generally be guided by several factors including your teaching philosophy and goals, your current level of teaching experience and responsibility, the teaching methods and strategies that you employ, the activities that you undertake in order to improve on your teaching, and the goals that you have for the future.

Teaching philosophy and goals. This will typically prove to be the foundation on which your portfolio is built, guiding you in the selection of work products for final inclusion. A teaching philosophy generally aims to answer one main question: *why is it that you do what you do as a teacher?* You would typically try to develop an answer to this based on four elements:
- Beliefs about how student learning occurs.
- Beliefs about how teachers can best help students learn.
- The ways that you put into practice your beliefs concerning effective teaching and learning.
- The goals that you have for your students.

Teaching experiences and responsibilities. When considering these, you will need to think about the courses that you are currently teaching, the ones that you have taught in the past, and perhaps the ones that you aim to teach in the future. Teaching activities that you have engaged in outside of the classroom are also important to consider here, and this may include the counseling, advising, or mentoring of students as well as things like preparing, chaperoning, and taking students on excursions, field trips, or camps.

Teaching methods and strategies. This means providing those work products that support your teaching philosophy and goals, and clearly showing an understanding of how they are effective in meeting them.

Activities undertaken to improve teaching. As you develop the portfolio, your reflections will begin to illustrate what has worked, what did not, and why, and how those things might be improved or changed to improve your effectiveness as a teacher. Consider what could be lacking (i.e., what you have not done but what can be worthwhile trying). This can include reflecting on how you could have revised or completed assignments differently, or how you may have participated better in the program to improve on your teaching.

Future goals. The penultimate reflection of the portfolio will see you needing to consider how all of the above (and all of your selected work products) come together to show how you need or want to move forward as a teacher, and to also briefly outline the steps that you can take in order to accomplish these things.

The Importance of Reflection

The process of reflective organization involved in the construction of a portfolio should illustrate how you have acquired your professional knowledge, and the proficiencies that you have gained by completing the program of study in which you have been enrolled. In other words, the reflection process is important because it requires you to review all of your work products in order to discover, understand, and then communicate what, how, when, and why they have helped you engage in learning throughout your program of study.

Some questions that Zubizarreta (2008) suggests that could help guide reflection, particularly when considering material to include in a portfolio, are:
- What have I learned? Why did I learn?
- What difference has learning made in my intellectual, personal, and ethical development?
- Has my learning been connected and coherent?
- Has my learning been relevant, applicable, and practical?
- When, how, and why has my learning surprised me?
- What have been the proudest highlights of my learning? What are the disappointments?
- In what ways has my learning been valuable?
- How does what I have learned fit into a full, continual plan for learning?

Model Portfolio

The following tasks and portfolio layout, along with the accompanying submission and evaluation procedures presented, are those that are currently used by the TESOL-MALL graduate program at Woosong University in the Republic of Korea.

Portfolio Tasks

There is a total of five tasks to complete for the practicum outlined here. It is important that you complete each task to the best of your ability, and adhere to the specific layout that is expected. This layout involves the following:
1. an introductory reflection,
2. a teaching English to speakers of other languages (TESOL) component,

3. a multimedia assisted language learning (MALL) component,
4. a culture in English language teaching (CELT) component, and
5. a summary reflection.

Portfolio Layout

The layout of a portfolio is typically very specific. The example discussed here uses the following structure:
1. Title page,
2. Table of contents,
3. Introductory reflection (Task 1),
4. Content components (Tasks 2 to 4),
5. Summary reflection (Task 5),
6. Checklist and declaration.

Guidelines to help you prepare the portfolio can be found in the photocopiable content section of this chapter.

Title Page and Table of Contents

The cover page, or title page of the portfolio, will have a specific style that needs to be followed, and this will be set by the particular university that you attend. It will typically see you include your name and nationality, the semester and years that you have spent in study at the graduate school, your advisor's name, and the semester and the year of portfolio submission. A template may have been provided to you by your graduate program, and it is the guidelines and specifications in that document that your advisor will check to see if you have laid out the cover page accordingly. An example is presented in the photocopiable section of this chapter, followed by an example table of contents.

Task 1: Introductory Reflection

The first section of the portfolio, following the title and the table of contents, is the introductory reflection. In this section, you will reflect on the circumstances that brought you to study at the graduate level. You would highlight the expectations that you had at the start of the program, as well as what you hoped to learn and do. You will also briefly introduce the other sections of the portfolio. The introduction to the portfolio should be completed in around 500 words.

Task 2 to Task 4: TESOL, MALL, and CELT Components

Each of the components in these tasks should begin with a short description of what you now know to be the focus and content of the component. These reflections should consist of a paragraph or two, and be in the range of 150 to 300 words.

Then, for each of the TESOL, MALL, CELT components include a minimum of <u>two</u> work products, and keep in mind that a total of <u>nine</u> work products is required in total for the portfolio. It is therefore advisable to focus on selecting three work products for each component. A work product would include any material that you have developed as a student throughout your course of study, and this may range from a conference, class, symposium, or workshop presentation; a literature review; an annotated bibliography; a research project; a published paper; or a pedagogy project/lesson plan. Following each of your nine work products will be a reflection of that work product in the order of 150 to 300 words. Things that you might reflect on for each of these work products may be:

- Why did you choose this piece?
- How does this piece expand or change your understanding of TESOL/MALL/CELT, yourself, your students, or some other element of the teaching profession?
- How will you use this piece, and what have you learned from developing it that might help you in the future?

Task 5: Summary Reflection

This section will see you reflect on all the material that you collected for presentation in the portfolio. It will also provide a summary of how your career has or might be shaped as a result of graduate level study. In other words, how do your experiences at graduate school aid in your future career path? This question would also be answered by presenting and considering your teaching philosophy and goals, and it should be in the range of 500 words.

Checklist and Declaration

In addition to the five core sections of the portfolio, you will usually be presented with a checklist and a declaration to sign and date. The checklist is provided to ensure that you have completed all necessary components, reflections, and sections of the portfolio. Then, by signing the declaration, you are affirming that all content is your own work, and that it is free of plagiarism. The checklist and declaration are to be submitted as part of your portfolio, and an example is included in the photocopiable section of this chapter.

Submission

Prior to final submission, for each work product that you choose to include, and for each of the necessary reflections that you develop, consider the following:

- Have you selected, organized, and presented the work product in a way that brings the most compelling evidence into focus for the reader (often your portfolio advisor)?
- Does each work product serve a purpose by supporting the points that you have made in your reflection?
- Do the reflections, and the supporting work products, give the reader a sense of who you are as a teacher?

Once you are happy with how you have prepared your portfolio, and your advisor has approved it, you are able to sign the declaration and finalize the formatting of the work for submission. Often this involves providing a bound project, and a certain number of copies (such as five) to your program department who will house this with the graduate team, the national and university library, and the department office. It would be your responsibility to check when the final dates for submission occur in each semester, and how many copies are required. The submission will also be accompanied by your advisor's evaluation. All of these serve as proof of ability to yourself, your friends and family, and to any future employer.

Evaluation

Although the portfolio is typically pass/fail, each section may also be assessed individually following certain guidelines or criteria. An example of the evaluation criteria, and the evaluation form used by the TESOL-MALL graduate program at Woosong University can be seen in the photocopiable section of this chapter.

Summary

This chapter focused on the importance of a portfolio, and the place for reflection in its development. Also considered were the place of the advisor and the time requirements for portfolio submission. It outlines the basics of what is involved in developing a portfolio, with particular emphasis on the kind of work products that might be included as well as the need to contextualize teaching philosophy and goals, teaching methods and strategies, activities undertaken to improve teaching, and future aspirations within those reflections. An example portfolio, with the means used to evaluate and submit it to one particular graduate program, was then presented.

Review

Content Quiz
Portfolio

To help solidify some of the concepts introduced by this chapter the following multiple-choice and true or false quizzes might be helpful for you to undertake. So that you can check the accuracy of your responses, an answer key can be found following the quizzes.

Multiple-Choice

Circle **a**, **b**, or **c** for the answer that best completes the sentence presented in each question.

1. A number of work products may be required for your portfolio. An example of a range of work products includes ...
    a) an activity photocopied from a textbook.
    b) a lesson plan that you have developed, taught, and evaluated.
    c) your professor's course syllabus and curriculum outline.

2. A choice of work products for a portfolio may be guided by ...
    a) your teaching philosophy and goals.
    b) the demands of your advisor.
    c) what you have found in a textbook.

3. Networking will help you develop a portfolio because you can …
   a) find someone who can develop it for you.
   b) talk to other students, teachers, and faculty about their teaching, which will help you reflect on their approaches and come to articulate your own much better.
   c) Talk to other students, teachers, and faculty about their teaching, which will allow you to improve your academic ability.

4. Filing is an approach to use regarding your academic work and assignments. It may help in the development of a portfolio by …
   a) keeping you busy.
   b) collating all of your work as duplicates, giving you a backup of everything you have completed in a course.
   c) collating all of your work products in one handy place, allowing you to categorize them into different record sets.

5. A well-developed teaching philosophy is a statement that …
   a) will get you in trouble with a school principal or advisor if they do not agree with it.
   b) is only useful to include on a curriculum vitae when looking for work, and serves no practical purpose.
   c) can help guide your reflection and selection of work products from a portfolio record set.

True or False

Circle **a** (true) if you think that the statement is correct, or **b** (false) if you think that the statement is incorrect.

1. Most commonly, portfolios are used to collect and evaluate student work that has been undertaken at key points throughout their academic career.
    a)   True.
    b)   False.

2. It is not the job of your advisor to guide you in the completion of your portfolio, or answer any questions that you may have about the process.
    a)   True.
    b)   False.

3. The process of reflective organization involved in the construction of a portfolio should illustrate how students have acquired their professional knowledge and the proficiencies that they have gained by completing the program of study in which they are enrolled.
    a)   True.
    b)   False.

4. Workshopping or presenting at a conference during your graduate program will help you develop critical and reflective skills that can prepare you to develop a portfolio.
    a)   True.
    b)   False.

5. The reflective narrative of a portfolio should only consist of a developed teaching philosophy, illustrating a range of teaching methods and strategies as well as engaging activities, as it does not need to focus on any other aspects of a student teachers academic development.
    a)   True.
    b)   False.

Quiz Answers
Portfolio

Multiple-Choice
1. b
2. a
3. b
4. c
5. c

True or False
1. T
2. F
3. T
4. T
5. F

Suggested Readings

Bullock, A., & Hawk, P. (2009). *Developing a teaching portfolio: A guide for preservice and practicing teachers*, (3rd ed.). Pearson.

Johnson, R., Mims-Cox, J., Doyle-Nichols, A. (2009). *Developing portfolios in education: A guide to reflection, inquiry, and Assessment*, (2nd ed.). Sage.

Kumaravadivelu, B. (2012). *Language teacher education for a global society: A modular model for knowing, analyzing, recognizing, doing, and seeing.* Routledge.

Lynch, B., & Shaw, P. (2005). Portfolios, power, and ethics. *TESOL Quarterly, 39*(2), 263-297.

Richards, J., & Lockhart, C. (1994). *Reflective teaching in second language classrooms.* Cambridge University Press.

Seldon, P., Miller, J., & Seldin., C. (2010). *The teaching portfolio: A practical guide to improved performance and promotion/tenure decisions*, (4th ed.). Jossey Bass.

Wyatt, R., & Looper, S. (2003). *So you have to have a portfolio: A teacher's guide to preparation and presentation.* Corwin.

Zubizarreta, J. (2008). The learning portfolio: A powerful idea for significant learning. *Idea Paper, 44*, 1-6.

Photocopiable Content
Portfolio

This section of the chapter includes a variety of material that is free to photocopy. Use it to help you complete a portfolio. It contains the following content:

- Portfolio checklist and declaration
- Portfolio title page
- Portfolio table of contents
- Portfolio guidelines
- Portfolio evaluation criteria
- Portfolio Evaluation Form

Portfolio Checklist and Declaration

Use this checklist to ensure that your portfolio submission is in good order. Then complete the declaration at the end of the page when you are ready to submit your portfolio for final evaluation. Include this section with your portfolio submission. The declaration should include your full name, as registered in the University system, your signature, and the date of your submission.

Cover Page
The portfolio cover page includes:
- ☐ Name.
- ☐ Nationality.
- ☐ Student number.
- ☐ Semester and years of study at TESOL-MALL.
- ☐ Advisor's name.
- ☐ Semester and year of submission.

Table of Contents
- ☐ Provides an outline of all of the items included in the portfolio.

Interior Sections
- ☐ All sections of the portfolio use appropriate headers, with page numbers at bottom center.

Sections included:
- ☐ Introductory reflection.
- ☐ TESOL – Teaching English to speakers of other languages component.
- ☐ MALL – Multimedia assisted language learning component.
- ☐ CELT – Culture in English language teaching component.
- ☐ Summary Reflection.

Photocopiable Content - Portfolio

Introductory Reflection
☐ Introduces the portfolio sections and provides a program reflection in around 500 words.

Content Components – TESOL, MALL, and CELT
☐ Each of the three content components (TESOL, MALL, and CELT) begins with a short description of what you now know to be the focus and content of that component in a paragraph or two (between 150 and 300 words).
☐ Each of the three content components should contain <u>at least two</u> work products.
☐ Each work product type is clearly labeled.
☐ <u>At least five</u> different genres of work products are included.
☐ <u>A total of nine</u> work products are included.
☐ A reflection is provided after each work product (150~300 words for each reflection).

Summary Reflection
☐ Contains a summary reflection of around 500 words.

Submission
☐ I will prepare five (5) hard copies for submission to the TESOL-MALL Graduate Program, and one (1) for my advisor.

Declaration
I, _____, state that all work in this portfolio is my own. I am submitting this portfolio as my capstone project for the Master's of Arts (TESOL) at Woosong University.

Signature: _____. **Date:** _____.

Portfolio Title Page

PORTFOLIO

for the Master of Arts

Name
(Nationality)
Student Number
Semester, Year – Semester, Year

Advisor: Name

TESOL-MALL Graduate Program
Woosong University

Semester, Year

Portfolio Table of Contents

Outline all of the items that you have included in your portfolio.

Section
1. **Introduction**
    1a. Introductory Reflection – [500 words]

2. **TESOL – Teaching English to Speakers of Other Languages Coursework**
    2a. TESOL: Focus and Content [150~300 words]
    2b. Work Product 1 – [*name the type included*]
    2c. Reflection on Work Product 1 [150~300 words]
    2d. Work Product 2 – [*name the type included*]
    2e. Reflection on Work Product 2 [150~300 words]
    2f. Work Product 3 – [*name the type included*]
    2g. Reflection on Work Product 3 [150~300 words]

3. **MALL**
    2a. MALL: Focus and Content [150~300 words]
    2b. Work Product 4 – [*name the type included*]
    2c. Reflection on Work Product 4 [150~300 words]
    2de Work Product 5 – [*name the type included*]
    2e. Reflection on Work Product 5 [150~300 words]
    2f. Work Product 6 – [*name the type included*]
    2g. Reflection on Work Product 6 [150~300 words]

4. **CELT**
    4a. CELT: Focus and Content [150~300 words]
    4b. Work Product 7 – [*name the type included*]
    4c. Reflection on Work Product 7 [150~300 words]
    4de Work Product 8 – [*name the type included*]
    4e. Reflection on Work Product 8 [150~300 words]
    4f. Work Product 9 – [*name the type included*]
    4g. Reflection on Work Product 9 [150~300 words]

5. **Summary**
    5a. Summary Reflection [150~300 words]

6. **Declaration**
    6a. Checklist and Declaration [checked and signed]

Portfolio Guidelines

The following is a concise guide to the elements that constitute the portfolio.

Cover Page
The cover page must include your name (and nationality), the semester and years you have spent studying at the Graduate School of TESOL-MALL, your advisor's name, and the semester and year of submission.

Table of Contents
Outline all of the items that you have included in your portfolio.

Interior Sections
Label all sections of the portfolio using appropriate headers, with page numbers at bottom center.

Section Contents
Each coursework section should contain <u>*at least two work products from each content component*</u>. The three content components include courses that start with TESOL, MALL, and CELT, although any work product with a focus on the content of the component is suitable for inclusion (regardless of the course to which it was originally submitted). A <u>*total of nine work products are required*</u> for inclusion in the portfolio. <u>*At least five different genres of work products*</u> need to be included.

Sections include:
1. Introduction
2. TESOL – Teaching English to speakers of other languages components
3. MALL – Multimedia assisted language learning components
4. CELT – Culture in English language teaching components
5. Summary

Portfolio Sections

Introduction
The introduction section sees you reflect on the circumstances that brought you to TESOL-MALL, your expectations for the program, what you hoped to learn and do, and other aspects along those lines. You should also introduce the sections of your portfolio here [about 500 words].

TESOL/MALL/CELT Components
a) For each of the content components, begin with a short description of what you now know to be the focus and content of that component in a paragraph or two. [150 to 300 words].
b) After each work product in a content component, provide a reflection on that work product. [Each reflection will be between 150 and 300 words]. Consider reflection on at least the following.
   - Why did you choose this piece?
   - How did this piece expand/change your understanding of TESOL/MALL/CELT, yourself, your students, or some other element of the teaching profession?

Summary
For the summary reflection, summarize the materials that you have collected, and write about your future aspirations for TESOL, how you intend to reshape or expand your career, and how your experience in TESOL-MALL will aid you along that career path [about 500 words].

Portfolio Evaluation Criteria

Cover Page, Layout, and Table of Contents
All satisfactorily laid out according to the guidelines and specifications presented within the provided template.

Introductory Reflection
Experiences are reflected upon in terms of how they relate to the program, the student as a teacher, highlighting current and future professional expectations and workplace situations, and consists of around 500 words.

Content Components
The short descriptions detailing the focus and content of each strand are accurate, and concisely articulated in 150 to 300 words.

Work Product Types
All work products included in the portfolio are clearly identified. There should be a minimum of two work products per strand, a maximum of five work products of the one type, and a total of nine work products all together. At least <u>five</u> different genres of work product are included in the portfolio.

Work Product Reflections
All work product reflections are clearly identified and come after each work product type. Each reflection is between 150 and 300 words, and covers:
    a) why the piece was selected for portfolio inclusion;
    b) how the piece expanded or changed your understanding of TESOL/MALL/CELT, your students, or some other element of the teaching profession, and
    c) how the piece may be used or learned from.

Summary Reflection
Adequately summarize in around 500 words the contents of the portfolio, identifying how the contents of the portfolio can contribute to your future aspirations, how study in the program has seen you reshape or expand on your career as an educator, and how program completion will lead to such outcomes.

Portfolio Evaluation Form

Student:		Number:

Section	Evaluation	Comments
Cover page		
Table of contents		
Introductory reflection		
TESOL component		
MALL component		
CELT component		
Summary reflection		
Required number of work products		

Summary Comments:

Grade:	Date:
Supervisor:	Signature:

12. Thesis

Overview
The thesis track in a master's graduate program typically consists of four basic components: successful completion of coursework, candidacy examination, the formation of a thesis committee and the writing and oral defense of a thesis project that follows a specific timeline. This track is also typically undertaken by those students who intend to go on to doctoral level studies or to engage in independent research on a topic of their own design. As such, the completion of a thesis as the capstone project to a degree serves as a means for prospective and in-service teachers to conduct an original study and perform critical analysis on a topic of their own interest.

Learning Outcomes
1. Understand the purpose behind writing a thesis, and the importance of developing an appropriate completion timeline.
2. Develop an appreciation for the role of advisors in master's programs, and understand the responsibilities of a student when undertaking a thesis.
3. Comprehend the importance of scholarly rigor and ethical considerations while gaining insight into what can constitute academic misconduct.
4. Gain insight into the purpose of the thesis proposal, its composition, and what to consider when creating one.
5. Become familiar with the thesis layout, the procedures of the defense, and what is involved with the binding and final submission of the thesis prior to graduating.

The Thesis Project
The purpose behind writing a thesis is for you to undertake original research, and to perform critical analysis of a topic while adhering to scholarly rigor. Your thesis manuscript should demonstrate the following abilities, and that you are able to:
- plan and carry out a research activity;
- correctly analyze the results of the research activity, and draw reasonable conclusions from the findings;

- develop a coherent written description of the research activity in a scholarly acceptable manner; and
- potentially deliver the research at a presentation or rework it for publication.

The steps to complete the thesis project typically involve finding and working with a thesis advisor, developing a thesis proposal, completing multiple drafts of the thesis prior to undertaking an oral defense, and then binding and submitting a final version of the thesis for submission to the university in a timely manner.

Completion Timeline

The completion time for a thesis may vary from one graduate program to another. You may have one year (two semesters) in which to complete it, or you may be given one semester (six months). It may be a part of your final class, or it may be an additional project that you need to complete. You will also be assigned a thesis advisor who will assist you in answering any questions that you may have while you work on the manuscript. An example *thesis track timeline (two-year degree, undertaking a six-month thesis)* can be found in the photocopiable section of this chapter.

Advisors

Academic Advisor

In most graduate programs, all master's degree students are assigned an initial advisor upon admission to a program. This academic advisor offers advice to students when they need it throughout the completion of their program. They may or may not become the student's thesis advisor.

Thesis Advisor

Your thesis advisor will typically have a specialization in either the topic that you are looking at completing or the research methodology that you will use to undertake the research. This advisor will be available to help guide you in the completion of your thesis, answer any questions that you may have about the process, and ensure that you have completed candidacy requirements, developed a proposal, completed an ethics form, and are ready to present a draft of your thesis manuscript to the thesis committee prior to defense. If you pass the defense, it will also be the responsibility of your thesis advisor to ensure that you understand any corrections that need to be made to the manuscript prior to final submission. The advisor will then perform a final check of the thesis manuscript, to ensure that everything has been completed satisfactorily, before allowing your thesis to go to binding.

Working with your thesis advisor. Ensure that you are able to schedule regular appointments with your thesis advisor. Provide work that has been spell-checked and proofread, and assume that you are not the only advisee that your advisor is working with, and that it may take up to two weeks for you to receive any feedback on your work. For an example of student responsibilities regarding the writing of a thesis, and working with an advisor, see the *listing of thesis student responsibilities* checklist in the photocopiable section of this chapter. Expect to write multiple drafts of each section of your thesis, and ensure that you are using the same revision system that your thesis advisor is using to review your work (e.g., the use of the track-changes feature in Microsoft Word).

Developing a Proposal

The purpose behind writing a thesis proposal is to demonstrate to your thesis advisor that you have:
- identified a specific problem on a certain topic to investigate;
- developed an organized plan that will allow you to collect, obtain, or work with appropriate data; and,
- identified a method of data analysis appropriate to the topic and nature of the study.

The research proposal should be written in a way that it describes what you will investigate, why it is important to investigate it, and the steps that you will follow in order to complete the thesis. An overview of what a thesis proposal might consider is laid out in the photocopiable section of this chapter as the *composition of a thesis proposal*. A *blank thesis proposal template* is also provided. While you develop the thesis proposal, it is important to cite any references that you rely on, and consider copyright issues as well as those involving ethics.

Ethical Considerations

Depending on the nature of your research, you will need to consider ethical issues and implications concerning research development and the way(s) in which you will conduct your research. Your responsibilities as a researcher are many and varied, and you have an ethical responsibility to safeguard those from whom you collect data as well as the data that you collect.

Provide information. Make the research aims clear to participants, and inform them of how the results will be used, and provide feedback to participants (including the opportunity for participants to verify the data collected about them).

Obtain permission. Written permission may be required, whether it be from participants or their guardians (especially from parents of school children); from principals (to carry out research at a school); and from teachers (allowing you to sit in on classes and observe students). Participants should also be made aware that they have the right to withdraw from the study at any time.

Privacy/Confidentiality. Provide a written guarantee of privacy and confidentiality to individuals and organizations from whom you collect data. Further, participants have the right to remain anonymous, and you will likely need to provide pseudonyms so that participants cannot be identified.

Consideration. Plan data collection so that there is as little disruption as possible for participants (e.g., no lengthy absences from class, or any considerable interruption of lessons). Cooperate with people where you conduct the research (e.g., determine ahead of time if you will sit in on a class to observe it, where you will sit, how and for what length of time you will record data, how you will be introduced, and so on).

Acknowledgements. The cooperation and contribution of all participants should be acknowledged in a way that retains confidentiality unless otherwise requested.

Necessities. It is also likely that you will need to gain ethical clearance from the university where you are undertaking your degree for which an example form is provided in the photocopiable section of this chapter as the *human research ethics application*.

Citation and Copyright

It is expected that you will be citing the literature at length in your thesis manuscript, and doing so from the time you start to develop your thesis proposal. This might include the findings from previous research, quotations from literary works, as well as that from surveys and other test instruments. You may either be quoting while you cite, or you may be providing the quote in your own words (paraphrasing). It is important that, in either case, you provide the correct citation. All citation references need to be included in the reference section, and adhere to a referencing system such as that of the American Psychological Association (APA).

In some cases, the copyright of particular material may be held by a corporation or an individual, and the rights to its use may need to be specifically acquired. You would need to provide proof of acquiring the right to use the material in an appendix to the thesis.

If you fail to cite work and present it as your own, or fail to gain the correct rights to the use of copyright material, then you may be held accountable for plagiarism or academic misconduct. These are both serious offenses in the realm of academia, and it may see you fail your thesis at best or receive an expulsion at worst.

Plagiarism

Many universities rely on plagiarism checking applications, and may also require students to run their manuscript (as well as their class assignments) through such software in order to produce an analysis of the work. Examples of websites that may be used for such purposes are Turnitin (https://www.turnitin.com) and Copykiller (https://www.copykiller.com). The level of plagiarism acceptable at universities may vary. An example of what may prove to be acceptable is listed in Table 3.1.

Plagiarism Acceptability Levels	
Level	Acceptability Percent
Secure	0 – 9
Caution	10 – 15
Suspicious	16 – 20
Risk	> 20

Figure 12.1 Plagiarism Levels

Depending on the results that you receive after analyzing your work (assignments, thesis, dissertation, and so on) you may need to rewrite elements, or provide a statement of why that level of plagiarism is acceptable. In particular, this may prove to be the case when submitting your thesis or dissertation for examination. You may be required to use a specific form in order to do this; see the *plagiarism analysis report* under photocopiable content for an example. You may also need to make a response after the plagiarism check.

If the level is *secure*, you may need to reexamine your manuscript carefully to ensure that all is in good order, and that it follows all of the appropriate ethical guidelines so that it can be submitted for grading/examination.

For the other levels, you should amend/revise the sections of the manuscript that have been flagged with the aim to lower the level to that of secure. If the level cannot be lowered, then a statement may need to be provided as to why this level of plagiarism is acceptable for the document that you will submit for grading/examination.

For the *risk* level, you may need to contact your course advisor or thesis supervisor for assistance in terms of reviewing the content and any steps forward. Any work submitted at this level is likely to automatically fail.

Thesis Layout

A handy reference guide for when you come to write a thesis, *a thesis cheat sheet*, is provided in the photocopiable section of this chapter. Although it does not aim to be comprehensive and to cover all types of thesis, it can serve as a reminder of what at the minimum may be required of you to include within each section of the thesis as you begin to write it up.

Keep in mind that there are a number of approaches to writing a thesis. These may involve qualitative or quantitative methods, or both in a mixed-methods study. This will see students conducting research projects that may involve anything from autoethnographic inquiry, to the comparison of groups and the running of tests, interviewing participants or using focus groups, through to project development and assessment. A generic sequential thesis layout has most or all of the following components.

Title Page
The title page will typically contain the name of your degree, your name, your advisor's name, and the year of thesis submission. Your graduate program will be able to provide you with the exact format to follow.

Signature Page
The signature page will contain the signatures of your oral defense committee members. It will list the committee chair, advisor, and the other members of the committee.

Abstract
The abstract is a summary of your study in very clear and plain writing. It should be no longer than half a page (try for no more than 300 words). State the research issues, the problem(s) that you want to examine, the way that you intend to conduct your research (meaning: with who, and how), what the outcome will be, and the goals and significance of your study. You may consider breaking the abstract down into the following:

Background: the shortest part which will outline what is already known about your topic and relate it to your research by detailing what is known about the subject and what the study intends to examine.

Methods: the second longest section of the abstract which will present enough information to understand what research was undertaken and how, with the significance of the research highlighted and rationalized.

Results: the most important part of the abstract, and it may be the longest as well as it provides details about the findings.

Conclusory remarks: the final sentences of the abstract which will serve to provide:
a) your take-home message,
b) additional findings or matters of importance, and
c) the real-world implications and significance of the findings to the field, the limitations of the study, and any future research possibilities.

Note that whatever appears in the abstract must also be present in the main body of the thesis. The abstract also needs to be read and understood independently of the thesis itself.

Definition of Terms

If your thesis requires definitions of terms, you may choose to highlight these on the abstract page, in the introduction, or in the glossary if there is one.

Acknowledgements

This page allows you to thank those who provided you with assistance and support throughout the completion of your thesis. You can also credit any companies that provided facilities free of charge for you to run interviews, testing, and so on. You may also add a dedication here if your graduate program does not allow for this on a separate page.

Introduction

Provide the purpose of the study. Follow this with justification of the study by clearly stating what makes it significant and why it is worthwhile to conduct, then provide the research questions. You may also need to include a definition of terms, and you can cover these either here or in a glossary, or list them under the abstract. It might also be applicable to mention any factors that you needed to control, those that were out of your control, and those that you assume are taken into consideration.

Background/Literature Review

A literature review should be developed to support the process and purpose of your study, and the conceptual model behind your study can be included here. Break down the literature review into important sub-topics relevant to your investigation, aim to explore the key concepts, theories, and studies, and identify key debates, controversies, and gaps in existing knowledge.

Methodology

This section will detail the methods that you will use in the study, and the rationale for using those particular methods over others. You would include information regarding participants, and the instruments that were developed or used to collect the research data. The reliability and validity of the instruments also need to be discussed and you will need to detail the procedures that you used so that another researcher would be able to replicate your study if needed. Describe any risks for the participants involved if there are any. A clear description of how the results are going to be analyzed also needs to be presented in this section of the thesis.

Findings
The findings need to be presented in the same order as you presented your research questions. You will need to provide all of the descriptive data that emerges from your analysis along with the results of the procedures that you used (e.g., statistical testing, coding of interviews), and offer a brief summary of the results with foundational interpretations of what the findings indicate.

Conclusion
Provide the inferences and implications of what the findings present, offering insight into what the study has done (and what it may not have done). Draw specific conclusions, and synthesize these with the literature/current knowledge in the field. Determine the limitations of the study, and provide recommendations for further research.

References
Provide a listing of all the material cited in the thesis in a scholarly format (e.g., APA citation style).

Glossary
If your thesis contains a large number of specific or unique terms, and/or a number of acronyms, it is important to detail them in a glossary section. List all the acronyms, terms, and key phrases in alphabetical order.

Appendices
Provide any additional data that is not included in the main thesis in this section. These may include ethics approval, survey examples, examples of thematic coding, examples of computer code, and so on.

The Thesis Defense

The Defense Committee

The thesis oral defense committee is responsible for reviewing your thesis manuscript. It is normally made up of a panel of three with one panel member being your thesis advisor, another, usually from your department, acting as the defense committee chair, and the third member either a member of faculty or an external examiner if required. The oral defense is pass/fail, and this is often the case for the thesis manuscript as well, although it might also be awarded a graded pass. Depending on your graduate program and the nature of the fail, you may have an opportunity to resubmit the manuscript for review by committee members in the following semester or be given an opportunity to resit the oral defense.

The Oral Defense

The oral defense is your opportunity to demonstrate that you are able to participate in a scholarly discussion regarding your research. The defense is typically one hour in length. It is advisable to plan for two hours, as you will need to arrive early to set up the room, and you will need to stay behind to engage in a debriefing session with your thesis advisor. You are welcome to bring guests to the defense if you require moral support, but you must obtain prior permission for this to occur from your thesis advisor. Otherwise, all guests will be required to leave once the proceedings begin.

Presentation. The defense will begin with you providing a short presentation regarding your research. This should be limited to around 15 minutes and it may involve PowerPoint or some other visual representation (e.g., the thesis conceptual model). The aim of the presentation is to provide a means of spring-boarding into a discussion regarding your research, and for the committee to see how well you understand the research that you have undertaken. You will need to do more than simply summarize your thesis. While preparing, consider answering questions like: *What led you to select this topic? What did you find particularly interesting or surprising as you investigated the topic? How is the topic of the thesis relevant to your current job or to future employment?*

Following your presentation, and perhaps some initial questions regarding the thesis by the defense committee, you may be asked to leave the room so that the committee members can discuss your presentation and the accompanying thesis draft.

Question and answer session. During the question and answer session of the oral defense, the thesis committee members will ask very direct questions regarding specific points about your thesis. Some may be very easy for you to answer, but others may prove very difficult. Remain calm, and take your time. If you do not understand a question, ask for clarification. Some of these sessions can be particularly difficult for students, and emotionally draining, because it is often the shortcomings of the thesis that are all brought to the fore over the many positives that may exist. Keep this in mind in order to help you get through this stage of the defense. The predominant aim of this session is to help make you aware not only of the positives of the thesis, but to draw attention to the negatives and to those aspects of the thesis that have fallen short. It is particularly important to do this, as the thesis committee members need to ensure by your responses that you are capable of addressing these issues in a redraft if necessary.

At the close of this session you will be asked to leave the room a second time, while the committee deliberates. You will then be called back to the room and informed if you have passed or failed the oral defense.

Evaluation

Your thesis, and defense of it, can be awarded one of several levels of evaluation. Each level will require a different response.

Passed defense. If your oral defense and thesis manuscript are both acceptable, and you address all questions posed by the defense committee in a satisfactory manner, then they will award a *pass for the defense*. You would then be able to proceed to bind the thesis, and officially submit it to the university.

Passed defense with minor revisions. If your oral defense is acceptable, you may still need to engage in some minor revisions before being able to prepare your manuscript for binding and official submission to the university, in which case you will be informed that you have been awarded *passed defense with minor revisions*.

Passed defense with major revisions. If your thesis manuscript has a number of shortcomings which you show that you are able to improve, then you will most likely be awarded *passed defense with major revisions*.

All of the revisions will need to be undertaken and reviewed by your thesis advisor prior to being allowed to submit the final version of your thesis to the university for binding.

Failed the defense. If the thesis manuscript is academically unsatisfactory (e.g., contains plagiarism), and/or you were unable to discuss your research adequately (i.e., indicating that you may not have written the manuscript), then you will not pass the oral defense. Additionally, if the manuscript has an excessive amount of inconsistencies or lacks academic rigor, and you are unable to demonstrate how the manuscript can be salvaged, then the oral defense will be awarded a *fail*. In any of these cases, the committee will come to a unanimous decision. They will then determine if and/or how you might address any shortcomings, and provide a timeline for you to do so. If permitted by the defense committee, you would then be able to undertake the oral defense a second time. The second defense will have the same guidelines as the first, with the oral defense allowed to be repeated only once.

Defense Debrief

After the oral defense you will meet with your thesis advisor. The thesis advisor will go over the decision made by the defense committee, ensuring that you understand it. They will then inform you of the next steps. If passing the defense this often means that they will help you understand all of the revisions that you need to perform, and set you a deadline to complete them. You will then provide a final draft of the manuscript for your advisor to review. If all is in order you will be granted approval to prepare the thesis for binding, and permission to ask the defense committee members to sign the signature page of the thesis. If failing the defense, the thesis advisor will help you understand why, and what you need to do in the timeframe provided in order to retake the oral defense if that is an option available to you.

Binding and Final Submission

Once you have passed the oral defense and made any required corrections to the thesis manuscript, your thesis advisor will perform a final check of the document. You may need to perform additional revisions before being permitted to officially submit your thesis to the university, and you will then need to work with the graduate program administrative assistants to adhere to all the requirements for this to occur (e.g., completing appropriate documentation and lodging the correct forms at the right times). Keep in mind that it will usually be your responsibility to check when the final dates for submission occur each semester, and how many copies of the thesis will be required. Depending on the graduate program that you are enrolled in, up to seven (7) copies of your thesis may be required, and they will go to such places as the university library, the national library, and to your thesis advisor. You will, at this stage, also be ready to format the thesis according to the university and/or government guidelines that are required. After formatting the document, it can then be printed and professionally bound for final submission to the university. Many universities require you to work with a particular print shop for this, and the administrative assistants of the graduate program in which you are enrolled will advise you accordingly. The bound copies serve as a record of your capability to perform research, and depending on the nature and quality of your material you may wish to rework it for journal article publication.

Summary

This chapter presented the rationale behind the writing of a thesis, and the need to follow a strict completion timeline. The role of advisors and students in the development of a thesis was also uncovered, as was the critical need to consider ethical implications when undertaking research. Scholarly rigor and academic misconduct were also discussed, along with what constitutes a thesis proposal. The typical sequential style thesis layout was then presented, along with stages of a typical oral defense, and the means of finalizing the thesis project for formal submission.

Review

Content Quiz
Thesis

To help solidify some of the concepts introduced by this chapter the following multiple-choice and true or false quizzes might be helpful for you to undertake. So that you can check the accuracy of your responses, an answer key can be found following the quizzes.

Multiple-Choice

Circle **a**, **b**, or **c** for the answer that best completes the sentence presented in each question.

1. The purpose of the title page of a thesis is to …
   a) present student academic information (e.g., name, student number, advisor name, name of degree, semester and year of submission).
   b) thank any of those who may have aided or supported you throughout the completion of your thesis.
   c) illustrate that the oral defense has been passed, and who comprised the thesis defense committee.

2. The purpose of the acknowledgements section of a thesis is to …
   a) present student academic information (e.g., name, student number, advisor name, name of degree, semester and year of submission).
   b) thank any of those who may have aided or supported you throughout the completion of your thesis.
   c) illustrate that the oral defense has been passed, and who comprised the thesis defense committee.

3. The purpose of the signature page of a thesis is to …
   a) present student academic information (e.g., name, student number, advisor name, name of degree, semester and year of submission).
   b) thank any of those who may have aided or supported you throughout the completion of your thesis.
   c) illustrate that the oral defense has been passed, and who comprised the thesis defense committee.

4. The purpose of the abstract of a thesis is to …
   a) illustrate that the oral defense has been passed, and who comprised the thesis defense committee.
   b) deliver a summary of your study in very clear and plain writing.
   c) compare and critique those studies that are most relevant to the research problem that you are investigating.

5. The purpose of the introduction section of a thesis is to …
   a) provide the purpose, justification, significance, and the rationale of what will be investigated.
   b) deliver a summary of your study in very clear and plain writing.
   c) compare and critique those studies that are most relevant to the research problem that you are investigating.

6. The purpose of the literature review section of a thesis is to …
   a) provide the purpose, justification, significance, and the rationale of what will be investigated.
   b) detail the methods and analysis applied to the study, along with the rationale for using those particular methods instead of others, while also discussing characteristics of the participants and the risks to them, the research instruments developed/employed, and the context of the study so that it can be replicated.
   c) compare and critique those studies that are most relevant to the research problem that you are investigating.

7. The purpose of the methodology section of a thesis is to …
   a) detail the methods and analysis applied to the study, along with the rationale for using those particular methods instead of others, while also discussing characteristics of the participants and the risks to them, the research instruments developed/employed, and the context of the study so that it can be replicated.
   b) compare and critique those studies most relevant to the research problem that you are investigating.
   c) provide all of the descriptive data that emerges from your analysis along with the results of the procedures that you used (e.g., statistical testing, coding of interviews), and offer a brief summary of the results with foundational interpretations.

8. The purpose of the findings section of a thesis is to ...
   a) detail the methods and analysis applied to the study, along with the rationale for using those particular methods instead of others, while also discussing characteristics of the participants and the risks to them, the research instruments developed/employed, and the context of the study so that it can be replicated.
   b) provide all of the descriptive data that emerges from your analysis along with the results of the procedures that you used (e.g., statistical testing, coding of interviews), and offer a brief summary of the results with foundational interpretations.
   c) present specific deductions, defining research limitations and providing recommendations for the future.

9. The purpose of the conclusion to a thesis is to ...
   a) present specific deductions, defining research limitations and providing recommendations for the future.
   b) provide all of the descriptive data that emerges from your analysis along with the results of the procedures that you used (e.g., statistical testing, coding of interviews), and offer a brief summary of the results with foundational interpretations.
   c) provide a listing of all the material cited in the thesis in a scholarly format.

10. The purpose of the references section of a thesis is to ...
    a) provide any additional data not included in the main thesis.
    b) provide, in alphabetical order, a listing of all of the acronyms, terms, and key phrases used throughout the thesis.
    c) provide a listing of all the material cited in the thesis in a scholarly manner.

11. The purpose of the glossary to a thesis is to ...
    a) provide any additional data that is not included in the main thesis.
    b) provide, in alphabetical order, a listing of all of the acronyms, terms, and key phrases used throughout the thesis.
    c) provide a listing of all the material cited in the thesis in a scholarly format.

12. The purpose of the appendix of a thesis is to …
    a) provide any additional data that is not included in the main thesis.
    b) provide, in alphabetical order, a listing of all of the acronyms, terms, and key phrases used throughout the thesis.
    c) provide a listing of all the material cited in the thesis in a scholarly manner.

13. The thesis oral defense committee is responsible for …
    a) chatting with you for an hour about your thesis manuscript.
    b) reviewing your academic and research skills along you're your development of the thesis manuscript.
    c) reviewing the spelling and grammar found in the thesis manuscript and to assess your citation use.

14. The thesis oral defense is your opportunity to …
    a) chat with faculty members for an hour about your thesis manuscript.
    b) demonstrate that you are able to participate in a scholarly discussion regarding your research.
    c) defend all of the choices that you made while in graduate school.

15. The aim of the thesis oral defense presentation is to …
    a) provide a means of spring-boarding into a discussion regarding your research, and for the committee to see how well you understand the research that you have undertaken.
    b) provide some entertainment to thesis defense committee members.
    c) take up time as the defense has to be an hour in length.

16. The aim of the question and answer session of a thesis oral defense is to …
    a) point out all of the thesis manuscript shortcomings.
    b) try and make the student cry.
    c) determine if the candidate is capable of addressing any issues in the thesis manuscript and is able to redraft it in a timely manner for final binding and submission.

17. Passing the thesis oral defense often means that you …
    a) will likely have a number of revisions to perform, and have a deadline in which to complete them, before being allowed to submit the thesis manuscript for binding.
    b) can throw a party to celebrate and then relax for the rest of semester, as the office assistants can now deal with the manuscript.
    c) feel a sense of accomplishment in completing the first draft of your thesis, and that you are able to now hand it over to the office assistants to deal with the binding process.

18. If you fail the thesis defense …
    a) your dreams of graduating are over.
    b) your thesis advisor will help you understand why, and what you need to do in the timeframe provided in order to retake the oral defense if possible.
    c) you will not be able to retake the defense, and will need to be moved to the portfolio track for degree completion.

19. When binding the thesis …
    a) many universities require you to work with a particular print shop.
    b) the graduate program office assistants will do everything for you.
    c) you can print it off at home and submit in a clear folder.

True or False

Circle **a** (true) if you think that the statement is correct, or **b** (false) if you think that the statement is incorrect.

1. The purpose behind writing a thesis is for you to undertake original research, and to perform critical analysis of a topic while adhering to scholarly rigor.
   a) True.
   b) False.

2. The steps to complete the thesis project typically involve finding and working with a thesis advisor, developing a thesis proposal, completing multiple drafts of the thesis prior to undertaking an oral defense, and then binding and submitting a final version of the thesis for submission to the university in a timely manner.
   a) True.
   b) False.

3. The role of the academic advisor is to supervise the progress of a college or university student as they undertake thesis research.
   a) True.
   b) False.

4. The role of the thesis advisor is to help students solve unexpected academic problems, resolve any class issues that might impact on their academic path, while also offering advice to keep students scholastically on track.
   a) True.
   b) False.

5. It is important to use the same revision system that your thesis advisor is using to review your work (e.g., the use of the track-changes feature in Microsoft Word).
   a) True.
   b) False.

6. The research proposal should be written in a way that describes what you will investigate, why it is important to investigate it, and the steps that you will follow in order to complete such an investigation.
   a) True.
   b) False.

7. Researchers have an ethical responsibility to safeguard those who they collect data from as well as the data that they collect.
   a) True.
   b) False.

8. It is important to make the research aims clear to participants, and inform them of how the results will be used.
   a) True.
   b) False.

9. It is important to provide feedback to participants (including the opportunity for participants to verify the data that is collected about them).
   a) True.
   b) False.

10. Written permission to participate in a study may be required for some participants (e.g., from a child's parent or guardian, from the principal, or from the teacher being observed).
    a) True.
    b) False.

11. Participants in a study should be made aware that they have the right to withdraw from the study at any time.
    a) True.
    b) False.

12. It is not necessary to provide a written guarantee of privacy and confidentiality to individuals and organizations from whom you collect data.
    a) True.
    b) False.

13. Participants may have the right to remain anonymous, and you will likely need to provide pseudonyms so that participants cannot be identified from your study.
    a) True.
    b) False.

14. The cooperation and contribution of all participants should be acknowledged in a way that retains confidentiality unless otherwise requested.
    a) True.
    b) False.

15. Prior to engaging in any thesis research, you may need to gain ethical clearance from the university where you are undertaking your degree.
    a) True.
    b) False.

16. There is no need to include all in-text citations in full within the reference section.
    a) True.
    b) False.

17. It is important to adhere to a consistent referencing system throughout the thesis. (e.g., APA style).
    a) True.
    b) False.

18. If you fail to cite work and present it as your own, or fail to gain the correct rights to the use of copyright material, then you may be held accountable for plagiarism or academic misconduct.
    a) True.
    b) False.

19. There are a number of approaches to writing a thesis. These may involve qualitative or quantitative methods, or both in a mixed-methods study.
    a) True.
    b) False.

Quiz Answers
Thesis

Multiple-Choice		*True or False*	
1.	A	1.	T
2.	B	2.	T
3.	C	3.	F
4.	B	4.	F
5.	A	5.	T
6.	C	6.	T
7.	A	7.	T
8.	B	8.	T
9.	A	9.	T
10.	C	10.	T
11.	B	11.	T
12.	A	12.	F
13.	B	13.	F
14.	B	14.	T
15.	A	15.	T
16.	C	16.	F
17.	A	17.	T
18.	B	18.	T
19.	A	19.	T

Suggested Readings

Celce-Murcia, M. (Ed.). (2001). *Teaching English as a second or foreign language* (3rd ed.). Heinle and Heinle.

Crookes, G. (2003). *A practicum in TESOL: Professional development through teaching practice.* Cambridge University Press.

Fraenkel, J., Wallen, N., & Hyun, H. (2018). *How to design and evaluate research in education,* (10th ed.). McGraw-Hill Education.

Joyner, R., Rouse, W., & Glatthorn, A. (2018). *Writing the winning thesis or dissertation: A step-by-step guide,* (4th ed.). Corwin.

Kornuta, H., & Germaine, R. (2019). *A concise guide to writing a thesis or dissertation: Educational research and beyond* (2nd ed.). Routledge.

Kumaravadivelu, B. (2003). Beyond *methods: Microstrategies for language teaching.* Yale University Press.

Kumaravadivelu, B. (2012). *Language teacher education for a global society: A modular model for knowing, analyzing, recognizing, doing, and seeing.* Routledge.

Lynch, B., & Shaw, P. (2005). Portfolios, power, and ethics. *TESOL Quarterly 39*(2), 263-297.

Rennie, L., & Gribble, J. (2006). *A guide to preparing your application for candidacy,* (Rev. ed.). Curtin University of Technology.

Richards, J., & Crookes, G. (1988). The practicum in TESOL. *TESOL Quarterly, 22*(1), 9-27.

Richards, J., & Lockhart, C. (1994). *Reflective teaching in second language classrooms.* Cambridge University Press.

Richards, J. & Renandya, W. (Eds.). (2002). *Methodology in language teaching: An anthology of current practice.* Cambridge University Press.

Scrivener, J. (2005). *Learning teaching: The essential guide to English language teaching* (3rd Ed.). MacMillan. [Chapter 16]

Ur, P. (2012). *A course in English language teaching* (2nd ed.). Cambridge University Press.

Woodward, T. (2001). *Planning lessons and courses.* Cambridge University Press.

Photocopiable Content
Thesis

This section of the chapter includes a variety of material that is free to photocopy. Use it to help you complete a thesis. It contains the following content:

- Thesis track timeline (two-year degree with six-month thesis)
- Listing of thesis student responsibilities
- Composition of a thesis proposal
- Blank thesis proposal template
- Human research ethics application
- Sample participant consent form
- Plagiarism analysis report
- Thesis cheat sheet

Thesis Track Timeline
(two-year degree program with six-month thesis)

First Year

Semester One
- Register for classes.
- Begin coursework.
- Meet initial academic advisor.

Summer/Winter Break
- Undertake readings for semester two classes.

Semester Two
- Continue with coursework.
- Meet with advisor as necessary.

Second Year

Semester Three
- Continue with coursework.
- Decide if you will complete a portfolio or thesis.
- If deciding upon thesis, meet with your thesis advisor.
- Decide on a preliminary topic for your thesis.
- Develop a thesis proposal and conceptual model.
- Complete the HREA (Human Research Ethics Application) form.
    Finalize members of the defense committee.

Summer/Winter Break
- Undertake readings for semester four classes.
- Finalize the literature review section of the thesis.
- Complete the methodology section of the thesis.
- Undertake any field work and data collection.
- Collate the data and begin analysis.

Semester Four (and Five if required)
- Complete program coursework.
- Finalize the discussion section of the thesis.
- Develop a conclusion and then introduction for the thesis, along with an abstract and a table of contents.
- Prepare the first draft of thesis that is to go to the defense committee.
- Prepare for the thesis defense.
- With advisor approval, distribute the first draft of your thesis to defense committee members.
- Sit for the oral defense of your thesis.
- Revise the thesis as required by the thesis defense committee.
- Submit the revisions as a final draft of your thesis to your advisor for review.
- After final approval from your thesis advisor, follow the graduate program procedures for submission of the thesis to the university.

Listing of Thesis Student Responsibilities

- ☐ I believe that my coursework writing experiences have enabled me to become familiar with how to write a research paper. If my advisor finds that this is not the case, I understand that I must put aside my thesis and first become familiar with the process of thesis writing before I can continue. (This might even entail enrolling in an approved writing course and/or needing more than one semester to write my thesis). It might also mean changing to the portfolio track (if that option is available to me).

- ☐ I understand that it is my responsibility to focus on form, and that my advisor is responsible for focusing on the content and assisting with developing an appropriate structure for the thesis. (e.g., my advisor should not be showing me how to use APA style, MS Word, or graphic aids. However, my advisor will notify me if the layout, the content of the tables or the thesis needs adjusting).

- ☐ I will make appointments to see my advisor during his/her regularly scheduled office hours whenever possible. I understand that this is why the university arranges for professors to have and maintain office hours.

- ☐ I do not expect my advisor to schedule special times to meet with me at my convenience; rather, I recognize my obligation to schedule appointments which are in all instances mutually agreed upon. Should I need to postpone or cancel an appointment, I will try within reasonable limits to provide my advisor with advance notice.

- ☐ I understand that it is also my obligation to arrange an agenda for scheduled meetings with mutual consent at least 5 days prior to the appointed date.

- ☐ I understand that it is my responsibility to provide specific updates to my advisor regarding the progress of my thesis, and to do so on a weekly basis, or as my advisor deems necessary.

- ☐ I understand that I must provide email documents/material to my advisor at least 5 days in advance of the receipt of hardcopies of sections of the thesis, unless my advisor waives this requirement.

- ☐ I understand that I should follow the research plan that my advisor and I have drawn up regarding my thesis, and that this research plan needs to be completed by the end of my third semester of study in the program. Any major modifications to this plan must be made in consultation with my advisor according to a mutually agreed upon and reasonable timetable for completion.
- ☐ I understand that, as a thesis student, I must make certain sacrifices, and that this includes working on my literature review and developing research instruments during summer and/or winter intersessions and that I will have to make a serious time commitment (including evenings, weekends, and holidays) if I intend to complete my thesis in a single semester.
- ☐ I understand that if I have neglected to prepare a study plan and thesis topic in conjunction with my supervisor in my third semester of study that I will need to do this as part of the thesis research course. Accordingly, I will then need to take advanced thesis research in a fifth semester and work on my thesis over two semesters and any intersessions.
- ☐ I understand that my advisor is assisting me voluntarily, and I need to respect the time and effort that they undertake to help me in the thesis writing process.
- ☐ I should consider all changes and recommendations offered, and understand that by ignoring any recommendations, I could fail my thesis defense, or I will need to resubmit the thesis in a subsequent semester.
- ☐ I have obtained and read the information on capstone projects prepared by the department faculty.

As a thesis student in the TESOL-MALL graduate program, I have read the above and by signing below, I indicate that I will honor my obligations and meet my responsibilities as outlined.

_____   _____   _____
Thesis Student   Thesis Advisor Signature   Date
Signature

Photocopiable Content – Thesis

Composition of a Thesis Proposal

Title Page
The thesis proposal title page may vary from one graduate program to another, but it should include your name and student number, your proposed thesis title, the name of your thesis advisor, the semester and year that you are lodging the proposal with your advisor, and the name of your graduate program.

Thesis Title
Your proposed title will be short (certainly less than 20 words, but aim for 15), and will attempt to accurately describe the research problem. The title needs to be as close as possible to the final title of your thesis.

Abstract
At this stage, you will need to develop a working abstract, and this document can help prepare the content of that abstract. State the research issues, the problem(s) that you want to examine, the way that you intend to conduct your research (meaning with who and how), what you think the outcome will be, as well as the goals and significance of your study. The abstract is a summary of your study (at this stage, the thesis proposal) in very clear and plain writing. It should be no longer than half a page (try for no more than 300 words).

Definition of Terms
If you need to define any specific terms used throughout the thesis you would go into detail regarding these here. However, you might instead prefer to include them in a glossary or incorporate them into another area of the thesis such as the introduction or the literature review.

Introduction

In this section, the research problem is outlined (what your research will aim to find out). This section must contain sufficient information to inform your advisor of what your thesis research will be about, and specifically what aspects your study will address. At a minimum, aim to consider providing a brief overview of the reason for your investigation, including the goals of your study and why these aims are significant or important. You should provide information under the following sub-headings:

Background and Context. Outline the topic and scope of the research to situate the reader.

Research Problem. Describe in detail the practical or theoretical research problem that you want to investigate or address. Consider what current literature knows about the issue here, and detail what is lacking from the literature. In other words, develop your research niche.

Significance. Indicate the relevance and importance of the research (i.e., how it adds to knowledge or makes an original contribution to knowledge). Clarify what new insights you will be able to contribute to the literature, to whom these insights are relevant, and why the research questions are worth asking, providing a summary of why and how the goals and aims of your thesis are significant and important. Indicate:

- how the results from your research could be used to help the target population;
- why the results could be important for other people in your field and how they might be used; and
- how the results could be important for other researchers.

You may wish to break the significance into two sections, practical implications and theoretical implications.

Practical implications. Will your findings help improve a process, inform policy, or make a case for concrete change?

Theoretical implications. Will your work help strengthen a theory or model, challenge current assumptions, or create a basis for further research?

Research Questions. State very clearly the research question and any subsidiary questions. (You should have at least three questions, but you may need to write down as many as you can to help you consider all aspects of the problem that you are investigating).

Background/Literature Review

This section contains a critical review of the literature concerning your area of study. Of note, this section must clearly relate to the research problem (outlined above). Further, references cited in this section must be in a scholarly format (e.g., APA style), and be included in a references section at the end of the thesis proposal. Here are some ways to structure a literature review.

Chronologically. This is perhaps the simplest approach, but it is not simply a listing of sources or citations in order. You will need to try to analyze any patterns that have emerged over time, and identify the key debates or turning points that may have shaped the direction of the field, and you would need to include some thoughts as to why these developments might have occurred.

Thematically. This structure will use a series of recurring themes to build the literature review. These can be the themes that you have identified in your conceptual model and have built your research questions on. For example, if you are looking at a topic such as the value of English in a particular country, then you may want to focus on social, economic, and educational aspects.

Methodologically. If you are looking at different disciplines that utilize a variety of research methods, then you might align the literature review with a discussion of each approach to research. You would then need to examine and present the research and conclusions that emerge from the different approaches (e.g., qualitative versus quantitative versus mixed-methods research; and empirical versus theoretical).

Theoretically. If the thesis is intended to discuss a theoretical framework or concept, then you can use it to present various theories, models, and definitions of key concepts. You might use it to argue the relevance of a specific theoretical approach to a practical problem, or combine a number of various theoretical concepts into a coherent argument for the development of a framework to support your research.

No matter the structure, the literature review should aim to compare and critique those studies that are the most relevant to the research problem(s) you are investigating. It is an extremely important part of a thesis proposal because it demonstrates that you have read the research available in your field of study and have utilized this research to be informed of the best way of attempting to resolve your research questions.

The literature review confirms that you have thoroughly searched the literature and understood what it means for your study. It proves that you have been able to distinguish good research from bad, as well as relevant research from irrelevant research. It must also provide what the literature supports as important in regards to your research problem or questions. In a literature review, you need to:
- give some background regarding the research problem;
- analyze what the literature says about the problem;
- define the meaning of important terms;
- explain how the research literature helps you to understand the problem under investigation; and
- provide any theoretical, conceptual or methodological framework that can help explain your problem.

Your advisor will point out if you have been able to provide the above to a sufficient standard.

The layout of your literature review may resemble the following:

Overview/Introduction. Explains how the review is organized.

Topic Headings. Organizes a critical review into topics associated with the research problem and questions. This might be based on the themes of your research questions or be organized using the following: key concepts, theories, and studies; key debates and controversies; or gaps in the literature.

Summary. Draw all of the main points together and describe what the review means for your thesis.

Research/Methods and Design

The methods section includes a statement as to the way(s) that you intend to investigate your thesis questions; design will indicate the steps for the methods process and provide further details. In other words, this is where you should explain your approach to the research and describe exactly what steps you took to answer your research questions.

This section is important because it shows that you have thought carefully about how you will carry out the research. That said, the structure and content of the research methods and design section of this document will depend on the nature of the research problem. There should be sufficient detail to enable your advisor to judge whether the study is likely to be successful or if some adjustments are required.

A further purpose of this section is to explain how and where you will carry out the data collection, and analysis. This will then determine the kind of ethics clearance that you may need before you can begin with data collection.

You need to give reasons as to why you have chosen a particular sample and method of data collection. You must also provide details concerning the data collection methods, including why and how those methods will be used and the site(s) where the data collection will occur. In this section you must:

- briefly outline your research method;
- state where your research will be carried out;
- describe what sample will be used, or who the participants will probably be;
- indicate the limitations that you perceive may arise when interpreting the results of the study;
- outline the steps that will be taken to overcome/minimize each limitation; and
- highlight any ethical implications or considerations that were taken into account.

Consider answering the following questions when writing this section:

- What kind of research design will be used? What are the advantages and limitations of that research design?
- What is the target population? Who will be my research participants? What and where are the research site/s?
- Will a sample be used? If so, how big will it be, how will it be selected, and will it be representative of the population?
- What instruments will be used? Do they include the researcher? How will they be selected/developed? What evidence will be given regarding their validity and reliability (or other standards)? Are they the best instruments to use?

- When will the data be collected or generated (in terms of time and relation to the research variables)? By whom?
- Will a pre-test or pilot study be used? If so, why? What action will be taken on the basis of the results?
- What methods of data analysis will be used? Why have these methods been chosen? Are they appropriate? Who will do the analysis?

An example layout might rely on the following sub-headings.

Research Design. Explain how you will design the research. Will it be qualitative or quantitative, or a mixed-method study? Will it rely on original data collection or primary and secondary sources? Will it be a descriptive, correlational, or experimental investigation?

Methods, Contexts and Sources. Describe the procedures, participants, instruments/tools, and sources of the research. When, where, and how will you collect, select, and analyze the data? Also take into account aspects of reliability and validity in this section, and show how you have met these factors in terms of your instruments and data collection.

Limitations of the Research. Address any potential obstacles, limitations, or other hindrances to the research in this section. How will you plan for these and work around them if necessary? If you are unable to generalize your results for any reason (e.g., use of a small sample of convenience), then explain that in this section, and state why your conclusions and research are still valid.

Ethical Issues. Depending on the nature of your research, you will need to consider ethical issues and implications concerning research development, and the way in which you will conduct your research. Regarding ethics, researchers have the following responsibilities.
- *Provide Information* - make the research aims clear to participants, and inform them of how the results will be used, and provide feedback to participants (including an opportunity for participants to verify the data collected about them).
- *Obtain Permission* - Written permission may be required. This may be in the form of an ethics clearance from the university, and/or from participants showing willingness to participate or from a child's guardian; from principles (to carry out research at a school); or, from teachers (allowing

you to sit in on classes and observe students). Participants should also be made aware that they have the right to withdraw from the study at any time.
- *Privacy/Confidentiality* – Provide a written guarantee of privacy and confidentiality to individuals and organizations from whom you collect data. Further, participants have the right to remain anonymous and you must change names so that participants cannot be identified.
- *Consideration* - Plan data collection so that there is as little disruption as possible for participants e.g., no lengthy absences from class, or any considerable interruption of lessons. Cooperate with people where you conduct the research (e.g., determine ahead of time if you will sit to observe classes, how and for what length of time you will record data, how you will be introduced, and so on).
- *Acknowledgements* - The cooperation and contribution of all participants should be acknowledged in a way that retains confidentiality unless otherwise requested.

Resources Required

Outline any special needs such as equipment or resources that is required to complete your thesis research, and if you have access to the required equipment or if you will need to secure it (e.g., particular software applications or recording hardware).

Data Storage

Ensure that you have a plan that sees you always maintaining a backup of data, both paper-based (such as original surveys) and electronic (such as a data repository). If you do not have a USB memory stick, you should obtain one and make regular backups of your thesis research on it. You could also use a cloud service such as Google Drive while conducting research as an interim storage solution or rely on more professional services like those of Figshare or Mendeley Data. You also need to be aware that the university where you study will have a policy regarding the length of time that you will need to keep all records regarding your thesis. This is so that your original data can be analyzed by a third party if required, and it is typically understood that you will keep these records for five to seven years.

Thesis Outline/Contents

Although different kinds of theses require different layouts, developing a guide to follow early on is important as it will help you maintain a research focus. The following is a common outline that you may include and develop with subheadings of your own:

- Abstract – 300 words.
- Definition of Terms – as required.
- Introduction – 3 to 5 pages.
- Literature Review – 15 to 20 pages.
- Research Methods and Design – 5 to 10 pages.
- Discussion and Results – 10 to 20 pages.
- Conclusion – 3 to 5 pages.
- References – in APA style.
- Appendices – as required.
- Glossary – as required.

Theoretical, Conceptual or Methodological Model/Framework

You may consider providing a graphical representation of how you intend to approach answering the research questions. Think of it as a blueprint, or the outline of how you plan to conduct the research for your thesis that also shows how your research sits/aligns within the larger field or scope of research. It is used to illustrate what you expect to find throughout your research, particularly how the variables that you are considering relate to each other.

There are many ways to go about creating a conceptual model. You may start with the main theme of your research broken down into three smaller themes (your research questions), with these then broken down into smaller concepts that you might then use to create survey or interview questions. These smaller concepts could all then be broken down further in order to develop interview questions from the survey, or follow-up questions from the main interview questions. The conceptual model or theoretical framework may simply show how all the variables of a study interrelate, e.g., what are the independent and the dependent variables and how they relate to each other and to the source of data or the context of the study. A graphical representation is an easy way for readers to see how things in your thesis relate to each other and how you will have undertaken the research.

Thesis Completion Schedule

Remember, you are not the only thesis student that your advisor works with, and in reality, a well-planned thesis and well-researched work should see you only need to meet with your advisor around four times if work is commented upon electronically and regularly. Keep in mind also that, without a schedule that you can commit to, you will not complete your thesis in the time allotted. Be realistic; don't think that you will complete your thesis in three weeks! By the time that you start your actual thesis research course, you will need to have a document like this one well and truly complete, and have already started to undertake research. You will likely have been engaging with participants (if there are any in your study), have had the method section complete, be reading to finalize the findings and conclusions, and be preparing for the oral defense.

You must remain constantly aware of the deadlines for submission of necessary documents, for example: the thesis defense period, the submission of first drafts to oral defense committee members, and so on. This information can usually be obtained from your graduate program handbook, from your department office assistants, and your thesis advisor.

References

Every reference that you cite must be included in a list of references at the end of your proposal, but do not include any reference which was not explicitly cited in your proposal. Ensure that the reference list adheres to the scholarly format decided upon by your graduate program, such as that of the American Psychological Association (APA).

Appendix (as required)

Add any additional items of importance in an appendix. At the thesis proposal stage, this might involve computer code, screen shots, or a listing of potential software that you need to narrow down for use in an experiment. It might also include samples of thematic coding and transcripts of audio interviews, and so on. A completed ethics proposal form could be placed here.

Glossary (as required)
If your thesis proposal contains a large number of specific or unique terms and/or a number of acronyms, it will be important to detail them all in a glossary section. List all the acronyms, terms, and key phrases in alphabetical order.

Common Problems
Some common problems found in the summary of the proposed research program could include:
- The abstract is not clear and precise, or it lacks information that an abstract should contain.
- The research problem/questions/objectives are missing or not defined at all.
- The background section is not clearly tied to the research problem.
- The significance of the study is confused with the background, or the significance section fails to define the significance clearly.
- The research method is poorly explained, or it does not clearly address the research problem or identify the questions.
- The research method is not feasible in the time or scope that the student has to be able to complete the thesis.
- The explanation or treatment of ethical issues is not raised or it is inadequate.

Remember!
This proposal, or more correctly the information within it, will ultimately become your thesis. Your advisor can assist in checking all parts of the proposal, but it is not their job to write the proposal for you or to sit with you while you come up with ideas to complete the thesis proposal. You must complete as much of this document as you possibly can *before* meeting your advisor.

Blank Thesis Proposal Template

Title of the Thesis

Thesis Advisor: Name

Semester, Year

Graduate Program Name
University Name

Your Name
Your Student Number

Abstract

Definition of Terms
If relevant, or placed into a glossary if not incorporated into the introduction or literature review.

Introduction

Background and context

Research Problem

Significance
Practical Implications

Theoretical Implications

Research Questions
1.

2.

3.

Literature Review

Overview/Introduction.

Headings
These should be research question-based, or those such as: key concepts, theories, and studies; key debates and controversies; and gaps in the literature.

Summary

Methodology and Design

Research Design

Methods and Sources
Procedure

Participants

Instruments

Context/Source

Practical Considerations
Limitations of the Research

Ethical Considerations

Other Considerations

Resources Required

Data Storage

Thesis Outline

Conceptual Model/Methodological Framework

Thesis Completion Schedule

Research Phase	Objectives	Deadline

References

Appendices

Glossary

Human Research Ethics Application

TESOL Graduate Program	Office Use Only	Received:	
Human Research Ethics Application (HREA)		Advisor:	
ETHICS REVIEW FORM		Ethics Review No:	

Purpose

The HREA was developed in order to assist researchers in considering the ethical principles of the Guideline for Establishment of Research Ethics (Instruction of the Korean Ministry of Education No. 153) in relation to their research.

Level of Ethical Review

Indicate the level of ethical review that is being sought for this application.

☐ **Full HREA Review**

Applies to all research involving more than 'low risk research'.

☐ **Low Risk Review**

Applies to 'low risk research' which is research that can generally be undertaken by an individual (e.g., involves one-site research: research across a single classroom or several of the researchers' classrooms, and conducted in a single country).

Section 1: Project and Researcher's Details

1.1. Project focus/objective (e.g., classroom observational process, developing vocabulary skills with *app name*, etc.)

1.2. Project timeframe (tick those that apply):
- ☐ Spring semester
- ☐ Summer session
- ☐ Fall semester
- ☐ Winter session
- Other (_____)

1.3. Main researcher

Name _____ ID: _____

Research Role _____

1.4. Others, such as research assistants, secondary investigators
If the research involves use of assistants, requires volunteers, or the participation of other teachers, please list them here.

Name _____ ID: _____

Research Role _____

Name _____ ID: _____

Research Role _____

Name _____ ID: _____

Research Role _____

Photocopiable Content – Thesis

Section 2: Nature of the Project

2.1. Rationale of the project (e.g., why are you undertaking the research? Filling gaps in literature, contribute new knowledge to field, research for CPD, research for a conference presentation.)

_____
_____
_____
_____
_____
_____
_____
_____
_____
_____
_____
_____
_____

2.2. Research interaction (e.g., describe the interactions between researchers and participants, such as teacher-student, or not involved as looking at data sets collected by third parties like administration)

_____
_____
_____
_____
_____
_____
_____
_____
_____
_____
_____
_____
_____
_____

Photocopiable Content – Thesis

2.3. Location(s) of the research (Include details of all sites and times where the project will be undertaken and locations of participants, e.g., classroom, in-office interviews, over six weeks during class/homework, conducted mid-semester three weeks prior to midterm and three weeks post-midterm.)

2.4. If the research is to be conducted with or about participants living outside Korea, outline any local legislation, regulations, permissions, or customs that need to be addressed before the research can commence. Outline the steps taken to ensure that this has been adequately considered and addressed.

Section 3: Participants and Recruitment

3.1. Who will be the participants in this project? (e.g., administration, teachers only, students only, students and teachers, a single GCT reading class.)

_____
_____
_____
_____
_____
_____
_____
_____
_____
_____
_____
_____

3.2. How does the research comply with participant consent? (e.g., permission granted by participants to record their images or voice for research purposes, right to decline participation has been granted.)

_____
_____
_____
_____
_____
_____
_____
_____
_____
_____
_____

3.3. What steps are being used to protect the anonymity of participants and the research data collected? (e.g., coding the data, obtaining pre-coded data, use of anonymous surveys.)

3.4. Will you obtain/do you have consent to use the collected data for research purposes? (e.g., a participation sheet has been provided to appropriate participants or those providing research data.)

3.5. What materials will be used to recruit participants and how will they be used? Provide details of any posters, flyers, participant information sheets, consent forms, advertisements, emails, and letters that will be used. Include a listing of any online or physical sites or advertisements that have been or will be used to collect the data. (e.g., a Google Forms account has been used to record student/teacher survey responses.)

_____
_____
_____
_____
_____
_____
_____
_____
_____
_____
_____
_____

3.6. How and by whom will initial contact between the researcher and participants be made? (e.g., teacher will ask in class, teacher will ask administration, administration will ask the teacher/students, teacher will recruit on Facebook/at a conference.)

_____
_____
_____
_____
_____
_____
_____
_____
_____
_____
_____
_____
_____

3.7. Describe how, when, and what information about the proposed research activities will be provided to participants and any third parties. (e.g., participants can publicly review the lead researcher profile on Research Gate and obtain the completed research product from such a site, research is made available to all faculty/students by the department website or university official blogs, research conducted and presented at a conference is made publicly available by sharing the notes/ppt as appropriate.)

_____
_____
_____
_____
_____
_____
_____
_____
_____
_____

3.8. For participants who are not fluent in English or who have difficulty understanding English, what arrangements will be made to ensure comprehension of the research information if any? (e.g., translation of surveys into native language.)

_____
_____
_____
_____
_____
_____
_____
_____
_____
_____

3.9. What research activities have been, or will be, conducted during the process of data gathering?

Research method/activity	Participant time	Research method/Activity	Participant time
Action research	☐	Interview	☐
Data linkage	☐	Observation	☐
Ethnographic	☐	Survey	☐
Focus group	☐	Textual analysis	☐
Intervention	☐	Use of data sets	☐
Other (_____)			

Section 4 Ethical Considerations

In addition to the ethical considerations pertaining to all research participants, researchers should be aware of the specific issues that arise in terms of the design, conduct, and ethical review of research involving various categories of participants as outlined in the *National Statement Section 4*.

4.1. Do you foresee any burdens or risks to participants or researchers? (Burdens include impact on participants such as inconvenience, e.g., those that are minor such as filling in a form, giving up time to participate in research, or those that are major such as anxiety induced by interview. Other risks may be emotional, social, legal, medical, or physical, and can include distress and harm.)

_____
_____
_____
_____
_____
_____
_____
_____
_____
_____
_____
_____
_____

4.2. Describe how the burdens/risks will be minimized or mitigated as necessary.

4.3. Describe how researcher(s) will protect the privacy and confidentiality of participants (e.g., anonymous encoding of research data.)

4.4. Will any inducement for participation be made available, who will provide it, and how will it be provided? (e.g., Starbucks coffee vouchers delivered by SMS paid for with a research grant; participation points provided to students to increase their grades.)

_____
_____
_____
_____
_____
_____
_____
_____
_____
_____
_____
_____
_____
_____
_____

Section 5: Data Confidentiality, Analysis, Reporting, Storage, and Future Use

5.1. Select the option that reflects the type of data that will be accessed throughout the research.

Note. For some research, the type of data received or collected may initially be different to the type of data that is stored. For example, interview data with names recorded is individually identifiable data. If names are *permanently* removed when the data is stored at the completion of the project, the data would be considered non-identifiable. Personally identifiable information is any detail that can be used to identify a particular individual. This may include name, email, phone number, student/employee ID, position, or rank.

Type of Data	Initially Received/ Collected	Stored (at completion)
Non-identifiable: participant data that is received or collected in a non-identifiable form, including data which has never had personal identifiers, e.g., an anonymous survey or a survey from which identifiers have been permanently removed before the researcher(s) receive it. It is not possible for the researcher(s) to identify specific individuals.	☐	☐
Re-identifiable: participant data from which personal identifiers have been removed and replaced by code(s). The data is either received with codes already attached with the personal identifiers removed or the researcher(s) remove the identifiers and replace them with code(s). It remains possible for at least one researcher to re-identify a specific individual by, for example, using the code(s) or linking to a different data set or to different data sets.	☐	☐
Individually Identifiable: participant data where an individual's identity can be reasonably ascertained via a (nick)name, student number, position in an organization, and so on.	☐	☐

5.2. How will the privacy and confidentiality of participant data, samples, and information be protected during the collection and/or recruitment phase? (Outline the de-identification processes, separation of roles of those responsible for the management of data, and any other relevant practices. Outline where data will be stored during the data collection phase and who will have access to it.)

_____
_____
_____
_____
_____
_____
_____
_____
_____
_____
_____
_____

5.3. How will the privacy and confidentiality of participant data, samples, and information be protected during the data analysis and write-up phases? (Outline the de-identification processes, use of pseudonyms, codes, or explicit consent, and any other relevant practices.)

_____
_____
_____
_____
_____
_____
_____
_____
_____
_____
_____
_____

5.4. How will participant data, samples, and information be analyzed and who will undertake this analysis? (e.g., t-test using SPSS conducted by the second researcher.)

5.5. What feedback of findings will be offered to participants? (e.g., access to transcripts of interviews, drafts, or final reports when they become available. If no feedback is to be offered, outline why. Note that it may be good practice to conduct member checking of any collected data.)

5.6. How will the project outcomes be made publicly accessible at the end of the project and in what forms (e.g., journal article, book, conference paper, in the media, presentation, stored in a library). If they will not be made publicly accessible, detail how the research will be applied (e.g., presented to a committee).

_____
_____
_____
_____
_____
_____
_____
_____
_____

5.7. Outline how the records, materials, and data from the project will be stored on completion and for how long, or if they will be destroyed. Include details of the storage location and who will have access. (Note that the <u>minimum</u> period for retention of research data is five years from the date of any publication, and that this varies depending on the specific type of research.)

_____
_____
_____
_____
_____
_____
_____
_____
_____
_____

5.8. Who will be the data custodian? (All data collections should have an identified custodian to enable access by researchers or participants to the data while maintaining it in a protected form. The custodian of the data may be the individual researcher, the agency that collected the information, or an intermediary who manages data coming from a number of sources.)

_____
_____
_____
_____
_____
_____
_____
_____
_____
_____

5.9. For future use of data and/or its re-issue, what type of consent will be obtained? Will consent be specific, extended, or unspecified? (Data collected as part of a research project can only be shared or used in future with the explicit consent of the participants. Ideally, if the data is collected and stored in such a way that it can be used in future research projects then the participant information sheet and consent forms should outline this and make that clear to participants.)

_____
_____
_____
_____
_____
_____
_____
_____
_____
_____

5.10. If specific consent is sought, justify why the data and information generated by this research should not be made available for future research. (e.g., Where a researcher believes that there are ethical reasons not to make research data or information accessible for future use, this must be justified.)

_____
_____
_____
_____
_____
_____
_____
_____
_____
_____
_____

5.11. Data custody: maintain the data from the project as data custodian. (If future use or sharing of the data is intended, participants are to be fully informed of this in the participant information sheet, in the survey that they complete, or during interview recording. Data custodianship will be the responsibility of the researcher.)

_____
_____
_____
_____
_____
_____
_____
_____
_____
_____
_____

Section 6: Conflict of Interest or Other Ethical Issues

6.1. Outline the source of any project funding.

_____

_____

_____

_____

_____

6.2. Outline any 'conflict of interest' issues that may arise during the project.

_____

_____

_____

_____

_____

6.3. Do the researchers expect to obtain any direct or indirect financial or other benefits through conducting this research?

_____

_____

_____

_____

6.4. Outline any other ethical or relevant issues not discussed on this form.

_____

_____

_____

_____

_____

_____

Section 7: Declaration by the Researcher(s)

I/we have read the *Guideline for Establishment of Research Ethics (Instruction of the Korean Ministry of Education No. 153)*.

I/we the researcher(s) agree to:
- conduct the project in accordance with our responsibilities under the Korean Ministry of Education and University guidelines;
- begin collecting data only after submission of the human research ethics application has been reviewed;
- only carry out this research project where adequate funding and personnel is available to enable the project to be carried out according to good research practice and in an ethical manner;
- notify the ethics committee in writing in the event of any adverse or unforeseen events occurring prior, during, or after the commencement of research, at the discontinuation of research, and changes to those involved in the research; and
- participate in an audit if requested by the ethics committee.

In addition, as researcher/applicant, I/we:
- accept responsibility for the conduct of this research project in accordance with the *Guideline for Establishment of Research Ethics (Instruction of the Korean Ministry of Education No. 153)*;
- certify that all researchers and other personnel involved in this project are appropriately qualified and experienced or will undergo appropriate training and supervision to fulfil their role in this project; and
- will take responsibility for the confidential maintenance of the research materials as per the *Guideline for Establishment of Research Ethics (Instruction of the Korean Ministry of Education No. 153)* and as required by legislation.

All persons named in **Section 1** are required to sign below:

Researcher's Signature: _____

Name: _____ Date: _____

Assistant's Signature: _____

Name: _____ Date: _____

Assistant's Signature: _____

Name: _____ Date: _____

Assistant's Signature: _____

Name: _____ Date: _____

Section 8: Checklist

The following documents (if appropriate) are attached to the main body of the application, and are clearly labeled using the appropriate number (i.e., Attachment 1, Attachment 2, etc.). Check Y for Yes, N for No, or N/A for not applicable.

Y	N	N/A	Item	Attachment
☐	☐	☐	Participant information including contacts for complaints either as an information sheet, verbal script, or survey preamble.	
☐	☐	☐	The standard consent form for a participant in a research project. (Written consent is required for the majority of projects.)	
☐	☐	☐	Consent by a third party to complete the participation form. (This is required where participants are under 18 years or a dependent adult.)	
☐	☐	☐	Other recruitment documentation including advertisements, flyers, recruitment letters, emails of introduction, copy of Facebook event pages, and social media event sites.	
☐	☐	☐	Procedure/protocol for interviews or focus groups including topics, questions, and themes.	
☐	☐	☐	Survey instrument/questionnaire. (Include a printed copy of the survey.)	
☐	☐	☐	Evidence of approval/rejection by other human research ethics committees, including comments and requested alterations to the application, if applicable.	
☐	☐	☐	Research with people outside Korea: evidence of permissions, approvals from overseas authorities, and so on.	

Section 9: How to Submit this Application

1. Print the completed form and obtain signatures from all researchers.

2. Scan the signed form including all labeled attachments as **one pdf file** and email it to the chair of the ethics committee.

3. <u>Submission deadlines:</u>
   Full HREA review: end of the semester prior to research commencement.
   Low risk HREA review: submit at any time.
   Allow for the possibility that a project submitted as a low-risk application may be deemed to involve more than low risk, or to raise other issues, which would therefore require a full committee review.

4. Be aware that in all cases, researchers may be requested to provide additional information, as well as a copy of their research results (e.g., journal article, presentation notes/ppt, thesis).

Note. References to the *Guideline for the Establishment of Research Ethics* throughout this form are not meant to be exhaustive but rather to provide a starting point for researchers to consider. Researchers should be familiar with these guidelines when conducting research from within Korea and during their time at the university.

Sample Participant Consent Form

Participant Name: _____

Research Project Title:
_____

Research Description:
_____
_____
_____
_____

- I have read the research description and have had the opportunity to ask questions about the purposes and procedures regarding this study.
- My participation in this research is voluntary. I may refuse to participate or withdraw from participation at any time without retribution.
- The researcher may withdraw me from the research at their professional discretion.
- Any information derived from the research project that personally identifies me will not be released or disclosed without my separate consent, except as specifically required by law.
- If at any time I have any questions regarding the research or my participation, I can contact the researcher by email at _____.
- If at any time I have comments or concerns regarding the conduct of the research or questions about my rights as a research subject, I should contact the advisor Dr. _____ by email at _____.
- I give my consent to be audio-recorded and/or video-recorded and/or for any written or electronic material that I have completed to be used for research purposes.
- My signature, or electronic statement, means that I agree to participate in this study.

Participant's signature: _____ Date: _____

\multicolumn{5}{c}{**Plagiarism Analysis Report**}
Author Details	Name			
	Student Number			
	Department			
	Major			
	Graduate Program			
Degree	☐ Master's ☐ Doctorate			
Course[1]	Name of course			
Title[2]				
Plagiarism	☐ 0-9% Secure	☐ 10-15% Caution	☐ 16-20% Suspicious	☐ >20% Risk
Comments[3]				
Attachments[4]	☐ Plagiarism report ☐ Other			
Student Signature _____				
Professor/Advisor Signature _____				
Date _____				

[1.] Complete if appropriate.
[2.] Assignment, thesis, or dissertation title.
[3.] Comments to be made by the course professor/thesis advisor in terms of recommendations for the student (if any).
[4.] Attach the plagiarism report provided by the application recommended by your school, and any other necessary documents as advised.

Thesis Cheat Sheet

Abstract

Background. Provide a link to the thesis purpose/problem.
Methodology. Include participant information, instruments, context, and design.
Results. Basic findings, conclusions, recommendations.
Final remarks. Additional findings of importance, real-world implications, limitations and future research possibilities.

Introduction

Introduce the topic. State the problem or area of focus with background information.
Significance. Explain why the research is valuable/important. Provide a statement of significance: *The research will be of value to/for ...*
Purpose of the study. Describe the purpose for undertaking the research. *The purpose of this thesis is to examine ... The specific research questions are ...*

Literature Review

Develop this section in order to support the process and purpose of your study – use peer-reviewed journal articles.
Breakdown the literature review into important sub-topics relevant to your investigation using headings and sub-headings.
Aim to explore the key concepts, theories, and studies.
Identify the key debates and controversies, and any gaps in existing knowledge.

Methodology

Rationale. Detail the methods and state why they best fit the research design, and the rationale for using those particular methods instead of others. The methodological framework or the conceptual model can be presented here.
Participant data. Information on those who form part of the study.
Instrument information. Detail the development and type used to collect the data, including any reliability and validity.
Context. Situate the study, and discuss and detail the context (e.g., school, environment of the study, and so on).

Findings

Restate the research questions. You could do this using the theme of each question as a heading or the major themes that emerge from findings.

Describe the data that answers the questions.

Present emerging themes, categories, and patterns in the data.

Detail the findings with tables, graphs, figures, and so on as required.

Summarize the results with foundational interpretations of what the findings indicate.

Conclusions

Overview. State what the chapter will cover.

Conclusions. Present these based on the findings.

Impact of the study in terms of what was learned, supported by the strengths of the study then follows.

Limitations of the study, including any problems you had, as well as what the results may not be able to tell us are then covered.

Implications for the field (practical ones), for theory, and for future studies are then highlighted.

Recommendations for further research, changes in academic concepts, knowledge or professional practice, modifications of accepted theoretical constructs, or changes in organizations, procedures and practice, behavior, policies, and so on are then presented.

Summary. Finally, provide a short summary of the answers to the research questions and ultimately what your thesis has achieved.

References

All works cited in the thesis must be listed using an accepted scholarly citation method (e.g., APA style).

Appendices

Include all supporting evidence that was not presented in the main body of the thesis here (e.g., instruments, transcripts of interviews, coding of interviews, software code, and so on).

Glossary

List all acronyms, provide definitions of terms or key words.

Photocopiable Content – Thesis

Basic Referencing
(APA Style 7th Edition)

In-Text Citations

A work with one or two authors
… Author and Author (Year) found that …
… (Author & Author, Year).

A Work by Three or More Authors
Author et al. (Year) argued that …
… (Author et al., Year).

Two or More Works in the Same Parenthesis
… (Author, Year; Author, Year).

In References

Periodicals
Author, A. A. (Year). Title of article. *Title of Periodical, volume number*(issue number), pages. DOI
Author, A. A., & Author, B. B. (Year). Title of article. *Title of Periodical, volume number*(issue number), pages. DOI

Proceedings
Author, A. A., & Author, B. B. (Eds.). (Year). *Title of Proceedings*. Publisher. URL

Presentations
Contributor, A. A., & Contributor, B. B. (Year, Month Day). *Title of contribution* [Description of contribution e.g., Keynote]. Title of Symposium/Conference, Location. URL

Book
Author, A. A. (Year). *Title of book: Capital letter also for subtitle.* Publisher Name.

Book in Another Language
Author, A. A. (Year). *Title of Book [Translation of book title]*. Publisher.]

Edited Book
Editor, E. E. (Ed.). (Year). *Title of book: Capital letter also for subtitle.* Publisher.

Chapter in an Edited Book
Author, A. A. (Year). Title of chapter. In E. E. Editor (Ed.), *Title of book*, (pp. #-#). Publisher Name.

Unpublished Dissertation and Theses
Author, A. A. (Year). *Title of dissertation* [Unpublished doctoral dissertation]. Name of Institution Awarding the Degree.
Author, A. A. (Year). *Title of thesis* [Unpublished master's thesis]. Name of Institution Awarding the Degree.

Website
Author, A. A. (Date). *Title of page.* Site Name. URL

YouTube Video
Uploader, A. A. (Date). Title of work [Description]. YouTube. URL

Note. There are a number of other basic rules to follow when using APA style. These include ways to format a reference list, how to format a paper, and how to accurately cite a range of other print and non-print sources.

Glossary

ABA — *See* **applied behavior analysis**.

Academic advisor — An academic advisor typically works with college and university students in a counseling role. They are available to help students if they experience any issues or problems with their classes, and to help them if they need it in regard to taking a portfolio or thesis completion track. They are also responsible for ensuring that the student is fulfilling degree completion requirements in a timely manner.

Accommodation — This occurs when existing **schema** does not work, and needs to be altered in order to deal with a new object or situation.

Acculturation — Assimilation to a different culture.

Achievement test — A test designed to determine the level of learning obtained by a student after the course or lesson has been completed. Also known as an **exit test**.

Acquisition/ learning hypothesis — This involves a distinction between learning and acquisition. Learning requires formal teaching, while acquisition is the unconscious process of learning.

Active learning — An approach to instruction that involves the active engagement of students with course content via discussion, problem solving, case studies, role plays, and other methods. It places a greater degree of responsibility on the learner over passive approaches such as a lecture.

Glossary

Adaptation processes	These allow transitions from one stage to another (**equilibrium**, **assimilation** and **accommodation**).
Advisor	The advisor role is to provide guidance, and to ensure that the tasks that need to be performed are understood. They will at times also be responsible for evaluating your performance.
Affective domain	This involves objectives that deal with the development of feelings, emotions, attitudes, appreciation, and preference.
Affective filter hypothesis	This relates to the emotional state or attitude of the learner that can make learning easier, impede it or block it entirely.
Allophone	These are any of the sounds of speech that represent a single phoneme (e.g., the aspirated *k* in *kit* and the unaspirated *k* in *skit* are allophones of the *k* phoneme).
American English	The set of varieties of the English language that is used in the United States of America (USA). *See also* **General American English**.
Andragogy	This refers to those theories and principles that apply to adult education. *See also* **pedagogy**.
ANN	Artificial Neural Networks.
Antonym	A word or a phrase that holds a different meaning as another in the same language.
APA	American Psychological Association
Aphasia	Loss of the ability to understand or express speech, typically from a result of injury to the brain (e.g., by accident, from neurological disease). It can also impair the ability to read and write.

Applied behavior analysis	This is a behavioral management theory that utilizes learning principles to assist with producing changes in student behavior. It relies on the assessment of the functional relationship between the targeted behavior and the environment to develop socially acceptable alternatives to any aberrant behavior. It is often abbreviated to **ABA**.
Arcuate fasciculus	The bundle of axons that connect **Broca's area** and **Wernicke's area** of the brain.
Army method	*See* **audiolingual method**.
Assertive discipline theory	This is an obedience-based discipline approach to classroom management which focuses on the teacher developing a positive behaviorist management strategy over being dictatorial.
Assimilation	Using an existing **schema** to deal with a new object or situation.
Attempt	Attempts occur when students make an effort to say something which they do not yet know how to verbalize correctly. They should be distinguished from **mistakes** or **slips** and **errors**.
Audio lingual method	This method of teaching foreign languages is based on behaviorist theory and relies on training through reinforcement. It emphasizes the teaching of listening and speaking before reading and writing, using dialogues as the main form of language presentation and drills as the main training techniques. The use of the native tongue discouraged during class. It is also known as the **army method** or **new key**.
Authentic learning	An instructional approach where students explore, discuss, and meaningfully construct

	concepts and relationships in context that involve real-world problems and projects that are of relevance to the learner.
Authentic materials	The term used to refer to content that is developed or written for native speakers of a language but used with learners of that language.
AWL	Academic word list. *See also* **new academic word list** *(NAWL)*.
Backslide	A relapse in language learning, or the attrition of an additional language.
Back chaining	Breaking down the sentence or word into parts, and then presenting it to the student in an order going from the end to the start.
Backwash effect	The positive or negative impact of testing on curriculum design, teaching practices, and learner behavior. Also known as **washback**.
Banking model of education	A term used by Freire to describe and critique the traditional education system. The name refers to the metaphor of students as containers into which educators must pour knowledge ('empty vessel').
BASE	*See* **British Academic Spoken English**.
Behaviorism	This theory focuses on the use of conditioning paradigms that are solidified by reward and/or punishment (stimulus-response) to deliver learning.
Behaviorist classroom management theory	This is one that necessitates the need for very clear rules and codes of conduct. It is also one that views the need for reinforcement decreasing as time passes, and one that changes the kind of negative reinforcer as students become desensitized to it.

Bloom's taxonomy	A framework that consists of a hierarchy that classifies educational learning objectives into levels of complexity and specificity.
BNC	*See* **British national corpus**.
Board plan	An example of how you intend the board to look by the end of the lesson.
Brain plasticity	The process where the brain reorganizes itself by forming new neural connections. This restructuring may also be referred to as **neuroplasticity** or **neural plasticity**.
British Academic Spoken English (BASE)	This is a text corpus consisting of 160 lectures and 40 seminars that were delivered at the Universities of Warwick and Reading from 2000 to 2005. It contains 1,644,942 **tokens**.
British national corpus	This is a 100-million-word corpus of samples of written and spoken English from a variety of sources, and it is often broken down further into different word lists. For example, the BNC 1,000 consists of the first 1,000 most commonly used English words, the BNC 2,000 consists of the first and second 1,000 most commonly used English words, and so on.
Broca's aphasia	Damage to **Broca's area** of the brain that may result in a person who is still able to read and understand spoken language becoming one who has difficulty in speaking and writing.
Broca's area	Located in the frontal lobe of the dominant hemisphere of the brain, usually the left, it is linked to speech production functions. It is linked to **Wernicke's area** by the **arcuate fasciculus**.
BSL	*See* **business service list**.

Glossary

Burnout	Physical exhaustion caused by job demands.
Business service list	This list consists of 1,700 words providing 97% coverage of general business English material when combined with the 2,800 words found in the **NGSL**.
CA	*See* **contrastive analysis**.
Capstone project	An extensive integrative educational task undertaken as a final project in an academic/degree program (e.g., practicum, portfolio, thesis).
Case grammar	A theory that stresses the importance of semantic roles in an effort to make explicit the basic meaning relationships in a sentence.
CBI	*See* **content-based instruction**.
CBLT	*See* **community-based language teaching**.
CCQ	Concept checking questions.
CELT	Culture and English language teaching.
Choice theory	A theory developed by Glasser where behavior is our best attempt at meeting our current needs. The aim of the teacher is to develop a classroom environment and to provide activities and materials that meet all of these needs.
Choral Drilling	The chanting of a pattern or vocabulary item all together.
Chroneme	A theoretical unit of sound that can distinguish words by the duration of a vowel or consonant.
Citation	A quotation or a reference to an article, book, author, or other periodical in a scholarly work.

Classical Method	The traditional teaching technique for the learning of Latin and Greek is the **grammar-translation method**, and as it was used as the standard method of teaching from the 17th to 19th centuries, it has also become known as the classical method.
Classroom management theory	This theory is concerned with the smooth integration and transition among learning activities, arranging the classroom, working with technology and other learning materials (e.g., texts, the board), working with learners, and managing their behavior.
Clinical observation	The process of being observed by a colleague or peer that can be trusted so that they can offer mentorship, feedback, and guidance on your teaching performance.
CLL	*See* **community language learning**.
Closed pairs	Pairs talking next to each other.
Cloze exercise	This involves the use of one or more gaps in a sentence, where every *n*th word is removed (e.g., every fifth, sixth, or seventh) Students need to fill in the space with an appropriate word or phrase (which may or may not be provided).
CLT	*See* **communicative language teaching**.
CNS	Central nervous system.
COCA	*See* **Corpus of Contemporary American**.
Code of ethics	Moral guidelines. Those values, principles, and standards that can impact decision making, and those that guide behavior and practice in personal and professional life.
Code mixing	*See* **code switching**.

Glossary

Code switching	Switching from the use of one language to another, or from one dialect to another or between two registers of the same language, to another. It occurs more often in speaking over writing, and is also known as **CS** and called **code-mixing** and **style-shifting**.
Cognitive compensation	The brain begins to use alternative networks and connections rather than the original pathways that have become damaged or destroyed.
Cognitive domain	This involves objectives and skills that assist with the processing of information.
Cognitive load	The amount of cognitive effort involved in performing the task itself (e.g., solving a math problem).
Cognitive load theory	A theory that posits that there is a certain amount of mental effort required to perform any task (**cognitive load**). There are three categories of this: **germane cognitive load**, **intrinsic cognitive load**, and **extraneous cognitive load**.
Cognitive wellbeing	This is associated with the sets of skills and abilities required for effective work/study to be conducted, mirrored in self-efficacy (the belief in the ability to perform).
Cognitivism	This theory focuses on inner mental activities as valuable and necessary for the development of learning. Knowledge development is seen as the construction of **schema** or symbolic mental constructions, with learning defined as a change in schemata.
Coherence principle	Students learn more deeply when extraneous material is excluded rather than included.

Communicative competence	A linguistic term that refers to a language user's **grammatical** (e.g., morphology, phonology, syntax, and so on) as well as their social knowledge about how and when to use the language appropriately. The term was later extended to include other **competencies** such as **discourse**, **sociolinguistic**, and **strategic**.
Communicative language teaching	**CLT** is an approach to language teaching, there is an emphasis on the four skills (listening, speaking, reading, and writing) with more of a focus on communicative competence than linguistic competence.
Community-based language teaching	**CBLT** focuses on outcomes of learning, and teaches to address what the learner is expected to do with the language that they are learning.
Community language learning	**CLL** is a language teaching approach where learners work together in order to develop the aspects of the language that they would like to learn. It is based on a counseling approach in which the instructor acts as a counselor and a paraphraser, and the learner is viewed as a client and collaborator.
Community of practice	A community of practice (**COP**) is formed from three components (domain, community, practice) where a group of people (the domain) who share a craft or profession come together (as a community) to distribute experience and information, and learn from each other (in practice) which leads to both personal and professional development.
Comparative grammar	The analysis and comparison of the grammatical structures of related languages. It is concerned with providing an

explanatory basis for how humans acquire their first language in order to develop a theory of grammar that is a theory of human language, and one that establishes a relationship among all languages.

Compensation Strategies — This involves finding synonyms in the context of reading, and relying on non-verbal cues when listening and speaking, when learners are attempting to communicate meaning and the exact meaning of a statement is not understood.

Competencies — Competence is the ability to be able to do something well, and a skill that is required to be able to perform a particular task. In language learning, competencies are what learners are expected to do with the language they are learning. These include **discourse**, **grammatical**, **linguistic**, **sociolinguistic**, and **strategic**.

Competency-based language teaching — This kind of language teaching focuses on outcomes of learning, and teaches to address what the learner is expected to do with the language they are learning. It is often abbreviated to **CBLT**.

Compound word — The result of two or more words being joined to form another word with a different meaning. E.g., *under + stand* → *understand*.

Comprehensible input — Language input that is understood, despite not understanding all the words and structures in it. This often varies from learner to learner, and is described as one level above that of the learner if it can only just be understood.

Conditioned response — A behavior that is learned by pairing a neutral stimulus with a potent stimulus.

Conditions of learning	Gagne developed this theory which describes eight kinds of learning, five types of learning outcomes, and nine events of instruction.
Connectionism	An approach in the field of cognitive science that explain mental phenomena using **artificial neural networks (ANN).**
Connectivism	Described as a 'learning theory for the digital age', it attempts to explain how internet technologies (i.e., browsers, search engines, wikis, online chat/discussion, and social networking) have created novel opportunities to learn from others and to share information with them.
Connectivist learning	This is a learning theory that applies **connectivism**. Learning occurs when knowledge is actuated by the process of a learner connecting to and feeding information into a learning community. It views the development of knowledge, or understanding, as the formation of connections between nodes of information (i.e., networks), with the ability to both construct and transverse those networks then considered learning. At its core, this is a form of experiential learning that prioritizes actions and experience over the notion that knowledge is propositional.
Connectome	A comprehensive map of neural connections, typically in the brain, but more broadly also a mapping of all neural connections with the nervous system.
Connotative meaning	The suggestive or associative meaning of a word or phrase, typically secondary meanings rather than primary or denotative ones. See also **Denotative meaning**.

Constructivism	This theory emphasizes the importance of the active involvement of learners in constructing knowledge for themselves, with novel information acquired based on the learner utilizing their background knowledge.
Content-based instruction	**CBI** is an approach to language teaching that focuses not on the language itself, but rather on what is being taught through the language being learned. In other words, the target language becomes the medium through which something new is being learned.
Contiguity principle	Students learn more deeply when printed words are placed near, rather than far from, corresponding pictures.
Continuous assessment	Measuring the learning constantly taking place throughout a lesson or course.
Contrastive analysis	Simply put, this is the systematic study of a pair of languages with a view to identifying the structural differences and similarities between them. It is often abbreviated to **CA**.
Controlled practice	This is the stage of a lesson where learners practice new language in a limited form. It can be compared to **free practice**, which involves student production of target language content on their own.
Cooperative language learning	The philosophy behind this approach is that heterogeneous classes (a mixture of strong and weak learners) can raise the achievement levels of all students if they work together in pairs or small groups. The intention is to establish a student-centered classroom where learners are able to benefit by supporting each other rather than competing against each other.

COP	*See* **community of practice**.
Copyright	An exclusive legal right that is given to an originator of a work, or an assignee, to print, publish, perform, film or record literary, articstic, or musical material, and to authorize others to do so as well.
Corpus callosum	The nerve fibers that connect the two hemispheres of the brain.
Corpus of contemporary American	The **COCA** is a 1.1-billion word corpus of American English from eight genres of content including academic texts, blogs, fiction books, magazines, newspapers, spoken words, web pages, and subtitles from TV and movies. It can be browsed by frequency up to the top 60,000 words, including word forms, parts of speech, and by pronunciation. Individual word searches are possible, as is a search for phrases and strings.
Correcting	Pausing to allow a student a chance to fix their slip or mistake before eliciting the answer from another class member.
CPD	Continuing professional development.
Creole	A stabilized natural language emerging from a **pidgin**.
Critical pedagogical theory	This theory, like poststructuralist theory, believes in the importance of critiquing how power operates in the classroom and how it harms minority learners.
CS	*See* **code switching**.
Culture	The social behavior and the norms found in societies, as well as the arts, capabilities, customs, knowledge, habits, and laws of individuals in those groups. It is

	communicated across generations, and although relatively stable, it is a dynamic system of rules that are implicit and explicit, and it has the potential to change across time.
D-needs	*See* **deficiency needs**.
Data-driven learning	The **DDL** approach consists of using the tools and techniques of corpus linguistics for pedagogical purposes.
Data-information-knowledge-wisdom paradigm	This refers to the **DIKW** paradigm which underpins the **data-driven learning** approach to foreign language learning, where language is treated as data and learners as researchers who undertake guided tasks.
DDL	*See* **data-driven learning**.
Declarative memory	This type of explicit memory involves the conscious and intentional recollection of factual information, previous experience, and concepts.
Deductive approach	A rule-driven top-down approach to teaching grammar.
Defense committee	This is a panel of experts that may convene at an oral defense for a college or university student's thesis completion requirements. It will typically consist of a minimum of a committee chair, the student's thesis advisor, and another examiner.
Deficiency needs	This refers to the most fundamental needs, as found in the **hierarchy of needs**, and includes esteem, friendship and love, security, and physical needs. It is also referred to as **d-needs**.
Deficit discourse	Disempowering patterns of thought, language, and practice which represent

	people or groups in terms of deficiency (absence, lack, or failure).
Defining vocabulary	A list of words that lexicographers use to write dictionary definitions.
Democratic classroom	One that promotes learner voice, with the learner regularly involved in the decision-making process in terms of establishing the classroom learning environment.
Denotative meaning	Literal meanings of a word phrase, or the dictionary meaning of a word, in contrast to a connotative or associated meaning of a word or phrase.
Dependency grammar	A class of modern grammatical theories based upon the dependency relation, as opposed to phrase structure (constituency grammars). Dependency is the notion that linguistic units (e.g., words) are connected to each other by directed links.
Descriptive grammar	The structure of a language as it is used by speakers and writers.
Desuggestopedia	Formed from 'suggestion' and 'pedagogy', the main idea of this language-teaching approach is to accelerate learning through the use of desuggestion to psychological barriers along with positive suggestion. Music and rhythm are key elements of the approach. It is also known as **suggestopedia**.
Developmental stage theory	This is a comprehensive theory put forth by Piaget that deals with the nature of knowledge itself, and how we as humans come to acquire, construct, and use it.
Dialect	Form of a language peculiar to a specific region or social group.

Glossary 717

Dialogue building	Using prompts to generate a dialogue.
Dictation	The action of speaking aloud words that are to be typed, written, or recorded.
Dictogloss	A classroom dictation activity in which learners are required to reconstruct a short text by listening and then noting down key words to use as a base when later reconstructing the text.
Digital discourse competence	The ability to manage an extended task, using several applications and/or types of equipment.
Digital immigrant	A term coined by Prensky to indicate those of us who have grown up without modern technology (or with old defunct technology), as opposed to **digital native**s.
Digital native	A term coined by Prensky to indicate those of us who have grown up with modern technology, as opposed to **digital immigrant**s.
DIKW	Refer to **data-information-knowledge-wisdom paradigm**.
Direct method	In contrast to the grammar-translation method, the direct method emerged near the turn of the 19th century. Rather than using the learner's **L1**, it relies on the **target language** or the **L2**. As a method for teaching languages, it was made popular by Berlitz (a chain of private language schools), and it has its roots in mimicking the process of first language acquisition. It is sometimes referred to as the **natural method** (not to be confused with the **natural approach**).
Discourse competence	The ability to produce coherent and cohesive utterances. Along with other competencies

(grammatical, sociolinguistic, and strategic), it comprises part of communicative competence.

Discrete item testing   The testing of one thing at one time, and it can involve integrative testing where students use a variety of language skills to complete a task successfully.

Dogme   This language teaching approach goes against resource-heavy classrooms and generally relies on material that is learner-directed and learner-generated, and it can be easily used and implemented, particularly in a one-to-one teaching context. The philosophy behind the method is that teaching should focus on learner needs and objectives, relying on real language stemming from a need to communicate, with grammar explanations arising naturally and in context.

Domains of learning   The three domains of learning are cognitive, affective and psychomotor.

Dual coding theory   This theory relies on verbal associations and visual imagery for deep learning to occur, with visual and verbal information processed differently and along distinct channels in the human mind.

EAP   English for academic purposes.

Echoing   Repeating what a student has just said, usually in response to a question that the teacher may have asked.

Eclectic era   Also known as the **post-method era**, this is one where we recognize that comprehensible input is important for practice and progress, and that many learners (aside from young learners) appreciate that an understanding of form and its use is extremely helpful to the language acquisition process. This sees instructors choose some or all of the elements from the various methods, approaches, and techniques that have come before to best benefit student learning, keeping in mind teaching style, aspects of student variables and readiness, and the type of content/lesson being taught.

Educaltional leadership	The process of enlisting and guiding the energies and the talents of teachers, students, and parents toward achieving common educational goals. It consists of a variety of roles that can be taken on formally or informally, and on a paid or voluntary basis.
Educational neuroscience	The practical application of neuroscience to education sees it able to analyze the biological changes in the brain that occur as a result of processing new information. Research involving educational neuroscience attempts to link understanding of brain processes with classroom instruction and experiences.
Eliciting	Asking the student(s) to provide answers, rather than the instructor giving them.
EFL	English as a foreign language.
EGP	English for general purposes.
EIL	*See* **English as an International language**.
Eliciting	Asking students to provide answers, rather than giving them yourself.
ELT	English language teaching.
English as an international language	This refers to the use of English by those who speak it as a second language, and to the use of English by those who speak one of the many varieties of English that are spoken across the globe. *Also known as* **EIL**.

Equilibration	The force that moves development along, with the learner seeking a balance by mastering any new challenges they are presented forming a learning loop: **schema** → **assimilation** → **accommodation** → **schema**.
Equilibrium	A state that occurs when **schemata** can deal with most new information through **assimilation**.
Error	**Mistakes**, or **slips**, are those things that students can correct themselves, once pointed out to them, but **errors** are not self-correctable and will need an explanation, while **attempts** occur when students make an effort to say something which they do not yet know how to verbalize correctly. Each will require a different approach to correction.
ESA	Engage, study, activate.
ESL	English as a second language.
ESP	English for specific purposes.
Ethical issues	Ethical issues and their consideration, particularly for educators and researchers, are those of privacy, respecting the anonymity and confidentiality of participants and their data, a need to acquire informed consent, and a need to ensure involve beneficence.
Ethics	A system of morality embraced by a person or a group, including invisible obligations: those ideas that are less tangible and observable than **laws**.
Ethnolinguistics	The study of the relationship between language and culture, and how different ethnic groups perceive the world.
Exit slip	*See* **Exit ticket**.

Glossary

Exit test — *See* **achievement test**.

Exit ticket — A question or activity that is posed to all students which needs to be completed before they are allowed to leave the room. It is often used to check students' understanding of the material studied during the lesson. Also known as an **exit slip**.

Extensive reading — Reading for enjoyment and the betterment of reading skills in general.

Experiential learning theory — This views knowledge as being created through the transformation of experience. It consists of a learning cycle and four associated learning styles.

Expertise principle — This sees many multimedia design principles become contradictory when used with those learners who have a greater prior knowledge of the subject matter under study than others.

Explicit instruction — A way to teach skills and concepts to learners using a direct, structured method or approach to instruction that can include a variety of teaching techniques.

Explicit memory — This type of memory involves the conscious and intentional recollection of factual information, previous experience, and concepts.

Extensive reading — Reading for enjoyment, and the betterment of reading skills in general.

Extraneous cognitive load — The mental effort arising from the manner in which a task is presented to the learner, such as sorting through other information for what is required to solve a problem.

False Beginner — A person that has a beginning level proficiency in a language, but has been exposed to that language for some time, and therefore knows the alphabet, the sounds of the language, and the use of basic survival phrases. As such, the person is not a true beginner who has zero knowledge of the language.

False friends Those words in two or more languages that look or sound similar, but differ significantly in their meanings.

Fidels These are color-coded pronunciation charts for the teaching of language, typically used in the **silent way**.

Finger stress A technique where a teacher may count out the syllables of word using their hand as a prop.

FLA Foreign language anxiety.

Fluency The ability to convey language in a meaningful, natural, and reasonably lengthy way without much hesitation.

Formative assessment A wide variety of methods, approaches, and techniques that a teacher can use to evaluate a student's comprehension, learning needs, and academic progress either during one particular lesson, a unit, or a course.

Fossilization This refers to linguistic features that have become a permanent part of the way that a person speaks or writes a new language, especially when not learned as a young child. This is also known as interlanguage **stabilization**.

Free practice This is the stage of a lesson which involves students producing target language content on their own. It can be compared to **controlled practice**, which is when learners practice new language in a limited form.

GA	*See* **general American English**.
Gap-Fill	This involves the use of one or more gaps in a sentence, with students needing to fill in or gap-fill an appropriate word or phrase (which may or may not be provided).
GenAm	*See* **general American English**.
General American English	General American English or general American (**GA** or **GenAm**) is the umbrella accent for the majority of American English speakers, and one that is perceived to lack distinct regional, ethnic, or socioeconomic characteristics.
Generative grammar	A grammar (set of rules) that indicates the structure and interpretation of sentences that a native speaker of a language would accept as belonging to the language.
Germane cognitive load	The amount of cognitive effort required to process information about the task itself, making sense of it, and accessing and/or storing information regarding it in long-term memory (e.g., see a math problem, identifying the values and operations required to solve it, and understanding that the task is to solve the problem).
Global Englishes	This refers to the recent spread of English due to globalization, and results from the use of **World English**.
Graded reader	A text that has been rewritten using appropriate language and vocabulary to suit a particular level.
Grammar-translation method	The traditional teaching technique for the learning of Latin and Greek is the grammar-translation method, and as it was used as the standard method of teaching from the 17th to

19th centuries, it has also become known as the **classical method.**

Grammatical competence
The ability to create grammatically correct utterances. Along with other competencies (**discourse**, **sociolinguistic**, and **strategic**) it comprises part of communicative competence.

GSL
General service list.

Guided practice
A teaching practice that involves three steps for the practice of new skills in the classroom. First, the instructor models how the task should be conducted. Then, the learner performs the task with guidance from the teacher. Finally, the learner performs the task by themselves. It is an *I do, we do, you do* technique.

Heterophone *or* **heteronym**
A word that has the same spelling as another but has a different pronunciation and meaning.

Hierarchy of needs
A theory proposed by Maslow to account for human motivation.

Homonym
A word that has the same pronunciation and spelling as another but has a different meaning.

Homophone
A word that has the same pronunciation as another but has a different spelling and meaning.

Horseshoe
This refers to the placement of classroom chairs into a U-shape, or the shape of a horseshoe.

Humanism
See **humanistic learning theory**.

Humanistic learning theory
The focus is on specific human capabilities including those of creativity, personal

growth, and choice. In this view emphasis is placed on learner potential over learner materials, and the role of the teacher is that of a facilitator. The theory posits that once the ideal learning environment has been established, free-willed learners who are fundamentally good, are capable of achieving their best. It is also known as **humanism**.

IcLL	*See* **Intercultural language learning**.
Identity	In sociolinguistics identity refers to the ways in which people position or construct themselves, or are positioned or constructed by others, in socio-cultural situations through language, with reference to variables comprising identity markers in each speech community.
IELTS	International English Language Testing System.
ILA	Initial language acquisition.
Image principle	Voiceover is adequate, and a moving image or a person's face is not necessary to see improvement in learning.
Implicit instruction	Teaching where the instructor does not outline goals and definitions or provide explanations, but instead presents information or content to learners who are then responsible for working with the material to create their own understanding and come to their own conclusions.
Implicit memory	This is a type of unconscious and long-term memory that aids in the performance of particular types of tasks.

Indirect test	The type of test that tests performance (e.g., how well a learner communicates).
Inductive approach	A rule-discovery approach to teaching grammar.
In loco parentis	Latin for 'in the place of a parent'. This term refers to the legal responsibility of an organization or person that takes on some of the functions and responsibilities that are normally undertaken by a parent. In the educational context, it is expected that schools (and teachers) act in the best interests of the learners in any way that they see fit in order to best achieve these interests.
Input	The process of comprehending language.
Input hypothesis	This hypothesis holds that language input plus content slightly behind current comprehension leads to acquisition ($i+1$).
Intake	Language that is remembered, subsumed, and internalized from various inputs (especially teacher input).
Integrative test	One that can involve both discrete and indirect testing in order to test more than one skill.
Intelligence quotient	A score that is derived from a set of standardized tests that are developed to measure a person's cognitive abilities in relation to their age group. It is also known as **IQ**.
Intensive reading	Reading that involves looking at a text in detail, and presenting it accompanied by specific aims and tasks.

Glossary 727

Interactive approach	An engaging way of teaching grammar that involves a variety of methods, approaches, and techniques.
Intercultural competence	The ability to function effectively across cultures, to think and act appropriately, and to communicate and work with people from different cultural backgrounds.
Intercultural language learning	An educative approach to language learning where students are provided with the knowledge and the skills to support them in the ability to both understand and interact with people from cultures other than their own. *Also known as* **IcLL**.
Interference	The influence of features from one language onto another. It can be either beneficial (positive) or negative.
Interlanguage	This is the idiolect developed by a learner of an additional language, which preserves some features of their **L1** with their **L2**, resulting in a unique linguistic organization.
Intrinsic cognitive load	The amount of cognitive effort involved in performing a task.
IPA	International Phonetic Alphabet.
IQ	A score that is derived from a set of standardized tests that are developed to measure a person's cognitive abilities in relation to their age group. It is also known as an **intelligence quotient**.
Jazz chants	An exercise where learners repeat short phrases or words to a beat or a rhythm, and generally to music. They are very useful when applying them to pronunciation and the practice of stress and rhythm.

KATE	The Korea Association for Teachers of English.
KCI	The **Korean Citation Index** is a listing of those peer-reviewed journals who are indexed at this scholarly level. It is often considered to be easier to publish at this level as opposed to that of **Scopus** or **SCI**. There are also other indexes such as SSCI. This allows academic researchers to identify the quality of articles being read, and the demands and rigors that were placed on the researcher during the publication process.
Keypal	Someone who emails another in order to engage in writing practice.
KOTESOL	The Korean Organization of Teachers to Speakers of Other Languages.
L1	First language, or **native language** (**NL**).
L2	Second language.
LAD	Language acquisition device.
Language ego	The identity that a person develops based on the language(s) that they speak.
Language faculty	The capacity to construct a mental grammar as a result of linguistic exposure.
Language family	Languages related through descent from a common parental or ancestral language (the protolanguage of that family).
Language group	Languages within a branch that share descent from a common parental or ancestral language.
Language planning and policy	The **LPP** field is concerned with those policies, explicit, and implicit, that influence what languages are spoken when, how, and by whom, as well as the values and the rights associated with those languages.

Glossary 729

Language transfer	The application of a linguistic feature from one language onto another by a bilingual or multilingual speaker.
Language variety	A general term for a distinct form of a language or linguistic expression, used to cover overlapping subcategories (e.g., dialect, register, jargon, and idiolect). Also called **lect**.
Law of effect	Stimuli that occurs after a behavior has an influence on future behavior (e.g., for example, behavior followed by positive responses is likely to be repeated, while behavior followed by negative responses is likely not to be repeated).
Laws	Explicitly written rules that members of a community must follow, and are often statements that have been formally produced by authorities.
Learner control principle	Students can learn more deeply when they are able to control their pace of movement through segmented content.
Learner management system (LMS)	An online software system to assist in the administration involved with grading learners, and providing them with learning content.
Learner variables	The unique learning needs of each student, or the things that may impinge or lead to their success. They include access to opportunities and mentorship, socioeconomic factors, intelligence, personality, beliefs, and preferences. It is often abbreviated to **LFG**.
Lexical approach	In this approach, emphasis is on the use of lexical units over grammatical structures. Students are taught with set phrases with a

	focus on fixed expressions that occur frequently in a dialogue.
Lexical functional grammar	LFG is a declarative, constraint-based framework for analyzing the various components of grammar, including, crucially, syntax.
LFG	*See* **lexical functional grammar**.
Lingua franca	A language that is used for communication between people who do not share a native language.
Linguistic anthropology	The interdisciplinary study of how language influences social life. Including how language forms social identity and group memberships, shapes communication, organizes large-scale cultural beliefs and ideologies, and how it develops a common cultural representation of the natural and social world, with influences of culture, power, and thought also considered.
Linguistic determinism	Although now considered a false hypothesis by modern linguists, it refers to the concept of language determining thought and linguistic categories determining cognitive categories. This idea was previously referred to as the strong version of the **Sapir-Whorf hypothesis**.
Linguistic imperialism	The imposition of one language on speakers of other languages.
Linguistic relativity	The concept that linguistic categories and usage influence thought and decisions. This idea was previously referred to as the weak version of the **Sapir-Whorf hypothesis**.
LMS	*See* **learner management system**.
LPP	*See* **Language Planning and Policy**.
MALL	Multimedia assisted language learning.

Markedness differential hypothesis	This states that areas of difficulty that a learner will have can be predicated by a systematic comparison of the grammars of the native language (**NL**) and the **target language** (**TL**), and the markedness relations that are stated in universal grammar.
Mental (competence) grammar	The grammar that is stored in the brain, allows a speaker to produce language that other speakers can understand.
Metamotivation	This describes the motivation of people who are able to strive to go beyond the scope of their basic needs in order to reach their full potential. Refer to **self-actualization**.
Michigan corpus of academic spoken English (MICASE)	A list that contains 1,848,364 words using 152 transcripts. It can be browsed by speaker and speech attributes, and searched by words or phrases in specified contexts.
Minimal pairs	Words or phrases in a particular language that differ in only the one phonological element but have distinct meanings.
Mistake	Mistakes, or **slips,** are those things that students can correct themselves, once pointed out to them, but **errors** are not self-correctable and will need an explanation, while **attempts** occur when students make an effort to say something which they do not yet know how to verbalize correctly. Each will require a different approach to correction.
Mistaken goals	This is the misbehavior of those who are striving to belong, and classified in terms of attention seeking, power seeking, revenge seeking, and failure avoidance.
Mixed-methods	This kind of research is an approach whereby an investigator will collect and analyze both

quantitative and qualitative data within the same study.

MKO — *See* **more knowledgeable other**.

Modality principle — Students learn more deeply when graphics are explained by audio narration over text on screen.

Modeling — Saying examples with natural speed, rhythm, and intonation.

Monitoring — Going around among students, assisting, and helping when required.

Monitor hypothesis — The process of using learned knowledge to help correct language production during communication.

More knowledgeable other — Crucial to the provision of **scaffolding** is the more knowledgeable other or the **MKO**. This is someone, or something (e.g., a software system), that literally knows more than the learner about what is being learned. The learner works with the **MKO**, operating in a **ZPD** which enlarges due to the provision of **scaffolding** which results in learner development.

Morphology — The study of the structure and meaning of words.

Multimedia principle — Students learn more deeply from words and pictures rather than just words alone.

Multimodal learning — A style of learning that engages a number of senses to help us better understand and remember more.

Multiple intelligences — This is an approach to teaching that is based on the belief that a learner's intelligence is not simply an **IQ** but that there are different types of intelligences, which some have

Glossary 733

	argued may be best called abilities. The intelligences initially identified are linguistic, visual-spatial, bodily-kinaesthetic, interpersonal, logical-mathematical, musical, intrapersonal, and environmental-naturalist, which have been extended to include spiritual and existential.
Native language	The first language (**L1**) of a speaker, often abbreviated to **NL**.
Natural approach	Teaching according to the natural approach involves focusing on learner communicative abilities, with more concentration on vocabulary than syntactic structures, and provided to the learner by comprehensible input and visual aids to assist in comprehension. The most important aspect of this approach is the use of teacher-delivered **comprehensible input**.
Natural method	*See* **direct method**.
Natural order hypothesis	This hypothesis views that grammatical structures are acquired in a predictable order no matter the language.
NAWL	*See* **new academic word list**.
Needs	Defined under **choice theory** as those that are genetically driven, psychologically driven, and survival driven.
Needs analysis	This involves learners undertaking an activity to inform about what they require from the course or are wanting to learn. This information can be used to better tailor courses to students.
Negative transfer	This refers to the interference of previous knowledge with new learning. See also **positive transfer**.

Negotiation of meaning	A process where interlocutors engage in strategies that clarify, rephrase, or confirm the meaning of what they have heard or read.
Neuroplasticity	*See* **brain plasticity**.
Neural plasticity	*See* **brain plasticity**.
Neutral stimulus	One that produces no specific initial response other than serving as a means of focusing attention. In classical conditioning, if this is paired with an unconditioned stimulus, the neutral stimulus then becomes a conditioned stimulus.
New academic word list	This list consists of 288 million corpora from academic text books, the British Academic Spoken English (BASE) list, the Michigan Corpus of Academic Spoken (MICASE) list as well as academic discourse, academic journals, textbooks, non-fiction works, and student essays. It is commonly referred to as the **NAWL**.
New general service list	This is a list of high frequency words for learners of English containing terms covering 92% of most general texts. It is commonly referred to as the **NGSL**.
New key	*See* **audiolingual method**.
NGSL	*See* **new general Service list**.
NL	*See* **native language**.
Nominating	Designating someone to perform a certain task.
Non-adversarial method	A classroom management method advocating positive rewards for learners exhibiting self-control, and utilizing preferred activity time as a means to leverage improvements in behavior.

Glossary

Noticing	Asking a specific student to answer or to perform or demonstrate a task. **Noticing the gap** allows the learner to internally process language and to restructure their internal representation of L2 rules in order to bring production closer to that of TL native speakers.
Noticing the gap	Allowing the learner to internally process language and to restructure their internal representation of L2 rules in order to bring production closer to that of TL native speakers.
Open-ended drills	Students repeat the modeled language, and complete the sentence that was modeled for them.
Open-pairs	Pairs talking loudly across a classroom.
Operant conditioning	A method of learning that occurs through a process of reward and punishment, resulting in associations being made between particular behaviors and their resulting consequences.
Operant	An operant acts with no observable stimulus, and is governed by the consequences that it produces.
Oral approach	This language-teaching approach is based on a structural view of language. That is, where speech, structures, and a focus on a set of basic vocabulary are seen as the basis of language instruction along with emphasis placed on the presentation of structures in situations. It is also known as **situational language teaching**.
Oral defense	An oral defense or **viva** is an oral examination in which a college or university student defends their thesis in front of a

panel of experts (the defense committee) as part of the process for fulfilling the requirements to obtain their degree.

Output — The corpus of utterances that a learner can actually produce, either orally or in writing.

PAT — Preferred activity time.

PCT — *See* **perceptual control theory**.

Pedagogy — This refers to those theories and principles that apply to young learners and children. See also **andragogy**.

Pedagogical grammar — The kind of grammar that primarily deals with word-level (morphology) and sentence-level (syntax) rules and order to provide descriptions (to foreign language learners) of how to use grammar to communicate.

Peer observation — Observing a colleague teach. Peer observation provides both the observer and the observee with the opportunity to mutually enhance the quality of their teaching practice.

Perceptual control theory — This is designed to assist in making sense of environment in order to construct a satisfying life.

Performance — Putting knowledge into practice (e.g., knowing how to pronounce a word, and demonstrating that the pronunciation is correct).

Performance grammar — The description of syntax as it is used by speakers in dialogues. The focus is on language production in the belief that production problems need to be dealt with prior to those of reception and comprehension.

Personal learning network	This refers to the combination of tools, people, and services that an individual utilizes as resources and approaches to learning (both personally for enrichment and for professional development purposes).
Personalization principle	Students can learn more deeply when words are presented in a conversational over formal style.
Phenomenon based learning	This is a holistic approach to education, and one where students learn through topics and themes as opposed to subject areas. It is a rejection of the **silo-based approach to learning**, which sees subjects taught in isolation from each other.
Phoneme	A perceptually distinct unit of sound in a specific language that distinguishes one word from another (e.g., *p, b, d,* and *t* in words such as *pad, pat, bad,* and *bat*).
Phonemic	The transcription of the sounds of a particular language.
Phonetic	The sounds of a language (e.g., those of all human languages).
Phonology	The study of the sound patterns of language.
Physical wellbeing	Physical wellbeing, refers to the health conditions that stem from work/study, including workloads that lead to exhaustion (**burnout**) or those that allow for a work-life balance.
Pidgin	A grammatically simplified language emerging for use as communication between people not sharing a common language.
Placement test	A test conducted to determine the level of the student so that they can be matched with others of a similar level.

PLN	*See* **personal learning network**.
PNS	Peripheral nervous system.
Portfolio	The portfolio is typically undertaken by those college or university students who do not wish to complete a thesis. It serves as a means for prospective and in-service teachers to showcase their learning, consider their competency as a classroom teacher, and engage in the reflection of their learning and of the coursework that they have competed while undertaking graduate study.
PosEd	*See* **Positive education**.
Positive education	The means by which schools and other educational settings apply the research and practice from positive psychology to their own contexts with the purpose of boosting wellbeing by building positive emotions, engagement, meaning, relationships, accomplishments, and health. Also known as **PosEd**.
Positive transfer	This refers to the positive interference of previous knowledge on new learning. See also **negative transfer**.
Post method era	*See* **eclectic era**.
Post-structuralist theory	This view focuses on discourse, truth, and power, with discourse meaning the way that language is used, truth being shaped by the dominant discourse presented, and power being in the hands of those who shape the truth of discourse and control that discourse.
PPP	*See* **presentation, practice, production**.
PPP(P)	Present, practice, produce, (personalize).
Practicality	Practicality in testing refers to the appropriateness of the applied aspects of an

	exam or quiz. An example is the length of time that a test will take a student to complete, or how long it will take for a teacher to correct.
Practicum	A practicum is a process that a student/practicing teacher will undertake in order to develop and practice the craft of teaching. It provides them with a means to put into practice what they have learned in theory. The goal is to have practicing teachers partner with supervising teachers. The practicum experience typically involves a combination of self-observation, peer observation, and clinical supervision.
Practicing teacher	A practicing, or practice teacher, also known as a student teacher, is a college, university, or graduate student who is teaching under the supervision of a supervisory teacher in order to qualify for a degree.
Pragmatic method	A psychoanalytic method of classroom management that relies on human beings striving to fit in with or belong to a social group. This views misbehavior as a result of the learner breaking rules in order to achieve, maintain, or protect their status within the group.
Pre-training principle	Students can learn more deeply when key concepts (which may include vocabulary) are presented prior to the processes or procedures related to those concepts.
Prescriptive grammar	A set of rules that refer to the structure of a language as people think that it should be used.

Presentation, practice, production	A communicative teaching technique that involves the teacher presenting language points, the teacher and students practicing together, and then the students producing the language points learned on their own. *Also known as* **PPP**.
Problem posing education	This is a method of teaching that emphasizes critical thinking for the purpose of learner liberation. It was proposed as an alternate to the **banking model of education**.
Procedural competence	Knowing how to use technology and the ability to manipulate it in terms of hardware and software.
Procedural memory	This kind of implicit memory is a type of unconscious and long-term memory that aids in the performance of particular types of tasks.
Processability theory	This theory posits that language learners are able to restructure their interlanguage knowledge to be in greater conformity to the language that they are learning.
Progress test	A test given periodically throughout a course to determine if students have learned particular points.
Progressive drilling	A form of drill-based exercise that continues with sentence practice by moving forward. That is, students do not come back to the original sentence but continue from the last.
Promise of multimedia	The promise involves students acquiring knowledge better from messages that consist of words and pictures over words alone, and includes all of the principles given in this glossary, namely those of **coherence**, **contiguity** (spatial-contiguity), **expertise principle**, **image**, **learner control**, **modality**,

multimedia, personalization, pretraining, redundancy, segmenting, signaling, temporal contiguity, and voice.

Psychological wellbeing	The emotions that arise regarding work/study, which might lead to depression or to increased commitment to work/study.
Psychomotor domain	This includes those objectives relating to the development of motor skills, coordination, and physical movement (kinesthetic action).
Psychosocial development theory	This identifies eight stages through which a developing individual should pass (from infancy to late adulthood). In each stage, there is a dilemma that we all face, and must resolve.
Qualitative	This kind of research is a method of scientific inquiry that relies upon non-numerical data, placing the focus on meaning-making. Examples might include diary accounts, ethnography, interview, as well as participant observation.
Quantifiers	Words that are used to indicate how much, or how many, of a thing we are referring to, e.g., a lot of, many.
Quantitative	This kind of research is a method of scientific inquiry that relies upon empirical investigation via computational, mathematical, or statistical techniques. Examples can include test data analysis.
Realia	Any material that is used in the classroom in the same way that it would be used in the 'real world'.
Received pronunciation	Standard British pronunciation, commonly known as BBC English. *See* **RP**.

Redundancy principle	Students can learn more deeply when graphics are explained by audio narration alone, rather than audio narration and on-screen text.
Reed-Kellogg system	A system for diagramming sentences that focuses on the function of words rather than sentence word order.
Reinforcement	A consequence applied that will strengthen an organism's future behavior.
Reliability	Something that is reliable provides a consistent means of producing an outcome (e.g., a test can be graded the same way by all who are tasked to do the grading).
Respondent conditioning	Behavior that is elicited by a preceding stimulus.
Response thinking process	This is a cognitivist method of classroom management stressing learner thought as a means for students to actively ponder their (mis)behavior and to develop a sense of responsibility and respect for their own lives and those around them.
Responsibilities	Things that one is required to do as part of a job, role, or legal obligation.
Rights	Moral or legal entitlements.
Role and reference grammar	A prose-like description of the major grammatical constructions of a language that is illustrated with examples.
RTP	*See* **response thinking process**.
RP	Received pronunciation, otherwise known as standard British pronunciation or BBC English. *See* **Received Pronunciation**.

Safe space	In the classroom, safe spaces are places where children can go to calm down, be alone, and recharge so that they are then ready to learn.
SAMR	A classroom technology framework categorizing four different degrees of technology integration, and standing for substitution, augmentation, modification, redefinition.
Sapir-Whorf hypothesis	A principle suggesting that the structure of a language affects its speakers' cognition or world view, and thus perceptions are relative to the language spoken. There have been distinctions made between a strong version (**linguistic determinism**) and a weak version (**linguistic relativity**).
Scaffolding	This refers to a variety of instructional techniques that are used to move learners progressively toward stronger understanding, and ultimately, greater independence in the learning process.
Schema	The building blocks of knowledge. It refers to a cognitive framework or concepts that help organize and interpret information, and it is primarily used to inform a person about what to expect from a variety of experiences and situations. The plural is schemata, but schemas is also commonly used.
SCI	*See* **science citation index**.
Science citation index	The **science citation index** is a listing of those peer-reviewed journal articles that are indexed at this scholarly level. It is often abbreviated to the acronym **SCI**. There are also other indexes such as SSCI, **Scopus**, and **KCI**. This allows academic researchers to identify the quality of articles being read, and the demands and rigors that were placed on

	the researcher during the publication process.
Scopus	A listing of those peer-reviewed journal articles that are indexed at this scholarly level. It is often considered to be easier to publish at this level as opposed to that of **SCI**. There are also other indexes such as SSCI, and **KCI**. This allows academic researchers to identify the quality of articles being read, and the demands and rigors that were placed on the researcher during the publication process.
Seating chart	A graphical representation of how the chairs in the room will be placed for the lesson.
Seating plan	A graphical representation of where students normally sit during the lesson.
Segmenting principle	Students can learn more deeply when content is broken down into smaller chunks.
Selective cloze	*See* **Gap fill**.
Self-actualization	This is the highest level of psychological development in the **hierarchy of needs**, and it occurs only after basic and mental needs have all been fulfilled. It is where full personal potential is achieved via **metamotivation**.
Self-observation	Observing yourself, or your performance as a teacher, can help you be reflective in terms of evaluating if what you are doing as a teacher is successful.
Semantics	The study of linguistic meaning.
Sensory stimulation theory	Traditional sensory stimulation theory posits that effective learning occurs when the senses

are stimulated – sight, hearing, touch, smell, and taste.

Sentence diagramming A visual mapping process that aims to show the relationships between parts of a sentence using **sentence trees**.

Sentence trees An illustrative example of a sentence that has been visually mapped using **sentence diagramming**.

SFI *See* **standard frequency index**.

SIG A **special interest group** is a community, online or offline, within a larger organization that consists of members who hold a particular interest in advancing a specific area of knowledge, learning or technology.

Signaling principle Students can learn more deeply when presented with auditory, visual, or temporal cues that draw attention to the critical elements of a lesson.

Silent way This language-teaching method is particularly famous for applying the strategic use of Cuisenaire rods and **fidels** for the teaching of language. The underlying premise is that the teacher should remain as silent as possible, limiting **teacher talk time** (TTT), with students encouraged to speak as much as possible. The learning hypotheses behind this method are that learning is facilitated by discovery and the creation of language rather than remembering and repeating things that should be learned; and that learning is facilitated by the use of physical objects and problem-solving approaches that focus on the content that needs to be understood.

SILL	Strategy inventory for language learning.
Silo-based approach to learning	Subjects are taught in isolation from one another, as opposed to the **phenomenon based learning** approach where students learn through topics and themes integrated from among a variety of subject areas.
Situated learning	Where learning is contextualized and individualized to a class as a community of practice that shares mutual engagement, joint enterprise, and a shared repertoire. It takes as a focus the relationship between learning and the social situation in which it occurs.
Situational language teaching	This language-teaching approach is based on a structural view of language. That is, where speech, structures, and a focus on a set of basic vocabulary are seen as the basis of language instruction along with emphasis placed on the presentation of structures in situations. It is also known as the **oral approach**.
SLA	Second language acquisition.
Slip	*See* **mistake**.
Social wellbeing	The levels of collaboration and support from peers, and which impact levels of performance and satisfaction.
Socio-constructivist approach	Social interaction assists learning progress through social interaction (group work where students learn from each other and support each other's learning).
Sociocultural linguistics	The broad range of theories and methods that focus on the study of language from a sociocultural context.
Sociocultural theory of cognitive development	Central to this is the notion that learner development, particularly of children, is

	advanced through social interaction, particularly with others who are more skilled.
Socio-digital competence	Understanding what is appropriate in different social contexts and knowledge domains in terms of both technology and language.
Sociolinguistic competence	Sociolinguistic competence. The ability to produce sociolinguistically appropriate utterances. Along with other competencies (**grammatical**, **discourse**, and **strategic**) it comprises part of **communicative competence**.
Sociolinguistics	The study of language in relation to social factors, including those of regional, class, and occupational dialect, gender differences, and bilingualism.
SPEAK	Speaking Proficiency English Assessment Kit.
Special interest group	A **SIG** refers to a community, online or offline, within a larger organization that consists of members who hold a particular interest in advancing a specific area of knowledge, learning or technology.
Speech community	A group of people who share a common language or dialect.
Spin-off	The effect of a test. E.g., *positive spin-off* could see the test being useful in remedial teaching and review, while *negative spin-off* could see it demotivate learners if they achieve a low score or they find the test too difficult to complete.
Spiral curriculum	An approach to education that involves regularly revisiting topics throughout a course and the academic career of a student, providing deeper learning on each revisit.

Stabilization	This refers to linguistic features that have become a permanent part of the way that a person speaks or writes a new language, especially when not learned as a young child. Also known as interlanguage **fossilization**.
Staff wellbeing	Although **teacher wellbeing** and **staff wellbeing** may be used interchangeably, staff wellbeing in terms of employee wellbeing refers to such considerations as the way employees' duties, expectations, stress levels, workplace environment, and workload affect their overall health, happiness, and commitment to an organization.
Stages of cognitive development	These involve sensorimotor, preoperational, concrete operational, and the formal operational stages.
Standard frequency index (SFI)	A convenient way to consider word frequency where an SFI of 90 could mean that a word can be expected to occur around once every 10 tokens; an SFI of 80 every 100 tokens; an SFI of 70 every 1,000; an SFI of 60 every 10,000; and so on.
State anxiety	Anxiety that is experienced due to being put into a particular situation, as opposed to **trait anxiety** (a predisposition to being anxious).
STEM	The Society of Teaching English through Media.
Strand curriculum	An approach to education that provides work on a given topic over a sustained and extended period of time.
Strategic competence	The ability to solve communication problems as they arise. Along with other competencies (grammatical, sociolinguistic, and discoursal), it comprises part of

Glossary 749

	communicative competence. In **constructivism**, it is the ability to repair problems and work around the gaps in technological knowledge and skills, and it refers to the ability to think of alternate routes or options (e.g., send an email if you are unable to contact a person by voice-call).
STT	*See* **student talk time**.
Structural approach	When a structural approach is taken to the teaching and learning of a language, learners are required to master sentence patterns. It includes the use of various modes in which clauses, phrases, or words may be used, and it assumes that learning is best done through a scientific selection and grading of the structures or patterns of sentences and vocabulary.
Structure of observed learning outcomes (SOLO) taxonomy	This model describes levels of increasing complexity in learner's understanding of subjects. Understanding is conceived as an increase in the number and complexity of connections that a learner makes as they progress from being incompetent to becoming an expert.
Student agency	Learning through activities that are relevant and meaningful to learners, driven by their interests, and often self-initiated with teacher guidance, giving them **voice** and choice in how they learn.
Student leader	Any student who takes on responsibility, particularly for spreading knowledge through inspiration, tutoring, and by applying for and being designated to undertake certain leadership roles.
Student leadership	Where a **student leader** takes on an active role in their education and in that of the

wider improvement of the classroom, school, school system, and community. It aims to develop positive skills in the process, to promote the opportunity for voice and agency in learning, and to allow meaningful positive changes to occur in the educational environment. At its core is the concept that leadership is inherent within all.

Student talk time STT is the time that a student spends talking during a lesson, and it can be compared to **teacher-talk-time** (**TTT**).

Student teacher A student teacher, practicing, or practice teacher is a college, university or graduate student who is teaching under the supervision of a supervisory teacher in order to qualify for a degree.

Student wellbeing The sustainable state of a positive mood and attitude, resilience, and satisfaction with self, relationships, and experiences at school.

Style shifting See **code switching**.

Substitution drilling Using flash cards or realia as stimuli to change sentence patterns as they are being practiced, perhaps as part of **choral drilling** or checking.

Subsumption learning This is concerned with how individuals learn large amounts of meaningful content from verbal/textual presentations in school contexts. It is based on the use of expository learning, or reception learning, which is an organized teaching method where information is presented in a specific order to focus attention and promote memorization (e.g., through the use of advanced organizers).

Suggestopedia Formed from 'suggestion' and 'pedagogy', the main idea of this language-teaching

Glossary 751

	approach is to accelerate learning through the use of desuggestion to psychological barriers along with positive suggestion. Music and rhythm are key elements of the approach. It is also known as **desuggestopedia**.
Supervisory teacher	A teacher who provides you with mentorship, feedback, observation, and guidance during peer and clinical observations, typically as part of a practicum experience.
Synonym	A word or phrase that has the same or nearly the same meaning as another word or phrase in the same language.
Syntax	The study of sentence structure.
Tabula rasa	Blank slate. This is a theory that was proposed by Locke which states that a human mind is born without rules for processing data, and that data is added and rules for processing are developed as a result of sensory experiences.
Target language	The language that a person wishes to learn.
Task-based Instruction	*See* **task-based language instruction**.
Task-based instruction *or* **Task-based language teaching**	Also known as task-based instruction (**TBI**), task-based language teaching (**TBLT**) revolves around the use of authentic language to undertake meaningful tasks such as seeing a doctor, conducting an interview, or calling a customer service center. The approach draws on a number of principles that also formed the **communicative language teaching** approach, such as those that view real communication as essential to language learning, that use of language that

	is meaningful promotes learning, and that language meaningful to learners supports the learning process.
Taxonomy	A scheme of classification.
TBI	*See* **task-based language instruction**.
TBLL	Task-based language learning.
TBLT	*See* **task-based language instruction**.
Teacher leader	Teachers who have taken on additional roles as facilitators within the school, and are important in the spread and strengthening of school reform and improvements. The process aims to promote the opportunity for voice and shared leadership.
Teacher leadership	This is where **teacher leaders** take on an active role in order to shape the culture of their teaching context. This is typically achieved by influencing peers, principals, and other members of the school community, with an aim to increase student learning and achievement through individual, collaborative/team, and organizational development.
Teacher talk time	**TTT** is the time that a teacher spends talking during a lesson, and it can be compared to **student talk time**.
Teacher wellbeing	When a teacher is flourishing in the workplace as an individual, and in their relationships with others, by maintaining a sense of balance between their emotional, physical, spiritual, and social needs.
TEFL	Teaching English as a foreign language.
Temporal contiguity principle	Students learn more deeply when words and images that support one another are presented simultaneously over sequentially.

TESOL	Teaching English to speakers of other languages.
T(G)G	*See* **transformational grammar**.
Thesis	A long, structured essay involving personal research that is written by a candidate for a college or university degree, typically a master's degree with a dissertation written for a doctoral degree.
Thesis advisor	This is the person who supervises the progress of a college or university student who is undertaking thesis research.
Thesis proposal	A thesis proposal is a document that a college or university student prepares which outlines their proposed thesis topic. It typically defines the research agenda and topic under investigation, detailing why the topic warrants research and how the student will undertake it.
Time on task	**TOT** is the time that learners spend with a particular activity.
TL	*See* **target language**.
TOEFL	Test of English as a foreign language.
TOEIC	Test of English for international communication.
TOEIC service list	A corpus of 1.5 million words derived from TOEIC textbooks, practice tests, and a range of other sources. It is often abbreviated to **TSL**.
Token economy	An approach to classroom management which relies upon reward and punishment to produce positive behavior. It utilizes a system of classroom currency where those who do the right thing are awarded points or

	tokens, while those who do not might be required to forfeit or rescind them. It is based on the principles of operant conditioning and behavioral economics, with tokens used as reinforcers, along with back-up reinforcers (what the token may be exchanged for) in order to encourage specific target behavior.
Toneme	A phoneme that is distinguished from another only by its tone.
TOT	*See* **time on task**.
Total physical response	TPR is a method to learn languages through physical (motor) activity.
TPR	*See* **total physical response**.
Traditional grammar	This is the type of grammar that is typically taught in schools. The basis of this grammar relies on imparting the prescriptive rules and concepts concerning the structure of language.
Trait anxiety	A predisposition to being anxious, as opposed to **state anxiety**.
Transformation task	Tasks that have students engage in changing the form of words and phrases.
Transformational grammar *or* **Transformational-generative grammar**	T(G)G is a part of a theory of generative grammar, especially of natural languages, where grammar is considered to be a system of rules that generate all of the combinations of words that form grammatical sentences in any given language, and involve the use of defined operations (transformations) to produce novel sentences from existing ones.
Transformative learning theory	This theory explains how humans revise and reinterpret meaning, while moving learners to a more inclusive, discriminating, self-

reflective, and integrative experience of learning.

True-false drills	Students repeat the modeled language, changing it to be true or false about themselves.
TSL	See **TOEIC service list**.
TTT	See **teacher talk time (TTT)**.
Twenty-first century core skills	This refers to the sixteen core skills that are required of twenty-first century learners, and may also include the eight key skills required for lifelong learning, the four digital competency proficiencies, and the need to develop **personal learning networks (PLN)** that include a **community of practice (COP)**.
Type	This refers to the number of distinct words in a text or corpus. For example, the sentence *I am bored in the house, and in the house bored* contains twelve tokens (twelve individual words) and seven types of token (seven words that are not repeated).
Unconditional positive regard	A humanist approach to classroom management involving basic acceptance and support of a learner regardless of what they say and do, believing them to be inherently good, and encouraging them to do good things.
Unconditioned Response	An unlearned response that occurs naturally.
UG	See **Universal grammar**.
Unvoiced sounds	See **voiceless sounds**.

Universal grammar	Proposed by Chomsky, Universal Grammar (also known as **UG**), refers to the genetic component of the language faculty.
Utterance	Spoken phrases, i.e., a word or group of words that a speaker has said before another speaker speaks.
Validity	A valid item, test, and whatever else, is one that does what it says that it will do.
VARK	A visual, auditory, reading and writing, and kinesthetic method of multimodal learning.
Verbatim memory	Memory for surface form, and it is typically detailed.
Viva	*See* **oral defense**.
Voice	The beliefs, opinions, perspectives, values, and cultural backgrounds of the people in a district, school, or school community, especially students, teachers, parents, and local citizens, and it includes how this is considered, included, listened to, and acted upon when critical decisions are being made in a district or school.
Voiced sounds	Vowels and those consonants that are sounded when air from the lungs pass through nearly closed vocal chords causing their vibration.
Voiceless sounds	The sounds that are produced without the vocal chords vibrating, so there is no vibration in the throat. Also referred to as **unvoiced sounds**.
Voice principle	Students learn more deeply when they are presented with learning content that is presented in a more human sounding voice than a non-human mechanical one.

Washback	*See* **backwash effect**.
Wernicke's aphasia	Damage to **Wernicke's area** may result in a condition where a person is able to make speech sounds but loses the ability to understand or express speech, and/or the ability to read and write.
Wernicke's area	Located in the temporal lobe of the brain, it is important for language development and for the comprehension of speech. It is linked to **Broca's area** by the **arcuate fasciculus**.
Word family	A group of words that share a common feature or pattern, e.g., words that share the same sound or letter combination such as *write*, *rewrite*, and *writ*.
World English	The use of the English language as a lingua franca in business, diplomacy, trade, and other spheres of global activity.
World Englishes	The different varieties of English and English-based creoles developed in different regions of the world.
Work product	A work product, in terms of a portfolio item, might include any material that a college or university student has developed during their course of study, and can range from a conference, class, symposium, or workshop presentation using PowerPoint, a literature review, an annotated bibliography, a research project, or a pedagogy project/lesson plan.
WTC	Willingness to communicate.
Zone of proximal development	The **ZPD** is a figurative distance between an existing developmental state and the potential where a learner who is not yet capable of independent functioning can

758 *Issues in TESOL*

achieve the desired outcome with relevant **scaffold**ed help from a more knowledgeable learner.

ZPD *See* **zone of proximal development**.

Useful Resources

As sites continuously go down, merge, and emerge, perhaps only a small selection of all appropriate resource content should be presented here. An attempt at keeping the number of resources to a select few for each type also provides a sample that is both comprehensive and extensive, but not overwhelming. Like any other instructor resource list, individuals will be able to add to the content as they find material that is useful, and over time, curate a vast resource library tailored to their individual teaching and learning context. Teachers who wish to record any additional resources that they come across might like to use the notes section that follows this chapter for that purpose.

The following content is covered:

- Associations
- Audio creation/editing
- Blogs
- Chatbots
- Citations
- Classroom management
- Comic strip generators
- Copyright
- Data-driven learning
- Dictation
- Dictionaries and Thesauri
- Digital assistants
- Digital story creation
- Flashcards
- Games
- Grammar
- Image editing
- image resources
- Interactive whiteboards
- IPA
- Journals
- Kids
- Lesson plans
- Listening
- Media timelines
- Music resources
- News
- Online short course providers
- Online teaching tools
- Plagiarism
- Podcasting
- Podcatchers
- Portfolio development
- Praxis tests
- Presentations
- Professional development resources
- Pronunciation
- Quizzes
- Reading
- Rubrics
- Screencasting
- Scripts
- Sentence diagramming
- Songs

- Speaking
- Storyboarding and scripting
- Story creation
- Stories
- Student response systems
- Testing
- Translation
- Vocabulary
- Video content
- Video editing
- Webquests
- Wikis
- Word lists
- Word webs
- Worksheets
- Writing

Associations

ACTA (https://tesol.org.au) is the Australian Council for TESOL Associations.

ALTA (http://altaonweb.org) is the African Language Teachers Association.

AsiaTEFL (http://www.asiatefl.org) is the Asian Association of Teachers of English as a Foreign Language.

EUROCALL (http://www.eurocall-languages.org) is the European Association for Computer-Assisted Language Learning.

TESOL International (https://www.tesol.org) is the Teaching of English to Speakers of Other Languages Association that is based in the United States of America.

IATEFL (https://www.iatefl.org) is the International Association for the Teaching of English as a Foreign Language, and it is based in the United Kingdom.

JALT (https://jalt.org) is the Japanese Association of Language Teachers.

KOTESOL (https://koreatesol.org) is the Korea Association for the Teachers of English to Speakers of Other Languages.

SinoTESOL (http://www.sinotesol.com) is the Chinese Organization of Teachers of English to Speakers of Other Languages.

ThaiTESOL (https://www.thailandtesol.org) is the Thailand Association of Teachers of English to Speakers of Other Languages.

Audio Creation/Editing

Audacity (https://www.audacityteam.org) is an open source digital editing program available for Mac and PC which you can use to record, edit, and mix narration and music.

Pocket WavePad (https://www.nch.com.au/wavepad/pocket.html) records, edits, and adds effects to audio for Mac.

GoldWave (https://www.goldwave.com) is a digital audio editor that provides simple recording as well as more sophisticated processing, restoration, enhancement, and conversion for Windows and Linux. A free version is available for evaluation purposes, after which a lifetime license can be purchased.

Twistedwave (https://twistedwave.com) is a browser-based audio editor that can record or edit any audio file.

Blogs

Blogger (https://www.blogger.com) will host your blog for free, and aside from being very easy to use, it allows some level of privacy so that it can be suitable for use as a class blogging site. From a single account, you can create as many blogs as you wish and determine who is allowed to comment on the content.

Edublogs (https://www.edublogs.org) allows teachers to create and manage their own and students' websites. There is room for customization of design and the ability to add various media to this private and secure platform.

Kidblog (http://www.kidblog.org) is an easy-to-use, safe, and secure publishing platform that is designed for students of all grades. There are a number of excellent features including privacy and password protection, and there is no need for student personal information to be collected, nor is there any advertising. It is free for up to fifty students per class.

WordPress (https://wordpress.com) is one of the most popular blogging and website platforms in use today as it is open-source and is easily customizable. The downloadable software for self-hosting purposes is much more flexible than that available on the blogging platform.

Twitter (https://twitter.com) deserves a mention here as it is useful for microblogging (posting short frequent updates). It allows users to post and read short 140-character posts called 'tweets'.

Tumblr (https://www.tumblr.com) is a blogging platform open to those over thirteen years of age, with most users using pen names over their real names when blogging. Users can post on their blog, follow others, and search posts. It is unique in that posts are divided into media types: text, photo, quote, link, chat, audio, and video.

Chatbots

A.L.I.C.E (https://www.pandorabots.com/pandora/talk?botid=b8d616e35e36e881) is the Artificial Linguistic Internet Computer Entity. It is a natural language processing chatbot which relies upon heuristic pattern matching rules when receiving human input.

Chatbots.org (https://chatbots.org) is a website dedicated to providing a listing of available chatbots, virtual agents, virtual assistants, conversation agents, and so on. Detailed information and a link to each are provided.

Mitsuki (https://www.pandorabots.com/mitsuku) is a chatbot that simulates an 18-year-old female, and is considered to be the most human-like AI. It has won the Loebner Prize Turing Test multiple times.

Replika (https://replika.ai) is a chatbot that serves as a personal friend, and one that you can have conversations with regarding daily life (and its ups and downs).

Wysa (https://www.wysa.io) is a chatbot designed to help people deal with mental health issues, including anxiety, stress, and depression.

Citations

Cite this for me (https://www.citethisforme.com) is a citation tool that can help you create a bibliography using the citation style of your choice.

EndNote (https://endnote.com) is a tool that is useful for managing and publishing bibliographies, citations, and references.

Refworks (https://www.refworks.com/refworks2) is a useful tool for managing and organizing bibliographies.

Mendeley (https://www.mendeley.com) is a good tool for reference management and for collaborating and sharing work.

Zotero (https://www.zotero.org) is a good tool for the management and organization of different resources and for the sharing of research.

Classroom Management

Class123 (https://class123.ac) is a behavior management tool for classes that allows teachers to make report cards and to keep track of student behaviour, and it includes additional tools like a chalkboard and timer.

ClassDojo (https://www.classdojo.com) is a classroom management and behaviour tracking app that can track rewards and demerits and allows any teacher with the app to award them to students. It also contains various management tools (e.g., timers), and allows for the uploading of student work for collation as a portfolio and for parents to see.

Comic Strip Generators

Comic Creator (http://www.readwritethink.org/parent-afterschool-resources/games-tools/comic-creator-a-30237.html) is a basic template-driven comic creator for use on a Windows computer.

Pixton (https://www.pixton.com) is an easy-to-use comprehensive online comic creator that supports narration, and offers a range of signup options from a free fun option to paid educator/business accounts.

MakeBeliefsComix (https://www.makebeliefscomix.com) is a basic comic creator that uses black and white images over a four-panel comic strip. An iOS version is also available.

Toonlet (https://download.cnet.com/developer/toonlet/i-6305727) allows for anyone to create their own cartoon characters and web comics.

ToonTastic (https://toontastic.withgoogle.com) is a wizard-based animated comic or cartoon creator for iPhones.

Copyright

Fair Use Evaluator (https://librarycopyright.net/resources/fairuse/index.php) is a website that will help you to understand the concept of 'fair use', and to also help you collect, organize, and archive any information you may require to support a fair use claim.

Data-Driven Learning

ANtWordProfiler (http://www.laurenceanthony.net/software/antwordprofiler) is a freeware tool that can be used to profile the vocabulary level and complexity level of texts. It can be downloaded for use on a Linux, MacOS, or Windows-based operating system.

Compleat Lexical Tutor (https://www.lextutor.ca) provides a range of tools that allow for the analysis of text so that you can develop data-driven learning content that can then be used with your students. Tools include vocabulary profiling, concordance, and so on.

English Corpora (https://www.english-corpora.org) provides links to widely-used online English language corpora.

Rewordify (https://rewordify.com) will reword any text that you provide into a simpler format that makes it easier for students to read. It identifies the language that it has reworded so that students and teachers know what has been changed. It also offers the ability to create quizzes from the content that you provide, including matching and cloze exercise types.

Word Families (https://www.enchantedlearning.com/rhymes/word families) is a useful resource that provides ready-to-print word wheels and word-family minibooks to use with learners.

Data Repositories

Figshare (https://figshare.com) is a free knowledge repository where users can make all research output available in a citable, shareable and discoverable manner.

Mendeley Data (https://data.mendeley.com) Allows researchers to upload their data, store it, share it with select users, make it publicly available and citable, as well as publish it.

Dictation

Dictation.io (https://dication.io) uses Chrome to provide speech recognition for dictation. It helps you to write emails, documents, and essays using only your voice.

Dictionaries and Thesauri

Acronym Finder (https://www.acronymfinder.com) is the world's largest and most comprehensive dictionary of acronyms, abbreviations, and initialisms.

Acronym Guide (https://acronym-guide.com) is a directory of common acronyms and abbreviations by topic.

American Heritage Dictionary (https://www.ahdictionary.com) includes definitions, pronunciations, etymologies, and feature notes.

Australian Slang Dictionary (http://www.koalanet.com.au/ australian-slang.html) provides definitions for those uniquely Australian words. Of note, it includes American and British slang that may also be of use in the Australian vernacular.

BeeDictionary (https://www.beedictionary.com/) gives definitions, audio, and IPA with spelled phonetics, usages, and personalization features.

Cambridge Dictionaries Online (https://dictionary.cambridge.org/) has corpus-informed dictionaries for English language learners of all levels and for those who are facing the Cambridge and IELTS exams. They also offer particular kinds of targeted dictionaries including those for business English, essential English, general learners, advanced learners, and those looking for academic content.

Chat Slang Dictionary (https://apps.apple.com/us/app/chat-slang-dictionary/id410672593) is a smartphone application that covers the meaning of the slang used in chat and the meaning of various emoticons.

CMU Pronouncing Dictionary (http://www.speech.cs.cmu.edu/cgi-bin/cmudict) is the Carnegie Melon University pronouncing dictionary which is a machine-readable pronunciation dictionary for North American English. It is useful for speech recognition and synthesis.

Internet Picture Dictionary (http://www.pdictionary.com) is an online multilingual picture dictionary designed particularly for learners of English and those beginning other languages.

Phrase Finder (http://www.phrasefinder.co.uk) searches for phrases rather than single words, and presents lists of phrases and sayings related to the topic or search term.

Rhyme Zone (https://www.rhymezone.com) allows users to search for words and find rhymes, synonyms, antonyms, homophones, for their search term.

SlangIt (https://slangit.com) is a slang dictionary that also provides acronyms, abbreviations, and emoticons.

Thesaurus (https://www.thesaurus.com) allows users to search for the synonym or the antonym of words. The site also provides a word of the day, word games, and other useful tools for learners of English.

Thinkmap visual thesaurus (https://www.visualthesaurus.com) is an interactive online tool that creates word maps complete with meanings and related words.

Tip of My Tongue (http://chir.ag/projects/tip-of-my-tongue) allows users to provide parts of the word, the meaning, or scrambled letters in order to perform their searches.

Urban Dictionary (https://www.urbandictionary.com) is written by users of the platform who provide definitions for new or uncommon slang terms. It is to be considered a 'not safe for work' product, and nor is it suitable for young learners.

Vidtionary (http://www.vidtionary.com) is a video dictionary that defines and expresses words through imagery.

Visual Dictionary Online (http://www.visualdictionaryonline.com/index.php) is designed to help people find words at a glance. It uses illustrations and labels and it is useful for learners when they know what *something* looks like but not what it is called in a foreign language. It is also useful for those who know the words but may not be able to picture the visual.

Visuwords (https://visuwords.com) is a visual dictionary, thesaurus, and an interactive lexicon search engine and display.

WordHippo (https://www.wordhippo.com) is a thesaurus and word tool that provides antonyms, definitions, rhymes, sentences, translations, and pronunciations.

Word Reference (https://www.wordreference.com) is a bilingual dictionary from English to many other languages.

Wordnik (https://www.wordnik.com) provides definitions from multiple sources.

Wordsmyth Premier Dictionary-Thesaurus (https://www.word smyth.net) is suitable for the beginner-, intermediate-, or advanced-level student.

Wordsmyth Illustrated Learner's Dictionary (WILD) (http://kids.wordsmyth.net/wild) provides a visual environment for promoting literacy among grades K-3.

Digital Assistants

Alexa (https://www.alexa.com) was developed by Amazon with an initial release in November of 2014. Alexa can be found in devices such as the Amazon range of smart speakers. The wake-word can be set by the user, with the default being *Alexa*. The assistant is also an application for smartphones and tablets.

Cortana (https://www.microsoft.com/en-us/cortana) was developed by Microsoft with an initial release in April of 2014. Cortana is the virtual assistant for Windows 10 and other related Microsoft products (including smartphones, tablets, Xbox, band fitness tracker, surface headphones, and Windows mixed reality). It also runs on the Invoke smart speaker, Android, and iOS. If always-listening mode has been selected in Windows 10, then the wake-phrase 'Hey, Cortana' can be used to activate the assistant.

Google Assistant (https://assistant.google.com) was developed by Google with an initial release in May of 2016. It is primarily accessible on mobile and smart home devices as well as Google smartphones and Android devices including Wear OS. It is also available as a stand-alone application for iOS, and it is integrated within Android Auto. The wake-phrases for the assistant include 'Hey, Google', and 'OK, Google'.

Siri (https://www.apple.com/siri) was developed by Apple Inc. with a release in October of 2011. Siri is the virtual assistant that became part of iOS, watchOS, MacOs, the HomePod and the tvOS operating systems. As an application, it was initially released in February of 2010 for iOS. It can also be accessed through the latest version of the MacOS and Apple CarPlay. The wake-phrase for this assistant is 'Hey, Siri.'

Digital Story Creation

Meograph (https://www.meograph.com) is a digital storytelling tool that relies on Google Earth to create map-based and timeline-based narrated stories.

WeVideo (https://www.wevideo.com) is a video editor that can mix images, text, video, and audio.

VSDC (http://www.videosoftdev.com) is a video editor that also offers screen recording and video capture capabilities.

Flashcards

Memrise (https://www.memrise.com) is a language learning platform that uses personalized flashcards in a spaced-repetition manner in order to increase the rate of learning. Users are able to create, upload, and share content with others.

Quizlet (https://quizlet.com) uses learning tools, flashcards, and games to help users to study. Users are able to create, upload, and share content with others.

Tinycards (https://tinycards.duolingo.com) uses a game-based technique along with personalized flashcards to promote learning of languages. Users are able to create, upload, and share content with others.

Games

Education.com (https://www.education.com/games/grammar) provide a range of interactive online grammar games by grade.

ESL Games World (https://www.eslgamesworld.com) contains interactive online and PowerPoint-based games, as well as a range of game-based printable worksheets.

Flippity (https://www.flippity.net) is a free website that allows you to develop online interactive games using data from Google sheets. Those available include word search, crosswords, word scramble, bingo, hangman, matching, quiz show, flashcard, and spelling games.

LearnEnglish Kids (https://learnenglishkids.britishcouncil.org/grammar-practice) provides a number of grammar games that are fun for all levels of learners, although they are targeted at young learners. The grammar rules that are presented align with online games. Handouts for the topic, the answers, and a practice test of the grammar rules are all provided.

Grammar

Grammar Girl's Quick and Dirty Tips for Better Writing (https://www.quickanddirtytips.com/grammar-girl) is run across various social media platforms. These include a YouTube channel, webpage, podcast, and a Facebook page that all offer quick and dirty writing, vocabulary, and language tips.

Grammarly (https://app.grammarly.com) is a free writing app that analyzes the text that you have written and provides feedback for clarity. It also offers a plagiarism checking service for a fee.

Linguapress (https://linguapress.com) offers free grammar online as well as printable resources for teachers and students, including readings and games. There is also an area for teachers who need a grammar refresh to brush up on their skills.

Image Editing

Phixr (http://www.phixr.com) is an online photo editor with various filters and effects, and it can connect to various social media sites.

FotoFlexer (https://fotoflexer.com) is an online image editor offering a number of effects, distortions, and other features.

Image Resources

Cagle Cartoons (http://caglecartoons.com) provides access to a number of political cartoons from around the world. The images are organized by topic with artists categorized by country.

Flickr Creative Commons (https://www.flickr.com/creativecommons) provides images that can be used for almost any educational project as long as proper citation is followed.

Morguefile (https://morguefile.com) provides a range of images that are copyright-free, and are available for use with few or no restrictions.

Pics4Learning (http://pics4learning.com) is a website that provides safe and free images for educational uses. Images here are copyright-friendly and can be used for classrooms, multimedia projects, websites, videos, portfolios, and other projects.

PicSearch (https://www.picsearch.com) allows you to search the internet for images, but be aware that the image may not be copyright-free, or that it may require permission to be used in projects or in any other educational contexts.

The Library of Congress Prints & Photographs Online Catalog (http://www.loc.gov/pictures) makes an attempt to ensure that as many of their images as possible are available online in a digital format.

Wikimedia (https://www.wikimedia.org) serves as a point from where all the images and video posted in Wikipedia can be viewed. Most of the images found here are either copyright-free or free for use with minimal restrictions.

Interactive Whiteboards

ExplainEverything (https://explaineverything.com) allows users to share their content by using an interactive screencasting whiteboard.

Miro: The Collaborative Whiteboard (https://miro.com) is a whiteboard in a browser that allows for collaboration among a number of users.

Twiddla (https://www.twiddla.com) is a web-based meeting environment that allows users to mark up photos, graphics, and websites, or to just start out with a blank canvas.

Web Whiteboard (https://www.webwhiteboard.com) is a simple way to draw and write together online by creating an online whiteboard with a click, and sharing it live or by sending the link to others.

IPA

Interactive IPA Chart (https://www.ipachart.com) provides a clickable website that pronounces the sounds using a vowel chart which indicates mouth positions along with consonant tables.

International Phonetic Association (https://www.internationalphoneticassociation.org) is the oldest representative organization for phoneticians. A number of resources are available from the website, including IPA charts under a creative commons license.

IPA Character Picker (https://r12a.github.io/pickers/ipa) is a website that allows you to click on characters to build words that are then provided in a unicode font for cut and paste into other applications or documents.

IPA Chart with Sounds (https://www.internationalphoneticalphabet.org/ipa-sounds/ipa-chart-with-sounds) lets you listen to each sound as you click on the phonetic symbols.

IPA Phonetics App (https://apps.apple.com/us/app/ipa-phonetics/id869642260?ls=1) for iPhone is a unique and intuitive touch interface for exploring the International Phonetic Alphabet (IPA), along with a number of voice qualities and articulations.

Pronunroid – IPA Pronunciation (https://play.google.com/store/apps/details?id=com.hoardingsinc.pronunroid&hl=en) is an android game-based app to help learners practice IPA transcription.

Seeing Speech Project (https://www.seeingspeech.ac.uk/about-the-project), undertaken by Scottish universities, contains a corpus of phonetic information from across the United Kingdom, Canada, and New Zealand. It provides the sounds along with corresponding ultrasound images of how the tongue moves in the speaker's mouth when producing that sound.

SIL – Sil Language Technology (https://software.sil.org) provides free IPA fonts. A number of other apps and programs are available including from those that perform linguistic analysis to those that can process ancient texts, and those that can assist in language development and translation tasks.

To.Phonetics (https://tophonetics.com) transcribes any word or phrase into the phonemics of American or British English with a variety of computerized voices available to render the pronunciation.

Journals

Computer Assisted Language Learning Journal (https://www.tandfonline.com/loi/ncal20) is SCI indexed and published by Taylor & Francis.

Journal of Education and E-Learning Research (https://www.asianonlinejournals.com/index.php/JEELR) is Scopus indexed and published by the Asian Online Journal Publishing Group (AOJPG).

Korean Citation Index (https://www.kci.go.kr/kciportal/main.kci) maintains a list of Korean peer-reviewed and KCI listed titles.

Language Learning and Technology (https://www.lltjournal.org) is SCI indexed, and published out of the University of Hawaii.

Scopus (https://www.scopus.com) maintains a list of peer-reviewed journal titles indexed in Scopus.

The Asian EFL Journal (https://www.asian-efl-journal.com) is SCI indexed and published by E.L.E.

The Journal of AsiaTEFL (http://journal.asiatefl.org) is Scopus indexed and published by the Asian Association of Teachers of English as a Foreign Language.

The Journal of Teaching English with Technology (https://www.tewtjournal.org) is Scopus indexed and published by the IATEFL Poland computer special interest group and the University of Nicosia.

The RELC Journal (https://journals.sagepub.com/home/rel) is Scopus indexed, and out of the Regional Language Center of the Southeast Asian Ministers of Education Organization.

TESOL Quarterly (https://onlinelibrary.wiley.com/journal/15457249) is SCI indexed and published by Wiley-Blackwell on behalf of the TESOL International Association.

Web of Science Master Journal List (https://mjl.clarivate.com/home) this list maintains SCI indexed journals.

Kids

English 4 Kids (http://www.english-4kids.com) provides a range of free teaching materials, such as worksheets, for use in EFL and ESL classes.

Lesson Plans

Breaking News English (https://breakingnewsenglish.com) offers a range of news articles broken down by levels, and it comes with a complete lesson plan for implementation.

Busy teacher (https://busyteacher.org) provides over 17,000 printable worksheets and lesson plans.

ESL Brains (https://eslbrains.com) publishes a variety of worksheets based around various videos, including those of TED talks. Lesson plans based on topic and level are also searchable.

Esllibrary.com (https://esllibrary.com) offers a range of lesson plans for EFL/ESL teachers to either use as is, or with some modification to suit their learners and teaching context.

ICALTEFL Lesson Plans & Activities (https://www.icaltefl.com/category/lesson-plans-activities) website offers a range of ideas, activities, and lesson plans that a teacher might choose to use with their learners.

One Stop English (http://www.onestopenglish.com) offers a range of materials for use with business and ESP classes for exams, for grammar, and a range of language skills, as well as for various ages. There is also a section on teacher resources and professional development.

Listening

English Listening Learning Library Online (ELLLO) (http://www.elllo.org) is a wonderful resource site that contains hundreds of recorded discussions in a variety of accents.

Randall's Cyber Listening Lab (https://www.esl-lab.com) provides graded online listening comprehension quizzes and activities for learners.

Media Timelines

Capzles (http://www.capzles.com) allows users to create rich multimedia experiences from videos, photos, music, blogs, and documents by integrating these into a timeline of sequential events, and then share them on various social media platforms.

Timeline (http://www.readwritethink.org/classroom-resources/student-interactives/timeline-30007.html) allows students of all ages to easily create a graphical representation of related items or events in sequential order and display them along a line using various images and text.

Preceden Timelines & Roadmaps (https://www.preceden.com) is a web-based timeline project creator that allows zooming and panning across timelines. Users are able to set the size of events as they relate to importance.

Tiki-Toki (https://www.tiki-toki.com) is a web-based timeline editor that allows viewing of timelines in 3D, and it allows for the integration of images and videos.

WhenInTime (http://ww7.whenintime.com) is a web application for creating and sharing media-based timelines.

Music Resources

300 Monks (https://www.300monks.com) provides a comprehensive source of royalty free music.

ccMixter (http://ccmixter.org) is a free music site that is community-based and promotes a remix culture. *A cappella* and remix tracks licensed under Creative Commons are available for download and use in creative works.

FMA (Free Music Archive) (https://freemusicarchive.org) provides access to a range of free music that is based on a wide variety of genres. The music is offered free under various licenses for use.

Find Sounds (https://www.findsounds.com) is a long-running service that can be used to search the internet for various sounds that can then be incorporated into various projects.

FreePlay Music (https://freeplaymusic.com) is a service that searches the internet for free music that can be used in YouTube videos and other projects.

Shazam (https://www.shazam.com) is an app that allows users to identify the music playing around them, and to discover song lyrics and other music related information and tracks.

News

Breaking News English (https://breakingnewsenglish.com) offers a range of news articles broken down by levels, and coming with a complete lesson plan for implementation.

Online Short Course Providers

Coursera (https://www.coursera.org) offers free courses in a variety of subject areas that are offered online from world-class universities and companies.

FutureLearn (https://www.futurelearn.com/) provides online study options from short courses through to postgraduate degrees across a wide variety of categories and from a wide variety of universities and organizations.

Study.com (https://study.com) is a site designed to deliver online courses for students, teachers, homeschool, college credit, and for test preparation.

Online Teaching Tools

Moodle (https://moodle.com) is a flexible open source learner management system that can be used by institutions as well as individuals.

Zoom (https://zoom.us) is a video conferencing system that allows multi-user conferencing, the ability to send files between users, and for holding a synchronous online class that allows students to share files and split off into breakout rooms to discuss topics before coming back to join the main conference.

Plagiarism

Copyscape (https://www.copyscape.com) is an online plagiarism checker that can be used to detect duplicate text on the internet.

Grammarly (https://app.grammarly.com) is a free writing app that analyzes the text that you have written and provides feedback for clarity and grammar. It also offers a plagiarism checking service for a fee.

Plagiarisma (http://plagiarisma.net) is a free online plagiarism checker for academics, students, and teachers.

Quetext (https://quetext.com) is an online citation generator and plagiarism checker. It will compare text to webpages, academic sources, news sources, and online textbooks.

Turnitin (https://turnitin.com) is one of the most widely used plagiarism checkers in academia, and it is often licensed by universities for faculty use.

Podcasting

Audacity (https://www.audacityteam.org) is a free multi-track audio recorder and editor with some very powerful features that include those for adding effects to files and conducting analyses of the audio recorded.

iTunes (https://www.apple.com/itunes) offers media on demand and a way to organize and enjoy music, movies, and TV shows, as well as accessing and subscribing to podcasts and screencasts.

LoudBlog (http://loudblog.com) is a content management system (CMS) for podcasts. This program automatically generates skinnable websites and RSS-feeds for audio and video podcasts, including provision for show notes and links.

ESLPod (https://secure3.eslpod.com) provides a range of podcast content tailored to second-language learners of English from specific topics through to test-taking guides.

FeedForAll (https://www.feedforall.com) allows for the creation, editing, and publishing of RSS feeds.

Feedity (https://feedity.com) is an online tool for creating an RSS feed for any webpage, with an option to upgrade to a premium account that offers additional features.

FETCHRSS: RSS Generator (http://fetchrss.com) is an online RSS feed generator that can create a feed out of almost any webpage, automatically updates the RSS feed when new content is added to the webpage, and generates an RSS for a social networking site.

OPML Viewer (https://chrome.google.com/webstore/detail/opml-viewer/injknmbdfficgcaedighapepbjdcdppi) allows users to view the contents of outline processor markup language (OPML) files.

PodcastGenerator (http://www.podcastgenerator.net) is an open source content management system for podcast publishing. It provides a comprehensive range of tools to manage all aspects of podcast publishing.

Podcast Alley (https://www.podcastalley.com) is the place to go if you are interested in podcasts, want to gain access to the top podcasts, and want to find out the latest news about podcasts.

PodOmatic Podcast Player (https://www.podomatic.com) provides the apps users with access to a wide variety of podcasts, listening in offline mode, and features such as a dynamic social feed so you can see the podcasts that Facebook friends follow and like.

Pod Gallery (https://podgallery.org) is a podcasting website where podcasters can share their episodes, and where listeners can subscribe.

QT-ESL Podcasts (https://www.qualitytime-esl.com/spip.php?rubrique20) provides a range of podcasts that cover oral grammar practice and includes scripts and worksheets.

SoundCloud (https://soundcloud.com) is a social sound platform where anyone is able to create and share audio.

Podcatchers

Cloud Caster (http://www.cloud-caster.com) is a web-based podcaster which works across all mobile devices. It syncs progress and playlists across platforms, and provides search and support for audio and video podcasts.

gPodder (https://gpodder.github.io) is an open source media aggregator and podcast client. It is able to store information in the cloud that has the shows that you have listened to, and it allows for the local installation of the client for download of content.

Juice (http://juicereceiver.sourceforge.net) is a long-standing cross platform no-frills podcast aggregator that is open source, and specifically designed to manage podcasts. Features include auto cleanup, centralized feed management, and, for Windows users, accessibility options for the blind and visually impaired.

Overcast: Podcast Player (https://overcast.fm) provides a combination of powerful audio and podcast management features. The iPhone application comes with a wide variety of features that allow it to download episodes, send notifications of new episodes, and play content offline or by streaming. It can also normalize speech levels, and speed through gaps and silence in podcasts.

Portfolio Development

Evernote (https://evernote.com) allows you to digitally organize a range of content, including notes and to-do lists, and to complete a range of task management activities and provide archiving for them all.

LiveBinders (http://livebinders.com) is an organization and eportfolio tool that allows you to integrate a variety of content into one location.

Seesaw: The Learning Journal (https://web.seesaw.me) is a versatile digital portfolio creation app that anyone can use to showcase their learning by uploading content and providing annotation.

VoiceThread (https://voicethread.com) allows users to import various media such as images, PowerPoints, and PDFs. It provides a means of making audio or video recordings concerning those media artifacts, and it also allows other users to reply to the initial comments by audio or video means.

Praxis Tests

Praxis Tests – ETS (https://www.ets.org/praxis) provides information on the test, and allows for registration to take the test.

Praxis ESL (https://study.com/academy/course/praxis-esl-practice-and-study-guide.html) is a short online course, which is free, and reviews the material found in the praxis test for teachers of English to speakers of other languages.

Presentations

Glogster (https://edu.glogster.com) allows students to create online multimedia posters, or glogs, from a combination of media types (audio, graphic, and video) and hyperlinks.

Google Slides (https://www.google.com/slides/about) allows those with a Google account a means of creating, editing, and collaborating with others on presentations.

LinkedIn SlideShare (https://www.slideshare.net) allows users to search for presentations, infographics, documents and other items on the topics of their interest.

Microsoft PowerPoint Online (https://www.office.com/launch/ powerpoint) extends the Microsoft PowerPoint experience to the web browser with OneDrive integration, and allows users to create, edit, and view files on the go.

Padlet (https://padlet.com) is a tool that allows learners to collaborate online by posting text, images, links, documents, videos, and voice recordings to their class page.

Prezi (https://prezi.com) is a visually-oriented presentation package that also allows users to upload PowerPoint slides and customize them, or use a variety of their own images, text, audios, and videos.

Slidebean (https://slidebean.com) offers a one-click presentation development system that incorporates a variety of templates into the design of presentations.

VoiceThread (https://voicethread.com) allows users to import various media such as images, PowerPoints, and PDFs. It provides a means of making audio or video recordings with those media artifacts, and it also allows other users to reply to the initial comments, by audio or video means, as the presentation progresses.

Professional Development Resources

Developing Teachers (http://www.developingteachers.com/index.htm) is a website that provides a range of resources for teachers to use, along with a variety of content that teachers can use to help make themselves better at their craft.

Ditchthattextbook (https://ditchthattextbook.com) is a website that offers various tips and insights into how to teach, and provides ways to use various technologies to assist in teaching.

Educational Technology and Mobile Learning (https://www.educatorstechnology.com) is a resource of educational web tools and mobile apps for teachers and educators.

Peachy Publications (https://peachypublications.com) provides a range of books for teacher development along with a range of lesson resources.

TEFLpedia (https://teflpedia.com) is a wiki that provides information on all aspects of teaching English as a foreign language.

TEFLVideos (http://www.teflvideos.com) is a dedicated professional development website for teachers of English to speakers of other languages that provides a range of content to help instructors improve upon their teaching.

Teaching English | British Council (https://www.teachingenglish.org.uk) offers a range of resources from their website, including those that focus on teacher development. The site also contains an ELT research database.

Pronunciation

ELSA Speak: English Accent Coach/ELSA – Pronunciation Training (*Android:* https://play.google.com/store/apps/details?id=us.nobarriers.elsa&hl=en *iPhone:* https://apps.apple.com/us/app/elsa-speak-accent-eductio n/id1083804886) is an app that helps learners to speak English like an American by indicating where improvement is required and how to do so.

Forvo (https://forvo.com) is the largest pronunciation dictionary in the world, and its aim is to have a database of all the words from all the languages in the world pronounced by native speakers of those languages. You can type in a word to then hear how it is pronounced.

Say It: English Pronunciation (*Android:* https://play.google.com/store/apps/details?id=com.oup.elt.sayit&hl=en *iPhone:* https://apps.apple.com/us/app/say-it-english-pronunciation/id919978521) is an app that assists users in pronouncing English using the Oxford model. Users can see the soundwave and record and compare their pronunciation. The free version provides 100 words, 4 tests, and 12 sounds.

Sound Pronunciation App (*Android:* https://play.google.com/store/apps/details?id=com.macmillan.app.soundsfree&hl=en *iPhone:* https://apps.apple.com/us/app/sounds-the-pronunciation-app-free/id428243918) by Macmillan Education uses three practice modes (listening, reading, writing) along with 650 high frequency words. It presents the IPA chart for English divided into three sections (consonants, diphthongs, vowels).

Speakit: English Pronunciation Checker (https://play.google.com/store/apps/details?id=com.eapp.pc&hl=en) shows Android users how the speech sounds of American English are formed, and checks pronunciation.

Voice Pronunciation Checker (https://voicenotebook.com/pronounce.php) helps learners to study the pronunciation, spelling, and meanings of words, and it provides a pronunciation-checking mechanism through text-to-speech transcription.

Quizzes

EDPuzzle (https://edpuzzle.com) offers the ability to turn any video content into a quiz.

Hot Potatoes (https://hotpot.uvic.ca) includes six applications that allow you to create multiple-choice, short-answer, jumbled-sentence, crossword, matching/ordering, and gap-fill exercises.

Kahoot! (https://kahoot.com) offers teachers the ability to create interactive games that are easy to make and fun to play. They require a tablet, PC, or a phone.

Socrative (https://socrative.com) helps you to visualize student learning in the classroom while providing on-the-fly assessment via multiple-choice, true/false, and short-answer activities as well as games.

Reading

BookRix (https://www.bookrix.com) allows access to thousands of books to read either online or to download as ebooks.

Children's Storybooks Online (http://www.magickeys.com/books) provides a series of illustrated stories for all ages to read.

Dreamreader (http://dreamreader.net) provides free resources so that learners can engage in reading practice from a variety of levels and topics.

Free Books (https://www.freebooks-app.com) features free access to 23,469 classic books for Android and iPhone users.

StoryPlace (https://www.storyplace.org) provides material that students might like to access for reading in their free time. It offers a range of stories with colorful videos and graphics that can also appeal to younger learners.

Wattpad Free Books (https://www.wattpad.com/stories/free-books) provides access to free stories and books that are written by aspiring authors.

Rubrics

Kathy Shrock's Guide to Everything: Assessment and Rubrics (https://www.schrockguide.net/assessment-and-rubrics.html) allows access to a wide range of rubrics that helps with the assessment of students.

iRubric (https://www.rcampus.com/indexrubric.cfm) allows teachers to create their own rubrics, or they can build off those that have been made available from other teachers.

RubiStar (http://rubistar.4teachers.org/index.php) allows instructors to create their own rubrics using templates that are designed for core subjects as well as art, music, and multimedia.

Screencasting

Screencast-O-Matic (https://screencast-o-matic.com) offers fifteen minutes of recording time for free, both for screen and webcam, and lets users save to places such as YouTube or as a video file.

TechSmith Camtasia Studio (https://www.techsmith.com/video-editor.html) is a comprehensive screen recording application that offers a free trial, and allows for audio and webcam capture as well as highlighting, adding media, and editing of recordings.

Scripts

Drew's Script-o-Rama (http://www.script-o-rama.com) offers over 10,000 free movie scripts, transcripts, screenplays, and teleplays.

IMSDB (Internet Movie Screenplay Database) (https://www.imsdb.com) is a database of movie scripts that is available for free, and touts itself as the largest collection.

Screenplays For You (https://sfy.ru) offers free movie scripts and screenplays.

Sentence Diagramming

Let's Diagram! (https://letsdiagram.com) assists in the learning of grammar and diagramming, but it requires signing up prior to use.

Diagram Sentence (https://www.conceptdraw.com/How-To-Guide/free-sentence-diagrammer) is a computer-based application that can be used during class to illustrate how to create sentence diagrams.

Sentence Diagrammer (https://www.microsoft.com/en-us/p/sentence-diagrammer/9nblggh10hzs) automatically analyzes and diagrams sentences using the Reed-Kellogg system.

SenGram – Sentence Diagramming (https://apps.apple.com/us/app/sengram-sentence-diagramming/id512943810) is an iPhone app that provides users with sentence-diagram puzzles to solve.

Songs

LyricsTraining (https://lyricstraining.com) is an app and website that offers students the ability to practice cloze (by typing) and multiple-choice gap-filling for songs.

TEFLtunes.com (https://tefltunes.com) offers ready-made song-based activities that teachers can use with learners.

Speaking

Drama in the ESL Classroom (http://esldrama.weebly.com) is designed to get students acting and speaking, and it offers a variety of free resources for teachers to use.

Total Physical Response (http://www.total-physical-response.com) is dedicated to providing a range of ready-to-use sequencing activities to engage students with TPR.

Stories

Agenda Web (https://agendaweb.org/listening/intermediate_advanced.html) provides a large collection of stories at levels that are suitable for all learners.

Many Things (http://www.manythings.org/voa/stories) provides classic American short stories that are listed by author. Stories are provided with MP3 audio and scripts, and they are available for advanced learners.

Rong Chang (https://www.rong-chang.com/mini-novels) offers a large collection of short narratives for beginner-level learners, and each comes with an audio component and script.

Storyboarding and Scripting

Penultimate (https://evernote.com/products/penultimate) provides, for iPhones, a natural feel of writing and sketching on paper, and connects to Evernote.

Storyboard Studio (https://www.educationalappstore.com/app/storyboard-studio) is a mobile storyboarding writing tool that is suitable for artists and non-artists alike.

Story Creation

Cartoon Story Maker 1.1 (https://cartoon-story-maker.informer.com) is a simple program that creates 2D cartoon stories with conversations, dialogues (recorded and/or speech bubble), and various backgrounds. Educators can edit and customize aspects of the program for their context. Backgrounds can be imported, but character templates are built in.

Littlebirdtales (https://littlebirdtales.com) provides younger learners the ability to create digital storybooks.

Storynet (http://www.storynet.eu/cms) is a website that aims at connecting people to and through storytelling.

StoryJumper (https://www.storyjumper.com) allows users to create illustrated storybooks from scratch or from existing templates.

Student Response Systems

Plickers (https://www.plickers.com) is a QR-based learner response system that takes technology out of the students' hands. The teacher uses a phone or table to scan the QR codes that students hold up to answer a multiple-choice (from A through D) question. Results can be viewed in real-time, and anonymously if desired, with scores recorded for later teacher review.

Poll Everywhere (https://www.polleverywhere.com) is an app that allows you to create a live poll in virtual and physical classrooms.

Testing

IELTS Podcast (https://www.ieltspodcast.com) is for those students who are preparing to undertake the official exam. It provides some tutorials, gap-fill exercises and quizzes that students can use to practice.

Translation

Google Translate (https://translate.google.com) allows you to type or speak words or phrases to be translated into other languages. It can also use cameras in devices to read the text of languages and provide real-time translations.

Papago (https://papago.naver.com) is a multilingual machine translation service that is popular in Korea.

Vocabulary

Vocabulary Spelling City (https://www.spellingcity.com) works with the content that you provide to present a spelling, writing, phonics, or vocabulary-based game. It provides a fun and interactive way to practice vocabulary items for review.

Video Content

Clipcanvas (https://www.clipcanvas.com/home) allows for the download of 600,000 royalty free HD and 4K video and film clips.

ESL Video (https://www.eslvideo.com) provides a large range of videos to engage learners in listening, speaking, grammar, and vocabulary skills with associated quizzes and lessons that are made by teachers.

Mazwai (https://mazwai.com) maintains a collection of free-to-use HD video clips and footage, and some unique time-lapse and slow-motion video footages which are provided under the Creative Commons Attribution license if used commercially.

Motion Elements (https://www.motionelements.com/?ref=6040ehxur) is a good source for premium stock videos, offering around 400 videos for free, as well as free After Effects templates.

Pexels Videos (https://www.pexels.com/videos) brings under one roof a video library of Creative Commons Zero licensed stock videos from a variety of different sources.

SaveTube (https://savetube.org) allows users to rip YouTube videos to their local computer in various audio or video-based formats.

Savevideo.me (http://savevideo.me) allows users to rip videos from a variety of sites to their local computer.

TeacherTube (https://www.teachertube.com) is an online resource that helps users to view and share videos, photos, audio, and documents on almost any topic.

TED (https://www.ted.com) provides more than 2,000 TED talks from various people by topic and mood.

The Peanut Gallery (https://www.peanutgalleryfilms.com) allows users to select short movies to subtitle with text produced from their speech.

Vimeo (https://vimeo.com) provides a variety of videos which are available across a wide variety of topics and genres. Users are able to upload their own content as well.

YouTube (https://www.youtube.com) allows for editing and uploading of videos, and one can subscribe to various channels that offer a wide variety of videos on various topics and genres.

Video Editing

Video Toolbox (https://www.videotoolbox.com) is an online video editing and conversion tool.

WeVideo (https://www.wevideo.com) is a comprehensive and easy-to-use web-based video editor that can mix images, text, video, and audio together to form compelling stories.

WebQuests

Creating a WebQuest (https://www.educationworld.com/a_tech/tech/tech011.shtml) is a comprehensive overview of the template to follow when there is a need to construct a WebQuest.

Having Fun with Reading (http://zunal.com/webquest.php?w=87555) is a webquest for college and adult-level learners of English who can interact with texts and complete activities that promote cooperative and collaborative learning along with reading narrative comprehension skills.

Idioms in Your Pocket (https://zunal.com/process.php?w=87183) is designed for high school and adult ESL students, and it allows them to discover the various meanings of English idioms.

OneStopEnglish WebQuests (http://www.onestopenglish.com/teenagers/topic-based-materials/webquests) provides a selection of webquests that cover major holidays.

QuestGarden (http://questgarden.com) was designed by Bernie Dodge, the creator of WebQuests, for use by pre- and in-service teachers, professional developers, other educators, and those who work with them. The site provides hosting and template creation of WebQuests that then become searchable.

WebQuestDirect (http://www.webquestdirect.com.au) is described as the world's largest searchable directory of WebQuest reviews.

WebQuest.Org (http://webquest.org) provides comprehensive information pertaining to the WebQuest model, and is run by Bernie Dodge, the creator of webquests.

Zunal (http://zunal.com) is a site for educators to create, host, and then share their WebQuests with others.

Wikis

DokuWiki (https://www.dokuwiki.org/dokuwiki) is a PHP based highly customizable and fully extensible wiki software platform. The advantage is that it requires no databases as all the data is stored in plain text, and for this reason, it is very popular and used by many sites. It has a variety of useful features, from locking to avoid edits through to a spam blacklist.

MediaWiki (https://www.mediawiki.org/wiki/MediaWiki) is open-source and it is the wiki software used by Wikipedia. It is available in a number of languages, released under a general public license (GPL), and written in PHP (Hypertext Preprocessor) which is a server-side scripting language. There are many extensions and plugins available for free, including a what-you-see-is-what-you-get (WYSIWYG) editor.

PBworks (http://www.pbworks.com) (formerly PBwiki) is a real-time collaborative editing system with several solutions including one for educators. It offers a single workspace where student accounts can be created without email addresses along with easy editing without the need for coding.

PmWiki (https://www.pmwiki.org) is a wiki tool that gives user-access control over individual pages so that they can be set for access by specific people with it being possible to set different passwords for each page. The software also allows for navigation trails through individual sections and insertion of tables, and it provides a printable layout.

Wikidot (https://www.wikidot.com) offers members the ability to create a wiki-based website with forums, where they can create a community or publish and share documents and content.

Word Lists

British Academic Spoken English (BASE) (https://warwick.ac.uk/fac/soc/al/research/collections/base) is a text corpus consisting of 160 lectures and 40 seminars that were delivered at the Universities of Warwick and Reading from 2000 to 2005. It contains 1,644,942 tokens.

British National Corpus (BNC) (https://www.english-corpora.org/bnc) is a 100-million-word corpus of samples of written and spoken English from a variety of sources. It is often broken down further into word different word lists. For example, the BNC 1,000 consists of the first 1,000 most commonly used English words, the BNC 2,000 adds the second 1,000 most commonly used English words, and so on).

Business Service List (BSL) (http://www.newgeneralservicelist.org/bsl-business-service-list) consists of 1,700 words that covers 97% of general business English material when combined with the 2,800 words found in the NGSL.

Corpus of Contemporary American English (COCA) (https://www.english-corpora.org/coca) is a 1.1 billion word corpus of American English from eight genres of content including academic texts, blogs, fiction books, magazines, newspapers, spoken words, subtitles from TV and movies, and web pages. The most frequent 5,000 words can be freely browsed at its website in lists of frequency, alphabetical order, and parts of speech.

Longman Communication 3000 (https://lextutor.ca/freq/lists_download/longman_3000_list.pdf) is a list of around 3,600 of the most commonly spoken and/or written words of English.

Michigan Corpus of Academic Spoken (MICASE) (https://quod.lib.umich.edu/m/micase) is a list that contains 1,848,364 words using 152 transcripts. It can be browsed by speaker and speech attributes, and searched by words or phrases in specified contexts.

New Academic Word List (NAWL) (http://www.newgeneralservicelist.org/nawl-new-academic-word-list) is a corpus of 288 million words from academic text books, the British Academic Spoken English (BASE) list, the Michigan Corpus of Academic Spoken English (MICASE) list as well as academic discourse, academic journals, textbooks, non-fiction works, and student essays.

New General Service List (NGSL) (http://www.newgeneral servicelist.org) is a list of high frequency words for learners of English containing terms covering 92% of most general texts.

New General Service List – Spoken (NGSL-S) (http://www.new generalservicelist.org/ngsls) is a list of 721 words that provides coverage of up to 90% of unscripted spoken English.

TOEIC Service List (TSL) (http://www.newgeneralservicelist.org/toeic-list) is a list of 1.5 million words derived from TOEIC textbooks, practice tests, and TOEIC corpora from a range of other sources.

Word Webs

MindMaster (https://www.edrawsoft.com/mindmaster) is a rather versatile mind-mapping tool that allows for collaboration and is available on a number of platforms to provide users with access to a wide range of clipart and templates.

MindMeister (https://www.mindmeister.com) can help teachers and learners develop word webs using images, links, notes, or vocabulary as they work either by themselves or in collaboration with others.

Mindomo (https://www.mindomo.com) is a mind-mapping tool that can be used to create concept maps, manage tasks, outline, and for collaboration. It has the ability to integrate a number of applications.

Worksheets

Busy teacher (https://busyteacher.org/) provides over 17,000 printable worksheets and lesson plans.

EFL4U (https://www.efl4u.com) offers a range of resources for teachers, including stories, games, and puzzle worksheets, of which only some are free.

English is a piece of cake (http://www.englishisapieceofcake.com) provides a wide range of teaching and learning resources for students and teachers alike.

ESL Activities (https://www.eslactivities.com/bingo.php) contains a number of tools, resources, puzzles, and games for learners and for teachers to use in class. This includes Bingo card makers.

ESL Brains (https://eslbrains.com) publishes a variety of worksheets based around various videos, including those of TED talks. Lesson plans that are based on topic and level are also searchable.

ESL Galaxy (http://www.esl-galaxy.com) is a comprehensive free resource site for ESL study that offers printable flashcards, worksheets, board games, lesson plan packs, and a range of PowerPoint slides, along with a number of ESP teaching materials.

ESL Printables (https://www.eslprintables.com/teaching_resources/lesson_plans) provides a range of downloadable worksheets that are categorized by age and learner level, and that teachers can print and use in their classrooms with learners.

Handouts Online (http://www.handoutsonline.com/index.php) offers a great deal of ready-to-use printable worksheets that are useful for a wide variety of levels and classes.

iSLCOLLECTIVE (https://en.islcollective.com) contains worksheets, PowerPoints, and video lessons which teachers can upload and be able to share the material that they have developed.

Quickworksheets (https://quickworksheets.net) offers free worksheet generators for word search puzzles, word jumbles and minimal-pair word trees. Teachers can input the desired target language, and the website generates pdf worksheets for printing or download.

TEFLtastic (https://tefltastic.wordpress.com) maintains over 2,000 printable worksheets that cover a range of language points and levels and are ready for class use.

Writing

ESL Writing Wizard (https://writingwizard.longcountdown.com/handwriting_practice_worksheet_maker.html) is for various grades to help them learn to write the alphabet. Although the materials are designed for the initial language learner, they are easily adaptable for use in the EFL or ESL classroom.

Purdue OWL (https://owl.purdue.edu/owl/purdue_owl.html) is the Purdue University Online Writing Lab, and it provides access to a wide range of writing resources and instructional content as well as access to the latest citation styles with examples that can help junior and senior researchers to adhere to academic standards.

About the Book

Serving as a general overview to the field, *Issues in TESOL: A primer for teaching English to speakers of other languages,* aims to deliver insight into the many varied concepts and practices involved in the teaching of English to speakers of other languages (TESOL). It focuses on those particular issues of TESOL that are important over the various stages of a career. Of significance, the book emerges to fill the needs of those who come to the education field from other disciplines; for those who may find themselves teaching without experience; for those interested in beginning a career in teaching English; as well as those in-service teachers looking to reground; or for those who are about to embark on TESOL certification. The intent is to provide insight that will assist readers in making connections between the various theoretical discourses, research, and teaching practices that are involved in the craft of teaching English to speakers of other languages.

The book consists of four parts, introducing readers to TESOL theories, methods, and approaches, along with the basics of classroom management and lesson plan development, to establish a foundation for teaching the four skills along with pronunciation and grammar, while also introducing how to benefit from engaging in classroom observation, professional development endeavors and leadership. Part one, *perspectives and practice* centers on aspects of second language acquisition and the place of educational theories in teaching. It also reviews the methods, approaches, and techniques applied to the teaching and learning of languages over time, particularly those that provide us with an understanding of how best to teach today. A variety of classroom management theories are discussed, with educational leadership, as well as the ethics, laws, rights, and responsibilities in teaching explored, with those influences affecting second language acquisition from language, planning and policy, to culture, identity, and intercultural communication also touched upon. Part two, *implementations* focuses on those practical aspects of concern to teachers. Such as how to frame lessons to engage students, the basics of classroom management, the delivery of appropriate teaching content, and the development of effective lesson plans. Part three, *sound, meaning, and form* then covers those concepts of most importance for teaching the 'what' of language. Part four, *capstone projects* highlights the expectations and steps required to complete some of the final projects often linked to obtaining accredited TESOL certification. A comprehensive listing of beneficial applications and worthwhile websites along with a comprehensive glossary of key terms used in the field is also provided.

About the Author

David Kent is an Associate Professor in the Endicott College of International Studies at Woosong University in the Republic of Korea. He provides teacher education through the TESOL-MALL graduate program where he currently serves as Head of Department.

David is also a long-standing member of the academic community with a principal research focus that revolves around the digitalization of language learning. Serving as conference plenary and keynote, as well as invited speaker, he has won a number of teacher association and conference presentation awards.

To date, he has published a number of books, including *Teaching with Technology: Integrating Technology into the TESOL Classroom*, *Internet in Education: Integrating the Internet into the TESOL Classroom*, and a *TESOL Strategy Guide* series that focuses on the use of specific digital tools for teaching. He has also authored a number of multimedia applications, as well as delivering and developing graduate online course material through the Korean open courseware (KOCW) system that focuses on TESOL and aspects of the place and integration of artificial intelligence in education.

Currently, he serves on the editorial board of several journals, and his research articles have been published at the Scopus and SSCI levels in such periodicals as *Teaching English with Technology* (IATEFL), *The Journal of Asia TEFL* (Asia TEFL), and *Language Learning and Technology* (NFLRC, University of Hawai'i at Mānoa/COERLL, University of Texas).

www.ingramcontent.com/pod-product-compliance
Lightning Source LLC
Chambersburg PA
CBHW071734020526
44116CB00043BA/962